Allan Mills.

THE QUESTION OF THINGS HAPPENING
The Letters of Virginia Woolf
VOLUME II: 1912—1922

THE QUESTION OF THINGS HAPPENING

The Letters of
VIRGINIA WOOLF

Volume II: 1912-1922

Editor: Nigel Nicolson
Assistant Editor: Joanne Trautmann

1976
THE HOGARTH PRESS
LONDON

Published by
The Hogarth Press Ltd
42 William IV Street
London WC2N 4DF

*

Clarke, Irwin & Co. Ltd
Toronto

ISBN 7012 0420 6

Printed in Great Britain by
T. & A. Constable Ltd
Hopetoun Street, Edinburgh

"There's the whole question, which interested me . . . of the things one doesn't say; what effect does that have? and how far do our feelings take their colour from the dive underground? I mean what is the reality of any feeling? . . . And then there's the question of things happening, normally, all the time."

Virginia Woolf to Janet Case
19 *November* 1919

Contents

Illustrations

Plates 1, 3a, 3c, 4a, 4b, 4c, 7a, 7b, 8a, 8b, 8c were loaned by Professor and Mrs Quentin Bell; 2a, 3b, 6a, 6b by Barbara Bagenal; p. 153 by Sussex University; 2b by the Greater London Council; 5 and 7c are the property of the Editor.

Editorial Note

THERE is no need to repeat from the Note attached to Volume I of these Letters every detail of our editorial method. It follows traditional lines. We have enquired widely for Virginia Woolf's letters in public collections in Britain and the United States, and persuaded her surviving correspondents or their descendants to search their desks and attics. The total haul now numbers over 4,000, and we hope that the publication of the first volumes will bring more to light. We have transcribed the letters either from the originals or facsimiles of them, adding dates and addresses where they were missing, and explaining obscure allusions. About twenty-five letters and postcards have been omitted from this volume, because they were notes of social engagements of no importance.

The editing of Volume II has been easier than that of Volume I, for two reasons. First, as the letters survive in increasing numbers and crowd more closely together, one provides clues to another, in date and subject-matter. Secondly, in 1915, and from October 1917 until her death, Virginia Woolf kept a diary, which fills in the chronology of her life and expands some incidents mentioned in the letters. By permission of Quentin Bell and Dr Lola L. Szladits, curator of the Berg Collection in New York Public Library, which owns the original, we have been able to examine it, but we have not quoted anything not already published by Leonard Woolf in his abbreviated version, *A Writer's Diary* (1953). The full diary is being edited for publication by Olivier (Mrs Quentin) Bell.

It has not been necessary or possible to explain and amplify everything which Virginia wrote to her friends. We do not wish to produce an edition of her letters in which a few lines of her text struggle, page after page, to keep afloat on a sea of footnotes. While that might be editorially impressive, it would destroy her fluency. We have confined our annotation to references which made us pause with the questions 'Who?', 'Where?', 'What?', on the assumption that the reader will do the same, and our answers have been given as concisely as possible. Even so, there are a few gaps. "I ran into Mrs Flower in the London Library. We merely spat at each other" (13 November 1918). Flower? There are several Mrs Flowers whom Virginia could conceivably have known, but which one was her target on that occasion? So with a sense of editorial incompetence, one surrenders: *unidentified*. There are other examples scattered through this volume. We are consoled, but not wholly, by the reflection that few readers will greatly care about Flower, and by the certainty that Virginia herself would have thought it foolish to subject her letters to feats of editorial archaeology.

Among those whom we wish particularly to thank are, foremost, Quentin and Olivier Bell. Professor Bell and his sister Angelica Garnett are the owners of the copyright in all the letters, and they have given us much of their time and help. But Olivier Bell has been the recipient of most of our enquiries. In preparing the material for her husband's biography of Virginia Woolf, she was the first to examine in detail Virginia's massive correspondence, and to place it in chronological order, often with only a 'Tuesday' to guide her. We have retraced her scholarly work, with the enormous advantage that she had done it first, and that we had other letters of which she did not know. In dating them we have rarely disagreed, and her unrivalled knowledge of Bloomsbury has filled many gaps in our own.

As before, this volume is published both in Great Britain and the United States. We wish to thank the Hogarth Press in London and Harcourt Brace Jovanovich in New York for their encouragement; and the printers, T. & A. Constable of Edinburgh, for their skill and care.

For their generosity in allowing Dr Joanne Trautmann to spend part of her academic year working on this volume, we are grateful to the Department of Humanities, the Pennsylvania State University College of Medicine, Hershey, Pennsylvania.

The following have also given us much help: George A. Spater; B. J. Kirkpatrick, author of *A Bibliography of Virginia Woolf*; Dr Lola L. Szladits, of the Berg Collection, New York; the librarians of Sussex University, and of the London Library; Paul Levy, of the Strachey Trust; Michael Holroyd; Benedict, Juliet and Adam Nicolson; Patrick and Mrs Heron; Gordon S. Haight; Dr Wendy Baron; Daphne Sanger; Richard Shone; Raymond Mortimer; Mrs Margaret Scott, of Wellington, New Zealand; Sybille Bedford; the staff of the National Gallery and National Portrait Gallery. Our other main benefactors, the owners of the original letters, are acknowledged at the foot of each.

Several secretaries (who should more correctly be designated sub-editors, so great has been their contribution) have typed the letters and prepared them for publication. We wish particularly to thank Pamela Kilbane, Jane Carr and Lyn J. Dunbar, in England; and in the United States, Gretchen Hess Gage, Valerie Henderson and Gwendolyn W. Pierce.

NIGEL NICOLSON
JOANNE TRAUTMANN

Introduction

BETWEEN 1912 and 1922 Virginia Woolf married, published her first three novels, twice went mad, and co-founded the Hogarth Press. The same years contained the First World War. It was a massive experience for someone so mentally frail. But the impression left by her letters is that she was stronger at the end of this decade than at the beginning, stronger in creative power, in social energy, in audacity. If this is true, it was due primarily to the happiness of her marriage.

When two people of independent minds marry, they must be able to rely upon each other's tolerance, affection and support. Each must encourage, without jealousy, the full development of the other's gifts, each allow the other privacy, different interests, different friends. But they must share an intellectual and moral base. One of them cannot be philistine if the other is constantly breasting new ideas. They cannot disagree wildly on what is right and wrong. Above all, their love must grow as passion fades—and Virginia never experienced much passion—particularly if they have no children. And if they face, as Virginia and Leonard faced, the ultimate calamity that she might at any moment go raving mad and turn upon him with vitriolic abuse, then he must draw upon all the reserves their marriage has accumulated, and expend them freely, knowing that they will be renewed by his very effort of sustaining both of them through her long ordeal.

All this Leonard Woolf did for Virginia. But for him she might not have lived until she was 40. Feeling the profoundest form of gratitude, thinking guiltily that she was ruining his life, she responded with a love that matched his own. "I assure you, I couldn't have married anyone else", she told Jacques Raverat in 1922. And to Leonard she wrote:

"Precious Mongoose. . . . I lie and think of my precious beast, who does make me more happy every day and instant of my life than I thought it possible to be. There's no doubt I'm terribly in love with you. I keep thinking what you're doing, and have to stop—it makes me want to kiss you so." (17 April 1916)

Their love was not at first sexless. For two or three years they shared a bed, and for several more a bedroom, and it was only on medical advice that they decided not to have children. It is not difficult to picture Virginia as a mother, particularly, one imagines, of a girl. She was jealous of Vanessa's fecundity, and freely admitted it. Her childlessness added to her sense of deprivation. It was another penalty imposed upon her. But there were compensations: greater freedom of movement, more time to work, and the delight she could take in the children of other people, coming to see herself as a natural aunt and god-mother, fascinated by the clarity of children's minds, and by childhood as a facet of human experience which no adult can recover nor properly describe.

Virginia did not ruin Leonard's life. He achieved all that he was capable of achieving, and it was much. There were periods when he must sacrifice his time to care for her, and the strains she underwent added to his own. Yet it would be difficult to identify a single instance when he was prevented by her illnesses from writing this article, that book, sitting on this committee, editing that journal. She made a brave show of sharing his interests, and throughout her life continued to accompany him to some of his political meetings. Never did she ridicule his preoccupation with problems of peace and social justice, although she did not hesitate to lampoon them in others. When Leonard stood for Parliament in 1922, he partly shared her hope that he would not be elected, for by nature he was still a civil servant with an exceptionally fertile and independent mind.

She looked to him for the big decisions of their lives. It was he who managed their finances, guided her through her traumas, conceived the idea of the Hogarth Press. Except in the choice of where they were to live (for Virginia had a nose for houses), she deferred to him in practical matters. There is no record that they ever had a serious quarrel, except when she was insane. They never experienced jealousy of another person nor of a talent unshared. She deeply respected his judgement on what meant most to her, her writing: and he, lacking the gift of soaring imagination and recognising that she possessed it, shielded her, watched her fluctuating health, nurtured her genius, and with instinctive understanding left her alone in a room of her own, while he remained always available in the common room between them.

One quality they shared with all Bloomsbury was dedication. This may seem difficult to reconcile with the wild parties in Gordon Square and Virginia's coruscating letters, but a serious intent always qualified their fun. Frivolity was not to be scorned, but it was an accompaniment to work, as wit was to conversation. There must be charitableness in their attitude to people, but not too much. No quarter should be given to women because they were women. "Purposely, perhaps," Virginia wrote in *Night and Day*, "Mary [Datchet] did not agree with Ralph; she loved to feel her mind in conflict with his, and to be certain that he spared her female judgment no ounce of his male muscularity." Standards were high; admiration grudging. Virginia compared Bloomsbury at this period to "the lion's house at the Zoo. One goes from cage to cage. All the animals are dangerous, rather suspicious of each other, and full of fascination and mystery" (Letter 1160). There must be imagination, originality, variety. It was more important to illuminate an argument than state it. What they required from their friends were periodic demonstrations of the best of which they were capable. It was a competitive society, with a streak of malice that could turn icy. They encouraged their children to adopt the manner, in order to sharpen their wits, and puncture their vanity which could balloon dangerously. Bloomsbury was a pressure-cooker which needed the safety-valve of constant mutual criticism.

Simplicity was not an obvious trait of Bloomsbury. But Virginia and Leonard were simple in that they did not require in their own lives the extravagance which they relished in talk and behaviour. Few of her letters deal with money or the want of it, though by the standards of their class they were poor. They spent a few days of their honeymoon in a Somersetshire inn, where their bed was menaced by low beams which reverberated to the sound of every passing waggon, every guffaw from the bar below, and thought it wonderful. At one moment they toyed with the idea of spending part of the year in a hovel in Cornwall. Asheham and Hogarth were elegant houses, but the rooms were simply furnished, and the earth-closets at Asheham, as later at Monk's House, were hellish cess-pits of which Virginia made no complaint. The food was plain, and there was seldom wine. Milk was one of the few foods that Virginia considered essential for good health. She could cook (even took cooking-lessons), but preferred not to. There must be servants. On this she and Leonard were agreed. It was the only way to buy time. But much of it was wasted in interviewing or reassuring the very maids who were engaged to save it. Lottie and Nelly, and Vanessa's servants, Trissie and Blanche, to mention only the most permanent, trip through these pages as regularly as Lytton Strachey or Roger Fry. Although Virginia's wavering relationship with them, sometimes amused, sometimes exasperated, may be of more interest to social than literary historians, it is important for an understanding of this side of her character. She was competent; she was solicitous; she was patient. She applied herself without resentment to the occupations of the majority of middle-class women of her generation. It is surprising that the backstairs trafficking and gossiping, which form a staple of her letters to Vanessa, reappear so seldom in her novels.

Virginia was mad, self-dangerously mad, for about three months in 1913, and attempted suicide by swallowing 100 grains of veronal when Leonard was temporarily absent from the house. Sixteen months later she had another attack, even more serious. These bouts of lunacy are represented in this volume only by huge gaps. She emerged from the tunnels weakened but sane. Her subsequent off-hand references to them give no idea of the agony she endured in passing through them. In September 1922 she wrote to Janet Case about "my remarkable nervous system, which, as everybody tells me, can't be beaten for extreme eccentricity, but works all right in the long run". With scarcely greater self-concern she wrote a few weeks later to Jacques Raverat: "I'm glad you are fat; for then you are warm and mellow and generous and creative. I find that unless I weigh 9½ stones I hear voices and see visions and can neither write nor sleep." She was aware of the danger that every new headache, every dose of flu (and she had many), besides symptoms of pneumonia, tuberculosis and heart-disease, might be signals of re-approaching madness, and none of the doctors could tell her whether the signals were long-distance or short. But she was un-frightened, almost as if she sometimes looked forward to re-entering that dream-world which she describes so vividly in *Night and Day*:

> Being a frequent visitor to that world, she could find her way there unhesitatingly. If she had tried to analyse her impressions, she would have said that there dwelt the realities of the appearances which figure in our world; so direct, powerful, and unimpeded were her sensations there, compared with those called forth in actual life. There dwelt the things one might have felt, had there been cause; the perfect happiness of which here we taste the fragment; the beauty seen here in flying glimpses only.

It has come to be accepted that the moments of greatest danger were when Virginia had just finished a difficult book. But the dates fit too loosely to establish a direct connection, except with her last, *Between the Acts*. Having completed *The Waves*, she was exhausted, but there was no manic reaction in the sense of a complete change in her personality: nor with *The Years*. If *The Voyage Out* produced the crisis of 1913, why was there a gap of more than a year between writing those dangerous final chapters and her attempted suicide? Was not *Night and Day* a 'difficult' book, if only for its length; and even more, *Jacob's Room*? Yet in 1919 and 1921 Virginia, though sometimes ill for other reasons, was never in higher spirits. The truth is that she and Leonard lived under continual threat, and anything might precipitate the crisis. Her manic-depression (I use the term loosely) could strike with terrifying suddenness. When she recovered, her letters soon regained their impetus; when she was ailing, they slumped, noticeably near the beginning of the present volume. There is one which I consider malicious beyond the point of sanity—and perhaps for that very reason the word 'malicious' is inappropriate. It was written to Lytton Strachey on 26 February 1915.[1] A few days later Virginia "entered a state of garrulous mania, speaking ever more wildly, incoherently and incessantly, until she lapsed into gibberish and sank into a coma" (Quentin Bell, II, p. 25).

One cannot overlook the First War as an incident in Virginia's life, although she did her best to overlook it herself. It had no effect whatever upon her mental state, except to confirm her suspicions of a male-dominated society. She was married to a man who would probably not have resisted conscription had he been declared fit enough, but thought the war "senseless and useless", and devoted much of his political energy to devising means for

1. Not published in Leonard's edition of the Woolf-Strachey correspondence (1956).

preventing another. Her brother-in-law Clive Bell was moved so passionately by the horror of it that his pamphlet against the continuance of the war was deemed a public menace, and destroyed by order of the Lord Mayor of London. Four of Virginia's relations, including one of Leonard's brothers, were killed. Friends were wounded; others, like Bertrand Russell, imprisoned for their pacifism, or ostracised. Virginia herself slept night after night in the cellar of Hogarth House, sheltering from the zeppelin raids. Yet so little did all this mean to her that her letters contain almost no reflections on it. Personal inconveniences like food-rationing are recorded, and she roused herself sufficiently to appeal to Lord Salisbury on behalf of Duncan Grant, one of the many conscientious objectors among her friends. But of the great battles in France (the very sound of the bombardment sometimes penetrated to Asheham), of America's entry into the war, of the revolution in Russia, there is no mention in her letters, although there is a little more in her diaries. Once she wrote of Gallipoli, but only to illustrate the ignorance of her nurse, who thought it was in France. Of the possibility of defeat, of the hope of victory, she says hardly a word. It might seem from these letters that the most important event of the war was the Omega Workshops; its finest product, semolina.

One can understand her attitude. She assumed among her correspondents a common level of concern, and did not bother to mention it. But it was more than that. She thought the war an inevitable outcome of male chauvinism, against which she had made her own futile protest by the Dreadnought hoax of 1910. She was incapable of patriotic reverence; contemptuous of it. If men were bent on fighting (even Rupert Brooke, who wrote that "Manliness in man is the one hope of the world"; even Maynard Keynes, who on occasions could express contempt for conscientious objectors), well let them fight, but it was worse than foolish: it was degrading, like the behaviour of "some curious tribe in Central Africa". She was far from insensitive to what was happening, but it made her angry. She would have nothing to do with "this preposterous masculine fiction". She would wait until they stopped, and then resume her normal life without a word of reproach or congratulation to those like Ralph Partridge and Nick Bagenal who had risked their lives in helping to win the war for her, not a single backward glance at something she regarded as absurd and obscene. On Armistice Day she felt "immense melancholy", finding it impossible to write the last chapter of *Night and Day* with "all this shindy" going on around her, and then she goes on to tell Vanessa about her tea with Nelly Cecil. She had washed her hands of the whole business. *Eminent Victorians* had said all that needed to be said about the way men behave.

It was typical of Virginia. Hard as she tried out of loyalty to Leonard she could not take politics seriously, until she came to write *Three Guineas*. "All phantasies and moonshine, only mud-coloured moonshine", she called the efforts of men to improve the world:

"She was convinced that society is man-made, that the chief occupations of men are the shedding of blood, the making of money, the giving of orders, and the wearing of uniforms, and that none of these occupations is admirable."[1]

Some public men and women she admired: Leonard himself; Margaret Llewelyn Davies for her work for women's emancipation; Asquith, Grey, momentarily. Lloyd George, Churchill, never. She was a Socialist, partly because Leonard was too, more profoundly because she believed that the privileges of her class were a social outrage. "Why the poor don't take knives and chase us out of our houses, I cant think", she wrote to Nelly Cecil from Manchester in 1913. But she hated cities like Manchester, and would not take a saw to the branch on which Nelly sat so comfortably, making only symbolic gestures for her Socialism, like handing potatoes to railwaymen on strike, or organising lectures at her house for the Women's Co-operative Guild of Richmond. It is a familiar dilemma: sympathy for the lot of the poor; tolerance for the lot of the rich. Particularly if one's own lot happens to lie between.

Virginia, I protest, was not a snob. She was an élitist. The distinction has never been properly made in discussing her attitude. A snob is a person who attaches exaggerated importance to the titular great, to birth and accent, to acquired or inherited wealth. An élitist believes that some people are born natural aristocrats, of mind and disposition, and that the world is a better place because of them. Virginia herself was one of these. She happened to have the advantage of birth too, as the child of cultured upper-middle class parents, but what mattered to her was that people should be 'distinguished' in character, whatever their backgrounds. That does not make her a snob. How could she be, living with Leonard? He would not even allow her to contribute a miniature manuscript to the Queen's Dolls House; and she, of her own volition, refused all decorations throughout her life. Of course she was class-conscious. She felt herself to be different in degree and kind from "the London poor, half drunk and very sentimental or completely stolid with their hideous voices and clothes and bad teeth" (987). But, equally, she disliked members of the upper classes who had no other merit except their birth, usually avoided their company, and despised their self-approbation. "I don't think them worth a damn", she wrote. And elsewhere: "They laugh at the things one cares about." They were "amateurish", unserious, even the Souls, the group of young aristocrats with intellectual interests which flourished before the First War. She would go occasionally to their parties:

"I've been meeting your friends, the Bibesco's. . . . I said all the most impossible things in a very loud voice; abused Lady Glenconner, and

1. E. M. Forster, Rede Lecture, Cambridge 1942.

then attacked Rupert Brooke: but at my age and with my habits, how conform to the way of the world? Hair pins dropped steadily into my soup plate: I gave them a lick, and put them in again." (To Molly MacCarthy. 4 December 1919.)

Unless one made some such gesture of defiance, one would be corrupted. Clive Bell she forgave for his socialising, because it amused her. But when Lytton Strachey allowed himself to be lionised, and even more when he was seen to enjoy it, she despaired.

When Katherine Mansfield told Middleton Murry that *Night and Day* "reeks of intellectual snobbery", she was nearer the mark. Here is one young man (Rodney) talking in the novel to another (Henry) about the delights of county society. Henry remarks that he had no wish to mix in it. "Oh but you should," replies Rodney. "They make one very comfortable, and the women are ravishing." Virginia goes on: "'The women', Henry thought to himself with disgust. . . . He could not help liking Rodney . . . [but] such words in another's mouth would have condemned the speaker irreparably." Why? Did Virginia believe that young men (or at any rate the young men with whom she would care to associate) never talked about girls when they were alone together? It is fastidiousness carried to intolerable lengths, the streak of puritanism which made her think Katherine Mansfield's sexual unscrupulousness fascinating but abhorrent, and at first reject *Ulysses* as "merely the scratching of pimples on the body of the bootboy at Claridges" (1277). But her attitude was not consistent. In her letters she could make scatological jokes of shocking nastiness, and flay the characters of her friends. Clive Bell called her "one of the best-bred women of her age". Sometimes she could be: sometimes.

Was she by nature unkind? In a memorial article about Virginia, Vita Sackville-West drew attention to the suitability of her married name: "Tenuousness and purity were in her baptismal name, and a hint of the fang in the other." When the fang showed, it could be merciless. About Will Arnold-Forster she wrote: "His little mongrel cur's body; his face appears powdered and painted like a very refined old suburban harlots; and his ridiculous little voice." About Sydney Waterlow: "My God! What a sight he looked bathing! like Neptune, if Neptune was a eunuch—without any hairs, and sky pink—fresh, virginal, soft." About Middleton Murry: "A posturing Byronic little man; pale; penetrating; with bad teeth; histrionic; an egoist; not, I think, very honest; but a good journalist, and works like a horse, and writes the poetry a very old hack might write." And those are not the worst examples in this volume. These fiendish opinions were not always confided to intimates. The first was written to Vanessa and the third to Janet Case; but the second (on Waterlow) she wrote to Carrington. Virginia often added the caveat, "This mustn't be repeated", but of course it always was. It was the same in conversation. Virginia came to be known among her friends (Quentin Bell thinks unfairly) as a security risk.

In her defence Leonard said to William Plomer after her death: "How can anybody with high critical standards fail to censure what seems trashy, trite, false or pretentious?" But her censoriousness went further than that. She enjoyed retailing harmful gossip, and in writing to one person, she would exaggerate the mental or physical deformities of another to whom she might be writing flatteringly by the same post. Sydney Waterlow was particularly vulnerable to this treatment, and few of Virginia's friends were totally immune. "Why", she jokingly asked Margaret Llewelyn Davies, "why is it so pleasant to damn one's friends?" She excused herself by telling Waterlow that it was 'her method', Bloomsbury's instinctive hyperbole. She did not mean the cutting things she wrote and said. Her opinion of people could fluctuate wildly, guided as much by the mood of the moment or an irresistible phrase as by her considered judgement. Ottoline Morrell is "like the Spanish Armada in full sail" in one letter, and "a foundered cab-horse" in the next. Indeed, her view of Ottoline is the best example of 'the method'. Virginia could not withhold admiration for her magnificence and courage, for her ability to remain afloat in the storms she generated at Garsington and in Bedford Square. Ottoline was an obvious target for Virginia's ridicule—flamboyant, rich, witch-like, a hunter of lions without the knack of taming them. But she had "an invincible spirit", "fundamental integrity", "an element of the superb", and these tributes come nearer to Virginia's true opinion of this remarkable woman than the mocking fantasies with which she amused herself at Ottoline's expense.

Let me place the 'Virginia' in her character alongside the 'Wolf'. She dropped only one close friend, Madge Vaughan, and only because Madge's husband was hostile towards Bloomsbury. She continued to correspond quite regularly with people like Violet Dickinson and Ka Arnold-Forster long after their ways had diverged. She never failed to answer a letter, and answer it in a manner that would give most pleasure, particularly if a friend were ill or in distress. She offered the love-lorn like Saxon Sydney-Turner the best of advice and consolation. Her bread-and-butter letters were so generous and charming that they risked a repetition of the invitation, just for the sake of receiving another. She was delightful to her new young acquaintances of the 1917 Club—Barbara Hiles, Carrington, David Garnett, Nick Bagenal, Gerald Brenan. In practical matters, too, she stood up valiantly for her friends. There was her intervention with the Cecils on behalf of Duncan Grant, which could have cost her Nelly's friendship. She supported the fund for Lytton Strachey to make him financially independent of journalism; and took the lead in another, for T. S. Eliot, young, American and unknown, when he was wasting his genius in Lloyd's Bank.

The most striking example of her concern for others—but this is about Vanessa—is the letter which she wrote to her cousin Dorothea Stephen on

28 October 1921. Dorothea had expressed disapproval of Vanessa's way of life, and asked to meet Virginia. Replying, Virginia discarded her pen for a flame-thrower: "I entirely sympathise with Vanessa's views and conduct.... If after this you like to come, by all means do, and I will risk not only my own morals but my cook's." Vanessa is the central figure of this volume, apart from Virginia herself: even more than Leonard. She was more than a sister. She was a mother too. There are scattered phrases in Virginia's letters to her which would fascinate a psychologist: "Why did you bring me into the world?" (1169); and elsewhere (1000) she describes herself as Vanessa's "first-born". Virginia's intimacy with her nephews and niece was not only a compensation for her own childlessness. She was one of them. She shared Vanessa with them. To Virginia Vanessa was a goddess, pagan but "with a natural piety"; a madonna capable of bawdiness; sometimes mysteriously withdrawn, but vigorous, splendid, iconoclastic. She could be Diana of the Ephesians: she could be Moll Flanders. Mute though she is in these pages, her personality is reflected by Virginia's letters as the sun is by a shield. She was a painter, and Virginia learned to understand painting through her eyes. She lived among the Sussex Downs, and shared their grandeur and serenity. But Virginia's version of her sister, as Angelica Garnett wrote so well,

> tended to soar into the Olympian regions, where she subconsciously felt that Nessa belonged. Like a highly coloured transparency held over the original design, sometimes it corresponded, sometimes not. . . . Vanessa's strength lay in her closeness to reality, to the everyday world. By comparison with Virginia she was calm, like a pool in which the coloured leaves slowly change their pattern. She accepted, rather than protested; was passive, rather than avid. She did not care deeply about abstract ideas, and was led by her sensibilities rather than her intellect. . . . Even if she said little, there emanated from her an enormous power, a pungency like the smell of crushed sage.[1]

Between 1912 and 1922 the record of the Woolfs' achievement is deeply impressive. Nearly three of those years were stolen from them by Virginia's illnesses and slow convalescence, and four were years of war. Leonard remade his life with nothing but the capital of his intelligence. He was an ex-colonial civil servant who had resigned in mid-career (for no other reason than his love for Virginia), without money, job, prospects, or friends in high places. Ten years later he was the acknowledged Labour expert on imperial and international affairs, on Co-operation and several branches of economics; he had published four political books and two novels, besides many pam-

1. Angelica Garnett in *Recollections of Virginia Woolf.* Edited by Joan Russel Noble. 1972.

phlets, translations and articles; he had edited, or helped to edit, three reviews; he had founded the Hogarth Press; he stood for Parliament.

Virginia's achievement was no less remarkable. Her bouts of manic-depression were interspersed by recurrent illnesses which presaged another. For months on end she lay in bed apprehensive and incapable of work. Her normal day was interrupted by domestic chores and crises, by unwelcome visitors, by the demands of the Hogarth Press. Yet she found time to revise one major novel, *The Voyage Out*, and write two more, *Night and Day* and *Jacob's Room*. For several years she wrote an almost weekly review for *The Times Literary Supplement*, unsigned and therefore unacknowledged except by very few, as well as many articles for other journals, all of a quality only attainable by a writer of great original gifts who is determined to let nothing pass, even anonymously, with which she was not satisfied. On top of all this, she led, when health allowed her, a scintillating social life, and wrote (from 1917 onwards) a regular diary and several personal letters a day. Yet she rarely complained of the pressure on her time, was seldom too exhausted by the day's work to face an evening's party. "I was aware", said Elizabeth Bowen,[1] "of an undertow often of sadness, of melancholy, of great fear. But the main impression was of a creature of laughter and movement." She was not indefatigable: but her resilience was astounding.

The most unexpected and fruitful of their joint-enterprises was the founding of the Hogarth Press. It was a bold decision. There was no necessity to load on their overburdened lives this additional encumbrance. If Virginia needed physical and mental relaxation, she could walk, or skate, or ride, and she did all three. While Leonard was a natural organiser, he was not a natural mechanic, as the crude early products of the Press testify. If the constant trembling of his hands decided the Army Medical Board that he was quite unfit to manage a rifle, still less was he capable of sorting tiny strips of lead and arranging them to form words on the printer's rule. Virginia, and later Barbara Hiles and Ralph Partridge, must do this work for him, while he 'machined'. The work was exhausting and distracted them from other things, although it was recuperative in the sense that it was absorbing and constructive, and Virginia enjoyed it. The whole venture was at first precariously unsound. They had no capital. Their office was their house: their printer's bench the dining-room table. They had no experience of producing or selling books, at first no salesmen except themselves, and the books they intended to publish were in any case almost unsaleable.

Yet it succeeded. It succeeded to such an extent that the story of the Hogarth Press is still one of the legends of publishing. The explanation lies in Leonard's determination, and in their choice of books. Their list proclaims their flair: 1917, *Two Stories*, by Leonard and Virginia; 1918, *Prelude*, by

1. In the BBC television film about Virginia Woolf, *A Night's Darkness, A Day's Sail.*

Katherine Mansfield; 1919, *Poems*, by T. S. Eliot; *Kew Gardens*, by Virginia; *Critic in Judgment*, by J. Middleton Murry; 1920, *Story of the Siren*, by E. M. Forster. Those were their first six books, all by authors (except Forster) then quite unknown to the wide public. Virginia was the chief talent-scout, recklessly imploring her friends to send her their verse and prose. They could have secured *Ulysses*. They did secure *The Waste Land*, and, later, Freud. Of course there were mistakes and strains. Leonard was a difficult man to work with, and often mean, while Virginia was obliged to spend hours of her time reading other people's manuscripts when she wanted to write her own. More than once they thought of abandoning it, but periodically their ambition soared. They would start a bookshop in a spare room of Hogarth House. They would open a combined bookshop, tearoom, and picture gallery in Bond Street. These day-dreams remained unsubstantiated.

Virginia's letters, as many as six a day, were written with affection, literary pleasure, and curiosity. "Life would split asunder without letters", she wrote in *Jacob's Room*. Her motives were to maintain, repair and extend her friendships, to nail the fleeting idea, to appeal for news and gossip. Her correspondence was lubricated by the rapidity of the posts, in both directions. She could not read a provocative phrase, no more than she could hear one, without wishing to retort immediately. She varied her approach from one person to another. In writing to Lytton Strachey, she gave rein to more malice; to Roger Fry, more deference; to Saxon Sydney-Turner, more affection; to Margaret Llewelyn Davies, more teasing respect. But for everybody the elements of her style were mixed. Its dominant note was banter, for she would seldom write seriously about serious things, far less than in her diary, and least of all about her own books. Her letter about *Jacob's Room* to Gerald Brenan (25 December 1922) is a rare exception, and perhaps she only brought herself to write it because she did not know him very well, because he was young, because he lived in Spain, and because it was Christmas Day.

So behind this frothing stream of written talk is quite a different Virginia Woolf. She was attempting the most difficult of intellectual exercises, to give an art a new form, "to create character without realism", as she explained it to Duncan Grant. E. M. Forster said retrospectively in his Rede Lecture that her friends were "tremendously surprised" by *Jacob's Room*. Her letters and conversation and first two novels had prepared them for her brilliant gifts of observation, her juxtaposition of detail. As one might return from a country walk with a handful of wild flowers and arrange them in a vase, neatly, to create something significant and beautiful out of a jumble, so Virginia could collect sights, sounds, smells and snatches of talk, and put them on a page before they died. What her friends did not expect was her discovery of the importance of "the things one doesn't say", of her deliberate lacunae—as when, on the last page, Jacob's death in battle is suggested only by the objects left lying about his room, and the delineation of his character less by his own words or Virginia's, than by the shapes formed around it by the behaviour of other people. The same might be said of her letters. She gives only part of herself to anybody. The lacunae are enormous. "There's the question of things happening, normally, all the time": too many, and some too private, to be explored.

Nigel Nicolson
Sissinghurst Castle, Kent

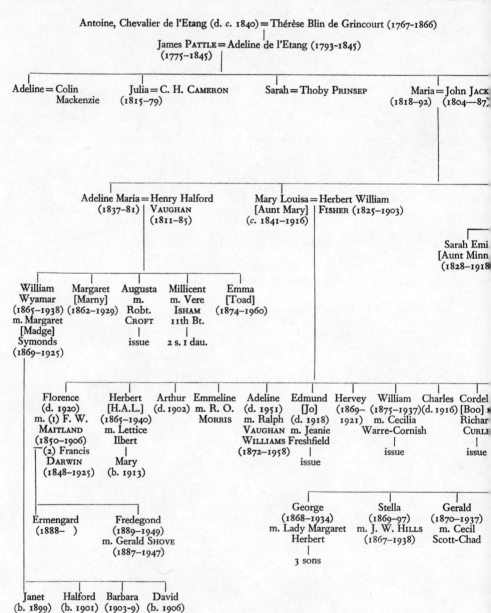

Based upon the Family Tree in Quentin Bell, Vol. I.

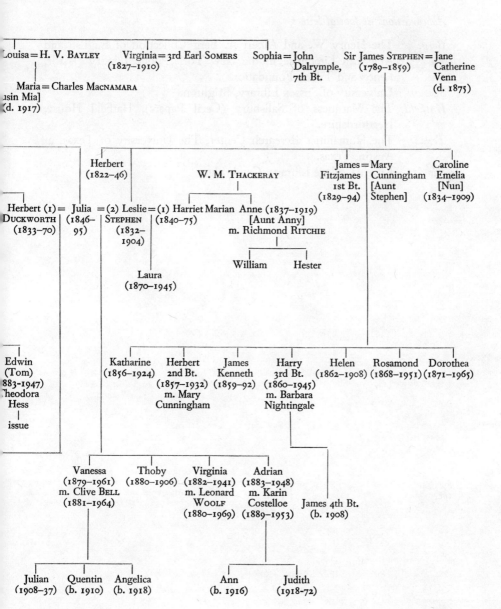

Louisa = H. V. BAYLEY   Virginia = 3rd Earl SOMERS   Sophia = John   Sir James STEPHEN = Jane
             (1827–1910)   Dalrymple, (1789–1859) Catherine
                                         7th Bt.   Venn
  Maria = Charles MacNAMARA   (d. 1875)
usin Mia]
(d. 1917)

Herbert   James = Mary   Caroline
(1822–46)   W. M. THACKERAY   Fitzjames | Cunningham Emelia
                                       1st Bt. [Aunt   [Nun]
Herbert (1) = Julia = (2) Leslie = (1) Harriet Marian Anne (1837–1919) (1829–94) Stephen] (1834–1909)
DUCKWORTH | (1846–‖ STEPHEN | (1840–75)   [Aunt Anny]
(1833–70)   95)   (1832–   m. Richmond RITCHIE
              1904)
                                       William   Hester
                  Laura
                (1870–1945)

Edwin
(Tom)   Katharine Herbert   James   Harry   Helen   Rosamond Dorothea
883-1947) (1856–1924) 2nd Bt.   Kenneth 3rd Bt. (1862–1908) (1868–1951) (1871–1965)
Theodora   (1857–1932) (1859–92) (1860–1945)
Hess   m. Mary   m. Barbara
issue   Cunningham   Nightingale

           Vanessa   Thoby   Virginia   Adrian
          (1879–1961) (1880–1906) (1882–1941) (1883–1948)
          m. Clive BELL   m. Leonard m. Karin
          (1881–1964)   WOOLF   Costelloe James 4th Bt.
                              (1880–1969) (1889–1953) (b. 1908)

Julian   Quentin Angelica   Ann   Judith
(1908–37) (b. 1910) (b. 1918)   (b. 1916) (1918–72)

Abbreviations at foot of letters

Berg: The Henry W. and Albert A. Berg Collection of English and American Literature in the New York Public Library (Astor, Lenox and Tilden Foundations).

Sussex: University of Sussex Library, Brighton.

Hatfield: The Marquess of Salisbury (Cecil Papers), Hatfield House, Hertfordshire.

Texas: The Humanities Research Center, The University of Texas, at Austin, Texas.

King's: King's College Library, Cambridge.

Letters 639-656 (August–December 1912)

Virginia Stephen married Leonard Woolf on 10 August 1912, at a registry office in London. A day or two later they went for the first part of their honeymoon to stay at a village inn in Somerset, and then to France, Spain and Italy. They were abroad for six weeks. Both had finished writing their first novels (Virginia's was The Voyage Out *and Leonard's* The Village in the Jungle*), but Leonard's future was uncertain, and they had not decided where to live on their return to England on 3 October. Temporarily they stayed at 38 Brunswick Square, Bloomsbury, where both had lived before their marriage, but soon moved to Clifford's Inn, off the Strand, spending some weekends at Asheham, Virginia's house near Lewes, Sussex. She resumed her reviews for* The Times Literary Supplement, *while Leonard took a temporary job at the Grafton Galleries as Secretary to the Second Post-Impressionist Exhibition, organised by Roger Fry.*

639: To Clive Bell   38 *Brunswick Square, W.C.*

[13 August 1912]

Dearest Clive,

Your letter made a great deal of difference to both of us.[1]

I dont think its only vanity that makes me glad that you should care—No, its because I do care for you that I want you to sympathise, and I can only say again you cant think how happy your letter has made me.

Leonard sends his love.

Ever your affectionate

V.W.

Quentin Bell

640: To Janet Case   38 *Brunswick Square, W.C.*

Tuesday [13 August 1912]

My dear Janet,

Its quite the nicest present I've yet had. I couldn't make out who had sent it and suddenly thought how cruelly I had misjudged some cousins living in Kent, which was the postmark. Then I found your letter and under-

---

1. Clive had written to Virginia immediately after her marriage: "You must believe that, in spite of all my craziness, I love you very much, and that I love your lover too."

I

stood the mystery. But how you found such a wonderfully beautiful brooch, and where it comes from I should very much like to know. Do remember to tell me. I've been wearing it all day. The box too is a most charming box for it—and who made that?

Well, I'm married—married since Saturday. We went down to Asheham and now we're staying the night here on our way through to Somersetshire. There we sit in the sun for a few days, and then go to Spain and Italy.

Please tell Emphie [Janet's sister] that she must get perfectly well without delay, because I want to bring my husband to see her, and have even been so bold as to promise him an egg with his tea.

How are you? I wish you were as happy as I am—and its quite clear that I shall never be ill again because with Leonard I get no chance!

It really was delightful of you to give me that brooch. Oh, if you could have seen the one that Margaret Duckworth[1] gave me! still unthanked for— a red and green crescent of precious stones!

Yrs affate
Virginia Woolf

Leonard asks me to send you his love and might you not by a stretch of boldness call him Leonard?

Sussex

641: TO LYTTON STRACHEY   [*Holford, Somerset*]

Postcard
[16 August 1912]

Here we are in the middle of divine country, literary associations, cream for every meal, but cold as Christmas and steady rain.

Leonard is learning Spanish and I am reading the Heir of Redcliffe.[2] We go to France on Sunday—I will send addresses.

Love to Henry.[3]

V.W.

Who lived at Alfoxton?[4]

Frances Hooper

1. Lady Margaret Herbert, who had married George Duckworth, Virginia's half-brother, in 1904.
2. The romantic novel by Charlotte Yonge, which was published in 1853.
3. Lytton was travelling through Scotland and Ireland with Henry Lamb, the painter.
4. On the reverse side of the postcard there was a picture of Alfoxton House, Holford, where William and Dorothy Wordsworth stayed in 1797 and 1798, while Coleridge was living nearby at Nether Stowey.

The Plough Inn, Holford, Somerset

Aug 17th [1912]

My Dearest Ottoline,

The great red cover came just before we left—it is most splendid. Whatever glum we get into, it will light up, and give us delight till the end of our days. Thank you again and again. Its the kind of thing one never gets tired of, or ceases to enjoy.

We were married on the 10th—quite suddenly, as Nessa and Clive wanted to be there, and they were going away. It was done in a Registry Office, in the intervals of a thunderstorm; the storm has practically never stopped, and we are sitting over a fire at this moment in the middle of the Quantock hills. But we are both as happy as we can be—at least I am—I suppose one oughtn't to say that of ones husband—but I think we do get an enormous amount of pleasure out of being together. On Sunday we go to Avignon,—snow storms are in the South, I hear.

Thank you again, and please believe—but that sounds conceited—I mean, I wish you would understand how very fond I am of you.

Your affectionate

Texas   Virginia Woolf

The Plough Inn, Holford, Somerset

[17 August 1912]

My dear Janet,

I meant to send you this [see postscript], but forgot.

Its really a very good way to be married—very simple and soon done. You stand up and repeat two sentences, and then sign your name. Nothing went wrong, the only disturbance was about Vanessa and Virginia, which the registrar, who was half blind and otherwise deformed, mixed hopelessly and Nessa upset him worse by suddenly deciding to change her son's name from Quentin to Christopher.

It thundered all the time, but we enjoyed it all. Afterwards there was a very odd lunch party—George and Gerald [Duckworth] in frock coats looking very suspiciously at Duncan [Grant], and an odd little painter,[1] who came in, and could only talk about pawning clothes. I suppose one oughtn't to enjoy one's wedding, but I did, and I enjoy the honeymoon even more. We've seen nothing of the Quantocks, except great shapes of mist, but we've walked to the top of them, and now we sit over a fire and read novels like

1. Frederick Etchells, who exhibited at the second Post-Impressionist Exhibition in 1912.

tigers. Now that we've done our own[1] its great fun to read other people's. Its not stopped raining once, I think since we came: tomorrow we cross to France, where there are snowstorms, so we see, and then we go on to Spain and Italy.

We are in treaty for rooms in Kings Bench Walk [Inner Temple]; but its uncertain whether we can get them, and anyhow we start for a week or two at Brunswick Square. Its great fun making plans, and we expect to be enormously busy, and never to have a real house. One was lent us with 5 servants,[2] which depressed us so that we have made this vow.

Leonard* instructs the world upon scientific management;[3] I think he's a fraud, but no one seems to know anything. My name is really *Woolf*, only to shops I shall be the ordinary animal, because its simpler.

What adventures my brooch had! But I'm very glad it survived so triumphantly.

Now I must get my husband to pack my box for me.

Yr aff.   V.W.

[*in Leonard's handwriting*]* Virginia says I'm to say that I'm not. She is just dropping off to sleep in a chair in front of the fire or possibly she might say so herself.

[*in Virginia's handwriting*] What I meant to send was the notice of our wedding in St Pancras Registry Office, but now I cant find it. If you ever want a most comfortable Inn, delicious food, cream for every meal, quite cheap, come here. Please take a holiday some time.

Sussex

644: To Lytton Strachey   *Tarragona [Spain]*

Sept. 1st 1912

Dear Lytton,

    I wonder if you got a card written at the beginning of our tour, from the

---

1. Before their marriage Virginia had completed, apart from revision, her first novel, *The Voyage Out*; and Leonard, his novel about Ceylon, *The Village in the Jungle*.
2. Possibly Lady Ritchie's house in St George's Square, London. She was the elder daughter of W. M. Thackeray, who had married Sir Richmond Ritchie in 1877. Or Dalingridge Place, Sussex, which belonged to Virginia's half-brother, George Duckworth.
3. Leonard published a series of articles on this subject in 1912, principally reviews of American books in the *Economic Journal* and *Co-operative News*.

1 Leonard and Virginia Woolf in 1912

2a Asheham House, Lewes, Sussex

b Hogarth House, Richmond from the garden. The right-hand half was Hogarth House, the left-hand Suffield House. The basement of Hogarth House served first as an air-raid shelter, and later as the printing-room of The Hogarth Press

home of Coleridge and Southey?[1] That is now remembered by us chiefly for its leg of mutton. We've travelled far, and beef has become mutton, chicken partridge—I should hardly know now if you gave me pork to eat. This is a sad state of things only balanced by the beauties of nature and the antiquities of man, upon which I would discourse if you would listen, but to tell the truth it is the food one thinks of more than anything abroad. When I tell you that the W.C. opposite our room has not been emptied for 3 days, and you can there distinguish the droppings of Christian, Jew, Latin and Saxon—you can imagine the rest. This is Tarragona; we go on to Madrid, and from Madrid to Venice. Our habits are simple; 2 days in a place, one day in a train; we walk in the morning, read in the afternoon, make our tea, which is the point we have just passed, then walk on the sea-shore; and after dinner sit by a café, and, as its Sunday tonight, listen to the military band. Several times the proper business of bed has been interrupted by mosquitoes. They bloody the wall by morning—they always choose my left eye, Leonard's right ear. Whatever position they chance to find us in. This does not sound to you a happy life, I know; but you see, that in between the crevices we stuff an enormous amount of exciting conversation—also literature. My God! You can't think with what a fury we fall on printed matter, so long denied us by our own writing! I read 3 new novels in two days: Leonard waltzed through the Old Wives Tale like a kitten after its tail: after this giddy career I have now run full tilt into Crime et Châtiment, fifty pages before tea, and I see there are only 800; so I shall be through in no time. It is directly obvious that he [Dostoievsky] is the greatest writer ever born: and if he chooses to become horrible what will happen to us? Honeymoon completely dashed. If he says it—human hope—had better end, what will be left but suicide in the Grand Canal. Have you been writing about him?

As you can imagine, we mean to be very various and active in the winter. Just about this moment, you're settling down over the fire, having returned from a brisk walk among the Scotch firs in a Scotch mist, and saying (something I can't spell—it's French) to the effect that life holds nothing but copulation, after which you groan from the profundities of the stomach, which reminds you that there is venison?—partridge? mutton?—for dinner, whereupon you take down Pope, your pocket copy, and proceed for the 150th time to read . . ., when the bell rings and the sandy haired girl, whom you wish was a boy, says "Dinner on the table". . . whereas I'm just off to walk by the shores of the Mediterranean, by the beams of the dying sun, which is still hot enough to make a cotton dress and a parasol necessary, while the military band plays the Barcarolle from Hoffman's Tales, and the naked boys run like snipe along the beach, balancing their buttocks in the pellucid air.

1. In 1794 Coleridge and Robert Southey (who married sisters) stayed together at Nether Stowey, and in 1798, when Coleridge and the Wordsworths were living in the district, Southey visited them from Bristol.

Please write to Brunswick Square: all the news; we've not seen an Englishman, or heard of London for a fortnight.

Leonard sends love.

Yrs.
V.W.

Frances Hooper

645: To Katherine Cox
Zara_zoga—Saragossa,
[Spain]

Sept 4th [1912]

My dear Bruin,

It seems to me about time that you took a pen in your paw and wrote to me. I find it more and more difficult to put myself in your position, not I hope on account of the encroachments of marriage—I don't condescend so far do I?—but because our climate has so completely changed. It is now 17 days since I have seen a cloud or a drop of water, other than man-made water. Whereas, when I wrote to an Aunt at Huntingdon [Lady Stephen], hoping that her rheumatism was better, she replied, "We leave the house in barges". It is true that she is very fat, but can it be possible?

I've not heard, practically, from any sane person since we went away. However, my State is independent of accurate news; we go from town to town, investigating the back streets and the rivers and the market places, wandering along the avenues at night until we find a place to drink at. We've seen 10 towns since we started; they get steadily more remarkable and highly coloured. This is certainly the best country I've ever seen, and we have it to ourselves. Finally we shall come out upon the coast and take a ship to Italy. I need hardly say that we talk a great deal; what is more remarkable is that we read with fury, having denied ourselves books until our novels were done. Had that thunderclap reached you—they are done? But at this very moment Leonard sits on a red plush chair about 6 feet away from me, opposite him my open box with drawers hanging out, and a handsome cupboard by his side, writing the first chapter of his new great work, which is about the suburbs.[1] I have thrown aside Crime and Punishment to write to you, having already read the Antiquary [Scott], Trespassers, Yonder,[2] the Heir of Redcliffe [Yonge], not all this afternoon, but since I lost my virginity.

Why do you think people make such a fuss about marriage and copulation? Why do some of our friends change upon losing chastity? Possibly my great age makes it less of a catastrophe; but certainly I find the climax immensely exaggerated. Except for a sustained good humour (Leonard shan't

1. His second novel, *The Wise Virgins*, which was published in 1914.
2. *The Trespassers* by D. H. Lawrence, and *Yonder* by Emily Hilda Young, were both published in this year.

see this) due to the fact that every twinge of anger is at once visited upon my husband, I might be still Miss S.

This is all very egoistical—I think I shall take another sheet however, from Leonard's novel, and begin it by saying what have you been doing, where are you, what are your plans? I heard of you last riding alone with Maynard.[1] No: being in Spain does not make me love him better.

I can't help supposing that you have been supporting James [Strachey] intermittently, and tending incipient paralytics, and telling Margaret [Ka Cox's sister] how to be honest with young Stockbrokers.

Leonard and I, I need hardly say, have a bees-nest of plans and theories in our heads; people in London found us a bore before we married. How I come back to egoism again. We have not let my two rooms. Being so far away, we feel helpless, and turn to you, not to do anything in particular, but if you could keep this in mind, please do. Possibly there are people coming down from Cambridge? Anyhow, we don't mean to stay longer in Brunswick than is necessary to find rooms. We may get some in the Temple. But we are both determined that to go back to joint life[2] would be impossible.

Do write when you get this, and if you send it to Brunswick Square there is a beetle headed woman living in the basement who forwards our things.

Leonard here looks up from his composition and sends his love; Come and see us about the 5th of October.

Yr V.W.

Mark Arnold-Forster

646: To Saxon Sydney-Turner   *Hotel Nettuno, Pisa*

17th Sept 1912

My dear Saxon,

I opened the enclosed letter, which was sent on here, having been returned to Brunswick Square by Frau Kanoldt.[3] As Adrian told me to write to Brunswick Square, I cant do anything further with it. Perhaps by this time he has sent them some address.

We have reached Pisa in our wanderings. We came up the coast of Spain in a little rusty iron ship[4] about the size of a large walrus; where I was sick,

1. In July and August Maynard Keynes had stayed with several friends, including Ka Cox and Rupert Brooke, at Everleigh on Salisbury Plain.
2. Before her marriage Virginia had shared 38 Brunswick Square with her brother Adrian, Maynard Keynes, Duncan Grant and Leonard himself.
3. Adrian Stephen was in Munich with James Strachey, and Frau Kanoldt was probably his landlady there.
4. A Hungarian cargo boat, in which they were the only passengers. They travelled in her from Valencia to Marseilles.

but Leonard triumphed, and we ate our meals off a packing case in our cabin
—sprats arranged in the form of a star with yellow oil for sauce.

I read Crime and Punishment, and Le Rouge and Le Noir. At Valencia I
found a really well printed edition, the first volume enchanted me but the
second hangs a little heavy. Is this as it should be?

The only fault we have to find with our journey is that it was a great deal
too hot at Madrid and Toledo, and that these southern skies are too invariably
blue. Occasionally we get an old copy of the Times, and there read of floods
and cloudbursts.

I think Spain is far the most magnificent country I have ever seen—and
we are planning the purchase of a great Spanish mule; if we had one, Leonard
thinks we could ride across it. The mule would carry our beds, and run
behind. We are both starved for music—have to trail about after town
bands.

We are now going out to see some pictures—

I hope your Sciatica is better.

Yours V.W.

Leonard sends his love, and thanks you for your letter.

Sussex

647: TO MOLLY MACCARTHY   *Casa Biondetti, Venice*
     FROM LEONARD WOOLF

28th Sept. 1912

My Dear Molly,

Virginia is very lazy, she's lying on a sofa eating chocolates and
reading and looking at pictures, including her own portrait, in the Strand
Magazine. She ought to be writing to you, but as I'm sure she won't before
tea, I'm doing it for her.

I'm very sorry you're giving up Hoxton in a way, though really I don't
much believe in that work after what I saw of it. Miss Booth wrote and asked
me to become Secretary but I had to refuse as I don't know yet what I shall
be doing or whether I'd have any time for it.[1]

I have, I believe, a considerable knowledge of your character, and one of
its characteristics is curiosity. Therefore if Virginia were writing this letter
she'd probably try to satisfy it. As I'm writing for her, have I got to try to do
the same? The first question you want to know about is how we get on

1. Imogen Booth, a daughter of Charles Booth, author of *Life and Labour of the
   People in London*, was working for the Charity Organisation Society in Hoxton,
   London.

together. I believe you'd rather have Virginia's version than mine, but there's no chance of your getting that today. I don't feel like a married man which I think is a good test of happiness. I believe it would be far easier to satisfy your curiosity, if the opposite were true and we had quarrelled and bored one another. It would be so much more amusing—but after all, you don't want to hear that I'm sorry we've got to be back in London next Thursday and that it's as pleasant to be with Virginia in the furnace of Spain as in the rain and biting wind of the Grand Canal of Venice. I never of course really did expect to be able to satisfy your curiosity.

We haven't yet got anywhere to go except two rooms in Brunswick Sq. But we hope to get rooms in the Temple and live a nomadic life. I expect you'll think that rather silly—but I hope when I die like a good Jew at 70 I shall still have no home.

Well, I'm now going to give Virginia her tea. She's made the great discovery that one can drink both tea and chocolate and coffee at the same time as buttered toast, cakes and ices for tea! I also benefit by this discovery.

L.S.W.

[in Virginia's handwriting]
Many thanks for your letter which was a great pleasure—though rather a shock too. I've finished the Strand Magazine and read Pendennis [Thackeray]. Like the letters of all married people, this is doomed to insincerity— However, I'm . . . That describes my state of mind. Very well. We've talked incessantly for 7 weeks, and become chronically nomadic and monogamic.

Yr. V.W.

Mrs Michael MacCarthy

648: To Violet Dickinson   38 *Brunswick Sqre, W.C.*

[9? October 1912]

My Violet,
   Yesterday, happening to go into one of the bachelor sitting rooms, I discovered a cradle, fit for the illegitimate son of an Empress. When I brought forth my theory however, they fathered the cradle on me. I blushed, disclaimed any intention and so on; and blushing leant my elbow on a table. "What a beautiful table this is anyhow!" I exclaimed, thinking to lead the conversation away from my lost virginity and the probable fruits of it. The table was disclaimed too. Bit by bit I pieced together the story—how a great packing case had arrived, how Miss Dickinson etc etc. Nobody but Miss Dickinson could deal with the facts of life so boldly of course. Nobody else ever routed old shops to such effect. My baby shall sleep in the cradle; I'm going to eat my dinner off the table tonight.

   We got back almost a week ago, and I begin to wonder if marriage is a sin, and makes one's friends not speak to one. You might write—I'm here

9

interrupted to unpack a golden cross, once belonging to Mrs Lushington[1]—weren't you supposed to be the Second? We had a splendid holiday—Spain, France, Italy. Now we're on the verge of moving into rooms in Cliffords Inn, I think; just off the Strand, but quiet, and a char will do for us. My husband sends his love—rather forward.

Yr VSW

Berg

649: To Violet Dickinson   38 *Brunswick Sq*, [*W.C.*]

[29? October 1912]

My Violet,

When will the presents cease? What other operation of nature can you provide for? Anyhow, we shall drink out of your glasses to the end of our lives, so long as we have a table to stand them on. They are perfect.

At this moment we are on the eve of our move to Cliffords Inn. I look forward to a week of intense misery, two weeks of profound discomfort, and finally, about Christmas, absolute happiness. Really our rooms are very nice. There's a little patch of green for my brats to play in; and a porter and a bedmaker, like a Cambridge College. I suppose you dont know of a bachelor wanting a charming bed room and sitting room, with service good coal and light for £150 a year? We're very anxious to let my rooms. Leonard spends his afternoons at the Grafton Galleries[2]—I'm writing hard.

I hope to see you—but in the present state of dissolution dont see what to suggest.

Yr Sp[arroy]

which is why I enclose this sheet [an announcement of the Post-Impressionist Exhibition].

Berg

650: To Emma Vaughan   13 *Cliffords Inn, E.C.*

30th Oct. [1912]

Dearest Toad,

All my nicest presents have come at the end, and yours is most lovely.

1. Wife of Vernon Lushington, K.C., and mother of Virginia's friends Susan and Kitty (Maxse). Mrs Lushington had died in 1884, and Vernon Lushington in January 1912. Violet Dickinson never married.
2. Roger Fry had invited Leonard to be Secretary of the second Post-Impressionist Exhibition.

Where did you get the beautiful pattern? I can hardly imagine the state of skill needed to produce it. I shall certainly wear it with great pride. We are just moving into these rooms and in such a state of chaos that I can hardly write. However, we hope to be straight in about a week and I hope soon you'll come and see us. It's the next turning after Chancery Lane. Thank you again.

Your loving,
V.W.

Sussex

651: To Katherine Cox   13 *Cliffords Inn, E.C.*

[November? 1912]

Dear Bruin,

As you can imagine it took me about 20 minutes to discover your note—then look on the floor. When I did I was in a state of keen joy—and at once fastened the embroideries first to a table, then a sofa, finally to our 2 arm chairs. Desmond [MacCarthy] chancing to come in, I put him against the purple one; my Jew had the one with the green border. I never saw two more handsome men. They are lovely—the embroideries, and in the daylight they will be better still. My life as you know is one long agony of emulation and envy, and I've already had the joy of hearing my rooms praised—very highly, more highly than Nessa's; on account of your present.

I came in 2 minutes I daresay after you went waddling across London with about 6 parcels—3 mutton cutlets, eggs, a cake, and a pound of potatoes. We had dinner in tonight off these, but I see that cutlets must be hung before eating, and the heart stays blooded long after the outside is brown. Karin[1] came to lunch, old Cousins half way through the afternoon, so I was late in going out, and thus missed Bru Cox; but she might name another day.

The world offers so much to say that I really can't even touch upon it in the remaining space especially as the geyser is alight.

Our servant shows extreme merit in not minding the sight of us naked which she has every morning. Indeed this is the kind of thing I hear. "And your husband, Mrs Worsley—now what Society is he insured in?"—"A postman? O well—they must give him a rise then after 5 years, in the Naval Reserve too"—and all this with Leonard naked in his bath—Mrs W. leaning on the W.C. door looking at him.

Yr. V.W.

Mark Arnold-Forster

1. Karin Costelloe, who married Adrian Stephen in October 1915.

[November 1912]

Dearest Mongoose,

Nothing has happened, I need hardly say—except a considerable amount of ferretting in the woods. Shot [dog] was taken out this morning—reeking of ointment. We were in fear of burglars last night, owing to the mysterious apparition of two lanterns among the trees late at night.

Were you very cold and uncomfortable? I've been reading the Village in the J.[ungle] which seems to me amazingly good. I hope Lytton insists upon publication, or at any rate puts some clear course before you.

I enclose a letter, which was sent with a pamphlet, for you. Quite cracked. Ka [Cox] and I stitch, gossip, grumble, as you can imagine. I read her article last night, which is very inarticulate and makes me think there's more in writing than one remembers. She's just off to [her] Cousin Emily.

Are you well? Shall you get any 'assions from Craig?[1]

Yr M[andril]

Can you possibly get some more powders for Shot in Lewes. If possible, also, bring typewriter—unless too difficult.

Sussex

653: To Lytton Strachey   *13 Cliffords Inn, [E.C.]*

Nov. 16 [1912]

Really, if you go on writing, you will vitiate John Bailey's[2] stock phrase "the art of letter writing is dying out—" Of course my objection to letters is that they were all written in the 18th Century, an age I find unlovable. Still, there seems no reason why we shouldn't write letters even upon the 16th of November—anyhow why you shouldn't. Of course for a wife and a woman the case is different. Do the race horses champ beneath you?[3] I dreamt of race horses all night which is partly why I take up the pen—when I ought to be reading and reviewing.[4] Isn't it damnable to have begun

---

1. Dr Maurice Craig, the neurologist. The word *'assions* may be a private word for contraceptives.
2. John Cann Bailey (1864-1931), the critic and essayist.
3. Lytton was staying in a farmhouse on the Berkshire Downs owned by a race-horse trainer.
4. She was reviewing *Frances Willard: Her Life and Work*, by Ray Strachey (*TLS*, 28 November 1912).

that again? and yet it's rather inspiriting. I feel like a child switching off the heads of poppies—it's such a joke now, writing reviews, and I once took it seriously. Poor old Desmond [MacCarthy] was here again yesterday, with his despatch box in which was a half written review of George Trevelyan's edition of Meredith's poetry—Out it came and we went through it with a pencil. "Now please suggest some alternative for 'revelling in romance'—I don't like 'revelling in romance'—'exalting in the magnificence?' No—that's not quite it—However, let's go on." On we went, defining youth, poetry and what precisely is meant by optimism. It was awfully gloomy—this poor man searching about in the roots of things at 2 guineas a column, and sweating and grunting and saying "If I had time, of course, I could do something better than this" and yet it was stiff with thought. He seemed to me altogether dismal. Starting for Biarritz where he is to help Paley with a book on Political Economy.[1] The kind of thing they debate is whether to call Disraeli Lord Beaconsfield, the late Mr Disraeli, or Disraeli pure and simple, which Desmond advises, provided the sentence will stand it.

Our great event has been that [Edward] Arnold has taken Leonard's novel with great praise. Of course he makes it a condition that certain passages are to go out—which, we don't yet know. It's triumphant to have made a complete outsider believe in one's figments. I don't suppose I altogether agree about the 19th Century. It's a good deal hotter in the head than the 18th. But you didn't shock my feelings as a daughter. The difference probably is that I attach more importance to his divinity "qua man" even in his books than you do. It always seems to me to count considerably. But my feeling for literature is by no means pure.[2]

Ottoline has been seen by several observers—not by me—passing through on her way South again, the gold streamers pendent from each ear, and trailing on the ground, amid a myriad of pointed foxes' tails—So Leonard, who's not given to exaggeration, describes her.

We are sitting over the fire, in complete quiet, save for an occasional van down Fetter Lane—L. half way through an immense Blue Book on Divorce, upon which he has to write an article, for that oozing officious man, Haynes.[3]

London is very nice—a trifle too rackety I agree—but we are off, thank God, tomorrow to Asheham, where we shall discuss the shepherd's morals—

1. G. A. Paley, whose only published book was *Paul Redway* (1923), to which Desmond MacCarthy contributed an introduction.
2. Lytton had written to Virginia about the Victorians: "They seem to me a set of mouthing bungling hypocrites"; and about Leslie Stephen: "Did I enrage *you*, by my rather curt remarks on ton père? . . . Of course I think qua man he was divine".
3. Edmund Haynes (1877-1949), the solicitor and moralist. In 1912 he published *Divorce Problems of To-Day*.

he's had a child at 60, and this gives rise to talk—with Mrs Funnell [shepherd's wife at Asheham].

Yr.
V.W.

Is this letter written upon Bumf? It looks like it. Isn't it a shame that Marjorie[1] is not going to be a publisher? We urged it all we could.

Frances Hooper

654: To Violet Dickinson

13 *Cliffords Inn, Fleet Street, E.C.*

[December 1912]

My Violet,

    We were fearfully sorry to put off coming last night. I had a headache and then Leonard developed an attack of malaria, and had to go to bed. He's better today, but its a beastly thing and we were very sorry not to come. I suppose you're going away directly. But will you and Ozzie [Violet's brother] come and dine with us at the Cock after Christmas. I'll write later.

Yr. V.W.

Berg

655: To Violet Dickinson

Asheham, Lewes,
[*Sussex*]

24th Dec. [1912]

My Violet,

    I think Nessa is better—though she never seems to have got rid of the effects of that miscarriage,[2] and I dont see how she's ever going to in the midst of all the rush at Gordon Square. They're coming down here for some time after Christmas. I suppose it will be better than London, but I wish she could have a month somewhere by herself without children or servants. She's had a good many bothers this winter, besides any amount of exhibitions and art.

    We're here for Christmas. We shall be back in a few days. Is it really possible to be inoculated for malaria? It would be well worth doing. Leonard hasn't heard of it. At this moment its raining hard, but we are very happy here—I think its best in winter. In fact I think it would be nice to leave all ones clothes in a great box in London, and turn into a kind of muddy turnip

1. Lytton's younger sister.
2. At Broussa, Turkey, in April 1911.

root, with Mrs Funnell to talk to. My husband wants to buy 2 cows, and 20 hens, which supplied with one cock would give us eggs and fowl, and the cows would give milk and butter, and eventually, from the butter we should create a pig; and then rent a little shooting. Do you keep wildstock of any kind, except the virgin goat?

Do you know of anyone wanting a Secretary? The Grafton [Post-Impressionist Exhibition], thank God, is over; artists are an abominable race. The furious excitement of these people all the winter over their pieces of canvas coloured green and blue, is odious. Roger is now turning them upon chairs and tables: there's to be a shop and a warehouse next month.[1]

Yr. V.W.

Please come and see us in London—we're now quite straight.

Berg

656: TO LYTTON STRACHEY

Asheham, Rodmell,
[Sussex]

Boxing Day [1912]

Dear Lytton,

I meant long ago to write to you, in London, but one can't write in London. In fact we're driven to think that the country is our destiny, partly led thereto by the charms of Mrs Funnell, Old Funnell, their son, and a soldier nephew who served in Egypt, who are all at this moment sitting in the kitchen, eating a great sugar cake, which I bore in and presented, amid subdued cheers. As for the boy he has the figure of a God—a very small, tightly curled head, set upon gigantic shoulders. That's the style I admire; and there he sits speechless, reading the cookery book.

We have just had dinner—Leonard is reading the poems of John Donne: I am half way through the Return of the Native, a novel by Thomas Hardy. We go back tomorrow, alas. Were there time I would tell you about Brighton on Christmas Eve; we spent 2 hours in the Aquarium. The common fish are perfectly wonderful. Soles laid flat on the bottom; cray fish crawling; mackerel shooting endlessly round and round, like torpedo boats; fat white anemones blooming from rocky corners. Then there is the monkey house. For some reason, the mackerel put me in mind of Ottoline and her troupe;

1. Roger Fry was about to launch the Omega Workshops, an enterprise for the employment of artists, and the design, manufacture and decoration of chairs, tables, pottery etc. His artists, like Duncan Grant and Vanessa Bell, were strongly influenced by the Post-Impressionist movement. The Workshops, in Fitzroy Square, opened in July 1913.

she ought to be put in a tank; it's absurd to expect her to stand scrutiny for ways and motives, which is her lot at present.

I suppose you have heard of various disasters in London—Nessa more or less broken down—Roger rampant, but at one point forced to sit with his head in his hands, giddy if he so much as saw a picture. They're starting on furniture now—have you heard? All good reasons for living in the country. Hom[1] turned up two days ago—but if one sees much of Sydney[2] one wants less of Hom, which does not mean that I don't find him large and serene and as satisfactory as a great big pigeon. This metaphor might be more fitting if I werent here interrupted by Mrs F: who says she can't eat curry; it repeats so dreadful—also how she saw her saucepan once float in at the back door—in a flood.

Are you writing? Have you despatched that wrinkled old hag?[3] and are you still interrupted by the champing of the race horses beneath? O I saw Walter Lamb[4] too; and if it weren't wicked could make you laugh—How anyone has the face to be so magnificently egoistical one can't conceive; he lives in the centre of domes upon domes of bubbles. His play has been refused. But he has hopes of a more brilliant future than falls to most of us—a Librarianship—(but this is a secret).

Yr.
V.W.

Frances Hooper

1. H. O. Meredith, a Fellow of King's College, Cambridge, and lecturer in economics.
2. Sydney Waterlow, who succeeded Leonard as Secretary of the Second Post-Impressionist Exhibition.
3. Lytton had recently completed his essay on Madame du Deffand for the *Edinburgh Review*.
4. At this time a Fellow of Trinity College, Cambridge. In 1913 he became Secretary of the Royal Academy of Arts. In 1911 he had proposed to Virginia, who refused him.

Letters 657-674 (January–June 1913)

During the first half of the year the Woolfs alternated between Clifford's Inn and Asheham, while Leonard, occasionally accompanied by Virginia, was studying Co-operation in Midland and northern cities. In late January they stayed at Studland, Dorset, in March with the Gills at Ditchling, and in June at Cambridge. Underlying Virginia's cheerful record of these excursions, and of her gardening and writing, was the fear that The Voyage Out *might be rejected by Duckworth's, and that she might once again become insane. Her novel was accepted on* 12 *April, though not published until two years later. But her illness, at first no more than recurrent headaches, led to the decision that it would be unwise for her to have children, much as she wanted them, and Leonard observed her failing health with increasing anxiety.*

657: To Violet Dickinson

13 Cliffords Inn, Fleet Street, E.C.

[January 1913]

My Violet,

I ought to have written before—We've been down at Asheham, which was very unfortunate to miss you and the young man—I didnt know we knew anyone who looked fashionable.

As far as one can tell in these complaints, Nessa is much better—but one cant tell very much, as down there she does nothing—and how she's ever to get absolutely right in the midst of family life I dont know. However, its no good interfering in the lives of others. I'm quite certain that 2 months of sensible life would cure her for ever, which is what makes one lose one's temper.

Will you and Ozzy dine with us at the Cock on Wednesday 22nd 8.? coming here first, not dressing. If Ozzy cant, will you? But both would be better.

Yr
V.W.

Berg

Friday [7 March 1913]

My dear Ottoline,

We've promised to go to the Gills[1] on the 22nd unfortunately; it would have been very nice to come down to you instead—I have the greatest difficulty in talking to artists and when they talk themselves its so philosophical and religious and profound.

We hope you'll ask us again.

London is very much like Hell and has been for the last 6 weeks. We disappear as often as we can to Asheham—however, London has a great charm too, especially the Strand. Are you coming back? What do you do. I suppose you've read every book worth reading, and I hope you begin to to consider writing a book. Everyone seems on the verge of having a book out—Desmond has them three at a birth. I'm told awful stories of Molly and Desmond up at 5 writing for 6 hours by an open window to keep their heads fresh.

Yr affate
V.W.

Texas

11 March [1913]

Dear Nelly,

Its no use for me to say that I'm glad you liked Leonard's book [*The Village in the Jungle*], as you know too well the profound and secret vices of Authors.

This is only to warn you against going to Cliffords Inn, just now, unless you like looking at names on doors, and milk jars—(by the way, the young lady who feeds pigeons opposite with chunks of bread flung herself in full light, curtains up, into a young mans arms the other evening, and as they remained like that for 10 minutes, we conclude that they love each other— L thinks it would be rash to say they are engaged)

I recognise the portrait of Beatrice [Thynne] with delight. If she got to the end of the book [*The Village in the Jungle*], she has now read 23—not counting the Bible, and the History of the Church, which she was made to read.

We are going about to see factories, and as we spent 8 hours walking

---

1. Eric Gill. At this stage of his career, he was designing inscriptions on stone and lettering for book titles. In 1904 he had married Mary Moore, and they lived at Ditchling in Sussex.

through them today, I'm very sleepy. Why the poor dont take knives and chase us out of our houses, I cant think. They stand for 8 hours tying up 6 gross of jampots.

We shall be back in 10 days and I hope then you will come and see us.

Yr affate
V.W.

Hatfield

660: TO KATHERINE COX   *Grand Hotel, Leicester*

[18 March 1913]

My Dear Ka,

Having lost my spectacles I can hardly see to write, but the female gynaecologist at the table and Leonard over the fire scribble scribble scribble so I suppose I must too. You would like to have my impressions of the condition of the working classes (the reason why I think she is a female g. is that when I came in she was pointing very low down in the body of a large diagram of the female body and saying to a sad elderly woman, "That's what we must have out"—ovaries, I presume).

We have been to Manchester, Liverpool, Leeds, Glasgow, and now end with the boot factory here. Many valuable things come into my head at once; it is as if the thaw were beginning—seeing machines freezes the top of one's head. It's the oddest feeling, providential, I suppose, so as to keep the poor quiet. The melancholy thing is that they seem perfectly respectable and content, rather like old gentlemen in Clubs, supposing they were worn down and out at elbows. I cant help thinking that fiery reformers fly completely over their heads. But my dear Ka, I see at a glance that nothing—except perhaps novel writing—can compare with the excitement of controlling the masses. The letters you'd get! The jobs you'd be sent on—and then people would always be telling you things, and if you could move them you would feel like a God. I see now where Margaret [Llewelyn Davies] and even Mary MacArthur[1] get their Imperial tread. The mistake I've made is in mixing up what they do with philanthropy. Why don't you force yourself into some post when you get back—in 6 months time you'd be driving about 6,000 helpless women in front of you. L. and I seriously consider branching out in some such line. I mean, he should branch: reviewing French poetry which is what he is now doing is only fit for crazy creatures, who have been in asylums.

We go back tomorrow. What are you doing? I'm glad you liked L's novel—(you can't see how insincerely I say that, and its no use grinning at

1. Mary MacArthur (1880-1921) was organiser of the Women's Trade Union League, and a champion of reform for women's working conditions.

me in Berlin). He gets a terrible lot of praise, and it seems to make no differ-ence. My novel[1]—but having said that, I'm now trained to stop short: isn't it wonderful? Its all Leonard's doing.†

Things in London were much the same as usual 10 days ago. A good deal of love, spite, art gossip, and opera. We dine at the Cock, and see the usual run. However, we shall probably retire after Easter and live sensibly. By the way, we want to buy a horse. How does one do it?

Yes, I'm *very* fond of you, and often think how I'd like to have my Bruin opposite. When shall I? Don't marry till you're 30—if then.*

Yr. V.W.

[*in Leonard's handwriting*]
    *No reflection on me. Vide†.

Mark Arnold-Forster

661: To Gwen Raverat   *Asheham House, Rodmell,*
                                        Lewes, [Sussex]
Sunday [23 March 1913]

Dear Gwen,

I didn't realise that you'd insulted me, or rather the people who live in London. Of course, your letters generally make me very angry, but thats because of the spirit of neo-paganism that breathes so fierce in them, and I'm sure you dont mean to apologise for that—utterly damnable though it is—(and perhaps the insult wasn't in a letter after all).

Anyhow, I wish I could see you on Tuesday, but we dont get back till about 7.30 which is too late, I'm afraid. Perhaps you'll be passing through again—if not, you and Jacques must come down here. I dont believe you've ever seen this place, anyhow not since it was lived in and had something like a garden—20 daffodils and $\frac{1}{2}$ a dozen crocuses. Its far the loveliest place in the world.

Yrs.
V.W.

We must have been just before you at Harbour View.[2]

Sussex

1. The manuscript of *The Voyage Out* had been delivered to Gerald Duckworth, the publisher, on 9 March.
2. At Studland, Dorset, where Leonard and Virginia had stayed from 25 January to 1 February.

[late March 1913]

My Violet,

We shall be delighted if you will come to tea on Wednesday. We've been away, or we should have been to see you.

I haven't seen Nessa for some time, but I hear she's much better, and they're coming back to London next week.

Yr
V.W.

Have you got a beautiful old edition of Jane Austen which you would like to lend me?

Berg

Tuesday [8 April 1913]

Sweet Mongoose,

I doubt that this will reach you—but I'm going down to Rodmell with M[arjorie Strachey].

It is very fine, but singularly dull without my little beast. I've spent the morning writing, the afternoon putting tulips in the pots. M. sat on the terrace making a genealogical table of the Austen family. At intervals we have wild discussions—she spits and I become vague as a woolly sheep.

She is of opinion that my book is lost, or rejected. God! I wish you were here. It would have been a splendid day. Your telegram came—I suppose there's no change—so I hope you will come.

We've discussed Clive's article, Jane Austen, novels, pessimism, Roger—I broke off abuse of Henry Lamb to write this. She says he's poisoning Lytton.

Now we must go—as with a wrung heel we shall be slow.

Yr darling Mandril

Love to everyone—your mother particularly.[1]

Sussex

1. Leonard was staying with his mother in Putney. He had been visiting his brother, who was in hospital with a cracked skull.

664: To Vanessa Bell

Asheham, [Rodmell, Sussex]

Thursday [10? April 1913]

Beloved,

I hope Clive is all right and that you haven't had to go down to Seend [Clive's parents]. This is to impose some miserable duties upon you, which however, you needn't do.

Could you send the Day Library books back to Days, 96 Mount St. W. I think you've got 3.

Could you give directions about bookcases, so that if we called we could get them. They are badly wanted here, but we dont want to buy more than necessary. We got one earthenware pot down with such labour that we shant attempt others. Also, Mrs F[unnell] buys breadpots which, if they had their bottoms pierced, wd. really do better.

The garden does you great credit—numerous daffodils, tulips, flocks, and nameless leaves—also a fine blue flower. We are now going to buy a Rhododendron hedge to put against the fence, and summer seeds.

Saxon [Sydney-Turner] is here, in difficulties with his teeth. He stays behind after every meal to rinse them.

An aeroplane has just flown over the house—it makes a noise like a motor bus.

We may meet again, or we may not, but I do not forget the scene of passionate love which you did not succeed in repressing—though you did your best.

Yr V.W.

Ransome refuses to pump unless we give him 5/ as you did—so the F[unnell]s have stepped in again—and they all seem violently at war.

Berg

665: To Violet Dickinson

Asheham House, Rodmell, Lewes, [Sussex]

Friday, April 11th [1913]

My Violet,

I was very glad to hear from you but you really must buy some great sheets like this to accommodate your lean long hand, if our intimacy is to live on ink. We come up to London this day, and wish you would ask us to tea, but I suppose you are now settled in at the [Burnham] Wood [Welwyn].

Perhaps you will invite us for 3 hours there.

We shall live here more or less this summer, but spend one out of 3 weeks in London.

We aren't going to have a baby, but we want to have one, and 6 months in the country or so is said to be necessary first.

However, on the whole, in spite of rain, there's nothing so nice as this place. We are wrestling with the garden. It is riddled with weeds, with roots a yard long, and finally we've had to dig a vast ditch, fill it with wood and straw, lay the earth on top, and set fire, in the hope that the nettles will be burnt out. After digging and fetching for 6 hours, until we both rained sweat and were the laughing stock of the yokels, we poured a can of paraffin on top and set alight—when a storm burst, and put the fire out, damped the earth, so that we must now begin again. We're also re-constructing the terrace and fighting moles rabbits and mysterious flower diseases, which attack tulips so that they never unfold. You *must* come here, and give advice. Will you?

We want to buy 2 horses. Can you recommend any? Isn't there a hunting peeress of your acquaintance who would part with a thoroughbred on condition we loved him? I only know one huntress, and she is now incapable, owing to marriage.

All the morning we write in two separate rooms. Leonard is in the middle of a new novel [*The Wise Virgins*]; but as the clock strikes twelve, he begins an article upon Labour for some pale sheet, or a review of French literature for the Times, or a history of Co-operation.[1]

We sew [*sic*] articles over the world—I'm writing a lot for the Times too, reviews and articles and biographies of dead women—so we hope to make enough to keep our horses. I've sent my book to Gerald, but have heard nothing so far, and expect to have it rejected—which may not be in all ways a bad thing.[2]

We are only waiting for £2,000 to start the best magazine the world has ever seen. Everyone agrees that it is the best idea in the world, but also hints that they cant support the bankrupt. Still, we go on looking up to Heaven.

We spent a fortnight moving from factory to factory in the North, getting as far as Glasgow and seeing every kind of horror and miracle. As you can imagine, I dont follow these economic questions very easily, but Leonard seems to be able to read and write and talk to enthusiasts without turning a hair. His book seems to be a great success—the reviews all compare him with Kipling—but I cant see that he has the vanity of the true author— which is a serious reason against his being one. *I've* never met a writer who didn't nurse an enormous vanity, which at last made him unapproachable like

1. Leonard's interest in the Women's Co-operative Movement was stimulated by his growing friendship with Margaret Llewelyn Davies, and his tour with Virginia of the Northern industrial cities in March. His book, *Co-operation and the Future of Industry*, was published in 1919.
2. She heard from Gerald Duckworth the next day that he had accepted *The Voyage Out*.

Meredith whose letters I am reading—who seems to me as hard as an old crab at the bottom of the sea.

Please write again. I suppose my character doesn't improve?

Aunt Minna [Duckworth] arrived at Cliffords Inn in a fly, and was unable to get out, so we had to stand in the Strand for half an hour with Angelo [her Italian manservant] dressed up as a footman—

Yr
Berg   V.W.

666: To Vanessa Bell   *Asheham House, Rodmell,*
                                                Lewes, [Sussex]

Friday 25th April [1913]

Beloved

I'm glad to find that you dislike Venice because I thought it detestable when we were there, both times[1]—once it might be due to insanity but not twice, so I thought it must be my fault. I suppose the obscurer reaches might be beautiful. There isnt much news to tell you, except of a very rural kind. The garden certainly does you great credit. Both the long beds are now full of flowers, mostly out, and every day new ones bloom—except the peonies, which are out in front, but not at the back.

We are undertaking tremendous labours. The large round bed has been thoroughly burnt for 2 days—mercifully the rain held off. I am terracing, and tomorrow we begin digging under the trees and planting foxgloves and wall flowers. However, much remains to be done—we mean to renovate the grass entirely. To our horror, when we came down, two raw new Christmas trees, each with a note tied to it, were planted in front of the windows, the work of Jean[2] and a lunatic, escaped from Eastbourne. The question is how to destroy them tactfully. No doubt you can suggest means. As they are to commemorate our marriage and novels, it will be difficult simply to uproot them.

We were invaded by Marny and Emma[3] two days ago. It was as hot as June, and they arrived in thick stuff coats and skirts, with mufflers made of white blanketing, for as Marny said, one never knows in April when it wont turn suddenly cold, although today it does seem fine at last—so unlike the past week—but last year if you remember. So she ran on for 3 or 4 hours, and Leonard was entranced, though so physically repulsed by Emma who became skittish at the sight of him that he couldn't sit near her. They said

1. First, in April 1904; second, towards the end of her honeymoon.
2. Jean Thomas, who was in charge of the mental hospital at Twickenham, where Virginia herself had twice been a patient.
3. Margaret and Emma Vaughan, Virginia's cousins.

24

that they dread the long summer evenings particularly—which are always so disappointing, and one cant light lamps, though it isnt really daylight. They have been lent a house, in the midst of George and Freshfields,[1] who all patronise them—lend them motors and so on. Lisa has not yet turned up.[2]

We saw Ottoline before we came here, and found her charming, with a bloom upon her cheeks, and certainly more life in her. She has bought a house,[3] 15th century, with enormous yew hedges, and everything in keeping. When she doesn't languish, I think she is well worth seeing. Tomorrow Sydney [Waterlow] comes here, to recoup for his divorce case, which he has invited Leonard to attend. We shall make him dig. Mrs Funnells daughter has now been taken ill; she has swollen to a great size, and Mrs F. suspects dropsy. Considering her symptoms I should say a child, but I suppose they wd. be on the lookout for that. I have just heard that the bookcases have come.

We have also heard that L. has sold 600 copies of his book, which is thought to be very good. We shall probably go up to London on Wednesday, and attempt again to buy a house. This place gets better and better—3 days so hot that we sat out in the shade. I lead a *very* healthy life. The clock now strikes nine, and I begin to undress, L. then fetches me a great tumbler of milk. wh. I wallop down. Then sleep 8 hours—then lie down in the afternoon—then bask in the garden where a snake 3 ft. long was killed today. There is a pest among the lambs. They creep up to the hedge and die.

Yr. B.

I am amazed to hear that you have fallen in love at last. I only hope you were smartly repulsed. Sydney says your and his and Shoves[4] stories were the best. I've heard great praise of yours from various quarters. Sydneys almost made me sick, throwing up blood over the bread and butter. He read it at dinner.[5]

Berg

1. George Duckworth and Douglas Freshfield both lived near Forest Row, Sussex.
2. Lisa Stillman, the artist, who drew portraits of Leslie and Julia Stephen. She was the daughter of W. J. Stillman, the American painter and writer, and lived at Ditchling, Sussex.
3. Garsington Manor, near Oxford. The Morrells did not actually move there until May 1915.
4. Gerald Shove, the economist, who had been at Cambridge. He married Fredegond Maitland, Virginia's cousin, in 1915.
5. These 'stories' may have been products of the Novel Club, which was formed with much the same membership as the later Memoir Club, and with the main intention of inducing Desmond MacCarthy to write the novel which he frequently promised but never achieved.

[May? 1913]

Dearest Clive,

You were quite right—Leonard when I told him it was Tuesday reminded me that we are going to a lecture upon management where L. may speak on Tuesday. Therefore it *must* be Thursday. Please dont think me too idiotic.

The exaltation of last night and Saxons sudden spiritual escape, as if his soul had been underground for centuries, flurried me considerably.

If not *Thursday*, then *Friday*. Until I hear, both shall be kept free, and please forgive if I've made you miss something.

Yr V.W.
great haste.

Quentin Bell

668: To Katherine Cox   13 *Clifford's Inn, [E.C.]*

May 16th [1913]

My dear Ka,

You seem to be a very famous person—the vaguest rumours are afloat about you—By some it is said that you have actually been seen in the Kremlin, which is thought to be a church—others, among them Helen Verrall[1], and an awful elongated woman called Graham report that you fed the swans in the Kaisergarten last Tuesday at four—Anyhow you wont get this letter I suppose, but as we are sitting over the fire together and Leonard wants to work, I shall write to you—Otherwise, as you know, I am always looking up and saying "now do tell me honestly, am I more clever than beautiful, or beautiful than clever, or good than either"—which is the very devil when you want to read economics.

We came up here 10 days ago to attend the Ring—and I hereby state that I will never go again, and you must help us both to keep to that. My eyes are bruised, my ears dulled, my brain a mere pudding of pulp—O the noise and the heat, and the bawling sentimentality, which used once to carry me away, and now leaves me sitting perfectly still. Everyone seems to have come to this opinion, though some pretend to believe still. We combined this with the sight of a great many people, whom you may still remember, and can now probably judge at their right value. Is it high or low, or, as I rather suspect, about middling? Then we have written many thousand words, and Leonard has undertaken to lecture and write and listen to people

1. Daughter of A. W. Verrall, the Cambridge classical scholar.

preaching in obscure but enlightened northern towns,[1] and they are to found a College, and I have hopes—I will not say more than hopes—of sitting on a Committee in 3 years time. All your friends write to you, I suppose, and you know far more of the inner history of the times than I can pretend to.

We meet James [Strachey] floating down the Strand at midnight, rather like a Chinese girl who has somehow gone astray, poor woman—His cheeks are a lovely pink. At Asheham the other day we saw a fine sight—old Marjorie [Strachey] in a short white skirt,—an orange jersey and knapsack, armed with a hunting knife, to repel accosters, limping, dead lame, on a walking tour which lasted 3 days, covered 15 miles, and ended in our arm-chair where she sat incessantly eating sweets—reading novels which she had acquired at Lending libraries on the way. That was what had struck her— you can get novels for 2d—She was to have gone to Gordon Craig,[2] but that is off, owing to his fault, as I suppose will be the case most often. The truth about Marjorie is that with the sweetest nature in the world, the human race are to her as fish—We swim past, divided by glass plates—its queer, considering her qualities, (but then it mayn't be true). Having to give up facts, you see, I may as well write psychology, only its dangerous. My words are always coming back to me, and in Russia I suppose, we must be careful.

Do write and describe Russia; and put in a little psychology too.

Tomorrow we go down to Asheham, where we have first to survive a visit from Lytton-Desmond, and then to relapse peacefully into a rural life, which now centres round a horse—to buy a horse seems to be as difficult as to write a novel, but I think we may be on the track of one now.

When are you coming back? I search the world for the like of you, but haven't found her; and if there's one thing I love it is female society. Are you happy—(that's a question you wont answer) and well? I liked the photo-graph, and Mrs Funnell rescued it from the fire once, where it fell by mistake, and pinned it in the middle of the wall. Public news I do not give—private is that Sydney is divorced—Nessa Roger and Clive still abroad—but seem uneventful this time.

Leonard sends his love, and hopes you will soon come back—a nice wise friendly Bruin, and so sagacious too, after seeing the world, but will she have forgotten me?

Yr
V.W.

Mark Arnold-Forster

1. From this time onwards, for several years, Leonard lectured on economics and politics to Co-operative Societies in London and various provincial centres.
2. The theatrical producer and writer on the theatre.

[17 May? 1913]

My dear Nelly,

Its very bad luck but we are going to Asheham today. Perhaps you will ask us another time—at least that is what we hope.

But please come to tea again—I've just got some new curtains and rearranged the room—said to be a great improvement.

The gentleman opposite has just got up in his pyjamas and fed his canary while the art student in the garret has got about 20 pigeons sitting on the sill.

Yr. V.W.

Hatfield

670: To Violet Dickinson   [*Asheham, Rodmell,*

[late May 1913]   *Sussex*]

My Violet,

Many thanks for your scrap of notepaper. Janet Case who is here has lent me her pen to try, but it slobbers like a week old baby.

Jane Austen[1] was received with pleasure by some, hatred by others. It has won for me the friendship of a tawny bitch in South Kensington, Edith Sichel,[2] who is black to the 3rd finger joint in ink.

We're down here, but come up for a few days, and then retire to New Castle on Tyne, to join the Cooperative Women. It seems impossible to foretell where life will take one.

Nessa I believe has come back, laden with works of indisputable genius bought off peasants in the Umbrian mountains. They are beginning to paint boxes and arm chairs in Fitzroy Sqre [the Omega Workshops]. Personally I dont feel in Roger Fry the inspiration of Morris, but no doubt I'm wrong.

Gerald has accepted my book[3] (I dont think he got through it) and I'm now correcting proofs.

I shall suggest later that you shd. come and stay with us.

We have bought a Broodmare, and I have a grey pony, so we ride on the downs.

Yr.

V.W.

Last night our charwomans daughter, aged 18, produced an illegitimate child without warning.

Berg

1. Virginia's article on Jane Austen was published in the *T.L.S.* on 8 May.
2. Writer on French and English cultural life, who died in the following year.
3. *The Voyage Out.*

28th May [1913]

My dear Molly,

I was very grateful for your letter, which made me also slightly envious. *I* dont meet such charming old ladies lying in their deck chairs when I go for walks. Have you read her poems, and what are they like? But we have given up walking—we ride on the downs and 2 days ago I was thrown off, ignominiously, but it is said that riding astride one must expect half a dozen falls, and they dont hurt. Only I'm so stiff at this moment that if one wrote letters with ones legs, I couldnt write this.

We have settled down to a country life, which is full of strange discoveries. For one thing the days shoot past so that there is scarcely time to take ones food before one goes to bed again. Did you find this—if so what a queer affair your life at Timworth[1] must have been—I'd never realised it before—perhaps that explains the tendency which we both observe in you to—dulness, in short.

I cant remember a single thing that we've done since Desmond was here. Mrs Funnell's daughter provided the only incident. At ten o'clock one night she began to have a baby, being 18 years of age, unmarried of course, and so far as they knew a virgin! with a tendency to dropsy. That was how she explained her figure. But it was a child, which has flourished, and after a certain amount of scolding she has promised not to do it again, and they've all settled down, and apparently feel none the worse which seems very much superior to us in such circumstances.

I wish I could tell you that we'd been thinking, of learning Italian, or doing anything likely to make you think well of us. The one thing that makes Monday different from Sunday is the morning post so do write again, and describe life in London, and help to preserve us from becoming dull too.

We come up to London on the 2nd, and I hope we shall meet, but I imagine somehow that you're whats called in a vortex. London altogether seems so strange; I believe our half in half existence is ideal—a taste of people, and then a drench of sleep and forgetfulness, and then another look at the world, and back again.

The only exciting thing I have forgotten—that Leonard caught two moles this morning.

yrs V.W.

Mrs Michael MacCarthy

1. Formerly the MacCarthys' country house near Bury St Edmunds, Suffolk.

Asheham House, Rodmell,
Lewes, [Sussex]

[28? May 1913]

My dear Nelly,

It isnt often that I address you upon public matters, and it is now only upon compulsion from Miss Llewelyn Davies who could compel a steam roller to waltz.

There is going to be a deputation to the Prime Minister on the Divorce Question.[1] It will go for getting the recommendations of the majority report. Is there any chance that you will join the deputation, or support it in any way? I could not describe your views, but thought it worth asking, and if you are opposed to such a thing, dont bother to take notice of this.

We are very hot, having chased a horse vainly round a field. It is a wonderful night, and you I suppose are attending some great ball; wearing a coronet, dressed all in pale green satin, with ropes of pearls, and diamonds on your brow. We come to London on Monday, and I shall try to see you, but I think of London now as a vast rabbit warren, and the rabbits pop in and out, and never stay still for more than 2 minutes at a time.

yrs aff
V.W.

Hatfield

673: To Katherine Cox   13 *Cliffords Inn, Fleet Street, E.C.*

Friday 13th July [error for 13 June 1913]

My dear Ka,

I was sitting alone and thinking of you with extreme desire and affection when your letter came.

You really are wanted back again—and there'll be such a set on you that I know I shall only grasp a handfull of Bruin fur.

We are here till Wednesday next, 18th, when we retire to Asheham again. We've been up for a week, but how small and provincial it must all sound to you—whereas, you're like a brilliant Cockatoo out of the desert to me—

Will you ring up (Holborn 5711) and suggest lunch, tea, dinner—

1. The Royal Commission on divorce, which had been set up in 1909, reported in November 1912, and by a majority recommended important changes in the law, including new grounds for divorce and an equal legal footing for men and women. However, the law was not changed until 1923.

Leonard sends love. We are both happy at the thought of seeing Bruin again.[1]

Yr
V.W.

Mark Arnold-Forster

674: To Molly MacCarthy

Asheham, Rodmell,
Lewes, [Sussex]

[late June 1913]

My dear Molly,

Do you remember promising at midnight under the archway of Clifford's Inn to come here on Saturday? I can quite believe that you've repented since, but this is to remind you. Are you groaning?

You will find [E. M.] Forster here, but he is going to be put on the brood mare, who has become very fresh, so we shan't see much of him.

We've been having [H. T. J.] Norton, who was charming and remarkable—so many ideas, and quite willing to be amused—Otherwise nothing but country life, so I cant write a letter—but you in the midst of frivolity might. Is it the fact everyone undressed at 3 A.M. in Brunswick Sqre and proceeded to act and James Strachey left the house in disgust? However, you'll be able to describe it when we meet.

Yr
V.W.

The 3.20 from Victoria is the best. Take week end [ticket] to Lewes and small train on to Southease, where you will be met. Love to Desmond. We enjoyed his last in the Statesman.

Mrs Michael MacCarthy

1. Ka Cox had been in Germany, Poland and Russia, to recover from the ending of her love-affair with Rupert Brooke.

Letters 675-682 (July–December 1913)

Virginia's mental health deteriorated to such an extent that in late July, when the Woolfs returned from a Fabian Society Conference at Keswick, it was thought advisable to send her for two weeks to her former nursing-home at Twickenham, where she was sane enough to write Leonard daily homesick letters. The crisis came after she left. On 23 August Leonard took her to the Plough Inn, Holford, Somerset, where they had stayed soon after their marriage, but she became so depressed that he telegraphed to Ka Cox to join them, and soon afterwards took them both back to London. There, on the evening of 9 September, Virginia attempted suicide by taking an overdose of veronal, and nearly died. Her recovery was very slow. For four months she was unable to write any letters —none, at least, survive between 5 August and 4 December—and she remained under the constant vigilance of Leonard and her nurses at Dalingridge Place in Sussex, which her half-brother, George Duckworth, lent them. She was alternately depressed and hysterically excited, slept very badly and was only with great difficulty persuaded to eat. At times she could turn violently against her nurses. In mid-November she was well enough to return with Leonard to Asheham, still under the care of two nurses.

675: To Leonard Woolf   *Burley, Cambridge Park,*
                                          Twickenham

[28 July 1913]

Darling Mongoose,

I got your two letters this morning. They made me very happy, but you shouldn't have gone out to the post again—poor tired little beast.

How are you, darling Mongoose? I'm very well, slept well, and they make me eat all day. But I think of you and want you. Keep well. We shall be together soon, I know. I get happiness from seeing you. I hope you've been out and not worked too much.

Darling I love you—

yr M.

Sussex

676: To Leonard Woolf
Burley, Cambridge Park, Twickenham

[1 August 1913]

Dearest,

I got up and dressed last night after you were gone, wanting to come back to you. You do represent all thats best, and I lie here thinking. I think of you in your white nightgown mongoose.

yr M.

I thought we were walking back to Cliffords Inn together Darling.

Sussex

677: To Leonard Woolf
Burley, Cambridge Park, Twickenham

[2 August 1913]

Dearest,

You cant stay in London any more in this heat. Do get away. Couldn't you go to Lytton until Thursday? Jean [Thomas] says she will keep me till then.

I want to see you, but this is best.

yr. M.

Sussex

678: To Leonard Woolf
Burley, Cambridge Park, Twickenham

[3 August 1913]

Dearest Mongoose,

I hope you got my wire this morning.

Are you well, are you resting, are you out of doors? Do you do your little tricks? Here it is all the same. . . . I've not been very good I'm afraid— but I do think it will be better when we're together. Here its all so unreal.

Have you written your review? How are you feeling? Is Asheham nice? I want you Mongoose, and I do love you, little beast, if only I weren't so appallingly stupid a mandril. Can you really love me—yes, I believe it, and we will make a happy life. You're so loveable. Tell me exactly *how you are*.

M.

Sussex

Monday [4 August 1913]

Darling Mongoose,

I did like your two letters this morning. They make all the difference.

But I wish you weren't working. I'm enormously fat, and well—very sleepy.

Have you ridden?

Nothing you have ever done since I knew you has been in any way beastly—how could it? You've been absolutely perfect to me. Its all my fault. But when we're together—and I go on thinking—it must be all right. And we shall be on Thursday—How are you? you dont say—I think about you and think of the things we've had together. Anyhow, you've given me the best things in my life.

Do try and get out, and rest, my honey mongoose. You did look so bad. When you say sleepy you mean tired, poor beast.

I have been trying to read American magazines which are lent to me by Miss Funk a tall American.

I do believe in you absolutely, and never for a second do I think you've told me a lie—

Goodbye, darling mongoose—I do want you and I believe in spite of my vile imaginations the other day that I love you and that you love me.

                                                    Yr *M.*

Sussex

[5 August 1913]

Darling Mongoose,

This is only to say Goodnight—Dearest, I have been disgraceful—to you, I mean.

Savage[1] was here today—says I may go on Thursday. Will you come tomorrow?

You've been working all day and I've been doing nothing. We went on the river.

Nothing has happened. I keep thinking of you and want to get to you.

                                                    Yr M.

Sussex

---

1. Sir George Savage, a specialist in mental illness, who had been a medical adviser to the Stephen family for many years.

Asheham, [Lewes,
Sussex]
Thursday [4 December 1913]

Dearest Mongoose,

To begin with, I am to say from nurse, that I have been very good. I add
that I have been very dull without you—I don't like being left with the
female creatures—still, they're both very kind.

We have been cleaning the drawing room. Its really rather fun, and makes
a wonderful difference, even in the smell of the air. Then I've been for a walk
—nurse has been to Lewes—lots of odd jobs have been done.

Still, I think of you a great deal, though you wont believe it, and resent
being kept with my head on a platter, like some gigantic sow, when you are
doing all the appalling drudgeries. I daresay you only snatch a bite and sleep
on boards.[1] D'you know, I believe I like you better and better? Feelings
arise in me, such as I have not had for long.

I keep thinking that you ought to be an independent man, doing things,
instead of wasting your life—but you'll be bored by this.

A good many parcels have come for you; your novel etc; but nothing to
forward.

Shot [her dog] is melancholy. Do if you can, stay over the weekend.
There's no reason why you shouldn't.

Its blowing great guns, and we are now going down to the Post Office.

Dearest Mongoose, I wish you would believe how much I am grateful
and repentant. You have made me so happy.
Yr old M.

Are you going to see Col. Banister [*unidentified*]? How are you?

Sussex

Asheham House, Rodmell,
Lewes, Sussex
Sunday [December ? 1913]

Immundus Mongoosius Felicissimus, I could write this letter in beautiful
silver Latin, but then the scurvy little heap of dusty fur could not read it.
Would it make you very conceited if I told you that I love you more than
I have ever done since I took you into service, and find you beautiful, and
indispensable? I am afraid that is the truth.

Goodbye Mongoose, and be a devoted animal, and never leave the great
variegated creature. She wishes me to inform you delicately that her flanks
and rump are now in finest plumage, and invites you to an exhibition. Kisses
on your dear little pate. Darling Mongoose.
Mandril

Sussex

1. Leonard was in London, moving their belongings from Clifford's Inn.

Letters 683-707 (January–July 1914)

1914 was a year of recuperation, which was scarcely interrupted by the outbreak of war in August. At first Virginia remained at Asheham, and the last of her nurses did not leave till mid-February. She was able to see a few friends, exercised her dogs on the Downs, did some typing for Lytton Strachey and read Leonard's Co-operative manuals, while Leonard, himself in need of rest after Virginia's long ordeal, stayed with Lytton and began gradually to involve himself more deeply in politics, initially with the Webbs and the Fabian Group. His second novel, The Wise Virgins, was accepted by Edward Arnold. Vanessa, Janet Case and Ka Cox took it in turns to watch over Virginia during his absences. The Woolfs spent most of April in the St Ives district of Cornwall, and then returned to Asheham. Virginia was still subject to alternating moods of excitement and despair. She rarely went to London, and the peaceful life which Leonard prescribed for her gradually restored her health.

683: TO LEONARD WOOLF   *Asheham, Rodmell,*
                                                          [Sussex]
Wednesday [7 January 1914]

Dearest,

Owing to curiosity I opened this letter. Old [Edmund] Haynes shows some sense.

Nothing has happened—Very fine—very cold. Ka, I suppose, is striding over the downs at this moment.

Dont you think it might be a good thing to go and see Arnold, and ask about the V. in J?[1]

It'll be very nice to see you again, I had your letter. O my dear little beast, I do think we care for each other.

Are you going to see your mother?

I must take this to the post.

yr M.

Sussex

1. By the end of 1913 *The Village in the Jungle* had been twice reprinted by the publisher, Edward Arnold.

36

3a Roger Fry and Vanessa Bell

b Saxon Sydney-Turner, a
portrait by Henry Lamb

c Sydney and Alice Waterlow

4a Katherine Cox in 1911   b Violet Dickinson in 1912

c (back row, left to right) H. T. J. Norton, Clive Bell, Mary Hutchinson and St John Hutchinson (front row) James Strachey and Duncan Grant

684: To Violet Dickinson

Asheham, Rodmell, [Sussex]

Thursday [15? January 1914]

My Violet

I was just writing to thank for the shoes when the jersey turned up. You couldnt have sent anything more timely.

There is a bitter wind directly one gets out beyond the trees.

It was good of you.

The boots are wonderful. They seem to send warmth all through.

I wish you'd ever send the name of a good book on a card if you happen to hear of one.

Yr
V.W.

Berg

685: To Lytton Strachey

Asheham, Rodmell, [Sussex]

[17 January 1914]

Would you be very kind and send me your articles, which I think you have bound together? I will be very careful, and return them. I am reading Lord Lytton,[1] and I think you wrote one upon him, and the others I'd like to read too.

V.W.

Frances Hooper

686: To Janet Case

Asheham House, Rodmell, [Sussex]

[22? January 1914]

My dear Janet,

This is in the first place to thank you for the tulips which enliven even this bitter cold day. But really I want to thank you for the pleasure which you gave by your visit. It was a delight—and makes me wish again that you'd

1. The First Earl of Lytton (1831-91), the poet, who became Viceroy of India in 1876. Strachey's article was published in the *Independent Review* of March 1907, and this, with other essays, was republished in *Literary Essays* in 1948. Lord Lytton's friendship with Sir James Fitzjames Stephen, Virginia's uncle, was one reason for her interest in him.

come long ago! But still—I eat up the black and doubtful pieces of meat in memory—

I wonder how Bristol went. What news is there to give you? Bitter cold—and the great excitement now impending of a visit to Seaford.

Thank you again for coming. It was a real pleasure.

your affate

V.W.

Sussex

687: To Lytton Strachey

Asheham, Rodmell,
[Sussex]

Jan. 29th [1914]

The one volume of essays has arrived—I still await the second—But this is really to ask you whether you have any manuscripts that want type-writing. I should very much like to do them if you have, supposing that you are not in a great hurry and it would save you 10d. a 1000. Can you lend us the Edinburgh [Review]?

V.W.

I'm ready to begin on typing now. I don't altogether agree about Miss N.[1] Is it true that you refused to do her? What a pity. I read nothing but biographies of statesmen—I wish you would recommend some.

Frances Hooper

688: To Lytton Strachey

Asheham, [Rodmell,
Sussex]

Feb. 7th [1914]

I shall be delighted to do [type] Esmeralda[2]—and anything else chaste or otherwise.

We hear that Arnold is glad to publish the Wise Virgins, if L. will cut out some sentences—finds it gives "fresh proof of your power as a writer."

Your second volume came this morning. Many thanks.

Frances Hooper

1. Florence Nightingale. Lytton had been asked to write her life, but refused. The Life was given instead to Edward Cook, and when Lytton read the book, he wrote to his brother James on 16 January 1914, "She was a terrible woman—though powerful".
2. *Ermyntrude and Esmeralda*, a fictional and comically erotic exchange of letters between two girls, which remained unpublished until 1969.

689: To Violet Dickinson

[11? February 1914]

My Violet

It was very nice to get a letter from you—tho' I find it hard to believe in the existence of Kitty [Maxse], or Nelly [Cecil] or Katie [Cromer].

Are you better?

Here, after a week of midsummer, it rains steadily. Leonard has gone to London to see Arnold about his book. Arnold is anxious to publish it, but the question is what L's. family will think.

We are starting a kitchen garden—with the hope one day of eating our own growing. Does this take long, and need great care? Any hints would be welcome, as there is no gardener. As to flowers, we have sown seeds in soap boxes filled with earth. Is this right?

We're trying hard to find a houseparlour maid.

It will be such a mercy to get rid of nurses and all this ridiculous nonsense.[1] Leonard will I hope get a holiday soon. Nessa was here the other day, with several fans which she was painting, and rugs she was designing. Have you been to the Omega? What do you think of it?

I suppose you dont know a man and wife who'd do for us.

Yr
V.W.

Berg

690: To Violet Dickinson

Asheham, [*Rodmell, Sussex*]

[18 February? 1914]

My Violet,

You're very good to write—But you mustn't enclose cheques.

We are not really very hard up, at this moment—If we ever are, I promise that we will come to you—anyhow its extraordinarily nice of you to think of it. I hope that we shall now lead an economical life—no nurses, and weekly books fairly low.

Did I tell you Arnold has accepted Leonards new novel?—and the Village in the Jungle has done very well.

I see Clives book [*Art*] announced—

Not much happens here, except adventures with the dogs and cats, who seem to feel the Spring in their bones, and behave according.

Are you recovered? I've got a funny old picture of you, taken by Beresford—d'you remember?

Yr
V.W.

Berg

1. The last nurse left on 16 February.

39

691: To Leonard Woolf   *Asheham House, Rodmell,*
                                Lewes, [Sussex]
[7 March 1914]

Dearest,

Everything all right—very quiet—pouring rain most of the time since you left.[1]

Janet works at Womens Suffrage—I read Clive, very laboriously, so as to be able to argue with you. At present, I'm inclined to think it good—anyhow very clear and brisk.

I must stop as Janet waits and the dogs are frantic.

How are you?

Yr. M.

Sussex

692: To Violet Dickinson   *Asheham House, Rodmell,*
                                   Lewes, [Sussex]
[7? March 1914]

My Violet,

The gardening things are very tempting, and just come at the right moment. But you shower too many gifts, and the next parcel will have to be burnt unopened.

We're planting vegetables, but have to war with fowls, and now a fold of ewes about to bring forth young. Leonard is in London, and Janet Case is here, who wishes me to send her love. She sits over the fire concocting lectures upon Divorce, Woman Suffrage, and Moral Hygiene.

Yr
V.W.

By the way, I wish you'd let me do typing of any kind for you.

Berg

693: To Leonard Woolf   *Asheham, [Rodmell,*
                                Sussex]
Sunday morning [8 March 1914]

Dearest,

If you could have seen my sorrow after you went you would have had no doubts about my affection. My darling old beast—I do wonder how you got on.

1. Leonard, who was feeling the strain of looking after Virginia during her illness, went to stay with Lytton Strachey at The Lacket near Marlborough for a few days.

We walked—our only excitement being that Mike [dog] ran out of the house at tea time, and wasn't back by bedtime, so that we had to go to the farm to ask for him—About eleven he appeared—from where we dont know. Otherwise all right.

I'm now waiting to begin porridge. Janet [Case] very nice and very moral.

Make Lytton take care of you—and stay in bed if your head aches, and dont get into long arguments but rest your poor pate.

I sent on Bella's [Leonard's sister] wire.

Old Mandril does want her master so badly and last night his empty bed was so dismal, and she went and kissed the pillow.

Yr. M.

Sussex

694: To Leonard Woolf   *Asheham House, Rodmell,*
                                        Lewes, [Sussex]

Monday [9 March 1914]

Dearest Honey,

I *was* glad of your letter this morning—It has poured practically ever since you left, and is now driving across the house, so that we cower over the fire, reading and gossiping. I shall take this letter to the post, and exercise the dogs. Three is a fair handful, but there have been no adventures, save two sharp quarrels between Mike and Shot. I dont like Mike—

Lord! I dont much envy you with such great intellects on either side of you. However, Norton is really nice—and I hope they cossett you, my pet brute.

By the way I gave Janet your Pearl Fisher story[1] to read—and found her in tears! She thought it very beautiful and impressive, and says you must publish it. What else is there to tell you?

I'm really very cheerful—in spite of the fact that Cascara [a laxative] has failed to work the 2nd day running.

I suppose you read Roger on Clive in the Nation—I also suppose you discuss that book[2] a good deal—But there's not much point in one's friends praises—poor old Roger—so humble and appreciative and eager that people should take Clive seriously.

I hope you get out, and to bed, and have some good weather. I've done Leicester, and am half way through Bradford.[3] Any gossip gratefully received.

1. *Pearls and Swine*, later published in *Stories of the East*, Hogarth Press, 1921.
2. Clive Bell's *Art*, in which he first expounded his theory of 'significant form', had just been published.
3. Manuals on the Co-operative Movement in these cities.

Love from Janet, who says we're having a very nice time.

Be careful, and come home cured to your dear Brute, and we shall have a happy spring. J. says "V. is a model of virtue, discretion, and reasonableness" Ha ha!

Yr. M.

Tell Lytton I shall start his work tomorrow when my typewriter comes back.

Sussex

695: To Leonard Woolf
*Asheham House, Rodmell,
Lewes, [Sussex]*

Tuesday [10 March 1914]

Dearest Honey,

There is not much news—but no news is good news—isnt that a fine sentence for the great Brute.

I'm glad you're staying on with Lytton, and if your head improves with him you must be recovering.

Janet went this morning, and Ka arrived 10 minutes before she went, so I haven't had a minute alone. Ka is very nice, full of people she's seen— Publishing is over for the present, and she's looking about for a new job. Arnold would take her but she thinks him such a bore that she wont.

O the dogs are uproarious! Shot crashed through the drawing room window this morning, but didnt cut himself wonderful to say. Mrs Bedford [cook] departed; a man came in a motor car, very smart, from Brighton to say that the typewriter will cost 10/- to repair, or £2.10. to do thoroughly, or they would give me a new one for £12.10. Meanwhile they have lent me a new one until the repairs are done, in the hope I suppose that I shall buy. It is a marvellous machine, with every kind of dodge, and I shall do Lytton's story on it. I wish he'd send me some more.

How are you, my pet beast? Your old Mandril cries so pathetically when it crawls into its straw, and sees your basket empty.

Yr. M.

Sussex

696: To Leonard Woolf
*Asheham, [Rodmell,
Sussex]*

Wednesday [11 March 1914]

Dearest,

It is now beautiful and sunny, and all the lambs are out in the field.

I had your 2 letters this morning, which was very nice.

42

The new cook [Annie] came last night, and she seems friendly and easy, and of course her cooking is at present very good. And now the prostitute[1] is arriving, and Ellen [maid] is gone. So I feel settled in. I've been typing Lyttons story—and now we're going to the post.

I do hope you're better. Once your head is right it'll stay right. I get no letters now that you're away. But I'm good and cheerful, though I should like to cuddle my dear little creature in my arms.

Is Lytton nice? or pernickety?

Yr. M.

Sussex

697: TO LEONARD WOOLF

[*Asheham, Rodmell, Sussex*]

Thursday [12 March 1914]

Dearest,

You are certainly *not* to come back here until Wednesday next—It really would be foolish to cut short your time. A day or two more will make all the difference. I'm very cheerful, very good, so there's no need for you—(I own I should like to have you to kiss, my dear little beast, and its very flat without you). O dear, you don't realise what a difference you make.

Ka is very nice, but as slow headed as an old cow. This household will be in apple pie order by the time you come back.

Lily has cleaned our room so that its like a new pin. She seems very nice, and they both say they like the place.

If I were you I'd stay all the time with Lytton. Its really more of a rest—and I wouldn't go to Bella at all this time. You could go to her for a week end later. *Must* you go to Kettering? There's no news, except that I want you, and love you more than you'd expect, and its very dull without you.

Yrs. M.

Sussex

698: TO LEONARD WOOLF

Asheham House, Rodmell, Lewes, [Sussex]

Friday [13 March 1914]

Dearest,

I had a good long letter from you today. Is your head *really* better, and keeping better, and do you tell me the truth, or rather improve upon it? Dont: but be my honest Beast—for which quality indeed, I bought you.

1. Lily, the new maid, was a Sussex country girl who had had an illegitimate child and was taken into a convent, by which she was recommended to the Woolfs.

43

Do you want to go to Bella—however, its no use asking, since you're already with her.[1]

I enclose a letter from Arnold, which I thought might be the Times proof.

Ka went this morning—Janet arrived. Margaret [Llewelyn Davies] you'll be glad to hear, is quite recovered, and welcomed the Labour leaders at the Docks. Otherwise, I dont think I've any news—except that I want very much to see you—and love every fur on your dear little thin fleasome body (you know Mongoose was a fleay beast, and I see that Scarlet fever depends greatly upon fleas.)

The taupe[2] is a marvel of consideration. I forgot to tell you that he praised the Village highly.

Love to Bella, and a kiss for M's snout.

Yr. M.

Sussex

699: TO LEONARD WOOLF   *Asheham House, Rodmell,*
                                                          Lewes, [Sussex]

Saturday [14 March 1914]

Dearest,

It was nice to see your little cramped claw this morning. I do hope Bella's over the influenza and not infectious.

Here it rains more or less steadily, and the downs are hidden in white mist. Perhaps Birmingham's better, but you certainly didn't get a good week for your holiday.

You see this card from [J. C.] Squire. I've looked in your room for the article, but dont see it. Wire if I can take steps.

We go on our way placidly. The cook is really a great improvement—she makes very good bread—and the whole house is much cleaner and nicer. Lily is a real servant in the way of brushing ones clothes etc.

All the morning I typewrite—then read your Co.op: books, and make futile notes I expect.

Do come back a brisk well mongoose, with a feather in your cap.

My pet, you would never doubt my caring for you if you saw me wanting to kiss you, and nuzzle you in my arms. After all, we shall have a happy life together now, wont we?

Yr. M.

Sussex

1. Bella Lock, Leonard's sister, lived at Streetly, Staffordshire.
2. French for 'mole', a nickname for E. M. Forster.

44

700: To Leonard Woolf   *Asheham House, Rodmell,*
                               Lewes, [Sussex]

[16 March 1914]

Dearest,

I dont know whether this will reach you—in any case its only a line, to catch the post.

We go on very smoothly—really its delightful to be so clean and sweet again—The servants are really good. You'll be amused to hear that the cook's young man is in the Newhaven Co.op: Says they work him very hard. To balance cleanliness, the dogs have begun to wet the stairs—An elm at the back was blown down. To our great excitement.

I am glad you're better in the head—I love your little ribby body, my pet. Dont get too tired.

                                                      Yr. M.

Sussex

701: To Janet Case   *Asheham House, Rodmell,*
                               Lewes, [Sussex]

[20? March 1914]

My dear Janet,

It's all very well to get rid of you, but then you turn up practically every morning in one way or another. Please, for Gods sake, Hell take you, *dont* send anything more—nevertheless, I'm very grateful—what a bother buying things for other people is—and you a busy woman. I'll keep everything— The gaiters fit perfectly—the knickerbockers I can never remember to try on, as they have taken lodgment in the drawing room. And then there's your hot bottle, off which a label has come.

Leonard is better, according to him, and to me too.[1] In fact I think if only I can behave now, he will soon be quite right. [Dr Maurice] Craig gave him a new medicine, and said he would get well if he was sensible. He's now fixed his mind upon weighing eleven stones, and so he certainly will.

By occupying myself with typewriting and Co-operative manuals, I keep cheerful, which I see does more to inspirit L. than anything else, and induces submission (on my part).

I gave Nessa your messages. She replied that she hoped to see you, and that Vanessa is equivalent to Janet.

The items of our life, as Mrs Bedford says, are various. As to dogs, I was met by a gamekeeper from the next farmer, who said Max and Shot had been

1. Leonard had returned on 18 March from his visits to Lytton and Bella, and had spent a night in London at Janet Case's house on his way back.

ranging the hills all morning alone, and would have to be punished. We seriously think we must get rid of one—as they're not to be trusted even in the garden—I also had a conversation with Annie [cook], about Gunn [local bailiff] and gentlemen visitors generally, feeling the greatest humbug; and ruled that Gunn should only visit once a fortnight, and the friend also— which she took with amazing docility, in fact I believe they like rules.

No one else would draw upon herself such details as these—but then you have your reward in being yourself, which must be so heavenly. Think of waking in the morning and finding oneself Janet!

Well—anyhow you've done a great deal to put us on our feet, I feel. I really think L. is better and happier.

What a table and what beds you keep! Three sorts of marmalade, porridge like cream, biscuits in a box by the pillow—these stories have urged me to begin making petticoats for all our washstands.

Yr. affate
V.W.

A cheque will follow—if you will add up these sums.

	£.	s.	d.
Hot Bottle		?	?
Knickerbockers		?	?
Gaiters		5.	9.

Please make Miss Emphie understand how much I thank her for letting you come, and I do realise what a piece of work it is to duty as Pest 2 weekends.

Sussex

702: To Clive Bell   *Asheham House, Rodmell,*
                                                    Lewes, [Sussex]

Friday [20? March 1914]

My dear Clive,

I ought to have thanked you before for sending me your book [*Art*], considering that I read it through at once, and enjoyed it very much—I liked the chapters of theory more than the historical chapters, which seem to me too much of a generalisation—and sometimes perhaps too smart, and of course there are a great many things I dont agree with, where I understand. But its great fun, and full of ideas and I suppose will put people's backs up like cats on a roof at night—but all this you will enjoy. What do the reviews say?

yrs
V.W.

Quentin Bell

46

Asheham House, Rodmell,
                                         Lewes, [Sussex]

[early April 1914]

Dearest Molly,

What a treat to get a letter from you! I wish it were possible to make a contract by which you should write once a month regularly. Perhaps when all your bothers have cleared up, you will. I do hope they're better. Well, I envy you all your bothers and your monkey life and the banderlogging etc— which is after all more normal than a life of milk, green fields, early bed, and contemplation. However its beginning to be very nice here, and I'm trying to titivate the house. We've let it to Keynes for a reading party next week, and we go off to Cornwall, while they're here. Perhaps you will see them. I gather they are to be mostly Apostles.[1]

By the way—we've been getting into hot water with the farmers over Shot. He is beautiful and charming, but we cant stop him from hunting, so do you think you could possibly negotiate for the people he came from to take him back? This seems very ungracious, and he's so charming that it is a great blow to part from him—but it seems the only thing to do. If you would give me the address I'd write.

Its very like living at the bottom of the sea being here—one sometimes hears rumours of what is going on overhead—reconciliations with Ottoline and so on. But oh dear, it is awful to be such a fool!

Do you think you'll retire to the country! Perhaps we shall meet some day—if you're still at Ford when we get back—It would be very nice.

                                    Give love to Desmond,
                                                yrs. V.W.

Do you remember the wonderful poetess in the conservatory at Freshwater?[2]

Mrs Michael MacCarthy

Carbis Bay Hotel, Carbis Bay,
                                         Cornwall

[mid-April 1914]

My Violet,

I ought to have thanked you for the book before—but it came as we were starting for this place—He's a queer card—no one less likely to write a romantic book about trees exists, I should think—

1. Members of the exclusive Cambridge intellectual society.
2. Virginia had been to Freshwater, Isle of Wight, in 1895, after her mother's death, to stay in her Aunt Annie Ritchie's house, called 'The Porch'. It was now lent to Molly. The 'wonderful poetess' is unidentifiable.

We are in great luck for weather, and we've been rambling over our old haunts—We crept into Talland House[1] itself yesterday, and found it wonderfully done up and spick and span, and all the garden brimming with flowers and rock gardens—very unlike what it was in our day.

I wonder where you are? and is your garden wonderful now? Nessa is at Asheham—or was—People all round me are talking golf—Thank you very much for your book. I wear your jacket daily.

Yr
V.W.

Berg

705: TO VIOLET DICKINSON

Godrevy, Carbis Bay,
Cornwall

[27 April 1914]

My Violet,

We have been moving about from one lodging to another. Its amazing weather here, and we've just been to some races, in the middle of the hills. As to Nina Lamb,[2] I think she is by this time a professional mistress. She has lived with various people. Last time I saw her she was in company with a little creature Adrian used to know—but I heard the other day that she had taken a house at Hammersmith, and was living with some one else.

I believe she's rather nice and pretty—but without any morals.

She began life in Manchester—her mother being apparently in the same line of life. She had a little money of her own, and she used to wander about London and Manchester (where a club was formed to protect her virtue) until she became H. Lamb's mistress, and then his wife. They separated soon after that, and when we were in Paris a year or two afterwards she was a well known character.

However, I dont think she's wanting, and she certainly was amazingly pretty. I think she moves from person to person—I could write pages of her adventures, because she used to appear at intervals with amazing stories of her doings, which were partly invented, but I think she was very attractive to a good many people.

Yr
V.W.

We go back to Asheham on the 1st.

Berg

1. The house above St Ives bay, where the Stephen children spent every summer holidays from 1882 to 1895.
2. Formerly Nina Forrest, who married Henry Lamb, the painter, in 1906.

706: To Violet Dickinson   *Asheham, [Rodmell, Sussex]*

June 2nd [1914]

My Violet,
    It was very nice to hear from you—We shall be here till August when we think of going to Northumberland, letting this to the Bells.
    Leonard is hard at work—reviewing for the Times and the New Statesman—my occupation is to renovate this house which is falling down, wilting and fading in every direction—but much can be done by polish.
    I'm very sorry about Lord Cromer[1]—but nothing appears in the papers. Is he very bad? Our excitement is a motor lorry overturned yesterday in our field—running away down hill and throwing 4 people over—but one only hurt.

                                                              Yr
                                                              V.W.

Berg

707: To Violet Dickinson   *Asheham House, Rodmell, Lewes, [Sussex]*

[June 1914]

My Violet,
    I'm afraid we can't come on Saturday, as we're only just back from an extravagant visit to London—but perhaps you would come here, either then or some other time.
    Leonard sends you his love.

                                                              Yr
                                                              V.W.

Berg

1. The 1st Earl of Cromer, a friend of Violet Dickinson, had suffered a severe stroke, and was reported to be 'at death's door'. He recovered, and did not die until 1917.

49

Letters 708-716 (August–December 1914)

The outbreak of war on 4 August found the Woolfs at Asheham and had no effect upon Virginia's slow recovery, nor on the plan which they had previously made, to take a month's holiday in Northumberland. They stayed in a hotel at Wooler from 6 August to 4 September, and then moved across the border to Coldstream. Returning to London on 15 September, their first concern was to find somewhere to live. Clifford's Inn had been given up early in 1914, and they moved first to Twickenham, and then in mid-October to temporary lodgings at 17 The Green, Richmond, which belonged to a Belgian lady, Mrs le Grys, while they looked for a house in the same district. It was towards the end of the year that they found Hogarth House in the centre of the Borough. Virginia was now well enough to enjoy a modified revival of her London life, and even to take cooking lessons, but not to write. Christmas was spent at Marlborough, near Lytton Strachey.

708: TO VANESSA BELL   *Asheham, [Rodmell, Sussex]*

Monday [3 August 1914]

Dearest,

Would it be possible for you to let us have half the rent—£15—before we go away? I'm afraid this sounds like poor relations, but we've got very little balance, and, if war breaks out, we shall probably be in difficulties for ready money. Of course, dont bother, if you are in the same state. We can always give up going to Northumberland, and stay here till you come, and so save railway fares etc.

We are just (4. P.M.) off to Lewes to get a paper. There were none at breakfast this morning, but the postman brought rumours that 2 of our warships were sunk—however, when we did get papers we found that peace still exists—save for a stop press message that England has joined in. It is rather like Napoleonic times I daresay, and being Bank holiday of course makes us more remote from life than ever.

The only difference here is that a great many special trains are being run to take English people off the boats from France; and there are no boat trains from Victoria. Duncan went off yesterday, hoping that war would make yachting impossible. Your jewels have not come yet.

50

It was a vision of pleasure to see you; I've thought of you 50 times each day—in fact you may be said to be a kind of running bass.

We shall come up on Thursday I suppose. I do adore thee.

Yr B.

Berg

709: To Katherine Cox   *The Cottage Hotel, Wooler,*
                                         Northumberland

Aug. 12th [1914]

My dear Ka,

We've been having an argument as to whether you really went to Ireland or not—so I write to find out, though it seems as unlikely as possible that you will ever get this letter. It is thought that you are probably doing service somewhere, either as a nurse, or part of the military. I never felt anything like the general insecurity. We left Asheham a week ago, and it was practically under martial law. There were soldiers marching up and down the line, and men digging trenches and it was said that Asheham barn was to be used as a hospital. All the people expected an invasion—Then we went through London—and oh Lord! what a lot of talk there was! Roger, of course, had private information from the Admiralty, and had been seeing the German Ambassadress [Princess Lichnowsky], and Clive was having tea with Ottoline, and they talked and talked, and said it was the end of civilisation, and the rest of our lives was worthless. I do wish you would write and tell us what you hear—They say there must be a great battle, and here, where we are 15 miles from the North Sea, they expect to be in the midst of it, but then so they did at Seaford.

Your future is practically blasted, because you will be on 20 different committees. The very earnest and competent are already coming to town, with their practical habits—but I never could see the use of committees.

We have struck about the most beautiful country I've ever seen here. Except that it has no sea, I think it is better than Cornwall—great moors, and flat meadows with very quick rivers. We are in an Inn full of north country people, who are very grim to look at, but so up to date that one blushes with shame. They discuss Thomson's poetry, and post impressionism, and have read everything, and at the same time control all the trade in Hides, and can sing comic songs and do music hall turns—in fact the Bloomsbury group was stunted in the chrysalis compared with them—But why did you never prepare me for the Scotch dialect, and the melodious voice which makes me laugh whenever I hear it?

Leonard is very well, I think, and gets a lot of information from the merchants.

We shall be here a fortnight anyhow.
A letter would be a great treat.

Yrs
V.W.

Have you settled about publishing?

Mark Arnold-Forster

710: To Molly MacCarthy   *Asheham House, Rodmell,*
                                 Lewes, [Sussex]

Thursday [1 October 1914]

Dearest Molly,
    You can't think what a difference it makes when one returns to life to
find you and Desmond waiting for one. You have been such a delight and
comfort.
    Here we are once more, and it's so lovely and fresh on a beautiful
autumn day that we regret having let it and London seems a boiling cauldron.
And this morning we hear that our charming £40 a year Twickenham house
is almost certainly let which is a great blow. Heaven knows how we are to
find another in 10 days, but still, one always does manage. Sydney Street is
too grimy and noisy I suppose.
    It was very bad luck to come in 10 minutes after Desmond went the
other night. Please give him our love and tell him I am sending back a parcel
of his books.
    Well, wherever we do settle, do please come and see us, as often as you
can. It was so nice to come and see you again.

Your affectionate
V.W.

I am sending a few relics of flowers—but *don't* write—they are only scraps.

Mrs Michael MacCarthy

711: To Lytton Strachey   *The Lacket, Lockeridge,*
                                 Marlborough

[8 December 1914]

Dear Lytton,
    We have both enjoyed ourselves very much here.[1] It has been perfect in
every way. Except for the house decoration and choice of books (a little

1. Lytton had lent his cottage to Leonard and Virginia for the weekend 5-8
December.

heavy, don't you think) and the weather too has been bad but not bad enough to keep us indoors. It is evidently magnificent country—to my thinking better—at least more solid—than Sussex—but L. don't agree. The cooking—the food—the discreet old lady [Mrs Templeton] who is as noise-less as an elephantine kind of mouse—all have been perfect. Shall you come and see us again?

Many thanks
Yr. V.W.

In spite of great temptation, your letters remain virgin.

Frances Hooper

712: TO MARGARET LLEWELYN DAVIES

17 *The Green, Richmond*

Wednesday Dec. 9 [1914]

Dear Margaret,

It was very good of you to write. I had a feeling that you were coming here somehow under false pretences—however, I can't explain it and it isn't worth explaining—anyhow, I don't feel that now.

I never see you without thinking of all that we once had—for Arthur and Theodore[1] seem to belong to it so much—and so do you—and you are different from other people because of that.

Do come on Friday—only when? Leonard thinks you mean Friday night,—we have to go out to a Chelsea evening but if its teatime, that will suit perfectly.

The Sidney Webbs ask us to dinner about once a week, and Leonard has got to go tomorrow, though it sounds too dismal. They've clawed him for a huge job[2]—but he'll tell you about it.

1. Margaret's brothers. Arthur Llewelyn Davies had died young, leaving five sons, who were adopted by J. M. Barrie. Theodore, who had been a close friend of Leonard and Lytton Strachey at Cambridge, was drowned bathing in a river in Westmorland.
2. The Fabian Society had asked Leonard to write a report on international relations, which was first published in a special supplement of the *New Statesman* (10 July 1915) under the title 'An International Authority and the Prevention of War'. Later Leonard wrote a second report, and they were published together by the Fabian Society in 1916 as *International Government: Two Reports*. The book had a strong influence on Government thinking about a future League of Nations.

He says he will give the lectures, but wants to ask what sort of thing you want.

Do publish those letters.[1] I wish they could all be in full.

Yrs.
V.W.

Sussex

713: TO CLIVE BELL   17 *The Green, Richmond*

9th Dec. [1914]

Dear Clive,

Would you mind lending me the first two volumes of your Michelets history?[2] I noticed that you had it. I can only get it in a miserable small type at the London Library. However, I well understand horror at lending books, so dont bother if you'd rather not.

I also noticed that you have No. 11 in the red edition of Ibsen—which is missing from our set. Is it possible that someone staying at Asheham, took it away with them? You seemed only to have odd volumes, so I thought it possible.

Yrs
V.W.

Nessa said she'd ring us up. Someone has been ringing up, while we were away—If its her, wd you say we're generally out this week till about 4.30.

Quentin Bell

714: TO JANET CASE   17 *The Green, Richmond*

10th Dec. [1914]

My dear Janet,

It was only the other day that I suddenly said to myself "Janet will soon be ill"—and here it is. If you remember, I also foretold the murder of the Archduke, and the death of Mrs R. L. Stevenson, so its not surprising. But how very foolish of you, and I can quite imagine the blouse and petticoat dodge: though I also remember something about doing things thoroughly while one's about them. Please do—you are so much more worth keeping going than almost anyone. You should hear Leonard and me going through

1. In September 1915 the Women's Co-operative Guild published *Maternity: Letters from Working Women*, with a preface by Herbert Samuel.
2. Jules Michelet, *L'Histoire de France* (1833-43).

your merits—and we are both very scathing as a rule: you would blush, I hope.

However, my views of humanity are changing, since I spent yesterday cooking at an institution in Victoria Street. The charm of the young English-woman is inconceivable. She has eyes like a dogs, and a great plait down her back, and she is really stupider than I am, but so adorable. Why did you never tell me that?

At one end of the room are sailors, and then there are a few greyheaded ladies of great culture and refinement, dabbling in the insides of chickens, and some very smart, come to improve their knowledge of dinner party soup. I distinguished myself by cooking my wedding ring into a suet pudding! Its really great fun.

Annie (our cook) is coming to the Garden City [Hampstead] in a few days. Might she call on your maids? But dont bother about that now—In fact, please do nothing but get well. I shall certainly come when you're better, but its foolish to be seeing outsiders now.

Have you read Thomas Hardy's new poems?[1] They're quite the most beautiful things I've read since—certainly since Meredith—Shall I send you them? Also Arnold Bennetts Price of Love [1914] is good—but I daresay you dont want books.
Only get well.
Yrs. aff.

Sussex
V.W.

715: TO CLIVE BELL   17 *The Green, Richmond*

13th December [1914]

My Dear Clive,

(You will be bored by these perpetual demands)—We rather think of spending a week at Marlborough at Christmas if possible in lodgings—I seem to remember that you once told me of some in the High Street, or other pleasant part. If you could put the name on a postcard, we shd. be grateful as lodgings are so much better than Inns. It seemed divine country.
Yr V.W.

Quentin Bell

716: TO MOLLY MACCARTHY   17 *The Green, Richmond*

15th December [1914]

Dearest Molly,

It would be most delightful to see you. We shall go off, I think, for a week at Christmas; so come either before that, or afterwards. I think Windsor

1. *Satires of Circumstance*, 1914.

is on the Richmond line—at the same time its amazingly easy to reach from most parts of London. I don't know where Berkely Gardens is, but I expect near some tube or underground. And we are about 3 minutes from the Station, this end. If you would ring us up, we are always in in the mornings.

I've just been taking a course of cookery lessons, at an institution in Victoria St.

I do hope you're going to have Rachel[1] taught plain cooking and needle-work, as well as Icelandic and Portuguese. It is dreadful how we were neglected, and yet its not hard to be practical, up to a point, and such an advantage, I hope.

Yes, that damnable book is coming out.[2] To my great relief, I find that though long and dull, still one sentence more or less follows another, and I had become convinced that it was pure gibberish.

We heard tell of Desmond, in various parts of London, as one hears of a shooting star, or an aeroplane. I do hope he's well, and not seeing things that will haunt his pillow for years.

Have you had a horrid winter? I must say I think you are the most unselfish and adventurous woman I know.

Yr. loving,
V.W.

Mrs Michael MacCarthy

1. Their daughter, who married Lord David Cecil in 1932.
2. *The Voyage Out* was eventually published on 26 March 1915. Publication had been postponed owing to Virginia's illness.

Letters 717-738 (January–December 1915)

In January Virginia was 33. She seemed recovered. She and Leonard intended to buy a printing-press (a plan revived and postponed for several years), and they were negotiating the lease of Hogarth House, Richmond, which eventually gave the Press its name. Then Virginia had another mental breakdown, the worst of her attacks. It first struck her in mid-February, and with renewed violence on 4 March. While she was taken to a nursing home, Leonard organised the move from The Green to Hogarth House, and Virginia first occupied it when she was mad. The Voyage Out *was published on 26 March, the day after Virginia entered the nursing home, and it received very favourable reviews, but she was scarcely aware of the event, which coincided with the most violent period of her lunacy. It seemed that her mind and character might be permanently affected. She would seldom speak even to Leonard, except to abuse him. Her letters are interrupted for nearly six months, early March to late August, but in June she began to recover, put on weight, and moved to Asheham in September, with a nurse, and then back to Hogarth House in November. The first 18 months of the war had barely affected their lives, but now Virginia became aware of its dangers—zeppelin-raids on London, and the threat of conscription.*

717: TO DUNCAN GRANT
17 The Green, Richmond

[3 January 1915]

My dear Duncan,

What hellish luck—to miss you—and all for the sake of a Queens Hall concert, where the patriotic sentiment was so revolting that I was nearly sick. We were so late that we had tea in London—And there was a delicious tea here, which you ought to have taken for yourself, of honey and Cornish cream. You would have been made to stay, however, and help entertain a Jewess,[1] who is now upon us, and I've not changed yet.

Will you come again? Any day to tea, if you'll say which. Please do. It was really abominable to find your note when I got back—

Yrs V.W.

Richard Shone

1. Flora Woolf, Leonard's sister.

57

[early January 1915]

Here is the book, which I hope will help the birth of many more Victorian lives. I have seldom enjoyed myself more than I did last night, reading Manning.[1] In fact, I couldn't stop, and preserved some pages only by force of will to read after dinner. It is quite superb—It is far the best thing you have ever written, I believe—To begin with, what a miracle it is that such a group should have existed—and then how divinely amusing and exciting and alive you make it. I command you to complete a whole series: you can't think how I enjoy your writing.

Yr.
V.W.

Frances Hooper

17th Jan. 1915

Dear Mr Hardy,

I have long wished to tell you how profoundly grateful I am to you for your poems and novels, but naturally it seemed an impertinence to do so. When however, your poem to my father, Leslie Stephen, appeared in *Satires of Circumstance* this autumn[2], I felt that I might perhaps be allowed to thank you for that at least. That poem, and the reminiscences you contributed to Professor [F. W.] Maitland's Life of him [1906], remain in my mind as incomparably the truest and most imaginative portrait of him in existence, for which alone his children should be always grateful to you.

But besides this one would like to thank you for the magnificent work which you have already done, and are still to do. The younger generation, who care for poetry and literature, owe you an immeasurable debt, and in particular for your last volume of poems which, to me at any rate, is the most remarkable book to appear in my lifetime.

I write only to satisfy a very old desire, and not to trouble you to reply.

Believe me
Yours sincerely
Virginia Woolf

Trustees of the Hardy Memorial Collection,
Dorset County Museum, Dorchester

1. Lytton had completed his essay on Cardinal Manning in December 1914 and sent the typescript to Virginia. She and other friends encouraged him to write more, and he began 'Florence Nightingale' in January. To these two he added essays on Dr Arnold and General Gordon, and published all four in 1918 as *Eminent Victorians*.
2. The poem was titled 'The Schreckhorn', and was written in June 1897.

Tuesday [26 January 1915]

My dear Janet,

What a damnable bore it all is! We *are* so sorry about Emphie [Case] and the Cook. Do you get any food? Do you stay in bed? Does anyone look after you? I shall come tomorrow about 5, and try to investigate. If you don't want to see me, you needn't—but influenza germs have no power over me, and Leonard has been sitting with an influenza patient without any bad results.

I wish you'd take me on as your cook. I'm sure I could manage perfectly, and I should like handling all those blue plates.

I feel a selfish desire as usual to see you, and get purified from a debauch of gossip.

Leonard came back from you the other day wondering whether you would let him come regularly and read to you—which he would love to do, for the sake of being with you—Would you like it, I wonder, or anything we could think of?

I do hope Emphie's not got it badly. Give her our love.

Yrs. aff. V.W.

Just got this letter from Thomas Hardy! I wrote to thank him for his poem about father—Will you keep it for me.

Sussex

22nd Feb [1915]

My dear Margaret,

I wrote to Gerald [Duckworth] about the letters[1] and here is his answer, (which I don't want back). We are sending them, and Leonard will go and see him if he wants to be seen. I do hope they will be printed—with lots of photographs. They are so amazing.

Have you heard about our Printing Press?[2] We're both so excited that we can talk and think of nothing else, and I think there's a chance of damaging the Webb influence irretrievably, (which is my ambition in life). Presses only cost £17.17, and can be worked easily.

1. See p. 54, note 1.
2. A month earlier Virginia and Leonard had discussed the idea of buying a small printing press. It did not materialise until 1917. The reason for the delay was probably the recurrence of Virginia's illness during February.

By the way—is there any chance that you have got the works of William Morris—and if so, would you lend me one called "The Pilgrims of Hope". There was a review of it in the Times last week and it sounds magnificent, but I can't get it at the Library. It came out in 1885-6 in the Commonweal, and has only been reprinted in America—but possibly you took in the Commonweal.

I do hope you'll come and see us often in our house—Hogarth House— Its far the nicest house in England[1]—and it would be so nice to see you there.

Your affate,
V.W.

Of course don't answer if you haven't got the Morris.

Sussex

722: To Margaret Llewelyn Davies

17 *The Green, Richmond*

Thursday [25 February 1915]

My dear Margaret,

Thank you so much for troubling about the Morris. I shd. very much like to see it.

I want just to tell you how wonderfully things have changed in the last few days.[2] I am now all right though rather tired. It is so wonderful that I can hardly believe it.

And I wanted to say that all through that terrible time I thought of you, and wanted to look at a picture of you, but was afraid to ask! You saved Leonard I think, for which I shall always bless you, by giving him things to do. It seems odd, for I know you so little, but I felt you had a grasp on me, and I could not utterly sink. I write this because I do not want to say it, and yet I think you will like to know it. Our happiness now is something I cannot even think about.

Please come. We have given up the [G. B.] Shaws, and Saturday after-noon about 4 would suit me. I cant do much but lie still, but I should like immensely to see you and gossip about Madame Tournier[3] and other friends.

1. They had first seen Hogarth House in Paradise Road, Richmond, late in 1914. It was a handsome 18th-century town house, which had been divided into two, one half called Suffield House, and the other, Hogarth House.
2. On the morning of 23 February, Virginia suddenly became very incoherent. The attack lasted two days, and she partly recovered her senses for a week. In this letter to Margaret she was remembering her madness of 1913.
3. This is probably Miss Tournier, who in 1892 had been President of the Women's Co-operative Guild.

Dear Margaret, I so often think of you, and thank you for what you have done for us both, and one cd. do nothing to show what it meant.

Yrs.
V.W.

I wanted to tell Janet what I have told you but Leonard thought better not. Her goodness was so great.

Sussex

723: To Lytton Strachey   17 *The Green,* [*Richmond*]

Friday [26 February 1915]

Dearest Lytton,

This is just to say that I am now well again and it is very wonderful, but I dont want to talk about it. I should like to see you. I wonder where you are. I want oceans of gossip. Ottoline's teeth for instance—has she got new ones?

Also a bright idea strikes me. Let us all subscribe to buy a Parrot for Clive. It must be a bold primitive bird, trained of course to talk nothing but filth, and to indulge in obscene caresses—the brighter coloured the better. I believe we can get them cheap and gaudy at the Docks.

The thing is for us all to persuade him that the love of birds is the last word in Civilisation—You might draw attention, to begin with, to the Pheasants of Saxby, which heard the guns on the North Sea before the Parson did[1]—We must interest him in birdlife of all forms; he has already a pair of Zests [Zeiss] glasses. The advantages of the plan are in the first place that Vanessa, in his absence, could put the Parrot in the basement, or cover the cage with a towel—and secondly, he would very likely after a year or two, write another book on Birds—The fowl could be called Molly or Polly. I commend this to you: get subscriptions. I head the list with 6d.

I have to keep lying down, but I am getting better.

Our happiness is wonderful.

Your loving
V.W.

Berg

---

1. On 28 January 1915 the vicar of Saxby, Lincolnshire, the Rev. W. L. Evans, wrote to *The Times* to say that the pheasants at Saxby Hall had begun clucking at an early hour when they heard the guns of the Battle of the Dogger Bank on 24 January. The bombardment had been inaudible to humans.

724: To Margaret Llewelyn Davies

17 *The Green, Richmond*

[*in Leonard's handwriting*]

28 Feb 1915

Dear Margaret,

Leonard is writing for me. Thank you for coming yesterday, when to have you there gave me extraordinary pleasure. I hope it did not tire you much. I meant to ask you for a photograph of yourself, as I am no longer afraid, and I look forward to the bread and the chocolate creams.

If you see Janet, would you give her my love and tell her that it is horrid that we should neither of us be able to move when I want to see her so much. Please come again.

V.

I write this in my own person. I think Virginia is decidedly a little better today. Your visit certainly did her good—she enjoyed it so much—and already last evening she felt more restful. It was so nice to see you.

Leonard

Sussex

725: To Margaret Llewelyn Davies

17 *The Green, Richmond*

[*in Leonard's handwriting*]

2 March 1915

Dear Margaret,

This letter is from Virginia. Thank you very much for the photographs. I have spent most of the morning looking at them, and I have come to the conclusion that the one with the japanese umbrella is one of the most beautiful things I have ever seen. However in case you should feel elated I must add that that is possibly due to the umbrella. (I am going to add three notes of exclamation to that sentence in order to show that it is a joke)

Did I tell you that I have decided to write all the novels of Mrs Humphry Ward and all the diaries of Mrs Sidney Webb? It will be my life work. (Leonard has not yet laughed at any of these jokes though I think them rather good)

But what I really want to tell you is that now I only see beautiful things, you and Janet and the downs. You must come to Asheham and we will sit and look at them.

V.

V. is still a little better I think. She would like so much to see you if you would come on Friday. Could you come to tea about 4-4.30 that day? I enclose a time table.

Leonard

Sussex

726: To Margaret Llewelyn Davies

[*Hogarth House, Richmond*]

Postcard

Tuesday [31 August 1915]

Your letter still delights me. I take it up at intervals to get into closer touch with Madame T.[1] But my dear Margaret, whats the use of my writing novels? You've got the whole thing at your fingers ends—and it will be envy not boredom that alienates my affections. I saw Forster, who is timid as a mouse, but when he creeps out of his hole very charming. He spends his time in rowing old ladies upon the river, and is not able to get on with his novel.[2] Also I saw Ray Strachey,[3] but alas, she makes me feel like a faint autumnal mist—she's so effective, and thinks me such a goose. If I were allowed a proper sheet, I would now explain how it is that you are so much superior as a visitor, and in every other way, to the rest. Please write if ever you have time. The potted meat has a lovely jar. I have not begun to eat it yet. I havent got the Meredith poem.

Sussex

727: To Lady Robert Cecil

Asheham House, Rodmell, Lewes, [Sussex]

Postcard

[13 September 1915]

Dear Nelly,

I am only now allowed to write cards, and this is to thank you for your letter and to entreat another. We came here 2 days ago, and to my delight I am allowed short walks in a kind of nightgown, and then retire to a bed which overlooks, or looks up to the Downs; and perhaps the ridge on which

1. Miss Tournier. See p. 60, note 3.
2. E. M. Forster's next novel, *A Passage to India*, was not published until 1924.
3. Rachel Costelloe, who married Oliver Strachey, Lytton's elder brother, in 1911. She was prominent in the Women's Suffrage Movement and other political causes.

you sit.[1] It is so lovely that one walk gives me something to see for hours. O do write a book for me to read! I read everything, but one's friends should certainly write novels. How are you, and what are you doing, and will you ask me to tea again someday? What has happened to your distinguished niece, Guendolen?[2] and Beatrice Thynne?[3] Your letter was such a delight; and with only one post a day I beg of you to sit down at once and reply, so that I may imagine you again. I often do think of you—you'll be amused to hear.

V.

Hatfield

728: To Lady Robert Cecil   *Asheham House, Rodmell,*
                                    Lewes, [Sussex]

29th Sept. [1915]

My dear Nelly,

This is merely to inveigle you into writing again. I'm only allowed to write to the end of the page, which has a paralysing effect.

I rejoiced to hear of you following the zeppelin in a taxi; such it is to have the blue blood of England in one's veins: my literary friends hide in cellars, and never walk at night without looking at the sky.

Your book must be about the aristocracy. I can't think what to tell you about my life. It passes much like old Lady Baths, checked by Waterbury watches. Bed-walk-bed-walk-bed-sleep. The downs however change perpetually, even in this rain drift. Sometimes we have a troop of cavalry in our orchard—at others a bat in the drawing room. I try to paint and embroider, but these arts are so vapid after writing.

I am reading Mrs Gaskell. What a modest, capable woman! It is so cold my fingers move like dry twigs: the Beagle, our dog, has got inside the fender; I wish you would turn your motor car up our drive and bring word of the great world. However, this is a very pleasant one: swallows, rooks, thistledown, men thatching ricks. Do I never miss anyone? I am 33, and have decided that I am completely misunderstood. So please write again, and say how very nice I am—

Yr. aff. V.

Hatfield

1. Nelly Cecil's country house was Gale, Chelwood Gate, about fifteen miles from Asheham.
2. Lady Guendolen Godolphin Osborne, daughter of the Duke of Leeds.
3. Daughter of the Marquess of Bath.

Thursday [30 Sept 1915]   *[Sussex]*

I suppose, Miss Davies, you are full of good works as usual. Did you see your very warm review in the Times?[1] Your Guild I find quoted everywhere.

The telegraphic style is needed as usual; only to the end of the page, Mrs Woolf, says Nurse. I am petrified with fear. Its odd how formidable you grow at a distance. The country makes one feel very pure—especially these cold autumn days. I have just drunk a large cup of hot cocoa: my fur cloak is over me, and my feet are wrapped in woollen jackets.

I am reading Latin, and French—and how I wish I could march round to an office and impose my will upon the mysterious Harris.[2] How I envy you—partly your face, and partly your intellect.

I hear from Vanessa that old father Bell threatens complete rupture with Clive if he writes more in the style of the pamphlet.[3] Vanessa is delighted, as she has her income safe, and need not stay with the Bells at Christmas! What a callous brood we are! I hear that Karin wants to remove Adrian from the U.D.C.[4] as his work there is elementary. Lowes Dickinson[5] wants Leonard to introduce him to the Webbs. A funny mixture. I still feel that Mrs Webb appreciates me more than old Ragbag Ll. Davies does.

Now I must stop. I am so flourishing in health that I stop here more for your sake than for mine. Please write—but I suppose you are too busy. Hah Ha!

                                                          V.

Sussex

730: To Vanessa Bell   *[Asheham, Rodmell,*
                                                        Sussex]

[October 1915?]

Dearest,

Here are two dismal letters which Madge [Vaughan] has sent me. I should rather like to keep Stella's [Duckworth]—miserable though it is.

1. Of *Maternity: Letters from Working Women*. Published by the Women's Co-operative Guild.
2. Lilian Harris, Assistant Secretary of the Women's Co-operative Guild, of which Margaret was General Secretary.
3. Clive's anti-war pamphlet, *Peace at Once*, published in the spring of 1915 by the National Labour Press, had recently been destroyed by order of the Lord Mayor of London.
4. The Union of Democratic Control.
5. G. Lowes Dickinson, the Cambridge historian, became very active during the war organising schemes for the future peace, including the Bryce group, which foresaw some of the actual provisions of the League of Nations.

How are you? I have heard nothing since the appendicitis scare. I hope you are being sensible. I don't see much chance of meeting at present, I'm afraid. My affairs have taken to coming back so that I scarcely go out. However I think they are now in hand.

The only news is that our hens lay eggs without shells. What does it mean?

Yr. B.

[*in Leonard's handwriting*]
I am sending you a product of our garden.

LW

Berg

731: To Lady Robert Cecil

Asheham, Rodmell,
Lewes, [Sussex]

14th Oct [1915]

My dear Nelly,

This is to wake you to your sense of duty to an old, though humble, friend. It seems to me inevitable that you and Lord Robert will one of these days rule England, and I shall smuggle into your Receptions and hide behind the vast pyramids of orchids and peaches. What fun it will be! My idea is to become a waitress, for which only a neat black dress is needed. Have you my passion for seeing the splendours of the world? I don't want to touch them or speak to them: as I'm afraid they would shiver. But I am often comforted to think that Lord Robert has some authority—

Leonard met Lloyd George the other day, and brought back a shocking account.[1]

Here the time passes too quick. Do you feel that the days in October melt into each other, the night being almost indistinguishable from the day? We begin with mist and end with mist. We have about 5 hours of soft sunshine in the middle.

We have just made pounds of blackberry jam; now we are going to pick mushrooms, and we have a tree which spills walnuts over our garden. I have never got so much out of nature before.

I have just read Conrad's book; with distant admiration, but no passion for his villains, who had much better shoot themselves, I think. And I have become rather bored by Sylvia's Lovers—although the substance of it is very satisfactory.[2] What I object to in the mid Victorians is their instinctive fluency—as if Mrs G. sat down to her writing with the cat on her knee—

1. Leonard had heard him speak at a public meeting in Bristol on 9 September.
2. Virginia had been reading Joseph Conrad's *Victory* (1915) and Mrs Gaskell's *Sylvia's Lovers* (1863).

But the nurse will not let me explain my profound wisdom to you—nurses are strange beings—After all, some things are better worth having than flawless health—Perhaps its the mushrooms she's after.

You must come to Hogarth one day—and sit in our small garden. It would be extraordinarily nice to see you again.

"A very long letter, Mrs Woolf?"

O —— so now we must go out.

Yr. affate
V.W.

I am *very* nice—getting nicer with age, too.

Hatfield

732: To Lytton Strachey   *Asheham, Rodmell,*
                                      Lewes, [Sussex]

22nd Oct. [1915]

Dear Lytton,

I think it is about time we took up our correspondence again. Surely you must have amassed a million adventures since we met. I can't feel altogether sure that you still persist in the flesh—my friends—ah, but Sydney Waterlow tells me I have none. By God! What a bore that man is! I don't know why exactly, but no one I've ever met seems to me more palpably second rate and now the poor creature resigns himself to it and proposes to live next door to us at Richmond and there copulate day and night and produce 6 little Waterlows. This house for a long time stank to me of dried semen.[1] And its only a kind of mutton fat in his case. You see what straits we are reduced to.

I am really all right again, and weigh 12 stone!—three more than I've ever had, and the consequence is I can hardly toil uphill, but it's evidently good for the health. I am as happy as the day is long, and look forward to being rid of the nurse soon (she is at present dusting the room, and arranging the books). We come up on the 5th; as the summer seems to have broken up.

I should think I had read 600 books since we met. Please tell me what merit you find in Henry James. I have disabused Leonard of him; but we have his works here, and I read, and can't find anything but faintly tinged rose water, urbane and sleek, but vulgar, and as pale as Walter Lamb. Is there really any sense in it? I admit I can't be bothered to snuff out his meaning when it's very obscure. I am beginning the Insulted and Injured [Dostoievsky, 1862]; which sweeps me away. Have you read it. But this will not lead you (O God, how this woman annoys me with her remarks "The Dardanelles,

1. Sydney Waterlow, who married Margery Eckhard as his second wife in 1913, had rented Asheham House in the winter of 1914/5.

Mrs Woolf, would they be in France?") to think that I am spending long hours with my favourites, as Ott. used to say she delighted to do, in the long country days. Have you seen her? Have you seen anyone? What are you writing? Please lend us your last Edinburgh [Review] article. Leonard is writing so many different books—one for the morning, another for the afternoon. His life, so he said yesterday, is to be spent on a History of Diplomacy, but as the Webbs have their claws fixed in his entrails, I see no hope for him.

Nurse now thinks I must stop writing. I tell her I'm only scribbling to a relative, an elderly spinster, who suffers from gout, and lives on scraps of family news. "Poor thing!" says nurse. "Arthritis it is", I remark. But it won't do!

Yrs.
V.W.

Frances Hooper

733: TO LADY ROBERT CECIL

Asheham, Rodmell,
Lewes, [Sussex]

25th Oct [1915]

My dear Nelly,

Far be it from me to say pleasant things, for the mere sake of giving pleasure—you will acquit me of that I'm sure. No, it is purely selfish with a view to getting further letters; but certainly you are cut out for a correspondent: far the best of those that write to me.

Of course, having access to the great official world of the "people who count" according to Mrs Humphry Ward, it is comparatively easy for you to be witty, instructive, and well packed. By the way, I've just read Eltham House, by that old mangy hack; and I wonder what you'd say to it. It seems to me the writing of a woman who has been accidentally locked in to the housekeeper's room of Longleat say for the past 20 years; and has done nothing but absorb family portraits and family plate. According to her, 12 people, all related, rule England. But its a vile book, and after gulping it down, I felt morally debased. My nurse however, is absorbed by it.

We are coming back to Hogarth House next week as the summer has toppled over, and the woods are ruined. For 6 days, the leaves flew past incessantly, and now only a few pure golden ones still hang, which is the loveliest time of all, though very muddy, for those elderly, like myself, who change their stockings.

Did I tell you that on part of the proceeds of the Voyage Out[1] we went

---

1. In *Beginning Again* Leonard records that in the 15 years after publication it sold only 2000 copies, and earned Virginia less than £120.

for a treat to Brighton; and had a delightful time—wandering into back streets full of most improper little shops, and past the great bow windows, where the old ladies and their pets were sunning themselves. I love seaside places, for about 6 hours. I wish you'd come with me some day. We had a grand luncheon.

How does Guendolen make out our relationship? I wish she'd tell me. I always mean to write a history of my Great Aunts, who are said in the family to have been incomparably beautiful and romantic, though I never heard of a Duke of Leeds.

Do you find any charms in the 1860's? They seem—my mother's family I mean—to float in a wonderful air—all a lie, I daresay, concocted because one forgets their kitchens and catching trains and so on. Still, they were beautiful anyhow, and French which used to make us so angry as children.

Leonard's view of Lloyd George was only from the pit of a hall; but he thought his appearance and views all very shocking.

Please come out one day and see us—Its so far that I hardly like to suggest it—I suppose I shan't be allowed to walk about in London much yet, though I'm ever so much stronger.

Yrs. V.W.

Hatfield

734: To Margaret Llewelyn Davies   *Asheham, Rodmell,*
                                                    [Sussex]

Nov. 2nd [1915]

Dearest Margaret,

I wish you would thank the great and mysterious Harris for her pamphlet. The human brain is amazing—first to have invented such complications, then to understand them. She must be powerful, I see. Do you understand all that too?

We have been having the Shoves [Gerald and Fredegond] to stay with us. He edits War and Peace [magazine], and she is a poetess and brought her poems. They are going to retire to the country and write books, and they seemed very young and incompetent, and I was filled with pity for them. We gave them good advice. In particular, I urged her to join her Co-op stores, but I could not rouse her enthusiasm. I quite understand that the cultured, enthusiastic but utterly scatterbrained young must be very trying.

The weather has been vile lately, but very beautiful none the less, if Nurse didnt attach so much importance to wet feet.

We have got a new parlour maid, grey haired, about 45, with no visible attractions, but seems sensible in the house. Annie seems to wish to stay on.

It has been very nice here—a great deal of reading and wandering about on the Downs. Leonard, of course, writes away at Cooperation,[1] and reviews so many books about the war that his brain ought to spin—but it doesnt. He has a whole shelf of odious mustard coloured volumes, with the Kaisers Head or Eagle on the back, which have to be tackled by degrees.

We are very happy, and both very much want to see you again. It is most delightful to think that you exist up at Hampstead, and I hope we may inveigle you to Richmond sometimes—No one is really (ah—but I mustn't say 'really' according to you) quite so inspiriting to see, as you are—and thank God. Those flashing half hours won't destroy us any more. (by which I mean that they were the saving of life to me but not to see you rush out of the room will be so pleasant)

Max is climbing over me, so I cannot write sense. Leonard who is scribbling away by my side, sends his love, and hopes to see you soon.

We come up on Thursday

Yr. V.W.

Sussex

735: To Katherine Cox   *Hogarth House, Richmond*

Sunday [14? November 1915]

My dear Bruin Cox,

It seems a very long time since I saw your nice furry body. I think it is greatly to my credit that I have left you at peace for so long. However, as I shant want your services in the medical line for 10 years I hope, we really might meet I think.

I am afraid that all my friends are dead. Most it is true I dont miss at all— I rather like snuffing their graves when I go into London—Ottoline and such like, I mean. But I dont want poor Bruin dead just yet. I am often seriously alarmed when I hear that the zeppelins have been over London, but accounts from Sydney and Nessa prove that you never turn a hair, but merely take a look at them, put the cowards in the cellar, and then walk the streets till you've seen all the fires! Poor Sydney took it very differently, and was so much disturbed by the notion of dying, I suppose, and his own cowardice, that he never stopped analysing his character at Asheham—when it wasnt his character it was Hom's [H. O. Meredith], which is rotting according to him. But I suppose all this sort of thing happens at your evenings— shall we be asked to them?

My difficulty is to find any clothes—my weight is 12 stones—Leonard says you weigh 13.10—but this I dont believe. Anyhow I'm very well, and enjoy sitting in this mound of flesh. I spend my spare time in bed, but I'm allowed out in the afternoons, and thank God the last Nurse is gone. I'm

1. *Co-operation and the War: Co-operative Action in National Crises.*

sure that the effort of keeping them going is a great strain on the nerves. We had to play cards every evening, but she was always beaten.

Are you still making socks for Queen Mary?—I make so many careers for you as I lie comfortably before the fire. I think you ought to knock down our present civilisation, with your great square head.

Will you dine with us one night? not to meet Walter Lamb this time. The house is really rather nice, or will be when I have done a few repairs.

L. sends love

Yr

V.

Mark Arnold-Forster

736: To Duncan Grant   [*Hogarth House, Richmond*]

Monday Nov. 15th [1915]

My dear Duncan,

I have always meant to ask you whether you left a coat and umbrella here last summer? There is nothing on them to prove it, but it has long been rumoured that they are yours.

I should very much like to hear from you an account of your doings, as it seems many a long age since I saw you. Someone said you had gone to Paris. I was meaning to call on you, but can't remember your number. Paris I daresay is full of interest—the streets, so I read, given up to prostitutes turned patriotic. Shall you escape conscription? The revelation of what our compatriots feel about life is very distressing. One might have thought in peace time that they were harmless, if stupid: but now that they have been roused they seem full of the most violent and filthy passions. Are the French better? This I gather only from newspapers as we haven't seen many people.

We are settled here again, and thank God, the last nurse is gone. So much of my energy went into making conversation that I feel better instantly. I am to be allowed to write, and gradually return to the world. However, I dont seem to know any of the young sparks who have sprung since my time. There is a man called Garnett,[1] and one Montague,[2] and another Allan,[3] so I

1. David Garnett was then 23. He had first met Virginia through her brother Adrian in 1910.
2. Paul Montagu, a zoologist and anthropologist. He had come down from Cambridge in 1913, and was a friend of David Garnett.
3. Clifford Allen, later Lord Allen of Hurtwood. At Cambridge he had been Chairman of the Fabian Society, and then Editor of the first official Labour newspaper, *The Daily Citizen*, until it ceased publication in 1915. He was also at this time Chairman of the No Conscription Fellowship, and was three times imprisoned for his anti-war views.

hear, and innumerable Miss Trees.[1] I daresay they are more lively than we old creatures used to be. Lord! what a strain the Cambridge intellect used to be! Does Noel[2] still exist, and the Stracheys? I hear from Sydney [Waterlow] that Gumbo [Marjorie Strachey] gives satisfaction in Manchester. He, poor man, has inadvertently begotten another child; and has no money, and therefore has taken a house in Gipsy Hill [S.E. London], where he is going to bury Mrs W: and her litter. The Zeppelins have frightened him away from London, and he lodges near us. The mange has attacked his head—a more depressing spectacle I have seldom seen.

I wish you'd come and see us. I should like to hear your views on many subjects. Richmond is certainly the place to live in, partly because London then becomes so full of romance. I am going up to the dentist this afternoon, and then I shall wander through the streets till I find a good place to have tea in, and then I shall read my newspapers, and find the way to the Underground. I suppose middle age makes one want only simple pleasures. How old are you? How is Aunt Hen?[3]—(I'm sure she'll be murdered one of these days)

May I come to tea with you one day when you get back?

Yrs V.W.

Duncan Grant

737: To Margaret Llewelyn Davies

Hogarth [House, Richmond]

[25 November 1915]

Dearest Margaret,

Far from being tired I was, as usual, much refreshed by you, but going home I thought of you climbing that hill in the dark again to a severe Harris waiting with her pen behind her ear among the papers.

Yes, Miss Davies, I enjoyed my visit, and my egg. I think you are a very nice person to see, and I quite agree to a weekly visit—Wednesday? Any day so far suits me.

Do think of Christmas or the days after Christmas at Asheham. We should both like to have you so much. I prescribe a change for you, and a roll down the hills, and sitting in the sun in our garden, and an unlimited

1. The three daughters of Sir Herbert Beerbohm Tree, the actor-manager, of whom Viola and Iris were the most socially prominent.
2. Noel Olivier, one of the four daughters of Sir Sydney Olivier, the Fabian Socialist.
3. Henrietta Anne Grant, paternal aunt of Duncan Grant. Her sister married Sir Richard Strachey, Lytton's father.

amount of talk with Leonard, and I should bargain for a certain amount of tenderness towards me.

I've just written with such appalling difficulty to old Bee Webb.

Yr. V.W.

Of course we use Pelaw polish. The Jewish Chronicle wants to interview L. on any Jewish subject.

Sussex

738: To Roger Fry   *Asheham, [Rodmell,*
Sussex]

Boxing Day [26 December 1915]

My Dear Roger,

The translations[1] are very interesting and have led to much discussion between James Strachey Leonard and me, though mostly upon the question of metre and rhyme. They think that theres not enough feeling for the metre in Apparition, and it should be rhymed, and more formal.* I myself felt the metre very strongly in your version and did not miss the rhyme. My only criticisms are that you might perhaps get greater richness of language if you were less literal—and also I dont like (as a matter of detail) 'beauty sleep' which reminds me somehow of a beauty specialists advertisement in a Ladies paper. But otherwise I think them very interesting, and I hope you mean to do them all. I'm sure you have a great gift in that way, and translations like these are exactly what people without much French like myself want, and never get, for translators are apt to be so entirely wrong in feeling.

I hope this is coherent, but I write in the usual Asheham chaos—Max has just been sick, having voided a large worm earlier in the day.

It was most delightful to see you, and I hope we may discuss everything under the sun before we die—though I'm sure you'll outlive us all, and only reach a kind of brilliant middle age when you're about 80, and the rest of us will hate you for not letting our poor old brains rest at the very end—

Leonard has just read aloud a passionate poem by Lawrence,[2] which perhaps made Max sick, but I expect you would have enlightened it somehow.

*They like the other one very much: so do I.

1. Roger Fry's translation of several poems by Pierre-Jean Jouve (b. 1887) from *Vous êtes Hommes* was published by Omega in February 1916, under the title *Men of Europe*.
2. D. H. Lawrence's *Love Poems and Others* was published in 1913.

We go back on Thursday. Won't you stay with us when you do the Hampton Court frescoes?[1]

Yrs ever,
V.W.

Sussex

1. Since 1910 Fry had been engaged intermittently in restoring the Mantegna paintings, *Triumphs of Caesar*, in the Royal Collection at Hampton Court.

Letters 739–756 (January–April 1916)

The increasing vigour of Virginia's letters indicate her complete return to normality, and she was not to have another total mental breakdown until she killed herself 25 years later. 1916 was on the whole a calm year for the Woolfs. Virginia continued to receive praise for The Voyage Out, *but she wrote little more than occasional reviews for the* TLS, *and began to learn Italian. The war had scattered her friends. Rupert Brooke died in Greece; Ka Cox was caring for refugees in Corsica; Duncan Grant was fruit-farming in Suffolk; Maynard Keynes and Saxon Sydney-Turner were busy at the Treasury. "Bloomsbury is vanished like the morning mist", she wrote to Ka Cox. But visits of friends to Asheham and Hogarth House, and Virginia's own "occasional dips" into central London, did something to keep its spirit alive.*

739: To Katherine Cox   *Hogarth [House], Richmond*

12th Jan [1916]

Dearest Ka,

I'm afraid we shan't be able to come tonight, as I'm rather headachy and have to stay quiet, and Leonard is going to the House to hear the debate. I wish we could come, though I daresay the room will be full of people wanting private last words, and cursing the others.

Yes—Asheham you must write with red ink in your book. Did I tell you how I mean to have a motor boat next summer?

I thought perhaps I was arrogant or scratchy in the way I talked of Rupert the other day.[1] I never think his poetry good enough for him, but I did admire him very much indeed, and he always seemed to me like a fully grown person among mummies and starvelings (which refers to the people I lived among). But it seems to me sometimes that our casual way of talking must sound silly to anyone like you who knew him really, and therefore understood what he might do. And I don't like my Bruin to think me silly, or to confound me with the artistic. Now, will she be a careful sensitive creature, and realise that her life is worth that of 20 Quakers? Besides, Quakers are notoriously long-lived and unsusceptible to shock. They stand any amount of strain, and have practically no feelings. Is this what you call a literary letter? (It suddenly strikes me, I should like to know what you mean by that).

---

1. Rupert Brooke had died on Scyros in April 1915.

Anyhow, please write occasionally, and for God's sake don't sacrifice anything to your country. Leonard sends his love, and you will believe in our deep affection.

Yrs. V.W.

Mark Arnold-Forster

740: To Margaret Llewelyn Davies

Hogarth House, [*Richmond*]

Sunday [23 January 1916]

Dearest Margaret,

It was very nice to get your letter, though we think scent a little luxurious—Ottoline scents her cigarettes. No doubt you are emulating her virtues. Kind acts from morning to night don't seem much in your line, I must admit. Do you ever get out onto your [Hampstead] Heath? I often think of you, as I pace beside my river, which surely surpasses anything you have.

The big mouthed red haired woman was, alas, my sister in law Karin. There can be no doubt of it. She sat 2 seats from L. at the [Bertrand Russell] lecture, and fills him with such physical repulsion that he can hardly endure to look at her. He says the lecture was interesting, though hard to follow. I hope to go next Tuesday, more to see the audience than to listen, I'm afraid. Then there'll be Mrs Sidney Webb, who attacks at great length. I don't see that there's much good in Lectures—clever people go home and gossip about them, and thats about all. But then, my dear Miss Davies, what does do good? You say sitting on Town Councils and upholding one's ideals. I incline to think that that merely improves one's own soul—still, I daresay the Women's Guild has done something; isn't it touching how I return to that achievement of yours always for comfort?

I've been reading Carlyle's Past and Present, and wondering whether all his rant has made a scrap of difference practically. But Bertie [Russell], according to Bob Trevelyan who lunched here, takes his lectures very seriously, and thinks he's going to found new civilisations. I become steadily more feminist, owing to the Times, which I read at breakfast and wonder how this preposterous masculine fiction [the war] keeps going a day longer—without some vigorous young woman pulling us together and marching through it—Do you see any sense in it? I feel as if I were reading about some curious tribe in Central Africa—And now they'll give us votes; and you say—what do you say Miss Ll.D? I wish I could borrow your mind about 3 days a week.

We're asking Miss Harris the great, and Miss Sheepshanks[1] the able to

1. Mary Sheepshanks, daughter of the Bishop of Norwich, and effective Principal from 1899 to 1913 of Morley College in South London, where Virginia had taught from 1905 to 1907.

dine—which is a bold step, I think. But Leonard's got to cope with them.

I enclose a poem,[1] in return for the immortal Bishop. The authoress, an insinuating elderly lady, called the other morning, and made me buy 4, at 3d a piece—and they don't rhyme or make sense—Lord Kitchener had thought them very pretty. Its rather a good idea—to sell one's works in person—

I'm quite well again, and hope to come up very soon, if you're visible. But this week is rather full. We saw the Dr, who says that in time I shall be able to do much more, but it will be a long time; still, I feel amazingly well.

Leonard sends his love.

Any roots will be most acceptable, though the garden is run wild.

Yr. V.W.

Sussex

741: To Katherine Cox   *Asheham, [Rodmell, Sussex]*

Feb. 12th [1916]

Dearest Ka,

We were very much delighted to hear from you. I think if the Serbians haven't got typhus, which you dont say anything about, you are happier among the Eucalyptus than here.[2] How long do you mean to stay? We came here yesterday, leaving London in fog and rain. We stopped at a small and peculiar shop, in Lewes, where Leonard buys his bleached socks, and we got you some stockings. If they suit, let me know, and I will get some more. We are here for a week, partly to see the spring come in, and partly to collect half the furniture in this house, which Miss [Jean] Thomas lent me and now claims—damn her soul. Needless to say, it is all broken, stained and damp eaten.

London goes on much as usual. I dip in occasionally, and shake my ears well when I get back to the purer air of Richmond. Nessa has had a picture show, which the Times critic says errs on the side of beauty, 'the national fault'. I predict the complete rout of post impressionism, chiefly because Roger, who has been staying with us, is now turning to literature, and says

1. *Kitchener's the Man*, by P. M. Gair. The first stanza reads:
   Kitchener's the man we all will trust
   To see us through this conflict first.
   Kitchener's the man we British adore,
   Give him his sway and he'll do more.
2. Ka Cox was in Corsica, caring for Serbian refugees.

pictures only do 'to look at about 4 times.' He has lent us two of his works.

Old Bob Trevelyan and Mrs B. have been ranging about London. They came twice to Richmond, having nothing whatever to do and Bob talked quite incessantly, asking after you, and Mrs Bob blew her nose in a great white handkerchief, and attended very carefully to all that was said, like a scrupulous Dutchwoman. Did you realise that all Bob's earlier works were written lying recumbent on the ground, with his legs supported on a tree trunk, so that the blood might flow to his head?[1]

Then one day we went to lunch with the Waterlows at Gipsy Hill. We saw a tall stout gentleman pacing up and down a suburban street, reading a book, which was Sydney, taking the air before lunch. Inside, Margery was very sleekly brushed, pregnant; and by God—what a house! Have you been there? The Omega curtains—hard bright blues—mustard coloured chairs— all very clean and cheerless. However, we agreed that after talking to Margery for some time,—forgetting her appearance, she is rather nice. It is a comic situation—to be perched on a bleak hillside, under the eye of the Crystal Palace, with an increasing family.

Leonard is very well, and working at his supplement and reviews, and lunching with the Webbs, who maintain that the war will end in October. Margaret suggests a new society or scheme on the telephone about every other day. Bertie lectures on Tuesdays, and thinks to issue a new constitution, so we are told, with the help of young Cambridge. I went to one lecture, and sat near the poisonous Widow Whitehead,[2] who wore tortoiseshell antennae in her hat, and looked more livid and snakelike than I can tell—the spirit of evil. Didn't she once say that I was a hard woman?

So we go on: personally, I am very happy and sanguine, because I think—I was going to say that even the purest are better than the state we were in, but that of course is a lie,—I suppose I am happy merely because it is so pleasant to be well again, and allowed to write for a little every day. I do think Richmond has great charms also, and now we have Roger's servants,[3] we keep clean.

We go back in a few days—and please, good Bruin, write again, and do, as you love me, keep well, and dont think that life is a thing to be thrown up into the air like a ball, which I'm sure is your present frame of mind.

Leonard sends love

Yr V.W.

Mark Arnold-Forster

1. R. C. Trevelyan had begun publishing his poems in 1898.
2. Possibly Evelyn, the wife of the philosopher Alfred North Whitehead, though he did not die till 1947. She had been scandalised by the dresses worn by Virginia and Vanessa at the Post-Impressionist Ball in 1910.
3. Nelly Boxall and Lottie Hope, who were to remain with the Woolfs for many years, arrived on 1 February.

Asheham House, Rodmell,
                                             Lewes, [Sussex]

15th Feb. [1916]

My dear Saxon,

There was a time when it would have caused you some pain to think you had not seen us for three months, but I suppose years and official splendours have much hardened your heart.

Will you come and stay with us this next week end?—Saturday the 19th, I suppose it is. We would take you along the river, and into Kew Gardens, where the rhododendrons are all in flower.

Why is it that nobody ever seems to see you now? Rumours are about that you have enlisted for garrison duty, in discharge of which you married a Sea Captain's daughter who can speak 6 languages—none of which I believe.[1]

We came here a few days ago for quiet and fresh air. The rooms were all a soft grey with mildew, and Leonard, sitting in a steaming arm chair, caught a cold in his head, which has just come to me.

Every night it roars with wind and rain, and last night we had to shout to each other in our bedroom about 3.A.M. and could only just hear, above the hail which rattled on the panes, and the wind which came pouring down the chimney. We had only a very small bit of candle, and Leonard's watch had stopped. Suddenly there was an explosion on the terrace—nothing to be seen, of course; but this morning we find two great trees have been blown down, and lie across the drawing room roof, completely blocking up the end window so that I write in semi darkness, looking into a kind of jungle. There is a great hole in the garden wall— tiles off the roof, our terrace uprooted, branches everywhere, and my great Italian pot smashed to atoms. Its a great pity, as the trees were very beautiful. Our servants, who were Rogers, were delighted to be out of the way of zeppelin raids, but are rather doubtful now. Still, the country is full of charms.

I am learning Italian, and want some help from you badly. Are there any easy, and not altogether insipid books to read?

We lunched with the Waterlows the other day. My God! What a neighbourhood! They spoke of you with awe and love. Owing to L. playing chess, we had to rush for a train, and took the wrong one, and circled round the Crystal Palace for about an hour, until we reached Gipsy Hill again.

Ka writes that she is in Corsica, washing verminous Serbians, quite well herself, very hot, and in need of white stockings.

1. Saxon Sydney-Turner was a Treasury civil servant all his working life. He never married.

Ring us up on Saturday morning, or Friday night and say you will come. We very much want to see you.

Telephone number, 496 Richmond

Yrs V.W.

Sussex

743: TO LADY ROBERT CECIL   *Asheham House, Rodmell,*
                                 Lewes, [Sussex]

Feb 18th [1916]

My dear Nelly,

It is a strange fact that I always think of you when I am down here. Yesterday was so clear that we could see the ridge where you sit surrounded by Freshfields, Duckworths etc., I cant help feeling that we are very superior in our isolation. We go back to Richmond this afternoon, having been here a week. The first two nights it was impossible to sleep owing to the gale, and when one did sleep, one dreamt of the traffic in Chancery Lane. About two o'clock the uproar was so terrific that we lighted a small stump of candle, and sat up in bed and listened, it being almost impossible to hear ourselves talk. Then there was a great explosion in the garden, and in the morning the maid pulled us out of bed to see a great tree which was blocking up the window. It had fallen right across our drawing room, and crashed through the garden wall, and brought down two trees under it! I sit and write looking into a deep tangle of branches and leaves, which Leonard says is exactly like the jungle. He went out next morning to chop up the branches for firewood, the gale still howling; and suddenly there was another explosion and a very high dead tree fell right on top of the others. I thought he must be crushed, but happily he had seen it shaking, and had moved away just in time. It was a great escape. Now we are cutting the branches into logs, and burning them. They make the room smell delicious and have lovely thin flames. The worst thing is that they are always falling out of the grate onto the carpet into the middle of a mass of dogs.

By the way, I meant to write and tell you how unreasonable your conduct was in that train, going back from Richmond. You see, if you had sat firmly in the one we put you into, you would have got to Charing Cross, without any change. Then there was the Bakerloo waiting for you. The story of your wanderings made us both feel very guilty. The same thing happened to us the other day, when we went to see some friends who have settled for some obscure reason at Gipsy Hill. We went round and round the Crystal Palace for an hour, and it was like a very long, bad dream. One goes through Tooting and Peckham, and Norwood, and Balling or Balham, and how we cursed our friends for living in such places!

May I now come and see you?

I have been reading Mr Strutts musical reminiscences[1], with interest. I must have seen him at every concert and opera I ever went to, and he often describes the same concerts. It is very outspoken criticism, which is refreshing. I have also been reading Mr Arnold Bennett[2] who depresses me with his very astute realism, and Miss Viola Meynell[3] who depresses me with her lack of realism—so perhaps I am hard to please. However, I am in the middle of 2 huge volumes by Mr Shorter upon the Brontës,[4] [which] rakes up every scrap of paper they ever wrote upon, so that it is something like a realistic novel, and, as usual, absorbing.

Now I must go and get ready.

Yrs. aff. V.W.

Hatfield

744: To Lady Robert Cecil   *Hogarth House, Paradise Road, Richmond*

[21? February 1916]

My Dear Nelly,

We should like very much to come to tea, and will come Wednesday week, 5 o'clock, 1st March, unless you stop us. I have rather muddled up my engagements, and possibly have arranged for something else on that day, in which case we will let you know. Therefore don't seclude yourself from Freshfields etc. and if we find them in possession we will behave with self restraint. Living in the suburbs one tends to set apart days weeks ahead, and then to get them all mixed (I speak for myself, not Leonard).

The Brontë book is edited by that reptile C. K. Shorter: however, it's mostly letters, and well worth reading. I only borrow it, or I should send it to you.

Yr. affate,

Hatfield   V.W.

745: To Lytton Strachey   *Hogarth [House], Richmond*

28th Feb. [1916]

Dearest Lytton,

What a treat to hear from you!—still it don't make much difference whether you write or not and I always feel you will turn up safe in the end,

1. W. M. Strutt, *The Reminiscences of a Musical Amateur*, edited by his mother, Lady Raleigh (1915).
2. Possibly *These Twain* (1916).
3. Either *Columbine* (1915) or *Narcissus* (1916).
4. C. K. Shorter, *The Brontës: Lives and Letters* (1908). Virginia was writing an article on Charlotte Brontë (*TLS*, 13 April 1916).

and in fact you never really disappear. Miss Berry[1] shall be sent off at once, and also a volume or two of Madame de Genlis,[2] which I always suppose to be yours.

Your praise [of *The Voyage Out*] is far the nicest of any I've had—having as you know, an ancient reverence for your understanding of these things, so that I can hardly believe that you *do* like that book. You almost give me courage to read it, which I've not done since it was printed, and I wonder how it would strike me now. I suspect your criticism about the failure of conception is quite right. I think I had a conception, but I don't think it made itself felt. What I wanted to do was to give the feeling of a vast tumult of life, as various and disorderly as possible, which should be cut short for a moment by the death, and go on again—and the whole was to have a sort of pattern, and be somehow controlled. The difficulty was to keep any sort of coherence, —also to give enough detail to make the characters interesting—which Forster says I didn't do. I really wanted three volumes. Do you think it is impossible to get this sort of effect in a novel;—is the result bound to be too scattered to be intelligible? I expect one may learn to get more control in time. One gets too much involved in details—But let us meet and have a long gossip—What about next Sunday? Will you come to dinner—or tea— and spend the night? I asked Pernel [Strachey] to come, but Duncan tells me she is away, and as I haven't heard from her, I suppose she doesn't mean to come. Ring us up—and if that day doesn't do, suggest another—We almost always have a spare room.

What are you about—are you in love?—are you writing?—I suppose you will come out brilliantly with the flowers of spring. I do wish you'd print all your works at once—Talking of which, I've just been sent an appeal to me as a 'passionate soul' to subscribe to a private indecency press called the Rainbow, for the production of that and other works—[3]

Yr.
V.W.

Frances Hooper

746: TO KATHERINE COX   *Hogarth House, [Richmond]*

Sunday, March 19th [1916]

Dearest Ka,

We are very sorry to hear about your disease. Dont you think that's a good reason for coming home? The night your letter came with (if you

1. The friend of Horace Walpole. Her correspondence was published in 3 volumes in 1866.
2. Félicité de Genlis (1746-1830), the prolific writer of popular romances.
3. This presumably refers to the suppression of D. H. Lawrence's *The Rainbow* in 1915.

remember) certain remarks, upon Waterlows and Eckhards,[1] Sydney was dining with us, and Margery Olivier,[2] and he was telling us with his usual ponderous devotion, how you had malaria, but were better. Next minute, there was a snuff-snuffling at the door, and Bruin's letter came in. I expect your present state gossip is most acceptable—not indeed that I ever write a letter about anything else. Do you suppose that Dora Sanger[3] writes letters about the Russian atrocities? In the 19th century, of course, they discussed politics and religion. Margery Olivier had not been in the room a minute before she said "I've just refused a proposal of marriage!" Nobody knew what to say. For some reason we all felt very awkward. She told us that the man is unknown to us, has £2,000 a year, and is employed in munition work: aged 32. Who can he be? Leonard inclines to think that she suffers from a disease of advanced virginity in which one imagines proposals at every tea party. Certainly, she's in a very odd state of mind.

We go on much as usual. It is with great difficulty that I can be routed from bed and sofa, where I make myself a kind of Bruin lair, snug from this damnable spring. A perpetual white or greyish fog has succeeded the snow. Old Margaret Davies and Janet are inclined to melancholy, and begin to feel very old. I think 50 must be the very devil—only one's decline into old age before one, and strength enough to realise the horror. You have heard how Duncan has become a fruit farmer in Suffolk with Bunny Garnett?[4] He came up after a week of it and says he finds it very soothing, and all his faculties sink to sleep. He is out picking Big Bug[5] off the currant bushes for 8 hours a day: sleeps all night, paints on Sundays. I daresay he will paint better, though I think he's very good; but sitting over one's work in Fitzroy Street, with a pat of butter turning yellow in a paint box seems to me infernally dreary. Nessa is going to keep house for him perhaps all the summer. So you see, Bloomsbury is vanished like the morning mist.

Leonard is as usual writing away at about 6 books, and he has now trained himself to compose straight on to a typewriter, without a mistake in sense or spelling. I feel like the owner of some marvellous dog who does tricks—there's pointing to my husband's gifts. Max had a fit in the drawing room last night: he rolled off his chair, lay twitching on the floor, then walked

1. The family of the second Mrs Sydney Waterlow.
2. Eldest daughter of Sir Sydney Olivier.
3. Wife of Charles P. Sanger, the barrister. Lady Ottoline Morrell writes of her at this period that she "lamented the war and . . . would devote herself to anyone who claimed her sympathies" (*Ottoline at Garsington*, p. 43).
4. Both were conscientious objectors. In order to establish a better claim for exemption from military service, they decided to work on the land. They went to Wissett, a remote village in Suffolk, where they took over a neglected house and orchard from a cousin of Duncan who had recently died.
5. Virginia got the phrase wrong. The black currant bushes at Wissett were infected with 'big bud'.

with great difficulty, and then recovered completely. Do you think it was a fit? Oughtn't they to foam green at the mouth?

Henry James is dead [28 February 1916]. His last words, according to Sydney [Waterlow], were to his secretary, whom he sent for. "I wish to dictate a few faint and faded words—" after which he was silent and never spoke again.

Ray [Strachey] is having her usual operation, with a view to a child. I am writing reviews. We go to Asheham for Easter—and wont you turn up one fine spring morning? Leonard has just come in, says this letter is absurdly long, sends his love, and says I cant write any more, so I must leave out about our Printing Press, and our motor Boat, and how I've sold 2,000 copies of the Voyage Out.

Write and take care.

Mark Arnold-Forster   Yr V.W.

747: TO DUNCAN GRANT   *Hogarth House, Paradise Road,*
                                                            Richmond
March 26th [1916]

My dear Duncan,

I hope this letter will arrive after you have spent 10 hours among the Big Bug—and I hope you wont have had any letters for a week, and then you will say, now, I must answer at once or I shan't get another. However I am also writing to thank you for the picture, which seems to me very massive and splendid. I like it immensely. It was all wrapped in the Westminster Gazette, I got safely with it into the Tube, when the paper slipped down, and all the old ladies began peering and squinting and looking at me with horror. Finally a very nice old Frenchman offered to hold it for me and so we got home.

You said you would like gossip. I collect what I can, and prick up my ears in company, but my opportunities are not what they were. People dont seem to trust me now, except poor old zanies like Margery Olivier, who ran into the room the other night crying "I've just had a proposal! I've just had a proposal!" Sydney Waterlow was there, and we were inclined to be ponderous. Who can it be? He has £2,000 a year: aged 32; very nice, but she wont have him. Leonard thinks its all imagination, a disease affecting the unmarried of her temperament.

The other day we went to tea with Nelly Cecil, and met old Beatrice Thynne, who is more like a sunburnt tinker who has just had a mug of beer than ever, notwithstanding the death of her mother and nephew.[1] She was as

1. Beatrice Thynne's mother, Lady Bath, had died on 31 October 1915; and Beatrice's nephew, John Alexander, Viscount Weymouth, was killed in action 13 February 1916, aged 20.

black as a rook, with one very large Bumble Bee, carried out in pearls and sapphires, attached to her throat. She is going to live in lodgings over St Johns Wood post office, in order to economise; she uses margarine instead of butter; and wears no underclothes. She spends all her time reading family letters, and tying them up in bundles, as they are too many to burn, and all perfectly dull. Nelly is going to economise by living in Henry James' flat. It is wonderful how entirely detached from sanity the aristocracy are; one feels like a fly on a ceiling when one talks to them.

Yesterday we went to the [Military and Appeal] Tribunal here, but there was only one interesting case—that of a young man who wakes up every morning 'wet to the ankles' 'which would quite unfit him for military life' his father said. There seemed to be a good deal of doubt about this however, and I dont think he got off. Did you see that 4 conscientious objectors were exempted on condition they worked at agriculture?—it was somewhere in the country, I forget where.

What happened at Wyndham Lewises[1] that afternoon? Did you feel that he was master of horrid secrets, or merely quite ordinary? I do hope other people haven't some secret about life up their sleeves, which makes me appear to them an innocent lamb. Henry Lamb (talking of lambs) always gave me that feeling. Thank God, he's now exposed.

Yrs
V.W.

Duncan Grant

748: To Margaret Llewelyn Davies
Hogarth [*House, Richmond*]
Monday [27 March 1916]

Dearest Margaret,
Wrong as usual. Miss Harris, right as usual. How could it be fish? It didn't taste of fish or feel like fish. It was Semolina (comes from flour, as you would know if you had been over the C.W.S. mill). I grant that it looked rather like the roe of cod, but you show how far you are from reality, and being a woman, not a lady—ha, ha! If it weren't for Semolina how should working women ever make both ends meet? Semolina is to us what cream, butter, eggs etc., are to you. We often eat nothing else for weeks. Try it with a spoonful of lard for supper.

Leonard says he has 4 brothers, none in the least like him, by which he means that they are all inferior. He was a strict Jew as a small boy, and he can still sing in Hebrew. Next time you come, we'll make him tell us all about it.

1. The painter and writer. He had exhibited at the Second Post-Impressionist Exhibition in 1912, and afterwards worked in the Omega Workshops. In 1913 he fell out with Roger Fry, and founded the Rebel Art Centre.

Lytton Strachey was here yesterday and described how he had to wait 4 hours at the White City to be medically examined. They then found that his right lung was diseased and exempted him immediately. Of course there is nothing the matter with his lungs, but he let this pass, —is now off to Ottoline, with a ticket exempting him for ever.

The classes are getting hopelessly mixed—when you speak of Janet at a lecture, do you mean the teacher or the cook? I hope it was Janet Case.

I want to go to Ireland, but we want to do so many things. Why cant one be turned back and live everything over again, perhaps rather more slowly?

I don't believe you for a second when you say you don't want your life over again.

Yrs. V.W.

We are always talking about Loonsdale.[1] How many servants did they keep at Loonsfield? Did they have a carriage? Did they have prayers? Did any of them go to the bad? I didnt ask many questions that I really wanted to ask, out of politeness. Leonard is very anxious to know more about the brethren.

Sussex

749: To Violet Dickinson   *Hogarth House, Paradise Road, Richmond*

Sunday [2 April 1916]

My Violet,

I daresay you want to drop us—if so, spit it out like a woman. If not, shall I come to tea with you one day? Are you still living on Manchester Street? Do you still think me very wicked for living at Brunswick Square with a household of young men? Does marriage purge one of impurity, or am I for ever contaminated?

I saw Nelly the other day and Beatrice as grimy as a coalheaver, what with mourning and the dust of old letters.

Leonard sends his love.

Yr

Sp.

Berg

1. Kirkby Lonsdale, in Westmorland. Margaret's father became the Rector there in 1889, when she was 28, and she organised the Women's Co-operative Guild from the Rectory. She had a number of women ('the brethren') to help her, including Lilian Harris.

Postcard

[5 April 1916]

I cant come on Friday, but I should like to come on Tuesday, 4.30. and hope to find a nice hot bun. Its your aristocratic aloofness that intimidates me—who always was so soft and attached, like an adhesive oyster—full of pearls, I need hardly say.

V.W.

Berg

751: To Vanessa Bell   *Hogarth [House], Richmond*

5 April [1916]

Dearest,

I was on the point of writing to you when your parcel of daffodils came in, which I suppose I may interpret as an embrace. (but you have to write as well) Are they wild ones? They look like it. I suppose they grow all about your lake, with blue flowers, and pear blossom,—and you're as happy as the day, and have quite forgotten the fleasome Singes? [Virginia]

I dont know what news there is to tell you—but I daresay one or two things have happened. I went to tea with old Janet Case the other day, and found her mending Emphie's mole grey blouse, with an edging of white frill, which took me back to the 1890ties. She is still more or less bedridden, and keeps her disease in the dark, though she was writing an article upon illegitimacy in Sweden for a newspaper. Downstairs, Emphie was playing very badly on the violin to a party of wounded soldiers. The house is crowded with photographs of old pupils, deceased parents and the Elgin Marbles, and they have covers to all the po's. Does this convey any of the spirit of Hampstead to you? They seem to float along very cheerfully, and with amazing sweetness of temper. I sat and gossiped, and Janet mended her blouse all wrong, and did it over again.

Then we went to tea with the [J. C.] Squires, who live at Chiswick; and we found a childrens party going on, and several gaunt prolific mothers, and we were much in the way, as Squire was out. So we walked up and down the embankment, and then went back, and were shown all his first editions. The children were very inferior to Quentin and Julian—such common lumpish brats, without any spirit—However, 2 were too young to talk. Squire had just bought a book for a shilling that was worth £10; and he had exchanged it for an ancient Breviary which seemed to me very dull. He is a thorough collector and journalist—but I rather like her.

By the way, I've got into touch with Violet again. I thought I'd write and ask her why she objected to my living at Brunswick Sqre., and whether she wished to drop me on that account. She writes back in the usual jocular style, doesn't mention Brunswick Sqre, and asks me to tea, which I shall do, and then I shall tease her.

Did you answer Madge[1]?—and what did you say? Nelly [Boxall] and Lottie [Hope] went to tea with Jessie [Vanessa's cook], and evidently had a terrific gossip about Sophie,[2] who is coming here tomorrow. Jessie said she had behaved disgracefully, and she would never go near her again, which was unfortunate, as I had been telling Nelly all Sophie's virtues, and want them to give her tea in the kitchen. Nelly is an odd character—she sits up every night till 1 watching for zeppelins, and so I said she had better sleep in the kitchen, as a joke. But she took it up very seriously, and is going to force Lottie to sleep with her in camp beds, among all the beetles. Do the zeppelins come near you?

What do you do? Happy? I'm going to write Duncan a criticism on his picture soon. What do you and he think of Turner? I've got to review a book on Ruskin. I wish you'd tell me something about Ruskin and Turner.

Write, Dolphin, and you'll then get an answer.

You cant think how I miss you. I'm going to the dentist, and if you were there, I shd. come in to tea.

Yr B

Berg

752: To Vanessa Bell   *Hogarth House, Richmond*

Friday [14 April 1916]

Dearest,

I am much better now[3]—in fact I got up yesterday for an hour, and I am to go out, if fine, on Sunday. Leonard is going to Asheham with Lottie on Monday to warm the house, and I shall go on Tuesday. We've got Lytton and [C. P.] Sanger coming on Thursday for Easter. [Dr] Fergusson says I shall have to be very careful for a fortnight, but I shan't trouble my head about visitors. It will be a mercy to get into the country.

I think you have a very great gift for writing. I enjoyed your description of country life immensely. But dont you miss that sweet voiced bright eyed Ape? Otherwise I think it must be heavenly to feel theres no telephone, and gossip is for the moment stilled. I've got absolutely no news, as I've not seen

1. Margaret Vaughan, married to Virginia's cousin William Wyamar Vaughan, who had been headmaster of Wellington College since 1910.
2. Sophie Farrell, who had been cook at Hyde Park Gate during Virginia's childhood, and since then with different members of the Stephen and Duckworth families.
3. Virginia had had influenza.

anyone. Violet Dickinson is coming to tea today, and I'll question her about you and Brunswick if I can. I had a long visit from Sophy the day I got ill. She has grown quite thin, and very small. She was very dismal and affectionate —doesn't at all like being with Aunt Minna [Duckworth], and lives on her memories of the past. She is almost doddering about St Ives, and old furniture and old days, and said she had nothing now to look forward to.

Then we had Gerald and Adrian and Karin. Gerald was very urbane, and grey as a badger. He asked after you, and was much amused to hear of your anticonscription work.[1] He treated us all as small children, and it made me feel how hopelessly in the minority we are. Sylvia[2] has been writing to Leonard about watching Tribunals—very official and pompous.

I am being very careful, as I dont at all want to have to go to bed at Asheham. I suppose I shan't be able to go to that house again[3]—but Leonard might. Your daffodils are most lovely, and there were such lots that the servants had some too.

Do write soon—I do like getting your letters. We shall be a fortnight at least at Asheham. I wish you'd come and stay with us.

Yr B.

Give my love to Duncan—I should much appreciate a letter from him.

Berg

753: TO LEONARD WOOLF   *Hogarth* [*House, Richmond*]

Monday April 17th [1916]

Precious Mongoose,

This is just to tell you what a wonderfully good beast I am. I've done everything in order, not forgetting medicine twice. Fergusson came this morning, and said it was the best thing for me to get away tomorrow. He had been seeing Craig, who had sent a message to tell me to stay in bed every morning, and always have a sleeping draught at hand, to take at the least wakefulness—and altogether to be very careful for a fortnight. Fergy said my pulse was quite different from last summer—not only much steadier, but much stronger. I am to go on spraying my throat. He seemed very pleased with me.

I had a letter and a poem from Lytton[4]—the poem very Lyttonian, but I'll bring it to show you—Also a letter from Janet who is in her farm house

1. Vanessa had been assisting at the offices of the No Conscription Fellowship.
2. Either Sylvia Woolf, the wife of Leonard's younger brother Edgar, or Sylvia Milman.
3. Virginia was looking for a farmhouse near Asheham, where Vanessa might live with Duncan and her children.
4. Both are published in *Virginia Woolf and Lytton Strachey: Letters* (1956), pp. 58-9.

in Herts. I rang up Molly and asked her to tea, as I thought my solitary afternoon without darling grey goose would be so dismal, and she's coming. Desmond suggested coming with her, but I said you were away, so I think he thought better of it. Thats all my news, but I lie and think of my precious beast, who does make me more happy every day and instant of my life than I thought it possible to be. There's no doubt I'm terribly in love with you. I keep thinking what you're doing, and have to stop—it makes me want to kiss you so.

Its quite fine, though windy, and I'm going out for a short walk. Fergy says its very good for me to go for a short walk every day.

I'm now going to write to Mrs Langston[1] about the room. I think I must subscribe to their Social, as we're not going.

It will be joyful to see your dear funny face tomorrow.

The Marmots kiss you.

Yr MANDRILL

Fergy is sending round some more sleeping draught.

Sussex

754: To Vanessa Bell   *Asheham, [Rodmell, Sussex]*

Saturday [22 April 1916]

Dearest,

Here we are sitting in the drawing room with the windows open and the rooks cawing. Sangers voice is to be heard bubbling up one bright remark after another. Lytton is rather languid and cadaverous, but as smooth as silk. I have to spend the morning sequestered, as [Dr] Craig sent a message to tell me to stay in bed till lunch. However, I rather like it, as I just dip in when I feel in the mood for conversation. Its no good worrying about one's visitors, and if they find it dull, I dont see that it can be helped.

Its been quite fine since Thursday, though to begin with we had gales and rain, and various misadventures. L. came down on Monday to find no fires lit, and he and Lottie had to set to and get the house ready. Bella Wooler [daily servant] burst into tears, and refuses to do anything more for us, partly I think because of the coal, so L. has to pump and do the E.Cs. Then Lottie said she thought she'd got influenza, and had to be put to bed— but she recovered at once, and works like a horse, and chatters to everyone without any fear.

London seems miles away, except for these damned newspapers— Sanger has awful stories about conscientious objectors shipped to France

1. Of the Women's Co-operative Guild, Richmond.

and there shot. He is very red eyed and wizened and overworked but he pumps up the most amazing quips and cranks, and his eyes glow and he looks like one of the dwarfs in the Ring. We went for a walk yesterday and he told me how his father was a chemist, and made a small fortune and bought a house at Dorking and longed for the county to call upon him, but they wouldnt, and then when Charlie was doing well at Cambridge, old Sanger got the asthma, and couldn't receive guests, so he died, and his life was a tragedy, and now the chemists business is going bust, owing to the war. Sanger trots about in white trousers with black stripes, like the deck of a ship, and a black coat on top. Lytton and I gossip about Ottoline and books, and last night he read us his Florence Nightingale, which is very amusing.

However, you say you want gossip about Gerald [Duckworth]. I plunged into the nineties last week—what with Gerald and Violet. The odd thing is that they haven't changed since Hyde Park Gate. Violet still very slapdash and jocular in a blue serge tailor made, slapping her thighs, and asking innumerable questions. Gerald paternal and white-haired and rather patronising. Ozzie [Dickinson] says Gerald is violently in love—but Violet couldn't remember who with. Then we heard all about Lady Bath's death, and her silk dresses hanging in the wardrobe, and lovely little Russian jackets for the boy who died,[1] and Beatrice [Thynne] counted out 50 matches and said the cook must make them last a week, and she has £2,000 a year, and a flat in Grays Inn, and Katie [Cromer] cooks the legs of rabbits in a keepers lodge at Welwyn, and Lord Cromer has the backs, and Katie wears a nightgown under her dress to save packing, and Ozzie dines with the Asquiths, and Mrs Drew[2] eats raw carrots and is cured of rheumatism, and Violet packs pyjamas in the Mile End Road and Lady Desborough[3] has had all Rupert's [Brooke] poems printed privately, and Violet Asquith[4] says she loved him as she has never loved any man, and Asquith is carried to bed drunk by Lillah MacCarthy[5]—Now in return for all this, for God's sake tell me how Ott: and Roger have made it up[6], together with any other items of Bloomsbury gossip.

1. Beatrice Thynne's twin brother John, 1867-87.
2. Gladstone's second daughter, Mary Drew (1847-1927), who had sometimes acted as his secretary.
3. Lady Desborough, the mother of Julian Grenfell, lived at Taplow on the Thames, and her house was a centre of political and literary society.
4. The daughter of the Prime Minister, later Lady Violet Bonham Carter.
5. The actress, who had married Harley Granville-Barker in 1906.
6. The quarrel between Lady Ottoline and Roger Fry originated in 1911, when Roger accused her of spreading the rumour that he was in love with her. Their relations worsened when Ottoline heard that Roger had been gossiping about her affair with Bertrand Russell. He was invited to Garsington for Easter 1916, but their friendship never fully recovered.

I saw Molly [MacCarthy], who was going to Ott. for Easter, rather brisked in the head by a Swedish doctor, but not very quick in the wits. By the way, Helen and Bernard Holland[1] have both become Roman Catholics.

Yr. B.

Berg

755: To Vanessa Bell   *Asheham, [Rodmell,*
                                        Sussex]
Sunday [23 April 1916]

Dearest,

I forgot yesterday to ask you what I wanted to ask you—which is, will you out of the overflowing generosity and superabundance of your magnanimous heart (in which I have always believed) design me a sketch for my summer cloak? I bought some grey silk and sent it to Miss Joy, who can't make it for lack of a sketch. What I want is something light and simple—I should think perhaps a kind of kimono. It is the colour of a young elephant, with a slight crinkle. I couldn't get what I wanted, owing to the presence of Amber Reeves,[2] who haunts me. If you could send the sketch straight to Miss Joy, I should bless your shadow.

She has just sent me my blue summer dress, which I like very much—in fact, I think even as an advertisement I should pay the Omega, as I'm always being asked who made my things. It's a superb spring morning, and Lytton and Sanger are in high good temper reading on the terrace. This is far the loveliest country in Europe.

Expecting a letter from you,

I am your faithful

Singe

Berg

756: To Violet Dickinson   *Asheham House, Rodmell,*
                                    Lewes, [Sussex]
Easter Monday [24 April 1916]

My Violet,

Here we are sitting with open windows looking onto the meadow in which a lamb has just died. We have been crawling about the downs, but we

1. Helen Holland was a distant connection of Virginia through the Duckworths. Bernard Holland held several minor official posts, and, among other literary work, edited the poems of Crabbe.
2. Amber Blanco White, a friend of the Webbs, Bernard Shaw and H. G. Wells, who had used her as the model for Anna Veronica in his novel of the same name (1909). She had published several books herself, and from 1916-19 was the Director of Women's Wages, Ministry of Munitions.

haven't found any plovers nests—Nessa has, but I thought only trained farmers knew where to look for them. It has been most lovely here, and I wish you would appear swinging over the gate with a dog. We have got a very much overworked barrister [C. P. Sanger] staying with us, and Lytton Strachey, and they moan and growl over the newspapers all day long. To make things worse, our meat supply has run out, because they eat such an enormous amount, and the spring chickens are only as big as thrushes, so today we've got to starve, and Leonards two sisters may turn up at any moment, and so we've got to knock up a village shop two miles off—

We are strewn with fallen trees, which L. chops up for the fire, but the garden, such as it was, is ruined. Plants are very odd things. Bulbs I planted 3 years ago suddenly come up in odd corners, and tulips with gigantic heads on very short stalks.

We come back again next week—and perhaps you will ask me to tea, or I shall ask you, and then we might gossip about our youth—Nessa is trying to breed rabbits, but discovered after buying that they are all varieties of the male sex!

Yr
Sp.

Leonard says he would like to see you again.

Berg

93

Letters 757-788 (May–mid-September 1916)

On 30 May Leonard, though not a pacifist, was exempted from military service on medical grounds, his doctor certifying that the trembling of his hands was uncontrollable, and that Virginia herself would suffer terribly, perhaps fatally, if Leonard were called up. Most of their friends were conscientious objectors, and the authorities treated them humanely. Virginia was particularly concerned for Duncan Grant, who was now living with Vanessa at Wissett in Suffolk, and pleaded on his behalf to Lord Salisbury, Chairman of the Central Tribunal. Duncan and his friend David Garnett were allowed to continue their agricultural work, but decided to move with Vanessa from Suffolk to Charleston, a farm four miles from Asheham. Soon after staying with them at Wissett in July, Virginia first conceived the theme of her second novel Night and Day, *in which Vanessa was to be the central character (No. 776). The Woolfs spent a weekend with the Webbs, where the Bernard Shaws were fellow-guests, but for most of the summer they remained at Asheham, and among those who visited them were Roger Fry and G. E. Moore. Two cousins of Virginia were killed, but the war still made little impact on their lives (neither having any form of war-service), although they could sometimes hear, from the Downs above Asheham, the pounding of the guns in France.*

757: TO VANESSA BELL　　　　　　　*Hogarth House, Richmond*

14th May [1916]

Dearest,

I was getting quite alarmed, not hearing from you, and remembering your promise to write at least twice a week. However, I guessed that you must have been having the devil of a time. I know nothing about the Tribunal beyond what I saw in the Daily News. It was headed 'A Follower of Tolstoy' who had been brought up by his mother to believe in Tolstoy, and there was an artist aged 31, also refused.[1] What steps will they take now? Do they mean to go to prison?

---

1. Duncan Grant and David Garnett had appeared before the Local Tribunal in Suffolk. Part of Garnett's case was that his mother (Constance Garnett, the translator) had been a life-long pacifist who had visited Tolstoy in Russia. The Chairman, thinking that Tolstoy was a town, rejected their claim for exemption. See Garnett, *The Flowers of the Forest*, p. 121.

94

Leonard went to Craig who said that he would give him a certificate of unfitness on his own account, as well as mine. He has written a very strong letter, saying that L. is highly nervous, suffers from permanent tremor, and would probably break down if in the army. Also that I am still in a very shaky state, and would very likely have a bad mental breakdown if they took him. He thinks they ought to give L. complete exemption on these grounds, and strongly advises him not to put in anything about conscience, which annoys them. It is rather difficult to know what to do, as the Tribunals are so erratic.

L. lunched with the Sidney Webbs, who of course professed to be behind the scenes; and according to them, the War Office has already too many men, and will connive at any gentleman getting off; so the thing to do is to produce letters from Harley St. doctors, or the peerage. They think that the war will probably be over before October, as Germany seems to be crumbling internally. L. went to a committee, where Buxton[1] said that we are now considering terms of peace, and only the amount of compensation remains to be settled. I daresay this is mere gossip, but there does seem some chance that things are changing. Also, the government seems to be thoroughly badgered by the number of C.O.s.

What is Clive doing? I suppose a rupture is about the best excuse one can have. I wonder what you'll do, if Duncan and Bunny are made to do some national work. I wish you'd leave Wissett, and take Charleston.[2] Leonard went over it, and says its a most delightful house and strongly advises you to take it. It is about a mile from Firle, on that little path which leads under the downs. It has a charming garden, with a pond, and fruit trees, and vegetables, all now rather run wild, but you could make it lovely. The house is very nice, with large rooms, and one room with big windows fit for a studio. At present it is used apparently as a weekend place, by a couple who keep innumerable animals, and most of the rooms are used by animals only. They say it only takes half an hour to walk to Glynde Station, through the Park, and you have Firle, with its telephone, quite near, so you would be more accessible than we are. There is a w. c. and a bathroom, but the bath only has cold water. The house wants doing up—and the wallpapers are awful. But it sounds a most attractive place—and 4 miles from us, so you wouldn't be badgered by us.

I suppose I must write and tell all this to Karin; but I'd much rather you had it than they.

Walking in Kew Gardens the other day, who should we run into but

1. Charles Roden Buxton, the Labour politician, who in 1916 published *Peace This Winter*. He and Leonard met at the Labour Party's advisory committees on international and imperial questions. Leonard became Secretary of both.
2. The farmhouse near Firle, Sussex, which Karin and Adrian Stephen later thought of taking. It was the house where Vanessa, Clive and Duncan spent much of their lives.

Watty [Walter Lamb], as spruce as a Bank Clerk, and as bald as an egg. He took us back to tea in his exquisite residence [on Kew Green], which has walls of ducks egg green, and delicately tinted engravings of 18th century buildings hang perfectly straight, and all his books polished and in order, and a green baize board with crowds of invitation cards. He goes to dances every night, and has become a sham man of the world. Art interests him less and less. And then he began upon the King and Queen, and the President [of the Royal Academy], and how wonderful the President thinks him, and his kidneys, and his rheumatism, and long long stories about Princess Mary and her Lord in waiting, whom she made wear a gas mask and then gave orders to his man, in a corner of the R. A—which Watty thought showed a fine wit—Poor creature! He knows he's but a slug, and all the time he tries to excuse himself.

We left Molly [MacCarthy] at Asheham, where she was to finish her novel[1]; once more verging on collapse, and, poor creature, resigned to her deafness, which the dr. says is permanent, as the nerve of her right ear is destroyed. People are much nicer when they stay with one—I wont say nicer, but more natural.

What do you think of a country life? James went before his National Service Com: and they said he must work on the land, which he refused to do; but we think if L. gets allowed that, we might retire to Asheham, and take service under Gun [local bailliff]. O God! I've got to go and see At. Minna [Duckworth], and At. Mary [Fisher]!

Yr B.

Leonard says that the caretaker at Charleston said that Mr Stacy to whom the house belonged, when he heard that Mr Ray the present tenant, wanted to sublet it, said he wouldn't let him sublet it. The Rays are very bad tenants and have let the house get out of repair; so you'd probably have to negotiate with Mr Stacy, but I shd. think he'd certainly prefer you as tenants.

Berg

758: TO MARGARET LLEWELYN DAVIES

Hogarth [House, Richmond]

Tuesday [23 May 1916]

Dearest Margaret,

Do come next Monday; and stay more than one night if you will—We do love having you.

Leonard has gone down to Janet [Case] today, but comes back tomorrow.

Yrs. V.W.

Sussex

1. *A Pier and a Band* (1918).

May 26th [1916]

My Violet,

I was much amused to hear of your meeting with Mrs [Neville] Chamberlain. She was very attractive when I last saw her; much nicer than Horace Cole, her brother. But I see occasionally that she has had another child, and I suppose being a Chamberlain is pretty stodgy.

I envy you your nightingales—We get them sometimes at Asheham. This afternoon we've got to go and see Aunt Mary Fisher. Doesn't it take one back to Hyde Park Gate days? She always gives L. a book of old photographs to look at, and half kisses him in the Hall.

Did you know old Samuel Butler? I have got to write about him.[1] I wish I'd known him—O and by the way, I'm told that you produced your life of your Aunt or grandmother, and made a tremendous success. *Please lend me a copy*—nothing is quite so nice as old family letters.[2]

Yr

Sp.

Berg

Saturday [3 June 1916]

Dearest,

Clive has just rung up and says that Duncan has had his questions put to him.[3] He seemed rather doubtful what I'd better do about Nelly,[4] but on thinking it over it seemed to me best to write to her at once, telling her about Duncan, and saying that if she thought she could do anything I would send her details in a day or two. So I hope you will let me have them.

I do hope it will come all right.

Yr B.

Berg

1. Review of *Samuel Butler, Author of Erewhon, the Man and his Work*, by John F. Harris (*TLS*, 20 July 1916).
2. These were *Miss Eden's Letters*. She was Emily Eden, Violet Dickinson's great aunt, and the daughter of the first Lord Auckland. The book was not published until 1919.
3. After the meetings of the Local Tribunal and the Appeal Tribunal at Ipswich, which had awarded them non-combatant service, Duncan and David took their case to the Central Tribunal, by whom they were required to fill in a preliminary questionnaire, giving their reasons for claiming exemption.
4. James Cecil, fourth Marquis of Salisbury, Nelly's brother-in-law, was Chairman of the Central Tribunal.

761: To Lady Robert Cecil   *Hogarth House, Paradise Road,*
Richmond

[3 June 1916]

Dear Nelly,

    I wonder if it would bore you or be in any way distasteful to you if I told you about the case of Duncan Grant the painter, who is a conscientious objector and will be coming before the Central Tribunal in a week or two.

    If you didnt mind, and felt that you could possibly say anything on his behalf to Lord Salisbury who is on the Tribunal, I would send you details in a day or two. He is perfectly honest in his objections, and also remarkable as a painter. But I dont want to become a pest to you, though I have a great wish to help Duncan if I can. I am told that the Central Tribunal enquires into the good faith of applicants—and I've known Duncan many years and very well, and could testify to his honesty—

Yours ever,

Virginia Woolf

Hatfield

762: To Vanessa Bell   *Hogarth House, Paradise Road,*
Richmond

[6 June 1916]

Dearest,

    This letter has just come from Nelly.

    If Lord Salisbury wants outside testimony, what had I better do? Get Roger or Clive or someone to write or see him? I'm writing to thank Nelly, and saying that theres any amount of testimony if Ld. S. wants it. I'll let you know if I hear again.

Yr B.

I suppose Lord S. will want testimony as to Duncan's conscience, and not as to his artistic genius. Please write, in case I hear again from Nelly.
Do you see that Charles Fisher [Virginia's cousin] went down on the Invincible!

Berg

763: To Lady Robert Cecil   *Hogarth House, Paradise Road,*
Richmond

[6 June 1916]

My dear Nelly,

    Thank you for taking so much trouble. It is very good of you.

    If Lord Salisbury should care to have outside Testimony there are many people who would like to give it—

By the way, being asked the other day if you would like an invitation to the Womens Co-operative Guild Conference which is to be held at the end of this month in London, I boldly said yes—so you will get a ticket, and if you liked to look in, we might meet there. It is worth seeing.

Have you taken Henry James' flat?

Yrs. aff.
Virginia Woolf

Hatfield

764: To Vanessa Bell   *Hogarth House, Paradise Road, Richmond*

Wednesday [7 June 1916]

Dearest,

I have just had the enclosed letter from Nelly.[1] Before it came, I had your telegram, which as you see, reads rather mysteriously. I think you must have written "outside evidence *sent* officially"—not *send*, as I haven't any to send.

I sent a messenger to Nelly before I got her letter (as she is away for the day) asking her to tell Lord Salisbury about Duncan at once, and repeating about his being very honest and a good painter. It sounds from her letter rather as though Lord S. didn't wish to be approached unofficially—but I hope she will at any rate send him Duncans name.

I am telephoning to Clive and telling him about Nelly's letter, in case he thinks we had better take any further steps.

Yr B.

Berg

765: To Vanessa Bell   *Hogarth [House, Richmond]*

Saturday [10 June 1916]

Dearest,

I'm afraid I cant come on Wednesday, much though I should like to. We are going out on Wednesday night, and we go to the Webbs on Saturday, so that wouldn't leave much time—only Friday really. But I hope you'll ask me—or us—again.

I think it was all right with Nelly, as I said the Tribunals had been very stupid which was our reason for asking her help, and we'd no wish to do

1. Nelly had replied that Lord Salisbury advised Virginia to write direct to the Secretary of the Central Tribunal.

anything underhand. I suppose it is probably true that Lord S. always does do his best for everyone.

Yr B.

Berg

766: TO VANESSA BELL   *Hogarth House, Paradise Road, Richmond*

[16 June 1916]

Dearest,

Nelly writes this, so I'm afraid its been not much good applying to her, but of course the Cecils are incredibly conscientious.[1] Do tell me what happens about Duncan.

I had this letter from Aunt Mary[2] who seems to me to be altogether wandering what with age and misery, poor woman—Now John, Millicents son,[3] is killed too.

Yr B.

Berg

767: TO LADY ROBERT CECIL   *Hogarth House, Paradise Road, Richmond*

[16 June 1916]

Dear Nelly,

I quite understand about Lord Salisbury, and of course it is what one feels to be right.

The first Tribunal was so prejudiced against C.Os. that one felt it was rather hopeless to expect a fair hearing, but I've no doubt the Central Tribunal will be quite different, and will see that Duncan is speaking the truth. Thank you very much indeed—It was very good of you to take so much trouble—One does hate writing to one's relations—at least I do.

The war is a nightmare isn't it—two cousins of mine were killed this last week, and I suppose in other families its much worse.

Yr.
V.W.

Hatfield

1. Nelly had written to Virginia: "It would be worse than useless my writing to Jem [Lord Salisbury], as he is one of those men who is so afraid of being biassed by personal influence that his conscience might make him lean the other way on a fine balance".
2. In reply to Virginia's condolences on the death of Mary Fisher's son Charles.
3. Aunt Mary's great-nephew, John Isham.

768: To James Strachey   *Hogarth [House, Richmond]*

Saturday [17 June 1916]

Dear James,

Margery not having answered, I suppose she can't be coming—anyhow do persuade Miss A.S.F.[1] (if those are her initials) to come—we shall be delighted to see her at last—you'd have to be very tactful, as we've never met her, and when here you would have to bridge all our gulfs—age and youth, I mean.

We're just off to the Webbs, possibly to meet the Shaws, and if it weren't for the boasting I should collapse altogether.

Yrs V.W.

Leonard has got complete exemption, did you hear, owing to his tremor.[2]

Strachey Trust

769: To Lady Robert Cecil   *Hogarth House, Paradise Road, Richmond*

[June 1916]

My dear Nelly,

We have been asked to get people interested in these Women farmers, and so I apply to you, though there doesn't seem much reason why you should again be bothered, I admit. Leonard went over their farm, and thinks they ought to do very well with a little encouragement. But dont trouble to answer this.

We were down next door to Gale last week end,[3] marching through woods with Mr and Mrs Sidney Webb, and Mr and Mrs Bernard Shaw, who all talked so incessantly upon so many different subjects that I never saw a single tree, and rather wished I could open your garden gate. Still, they were very kind.

I hope we may meet on Tuesday.

Yrs. V.W.

Duncan Grant has heard nothing of his case so far.

Hatfield

1. Alix Sargant-Florence, an ex-Newnham student, whom James Strachey had recently met and was later to marry.
2. See letter No. 770.
3. The Woolfs spent 17-19 June with Beatrice and Sidney Webb at their house near Turners Hill, Sussex, which was near Nelly's house, Gale, Chelwood Gate.

June 25th [1916]

Dearest Ka,

It was a great pleasure to get your letter. I had become so much in want of news of you and there were such rumours about your state, that I actually wrote to Mrs Wilson [Ka's sister Hester], who agrees with me that you are a desperate spirit, bent on destruction. I wish you'd say more exactly how you are though—do you have to be very careful and wear wool, and sleep between blankets, like Saxon? You needn't think that you're forgotten here. Last week I saw James [Strachey], Miss Alix Florence, Margery Olivier, and Olive Heseltine,[1] and they all asked warmly after you: indeed it was proposed to send you a Round Robin, to make you come back. Still I daresay I'm fonder of you than they are, with my warm heart. Anyhow I often wish I could see anyone as nice and sensible and courageous as my Bruin is.

It is very difficult to collect the wrecks of life and describe them to you. Bloomsbury is pretty well exploded, only Clive and Mary Hutchinson[2] remain; Adrian and Karin have taken a house in a dismal sounding place called Tanza Road, somewhere behind Rays [Strachey] in Hampstead. Nessa and Duncan remain at Wissett, waiting for the Central Tribunal to decide whats to be done with Duncan. Leonard has been completely exempted from serving the Country in any capacity. He went before the military doctors trembling like an aspen leaf, with certificates to say that he would tremble and has trembled and will never cease from trembling. It's a great mercy for us. But the whole of our world does nothing but talk about conscription, and their chances of getting off; and they are all taken up with different societies and meetings and wire pulling—Clive having breakfasted with Lloyd George, and even I got in touch with Lord Salisbury! The latest rumour is that all C.Os are to be interned as Alien enemies—You're very lucky to be out of it all, I think, especially as we have had a perfectly unalterable black cloud over us all through June, and a hot dusty wind which has turned the trees dark green already.

Last week end we spent with the Sidney Webbs, in Sussex (next door to Dalingridge) and there were the Bernard Shaws, and they all talked incessantly. I liked it better than I expected. At anyrate one can say what one likes, which is unusual with the middle aged; indeed I felt much more of a mature woman with a passionate past than Mrs Webb, who seemed to me astonishingly young and crude and without atmosphere, and as keen as a knife—rather like [H. T. J.] Norton or Hawtrey[3] or [Maynard] Keynes indeed, and

1. Previously Olive Ilbert, who had been in love with Hilton Young (later Lord Kennet) in 1909, when he proposed to Virginia.
2. Wife of St John Hutchinson, the barrister. Clive was in love with her for many years.
3. Ralph Hawtrey, the economist.

so is Sidney, except that he is rather more pompous. This doesn't apply to poor Mrs Shaw though, who is very stupid, and has rolled herself up in Indian mysticism, like a caterpillar in a cocoon, in self defence. When she got me alone she tried to convert me, and lent me little books about the Seutras, which she had to hide from Mrs Webb. Bernard Shaw is rather more remote than the others, but when stirred up he told stories, all about himself, without stopping—at intervals he wrote letters to the newspapers, which he read aloud.

Two nights ago we dined with Olive [Heseltine], and there was a little private secretary called Davies[1], who had been to one of your evenings in search (did you know?) of a wife, but found none presentable in Downing Street. It was all incredibly mild and Oxford and worldly, and Leonard was almost sick with disgust. We stayed with Roger too, though it seems a long time ago. Lady Strachey [Lytton's mother] was there and Pippa, and we made Lady S. read Pope aloud to us, until her nose bled, which shows what a spirited old creature she is. Roger I thought rather melancholy. He talked a lot about old age, and the horrors of loneliness; the poor man can't make up his mind to have done with youth, and his attempts to keep with the young are rather pathetic.[2]

Leonard is very well (so am I) and has a book [*International Government*] coming out next month, which I may send to you: but I think I shall keep it for you—seeing that you *must* come home, my dear Bruin; there is nobody who takes your place at all.

We go to Asheham in August, and plan to have a fortnight in Cornwall in September. Do come with us. Sydney [Waterlow] is said to have had a child, but no one knows the sex.[3] Bryn has one—a daughter.[4] Poor Molly MacCarthy is about as deaf as Karin: and so melancholy one doesn't know what to do with her and the Dr says its incurable.

Please write again soon. Love from Leonard.

Yrs. V.W.

Mark Arnold-Forster

771: To Vanessa Bell   *Hogarth House, [Richmond]*

28th June [1916]

Dearest,

It's very odd about Duncan, isn't it? We dined with the Heseltines the other night and there we met one of Asquith's secretaries, who said, in

1. J. T. Davies, one of Asquith's personal secretaries, who remained at Downing Street to serve Lloyd George.
2. Roger Fry was then aged 50.
3. John Waterlow was born on 13 June.
4. Anne Olivier Popham, who married Quentin Bell.

confidence, that all C.O.s in future who are imprisoned are to be interned as alien enemies. If this is true, I suppose Asquith will say so in the House today.

About coming to you—we should like to very much, but we are going to Asheham on the 7th for a fortnight, so our best time would be between the 21st July, and 7th August. I daresay you'll have other plans for that time, so would you say what time suits you. All are equally good for us, I think.

I always keep a sort of pouch of gossip for you in my mind—I imagine you have a very soft trembling silken nose—but let me think now about our weekend with the Webbs. The Bernard Shaws were there. We talked quite incessantly—we were taken for brisk walks, still talking hard, through kind of Dalingridge country. Mrs Webb pounces on one, rather like a moulting eagle, with a bald neck and a bloodstained beak. However, I got on with her better than I expected. She seems very open minded, for an elderly person, and with no illusions or passions, or mysteries, so I daresay one would find her rather dull in the long run; she reminded me of one of the undergraduates of our youth. Shaw went fast asleep apparently, in the midst of all the talk and then woke up and rambled on into interminable stories about himself, and his backbone which is crooked, and his uncle who tried to commit suicide by shutting his head in a carpet bag, and his father who played on the ophicleide and died insane as they all do, and so on and so on. Poor Mrs Shaw was completely out of it, and she took me for a motor drive, and confided to me that Beatrice and Sidney, though wonderful people, had no idea of religion; and then she told me all about her conversion to Indian mysticism, and lent me little books, which unluckily, Mrs Webb got hold of, and she jeered at poor old Mrs Shaw, who sat in her corner, like a fat white Persian cat, making straw mats. I think I should be driven to mysticising if I saw much of the Webbs.

I wish you'd tell me more about your visitors—Lytton and Norton—is Norton just the same? We've sent in our income tax papers, but so far we haven't got any money. I hope we shall get the press this summer, and start in the autumn. The question now is, who will write for us? Will you? We shall certainly want some endpapers.

By the way, we're in the middle of spring cleaning, and Lottie unearthed the Watts drawing of mother and an early work of yours—Hayle harbour [Cornwall]. It is so good—grey, pink and buff colour (in my opinion) that I have hung it up. I should like a great big one of yours, to put in the stair-case.

Olive has become rather smart, and as brisk as a well groomed hunter—hair all glossy, and cheekbones bright red—and a lot of chains and bits of green silk. She talks of Michael as if he were a pet dog. The little private secretary [J. T. Davies] is the son of a Bayswater boardinghouse keeper, and so he never gets asked out, except by Olive, and he wants to marry a wife, so Olive took him to Ka's but he thought none of the young women there would do in Downing St. I heard from Ka, who seems to be staying on, and is apparently all right—and also from Aunt Anny [Ritchie], but it's all about books and rather dull. Sydney Waterlow has a son; Bryn a daughter. I liked Miss Sargant Florence, who was brought here by James. Now I've got to go to the Womens Guild Congress. Dont you wish you were coming?

If I stay with you, shall I get special attention? petting and free rights of kissing and stroking the ladies mile.[1] Eh?

Yr B.

Berg

772: To Margaret Llewelyn Davies

*Hogarth House,
Paradise Road,
Richmond*

[end June 1916]

Dearest Margaret,

We go to Asheham on the 7th till the 21st. We are hoping you will be able to come—the sooner you come and the longer you stay the better we shall like it—

This is only to tell you the dates—dont bother to fix on dates if it isn't easy to now. A line the day before is all we want.

Yrs. V.W.

[in Leonard's handwriting]

I hope you will come. I enjoyed [the Women's Guild] Congress enormously. I thought yesterday morning was better almost than I had ever heard it before. They really are wonderful. The boy who brought in the Press telegrams became so absorbed in listening to the speeches that some one had to prod him in order to make him realise that he had to go off to the post with one.

Sussex

773: To Katherine Cox

*Asheham, Lewes.
[Sussex]*

Wednesday [11 July 1916]

Dearest Ka,

I hope there was a real live Bruin at the end of the telephone the other morning, but I begin to doubt it. Perhaps you died that very moment in Corsica.[2] However, this is merely to say that we shall be here till the 21st, so

1. The inner arm, between wrist and elbow.
2. Ka Cox had returned to England from Corsica at the beginning of July.

come any time, but dont let it be a beggarly week end, and this doesn't count as your proper visit. Would you like to meet anyone—or to bring some one down with you? We have plenty of room.

I suppose you are now in the midst of a swarm. How do you feel?

The maggots got into the mutton today—otherwise no adventures.

Yr V.W.

Mark Arnold-Forster

774: To Vanessa Bell   *Asheham, Lewes,*
                                        [Sussex]

Sunday [16 July 1916]

Dearest,

Would it suit you if we came next Friday to Monday? That seems the only time. Could you let me know as soon as possible if this suits you—and if so, what your station is, and which afternoon train is best. We should come straight from here, and I hope you wont mind my having no clothes.

I'd better keep such fragments of gossip as I have till we meet—but nothing much has happened down here. Did you see Ka in London? She rang me up just as we were going to say she'd come back, in order apparently to be inoculated. I'm very glad Duncan has got off.[1] They'll certainly let him stay on, I suppose; but what a farce it all is!

I rather hope you wont settle at Wissett. I miss your company very sadly. Yesterday a great wad of matted hair had to be cut from my head, so I'm nearly bald.

I make bread every morning here, but I haven't mastered the art yet. Can you do it.

O the Apes [Virginia] are so excited at the thought of seeing you.

By the way, have you invited Leonard, or haven't you? Perhaps there isn't room.

Yr B.

Berg

775: To Lytton Strachey   *Hogarth House, Richmond*

25th July [1916]

We've been wandering about from Asheham to Wissett, and I'm so stiff with weeding and herding geese that I can hardly walk. Could you come to

1. Duncan Grant and David Garnett were exempted from military service on condition that they did farm work for the rest of the war. They were not allowed to continue working at Wissett because there they were self-employed. This led to their decision to move from Suffolk to Charleston, and take jobs with a farmer.

Asheham from the 15th to the 21st? Moore[1] will be there then I think. Please bring the dialogues,[2] and any other pieces lately composed, and then we will set you to read aloud after dinner. My industry has the most minute results, and I begin to despair of finishing a book on this method—I write one sentence—the clock strikes—Leonard appears with a glass of milk. However, I daresay it don't much matter. Wissett seems to lull asleep all ambition—Don't you think they have discovered the secret of life? I thought it wonderfully harmonious. The Inn, by the way, is The Plough Inn, Holford [Somerset]. The man's name I can't remember—but I daresay it isn't needed.

Katherine Mansfield has dogged my steps for three years—I'm always on the point of meeting her, or of reading her stories, and I have never managed to do either. But once Sydney Waterlow produced Middleton Murry instead of her—a moon calf looking youth—her husband? Do arrange a meeting—We go to Cornwall in September, and if I see anyone answering to your account on a rock or in the sea I shall accost her.[3]

Duncan was very bitter against your—what shall we call her?—but you know who(m?) I mean [Ottoline Morrell]—He said she was raddled and putrid and kept him on the stretch for 48 hours. I wonder if you've got your cottage.

Leonard sends his love—he is reading the proofs of the French translation of his book,[4] in which every word is rendered literally.

Yr.
V.W.

Frances Hooper

776: To Vanessa Bell   *Hogarth House, Richmond*

Sunday [30 July 1916]

Dearest Creature,
    Before I forget, did I leave my umbrella at Wissett and take away one almost identically like it, only larger? When I got into the tube I found

1. G. E. Moore, the Cambridge philosopher, author of *Principia Ethica*.
2. Probably *Old Lytoff*, which had Wissett as its setting (see Michael Holroyd, *Lytton Strachey*, II, p. 145).
3. Katherine Mansfield had been publishing stories since 1910, and had been living with John Middleton Murry, the critic, since 1911. They did not marry until 1918. Lytton had just met her at Garsington, where she spoke enthusiastically of *The Voyage Out*, and told him that she wanted to meet Virginia. Mansfield and Murry had gone to Cornwall, to stay with their close friend, D. H. Lawrence, who was living in a cottage at Zennor.
4. *International Government*, translated by Louis Suret, with an introduction by G. B. Shaw.

myself with a strange umbrella, not so refined as my own, which I am ready to return, but I fear it really belongs to a very smart tradesman who travelled with us.

Also, we never paid for our trap—what was it?

We came back to the usual run of small incidents, which I think you are lucky to avoid. You heard about Adrian and Gerald [Shove] I suppose? I met Fredegond and Gerald in a teashop in the Strand, and they were thinking of appealing, as they dont want to become agricultural labourers. Having ones own land of course, makes all the difference, and I daresay they'll all try to come to Wissett, but I suppose you dont much want them. I said I thought there wasn't much room. Fredegond is really rather beautiful I think, though a little too austere and reminiscent sometimes of Aunt Mary.

I've seldom enjoyed myself more than I did with you, and I cant make out exactly how you manage. One seems to get into such a contented state of mind. I heard from Lytton who feels the same, and says he would like to live with you forever. He's rather off Ottoline, I gather—at any rate he doesn't mean to live with her, and is looking for some other lodgment. He is off to Wales, so I dont suppose we shall see him.

I talked to Ka on the telephone—she wasn't well enough to come here, and has gone to Aldbourne, rather ill I think, with bad earache. She is coming to Asheham—but I suppose she is in need of a rest cure. England is too horrible to stay in she says, but so it would be if one only saw Dominic [Spring-Rice] and Dudley Ward[1] and had to soothe their miseries all day.

I sent you some velvet slippers, which cost 4/11—but I dont know if they'll do. They will change them if they are too large—Sears, George Street, Richmond. But I will take them off you, as I really want a new pair. Their toes looked a little odd.

I greatly envy you your brats. They are very interesting. How odd it will be when Julian is a very clever, severe, undergraduate as I see he will be.

I think you ought to take a holiday sometime; you do keep at it so, and having responsibilities is a great strain. Desmond dined with us last night, and said he supposed you were perfectly happy, in a state of complete mental suspension, like a big dog—whereas you're as active as a grasshopper. I hope to go to Seven Dials and get the silkwinder tomorrow. The Stores dont keep them. We go to Asheham on Tuesday. The servants [Nellie Boxall and Lottie Hope] now propose to stay with us forever.

Please write, and tell me what flowers to plant. I want to begin at once. I have made your rolls, not so good yet as yours, but better than Nellys. That egg savoury is made by boiling the semolina in milk, not water.

1. Cambridge contempories of Ka.

I am very much interested in your life, which I think of writing another novel about.[1] Its fatal staying with you—you start so many new ideas.

Berg

777: TO SAXON SYDNEY-TURNER   *Asheham, [Rodmell, Sussex]*

Aug. 10th [1916]

My dear Saxon,

Is there any chance that you could come here for a week end? Would the 8th suit you? Do come if you can.

I am reading Count Carlo Gozzi[2] in his own tongue, and dont find it very difficult, but then they only use about 16 words.

It is very nice here—grass being cut down by Leonard, mice caught in traps, and Hawks falling dead at my feet—

Tomorrow we go for a treat to Brighton.

Yr. affate,
V.W.

Sussex

778: TO VANESSA BELL   *Asheham, [Rodmell, Sussex]*

16th August [1916]

Dearest,

I suppose you are still in the flesh at Wissett—such as there is of it. I do think you ought to drink more milk. Leonard thought you had grown much thinner—so did someone else. You are always on the trot, if not gallop. Please take 2 glasses, and keep well, for love of me. Duncan also is said to look ill. Your life may be tiring without your knowing it, owing to the difference between it and Gordon Square. Here I lie in bed, 12 AM, a glass of milk by my side. [G. E.] Moore and Leonard on the terrace, and Pernel [Strachey] deep in the very latest book.

We are once more in domestic difficulties. After saying she was quite content, Nelly told me two days ago that she finds Asheham too depressing to stay, and, though Lottie would stay with her, she wont without her. They like Richmond, and its only a question of Asheham, but it seems to me too difficult to arrange to get different people every time we come here; so I must find a new couple by Oct. 1st. Do you think there is any chance that Blanche and Jessie [Vanessa's maids] would come, if Maynard doesn't take Gordon

1. This was her first conception of *Night and Day*, in which Vanessa appears as Katharine Hilbery.
2. The Italian dramatist (1720-1806).

Square? Or, if he does, what sort of person is Miss Chapman?[1] Would she come as cook?

I should be very grateful if you would answer as soon as possible about Blanche and Jessie, as I foresee we shall have difficulties in getting anyone.

I have been considering the question of having Sophy [Farrell] back. She wrote me another melancholy letter the other day, but I daresay she would prefer to stay with Aunt Minna in H. P. G. [Hyde Park Gate] to coming out to Richmond, and being rather humble. Also, I dont know whether she would be very expensive—in weekly books I mean, for the expense of a slopper isn't much—and very tyrannical.

I wish you would give me your sage advice on the subject. Lottie cheerfully says we shall find no one who likes Richmond and Asheham; and of course Asheham, without the train, and no shops sending out, is very lonely, if one doesn't care for the country.

Sydney Waterlow has invited himself to stay here at the end of the month, so I will tell him about Gower St—but you'd better tell me the rent, and the exact address.

Adrian and Karin were here the other day, and went to see Charleston, which they liked so much that they are going to take it, and let it for the first year, probably to the Squires. I wish you'd taken it. I suppose you've heard that they've settled at Cheltenham, with 6 C. O.'s, near the Milmans.

Leonard has just been offered the Secretaryship of the National Council for Liberty (that isnt quite the right name)—the thing Langdon Davies runs;[2] they offer £3 to £400 a year, but it doesn't seem worthwhile if he has to go there all day and every day. I think he is going to offer to run it with a secretary under him, going 3 days a week; but that mayn't be possible. I should find it very dull if he were out all day, and it would mean that he gave up all his other work.

Then we have heard of a house in Maids of Honour Row on the [Richmond] green, and Leonard is a good deal in favour of moving, because they are lovely houses with gardens, and perfect quiet, no further from the station than we are; but I dont know that they are really so much better than Hogarth to make the move worthwhile.

Alix S[argant]. F[lorence]. was here the other day. She seemed to me to talk without ceasing, very positive and intelligent, and liking serious arguments, as we did in youth, and letting no vague statement pass without examination. I gathered a few crumbs for you—chiefly about Dobbin,[3]

1. Housekeeper for Maynard Keynes in Gower Street.
2. Bernard Langdon-Davies (1876-1952) was Chairman of the Council for Civil Liberties. Leonard turned down the offer of the Secretaryship.
3. Mary Creighton, daughter of Mandell Creighton, Bishop of London. Virginia and Vanessa had known her in their youth.

who was set to paint frescoes with Mrs S. F [Alix's mother]: and bored her to death. Dobbins work had to be painted over mostly when she left. It is thought that she is taking up literature instead of painting, having married a literary and very nervous man, who has to live in the country.

My God! What colours you are responsible for! Karins clothes almost wrenched my eyes from the sockets—a skirt barred with reds and yellows of the vilest kind, and a pea green blouse on top, with a gaudy handkerchief on her head, supposed to be the very boldest taste. I shall retire into dove colour and old lavender, with a lace collar, and lawn wristlets.

Please write as soon as you can.

Yr B.

Berg

779: To Vanessa Bell   *Asheham, [Rodmell, Sussex]*

Sunday [20 August 1916]

Dearest,

I went into the shop at Firle the other day, and the man took me for you, and said you owed him 17/6 for butter which he sent you to Gordon Sqre 2 years ago. He was rather cross, and I said I would send you the bill, and that you would certainly pay at once, if correct.

Adrian and Karin, Leonard and Alix S. F. are all playing Bridge and making such a gabble I can hardly write.

I sent Julian a silkwinder, which I hope will make silk dresses for us all.

Yr V.W.

Berg

780: To R. C. Trevelyan   *Asheham House, Rodmell, [Sussex]*

Aug. 21st [1916]

Dear Mr Trevelyan,[1]

We are very glad that you can come on Saturday.

When you get to Lewes you can either wait till 5.7, when there is a train to Glynde, which is 2 miles from us; or you can take a taxi out here, 4 miles. If you only bring a knapsack, Leonard would meet you at Glynde, and carry it out for you. But in this case, would you send a card?

Otherwise, we shall expect you about tea time—Needless to say, we do not change our clothes.

Yours sincerely,
Virginia Woolf

Sussex

1. Robert Trevelyan (1872-1951), a friend of Roger Fry. He wrote many volumes of verse, and two of essays, and translated from Greek and Latin.

Friday [25 August 1916]

Dearest,

Its no good sending me a postal order which I can only cash at Wissett, you foolish animal! Will you give it to Quentin for a birthday present, as I had meant to send him one; and then we shall be quits.

I wrote to Sophy, asking her to come back, and offering a kitchen maid, and got a fearful snubbing! She said she had been very unhappy when Mr Adrian sent her away, and Miss [Minna] Duckworth had taken her when no one else wanted her, and she thought it her duty to stay. I think she has washed her hands of us, and will never come back—I feel I've done my duty anyhow, though in many ways, I wish she had come back. Servant hunting is such a bore; and they'll all leave again, I suppose. However, there seem to be any number going at Lewes; I shall try for an elderly cook, and saw one most charming old lady, who was of course, just engaged. I cant help being selfishly rather glad that you may spend part of the winter in London, especially with these raids going on. We actually had a zeppelin over the house here—in broad daylight. We were away, but the servants say the sound is unmistakable, and were in a panic; Nelly hiding in the wood, and Lottie running to the Woolers, where Mrs Wooler did nothing but dash into her house and out again. But it was so high up that no one saw it. Eleven aeroplanes chased it. I cant help thinking it was really English.

Moore and Pernel were a great success, though we poisoned Pernel with sour milk, and she looked rather cadaverous. Moore sang to us every night. He is quite easy, and much more human than his followers; but one can see how they've copied him, but he has much more vigour than they have. Perhaps they no longer exist though. Karin thinks that B. B. is going to cut off her allowance,[1] owing to being a C. O, so they cant take Charleston after all.

Sydney W: comes next week, so you'd better tell me anything about the house that you think necessary.

What old wives letters these are! All about cooks and plans. We ought to be walking up and down making our winter plans now, but I suppose you dont want me as much as I want you. Write. Do you take milk?

B.

Berg

1. Karin's mother, Mary Costelloe, married Bernard Berenson, the art historian, in 1900.

Saturday [26 August 1916]

Dearest Molly,

We are much disappointed at not having you. The worst of it is that I'm afraid we're already full up on 9th Sept: which is our last week end here, as we go to Cornwall for the end of the month. I wish I'd known before and I would have swept everyone else away with a broom.

What a life you lead, to be sure! And here am I sitting up in bed, with large glasses of milk—however, both my servants are leaving, and I have had to write already one dozen letters. Jane Blackman—I hear that you want a situation—etc.,

Now we are setting off to meet Bob [Trevelyan] and James S[trachey], who suddenly says he is coming, and I wish you were going to be found in Lewes station too.

We shall be in Richmond on Oct 1st, if we can find anyone to cook and make beds.

Do you hear that Clive is settled as farm labourer at Garsington? The war at anyrate has done some funny things among our friends.

I've just read Mrs Mordaunts latest novel "The Park Wall",[1] very good I think, and if it weren't for you, I should again attempt to write to her. Have you ever read Cashel Byron's Profession? [1886] much the best thing Shaw ever wrote, to my mind.

Your loving,
V.W.

Mrs Michael MacCarthy

Monday [28 August 1916]

Dearest

Do you see that Aunt Mary[2] has been killed by a motor car?
Bob Trevelyan is here, and his wife had just heard—
(I see it is in the Times this morning.)

Yr B.

Berg

1. Virginia's review of Elinor Mordaunt's novel appeared in *TLS*, 31 August 1916.
2. Mary Louisa Fisher, the sister of Virginia's mother, was born about 1840. She was killed by a car on 24 August.

Sunday [10 September 1916]

Dearest,

Look, what promptitude I show! The thing is this—if you want me to do anything about the farm, you must send instructions at once, as we go away next Saturday.

I've not seen Gunn, but I daresay he has written to you. As far as I can make out the farm [Itford Farm] has probably 6 bedrooms, and 3 sitting rooms. Nelly was shown over the house, and say its much darker and lower than this. It was I, with my usual spurt of intelligence, who suggested the plan to Roger; so I quite approve of your being here, and only stipulate for the usual rights, in precedence of the legitimate brats. Gunn has laid by money, and has bought a farm at the foot of Mount Caburn, by Glynde, where he moves at the end of the month. I think it might be worthwhile for you to suggest taking that, if this one isn't feasible; he might let it for the war, I should think. If these dont do, what about Charleston? Mr Stacey has a large farm there, and I've no doubt wants labour, though I know nothing of his views about C.Os. The house is furnished in a kind of way, I think. Limpsfield[1] must be swarming with your friends; and Cheltenham,[2] with that solid breezy woman [Karin] would drive me to drink at once.

I thought Aunt Mary's death a positive stroke of genius—I mean the discomfort and self sacrifice of it—no trouble to anyone; and yet done out of life by the inhumanity of someone else. I believe a woman motor driver was driving at 30 miles, some people said; but others said only 6. Of course At. Mary wouldn't be able to get out of the way, if she were alone. I wrote to Adeline[3] with great difficulty, and like all my mortuary letters, it was a great success. As she was perishing by degrees, I think its a great mercy for her, poor old creature; though really one can hardly think of her as a live human being.

Sydney [Waterlow] was here with Roger, and was anxious to know how the report of their leaving Gipsy Hill had got about, as they've no idea of doing so. After listening to our talk for an hour or two he said "Its no use my going to bed tonight. I shan't be able to sleep after this excitement." When asked what excitement, he said "The excitement of seeing you all again."—which I thought threw a ghastly light upon their evenings at Gipsy Hill.

At this moment I am doing my duty by having my family in law to

---

1. In Surrey, the home of the Garnetts and Oliviers.
2. Where Adrian Stephen was doing agricultural work.
3. Aunt Mary's daughter, who had married Ralph Vaughan Williams, the composer.

spend the weekend—Bella and Herbert. Bella is dressed all in black silk, with long widow streamers. She goes to Bexhill to run a Little Folks childrens hospital, where she meets Lady Egerton, Aunt Stephen's sister, who seems to know all about us. I spend my time in trying to see which of Bella's eyes works, and she talks incessantly, and is always making jokes, though I gather she is really much depressed by the loss of her husband, who was practically the same thing as a cauliflower (he was a botanist) and he died in his bath.[1]

We are going to

Gwel Marten,

Carbis Bay [Cornwall]

next Monday for a fortnight. Margaret Davies has asked to come too, in order, partly, to discuss her future, which is very complicated owing to cancer etc; and I hope to upset all her plans, and attack her in every possible way, so as to keep things brisk. I believe its the only way of keeping these ardent spirits from overwhelming one entirely.

Ka writes that her doctor wont let her go back to Corsica till the end of October. Leonard has suggested that she should take on his job at the Civil Liberty Society, as he thinks its too great a bore to do himself; and Ka would suit it exactly.

Nelly and Lottie are now very anxious to stay on, though I'd almost got a cook; we are getting a slopper.

Now answer at once, and do tell me about Otts: visit, and Bertie's [Russell] letter.

I will go to any house, before Saturday, and use my sagacity, as I should much like to have you.

Yr B.

Berg

785: To Roger Fry

Asheham House, [Rodmell, Sussex]

Sunday [10 September 1916]

My dear Roger,

I've been trying in vain, I need hardly say, to collect ten penny stamps for you in return for the Cigarettes, which came in the nick of time—Thank you very much for them.

I meant to ask whether you have a list of possible buyers at the Omega which you would lend us when it comes to sending post cards about the press. However, this can wait.

1. Bella Woolf had married Richard Lock, who had been Assistant Director of Peradeniya Botanical Gardens in Ceylon. He died in 1916, when Bella was 39. She married again later.

Our address in Cornwall, by the way, is
Gwel Marten,
Carbis Bay,
Cornwall,
if by any chance you could come.

The Club I'm sure would take wing in 10 seconds if you think it a feasible plan—I wonder what fire and light would come to: and the room you must charge for of course. I think a life of three months is about right for that kind of thing, and no host or hostess, but you have to have the right of producing some entertainment, such as reading, or magic lantern, if you could. I think there's a lot to be said for something of the sort.[1]

Nessa seems enthusiastic (for one of her temperament) about coming to the farm, but I dont know whether Gunn is agreeable, and whether the farm is large enough.

I think one way or another we shall rake together some sort of civilisation, independently of Ottoline, so as to make Geneva unneccessary.

Anyhow, do light upon us whenever you can.

I imagine you sitting on this misty morning with the great white Chigaco [sic] teeth flashing incessantly[2]—And I've got my relations in law!

Yrs.
V.W.

Sussex

786: To Vanessa Bell   *Asheham, [Rodmell, Sussex]*

Monday [11 September 1916]

Dearest,

I forgot to say, will you be careful not to tell anyone about the farm being to let, if you dont take it? So many of our friends have been asking about houses here, and we're not at all anxious to have neighbours (unless you).

Did you see this in the Times?[3]

Yr. B.

Berg

1. The plan materialised early in 1917 in the founding of an evening club at the Omega Workshops. It met once a week, and among those who visited it were non-Bloomsbury people of distinction, like Yeats and Arnold Bennett.
2. Helen Dudley, the American girl with whom Bertrand Russell fell in love. (See *Letters of Roger Fry*, ed. Denys Sutton, II, p. 402).
3. A previous report had incorrectly announced the death in action of J. W. Hills, M.P., the widower of Virginia's half-sister, Stella Duckworth. The newspaper cutting which Virginia enclosed stated that it was his nephew who had died.

Asheham, [Rodmell, Sussex]

Tuesday [12 September 1916]

Dearest,

I have been talking to Nelly about your taking the [Itford] farm, and she says it is said to be very unhealthy. The Mockford children are always being ill there, and the little boy has just been having tonsilitis very badly. The doctor said that the house was much too low. Also the Woolers who used to be there say that their children were never well there. Mrs Mockford doesn't know that you may take it, so I dont think this was said to put you off. I thought I'd better tell you, though one never knows how much faith to put in these people. If you could get work on Staceys farm, I expect the Charleston house would be a much better one.

Yr B.

Berg

788: To Vanessa Bell   *Hogarth House, Paradise Road, Richmond*

Saturday Evening [16 September 1916]

Dearest,

We have seen a very nice house, which we are much tempted by; and now it strikes us that we must let Asheham for the winter. Would it be any good to you? We thought of asking £2.2 a week. We want to let it until 15th December anyhow—possibly till the spring, but that we can't settle now. If Madame Vandervelde¹ takes it, she will be there possibly till Oct. 1st —certainly not longer, so you could go there on the 1st—or if you only wanted it for 2 or 3 weeks while getting into another house, we would let it.

Its a miserable state of things that I shouldn't see my dear old Dolphin,²— I did want to extremely, but perhaps we can [arrange] to meet before long. We shall be in Cornwall till Oct. 1st.

It seems to me a great thing that Gunn will take D. and B.³ on to work for him—and I should think you could certainly get some sort of house in the neighbourhood. Do stay on as long as you want to (if M. Vand. doesn't come—and I dont think she will) Mrs Attfield [caretaker] seems very willing —I hope you'll be decently comfortable.

Yr. B.

Berg

1. Lalla Vandervelde, the wife of Emile Vandervelde, the Belgian Socialist politician, and a friend of Roger Fry.
2. Virginia's pet name for Vanessa, said to be derived from her undulating walk.
3. Duncan Grant and David ('Bunny') Garnett.

Letters 789-813 (mid-September–December 1916)

On 18 September Virginia and Leonard went to Carbis Bay in Cornwall for a fortnight, accompanied by Margaret Llewelyn Davies and the Assistant Secretary of her Guild, Lilian Harris. On returning to Richmond, Virginia led a quiet life. She paid occasional visits with Leonard to inner London, and began to hold a monthly meeting of the Women's Co-operative Guild's local branch at Hogarth House. They kept in touch with Bloomsbury friends mainly through Roger Fry's Omega Workshops, and with politics through Maynard Keynes and Leonard's Fabian friends, with whom his influence was becoming increasingly important, especially in the field of international relations. In October Vanessa, Duncan and David Garnett made their planned move to Charleston. Two Slade students, Dora Carrington and Barbara Hiles, now entered their lives, the former owing to her friendship with Lytton Strachey, the latter because Saxon Sydney-Turner was much in love with her. The idea of a printing-press had not died, but they were too poor to afford one.

789: To Vanessa Bell   Gwel Marten, Carbis Bay,
                                         Cornwall

Sunday [24 September 1916]

Dearest,

It is very exciting to think that you may get Charleston. I hope you will. Leonard says that there are certainly 8 bedrooms, probably more, and very good ones, two big sitting rooms on the ground floor and one small one; and very good large rooms on the first floor. He says the garden could be made lovely—there are fruit trees, and vegetables, and a most charming walk under trees. The only drawbacks seemed to be that there is cold water, and no hot, in the bathroom; not a very nice w.c, and a cesspool in the tennis court. But he thought it almost as nice as Asheham. Whatever you may say, I think the country there is superb to live in—I always want to come back again, and one never feels it dull, but then, not being an artist, my feelings are not to be considered ha! ha!—As to the beds etc—you did once send me a list, which may be in existence. Perhaps Jessie might know. Anyhow you shall have your dues. The green china certainly shall go, as we have enough. But could we arrange to send it by some carrier already bringing things?—they charge so tremendously for carting now. I do envy you, taking a new house— Nothing in the world is so exciting. And I shall remind you of my services in getting it from time to time; and you will then always have to give me complete rights for 5 minutes by the clock.

The romance of Cornwall has once more overcome me. I find that one lapses into a particular mood of absolute enjoyment—which takes me back to my childhood.

I hope Quentins cut is better. I think one was rather proud of being cut—my legs are all over scars, but not so good as his.

We are a very funny party. Miss [Lilian] Harris has turned up, Margarets secretary, an old creature of 50, extremely sensible and unselfish, and independent, who smokes a pipe, and lives alone in lodgings, and reminds us both so much of Saxon in her sayings and habits that we frequently disgrace ourselves. When Margaret gets excited she calls her "John", and Miss Harris calls Margaret "Jim". They go out sketching all day, and produce their sketches, and want to be praised. They think it is a very bad thing to use Chinese white in water colours, and that real artists leave bits of white paper, so I said I would ask you. I have had several arguments about art and morality with Margaret, and I hope I have done some damage, but a life rooted in good works is hard to injure—especially as she always assumes that I think what Oscar Wilde thought in the 80ties.

I wish you were here—as only the Cornish bred really see its stupendous merits—not but what Leonard is very appreciative, and Margaret gets her aesthetic emotions roused in great outbursts, when the clouds have reflections in the sea.

Please write soon and say what happens. I'm sure, if you get Charleston, you'll end by buying it forever. If you lived there, you could make it absolutely divine.

Yr B.

We are here till Oct 1st—then Richmond.

Berg

790: To Saxon Sydney-Turner   *Gwel Marten, Carbis Bay, Cornwall*

Sept 30th [1916]

My dear Saxon,
     I cannot help thinking of you coming into the dining room at Carbis Bay with your bag weighed down with books [in 1905], which was the foundation of my reverence for your character.

We are next door to that house, and I wish you were here to read a little Leopardi with me—not that I find him very difficult so far. We have been here a fortnight with Margaret Davies and an elderly secretary of hers, by name Lilian Harris. The secretary is a most interesting and sensible person, and I think you would have much in common—In fact you are very like her when you smoke your pipe and say nothing. She lives alone in lodgings at Hampstead, and smokes about 8 pipes a day, and is very fond of good wine and cigars. She has asked me to bring you to tea—Will you come?—her other taste is for statistics.

We had [G. E.] Moore to stay with us at Asheham. He, too, came with a box like lead, and it was full of music books, which he meant to sing to us, but we had no piano, so he sang without one—some very nice old German and English songs. Do you know one about the "foggy foggy dew", and another about "lost in the Lowland seas"? He is a very great man, I think, so solid and direct: and not the least hard to talk to. He knows all the wild flowers and butterflies. He spent his time writing a review, and when he went he had scratched it all out and begun a new one.

We also had Bob Trevelyan: you can imagine what it was like walking on the top of the Downs in a high wind, with him talking quite incessantly about poetry religion etc. beside one. At last, about 11 o'clock at night, he stopped and said he really didnt know what he was talking about.

Have you heard whether Nessa has finally taken Charleston? Adrian writes that he has 30 cows and 6 C.Os. under him, near Cheltenham.

We come back on Monday, and the first thing we do is to go to the city and buy our own press—so please look and see what old manuscripts you have. We shall begin with short poems.

It is a perfect day, and we are going to the Gurnards Head.[1]

Yrs
V.W.

Leonard sends his love.

Sussex

791: To Lady Robert Cecil   *Hogarth House, Paradise Road, Richmond*

Monday [October 1916?]

Dear Nelly,

I'm afraid this Wednesday will not do after all. May we come *next* Wednesday week, about 5? We shall come then unless you prevent us. Leonard would very much like to come too.

We are thinking of starting a printing press, for all our friends stories. Dont you think its a good idea?

Yrs
V.W.

Hatfield

1. A rocky promontory on the north coast of Cornwall near Zennor.

792: To Roger Fry   *Hogarth House, Paradise Road*
                                      Richmond

Sunday [8 October 1916]

My dear Roger,
    The photographs certainly are masterpieces—the one of Leonard is far
the best that I've ever seen of him—How does that minute camera produce
such large pictures?
    We are back, and should like it very much if you can come. Would
Wednesday and Thursday this week suit you? You might ring up and say if
they do—
    Tim [dog] has just been found to swarm with nits—I'm not sure that
my own head is free from them—but its no good looking into the future.
We have rubbed him with paraffin.

                                            Yours ever,
                                            Virginia Woolf

Sussex

793: To Vanessa Bell   *Hogarth House, Richmond*

Monday [9? October 1916]

Dearest,
    I saw Lytton yesterday, who told me he had heard that you and Duncan
and possibly others had all got influenza at Wissett. I should be very grateful
if anyone who hasn't got it would send a line to say how you are. I hear
Clive had it, and Adrian too, and Nellie went for a holiday and was in bed
with [it] all the time; and Ott's got it.
    Both the dogs have got nits.
    Gwen Raverat[1] is going to have a baby. So is Frances Cornford.[2]
    I saw Ka, who seems rather feeble still. I do hope you are all right.
Please dont start a move with the germs still in you.
    Have you got Charleston?

                                            Yr B.

Berg

794: To Janet Case   *Hogarth House, Paradise Road,*
                                      Richmond

Oct. 10th [1916]

My dear Janet,
    Words fail me to express my thanks and admiration—It is not only a

1. Gwen Darwin had married Jacques Raverat. Both were artists.
2. Frances Darwin, the poet, who had married Francis Cornford.

miracle of work ("Thats a gift that comes from nature—well, one cant have everything!", Lottie said looking at it) but it comes when I was completely out of nightgowns—they hang in loops about me. How did you make this one? Did you have a pattern? Is it thinkable that I could ever make one like it—so open at the neck—so beautifully shaped on the shoulders—and with all those wonderful small stitches.

My dear Janet, you are too good to think of doing such a thing—and then to go and do it! Now what I pray for is a mild attack of influenza, so that I may really look like a lady in bed—But I cant get over your skill— Nice you always were—If you want work, why dont you open a shop for underlinen? The ladies who merely flirt with Greek[1] take underclothes seriously—But I'm very proud that you made one for me.

Yr affate and grateful,
V.W.

Sussex

795: To Dora Carrington   *[Hogarth House, Richmond]*

Sunday [15 October 1916]

Dear Miss Carrington,

Roger Fry says you are doing some work at Hampton Court [on the Mantegna paintings]. Could you dine with us on Thursday next, 7.30—of course without dressing? I am very anxious to hear what state Asheham was in the other day—were there trays about, that hadn't been cleaned?[2]

We hope you may be able to come—We are about 5 minutes walk from Richmond Station—anyone will tell you the way.

Yours sincerely
Virginia Woolf

I think James Strachey is coming.

Robert H. Taylor

1. Janet Case was a teacher of Greek, and had taught Virginia.
2. Virginia had only recently met Carrington, although Lytton already knew her well. At the beginning of October, she, Barbara Hiles (a fellow student at the Slade) and David Garnett had been on their way to see Charleston, where Garnett and Duncan were to live with Vanessa while they worked on a neighbouring farm. Finding themselves without a lodging for the night, they went to Asheham, and broke in. When the Woolfs heard about this escapade from the Asheham caretaker, they were indignant, and asked Carrington to dine with them and explain what had happened.

Hogarth House, Paradise Road,
                                          Richmond

Tuesday [17 October 1916]

Dearest,

We are going to Asheham this Friday, till Tuesday. Shall you be at Charleston? If so, perhaps you'd come over. Anyhow, I'll try to find the list of furniture, and show Mrs Attfield which it is, so that if you send for it, she can show the man which it is.

Yr B.

Berg

Hogarth House, Paradise Road,
                                          Richmond

[19? October 1916]

Dearest,

Do come over on Monday. We shall expect you for lunch, at 1, and tea, and dinner if you will. The furniture is certain to take some time.

Your best way to come, if you bicycle, is to take the path to Firle, under the Park wall. Then you may have to go down into the main road; but if you are clever, you will find a turning to your left (There is a signpost saying "To the Hill") which leads you up to a machine for pumping water—and then the path goes straight on, beneath the downs, till it joins the main Beddingham road to Asheham. This cuts off at least 2 miles from the main road way. Or would you sleep the night, and go home next day?

I see you're going to say that Charleston is better than Asheham— It cuts me to the heart. I dreamt I was sitting in a kind of portable w. c. at Charleston, painted grey, like a Beehive to look at.

B.

Berg

Asheham, [Rodmell,
                                          Sussex]

Saturday [21 October 1916]

Dear Mr Garnett,

As a matter of fact, we are not at all annoyed [by the Asheham escapade] —It seems a very sensible thing to do—The caretaker (who saw you vanishing) was a good deal alarmed, thinking we should blame her, and gave such an account of tables upset, beds stripped etc; that we thought strange villagers must have been playing a joke. So its a relief to find it was you—

123

It flatters us a good deal to see what a reputation for temper we've got—I telephoned to Miss Carrington, and heard her quake at the sound of my voice miles off!

Leonard is reading your poems [in manuscript], and says they are the best return you could make for the raid.

Yours Sincerely
Virginia Woolf

Berg

799: To Vanessa Bell   *Asheham, [Rodmell, Sussex]*

Tuesday [24 October 1916]

Dearest,

It was a great disappointment that you didn't come—but it would have been perfect madness—think of bicycling 9 miles on the first day of one's affairs! I half thought of coming over, but it struck me you might be out on business, or have some one—I dont know when we shall be here again—anyhow for Christmas—perhaps for a weekend before.

I could come and see you at Gordon Sqre. on Thursday, but I suppose this wouldn't suit—Friday we dine out, so I suppose I mustn't—God damn!

I have looked for the list but can find it nowhere. There are now 7 beds here (not counting a camp bed—) and a cot. Can you remember whether you sent your beds when I was at Firle or at Asheham? I know I had 4 beds (not counting Jeans) at Firle; last year we bought 2 more—That only leaves 1 bed, a camp bed, and a cot for you. If you sent the beds to Firle, however, then others belong to you. Perhaps you can tell yours by looking at them. Mrs Attfield thinks that her husband could take the furniture for you, if Gunn let him have a cart, which she thinks possible. I have told her to ask Gunn at once, and to send you a card. I have also said that you will come over on Monday next, and show her the furniture. If you cant, you might send a line to Mrs Attfield, Asheham Cottages—The rest of the things you will find easily—When you have taken the furniture would you let me know what it amounts to, as we might have to get more, before Christmas.

Would you ask Bunny if he took The Oxford Book of Poetry when he came? It was in my bedroom; I can't find it—and possibly he did—I always read it while I'm waiting for breakfast—and I cant find anything else to read.

How pleasant it would be to see you here, or to roll on the downs together, and the Ape would steal kisses from the most secluded parts!

I hope we shall get our press now, as we've just heard that they are soon sending our money.[1]

---

1. The Inland Revenue were due to pay them a refund of income tax.

I keep dreaming of Charleston—I shd. like to see it. Perhaps we cd. arrange a meeting here one weekend.

Yr B.

Berg

800: TO VANESSA BELL   *Hogarth House, Paradise Road, Richmond*

Thursday [9 November 1916]

Dearest,

My affairs have just come on, so I'm afraid I shan't be able to come up until Saturday, when we thought of going to Maynards party—Damn it all! I had meant to go to the Omega show tomorrow,[1] but I suppose I mustnt. Shall you be at the party? If so, I could possibly settle to come on Sunday some time—

We had an awful time with Jean [Thomas] about the furniture—however I'll tell you about it when I see you, as I hope I may do.

If we come to the party we shall come very early and go very early.

I will keep Sunday afternoon free on the chance that you will stay on.

Yr B.

Berg

801: TO VANESSA BELL   *Hogarth [House, Richmond]*

Monday [13? November 1916]

Dearest,

I think, from what Leonard says, that I must have given a wrong account of what Maynard said about having a room at Charleston. L. says he only said that he *hoped* he might have one; but was quite doubtful.

I expect L. is right, as you know I don't attend very carefully—

Yr B.

I've just had a wonderful letter fr. Aunt Minna, saying that in your pre-cubist days you might have liked to paint a fallen tree in her garden, but not now—Also, did she give us a silver tea pot for a wedding present, as one is missing, in her chest.

Berg

1. The Omega artists were exhibiting at the arts and crafts show at the Royal Academy.

802: To Barbara Hiles

Hogarth House, Paradise Road, Richmond

Friday [24 November 1916]

Dear Barbara

(I hope you wont mind my calling you so—)

Is there any chance that you would come and see us? We should like it so much. Could you come next Wednesday to tea and stay to dinner.

Your best way to come is to get the train at Finchley Road Station direct to Richmond.

A train leaves Finchley Road at 4.8 which would bring you here in time for tea. We are about 5 minutes from the station. Anyone would tell you the way.

Yours
Virginia Woolf

Berg

803: To Saxon Sydney-Turner

Hogarth House, Paradise Road, Richmond

Friday [24 November 1916]

My dear Saxon,

I was just going to write when your letter came this evening—not that I have much to tell you except that I have been feeling oddly happy all day, because somehow I think that you are. And as you ought to know, that does seem to me one of the very best things that could happen.

I've a feeling that I want somehow to give you back or that some one else should give you back what you lost in Thoby.[1] For I've often thought that you were the one person who understood about him—I mean his death meant almost more to you and me than to anyone, and I think we shared together some of the worst things. I know anyhow that you helped me then —and often I've known that we both kept him with us, though we did not talk of him. But this is not what I meant to say.

I never dreamt that you had been *selfish* about Barbara. I had an idea that she was extremely young and so might not perhaps understand the situation unless you explained it. But on thinking it over I dont see there is any reason to think this—in fact its absurd.

I wrote and asked her to tea and dinner on Wednesday. I do wonder what I shall think of her. Of course I hope you will marry her if she's what I think she must be—because I do want someone to explore all the exquisiteness of your nature—and then after all, to love is so much the best of all things. I'm

1. Thoby Stephen, Virginia's brother, who had died aged 26 on 20 November, 1906.

often amazed to find what it means, and I believe no one has more power of caring than you have. Shall I be very jealous? Ah—but I think I know some things about you that no one else does.

I wonder how your dinner with Nick[1] is going off. I'm in the train, since I took to purple ink, so I daresay I'm writing nonsense, but its my way of kissing you as I should like to do—dear old Saxon.

Please write if it doesn't bother you; or do come and have a walk in the Park.

Yr. loving V.W.

Sussex

804: To Mary Booth

Hogarth House, Paradise Road, Richmond

26th Nov [1916]

Dearest Mrs Booth,

I think nobody can have given more to other people than you and Mr Booth did, and so I cannot help writing one word to you, and think you will not mind it.[2]

So often when Thoby died it was like finding our own home again to come into yours, and the thought of you has always been an extraordinary comfort.

Your loving,
Virginia Woolf

University of London

805: To Saxon Sydney-Turner

Hogarth House, Paradise Road, Richmond

Monday [27 November 1916]

My dear Saxon,

Whatever your state of mind, you must say I'm an obedient creature to sit down and write to you, directly I've finished tea—However, I admit I like writing to you very much, though its rather like writing to an elf bathed in moonlight on the top of some hill. And I've nothing to say—except that I owe you 5/5 for the chess book, which I will send you tomorrow, if I can remember, as I think I shall.

1. At this period two men were hoping to marry Barbara Hiles. One was Nicholas Bagenal, who was serving as an officer in the Irish Guards in France; the other was Saxon Sydney-Turner, who was working in the Treasury.
2. Her husband, Charles Booth, the writer on social questions, died on 23 November.

Probably I ought to insist upon rest and food at this juncture. If you dont sleep or eat, your feelings will become so much of a puzzle that you'll waste these exquisite days merely scratching your head. For I'm convinced they *are* exquisite days—more entirely exquisite for you than for most, because all your feelings are so true. Have I ever heard you say an insincere thing? Never. Now I think you can trust yourself because you have made a habit of honesty. And, dear me, one never regrets *feeling* things in this life; not even if mere disappointment follows, which I think utterly impossible in this particular case. You will say I know nothing about it; and very properly give me one of your slight raps on the nose, but in spite of being in some ways foolish, I am sensible in others. I know, being civilised as we are, we can't help watching our feelings, and being incredulous of them. But that I believe to be the proper way to feel, and later when things are less new, one loses this self-consciousness, and enjoys the fact that our feelings have been so watched, and are therefore so good—I've never had to go back on any of mine for Leonard, or indeed for any of my friends. I dont think this is very well expressed, but no doubt you will see what it means.

How delightful it is to think of you. Are you writing any poetry? I am reading Mendel,[1] which is rather interesting, and makes me think of Barbara, not that she occurs in it, I suppose, but all the young do, and I wonder if they're so very different from us. I think life for us was more complicated at that sort of age—

We went to a concert on Friday, and met Gertler and Carrington, and Walter Lamb, who came home with us—O dear! But the main point is that I hope you will write to me; and I think you a most adorable and tender hearted sprite? no, spirit.

Yrs.
V.W.

Sussex

806: TO VANESSA BELL   *Hogarth* [*House, Richmond*]

Sunday [3? December 1916]

Dearest,

We have now got £15 from the income tax, instead of the £35 we hoped for—As the press costs £20, and we are rather hard up just now, I'm afraid we shall have to wait to buy it until March, unless we can raise some money on the Vanity Fair page.[2] D'you think there's any chance of selling this

1. *Mendel*, a novel by Gilbert Cannan (1916), based on the character of Mark Gertler, the painter, who had been deeply in love with Carrington since they first met in 1911.
2. The Stephen children had inherited some Thackeray manuscripts from their father, whose first wife was Thackeray's daughter.

before Christmas?—I don't remember what you settled to do—Of course, if its better to wait, we must. My fear is that the £15 will be used for house expenses, and the hope of the press disappear—

Saxon is here, saying he feels that he must now look after his body, as his mind is more settled, now that he sees he cant get what he wants. He reads Jane Austen to Barbara, and says she is extremely natural and nice to him; but I think he's pretty hopeless—However, one can't be sure whether he's really in love, as other people are; perhaps he would be content if B. married Nick, and he became a member of the household. I think he means to stay some time with you.

I've had a letter from Mrs Booth, describing Charles' death, which was very peaceful, and he knew them all and only died because his body was entirely worn out—so it seems to be a typical ending for that family—she seems to have the deepest feelings for us all.

If you ever feel lonely, which I dont suppose you do, I could always come down for a night or two in the middle of the week—But I suppose you will be having Snow[1] and Saxon—We heard Desmond introduce Shaw's lecture; and he spoke so long that the audience coughed him down, which was rather terrible. I saw old Dobbin [Mary Creighton] and her husband—much alike, and quite unchanged.

Yr B.

Berg

807: To Barbara Hiles   *Hogarth House, [Richmond]*
Postcard

Monday [4 December 1916]

Will you come to tea—stay to dinner on Thursday next, catching the same train? We should like it very much.

V. Woolf

Bring your sewing, and I will do mine!

Berg

808: To Vanessa Bell   *Hogarth [House, Richmond]*
Tuesday [12 December 1916]

Dearest,

I'm afraid I can't come, because we have people dining here on Wednesday, and we dine out on Saturday.

1. Margery Snowden, a painter, who had been Vanessa's greatest friend in her youth.

However, I hope I shall see you next week, and perhaps you'll ask me later. We shall be coming down next Thursday to Asheham, and I think we shall stay a fortnight, so I daresay you'll see as much of me as you want to.

Its very exciting about your new children.[1] I suppose Amber's brat is the bastard, which is said to make them interesting. Do you think Saxon has any chance [with Barbara Hiles]? or what is their relationship? I think we have Ka for Christmas, and perhaps Desmond, but as the servants aren't coming we shall be alone for the most part.

I very much want to see Charleston. It is said the Apes have a special sunny room there kept for them.

Yr B.

Berg

809: To Duncan Grant *Hogarth House, [Richmond]*

Sunday 17th Dec [1916]

My dear Duncan,

I began a letter to you, in my head at least, some days ago, after seeing your pictures at the Omega. I liked the one over the fireplace immensely: the green and blue one, I mean; which seemed to me divinely romantic and imaginative. Lord! how tired I got of those sturdy pots and pans, with red billiard balls attached to them! I daresay I am saying all the wrong things—I was taken round by Roger, and felt innumerable eggs crack beneath me. I was very much struck by his sensibility: he showed me minute patches of black, and scrapings of a sort of graining upon which the whole composition depended. And I believe it did too. Certainly, it is a most remarkable art. I can't pretend to "buy" another picture of yours, but I wish I could. However, when we have a success with our press, I shall make a little hoard with a view to a picture.

I am involved in the romance of Saxon and Barbara. I dont know what to think of the state of things—if I had Saxon attached to me indefinitely, madness would be the least of my sensations. Surely she must think him a possible husband? Anyhow they dined here the other night, and after dinner what with the cold and the silence I committed some hideous breach of manners,—how I dont know—and was rung up next day by Saxon, and told I had been very unkind to him!—What I said, as far as I can remember, was that people ought not to be reserved about their emotions—He ought to have thought this a compliment; only I wasn't thinking of him at all. But

1. The two daughters of Amber Blanco White (*née* Reeves), who had sent her children to Vanessa for a few months. The elder was her illegitimate child by H. G. Wells, born after her marriage to G. R. Blanco White.

of course his state is for him what ours would be if we discovered a tremendous pair of white wings sprouting between our shoulder blades.

Last night we dined with the [J. C.] Squires on Chiswick Mall. O my God! what an evening! All the lights went out, dinner an hour late, pheasants bleeding on the plate, no knives, tumblers or spoons; poor Mrs Squire thought to laugh it over, but became distracted; Squire ferocious. Strange figures wandered in and out, among them Mrs Hannay, an artist[1]—Pike an inventor, Scott a don. Stove smoked, fog thick. Trains stopped. Bed.

Yrs V.W.

Duncan Grant

810: To Saxon Sydney-Turner   *Asheham, [Rodmell, Sussex]*

Christmas Day [1916]

My dear Saxon,

I hope to go and see your mother[2] one day soon, but would you send me the number of the house, as I stupidly left your letter at home. But your implied stricture makes me rather doubtful as to my power of being useful to you by seeing people.

I did not 'obviously mean to be very charming' at your expense the other day—I thought twice before telling the story of the organ grinder, and decided to tell it because it comes natural to me to behave in that way, and to be tongue tied on these occasions lands me in insincerity. In fact, I expect I am the worst possible confidant for many reasons—but I think they *are* reasons and not merely the desire for admiration—But this applies rather to Barbara than to your mother, with whom I shall naturally be on my guard.

Except for the wind, it might be April here. Duncan and Maynard came over yesterday, as Maynard has been sent for by the Treasury, and so cannot stay here. The rest of the time I think we shall be alone.

I am quite well—I was rather depressed at being told to rest again, but it is very difficult to keep at the weight which [Dr] Craig thinks necessary[3]—However he was very encouraging about the future—if one is careful now. Certainly, you were not to blame—

Ka and Leonard send their love. She goes early tomorrow, and we are going to try and get the train stopped for her at Rodmell.

Yrs.
V.W.

Sussex

1. Wife of Alexander Hannay, the art-critic of the *London Mercury*, 1920-34.
2. Saxon's mother lived at Hove, Sussex.
3. Virginia now weighed 11 stone, having lost a pound during this year.

Asheham, [Rodmell, Sussex]

Wednesday [27 December 1916]

Dearest,

Would it suit you if we came over on Monday, and I spent the night? We should arrive about tea time, and Leonard would fetch me the next day.

I'm very well, but Craig thinks I've been losing weight too fast, and wants me not to walk much; and as I very much want to avoid having to go to bed, I am being very cautious. But he was very cheerful—

I think we go back on Thursday next—but its perfect down here. If I dont hear, we shall turn up on Monday afternoon. I am longing for a good gossip with my dear Dolphin.

Yr B.

Berg

812: To Margaret Llewelyn Davies *Asheham, Lewes, [Sussex]*

Friday [29 December 1916]

Dearest Margaret,

There isn't much news to tell you; however I should like to get a good thick letter from you, so I must write.

Perhaps you are in the midst of moving to the cellar—Do you know that if people live in the dark, they become bleached all over and very likely their eyes turn pink? I should mention this to Lilian [Harris]. But from the papers I see that you have all been in deep fog. Here of course the sun has been such that lying in bed I've had to pull the curtains; frost on the ground, and the downs most lovely. We found a hare dying the other afternoon, and then a green plover, turning its head from side to side, with its eyes shut. Today we meant to go and have a treat at Brighton, so of course the wind has risen and covered the whole place with sea mist. Nevertheless we are full of small occupations which keep us so busy that the time flies.

Leonard is writing an article about beasts in Ceylon for the New Statesman; I am—or was—reading Greek! I can't make out what the fascination of Greek is, seeing that I have to look out every other word, and then fit them together like a puzzle.

The voice of the Webbs has reached us even here—Sydney much aggrieved that Leonard doesn't jump at his offer,[1] seeing that the Committee were unanimous, and asking us to dine and discuss it at length, which of

1. To become Secretary of the Labour Party's advisory committees on international and imperial questions. Leonard eventually accepted.

course I should like to do for the sake of squeezing a compliment, addressed to me but intended for my husband, from that barren woman. But compared with Widow Whitehead,[1] how she shines! Widow Whitehead was one of your very worst—

We had Ka for Christmas, and Maynard Keynes and Duncan came over, and tomorrow I'm going over to spend the night at Charleston, which they've covered with various bright shades of Distemper. I shall note down the effects for you.

Maynard thinks that we may be on the verge of ruin, and thus of peace; and possibly [President Woodrow] Wilson intends to cut off our supplies and altogether he was quite hopeful. He dined with the Asquiths two nights after their downfall;[2] though Asquith himself was quite unmoved and most magnanimous, Margot [Asquith] started to cry with the soup, sent for cigarettes, and dropped tears and ashes together into her plate—utterly overcome. Maynard has a great admiration for Asquith who had perpetually to stand buffer between [Lloyd] George and McKenna,[3] who hate each other like poison.

I've just finished Bertie upon Reconstruction,[4] with a melancholy feeling that this sort of lecturing does me no good, but only exasperates me with the rest of the world. However, others say they think it does good—to the working classes perhaps—

Give my love to Lilian, and tell her that it needn't necessarily be beetles; it might be butterflies, or even wildflowers, or heraldry, or old china; the main point is it mustn't be for the good of the race—

We come back on Thursday and then hope etc, etc,—If you do any painting, you will let me help wont you? or moving books.

L. sends his love

Yr

Sussex   V.W.

813: TO SAXON SYDNEY-TURNER   *Asheham, [Rodmell, Sussex]*

Sunday [31 December 1916]

My dear Saxon,

I am much relieved to find that no stricture was implied; and hereby declare you forgiven. But I would point out that my sensibility is a tribute to you—there's nothing I should dislike more than to hurt you in a matter of

1. See p. 78, note 2.
2. The Prime Minister had resigned on 5 December, and was succeeded by Lloyd George.
3. Reginald McKenna, Chancellor of the Exchequer, who resigned with Asquith.
4. *Principles of Social Reconstruction*, by Bertrand Russell.

this sort; and that is what I thought I must have done. And I was hurt to think that you could have been hurt.

Yesterday we went to Brighton and thinking it possible that your mother might see me, I rang them up. Your father answered, and I had the greatest difficulty in making him understand who I was. After repeated spelling he grasped the name of Woolf, and Asheham—but neither conveyed anything to him—I was about to ring off, when suddenly it occurred to him that I was "Virginia" by which name and no other he said he knew me. He thought I had better not come, for fear of infection, though your mother is much better. He was so decided that I agreed not to come, though I'm afraid I shan't be able to go over again before we leave. I go to Charleston tomorrow, which only leaves one day possible, and though I myself would go, I find Leonard is against it—as it means a four mile walk to Glynde and back?— Would it be any use to suggest to Nessa that she should go one day? I suppose she sometimes does leave Charleston—or I could write to your mother. Your father wanted news of you, and said there had been a death in the house,[1] but things were now rather better.

We have done nothing except visit Brighton and fetch the milk from Beddingham. Almost every day has been lovely for some reason or other— all different—and only one actually wet. Duncan and Maynard—but I think I told you they had been over. I think the maledictions against Ka are quite unfounded in fact, though she has some mannerisms—like the rest of us, only not quite the same ones—

Now I am going to read the Greek Anthology (in a copy you gave me once) which I find very hard and quite absorbing. I beg to point out that there is time for me to get another letter; and I want news of Barbara; in default of news, reflections about her!

Yr. V.W.

'Ηδη λευκοιον θαλλει, θαλλει δε φιλομβρος
ναρκισσος, θαλλει δ'ουρεσιφοιτα κρινα.
ήδη δ'ή φιλεραστος, έν άνθεσιν ώριμον άνθος,
βαρβαρα Πειθους ήδυ τεθηλε ρόδον.
λειμωνες, τι ματαια κομαις έπι φαιδρα γελατε;
ά γαρ παις κρεσσων άδυπνοων στεφανων.[2]

Sussex

1. The family cared for mental patients in their own home.
2. Virginia wrote this quotation (*from The Greek Anthology*, v. 144) in Greek letters but omitting the accents, and changed the first word of line 4 from Ζηνοφιλα to βαρβαρα. *Translation:* "Already the white violet is in flower and narcissus that loves the rain, and the lilies that haunt the hillside, and already she is in bloom, Barbara [Zenophila], love's darling; the sweet rose of persuasion, flower of the flowers of spring. Why laugh ye joyously, ye meadows, vain-glorious for your bright tresses? More to be preferred than all sweet-smelling posies is she" (*Loeb edition, translation by W. R. Paton*).

134

Letters 814-855 (January–July 1917)

The plan to buy a small printing-press, frequently postponed, materialised in March, when they acquired a hand-press and set it up on the dining-room table at Hogarth House. Leonard later explained that their main purpose was to give Virginia a manual occupation which would ease the pressures on her mind, and they also foresaw with pleasure the possibility of publishing their own work free from the comments of editors and publishers, and the work of their friends. They first printed Two Stories, *one by Leonard and one by Virginia (The Mark on the Wall), and issued an advertisement appealing for subscribers to the Press, even before Virginia had begun to write her contribution to its first publication.* Two Stories, *illustrated by Carrington's wood-cuts, was published in July. Virginia had also begun to write* Night and Day (*though no mention of it is yet made in her letters), and contributed frequently to the* TLS. *The Woolfs moved between Richmond and Sussex in what had become an established rhythm, entertaining a few friends at Asheham and lending it to them for short periods. There were infrequent visits to Charleston (Leonard had bought Virginia a bicycle in 1914), but she maintained with her sister a brisk correspondence, in which each commiserated with the other on their servant troubles. Leonard was again exempted from all forms of war-service, even agriculture, and became a leading socialist authority on international affairs.*

814: To Saxon Sydney-Turner

*Hogarth House, Paradise Road,
Richmond*

Tuesday [16 January 1917]

My dear Saxon,

It was very pleasant to get a letter from you, in spite of your asperity about my Greek—I maintain though, that right or wrong the quotation was a very good one.

Would it suit you to dine on Sunday here? I find that is better for us than Saturday, and I am writing now to ask Barbara. This morning I heard from Carrington, who says that Barbara is delighted by the idea of Asheham, and they hope to go in about a fortnight. I should suggest your going too. It is a place that makes me feel completely natural—which, whether one is anxious or not, always makes life easier. This afternoon we are going to a Beethoven concert, opening Wigmore Hall (the old Bechstein)—I am glad that Barbara is busy, for after all, people have to help themselves through these things;

and after her work, I am sure you are the person best able to help. I shall concoct a few more stories for her. I wonder if she would be interested by the amazing story of Sydney Waterlow? We have been having a crisis with him, really unthinkable with any one else, and its not yet over.

By the way, I must seriously lecture you upon late hours. Twice you date your letters 2 a.m. and if so, how can you possibly be well? Even if you dont sleep, try going to bed at 10. I find nothing makes so much difference. One late night is sufficient to start a headache. However, I shall speak to Barbara.

Yr.
V.W.

The snow is beginning to drip through my roof again.

Sussex

815: To Barbara Hiles   *Hogarth House, Paradise Road,*
                               Richmond
Tuesday [16 January 1917]

Dear Barbara,

Will you come to dinner next Sunday? I have asked Saxon to come.

I am coming to the Omega on Thursday, to be slightly altered,[1] but it is really a great success, and such a mercy to creep into ones fur like an animal.

Please make Saxon keep earlier hours. He writes to me at 2 in the morning. It is absolute ruin to the health. I hope you are sensible too—but how dangerous it must be to live with a packet of pins in one's mouth, year in, year out.

I am longing to hear about Kenilworth on Christmas day, and whether it was as we imagined it—Or is it really a sink of iniquity? I can imagine most lurid military amours taking place under the Elizabethan ruins.[2]

I heard from Carrington that you may be able to go to Asheham in a fortnight. We shall like you to be there—which is more than we can say of some of our friends, but I will not be so indiscreet as to say which.

We were divinely happy there at Christmas; the weather like spring, and not a soul to be seen. You must make Saxon go with you; then take him to the top of the downs; while Carrington asks him something about the man on the moon, you run behind, give him a shove, and send him rolling to the bottom. We used to do this with Vanessa, and it made a new woman of her.

Your affate
V.W.

Berg

1. Virginia was having a dress made at the Omega, where Barbara occasionally worked as a dressmaker.
2. Barbara was not visiting the great Warwickshire mediaeval-Elizabethan house. She was staying in the village with her parents, who were working there during the war.

Hogarth House, Paradise Road, Richmond

Wednesday [17 January 1917]

Dear Carrington,

I hope you will be able to go to Asheham. It doesn't matter when, so long as you let me know in time to warn the caretaker. I shall have to explain a good many things, about food, as our arrangements are now very difficult there, without trains.

Could you dine with me on Friday next, 7-30? Perhaps you would spend the night. There are trains up early in the morning.

I shall be alone, and it would be very nice.

As letters seem to take so long, would you ring me up tomorrow morning.

Yours affate
Virginia Woolf

Robert H. Taylor

817: To Vanessa Bell   [*Hogarth House, Richmond*]

Monday [22 January 1917]

Dearest,

You didn't send me the recipes—but never mind—perhaps you will one day—We had Saxon and Barbara and Adrian and Saxon [error for Karin] last night; and Saxon wanted to know whether he might suggest a visit to you on Tuesday, till Saturday. He is ordered a rest; and we have lent them Asheham. Carrington is going with them.

But he told me that Roger said you were overworked, and was therefore doubtful about coming. I think its most likely that you are overworked—and I do think it a most ridiculous thing, knowing what horror illness is. I now take 3 glasses of milk daily. If you would take one, some good would be done. You use every part of you, so incessantly. I cant think how you manage visitors. But I wish you'd send me a line to say how you really are. If you'd ever like comparative quiet here, we both wish that you'd come. My husband is nursing a hopeful passion for you—and as for me!

Adrian and Karin have got a place in Hertfordshire, much to their delight. Saxon and Barbara seem both of them on the verge of some form of melancholia, and I think you'd better not have him, as his silence and look of disease infect one after a time. However, I'm sure he meant to come. Then you'll have them all over from Asheham.

I wonder how the Amber brats are doing.[1] Personally, I think its better

1. See p. 130, note 1.

not to teach one's own children;—are you sure you couldn't bed out one of our enlightened virgins, an Olivier say, (Daphne might do) in Firle, and make her teach everything? I meant to write a long, passionate, and interesting letter, but Saxon has just rung me up, and kept me so long talking, that I must now dress. He says he's going to you—and you say you're all right. But I dont much believe it. The fog is permanent here; by night we have the Aurora Borealis, which a man in the street took to be zeppelins, so shouted out loud under the servants window. At midnight we heard them carrying their bedding to the kitchen, there to lie on the floor till day—With great difficulty we got them up again, and lectured them on the nature of northern lights. I think I must write the stories of our youth for Julian. Aunt Ena[1] is dead.

Yr B.

I should very much like to stay with you—but I don't know when.
I found this letter.
Leonard saw Sydney [Waterlow]—we had him here—but not much result—
I think he's hopeless—not being chosen an Apostle[2] wrecked his life he says.

Berg

818: To Margaret Llewelyn Davies

Hogarth House, Paradise Road,
Richmond

Jan. 24th [1917]

Dearest Margaret,

I hope you are better. Leonard never went to that Committee. Would Saturday suit you as well as Sunday to dine here? On Sunday we have Roger, I think, and it would be perhaps nicer for you and for us to meet alone.

We had a very remarkable Guild meeting[3] last night, which I must tell you about. A speaker [Mrs Bessie Ward] from the Civil Liberty Council, lectured us upon Venereal Diseases, and moral risks for our sons. I felt that the audience was queer, and as no one spoke, I got up and thanked her, whereupon two women left the room, and I saw that another gigantic fat one was in tears. However, they all went, except Mrs Langston who told the

1. The mother of Helen Holland, a distant Duckworth relative.
2. The exclusive intellectual club at Cambridge, of which Leonard, Lytton, Saxon, Desmond, Maynard, Roger Fry, E. M. Forster and Bertrand Russell had been elected members as undergraduates.
3. The Richmond Branch of the Women's Co-operative Guild, of which Virginia had become an active member in the autumn of 1916. For the next four years she provided speakers for the monthly meetings, which were held at Hogarth House.

lecturer it was a most cruel speech, and only a childless woman could have made it "for we mothers try to forget what our sons have to go through". Then she began to cry. Did you ever hear such—nonsense it seems to me. The poor speaker said she was used to it. I do think its odd—the servants tell me that great indignation was expressed by most of the women at the mention in public of such subjects—however, I must stop—

Are you really all right? I will come and see Miss Kidd of course if she would ever like it.

Yr. V.W.

Sussex

819: To Margaret Llewelyn Davies

Hogarth [House, Richmond]

Friday [26 January 1917]

Dearest Margaret,

I expect that, writing in a hurry, I gave you rather a wrong impression of what happened at the meeting. I have asked the servants since what the women who objected said about the lecture. Their chief objection seems to have been that she spoke in the presence of two girls—Gladys, our tweeny, aged 16; and Mrs Reed's daughter, 16 or 17. They thought this very wrong. But then Mrs Ward (Mrs Bessie Ward) specially noticed the presence of girls, said that she was going to speak on moral questions, and asked whether she was to go on. They all agreed; at any rate none objected. As a matter of fact, Mrs Reed, the girl's mother, thought the lecture splendid, and did not mind her daughter hearing it. Mrs Miller also said it was the best lecture we had ever had, and offered to do anything, wished us to affiliate to the Council of C[ivil] L[iberties]; etc. There were three who objected strongly, (partly because of the presence of girls) only one of whom I spoke to, Mrs Langston. I thought her unreasonable, because she seemed to take it as a personal insult on the part of Mrs Ward—and I was surprised because Mrs Langston is on a good many local Committees, I think, and is by way of being among the most broad minded. But I quite agree that their point of view about their sons is quite easy to understand and sympathise with—I thought Mrs Ward a nice woman, evidently trying to make her remarks as general as possible; half the lecture was about the conscription of women; only a small part was devoted to Venereal Diseases.

I think that the objection raised by other branches to whom she had spoken was patriotic—certainly in one case; they said nothing but sang God Save the King. It is queer though, that that class shouldn't discuss these questions openly, considering how much more they are affected by them than we are. I spoke to Nelly (the cook) afterwards, and after being a little shocked, she agreed that it was most important that women should have knowledge in such matters—and then she told me stories of friends and relations, and how they'd suffered, and so on.

Dont bother to answer.

Yr. V.W.

Sussex

820: To Vanessa Bell

Hogarth House, Paradise Road,
Richmond

[end January 1917]

Dearest,

Would you be so good as to explain on the enclosed card in what proportions one mixes the size and the paint and water. The people at the shop didn't know. If you could answer at once, we should be grateful as we want to paint the dining room on Sunday.

Give my love to Saxon.[1] I saw Barbara yesterday, and explained everything about Asheham.

Yr
V.W.

Berg

821: To Saxon Sydney-Turner

Hogarth [*House, Richmond*]

Saturday [3 February 1917]

My dear Saxon,

You must put it down much to my credit that I write, as the cold is nipping my fingers. However, I daresay its nothing to what you have been suffering. I am very sorry about the pipes and Mrs Attfield [caretaker]. I hope you now use her, and there's no need for you to make beds and break ice, which will undo the good of the air. Your praise of Asheham pleased us very much. I don't think Charleston can hold a candle to it, and that, owing to the vileness of human nature, pleases us too.

What is the truth of the rumour that Barbara is going on the Music Hall Stage?[2] I went to hear a new Debussy sonata for the harp flute and viola yesterday, and there met Adrian and Karin, who told me she had accepted an offer—I hope its not true, because I want to feel that for ever and ever

1. Saxon, Barbara and Carrington were now arriving at Asheham.
2. Barbara Hiles had been auditioned by the manager of the Palace Pit, who had seen her dancing at a party, but she was not offered a job.

she will make my clothes*—and in fact I had a vision of some adaptation of dress contrived by her and Faith[1] to do away with underclothes and be attached by a solitary button.

I went to tea with Roger yesterday, and there met his Belgian Vander-velde,[2] and Lady Constance Stuart Richardson.[3] Save that the titled lady wore top boots, such as the foresters in Shakespeare wear, I saw nothing strange and even improper about her; but we all made believe that the whole of life was an unsealed book to us. I rather liked the Sonata (this is in your later manner).

We are going skating today on the Pen Ponds [Richmond Park] and tomorrow we have induced Lytton to come too. As to the William Watson,[4] I prefer his pomp to his wit. The epigrams are like crackers that dont go off— As to Aeschylus, on the other hand, I've been reading him in French which is better than English; I dont think I have read anything else. Aeschylus however excited my spirits to such an extent that, hearing my husband snore in the night, I woke him to light his torch and look for zeppelins. He then applied the Freud system to my mind, and analysed it down to Clytemnestra and the watch fires, which so pleased him that he forgave me. All the morning I have been reviewing with great labour an American essayist;[5] and therefore I can't think of any good jokes. But from Adrian's account you are all like rosy elves; and I seriously hope that you have rested and not worried. After all I think your situation must be extremely good, from all points of view, and you will have a solid experience to look back upon, more satis-factory than visits and journeys in the Tube.

Please write again and give my love to Barbara and Carrington, and I hope we shall all meet as soon as you come back.

Yr. V.W.

*Tell her the dress has come back, altered, and greatly improved. Many thanks.

Sussex

1. Faith Henderson, sister of Nicholas Bagenal.
2. See p. 117, note 1.
3. Lady Constance Stewart-Richardson, daughter of the Earl of Cromartie. In 1904 she had married Sir Edward Stewart-Richardson, who died of wounds in November 1914.
4. William Watson (1858-1935), who was knighted in this year for his patriotic poems, was well known as an epigrammatist.
5. *An Apology for Old Maids*, by Henry Dwight Sedgwick (*TLS*, 8 February 1917).

Hogarth House, Paradise Road, Richmond

Sunday [4 February 1917]

My Violet,

I have been meaning to ask whether I might come to tea one day; also I have been meaning to thank you for the fur boots, which I am still wearing —the third winter I think—They're quite unapproachable. As our coal gave out the other day, they were my chief support for a week.

How are you? Are you writing (as is rumoured) a History of the Eden family since the Fall[1] I suppose you have been charged with all the horrors of the death of Lord Cromer,[2] arranging everything—If you are in London I hope I may see you. We have been at Asheham, where the entire garden has been crushed out by fallen trees, and we have to start all over again. Nessa is settled about 4 miles off, and has adopted two small girls. Aunt Mary (did you see) was run over by a taxicab. Let me know some afternoon when you wd be in.

Yr

Sp:

Berg

Hogarth House, Richmond

Monday [5 February 1917]

Dear Carrington,

I wonder whether you are still at Asheham.

This is to ask you whether, if you are, you will be so very kind as to bring back my Kodak with you. It is in the drawing room, and has some films wh. ought to be developed.

I hope your difficulties are less—they cant be over so long as this frost holds—our sufferings here are very great; one day last week we had no coal, no milk, no telephone.

Please come and dine and bring the Kodak when you get back.

Yr

V.W.

Love to Barbara and Saxon.

Robert H. Taylor

1. A collection of family papers which Violet had edited. They survive only in typescript.
2. The first Earl of Cromer, whose second wife was Violet's and Virginia's friend Katherine Thynne, died on 29 January.

Sunday [11 February 1917]

Dearest,

We shall be very glad to sell you the apples, at whatever price is their due, as I don't think they'll keep till Easter.

But I dont know how you're to get them—or the carpet. Do you deal with Bannisters? If so, his cart might bring them. If not, shall I ask Mrs Attfield if she can manage it?

I wish you would send me details of your housekeeping. My books run to about 17/- a head; but then I suppose 5 cost more to feed in proportion than 9. I believe the only way to be cheap is to get rid of respectable servants; for there's no checking them, short of dismissing them altogether. Have you any cheap dishes you could recommend? It would be a great comfort to get rid of the feeling of waste, let alone spending so much on such dull things.

London always seems to me rich in romance when I dip into it, which I do about twice a week, but thank God I don't live there. I find that when I've seen a certain number of people my mind becomes like an old match box—the part one strikes on, I mean. But its pleasant seeing our friends a-hopping in the frying pan. I met Vandervelde and Lady Stuart Richardson last week—rather elderly both of them, and without obvious attractions. We went up yesterday, and at once ran into Ka, and Roger, separately—Ka flying to Wimbledon, as her pipes are burst, Roger returning from Lady Constance. And we dined with the [Desmond] MacCarthys, and met Alix [Sargant-Florence] and that strange phantom Abbott,[1] with the disease which makes the touch of human flesh repulsive to him.

I must consider what gossip I put in my pouch for you. Dr Seton[2] is dead, aged 90, and lived in the next street to us here. I saw Mrs Cole in the park. Leonard knew her. I only saw a great proboscis flash by. Molly's [MacCarthy] ear specialist (a new one) seems to think her case hopeless; but she was very sprightly, and her children are certainly very charming—I wont say more charming than yours—which reminds me—did Julian get a parcel of various toys which I sent at the same time as the book? If not, I had better ask—Here I was rung up by Saxon; seems in the depths of depression, about his health, as far as I could gather. The doctor, whom he had just seen, may send him away for a long time. However he's coming to tea, and he was so testy that I think he must be rather bad, or Barbara changed. He wrote to me that he was always repeating to himself "The happy ghost"—which I recognise among the signs of mania. He wanted Barbara to stay at Asheham for the rest of the war, which we dont at all wish for—In fact we may come down

1. Possibly Edwin Abbott (1838-1926), the teacher and scholar, who had made his reputation as Headmaster of the City of London School.
2. The doctor who had cared for Sir Leslie Stephen in his last illnesses, and was also doctor to Leonard's family at 101 Lexham Gardens.

next week, as our domestic difficulties are likely to be great. Last week we ran out of coal, and managed to get one ton, which is now almost finished, and it seems impossible to get any more. During the worst of the frost we had to live on coal bricks, bought from an old woman in the street; then our milk gave out, and then the telephone.

However we have had amazing bright sun, and skating at Hampton Court. I bought a pair, and found I could get along, and enjoyed it very much, but now its thawing hard. Old Lady Strachey has taken to reading us plays, which is rather amusing. She reads for 2 1/2 hours without stopping, acting every part (cutting out obscenity alone) and has only one eye; she is far the best reader I have ever heard. There was a woman there called Miss Ammonia. I have had a slight rapprochement with Katherine Mansfield; who seems to me an unpleasant but forcible and utterly unscrupulous character, in whom I think you might find a 'companion'—

What are the Amber Brats like? I can't remember a word of tonic-sol-fa— I could get you books if you like.

Yr B.

Berg

825: To Duncan Grant   *Hogarth House, Paradise Road, Richmond*

Tuesday [6 March 1917]

My dear Duncan,

I hope by this time you have got all covered with mud and manure again, so that a letter from a suburb even may have some romance. You were like a beautiful but rather faded moth, the other day, after your nights debauch among the red hot pokers and passion flowers of Hampstead. Directly I left you, by the way, I ran straight into Lord Ribblesdale, the very image of his picture[1]—only obviously seedy and dissolute. Then I had my tooth out, and dreamt such a terrifically exciting and somehow sexual dream that I woke up laughing, upon which the military doctor said "I declare you are laughing Mrs Woolf! Now do tell us what your dream was about?" which I could not do.

It is very difficult to get in to touch with people who live in the country. I am sitting alone by myself over a large fire after dinner, Leonard having gone up to see Mrs Hamilton;[2] and if you were opposite we should soon be wagging our tongues like a pack of hounds. As for gossip, I daresay I had better think what there is, though I expect the true version of every single

1. The portrait of the last Lord Ribblesdale (d. 1925), by J. S. Sargent (1902), now in the Tate Gallery.
2. Mary Agnes ('Molly') Hamilton, the politician and biographer, later a Labour M.P.

thing is known at Charleston long before it is here. In fact, I always think of you and Nessa like the young women at the telephone exchange, with the wires ringing little bells round them, as loves, divorces, and copulations and insanities blaze out in London.

Last night the Hawtreys dined here—an odd couple. Almost her first words were "Do you like Lady Ottoline?". As far as I can make out Mrs H: must have failed in that circle, for her disapproval of their ways went on practically the whole evening. It was odd to see Hawtrey as a married man— especially married to a practically barbaric Pole[1]—or so she seemed to me, with ungoverned passions and the brain of a yellow cockatoo. She described his proposal, which took place in the middle of a Beethoven quartet. "I love you" he said "and I didn't know at first whether he meant me or another girl" upon which Hawtrey tapped her archly upon the nose (in our house, I mean—he was very arch and sprightly with her, and she very amorous). Then I had tea with dear old Violet Dickinson, who, I must say, has more of the flesh of humanity about her than those rather disembodied young women at the Omega. However, I see I am getting as crusty as old Nessa; but I get on better with mellow spinsters like Violet, who have had their noses in every cesspool since about the year 1870. When I was there a young woman arrived to ask her advice about a paralysed doctor to whom she (the young lady) is engaged; and that has been going on without ceasing since the days of the first Jubilee, at least. She had been consulted by the Turtons, parents of Nina's[2] Turton; old family friends of course, Nina has now taken away the baby. She knew Turton himself, who had only one fault—his chivalry; and he believed Nina to be the deserted wife of an officer who only wanted a chance to reform; at least so he told the Dickinsons, just before he went to the front. And then I heard about Katie [Cromer], who makes a beautiful widow; and how Violet met Helen Holland roaming about a railway station all in black, and saying when spoken to "Mother has just gone home", which meant that Aunt Ena's coffin was in the van.

However, I daresay all this will sound very unreal, when it gets among the sheep and the downs; and old Nessa (who has become a Shakespeare character in my mind, so that I often put her into action for my amusement) —she, I suppose, is long past reading letters by this time—what with the dirt, the itch, the brats, the paints; and is it true, by the way that she said the other day "Its the last feather in the Camels Cap", meaning, it is thought (Heaven knows why) that she was unable to break the ice in her Po? And I suppose speech will be beyond her soon; Maynard seemed to think so, not that she ever had a complete vocabulary—I wish when you write me that very long letter which you will do this evening you would tell me what her

1. Ralph Hawtrey, the economist, had married Hortense Emilia, the pianist, daughter of Taksony d'Aranyi of Budapest.
2. Nina Lamb. See p. 48.

habits are. People are always asking after her; indeed one of the concealed worms of my life has been a sisters jealousy—*of* a sister I mean; and to feed this I have invented such a myth about her that I scarcely know one from tother.

I saw Sylvia Milman[1] and her husband the other night; at least Sylvia M: and a kind of Belgian Shakespeare in brown velveteen, whom I took to be her husband, but they are dining with us, so I shall see.

I wish I could stop writing this letter—it is like an extremely long visit to the W.C. when, do what you will, fresh coils appear, and duty seems to urge you to break off, and then another inch protrudes, which must be the last; and it *isnt* the last—and so on, until—However—I must not tell you about Sydney Waterlow; or Leonard's misconduct in the Strachey drawing room; but do tell Nessa this one flaming invention of mine—I make my own sanitary towels, and save at least 2/6 a month.

I hope you get half a day off, and will spend it in writing a long letter to me.

Yr V.W.

Duncan Grant

826: To Vanessa Bell   Hogarth [*House, Richmond*]

Friday [23 March 1917]

Dearest,

I write to suggest that you should pay us a little visit at Asheham. Do you think it would be possible? Our visitors go on the 10th, and then we shall be there alone for a week—and we should needless to say, be extremely happy if you would come for that week. The brats would be near enough for you to keep an eye on them, and you could paint, and be alone most of the day, and call me in for a gossip when wanted.

I did think you looked in want of a holiday—and coming to London is only the fire after the frying pan, as you would say.

The spring season is full of disease; and a small break in your life might keep you healthy for a year. However, I admit I really dont ask you for any unselfish reason, but because it would be such fun if you did come, and we shan't be having any one else then.

I think we come down on the 3rd. Marjorie [Strachey] and [C. P.] Sanger arrive on the 5th. So do think it over and say you will.

Have you got rid of the Ambers? I hope so.

I gather you didn't see Walter [Lamb] after all—

1. The daughter of Arthur Milman, the barrister. The family had been friends of the Stephens for three generations. Her husband was John Mills Whitham, the writer.

146

I must stop—as we are going to the Farrington Rd. [error for Farringdon St] to buy our press.

Love to Duncan.

Yr B.

Berg

827: To Violet Dickinson

Asheham, Rodmell, Lewes, [Sussex]

Tuesday [10 April 1917]

My Violet,

It was very nice to read—or rather decipher—your very distinguished hand again. I wish you would write oftener; but its almost impossible to write letters. I can only just manage it now that our visitors have gone. We have talked incessantly for 5 days; one was a very minute, half starved barrister, with views upon every political question—indeed upon every possible question; the other was one of the Stracheys who has taken to board school teaching, and had to argue the whole question of Education. What a mercy it is when one's friends go! But we were hoping that you would come down to Richmond. Could it be arranged, or are you settled now for the summer?

I didn't honestly think that Lady Newton had made the best of her Lyme papers;[1] the truth was that the Legh's were almost invariably stupid—which accounts, I suppose, for their centuries of life on the same spot. Do you know them in the flesh? I should like immensely to write a book of that sort, if someone would trust me to tell the truth about their relations. It's so queer the sentiment she had for them. If you have got Mrs Lyttelton, do hand her on to me.[2] I know its a base pleasure that one takes in these indecent revelations—why do they do it? But if they enjoy it, I dont see why we shouldn't. Was Alfred a fraud?—half a fraud, I suppose; a sort of glorified George [Duckworth]; a much nicer George—but still in that line of business. But I know nothing about it.

Nessa and Duncan came over yesterday, having previously washed themselves; and then went back in a storm late at night to help ducklings out of their eggs, for they were heard quacking inside, and couldn't break through. Nessa seems to have slipped civilization off her back, and splashes about entirely nude, without shame, and enormous spirit. Indeed, Clive now takes up the line that she has ceased to be a presentable lady—I think it all

1. Violet had read Virginia's review of *The House of Lyme from its Foundation to the End of the Eighteenth Century*, by Lady Newton (*TLS*, 29 March 1917). Lyme Park, Cheshire, had been the home of the Legh family for over 500 years.
2. The Life of Alfred Lyttelton, the lawyer and statesman, by his widow, Edith Lyttelton (1917).

works admirably. The wind rages incessantly, and Leonard spends his day cutting up the fallen trees. We live on the wood, which smells so delicious. I am trying to read Conrad's new book[1], but owing to endless talk, I haven't got far. Now we are going to Lewes to buy some plants—for the summer. Potatoes there are none. However, the old ewes give birth nightly behind hurdles at the back of the house. And all day the lambs keep up an extraordinary loud noise.

I hope I shall see you again soon—We have bought our Press![2] We don't know how to work it, but now I must find some young novelists or poets. Do you know any?

Leonard sends his love, and says he hopes you will come and see us. I liked my tea with you so much—

Yr
Sp.

Berg

828: To Lady Robert Cecil

Asheham, Rodmell, Lewes

Saturday 14th April [1917]

My dear Nelly,

Whenever I come here, I think of you—I don't exactly know why, but I feel its a great compliment to you even when its pouring with rain and the downs are half covered with mist. I saw Violet the other day, and she said something about your being on the move. Is it to the flat in Victoria or to Henry James' sister in law's flat?

Its melancholy to think that you have left St John's Wood, with that square garden, and the trees which I always think of bare, as trees ought to be. However, Violet is so much of an enchantress that I daresay she made this all up in her head. Dont you know the sort of unreal haphazard air which meets one on the staircase in Manchester Street [Violet's London house]?

We came here for Easter, and every day we had either a gale or a snow-storm. We had two visitors [Marjorie Strachey and C. P. Sanger], one a barrister, and such a lot of talk that I used to go up to my room and fall upon a French novel like a starving dog. They were both very nice; and I suppose being both hard at work the rest of the year their minds ran away with them with no work to do. Or do you find that barristers are always like that? The world seems so definite to them—so full of information.

When I'm in the country I like sitting over a great wood fire and reading

1. *The Shadow-Line* (1917).
2. Their first hand-press, which they bought at a printer's shop in Farringdon St, Holborn.

—or thinking I'm going to read. I've just read Conrad's latest. Have you? Its very beautiful and very calm. I wish I knew how he gets his effect of space.

By the way, we've bought our printing Press. We are going to start work directly we go back, next Tuesday. Heaven knows how one prints— but please consider whether you haven't a page or two of practically faultless prose in some desk. We want to start on something very short and very sublime.

May I come to tea with you some day, if you're in a house where that is possible. I must send this to St John's Wood.

Nessa is 4 miles on the other side of the down, living like an old hen wife among ducks, chickens and children. She never wants to put on proper clothes again—even a bath seems to distress her. Her children are for ever asking her questions and she invents all sorts of answers, never having known very accurately about facts.

Yr.
V.W.

Hatfield

829: To Vanessa Bell   *Hogarth House, [Richmond]*

April 26th [1917]

Dearest,

I went to Bumpus [book shop] the other day, and the man seemed to think that books about making things are to be had, but was out of them. Perhaps you could say, more exactly what you want—I'm not sure I've got it right. I got a book of Bucklands,[1] which Leonard used to know by heart, as a small present.

Wouldn't bugs be a good thing to start?—what fun to sugar the trees again. When Moore was with us last summer he discovered several varieties of Blue [butterflies] on the downs.

It was disappointing not to see you, and we had a fine roast fowl for dinner, but I hardly thought you would come. I must now bethink me as usual of my gossip, though I maintain its a case of coals to Newcastle. Various Stracheys have descended upon us. That letter from Jos[2] set the affair going again—at least Marjorie [Strachey] spent two days with him, and left a brooch in his room, which had to be telegraphed for, and it is thought her character is gone. What happened no one knows—but she appeared on Sunday saying that either she must get a letter delivered at once, or go to Staffordshire by the next train. They are filled with disgust. Lytton

1. Francis Buckland, the 19th century naturalist.
2. Josiah Wedgwood, the politician, of the famous Staffordshire family.

has had his exemption taken away by the Tribunal, and is going to appeal.[1] Rodker[2] has been arrested, and declared insane (but something may have happened later). So far, nothing has been done to us. I collected this at dinner last night with Alix and Carrington, where there was also a most singular speckly eyed young man—Aldous Huxley—who owing to Ka, has got put into a government office.[3] I warned him of what might happen to his soul; however, he spends his time translating French poetry.

Did you hear of Maynards terrible outburst at Easter, when he said that Asquith is more intelligent than Lytton? Lytton thinks this a very serious symptom. I had a wonderful plunge however from this exalted society to—what? Imagine Marny,[4] all black, incredibly faded and genteel, on the platform at Victoria!—carrying a small bag, with gold rimmed pince-nezs! There was no escape; she asked about 20 questions. "Where is Nessa? Does she live at Asheham now? How are her children? Have you got a house? Isn't Richmond very pretty?"—happily her train came; but next day I was rung up by Toad,[5] who seemed quivering with excitement, and insists upon dining here. But I know I shall enjoy it. I rather gather that Marny disapproves of her [Emma's] work for the Germans [prisoners of war].

Our press arrived on Tuesday. We unpacked it with enormous excitement, finally with Nelly's help, carried it into the drawing room, set it on its stand—and discovered it was smashed in half! It is a great weight, and they never screwed it down; but the shop has probably got a spare part. Anyhow the arrangement of the type is such a business that we shant be ready to start printing directly. One has great blocks of type, which have to be divided into their separate letters, and founts, and then put into the right partitions. The work of ages, especially when you mix the h's with the ns, as I did yesterday. We get so absorbed we can't stop; I see that real printing will devour one's entire life. I am going to see Katherine Mansfield, to get a story from her, perhaps; please experiment with papers.

Nelly gave notice our last day at Asheham—as I expected. Neither she nor Lotty feel they can face 6 weeks there in the summer; so I'm speculating on a complete change—one servant, and meals from the communal kitchen, which is going to be started, near us I hope. What do you think?

We shall count upon your coming here. I think I shall invite a small, and select party to meet you—or would you like a drunken riot? I want to give a party. We might take float upon the river—I hear from Lytton that the

1. The Government was reviewing the cases of all those who had previously been exempted from military service. Lytton's appeal was successful.
2. John Rodker, the poet and translator, who later founded the Imago Press.
3. Huxley had been working on the Morrell farm at Garsington, having been rejected for military service as physically unfit. From April to July he had a clerical job at the Air Board.
4. Margaret Vaughan, Virginia's cousin.
5. Emma Vaughan, Margaret's sister.

Omega Club is doomed—very few go, and only the dullest—I did an awful thing on Sunday—lost poor old Tim [dog]—I've done it hundreds of times, but he never came back, and we can hear nothing of him. The police say he cant be run over—

Promise to come for 2 nights at least—I particularly need to inspect you.

Love to Duncan.

B.

Berg

830: To Lady Ottoline Morrell
Hogarth House, Paradise Road,
Richmond

[end April 1917]

My dear Ottoline

It was a great surprise and pleasure to see your hand again. I haven't forgotten you—indeed you have become one of the romantic myths of my life, and when I hear of other people seeing you, I don't believe them. I daresay this is a form of jealousy though.

Anyhow, I shall like very much to come to tea on Thursday.

Your affate
Virginia Woolf

Texas

831: To Margaret Llewelyn Davies
Hogarth House, [Richmond]

Wednesday [2 May 1917]

Dearest Margaret,

It is a damned bore (as Lilian [Harris] would say) that you should be so weak still. I daresay you have deserved it, what with one thing and another, if that is any consolation to you. You must keep us all at bay, until you are prepared to fling yourself into the most absorbing of all pursuits. After 2 hours work at the press, Leonard heaved a terrific sigh and said "I wish to God we'd never bought the cursed thing!" To my relief, though not surprise, he added "Because I shall never do anything else". You can't think how exciting, soothing, ennobling and satisfying it is. And so far we've only done the dullest and most difficult part—setting up a notice, which you will recieve one day. We cant print it off yet, because, to our horror, the press arrived smashed, and it will take some time to get it mended. Meanwhile our brains buzz with all sorts of works—but the great thing is to annoy the secretive and reticent—Lilian, Janet, Emphie, Mrs Copper; they must all take to the pen.

This has rather swamped everything else. I dont know what I've been doing since we came back—thats to my credit I mean. Two meetings of the Guild I've presided over. We are trying to set up a Bread Shop here; we held a committee to decide about it, at which we all told stories about our house-hold difficulties. Mrs Langston is helping the ladies of Richmond to found a Communal Kitchen. She says "What can you expect of ladies? They dont know anything"—"And Lady Yoxall[1] isn't a real lady—she was only a school teacher before she married". Anyhow, according to Mrs Langston they're going to make a mess of it. I propose to get our food there.

I've been exchanging compliments with Ottoline. She protests that I must have forgotten her. I say No, that's quite impossible. I'm to go to tea with her tomorrow. I am told that she is deserted and despised, and claws you like a famished tigress to go to Garsington, where no one will now stay, save the C.Os, who have to; but I've heard this story so often, and no one has the strength of mind to stop going. But I feel as if I were stepping into a Tomb. Please recover at once, and come and see us. Its such an age since we met.

Yr. V.W.

Sussex

832: To Margaret Llewelyn Davies

[Hogarth House, Richmond]

[7 May 1917]

Dearest Margaret,

I will come on Thursday, 4.30, with great pleasure (unless you stop me) Here is the first proof from the press[2]—We did it by hand, as the machine is still broken, so its not a fair sample. We've been staying with the Trevelyans for Sunday—very nice both of them, but how I hate Surrey!

Your,
V.W.

Sussex

833: To Violet Dickinson

Hogarth House, Paradise Road,
Richmond

[May 1917]

My Violet

I hope you're still in London. Would you come to tea next Tuesday,

---

1. Wife of Sir James Yoxall, M.P. for West Nottinghamshire 1895-1918. They had been married in 1886, and lived in Kew Gardens Road.
2. See the reproduction opposite.

HOGARTH HOUSE
RICHMOND.

THE HOGARTH PRESS.

It is proposed to issue shortly a pamphlet containing two short stories by Leonard Woolf and Virginia Woolf,(price,includ--ing postage 1/2).

If you desire a copy to be sent to you,please fill up the form below and send it with a P. O. to L. S. Woolf at the above address before June .

A limited edition only will be issued.

Please send   copy of Publication No. 1 to

for which I enclose P. O. for

NAME

ADDRESS

15th, and stay to an early dinner? We should enjoy seeing you very much. I've just finished Alfred Lyttelton. I suppose the only excuse is that it was a relief to her feelings to write it, but the horror of having that sprawling and emotional stuff written about one, and all ones private papers hung up in public, seems to me considerable. Poor Laura![1] And Alfred himself seems to have [been] against lives on the whole. The truth is that those very sentimental and adoring circles dont last very well—after 20 years, only the gush still gushes: and then I was roused to anger by Alfreds ecstasy over a dead lion, and rhapsodies at communion 2 days later. Poor man! I suppose she drove him on to be a celebrity and a politician, which wasn't his line— However, all his sins are paid for by this sort of monument. We're sitting in our backgarden after tea enjoying the sun.

I hope you'll come.

Yr
V.W.

Berg

834: To Lady Ottoline Morrell

Hogarth House, Paradise Road,
Richmond

[May 1917]

My dear Ottoline,

I should like to come very much—but whether I can persuade Leonard to get over his quite unreasonable terror of a week end, I dont know. Would some week end in June, the 23rd or 30th suit you?

We go away for Whitsun and may stay away for a bit, so I put it late.

My images, after leaving you, were all of the depths of the sea—mermaid Queens, shells, the bones of the shipwrecked. I was incapacitated for normal life for some time after seeing you. It was a great pleasure, and reassurement to find that my memory had not been nearly mythical or romantic enough. But in what condition you are when the clock strikes 11 in the morning, I cant conceive—or how you order dinner;—or, in short, I shall follow you with my mouth agape. I've just sent you a halfpenny envelope containing a notice of our first publication. We find we have only 50 friends in the world —and most of them stingy. Could you think of any generous people—they need not be very generous—whose names you would send me? If so, I should be very grateful—

Your ever affate
Virginia Woolf.

Texas

1, Laura Tennant, Alfred Lyttelton's first wife who died a year after their marriage.

835: To R. C. Trevelyan   *Hogarth House, Paradise Road,*
                                 Richmond, Surrey

May 20th [1917]

My dear Bob,

I am writing to ask what of course you must refuse if inconvenient—would you come and speak to my Guild of Co-operative Women (Margaret Davies' affair) on Tuesday, 5th June? Any subject does—not literature perhaps, but travel, or politics. The talk should last half an hour. The audience consists of about 12 mothers of families. They listen with great attention.

If you could, as I much hope, would you dine here at 7 first, and spend the night.

Yours ever,
Virginia Woolf

Sussex

836: To Violet Dickinson   *Hogarth House, [Richmond]*

[May 1917]

My Violet,

Here are some of our new notices, in case you are able to distribute them among the great. There is nothing in the stories to shock the King—in fact they are very mild. We've just stopped printing after three hours—it is so fascinating that we can hardly bear to stop.

Do come and see us again whenever you have time. We both so much enjoyed it, and you should be made to lend a hand.

Leonard sends his love

Yr
V.W.

We've got 50 people now.

Berg

837: To Vanessa Bell   *Hogarth [House, Richmond]*

May 22nd [1917]

Dearest,

We are coming to Asheham on Friday till Tuesday, so I hope we may meet. Perhaps you would say what suits you—We shall be alone. I suppose you wouldn't come for the night?—and Duncan?

We've been so absorbed in printing that I am about as much of a farm-yard sheep dog as you are. I can hardly tear myself away to go to London, or see anyone. We have just started printing Leonards story; I haven't produced mine yet,[1] but there's nothing in writing compared with printing. I want your advice about covers.

We've got about 60 orders already, which shows a trusting spirit, especially as most of them come from old ladies and poets in the North, recommended by Bob Trevelyan, whom we've never heard of. Not one of our intimates has yet bought a copy (this arrow is not aimed at you.)

However, I did rouse myself to go and see Ott. I was so much overcome by her beauty that I really felt as if I'd suddenly got into the sea, and heard the mermaids fluting on their rocks. How it was done I cant think; but she had red-gold hair in masses, cheeks as soft as cushions with a lovely deep crimson on the crest of them, and a body shaped more after my notion of a mermaids than I've ever seen; not a wrinkle or blemish—swelling, but smooth.

Our conversation was rather on those lines, so I'm not surprised that I made a good impression. She didn't seem so much of a fool as I'd been led to think; she was quite shrewd, though vapid in the intervals. I begged her to revive Bedford Sqre and the salon, which she said she would, if anyone missed her. Then came protestations, invitations—in fact I dont see how we can get out of going there [Garsington], though Leonard says he wont, and I know it will be a disillusionment. However, my tack is to tell her she is nothing but an illusion, which is true, and then perhaps she'll live up to it. She was full of your praises. "That exquisite head, on that lovely body—a Demeter—promising loaves and legs of mutton for us, and such *sympathy*, more *feeling* for others now. I *did* so enjoy my time at Wissett."[2]

Emma Vaughan came; and I was plunged fathoms deep in St Albans Road [the Vaughan house], and Sunday tea. She is rather more set, and has a blankness in the eye which is precisely that of a toad glutted with large moths. Do you remember the look—how desperate it makes one feel—and then some perfectly banal remark or laugh in the manner of Aunt Virginia.[3] She woke up however about the war, and was very pro-German within limits. She visits wounded Germans in camps, and works from 10 to 7 every day, and has a great many sensible things to say, so I daresay she is going to become a respectable middle aged person. Then we had a visit from Violet [Dickinson], who assured us from private sources that the war will be over in August—but really the ramshackleness of the aristocratic mind is a marvel. They seem to be incapable of thinking and skate along from one extraordinary rumour to another. She said the King would certainly buy copies of our pamphlet—and I got her to tell me a series of death bed scenes of the Lyttelton family—the poor old Bishop Arthur L.[4] was pestered to

1. Leonard's story was *Three Jews*, and Virginia's, *The Mark on the Wall*.
2. Ottoline had visited Vanessa, Duncan and David Garnett at Wissett Lodge, Suffolk, in August 1916.
3. Countess Somers, Virginia's great-aunt.
4. Arthur Lyttelton (d. 1903) was the Bishop of Southampton.

death by them. "Now you're practically dead, Arthur, you *must* collect yourself and tell us what you see. Dont you feel anything like immortality coming on?" and so on, till he was forced to say that [he] was merely bored and nothing else.

Lytton has just rung up to say that he goes before his Tribunal tomorrow, and expects the worst. So far, we have escaped; but I suppose our minutes are numbered.

I've still got some gossip left, so you had better not make up your mind, as I see you doing, that the Apes [Virginia] are too fleasome a brood to visit when one can get their news without.

Do you really love me? How often a day do you think of me? How is Julian's foot? Why dont you get Saxons cousin (the son of the ichthyologist) to live with you!

Yr

B.

I daren't go to the Omega, for fear I shall be made to buy a hat. Miss Gill[1] knows nothing about the pictures you said I could have.

Berg

838: To R. C. Trevelyan   *[Hogarth House, Richmond]*
[late May 1917]

My dear Bob,

It is very good of you to say you will speak on the 5th.

Morgan [Forster] and someone else have already spoken about India, so perhaps Java and China would be better—or, if you prefer it, choose any labour problem, or social question. I didn't mean to limit you to travels.

Though apparently apathetic, the audience is really very keen, and of course, labour in its sympathies.

There's no need to tell me the subject beforehand.

Dinner is at 7.

Yours ever

Virginia Woolf

Sussex

1. Winifred Gill, who was employed at the Omega Workshops.

839: To Lady Ottoline Morrell

Hogarth House, Paradise Road, Richmond

June 5th [1917]

My dear Ottoline,

Thank you for sending Mr Sassoons letter. I am so glad he liked the review.[1] I've reviewed so little poetry that I was rather nervous, and I liked his poems very much.

We will come with pleasure on the 23rd, in spite of the fact that Garsington is a dull conventional place to stay at.

Please dont treat me as an invalid—save for breakfast in bed (which is now a luxury and not a necessity) I do exactly as others do.

Have the Shoves gone? I heard from Fredegond that they were off, but she didn't say where to.

Your affate
Virginia Woolf

I never thanked you for the Palatine Review.[2] I liked Mr Huxleys story (part of it at least) Poor Bob is as large as life—even the facts were true, I'm told. It will be very nice to see you again.

Texas

840: To Vanessa Bell

Hogarth House, [Richmond]

Friday [8 June 1917]

Dearest,

It will be great fun if you and Duncan will come next week end—the 16th, it is, I think. Dont make an engagement for Saturday night, and we will get some one to dine. Who would you like to meet?

We dont go to Ottoline until the end of the month.

I should like to come to Charleston very much—perhaps in July, some time?—only Julian must take my fish off the hooks, and put my worms on. I will do the rest. Tell him he needn't write and thank for the book if he ever thought of doing so—It was a very dull one we happened to have, but I thought the pictures might amuse him, and I know dull books were rather impressive when one was a brat.

I hope his foot is all right. It sounds too fearful—the agitation of having those limbs (of Satan) loose in the house.

1. Of Siegfried Sassoon's *The Old Huntsman and Other Poems* (*TLS*, 31 May 1917).
2. A literary magazine started by Aldous Huxley and Thomas Earp while they were still at Oxford. Huxley's story was *The Wheel.*

I must keep such gossip as I have (very little, as I do nothing but print) till we meet.

I have heard of a shop where you can get wonderful coloured papers. We're half way through L's story—it gets ever so much quicker, and the fascination is something extreme.

Yr B.

Berg

841: To Vanessa Bell   *Hogarth [House, Richmond]*

Wednesday [27 June 1917]

Dearest,

I saw Katherine Mansfield last night, and asked her about the chance of getting reviewing. She thought it would be far best for Bunny [Garnett] to get work on The Daily News, as Desmond, the man who wrote on land and country things has been made prisoner. [Middleton] Murry knows [Robert] Lynd the Editor; and if Bunny would write a specimen article on some country subject, and also explain what sort of work he wants, Murry would speak to Lynd. She thinks he had better do this as soon as he can. I should send it to Murry, c/o Katherine Mansfield, 141A Church Street, Chelsea, S. W. 3. Leonard will talk to [J. C.] Squire when he sees him. K. seemed to think there was a good chance now for anyone who is a specialist about agriculture.

I haven't been able to see the C. O.[1] yet, as she has had to keep a place open for her sister. The worst of it is that our domestics seem determined at last to settle in for ever; but our books are so high, and the difficulty of Asheham so great, that I think anyhow I must change. If the C. O. says she can't come, I shall go straight to Mary H[utchinson]. I shall make it plain to the C. O. that I can't do a stroke myself—

What about coming to you for 2 nights at the beginning of August, and going on to Asheham? But perhaps you will be full up.

We have just got a handsome sum back on our income tax, which we mean to spend on a press (I need hardly say) which will print 8 pages at a time, and then we shall be very professional.

I had an odd talk with K. Mansfield last night. She seems to have gone every sort of hog since she was 17, which is interesting; I also think she has a much better idea of writing than most. She's an odd character—admired what she could see of you, of course.

L. says the [Apostles] dinner was rather better than usual last night. Desmond [MacCarthy] made a very good speech; and rang us up at 8.30 this

1. A possible new servant. The initials are not now identifiable, but may refer to Keynes's Miss Chapman (see letter 778).

morning to ask if he could come round at once with Moore and spend the day. Its now 12.30; and I think they've just arrived, so I must take a bath.

It was a pleasant sight to see my Dolphin disporting, and the lovely creature asleep in bed that morning was almost irresistible.

Yr
B.

Is there any chance that you'll come again? Tell Quentin I like my necklace very much.

Berg

842: To Vanessa Bell   *Hogarth House, Paradise Road, Richmond*

Tuesday [3 July 1917]

Dearest,

This must be a dull, domestic letter. First a million thanks for the potatoes and greens. We still live upon them, and they have far more potato in them than shop ones—But you mustn't be so generous.

I am sending back the hamper today. We were able to get you 2 lbs. of icing sugar, which I am sending. I dont think we can get more than 1 lb: a week for you regularly—in fact they may put an end to this, but I will get it and hoard it, unless you think its too expensive—9d a lb.

I have had a long talk with Nelly, and she agrees that they will never like Asheham, and so had better go. I then told her about Mary H[utchinson]: and drew the most inviting picture I could of the place, but she said she did not wish to go there. It came out finally that Jessie [Vanessa's maid] had told her that Mary had been rude to Ethel [Mary's maid]—for God's sake, dont tell this to Mary: I merely told her they wanted to live in Guildford. Anyhow, Nelly thought it wasn't a good place, and also they don't want to be in London, and nothing I could say would change them. I cant get any answer from the C. O. who is now in the country, so I have asked Ethel to wait a week, in case I want her to come—She says she will wait as long as there is any chance, as she has a passion apparently for Asheham; so I expect I shall get her and the cook in the end—That will be cheaper anyhow than our present system, and I daresay the other idea wouldn't have worked. It was very clever of you to think of this arrangement; though I'm afraid poor Mary H: is left in a hole. Evidently there is a secret society among servants; I believe Nelly knew perfectly I was going to give her warning, and she didn't seem at all surprised when I told her that Ethel wanted to come. You had better put this letter down the W.C. That is the only safe method, we find.

I saw Lytton the other night. He says that Charleston runs Asheham close—Damn him! I think he wants to spent [*sic*] August between the two of us. Carrington is doing us some woodcuts for our pamphlet [*Two Stories*], but they're not done yet. Are you coming up any time? I do look forward to Asheham this year. Ask Julian why he has never written? I think it a great pity that he doesn't practise writing, as he has such a gift for it.

Yr B.

Jessie said that she was going to complain to you of Ethels treatment— Did she?

If you would prefer it, I could send your sugar every week instead of waiting.

Berg

843: To Vanessa Bell   *Hogarth [House, Richmond]*

Friday [6 July 1917]

Dearest,

To continue the great story of the servants. After talking to Nelly, and thinking all was happily over, Lottie came to me, and said they had never meant that they would not go to Asheham; in fact they were quite ready to go, and couldn't think why I had given them notice for that reason. So I had to talk to Nelly, and she accused me of plotting behind her back with Ethel, and protested that though she disliked Asheham, she would go there— or *would* have gone there, but now of course, she saw I was better suited elsewhere etc—So I put it to them whether they would come whenever we wanted, and whether they would do without a tweeny—and offered to keep them on these conditions—but they are now convinced that I want them to go, and Lottie (who is quite sensible) says that Nelly would always object to Asheham, and she thinks it would be more sensible to make the break now. I rather agree with her, but of course its very uncomfortable, and they won't believe that I really thought they wouldnt come and will have it that I've been scheming to send them off.

Meanwhile, Mary H: says that there are certain things she would like me to know before engaging her domestics—wh. sounds rather mysterious. I am to see her on Tuesday, and then I hope it will be settled.

The worst of it is that Lottie wd. evidently stay on and like Asheham, if it weren't for Nelly and it seems a pity to lose her—but Nelly makes things too difficult with her boredom at Asheham.

We put off going to Ottoline last week end because I had rather a head-ache and now I hear from Philip that she's got measles. I've been extremely sensible, and I'm all right again. Its possible that we shall come down to Asheham next Friday till Tuesday, but I will tell you if we do.

I dont think Mary H's difficulties arise from a lack of virginity, but from her temper—anyhow I did my best to persuade N. and L. and they were quite resolute partly owing to Jessies account of her [Mary Hutchinson's] dealings with Trissie [Vanessa's cook, previously Mary's] and Ethel, and partly to their dislike of London.

I shall be guided by what you say about Ethel however. I had a most charming letter from Julian yesterday. I will write to him soon. He must not tell the farmer about the fox or it will be poisoned as ours were. Did Bunny have any success with the Daily News? L. hasn't seen Squire yet.

Berg

844: TO DORA CARRINGTON   [*Hogarth House, Richmond*]
[13 July 1917]

Dear Carrington,

We like the wood cuts immensely.[1] It was very good of you to bring them yourself—We have printed them off, and they make the book much more interesting than it would have been without. The ones I like best are the servant girl and the plates, and the Snail.

Our difficulty was that the margins would mark; we bought a chisel, and chopped away, I am afraid rather spoiling one edge, but we came to the conclusion at last that the rollers scrape up the wood as they pass, as sometimes the impression would be clean to start with, and end with smudges. Next time we must have them cut exactly round the picture by a shop. Nevertheless, we are both very much pleased, and think them a great acquisition. and they print very well. Will you let us know what your expenses (including fare, and one halfpenny newspaper) come to, so that your pittance may be doled out to you. We are just off to Asheham, and can't get the books sewn to send out before; but we shall finish next week.

Are you in the country with Alix? Give her my love; tell her Margaret Ll. Davies was asking after her last night, and it occurs to me that if Alix liked to work for her instead of for us,[2] she would be delighted, and the work (for Womens Cooperative Guild) no doubt more amusing. Still, I hope she's thinking over our offer.

We both find that printing far cuts into every other occupation. We are in treaty for a press, once costing £100—so it looks as if your friends figures

1. Carrington did four small woodcuts to illustrate *Two Stories*, for which she was paid 15/-. They printed about 150 copies, of which they finally sold 135.
2. They were already thinking of employing an assistant at the Hogarth Press, and had discussed the job with Alix Sargant-Florence.

would come true. It is specially good at printing pictures, and we see that we must make a practice of always having pictures.

Ring us up and come to dinner when you come back—

Yr affate
V.W.

Robert H. Taylor

845: To R. C. Trevelyan   *Hogarth* [*House, Richmond*]

[*Leonard's contribution typewritten*]
13 July [1917]

Dear Bob,

Why Minna is Minna I do not know but she is. She is about 90 years old, and a very sporting old lady who paints little water colour sketches of trees and flowers. She is, I imagine, a sister of George Duckworth's deceased father and therefore of Virginia's mother's first husband. At any rate we call her Aunt Minna, though she also answers to the name of Miss S. O. Duckworth.

Your idea about Roger's essays is a very good one. We have finished printing the pamphlet and are off to Asheham until Tuesday. We shall get them sent out towards the end of next week.

Yours
Leonard Woolf

[*in Virginia's handwriting*]
Aunt Minna's baptismal names are Sarah Emily (*not* Olivia). On attaining the age of puberty she christened herself Minna—I have always supposed after a herione in one of the Waverley novels—anyhow, as she is rather the Robin Mayor type, it exactly suits her.

V.W.

Sussex

846: To Vanessa Bell   *Asheham,* [*Rodmell,*
Sussex]

Saturday [14? July 1917]

Dearest,

I really don't think its worth while for you to come all this way for such a short time on Sunday—especially if you've not been well—Are you better? Do take care.

I would offer to come to Firle and have a picnic, but I've promised not to walk at all, and I suppose I must abide by it.

Of course we could give you a bed on Monday if you could come, but I suppose you can't—Its a great nuisance altogether, but I'm sure you'd better not bicycle all those miles in this heat.

I'll send your sugar by post.

Have you been doing too much?

I've finally taken Ethel and the Cook [servants of Mary Hutchinson]—after a good many difficulties with the others.

Yr B.

Of course we shall be in on Sunday if you should come, but don't make any effort.

Berg

847: To Margaret Llewelyn Davies   [*Asheham, Rodmell, Sussex*]

[15 July 1917]

Dearest Margaret,

The place we told you of at Southease hasn't got a room free till Aug. 18th, but we could get you rooms at the farm (15 minutes walk from here) on 8th August. There is a good big sitting room, 2 bedrooms opening out of each other. The woman would cook for you. The rooms are rather rough, and the beds looked hard, but clean, and the farm is a nice old house. She would charge 25/- a week for everything including sitting room. We looked at the farm when we sat on the edge of the down that afternoon. It is a good deal nearer us than Southease—not quite so comfortable I should think.

I said you would let her know at once if you wanted the rooms, as other people are after them.

The address is,

Mrs Woolgar,
Itford Farm,
Rodmell,
Lewes.

We've been having a perfect time—and go back tomorrow.

Yr. aff.
V.W.

Would you settle a time to come to us *before* the 17th [August]—We come here on the 3rd—Perhaps Janet could come too?

Sussex

Postcard
[18 July 1917]

"Moorland Cottage near "Gurnards Head"; wild and remote; 2 guests
30/ each weekly, full board, private sitting room if desired.—Miss Hardwicke,
Ninnis Manning Cottage; Newmill, nr Penzance"
    from this weeks Cambridge Review—the best part of all.

                                                              V.W.

Robert H. Taylor

849: To Katherine Cox   *Hogarth House, [Richmond]*

[18 July 1917]

Dearest Ka,
    Do come to us for that week end. You don't like company I remember—
and I don't think you'll have any. I'm settling in a new cook and maid, and
therefore asked no one—but you don't count.
    It was so divinely lovely that I can't feel contented here—We had a
swarm of bees in the attic and a nursery of swallows in the E.C. German
prisoners on all sides with absurd little soldiers guarding them and now
we're to have a real fur coated Bruin. Did it ever strike you that *that's* why
you feel the heat so? A visit to the Barber once a month might help you—
They have some very nice patterns too—a bald rump, with two rosettes left
on the flanks (something in the poodle style, but with more dignity—)
    May we come to supper next Monday—7.30 I suppose—

                                                              Yr
                                                              V.W.

Mark Arnold-Forster

850: To Violet Dickinson   *Hogarth House, Paradise Road,*
                                  Richmond, Surrey

July 21st [1917]

My Violet,
    We are very glad you like the book [*Two Stories*]. It is tremendous fun
doing it, and we are now in treaty for a much larger press, and mean to take
it up seriously and produce novels with it. And we are even getting an
apprentice!
    We are nearly at an end of our copies, and have raised the price from
1/6 to 2/—
    If you want 4 in spite of the price, we will send them to you. It has been

quite a success. One of the greatest helps in doing it was that table you gave me, which rears up, so that one can put the drawers of type on a slope, and sit in front of it. I dont know what we should have done without it.

We go to Asheham on the 3rd. Shall you be in Sussex at all? If so, couldn't you drop in upon us?

Leonard sends his love.

Yr
V.W.

Berg

851: To Roger Fry

Hogarth House, Paradise Road,
Richmond, Surrey

22nd July [1917]

My dear Roger,

Would you say what time in Sept. would suit you best. It would be very nice to have Pamela [Roger's daughter]. The only difficulty about August is that we've asked people who wont answer. Lytton is coming on the 17th to 24th—and we've asked Katherine Mansfield, but if she cant come, would that suit you and Pamela? Anyhow, you must come—so please consider a way of doing it.

How damnable people are about doing the sensible things! I still believe though that the loan scheme will succeed;[1] it only wants time to sink in. I sent my form off. Would it be possible to change oftener than once a year?

I'm sending a copy of the book to Durbins;[2] and 4 to the Omega, but we're very nearly sold out, so if you dont want them there, we shall be quite glad to have them back. You will see lots of mistakes, but we're rather proud, considering we learnt as we went.

Tomorrow we are going to see a £100 press which we are told is the best made,—particularly good for reproducing pictures. This opens up fresh plans, as you will see. Wouldn't it be fun to have books of pictures only, reproductions of new pictures—but we must get you to tell us a little about how one does this. Carrington is swarming with woodcuts. Its most fascinating work.

By the by—we have been talking of a book of your old articles—what do you think?

Yrs in haste,
V.W.

Sussex

1. Possibly a scheme for hiring out Omega pictures on loan.
2. Roger's house, near Guildford.

Hogarth House, Paradise Road, Richmond, Surrey

Tuesday [24 July 1917]

My dear Clive,

I've always thought it very fine—the way you run risks, though I don't see that there's much risk in sending such a letter to such a woman. You know you always told me I was notorious for vanity, and its still a fine plant, though growing old.

But please dont put it all down to vanity. I do like you to praise me,[1] not only because of your gift for knowing whats what, but for what you would call sentimental reasons too—as for instance that you were the first person who ever thought I'd write well. We talked so much about writing too. I should like to discuss this with you, and see *why* you think it good—Its an absorbing thing (I mean writing is) and its high time we found some new shapes, don't you think so? As for Mr Joyce,[2] I can't see what he's after, though having spent 5/- on him, I did my level best, and was only beaten by the unutterable boredom—As you don't waste your time on reviews, but sit in a farmhouse [Garsington], and occasionally turn over a vegetable marrow—why don't you try a few experiments—our press you know, is to give birth to every monster in the vicinity.

It was very nice of you to write—If you're at Charleston this summer, won't you come and see us?

Yr. aff.
V.W.

Quentin Bell

Hogarth House, Paradise Road, Richmond, Surrey

26th July [1917]

Dear Bunny,

I hope you dont mind, but as I always hear of you as Bunny and you of me as Virginia, I think we might venture—

Thank you very much for writing. I'm very glad you liked the story. In a way its easier to do a short thing, all in one flight than a novel. Novels are frightfully clumsy and overpowering of course; still if one could only get hold of them it would be superb. I daresay one ought to invent a completely new form. Anyhow its very amusing to try with these short things, and the greatest mercy to be able to do what one likes—no editors, or publishers, and only people to read who more or less like that sort of thing. We've been

---

1. Clive had written to Virginia praising *The Mark on the Wall*.
2. James Joyce's *Portrait of the Artist as a Young Man* was published in 1916.

seeing a Russian called Koteliansky[1] who says that to write for a small public is damnation. However, I dont like writing for my half brother George [Gerald].

We had a second swarm of bees. They went down the chimney of the attic; we shut the door and left them swarming in the grate. What ought we to do? Any advice would be welcomed. We go down tomorrow week. Have you any honey to sell?[2]

By the way, you dont enclose a postal order—and I must tell you the terrible fact that we have raised the price to 2/- We have only got 9 left; do you want one or 2 or none at all?

Would you come over and spend Saturday night, Aug 4th, and tell us what to do about the bees—Ka will be there.

Yours
Virginia Woolf

Berg

854: To Vanessa Bell   *Hogarth House, Paradise Road,*
                                        Richmond, Surrey

Thursday [26 July 1917]

Dearest,

We should very much like you and Duncan to do a book of wood cuts— in fact we are getting a machine that is specially good for printing pictures, as we want to do pictures just as much as writing. Of course they would take much less time to do. At present we've promised to do Katherine Mansfields story,[3] but Alix is probably coming as apprentice, so that we could get on quicker, and might do your book before Christmas. However, there will be many details to discuss, which we could do when we meet. The difficulty with Carringtons wood cuts was that she didn't cut the margins low enough, and we hadn't the proper tools for doing it, so that we had to take very light impressions, in order not to get black marks on the margin—which even so we didn't altogether avoid. But do go ahead, and get your book arranged. We went to see the head of a great printing school in the city the other day, and he is going to look out for a press at a sale, and we shall get it by the autumn. It will be quite easy to print a large number of copies on it—as one does at least 4 sheets at a time.

1. S. S. Koteliansky ('Kot'), the translator, whom Virginia and Leonard had met through Katherine Mansfield and Middleton Murry.
2. David Garnett kept bees at Charleston.
3. They did not buy a larger press until a few years later, and printed their second publication (Mansfield's *Prelude*) in 1918 on the press belonging to a jobbing printer in Richmond called McDermott.

I suppose the size would either be the size of our book, or twice as large—however, we could tell you more later. It is tremendous fun, and it makes all the difference writing anything one likes, and not for an Editor.

The servant problems are really more interesting than anything else. On Monday night, I got a letter from the cook, saying she did not like a basement, and would not come. I thought this very odd, as after seeing the kitchen she had told me she thought it perfectly all right, and she had told Nelly the same thing. Also, it seemed queer that she had waited a week before telling me. The question then was whether to get another cook, or to ask Nelly and Lottie to stay on. It seemed absurd not to ask them, as they were so sorry to go, and so I did; and find them delighted to stay, even though it means going to Asheham, and having no tweeny. I didn't like Mary H's. cook at all, when I saw her here, so I am extremely glad to be rid of her. It seemed very hard on Ethel, but I wrote at once explaining and sent her a months wages. Yesterday she rang me up (from a post office) and said that she was completely taken by surprise; the cook had never told her she wasn't coming until the night before, and then had told her that she was going to be married and therefore would not take a new place for a short time. I said that she told me it was the basement; but Ethel said this was quite untrue, as she had found no fault with it. I also told her that the cook was staying on with Mary H. (as you said)—which was entirely new to her, and made her very angry. She said Mrs H: had spoken to her that morning, seeming very confused, but had said nothing about the cook staying. However, Ethel most wanted us to realise that she hadn't any share in it—and also to thank you for having taken so much trouble. I'm afraid she wanted to come to Asheham, but she was very nice about it.

I think its probable that Mary H. offered the cook a rise, and persuaded her to stay on; anyhow I'm thankful, as its much nicer to keep Lottie and Nelly, and they have made up their minds to put up with Asheham. The amusing thing is that they had decided to go to Mary H: after all, if on seeing the cook and Ethel, they came to the conclusion that there wasn't anything in their stories against her. However, the first words they said (which they wont repeat) determined them to have nothing to do with it, and the cook in particular said that she strongly advised them not to, and though she had only been 6 weeks there, it seemed like 6 years!—so I dont suppose she'll stay very long. I feel slightly cross and malicious against Mary H: as they didn't leave me much time to get a cook, supposing Nelly and Lottie hadn't been ready to stay on. But isn't it all fascinating?

We're coming down on Friday—and old Ka has asked to come for Bank Holiday and Alix after that, so I'm afraid I shan't be able to come to you that week. But I expect you'll be overflowing. People simply clamour to be asked now—I suppose we make a very nice centre. I'm afraid I shall have to be rather careful about coming over, as Leonard has been in rather a state again, and I've promised to be very quiet. I feel all right, but I've gone down rather in weight though I still weigh only just under 10 stones, which is half a stone and more beyond what I've ever weighed. I dont see how one can expect to keep the results of a rest cure permanently. But I shall come and stay the night some time.

Tell Saxon the Squires aren't at Asheham, so he can get blankets and stay there if he likes. It will be empty till we come. Leonard started to go and see you, but found both his tyres punctured and so had to come back.

We had another swarm in the attics—but I must ask Bunny about them.

We shall expect any one who likes to come on Sunday or Monday.

Yr B.

Berg

855: To Violet Dickinson   *Hogarth House, Paradise Road,*
                                  Richmond, Surrey

July 26th [1917]

My Violet,

I am sending you one copy today. There's no reason on earth why you shouldn't have 3 more if you want them. We have about 10 left, and if you want any more, will you write at once, as we are still getting orders, and shall be sold out (we have broken up the type and can't print any more)

By the way, they are only 2/ a copy, not 2/3—

Give my love to the Wicked Walter [Crum] if you ever see him—I wish I ever did—I'm sure my morals would have been worse—

Yr
V.W.

Berg

Letters 856-899 (August–December 1917)

At first the Woolfs managed the Hogarth Press alone, setting the type, machining, binding, advertising, packing and despatching without help. In October they engaged Alix Sargant-Florence as an assistant, but she found the work tedious and left after a single day. She was replaced in November by Barbara Hiles, who began to set the type for their second publication, Prelude by Katherine Mansfield, whose friendship and literary stimulus came to mean much to Virginia during 1917, and it is sad that almost none of Virginia's letters to her appear to have survived. Virginia was writing Night and Day as well as weekly journalism, and in October began to keep regularly the diary which she continued for the rest of her life. There were no holiday journeys during this summer and autumn, but the Woolfs spent the weekend 17-19 November with Lady Ottoline Morrell at Garsington. Air-raids over London drove Virginia to the cellars night after night, and often she escaped to Asheham, where she spent a few days with Saxon Sydney-Turner while Leonard was lecturing in the North. Towards the end of the year the 1917 Club was founded largely at Leonard's instigation, and it provided Virginia with a new source of friends and entertainment. In one of her many letters to Vanessa (894) she enclosed a long satirical sketch of a meeting with her cousin Margaret (Marny) Vaughan, which well illustrates how far she had moved from the companions and attitudes of her youth. In December the Woolfs heard that of Leonard's two brothers serving at the front, one had been killed, and the other wounded, by the same shell.

856: TO VANESSA BELL

Saturday [4 August 1917]

Asheham, [Rodmell, Sussex]

Dearest,

We hope you may come to tea and stay to dinner tomorrow. If you dont, I will *try* to come to tea and stay dinner and go home early on Monday—but I dont know whether I shall be able to.

I want to hear about Chapman [maid], also, why can't I have your pictures?

I cant get over the perfection in River House.[1]

Yr
V.W.

L. thinks it too far for me to bicycle, wh. is absurd, but I cant very well do it

1. The house at Hammersmith belonging to Mary and St John Hutchinson, which Vanessa and Duncan Grant had decorated.

if it makes him in a state. I think its quite unreasonable, so I shall do my best if you dont come.

Berg

857: To Vanessa Bell   *Asheham, [Rodmell, Sussex]*

Sunday [5 August 1917]

Dearest,

We thought of having a picnic at Firle tomorrow, Monday. We shall be at the Post office there at 4 (or shortly before) and we shall bring some food and tea. It would be very nice if you could meet us at the P. Office, and we could go up into the wood. I find that Leonard thinks this much less tiring then for me to go to Charleston!

I sent a wire which I daresay won't get to you. However that old servant, Emily Hunt, has suddenly turned up, and is posting this in Lewes.

We cant bring enough tea for more than 2, but we could bring enough eatables for more, I expect.

We shant wait beyond 4.15 if you dont turn up, but I hope you may be able to, with the brats.

I'm taking it for granted your not coming today, as I dont much expect you will.

We've asked Pierpont [Morgan] £200 for the page.[1] Do you think thats about right?

B.

Berg

858: To Dora Carrington   *Asheham House, Rodmell, Lewes, [Sussex]*

Sunday [12 August 1917]

My dear Carrington

It wasn't Alix's fault that I asked you for the weekend, but your own remark, in your letter that *next* week you went with your brother.

The nuisance is that any other date seems impossible for us. Katherine Mansfield comes on the 17th, and we are full up till the 24th, which is I suppose about the time you go to Charleston.

Anyhow, you might come over and see us from Charleston. September of course, is no good for you.

1. See p. 128, note 2.

We want to hear about the letters, and the design for the cover.[1] We are undertaking a book of woodcuts by Nessa and Duncan. They thought the printing quite good enough, in fact Nessa says that the greyness of the wood cuts seems better to her than the extreme blackness: your wood cuts have certainly been a great success.

We are waiting to hear of a sale of presses, which should be soon. We are sold out, and more: offers have even been made for our spoiled copies!

Yr aff

Virginia Woolf

Robert H. Taylor

859: To Lytton Strachey

Asheham House, Rodmell, Lewes, [Sussex]

Aug. 14th [1917]

Naturally, we are much grieved,[2] but if Gordon comes to birth and is read regularly after dinner, we forgive. We all retire to compose after breakfast, the sheep occasionally come into the field, but that's about all. The trains are these: 2.13 from Guildford to Brighton; arrives Brighton 4.14: catch a train arriving Lewes at 4.46. Or go to London, and take 3.20 from Victoria. The only way out is a taxi, or fly, unless you walk.

I have been sent 20 of these leaflets by old Mrs Hobhouse.[3]

Yr.

V.W.

Frances Hooper

860: To Lady Ottoline Morrell

Asheham House, Rodmell Lewes, [Sussex]

Aug. 15th [1917]

My dear Ottoline,

I couldn't help feeling rather relieved when I heard that you had the measles, because then all the blame wasn't on my head—but it certainly was a most malicious freak on the part of fate—I'm quite well again and hope I've earned some sort of reward by being so good. Leonard wants me to say that he does not think Garsington too tiring, and will you ask us in the autumn?

1. Carrington was experimenting with lettering and linocuts for the Press.
2. Lytton had postponed his visit because he was struggling with 'General Gordon', the last essay in *Eminent Victorians*.
3. Mrs Henry Hobhouse on the treatment of conscientious objectors.

173

We are here till October, and have various people staying with us (Goldie [G. Lowes Dickinson] at this moment)—In October we have promised to go North, for Leonard to lecture for the League of Nations, but the date is not yet settled.

You are again becoming almost too mythical to be believed in any longer; I catch scraps about you and the garden and keep you going in my mind. Clive's visit was quite innocent; I dont think any mischief was made about anyone. I've been out of that particular society for so long, that I've rather lost my bearings in it.

What is happening to Sassoon? Can they keep him shut up indefinitely? We thought his letter a very good one.[1] It was a splendid thing to do. I ran into Mrs Hobhouse the other day, and had these notices of her book pressed on me. I send one though you are sure to have seen it.

It is very lovely here, and we meet Nessa and Duncan and have picnics on the downs; they seem perfectly happy, painting, making jam, getting all their own vegetables, and yesterday Nessa went to Brighton and bought a donkey.

Please write again some time—Katherine Mansfield describes your garden, the rose leaves drying in the sun, the pool, and long conversations between people wandering up and down in the moonlight. It calls out her romantic side; which I think rather a relief after the actresses, A.B.C's. [teashops] and paint pots.

Yr affate
Virginia Woolf

Texas

861: To Katherine Cox

Asheham House, Rodmell,
Lewes, [Sussex]

Wednesday [15 August 1917]

My dear Bruin,

I'm very glad you're going—but how penny-wise to take only one week! Why not 3 while you are doing it?

However this is to hand you Mrs Hobhouse's leaflet. You can read the book in the train, full of ghastly details.

Goldie is here, has borrowed a typewriter, is clattering out articles all day long, so illegible even he can't read them, even on a typewriter, owing to his habit of striking 3 letters at once.

1. Siegfried Sassoon, when recovering in England from wounds in 1917, wrote a letter to his Commanding Officer protesting against the continuation of the war. He had been encouraged in his action by Ottoline, Bertrand Russell and Middleton Murry. Instead of being court-martialled as he had hoped, he was sent to a hospital to recover.

All Charleston is expected to tea: so I must go and make bread.

We note (as they say in Government offices) invite to Aldbourne, prox: but we don't know if circs permit.

Yrs. V.W.

Enclosure.   1 circ for self
              1 for distribution

Mark Arnold-Forster

862: To Saxon Sydney-Turner   *Asheham, [Rodmell,*
                                              Sussex]

Friday [17 August 1917]

My dear Saxon,

Do you think in memory of our old friendship, you would buy me 3 packets of Bastos cigarettes price 1/- each. (They are in a blue packet, with a red rosette) and send as soon as you can. The younger generation (Alix) has failed, and I am running out. I will faithfully send P.O. tomorrow. Lytton and Goldie are talking over my head, and Leonard getting out his chess men—I wish you were here, but its too confusing to write.

Yr
V.W.

The enclosed scrap will show you the right kind; Alix got them wrong. Salmon and Gluckstein keep them.

Sussex

863: To R. C. Trevelyan   *Asheham House, Rodmell,*
                                        Lewes, [Sussex]

Postcard
Sunday Aug. 19 1917

We the undersigned, wish to say that we have read the Pterodamozels[1] with great pleasure, and wish to thank the author.

Virginia Woolf
Katherine Mansfield
Lytton Strachey
Edward Garnett[2]

Sussex

1. *Pterodamozels, An Operatic Fable* (1917). It was a play in two acts.
2. David Garnett's father, the author and publisher's reader.

864: To R. C. Trevelyan   *Asheham House, Rodmell,*
                                           Lewes, [Sussex]

Postcard
[27 August 1917]

We have sold all our copies of the two stories; we did send Morgan
[Forster] a notice—We have promised to print one or two things, so that
we shouldn't be able to undertake anything just now, and of course it would
be much better to have the Greek done with your translation.

                                                            V. Woolf

It was Garnett, the father, not son.

Sussex

865: To Vanessa Bell   *Asheham, [Rodmell,*
                                           Sussex]

Thursday [30 August 1917]

Dearest,

We didn't start on Sunday, as it seemed hopeless. Our trees are almost
like winter now.

We live almost entirely upon roast apples.

I'm afraid its not much good your bringing Roger over on Sunday, as
we have Mrs Woolf, Bella, Herbert,[1] and a Norwegian whom I've never seen.
On Monday we shall be alone (Thank God!) and it would be very nice if he
and you could come (any time); if he hasn't already gone. Tomorrow
(Friday) we shall be alone, and in about 5.30 (we go to Eastbourne to buy
Glidine) if it were fine, and you could come over.

We shall be alone most of next week, until Friday, when we have Pernel
Strachey, Philip Morrell, and Sydney Waterlow. However you'd better
come whenever you can.

God! its now raining again—we thought it was really fine at last. I
suppose Barbara will now be permanently indoors and Nick too.

I think donkeys are the nicest animals in the world.

I wish the children would come again. We could stable the beast.

                                                            Yr V.W.

Berg

1. Leonard's mother, sister and brother.

Asheham House, Rodmell,
Lewes, [Sussex]

Friday [7 September 1917]

Dearest,

We really might be in London for all we see of each other, but I see it can't be helped—These damned people always seem to flock.

If it's fine on Sunday, we thought we might try and have a picnic, at the usual place, at 5. Sydney and Philip would both much like to see you I'm sure.

Pernel comes today, and I'll bring her too, if she doesn't think it too far. They go on Tuesday; and I think I could bicycle over to see you on *Wednesday* if that suits you. Might I come for lunch, and go back after tea? Please say if you have other occupations. I could come for 2 nights when Duncan and Bunny go; in fact, our people are only coming for the week ends now, so I shall be much more free. But I dont suppose this applies to you. I'm afraid you've had an awful doing. Has Barbara come back? I made such a pointed remark to her about staying at Charleston (not thinking of her but of Alix) that I hope she won't settle down again. I hear from Alix that she's gone to Ireland for a month with [H. T. J.] Norton. I think it would be a most suitable match. She is determined to do the printing, I'm afraid.

You might send a line if you *cant* come on Sunday; otherwise we shall come to the same place.

My servants say that they have actually enjoyed Asheham this year—but they say its all owing to Charleston!

Yr B.

Berg

Asheham, Rodmell,
Lewes, [Sussex]

9th Sept. [1917]

Dearest Margaret,

I wish you wouldn't withdraw into the clouds in the way you do. We are now without even your address, and have to make you up entirely fresh in our minds, and then you become so alarming—such flashing eyes, such scorn, such majesty in every joint, that I can hardly dare write to you. Did you refuse an honour? or are you now a Dame? At this moment we've got Sydney Waterlow (the man who confides in Leonard) and Philip Morrell and Pernel Strachey (of Newnham) staying with us. We were told that Philip was so lonely, and had never once been asked to stay away by himself, that Leonard insisted upon asking him; I rather think it is true. It must be fairly crushing to live in the shade—at least in the atmosphere—of Ottoline. I dont think he's ever had his opinions listened to before; he is now sitting on the terrace and holding forth at a great rate about politics. He says that opinion in Burnley[1] has so changed about the war, that its quite possible they may ask him to stand again. The local papers print strong pacifist articles. In fact he thinks that if someone in power now demanded peace the whole country would back him. But oh dear, how little one believes what anyone says now. I feel we've sunk lower than ever before this summer.

And then we've seen a lot of the younger generation, who seem to me the essence of good sense, honesty, sobriety and kindliness, without that romance, that flash of lightning splendour which mark—well, Miss Davies, and Miss Case. How is Janet?, but she too has vanished into the past. The younger generation walk across the downs in brown corduroy trousers, blue shirts, grey socks, and no hats on their heads, which are cropped, so that as I sit on the terrace, I really don't know Barbara Hiles from Nick Bagenal, who is in the Irish Guards. It seems to me quite impossible to wear trousers.

We are going to attempt a picnic today with Vanessa, and her 5 children; she has now got the 3 little MacCarthy's staying with her, and can scarcely leave them, as Julian is so powerful, and they are very gentle. However, our weather is thoroughly broken; I suppose it will rain.

Now isnt this a good long letter?—and doesn't it soften even your heart? Are you having a holiday or have you constructed a few more new systems, sitting over the fire, with your pipe? I am upsetting my inkpot, so I had better stop, though I have a great deal to discuss with you, and we should both be much happier if we saw you coming up the drive. Leonard sends love. Please give Lilian our affectionate respects. Has she read Trents Last Case?[2] What did she think of it?

Yr aff.
V.W.

Is there any news of William Sheepshanks?[3]

Sussex

868: TO VANESSA BELL   *Asheham, [Rodmell,*
                                                        Sussex]

Friday [14? September 1917]

Dearest,

I have another suggestion to make about the wood cuts. Mightn't we print them, not in a book, but as separate sheets, one wood cut to one sheet?

1. Philip Morrell was Liberal M.P. for Burnley from 1910 to 1918.
2. The detective story (1913), by E. C. Bentley.
3. The ninth son of John Sheepshanks, Bishop of Norwich until 1910. Virginia had been a friend of William's sister Mary.

We would get a certain number of people, the ones you suggested if possible, to do two or three wood cuts each; we would send out notices to say that we were printing a set of wood cuts by different artists, which we would sell in sets, in envelopes. Then it would be open to the buyer of the set to order more copies of any single wood cut. By this method, all difficulties of binding, cover, title page, would be got over, and one would probably do more justice to the wood cuts if they were on separate sheets; also I think people would prefer them in this form, as they could easily be framed, or pinned up. Also I expect many people would want to buy extra copies of one of the wood cuts, without having to buy a whole book over again. In addition, it would be much simpler and considerably cheaper to do, and after issuing the sets we could print off separate copies as they were ordered, so we should run less risk. The artist whose work was liked would make more profit, which seems fair.

This only occurred to me yesterday, and I haven't thought out any details of payment etc; but Leonard thinks favourably of the plan, which seems to involve no aesthetic judgment on our part, and we would like to know if you think there is anything in it.

I hope you will consider it, not only because I think there is a good deal to be said for it, but also because I should very much like to produce your and Duncan's pictures.[1]

Yr B.

We shall be at Firle post office on Sunday, at 3.30, as we want to have a picnic in those woods. If you could come it wd. be very nice and we cd. discuss it. We will anyhow bring a tea cup and enough tea for you in case you come, but don't bother, as we are going anyhow—only if fine, of course.

Berg

869: To Clive Bell

Asheham, Rodmell, Lewes, [Sussex]

17th Sept. [1917]

My dear Clive,

As to the K. M. affair,[2] I expect the most sensible thing for me to do would be to keep silent. I have torn up a letter in which I gave my version.

1. This plan never materialised, although woodcuts by Vanessa Bell and Duncan Grant were used in later Hogarth publications, and in 1923 the Hogarth Press published a volume of Duncan's pictures.
2. Clive believed that Virginia had repeated to Katherine Mansfield some unflattering remarks which he and Desmond MacCarthy had made about her. The gossip had reached Garsington.

179

But I really do not wish to become further involved in it, or in a discussion of it, so I think all I'll say is that I deny entirely that I said what I'm reported to have said. When I see K. M. no doubt we shall be able to arrive at a more correct version of the facts. The present one, I should have thought, is on the face of it absurd. The only thing I really regret is that there should be any rupture between Philip [Morrell] and [Middleton] Murry.

I very much want to keep out of these affairs in future. So I think you can have more trust in me than usual about the gossip of Garsington.

Yes—I certainly think its time the feud was buried. I didn't feel even the most distant rumours of it the other day, and I'm glad you didn't either.

Yrs ever,

Quentin Bell   V.W.

870: To Katherine Cox   *Asheham, [Rodmell,*
                                                                                                    Sussex]
18th Sept [1917]

Dearest Ka,

Its a great pleasure to feel that we've really been asked, though I'm afraid we cant come. Desmond is coming today, and when he goes I'm going over to Charleston for a night or two, and then to wind up we have Roger, and I'm trembling on the verge of asking your Mrs [Molly] Hamilton, whom I've never seen, and don't know that I shall ever want to see, after one weekend. We go back about the 3rd Oct. when printing will begin upon a story by Katherine Mansfield [*Prelude*].

Do you mean that you might have been taken (disguised as the stuffed umbrella stand) to America on a destroyer with Lord Reading?[1] You might be more explicit. Have you become Matron of the British Empire, and must one call you Dame Bruin in future?

It is now setting in wet, but we seem to have done far better than the rest of England.

Did Dawks Waterlow[2] tell you that we are going to stay with her mother in Manchester? I'm afraid we shall be there early in November. Have you only got one week off in the whole summer?

Yrs V.W.

We have been out, and got wet through, come back, and now sit over a log fire hoping for tea. Perhaps you will ring me up.

Mark Arnold-Forster

1. Daniel Rufus Isaacs (who was created Marquis of Reading in this month) went to the United States as High Commissioner in order to take charge of discussions on Anglo-American finances, following America's entry into the war in April 1917.
2. Margery Waterlow, Sydney's wife.

Asheham House, Rodmell, Lewes, [Sussex]

Tuesday [18 September 1917]

My dear Saxon,

I ought to have thanked you for your efforts about the cigarettes, I hear that its almost impossible to get them, and it says much for Barbara [Hiles], and rehabilitates (in part) the intellect of the younger generation, that in spite of this she found out the last 2 packets in England and ran them to earth; but I was pleased to hear how the tobacconist spotted her youth and innocence and warned her against such strong smokes. Its really no good wearing corduroy trousers when even a tobacconist sees through one.

As you have perhaps guessed, this is not a letter of gratitude at all, but a letter of self defence. Its been raining all day; we set out to walk to Glynde, in order that Leonard might get his hair cut, and were driven back at the corner by the watermill, (the skeleton thing thats in the corner of the field belonging to the two old ladies who keep the Alderney cows and the coffee coloured collies). It is too hot to light the fire; too early for tea. It is true that I might read the Sense of the Past,[1] or practically any one of the works of Shakespeare, Scott, Balzac or Swinburne. I should much prefer to talk about them and if I had a ring, I would rub it and you should gently well up in the yellow arm chair, with your usual expression of sapient composure! We expect Desmond at any moment; but then we expected him (and Molly into the bargain) all yesterday. Molly evaporated in the course of the day, having reached, according to her telegram, a railway station in Portsmouth; but Desmond is still on the road. Whenever I hear a wheel I get up and look out of the window. As a large beer lorry has broken down and is being hitched on to another van there is a good deal to look at.

What is there to say about The Sense of the Past? I'm afraid my old image must still hold good as far as I'm concerned—the laborious striking of whole boxfulls of damp matches—lovely phrases of course but—but— but. Sydney Waterlow sat on me with all the solemn weight (which is after all so light) of his portentous haystack for saying this; but we made it up, you'll be glad to hear, and his eyeglasses are fixed upon me not without some melancholy hope that I shall escape the doom of my sex and prove quite worth talking to (if one discounts the inevitable insincerity) one of these days. His absurdity is really delightful and even lovable.

O My dear Saxon, they're laying tea! We come back about the 3rd and I hope you'll take the hint, and come soon. I thought Barbara looked very well. Nick [Bagenal] seemed to us both very charming. I hope he's all right.   Yr V.W.

Sussex

1. *The Sense of the Past* was left unfinished at Henry James' death, and was published in fragments in 1917.

Asheham, [Rodmell, Sussex]

[21? September 1917]

Dearest,

The weather has been too vile for anything. Desmond is still here—in fact, I think he means to stay till Monday.

I am full of envy of Roger. How crafty of him to slink in and have a whole week of you to himself! I dont quite know what to do about coming. I have promised to write a long article upon Henry James,[1] and the book may arrive in a day or two, in which case I should have to spend next week doing it, and it means such a lot of reading as well as writing that there wouldn't be much point in coming to you—Or it mayn't come till the end of the week.

Would it suit you if I came on Monday 1st for one or 2 nights? Of course it would be ideal to see you alone, but I see that can't be managed, unless indeed Roger didn't come to you till Wednesday, and I could come this next Monday? You might let me know if there's any chance of this.

I'm very sorry about your domestic worries. I spoke to Mrs Hammond this morning, and she said she would like to think it over. I think it wd. be a good thing if you could tell me when you want her, and if you want her permanently, and what wages you pay. She is very nice and clean, I think, and was a housemaid, though she's not much of a cook. She seemed quite favourable, but she's very silent. I will certainly ask Nelly if she falls through. I think one ought easily to be able to find some one among their friends.

Couldn't I see about a governess in London? The Cases might know of one. Shall I write to them—a nursery governess, do you call her?

I'm glad the Kodak was all right; I thought it would be, but on the other hand, I'm sorry that my idea about the woodcuts won't work. Couldn't we invent another?

Yr B.

Berg

Asheham, [Rodmell, Sussex]

Monday [24 September 1917]

Dearest,

I have just seen this advertisement in the Times today.

No salary: Young lady with Oxford senior certificate wishes to teach and take care of children, in family or school. Time for study required.

Advertiser, Box F. 95, The Times,

Printing House Sqre.

London, E. C. 4.

1. Review of *The Middle Years*, by Henry James (*TLS*, 18 October 1917).

She could be shut up to study in the evenings, and so be no bother at all.

I've just come back from Lewes, where I sent you a card, which I daresay you won't get, though I posted it myself. I met Duncan at Glynde; I hope we shall be able to arrange a meeting before we go. I think we stay until about the 4th. My difficulty, as I explained in the last letter, is about a review, which I may have to do this week—but this is uncertain, so you'd better say what suits you, and then I'll try and manage it.

Mrs Hammond asked whether I'd heard from you about wages and when you want her, so I think she is probably considering it. She is very nice, silent, clean, and has a large sheep dog. She does for us and Desmond entirely without help, and manages very well—in fact I think its much nicer than having 2.

Yr B.

Berg

874: To Vanessa Bell   *Asheham House, Rodmell,*
Lewes, [Sussex]

Wednesday [26 September 1917]

Dearest,

What an age it takes to get a letter from Charleston to Asheham! I got yours this morning.

About our plans of meeting—we should of course be delighted if you and Roger would come to tea and stay to dinner tomorrow (Thursday).

If you dont, I could come on Friday and spend the night, though I feel this is rather hard upon Roger, who has already had one of his days taken from him.

Or I could come for lunch and go back after tea, on Friday. What I had meant was to stay a night with you on our way back—say Thursday night next week—but I daresay this would not fit in.

I spoke to Mrs Hammond, who says that she has promised to stay with a sister in law and therefore only wanted a temporary place. I told her I thought you could probably arrange for Ivy to stay a week or 2 longer, if that would do. She said she would like to think it over. I daresay it would be a good thing if you could see her yourself (as you could do if you came on Thursday) as with a little management I believe she would come. She is certainly very clean and hard working, a very sensible nice sort of person, as far as I can tell.

I talked to Duncan about the wood cuts, and he said he would like to do some, if we undertook the whole thing. Would you think this possible for yourself?

However, we could talk this over, if, as I hope, we manage to meet.

183

I'm taking this to catch the evening post, and have hope it may reach you by the second post tomorrow.

If I come on Friday, I will come to lunch if I'm going back after tea; and to tea, if I'm going to stay the night.

Yr B.

Berg

875: TO VANESSA BELL   *Asheham, [Rodmell, Sussex]*

Wednesday [3 October 1917]

Dearest,

I have looked through the governesses in the East Sussex News, but there aren't any this week—except a Tutor at Eastbourne. So I will tell them to send you a copy on Friday, which is the day it comes out.

I think it would be worth your while to go to the Sussex Registry Office in Friars Walk, about 5 minutes from the station in Lewes; first turn to the right, past the Churchyard. There is rather a nice woman there and though she deals in servants, very likely she would have someone just above a servant, or anyhow could tell you the best way of getting hold of a governess.

By the way, if you do want that carpet, we shall be very glad for you to have it, as it is probably only getting the mildew. I will tell Mrs Attwood that you may call for it some day.

I think you had better call at her house for the key, if you do come, as she gets rather alarmed, if people get in without her knowledge. I enjoyed myself very much, I need hardly say, and I think my behaviour was irreproachable.

I tried to sing the Wolf song this morning, tell Quentin.

Would you send me (to Hogarth) the recipes? I did the tea cakes from memory today, and they were a great success.

Yr B.

Mrs Attwoods hen has started laying, so perhaps a red comb does foretell it.

Berg

876: TO DORA CARRINGTON   *Hogarth [House, Richmond]*

[5 October 1917]

Dear Carrington,

I hope this cheque wont seem to you to prove that we are slave drivers—it is very small—but our profits [£6.7.0.] aren't much on this venture.

Anyhow, I'm sure your pictures will attract lots of people who are repelled by print (very rightly too).

As you will see from the form I send, our prices have already gone up 6d.—They will rise steadily as the copies give out—and I daresay the last and worst will sell for over a sovereign—in a hot competition too of elderly ladies who never read a line just because it is the last—

Leonard has been rung up by Kabotinsky (?) [S. S. Koteliansky], and we're asking him to dine on Sunday. Will you come too? I've asked the price of Salmon, but its much too dear. Never mind: the welcome of the heart—that is what you'll get, and think it sufficient, I know.

The truth is, there was something I had to remember to ask you, and its gone clean out of my head, and thats why I go on writing this letter—Cant think what it was—Something very important and interesting too—We had such a divine time at Asheham, except for one terrifying moment. A swarm of bees conglobulated suddenly over our heads on the terrace—in an ecstasy of lust—drove us in—then made for the chimney, and all settled in the attic. Please tell us what to do. We want the honey; the males were all dead—But I forgot: you dont like the fact of copulation, only the theory—What an odd generation yours is! but this isn't the interesting thing. Give my love to Alix.

Yr
V.W.

Robert H. Taylor

877: To Vanessa Bell   [*Hogarth House, Richmond*]

Saturday morning [6 October 1917]

16 German aeroplanes have just passed over Richmond—They haven't done us any harm—We went and sat in the cellar and listened to them, and Nelly nearly had hysterics. The people next door saw them perfectly from the top window. A man in the street says one has been brought down in the Park—They sounded quite near, but I dont know if they dropped bombs, or whether it was only our guns. Carrington has just rung up to say there were 35 over Gordon Sqre but didnt drop bombs.

Berg

878: To Emma Vaughan   *Hogarth House, Paradise Road,*
Richmond, [Surrey]
[7? October 1917]

Dearest Toad,
   We would like *everything*![1] In fact, if we have anything, the remains

1. Emma Vaughan shared with Virginia in their youth an interest in bookbinding. She had kept all her equipment, and now sent it to Virginia.

wouldn't be much good to the Isle of Man.[1] It is most angelic of you; I
think the presses will come in most useful, though what a "Kipping" press
is, I don't know.

The sending them here ought to be quite simple. All you have to do is to
stick a Carter Paterson card in the window. The smaller things need only be
tied in a bundle with a label; and the bigger ones not packed at all. I expect
the Porter and the C.P. man between them could easily lift the presses as
they are downstairs; then we would pay him when he delivered them here.
We deal with C.P. a lot, and haven't found any difficulty in getting them, in
spite of the war.

What luck I stepped in and frustrated the Isle of Man! But are you sure
you couldn't get a pound or two on them?—We would like to give whatever
you might have had.

Love to Marny. I suppose the bombs on Hoxton respected her Saintly
body—We had 16 Germans over our house, but they did no harm.

Yrs.
V.W.

Sussex

879: To Emma Vaughan   *Hogarth House, Paradise Road,*
Richmond, Surrey

Wednesday [10 October 1917]

Dearest Toad,

I should never have suggested such a gift if I had known how magnificent
it is. All the things came safely yesterday, and they will be of the greatest use
to us. I do feel sorry for the prisoners, and only hope they never saw what
they have lost. The cutting press is exactly what we want—Wont you come
and dine with us one night and see them? We are only just back from
Asheham, having missed all the raids. Give my love to Marny and tell her I
think she might come too, but I believe you prefer to be apart and I suppose
you are both out all day, eating sandwiches in the park, or, as I imagine,
forgetting to eat anything at all. Don't forget to send the bill, and don't
forget to put in everything, including Oliver's [the porter] time, and any
damage done.

Yr.
V.W.

Sussex

1. A main centre in both wars for enemy aliens and prisoners of war. With her
   concern for the German prisoners, Emma Vaughan had offered them her
   equipment.

Hogarth House, Paradise Road,
                                    Richmond, Surrey

[17 October 1917]

Dearest,

I wonder whether it would suit you to have me for 2 nights from Wed. 31st to Friday 2nd Nov:? I rather expect it won't, as your governess must be coming about then, and visitors would be a nuisance. We have decided that its more sensible for me not to go north with Leonard,[1] as its sure to be rather exhausting, let alone the expense. Therefore I thought it would be a good chance to come, but I could go either to Ka at Aldbourne, or to Roger, I think, if I didn't want to be here, or to Asheham, so dont consider for a second anything but your convenience. I should bring some work, and write in my bedroom.

I've just been to see the pictures,[2] and to tea with Ottoline and Roger. I didnt see much of the pictures—but I was much impressed by one of yours —a brass pot on its side, or something of that sort. In fact I think you're about our best painter—such imagination; such a way of seeing, so that the thing seems a beautiful, queer, whole. But as I say I met Aldous Huxley, and to look at pictures was useless. Besides, Ott: and Roger were very awkward.[3] I've fallen from my height with her. She was rather distant—though I think this was partly due to the discomfort with Roger. She told me they couldn't get on at all.

We went to Kingston Barracks, and after saying, I suppose to insult him, that L. had senile tremor, and suspecting a sham, they gave him complete exemption which they said was probably permanent.[4] It was only due to [Drs] Craig and Wright though.

Alix came to print one afternoon, and was so bored that she has given it up—rather a relief. I'm now asking Barbara.

Could you let me know rather soon whether I could come, as I had better settle something or other.

I enclose the films.

                                              Yr.

                                              B

Berg

1. He was to lecture in Bolton, Manchester and Liverpool.
2. The Omega show at Heals, Tottenham Court Road.
3. Due to their quarrel. See p. 91, note 6.
4. Leonard was re-examined in the general comb-out in 1917 of those previously exempted from military service.

Hogarth House, Paradise Road,
Richmond, Surrey

Thursday [18 October 1917]

My dear Ottoline

I've just telephoned to say that I'm afraid I shan't be able to come tomorrow. I expect I shall be in London, but I don't see how I can get to Tilney St. before 5.30—and you wanted me to come early I think. Besides, I should have to leave at once—thats the worst of Richmond. After leaving you I spent over half an hour wedged in a crowd, at Charing Cross, and only got back here at 7.30.

If you come up again, do (if you would like to see me) let me know and then I could arrange it—you don't realise, at least I sometimes think you dont, how nice it is to see you—not only romantic, but nice. My flowers, which I saved in the crush, still breathe of Tottenham Court Road in the rain—

Yr affate
Virginia Woolf

Texas

882: To Vanessa Bell   *Hogarth House, [Richmond]*

Saturday [20 October 1917]

Dearest,

I am very sorry to hear of your domestic worries—I thought I'd better stir up Mrs Hunt myself, so I went there yesterday, and was told they had no h. parl's [house parlourmaids] on their books at present; but would ring me up directly there was a chance of one. I've also been to two agencies here; the first had one, but she wouldn't go to the country. The second also had one, and she wouldn't go either. As I was there however, a servant came in, who wanted to be houseparl. and didn't mind the country, but I didn't much like the looks of her. She was leaving because the gentleman said she coughed too much, but has a character from another place. I said I'd see it; but I don't think she is worth having really, as she looked very ill, and also rather shifty and dirty and the sort of person who might drink.

By a miracle, I've kept the address of a very good agency in Chelsea, recommended by Pinkie Ritchie, where I'll go if I can on Monday. It would be too awful if Trissie [Vanessa's cook] went—but I feel pretty sure I can get you someone from one of these places. Meanwhile Nelly is routing about among her friends and the servants where they are. She strongly advises you to advertise in the West Sussex Gazette, which one can get at Lewes. She says that all the servants round Guilford go to it for places, and its much better than an agency. It must be an awful nuisance with Eva Edwards[1] arriving and all the rest of it. I suppose a temporary would be no good? I expect its much easier to get a permanent one in the summer. Also I expect it might be worth trying the agencies in Brighton and Eastbourne.

We had Zeppelins over last night. They are said to have destroyed Swan and Edgar at Piccadilly. We only heard the guns at a distance, and never heard the warning at all.

Have you seen this from the Cambridge Magazine?

I will write if I discover any one, as I hope to—its rather like hunting a Swallowtail [butterfly]—I get quite excited.

Yr

B.

Berg

883: To Vanessa Bell   *Hogarth [House, Richmond]*

Monday [22 October 1917]

Dearest,

I'm very glad that you've caught your servant. It certainly seemed rather hopeless here.

I've just rung up Saxon and offered him and Barbara Asheham. She is away at this moment, and he thinks that Nick may be back soon, in which case B. would stay in London. However, if not, they would like nothing better than Asheham—in fact he wants to go there on Monday anyhow, and to spend his holiday there. Possibly I shall go there on Monday, and he rather wants me to stay and keep him company, if Barbara doesn't come. I daresay as a matter of fact, you'd be well pleased to be without visitors while you're starting your new arrangements. Anyhow, you're quite free from Barbara and you can see how you get on and let me know anytime about coming, as I shall certainly either stay here or go to Asheham.

We are plunged in (temporary) difficulties: Liz [Nellie Boxall's sister] has at last had her baby and her husband has been wounded at the same time, so that Nelly has had to go and look after her—however, I suppose we shall manage all right. We had 6 hours of Walter Lamb the other day—his qualities are such that in spite of everything it is really worth while, once a year.

Yr

B.

Berg

1. A governess whom Vanessa had obtained for her children at Charleston. She was beautiful, but the whole household found her an intolerable bore. (See David Garnett, *The Flowers of the Forest*, p. 178.)

Hogarth House, Paradise Road,
Richmond, Surrey

Oct. 25th [1917]

My dear Ottoline

I think your quarrel with London is much more the result of being tired than of being old, ugly, or useless. But I'm not going to run down London, because as you know, my perfectly selfish ambition is to have you at Bedford Sqre. again. But coming up for a day or two one gets, I used to think, violent and exaggerated impressions; *my* impression was of beauty mixed with the usual melancholy misunderstanding of all complex and sensitive people, the other day. I'm talking of Rogers tea party. The walk in the rain was romantic and so satisfactory from my point of view—but then I like you yourself, beneath the depressions and agitations and varieties of the surface. By this time surely, our degree of polish is scratched through, and we have come upon something—I have, anyhow—human and true beneath.

I'm very glad you saw Desmond; I think his mixture of intelligence and standard combined with sympathy is rare among us—I couldn't have come, for after a wretched hunt for servants in London I was degraded by tea time.

We are just starting for the North—at least Leonard is. The difficulty of going was so great that I'm staying here or going down to Asheham and Charleston till he comes back. I feel that he'll be too tired to go anywhere for a bit; but would the 17th Nov: suit you? Do you mind our having no clothes? Philip will have told you how we live like superior mechanics.

Dont—if you can have us—bother about Clive. That difficulty is formally buried.[1]

Your carnations are still in front of me!

Yr very affate
Virginia

Texas

885: To Vanessa Bell   *Hogarth [House, Richmond]*

Saturday [27 October 1917]

Dearest,

I have settled to go to Asheham on Monday with Saxon, and then to come to you, if I may, on Wednesday, till Friday. I think Saxon is going to Brighton on Wednesday; we have lent the house to him, Barbara and Nick for Nicks leave, and B. and N. come down on Friday I think.

Of course if you liked to come over to see us, we should be delighted, but

1. The falling-out over Katherine Mansfield.

anyhow I'll turn up for tea on Wednesday with great joy. By the way, if a parcel should come for me from the Times, do you think your servants would re-address it to Asheham and give it back to the postman? Its just possible they'll send it to you; and I'm in rather a hurry.

Barbara seems very anxious to do the printing, and evidently she's much more capable than Alix, but as long as Nick's in England she has to be with him.

I shan't bring any clothes. I hope Miss Edwards [the governess] won't mind but I'll try to make up by the elegance of my conversation.

Yr B.

I'm also having my letters sent to Charleston, but will you keep them—its only the parcel I should like forwarded to Asheham.

Berg

886: TO LEONARD WOOLF [*Hogarth House, Richmond*]

[29 October 1917]

My Darling Goose M;

Here I am, just having had a very good luncheon, ending with an apple. I did my business this morning, and bought a fine pair of check slippers, which fasten with a clip. I couldn't find Miss Kelley, so I had to bring my cloak home again. I bought 2 torches, 1/11 each for the children; I dont suppose they're good, but then they'll be smashed. I am now practically ready to start—I am taking my basket, and its as light as a feather. I suppose at this moment you're cracking your bone, poor little darling, and some old woman being overcome by your sweet appearance, is offering you a piece of biscuit. I copied out the notes[1], have put them all in order on your table (this is a lie, but I will do so) and sent the book off.

I'm going to catch the 2.30 and its now nearly 2, so I'd better finish off my small jobs.

I promise faithfully to do everything as if you were there, but you wont be there, and I shall find Saxon such a stick and such a pussy cat after my own passionate and ferocious and entirely adorable M.

Yrs.

Thank Mrs E.[2] from me. M.

Sussex

1. From consular documents on colonial trade, for use by Leonard in the book which eventually became *Empire and Commerce in Africa*.
2. Mrs G. Eckhard, mother-in-law of Sydney Waterlow, with whom Leonard was staying at Didsbury, a suburb of Manchester.

Tuesday [30 October 1917]

Darling Mr Mongoose,

Thank God, one day is over. I keep wondering how you've got on—what people said about the lecture, whether you were nervous, wetted, etc etc—but I must wait till tomorrow morning.

I met Saxon at Victoria; he had already taken our seats, and bought 1st class tickets, because, having made up his mind to economise, he had carried his own bag, and found it so heavy that he couldn't, and so he thought it was better to not to attempt travelling 3rd. I explain this for the benefit of that generous old gentleman Mr Household [Leonard]—of course our carriage was quite full—golf playing stockbrokers who began by saying that it was the poor who did all the eating and over eating and then fell asleep—disgusting hogs. We did our shopping successfully in Lewes, found our taxi—a new man who had to have a boy as he didn't know the way—and came home. By the mercy of providence, I bought eggs butter and milk in Lewes; the Killicks had none over. When we got to Asheham all the windows were dark, and the door locked; so we had to go down to the cottage, where we found a party going on in the Attfields, and Mrs A. declaring I had never said what time, and therefore she had not lighted any fires. However all the beds had been thoroughly aired. I said we must have dinner at once, so Will was sent up with us, and it was managed all right though rather late. The truth was she hadn't expected me, and didn't much mind what happened to Mr [Sydney] Turner and the young ladies.

We had a very good dinner—and she was extremely apologetic. The house was perfectly dry, and looks very clean—but of that I'm no judge. Saxon and I had a splendid fire, and he talked a great deal about marriage and Barbara, and said how our marriage seemed the best of any he knew, and how coming to see us one night, he had understood for the first time the advantages of being married, which I thought a pretty compliment. He has brought French and Italian novels, and he produced a bottle of Brandy at dinner and made me have a sip. It was wonderful stuff, and cost 25/- a bottle. I see why Desmond likes it. I had a very good night, and didn't need any aspirin. Of course I had no letters this morning, and Saxon prefers not to take in a paper, so it was rather dull and I feel very much buried—but thats being without you really.

This morning I did a little writing in my room. The first thing was that Saxon cut 2 fingers opening a bottle of patent medicine; but as he had cotton wool, sticking plaster and ointment, we hope it wont mortify. He is incredibly timid and uniniatived [sic] (a very long word that). He cant make up his mind about anything—He takes as long to decide whether to order beef or coals as you do to write an article. I find it very odd and rather irritating. However, he's extremely nice and very attentive.

We must now go to the Killicks for the milk. It has poured all the morning, but I foretold a fine afternoon and so it is. Will has done nothing to the garden. The sunflowers are dead. The wall flowers look very healthy. Will has got off again. This is a hideous dull letter I know. I have rested, and done everything as if you were here.

Its no good repeating that I adore you, is it? That seems to be a well known fact. Its so frightfully tame without you.

For Gods sake don't get overtired; or a chill; the little beasts have all crept out and kiss the page.

Yrs.

Sussex   M.

888: TO LEONARD WOOLF   *Asheham*, [*Rodmell,*
                                                                                    Sussex]
Wednesday [31 October 1917]

My darling Goose M,

I got your card this morning which was a great relief, as I forgot to tell the Post Office at Lewes to forward letters. However they've sent them all on; but I only wanted yours, and I'm longing for a proper one, with a full account. The rumour is that there was a raid on Monday night—I've no paper, but I can't think it went to Bolton. I'm forwarding Norgates and Unwin's [publishers] letters. I wonder what your agreement with Norgate was. Its clear that they're determined to keep your book,[1] and I'm amused to see how the publishers squabble for you—you must admit its rather a compliment. All I had was a card from Aunt Minna [Duckworth] asking us any week end—

There is very little in the way of news. We fetched our milk, and Saxon carried it back, and then we settled down to gossip, in the usual minute way. We spend a great time working out infinitely unimportant details—whether he shall go to Brighton, where he shall buy coal—his indecision and meticulousness rather surprise me. Its so odd, after my rapid bold Mong[oose]. I have to make up his mind, but I can't get him to settle whether he means to stay here or go to Brighton. They're very anxious for me to come [stay] here till Saturday, but I shan't; I dont want to lose the chance of your coming; in fact I couldn't bear to be away an hour more than's necessary. I've ordered my taxi for Friday.

1. *Co-operation and the Future of Industry*, originally commissioned by the Home University Library (Norgate) and published by Allen and Unwin Ltd. 1919. Leonard had threatened a suit against Norgate, who then surrendered the copyright to him.

Then I said I must read my book, and he got out Aristotle, but the poor old creature really wants to discuss himself and Barbara more than anything, so I didn't read much. He consulted me upon what he calls "the moral question" of whether it is right for him to go on seeing B. in Nick's absence, supposing that by so doing he may make her fall in love with him—"although that possibility is hardly a serious one. I must seem to her very dull, I think I am very dull—Well, I'm middle aged; in fact I dont at all suppose I shall live to be twice my present age. My landlady hopes I shall stay another 13 years with her; then I shall be 50. I've been 13 years with her already. . . . . I think a difference of 11 years is too much—between me and Barbara I mean. I saw Nick in his bath the other day. It struck me that he was much more suitable. However, I don't worry about that—I shouldn't *mind* if he did marry her". etc, etc, etc. He's a dear old creature—but what a frightfully vivid view of a person's peculiarities one gets by staying with them! No, mongoose, he wouldn't at all have done for a Servant! We've discussed that too; and he concluded that the reason he'd never been in love with me was that Thoby's death had made us so intimate that it wasn't necessary—besides he had always thought I should marry you.

Its a lovely still day—perfect for bicycling and I shall start after luncheon. I'm drinking my glass of milk and ovaltine as I write. I've not done any work this morning, as I must finish my Review book, which it is impossible to do with Saxon in the room. I feel extremely well, and slept perfectly, and stayed in bed rather late with my window open, and then had a hot bath; and then walked for 5 minutes on the terrace, and then made my bread, which I must now go down and knead. Saxon I hear wandering from room to room; in a way which would madden you.

By the way, I travelled up from Richmond with Jean [Thomas]! She was in the next carriage, through a glass door, and didn't see me—at least we made no signs—She got out at Hammersmith.

God, how I want to know what you're up to—Please tell me honestly if its very tiring, and cold; and if you're *perfectly* well in every way—no headache, or ears bad; or inside; and as cheerful as can be expected. I'm perfectly honest; I eat exactly as if you were here, and I think its done me good. Its so quiet and lovely. When do you get back at night after the lecture? Do they question you much?

Darling love I kiss thee.

M.

Sussex

889: TO SAXON SYDNEY-TURNER   *Hogarth [House, Richmond]*
Friday [2 November 1917]

I found this letter waiting here. I can't think why they've sent it back. I

194

never gave any orders to the Post Office about my letters. Perhaps you ought to explain that you're staying on at Asheham.

Love to everyone. I shall expect a nice long letter some day, when you feel in the mood for writing. I enjoyed my evening with you, my dear Saxon, and it was *not* due to Brandy (though that was a divine pleasure) but to your exquisite nature.

Sussex

890: To Vanessa Bell   [*Hogarth House, Richmond*]
[11 November 1917]

Dearest,

The boots were sent off; Julian's cost 4/6 which seems absurd, but the others were old stock and his were new, so they cost more. Wouldn't you like a pair for your own feet? They are amazingly comfortable.

I went off [from Gordon Square] the other night forgetting your pictures and my umbrella of course; but I shall go tomorrow if I can. I think you're very generous. My opinion of your art is so high that I suppose you think it worthless. Of course I only saw the [Omega] Show in half light the other day; but I got some quite strong feelings from it, good or bad. I think you exaggerate the lack of sensibility; you see the worst of art is that it appeals solely to the aesthetic faculties, and one's extremely shy and snobbish about giving away ones deficiency or eccentricity about them. Of course, I committed myself all wrong to poor old Roger, about his cold hard little compositions and called them literary, which he said they aren't. I was a good deal impressed by Gertler, much more at this Show than at the other.

What a divine hour I had at Gordon Sqre! I enjoyed it, like Saxon's brandy—the unreality, and bloom of the sensations went to my head, but of course if I'd stayed I should have run to ground. Was it great fun all through? I hope not.

The real point of this letter is to say that you owe me 11/—but I think you ought to deduct something for the port. Then we want to make a stove for the drawing room. If you could give us any hints we should be grateful. We're buying 10 tiles and arranging them like yours, but I can't remember how the hood on top went.

I suppose you're dining at Asheham today, to meet Faith [Henderson]. I'm sure she'll have our letters out.

I must now get ready to lunch with the Webbs. Do tell me how your educational plans work out. My feeling is that excessive masculinity has to be guarded against; I mean young men do seem to me so selfish and assertive; which tends to my thinking to be frightfully boring, (but I wont go on, as I know you dont agree, and also I've no time.) Anyhow, Julian's a very attractive brat, and as full of brains as an egg (this is really a compliment).

Yr
B.

Berg

891: To Barbara Hiles

Hogarth House, Paradise Road,
Richmond, Surrey

Tuesday [13 November 1917]

Dear Barbara,

I'm glad to hear that you've enjoyed yourselves; I was afraid from Faith's account that the difficulties were rather great. I wonder if you're coming back on Friday (do stay on as long as ever you want to, short of Christmas)—and if you are whether you would be so very good as to bring us back a little *tea*. When I was in Lewes one could get it easily at Roberts; 2 lbs; or less would be very welcome. I daresay the Coops: dont allow any. Here we are reduced to our last spoonful, which has hit the servants more than any disaster in the course of the war—We bear up, because we like coffee.

We are starting printing [*Prelude*] in earnest, having just got our paper. Love to everyone.

Yrs.
V.W.

Berg

892: To Lady Ottoline Morrell

Hogarth House, Paradise Road,
Richmond, Surrey

Wednesday [21 November 1917]

My dear Ottoline,

It is quite impossible to write with Barbara taking her first lesson in printing, and Leonard mending the machine which has broken of course; but we did enjoy ourselves immensely. I hope this simple and sincere statement will not be brushed aside by you in a cynical way. As an artist, I suppose I ought to quarrel with you—to put the aristocracy beneath my feet. I'm sure thats why they are so disagreeable—I mean the artists.

Anyhow Garsington struck me as quite enough of a work of art to justify you in casting us off—But dont do it just yet.

We took about 6 hours to get back; but we stopped at Oxford, where I bought 2 lovely writing books, not so gorgeous as Brett's[1] but more practical; and then we lunched at Reading, and then we got out at Ealing, and home at last to find Alix waiting.

Leonard wishes to be remembered to you. We both feel freshened up and set going by all the enjoyments you gave us. I couldn't put half of them in my diary.

Your affate
Virginia Woolf

Texas

893: TO VANESSA BELL   *Hogarth House, [Richmond]*

Tuesday [27 November 1917]

Dearest,

I'm sorry I haven't been able to go to the Bead Shop yet, but I will do my best tomorrow when I'm going to the dentist. I dreamt about you and Duncan all night; how you were going off to live on a ranch in California because it was the only way to paint—and you were very bitter—didn't want ever to see me again.

The following conversation took place a few nights ago at Rogers:

R. "Vanessa really gets more and more amazing—I mean her character.

Clive: Yes. She's quite sublime.

V. W: Her natural piety has greatly increased.

R: And then her painting. Sickert says he'd rather have her picture of apples than a Chardin. She's gone miles ahead of any one.

Clive: That picture is what one may call a diploma picture. It marks a stage.

V. W: Thats the one I wanted to buy.

Roger: You cant now, for Lalla [Vandervelde] has bought it.

V. W. Damned old Jewess!

Clive: But you know its her character!

Roger: The greatness!

Clive: The originality!

V. W: We've talked enough about Nessa—

In fact there was much more in this loathsome strain, which I cant bring myself to write down. I said the truest thing though—about natural piety—

I suppose the whole of our weekend has been told you in detail before now. There wasn't very much to tell. The worst of a week end on that scale is that one gets rather stupefied before its over. I had a private talk with Ott; and on the whole I think that she has been slightly maligned. At least she was more vivacious and malicious and less vapourish than I expected. She said

1. The Woolfs had met Dorothy Brett, daughter of Lord Esher, at Garsington, where they had been spending the weekend. Brett, who had been a fellow-student of Carrington at the Slade, followed her friend's example by using only her surname.

that she was now happier than ever before, though she had had many bitter disappointments in friendship; and couldn't understand why Lawrence and Murry and Katherine all turned against her. I said it was a form of inverted snobbishness; and she quoted long passages from L's novel [*The Rainbow*], and was very discreet about Katharine—in fact she was rather reserved, thinking most unjustly that I do sometimes let things out. There were endless young men from Oxford, and Brett and Lytton and Aldous Huxley who talks too much about his prose romances for my taste, and falls into deep glooms, when, according to Ott: he is thinking of Maria.[1] I saw Fredegond [Shove], and we had a family gossip—all I remember of interest is that Ermengarde [her sister] has just become a Quaker. At least Fredegond was sending her a post card to ask if this was true. Gerald [Shove] poured out his miseries to Leonard, and is secretly trying to get moved. They have a dismal little cottage, I thought, and the whole situation for both parties seemed to me intolerable. Brett is a queer imp. She took me to her studio and is evidently very proud of a great picture full of blue umbrellas, which seems to console her for being deaf. There was a poet called Evan Morgan,[2] in black velvet with a scarlet ribbon and a ruff: a twitching man called Earp:[3] Philip all gaitered and very well-meaning but I should fancy a dreary old death's head in the long run.

I had my period 2 days ago and spent one morning reading old letters. Needless to say yours beat the literary gents quite hollow. I was amused by your account of meeting "Barnes"[4] at Florence in the year 1909. I must copy it for you.

"On our evening walk we met the Barnes'. I dislike her. In fact I came to the conclusion that the new generation of females is not a patch upon the old. They have the hardness of youth and the self-possession of age—a horrid mixture. They have none of that endearing gaucherie which you and I must have possessed in abundance. Adams, Meynell, Barnes, all are alike, but Barnes and Meynell, on account of their upbringing are also aesthetic. On the whole I prefer the unaesthetic Adams, who might I think have been shaken out of her self-possession." That pretty well does for Barnes!

Barbara is constantly bursting into my room for help in printing. She comes 3 days a week and has lunch and tea, and has already told me that I am to tell her honestly if I ever want to be rid of her—so what is one to do?

Yr

B.

Barbara says that your getting rid of Miss E[dwards, the governess]. I rather

1. Maria Nys, a Belgian girl, who stayed at Garsington for much of the war, and married Aldous Huxley in 1918.
2. Later 2nd Viscount Tredegar (1893-1949).
3. See p. 158, note 2.
4. Mary Barnes, the maiden name of Mrs St John Hutchinson.

thought you would. Let me know if I can be of use. I could easily go and see any at Mrs Hunts or elsewhere.

Berg

894: TO VANESSA BELL   *Hogarth [House, Richmond]*
Sunday [9 December 1917]

Dearest,

I enclose a sketch—in fact it's word for word true—of Marny's[1] conversation, as a thank offering for the loan of your picture; and if you think it a fair exchange, we might do traffic on these lines. There was a great deal more of Marny, as you may suppose, since she spent 2 1/2 hours here. She sent you her love and I told her you had particularly wished me to give her yours, when I told you she was coming. This gave her immense pleasure; and I think you ought to ask her to stop and lunch with you next time she goes to Hastings. We are now corresponding about bread making.

I'm afraid the chances are that I shan't be able to come to your party—my affairs will probably choose that day. The servants are already half tipsy at the idea, and have planned all sorts of assignations by moonlight with Sid and Will. Noel [Olivier] can't get away, and James [Strachey] wants to stay in London to see her, so I think we shall be alone for Christmas itself. Then Ray [Strachey] is coming for a few days, and Ka I think—Shall we meet at all?

Could you tell me if Julian would like Scotts Tales of a Grandfather? I've got our old copy which I would give him—but I want to find a lighter book too, but I dont know what. Have you any photographs of father? A man who is writing a book on Meredith has written to ask me for one, about 1870-9—I can't find any; but I suppose Aunt Julia's[2] is in existence—

I hear you took Widow Brereton.[3] Do take care what you say about death, separation, divorce and concubines—Be tactful about her children's faces; say nothing about the Church, for you can't be sure that she is an atheist, merely because her husband is a clergyman. I can see you whisking

1. Margaret Vaughan (1862-1929), Virginia's first cousin, never married, and spent a large part of her adult life doing social work among the poor in Hoxton. Marny and her sister Emma ('Toad') had been intimate friends of Virginia in her childhood and early youth, but they had drifted apart from her.
2. Julia Cameron (1815-79) was an aunt of Virginia's mother, and achieved great fame as a photographer of her distinguished contemporaries.
3. Mrs Brereton came to Charleston from Roger Fry as governess to Julian and Quentin, bringing her daughter Anne with her. She was separated from her husband.

your tail on her innermost entrails and then asking why she minds, seeing he's dead—which he isn't of course, or has that point been established?

Yr

B.

I'm *not* giving you a [Christmas] present. I trust to your honour not to give me one. (or merely a passionate outburst of embraces)

Typewritten

SATURDAY, 8th Dec;—

Today, Saturday, we walked to Twickenham where L. took the train for Staines, and I got back late to find Marny waiting. I found her sitting bolt upright, away from the fire, as if she wouldnt encroach upon it, dressed in a sleek black coat of some fabricated fur; large muff; little bit of lace at her throat; thin gold chain; all infinitely decorous and after the pattern of the spinsters of breeding who buy their goods at Barkers, and wait to be served in Kensington Post Office, and are always kept waiting, and then become plaintive, but never angry. Her face is more than ever the face of the emaciated saint with a dash of the sheep, and the eyes of a child. So we greeted each other.

V. . Dear Marny, how nice to see you—after all these years!

M. . . O Goat dear, how charming to see *you*, and Ive been using up your lovely fire, for I caught my train, which one cant be sure of doing in these times; and I found my way up so beautifully. I'll take off my gloves but not my coat, and I've such heaps of things to ask and to hear—

and so we sat down to tea; and straightway lighted—(it didnt seem to matter where one lighted—) upon Florence Bishop.

M. . . O but you mustn't call her Bishop. Shes married a naval doctor and her name's Burke. Yes, she still keeps up with us, for we met in the street one day and she asked us to tea. She lives in a little flat in the Earls Court Road, for she's not at all well off, you know; I fancy old Mr Bishop was a foolish old man. But she gives you Tiptree jam for tea, and she looks like a picture. Such a pretty flat, and her white hair so becoming, and everything as nice as possible . . . But not as nice as this; no, Goat dear, no one ever has tea's like your's. We havent had butter (this *is* butter isnt it?) for a long time, and sometimes we can't even get the nice kind of margarine; but I won't deal at Barkers, no I dont think its *right* to deal at Barkers, after the evidence at that dreadful fire—I thought it gave one a dreadful idea of him. And we seem quite in the region for fires. Wright's coal shed burnt down behind us the other night—all that good coal wasted; it seemed such a pity, didnt it? and last winter we quite ran out of coal. It was a Saturday too, and I went from shop to shop begging—even a scuttlefull will take us over Sunday I said, but

200

they hadnt got any, and who should I meet at Knightsbridge but Kitty Maxse? and she said, "O I'll give you some coal; I've got two cellars full, and sure enough, though I begged her not to, that very afternoon up she drove in a taxi with a sack full, and that saw us through, but I've not seen her since that day, so distinguished looking and not a year older, though she must be going on for fifty. Why, I'm 55, and Toad 43—but one forgets peoples ages, and I'm sure I dont feel old, and you look like 25, and Nessa as lovely as ever I suppose! with those great blue eyes—

(here followed the whole history, very skillfully concocted by me, of the more reputable side of Nessa, Clive, Adrian, Duncan, Bunny, and ourselves —also, the Shoves came in, and how Ermengarde [Maitland] has turned Quaker, and probably has more in her than Fredegond, though she's not attractive, or beautiful in the family way—"Still, Goat dear, looks arent everything . . .")

M. . . . Dear me, how we all move about, partly owing to the war to be sure; though I do manage to see some of my old friends still, like Miss Harris; Nessa would remember her; she paints really remarkably well, but she won't exhibit, because she thinks she's not worthy, and she's given it up now, like most people, for war work. And Hilda Lightbody, I see her sometimes. Yes, she's a widow—oh, for years now, and Mr Lightbody was always a great invalid, and now she makes papier maché splints down in Westminster, and I believe we're going to tea with her next Wednesday. Yes, I keep up with Adeline [Vaughan Williams]; I'm not so naughty about the Fishers as you and Nessa are; and she hasn't changed at all—such lovely golden hair, not a white hair in her head, though she has this dreadful arthritis, and can't get out of her chair without a stick. She took Hervey [Fisher] to Hastings for a change, and theyve stayed on, for there wasn't any reason why they *shouldnt* stay on, and the lodgings suited them, and Hervey liked the air, and Millicent isn't very far off. Poor Millicent [Marny's sister]— she suffered terribly over poor John [Isham]. It was the camp, bad drains we think—though no one knows and he'd always meant to be a soldier anyhow, which makes it rather better perhaps . . .

And Virginia [Isham] milks cows at Lord Rayleighs place in Essex. She prefers horses, but she couldnt get horses, and she's very fond of cows. No, I dont think they'll ever leave Hastings, though Millicent would rather be in the real country or in the real town; but then they know people and she does a lot in a social way. Last winter she got up dances though she didnt feel like dancing I'm sure, but she thinks young people ought to have their gaieties, in spite of this dreadful war. What a terrible tragedy it all is, Goat dear! And what does Leonard think of it all? I suppose he cant say for certain when we shall have peace—nobody seems able to tell one that. And the children grow up—its quite wicked *how* they grow up, and Nessa's children just the same I suppose, big boys, both of them, and I hope they look like her. Yes, Halford [Vaughan] is quite a man, with a poetic side but very practical in other ways,

I'm glad to say; and Janet [Vaughan] so like Madge [Vaughan, née Symonds, their mother] to look at, but I dont think she'll take to writing—but I wish you *could* make Madge write. Perhaps she'd be happier then, though I dont think anything could make Madge really happy; its not in the Symonds nature, though theyre such wonderful people in their way . . and I was so glad to hear that Katharine [Furse née Symonds] has quarrelled with that odious Northcliffe. I'm told they never see each other now. And I do feel that he's at the bottom of all our troubles, though the Prussians seem to have acted in a very high handed way, I must say; but the fault can't be entirely with them as people make out. I believe the south Germans want peace just as much as we do . . . Yes, we had the raid the other night, and we went and sat in the Wales' room on the ground floor. We all sat in the passage till it was over, and then we went to bed. And Toad had dropped off to sleep, when I heard a dreadful moaning noise, and I knew it couldnt be the raid, so I didnt wake her up. And then it came again, and I wondered whether it could mean that the Germans were actually *there*; so I put on my dressing gown, and looked out of the window and saw nothing, and suddenly it sounded just beneath my windows, so I thought, "well, this time I will make sure, for if its any thing queer we oughtnt to be up in the roof like this", and I went out on to the staircase, and I met a lady dressed for walking and she said, O 'theres nothing to be frightened about, Thats the all clear Bugle" So I went back again, but I think the authorities ought to tell one, dont you?"

Berg

895: To Vanessa Bell   Hogarth [*House, Richmond*]

Wednesday [19 December 1917]

Dearest,

I think it would be a pity to put your party on to Saturday, as my affairs are quite undependable, and anyhow it might pour. But leave it on Monday, and if I can and its tolerably fine I'll come to lunch and Leonard will come to tea and we'll go home afterwards.

I'm sending Quentin's present addressed to you today, as its too bulky to pack. We had a raid last night—Bob [Trevelyan] was dining with us and talked so loud that we couldn't hear the guns; but Saxon says it was rather bad in London. We ate most of our dinner in the coal cellar.

Yr

B.

Berg

896: To Clive Bell

Asheham, [Rodmell, Sussex]

Saturday [22 December 1917]

My dear Clive,

It was unanimously agreed at a party of your democratic friends the other night that you could only fitly be answered in verse[1]. I wait the rhymes and they won't come. I compare my dumbness with your exquisite larks carolling. And then I remember how its been said that I cant even criticise verse—which are reasons enough you will agree to keep me silent. But in some capacity or other I was so much enchanted by the pirouettings of the scarlet elf upon my breakfast plate the other morning that I can't forbear to croak a kind of frog's chorus in which the note of envy is plainly to be heard.

He is an exquisite original—this elf. Criticism, I repeat, is not for a Times reviewer, and who am I to predict which of these pages will be found in the anthologies of the future? I know which particular one I would back with some confidence, and V.S. [Virginia Stephen] 1909 a good second. But leaving the actual selection for better eyes I will only express the view that to my feeling you have quite undoubtedly twitched aside the veil and penetrated to the heart which perversely enough resists the solemn and premeditated assaults of Eddie's strenuous young men.[2] I read them in the coal cellar the other night during the bombardment and turned to you when the explosions had subsided. I suppose that you have enjoyed making exceptions among your friends; Gumbo [Marjorie Strachey] was complaining bitterly; Bob T: not without foreboding. Might I buy a copy to send to an elderly philanthropist [Margaret Llewelyn Davies] in bed with a cold? I will send a P.O. if you will tell me how much.

Yrs. V.W.

We are just off for a day on Brighton front.
Did you ever pull off the hood of a scarlet flower whose name I forget? Thats what I see you doing, and letting loose scores of them in the fog and frost too. I daresay they were called pimpernels [Eschscholtzia]; they had long green hoods shaped like extinguishers. The flower was folded up inside—then came loose.

Quentin Bell

1. Clive had sent Virginia a copy of his privately printed book of poems, *Ad Familiares*, which included a poem 'To V.S. with a book'.
2. Between 1912 and 1922 Edward Marsh edited five volumes of *Georgian Poetry*, an anthology which included poems by Rupert Brooke, D. H. Lawrence, Robert Graves, W. H. Davies and others.

897: TO VANESSA BELL   *Asheham, [Rodmell,*
                                        Sussex]

Wednesday [26 December 1917]

Dearest

I've found out that I can borrow a mattress from Mrs Attfield, so that we shall have 2 beds free on Saturday, unless by any chance Ray, who's not come, should want to stay over Sunday. But I would send a wire if that were so.

If not, do bring the children—wont you come to lunch? Roger, too, if he's there.

I think we can manage enough milk—you might let me know what meals they usually have.

Its quite all right that Barbara should go to you, if its only till the 10th.

Its very melancholy how life is disposed of by periods.

Do come on Saturday if you can.

                                        Yr
                                            B

Berg

898: TO VANESSA BELL   *[Asheham, Rodmell,*
                                        Sussex]

Friday [28 December 1917]

Dearest,

It will be quite all right for the children to come this weekend. Ray is ill, and can't come. The only thing we're short of is sugar. If they could bring what they would have at home, everything else is quite easy.

We shall expect you, and children and Roger if possible, for lunch tomorrow.

I never thanked you for the flowers which are lovely.

Would it be a good plan for me to bring the children back—on Monday and possibly stay the night?

                                        V.W.

Berg

899: TO LYTTON STRACHEY   *Asheham, Lewes,*
                                        [Sussex]

Friday [28 December 1917]

It was a great treat to get your letter, which, you know, is the first of a series, gradually becoming more and more indiscreet, until every dot has given place to fact. Besides, how can you be indiscreet with me? Don't I live in the middle of padded walls, through which not a sound escapes but what is to everyone's credit? Remember my blazing testimony—the Mansfield affair.

I suppose, not altogether hope, that some of our blessings have reached the Mill on the Pang[1] by now: sun, light, running taps, frisking cowherds etc; but I can't believe that your spiritual level is quite up to ours. We had Maynard and the author [Clive] of *Ad Fam* [*Ad Familiares*] the other day— both extremely agreeable, and the author so modest—though he had a bundle of compliments collected in a large envelope—that I couldn't find it in my heart to be clever at his expense, though as you say—Leonard is seized with a spasmodic clutch at the mere sight of the affair. I confess that I fairly cut adrift, and mounted in my litter, produced a crowing and cocking imitation of his own foppery. Do you call it foppery, or turkery? Its the only way, I assure you, and whatever you do, don't discourage an annual exhibition.

Gordon,[2] as I knew he would, cast a gloom upon my festival. I thought him masterly—indeed, it's amazing how from all these complications you contrive to reel off such a straight and dashing story, and how you weave in every scrap—my God, *what* scraps!—of interest to be had, like (you must pardon one metaphor) a snake insinuating himself through innumerable golden rings—(Do snakes?—I hope so) I don't see how the skill could be carried further. My only criticism, which I ought to hesitate to give until a second reading, is that I'm not sure whether the character of Gordon altogether "convinces". I felt a little difficulty in bridging the gulfs, but I rather think this is inevitable from the method, which flashes light and dark this side and that—and then the crowd of facts to be found room for—and so perhaps one can't get that shifting and muddling which produces atmosphere. I daresay I'm really putting in a claim for the novel form; and it doesn't read very lucidly. The writing I thought more than usually unadorned, and surely the most flawless example of the master's style in its maturity. I will read it once more—unless you want it back at once?—with a pencil.

We go back on Thursday. Shall you be passing through, and will you come to tea or something? I saw Molly the other day, and she, on the advice of Arnold Bennett, has sent her novel[3] to Chatto and Windus, who are, he says, the most intelligent publishers in London. Have they answered?

It's now Sunday; this letter has hung about, and Julian has splashed cocoa over it, and if I don't write it again it's because my fingers refuse their office. Cold has set in; Ka is here; Bunny imminent; Julian and Quentin are

1. Lytton and Carrington had taken the Mill House at Tidmarsh on the River Pang, Berkshire.
2. 'The End of General Gordon', the last essay in Lytton's *Eminent Victorians*.
3. *A Pier and a Band*, 1918, by Mary MacCarthy.

spending the weekend. I meant to tell you about the 17 Club[1]; (but now it's too stale), and how I surprised the secret of Jos's[2] fascination; it's *virility*; (perhaps to lose one's parts sends the semen to the surface—it seemed to splash and sparkle like phosphorescent cod's roe from every glance)— Marjorie [Strachey] all a tremble at one corner, and Miss Dudley[3] immensely receptive at the other—I thought him a random untrustworthy mongrel, utterly incontinent.

This must go, I suppose to Garsington. My love to Ottoline. By God's prevision among my presents was a box of sealing wax, to unstick which warmth must be applied, and warmth is rare. Look for the impression of a perfect rose.[4]

But then, as you justly say, what is there that needs sticking or unsticking? . . . [dots in original] (that's cribbed from you).

Please write,

Yr. V.W.

Frances Hooper

1. A club which had been founded in October, after long discussion. Its premises were in Gerrard Street, Soho, and its membership consisted partly in left-wing politicians, from Ramsay MacDonald downwards, and partly in Bloomsbury intellectuals, including Leonard, Virginia and Lytton. The Club's first general meeting was held on 19 December.
2. Josiah Wedgwood, with whom Marjorie Strachey was in love. He had been seriously wounded in the groin at Gallipoli in May 1915. He made the speech at the Club's inaugural meeting.
3. Helen Dudley, an American who studied at Oxford under Gilbert Murray, and was briefly engaged to Bertrand Russell.
4. On the back of the envelope.

Letters 900-932 (January–mid-May 1918)

Vanessa's plan to start a small school at Charleston made no progress, and Virginia spent a vast amount of her time and energy organising her own and her sister's domestic affairs, interviewing and exchanging servants, whose changeful moods alternately amused and exasperated her. She was writing Night and Day *rapidly, and by March had finished over 100,000 words. In the intervals she wrote many reviews. The air-raids almost persuaded the Woolfs to spend the rest of the war at Asheham, bringing the Hogarth Press with them, but there was much to compensate them for long nights in the cellar at Hogarth House— Leonard's political activities and his acting-editorship of the monthly magazine* War and Peace, *and Virginia's enjoyment of the society of the Omega Work- shops and the young people of the 1917 Club. Among the latter, Barbara Hiles finally made up her mind to marry Nick Bagenal, and Virginia had first to console Saxon Sydney-Turner for his loss, and then Nick himself when he was seriously wounded in Flanders on 30 March. In April the unfinished manuscript of* Ulysses *was offered to the Hogarth Press for publication.*

900: To Vanessa Bell

Asheham, [Rodmell, Sussex]

Wednesday [2 January 1918]

Dearest,

Nelly [Boxall] is coming to say good bye; so I am sending the paints and 2 boxes of pens by her.

Would you be so kind as to give her my umbrella, which you forgot to remind me to take—having designs of your own, I daresay.

I enclose Aunt A's:[1] letter in case it may amuse you—but would you send it back. It was very melancholy not to see more of you but the little I did see seemed in fine feather, and I had some difficulty in restraining poor B's [Virginia's] amorosity, which became at moments violent—Never was there a more lovely creature—and I'm afraid the children mean to make me jealous. I enjoyed myself greatly, and hope you will ask me in Feb:

Love to Poor Bun [David Garnett]

Yr
B.

Berg

1. Anne Ritchie, the elder daughter of W. M. Thackeray.

Wednesday [2 January 1918]

Dearest Margaret,

It is a proof of great devotion on my part to write a letter—but I see that its the only thing to do. We must try to write once a month, and then when we meet at the end of 25 years or so, it will be very interesting to see what sort of people we really are. In fact, that might make a good story, don't you think? I know what sort of idea I should have of you. But the reason I am now writing is to send you a copy of Ad Familiares. When I saw it, I thought at once how you'd relish it, and so I persuaded Clive to give me another copy. What do you think of it? Here is a text for your next letter.

The time passes with such speed that now we're at our last day, and I've not done a thing I meant to do, except read one or two books. All our visitors failed us at Christmas, rather to our relief, though it seems selfish to enjoy our chicken and be in the sun here all alone. Then Ka Cox came, and Nessa's children. I've been spending the night at Charleston, and organising a small boys' school with Vanessa. She wants to take in 8 small boys, a tutor and a governess next summer, so as to avoid public schools, and has already both tutor and governess in view, and now only wants small boys, but that's the difficulty, because one can't imagine any morbidly careful parents—say the Trevelyans—trusting their children to grow up in a happy state without passing examinations, and only learning sensible things. She's got a Mrs Brereton to make a start—a wife separated from a husband who's a clergyman.

Isn't it appalling to find what wits the younger generation have? They begin asking questions about the Roman Empire, and whatever one may say, there's something about a mind which hasn't been used at all which makes one shudder at the degradation of human beings. In fact I believe the only hope for the world is to put all children of all countries together on an island and let them start fresh without knowing what a hideous system we have invented here. All the things they're interested in seem to me sensible and not half pretence, as ours are for the most part. I mean honours, degrees, and governments and so on. Or would they hark back to the same ways of their own accord?

We've had our usual prophecies from Maynard Keynes, but these officials have to knock up something definite to say and so are always proved wrong—He says L. George is on his last legs, only no one can stand up to him, such is his fascination; and the country is practically ruined, and no one, after another year, will have more than 2,000 a year—but what does it amount to? We did our best to persuade both Maynard and Ka that if they stay any longer in offices they will be lost to humanity—as indeed I think they almost are. They can't help believing in a system which pays them £700, or whatever it may be.

However, I must stop; why is it so pleasant to damn one's friends?

Love to Lilian.

Yr. V.W.

Sussex

902: To Violet Dickinson   *Hogarth House, Richmond*

Jan. 14th [1918]

My Violet,

Leonard's brother has gone on very well—in fact I think he's leaving his convalescent home this week—I'm afraid he's pretty wretched.[1]

They [Cecil and Philip] had always done everything together and I don't know how he'll get on alone.

We are hard at work printing a long story [*Prelude*] by a woman called Katherine Mansfield. I think it'll be out by Easter, and I shall come round with my wares like a peddlar. It's very good I think; but the publisher wouldn't take it.

I hear about once a month from Aunt Minna. She is generally under the impression that we're coming to stay with her for the week end. Why should she ever die? It seems to me that no Duckworth need ever give way.

Shall you ever come and see us again? We are increasing our printing stock largely.

L sends his love, and hopes to see you.

Yr
Sp:

Berg

903: To Vanessa Bell   *Hogarth House, [Richmond]*

Jan. 17th [1918]

Dearest,

How nice it will be for you if I fill this entire page with gossip, as I mean to do. Before starting, I may tell you all the kind unselfish acts I've done in your behalf—some fruitless its true, but what is an act if judged by its fruit? Often no better than a rotten quince. Well—yesterday I went to Robersons and bought 3 1/2 lb: tubes of white paint. Mr Roberson was most attentive

1. On 2 December 1917 the Woolfs had heard that Leonard's brother Cecil had been killed, and another of his brothers, Philip, severely wounded. They had been hit by the same shell.

and charming, and remarked that several people had been in for white paint lately, which he would sell as long as he had any. The difficulty about paints is that they're made with oil, "Now you may not know that every gun when its first cast has to be dipped in a bath of oil, or after the first or second shot, I daresay, it would explode, for the outside cools quicker than the in. That means one thousand gallons of oil for each gun—and when the guns dipped in the oil, d'you think much oil is left? No, not a drop—But you come and ask me for what you want and I'll let you have it—"

Your brown paper books are sold out, but there may be others in a fortnight. As Mrs Grant refuses to tell me her watchmakers name, being doubtless a good deal upset still by the burglary and the Bird, I can't take any steps about your watch. Duncan's continues to go—only after being wound up though, I could of course ask if there's anything odd about that— How I've enjoyed that story! It shows signs of growth too. It is passing into the currency. I may say that the current into which I now drop my little . . (I *must* and *will* avoid what shocks Julian—although it would be vivid and picturesque to bring in here the [lavatory] seat which is always frozen at Charleston)—The centre of life I should say; is now undoubtedly the 17 Club. I'm going to give you tea there; and you may write a letter on stamped paper, and they have nibs, and real ink—the sort that runs, I mean. The chief disfigurements, if one dislikes ones friends, are Babs Hanning in a crimson dress like a servants petticoat, and you don't care about Faith [Henderson] I believe, but she's only sometimes there. Alix[1] however is quite invariable, and I suppose permanent now that she's been finally ousted from Gordon Square, which operation, she told me yesterday, was firmly carried out by Norton or Maynard or both. She is now trying to fix herself upon Fredegond [Shove]; and its like watching a poor silver fish enveloped by a mass of jelly fish, to hear them debating about a house which Alix wants to share, and Gerald [Shove] won't let Fredegond take with Alix, and Fredegond of course half promises, and Alix intones like a funeral bell, and becomes more and more insistent, though incapable of making up her own mind, or doing anything but cloud the entire aquarium for miles around. At length (this is a perfectly true scene, and happened yesterday) F: lost her head completely, beckoned me out of the room, and begged me to tell her whether she was to tell Alix the truth, or shift along with lies. My candid spirit had no doubt whatever. I said Alix must know the truth. I left F: to tell it her. It will be a blow; but Alix bears no malice, and I have a plan on foot for establishing her in Ormond Street above Saxon. Who knows? His gloom and her despair meeting may build a rainbow.

Saxon's gloom has now passed beyond a joke. And it is all connected with another scene on another day at the 17 Club. Now here we come to

1. Alix Sargant-Florence had been staying at 46 Gordon Square with Maynard Keynes and H. T. J. Norton.

delicate matters which must *not* be shouted across the table next time Barbara stays with you. I had just finished my toast, bought my cigarette, and dared Lytton to break up a party of Cambridge intellects gathered round the other fire—yes, you must be told about them. First theres Hogben the poet;[1] a youth of genius; a shock headed but fresh coloured ardent man of perhaps 22, either hiding from the Police or a C. O. He is always at the Club, and he always has a play in a despatch box by his side; and when more than four are gathered round him, he will take this play out of the box, and after a little persuasion will lend it to a stout girl with a very large pipe. This being done, a second girl with an enormous cleft in one cheek, coloured grey, since identified, (and I've no doubt the fact's responsible for the cleft,) as Jos Wedgwood's daughter, throws herself on her knees and begs to be lent the play too. Hogben lends it. Next time they all get together and say how unconventional it is, and how the public can't be expected to understand, though to my elderly and sarcastic view, the public would swallow the whole of them without turning a hair.

Well, I dared Lytton to break in upon them, which he did, by lingering ostentatiously in the background, and was soon in the chair next Hogben, whose hair by the way practically grows into his left eye, so you'll know *him* when you see him.

This being arranged Faith, Fredegond and I had some intimate discourse about Barbara and her faithful troop. Poor Nick, they say, is moping and pining and longing to pull out all Saxon's feathers, and no wonder. Under the shield of immaculate altruism, that old wretch has won the prize, and refuses to own that he has, and makes an elaborate pretence of sharing, which is vinegar to Poor Nick, who is too high minded to protest, and has to agree to be a disembodied Saint. Barbara ended the time at Asheham by refusing Nick once more, and takes no pains to hide the fact that she prefers Saxon, always has Saxon about when Nick comes to town, and means to marry neither. I've no doubt that Faith makes this blacker and bitterer than it need be, and if one should prefer Saxon, then there's no help for it; but at the root of it, still according to Faith, there is nothing but a perverted wish to do what Bloomsbury approves.

The Bloomsbury hypnotism, I may say, is rank, and threatens the sanity of all the poor Bunnies,[2] who are perpetually feeling their hind legs to see if they haven't turned into hares. I tried tactfully to explain to Faith that once a Bunny, always a Bunny; and what great Bloomsbury respects is the

1. Lancelot Hogben, the scholar and writer of popular scientific books, including *Mathematics for the Million* (1936). As a very young man, he also published a book of poems, *Exiles of the Snow*.
2. The 'Bloomsbury Bunnies', or 'Cropheads', was a current term among them for their younger women friends, including Carrington, Alix Sargant-Florence, Brett, Barbara Hiles and Faith Henderson.

recognition by the B's that they are Bs. But they're going through a terrible season of delusion. Barbara can't bear that Nick should be seen with her in Bloomsbury. That is the height of his ambition; a dinner with Maynard would glorify him for ever. He is very humble, a devout admirer, and has taken to reading hard in order to qualify. For my part, I'm going to ask him here, to show my deep respect for him, and then casually and tactfully to assure Barbara that she's worthy of him neither in brain nor in education. You and Duncan can imagine how gracefully this will be done. Now Saxon droops because he's discovered that human nature is fallible; if only she didn't prefer him, he'd be quite happy. I can't help thinking that there *is* something rather sublime about us. I often feel very sublime myself—Odd, disconnected thoughts of undoubted spiritual beauty come upon me unawares.

Your lost Cockatoo [Clive] (a lady in Hammersmith[1] is offering a suitable reward for a lost Green Lovebird) came here last Sunday, with Gerald and Fredegond and we had a fine gossip. They carry out all I say about Bloomsbury hypnotism. F. and G. went over to Tidmarsh the other day, and after tea Lytton and Carrington left the room ostensibly to copulate; but suspicion was aroused by a measured sound proceeding from the room, and on listening at the keyhole it was discovered that they were reading aloud Macaulays Essays! Barbara herself has finished vol. 2 of Tom Jones, and hopes by persevering to see it through next summer in the tent at Charleston.

Sunday.

Barbara and Nick came last night, and its perfectly true what I say about his intelligence and education. He described Erasmus. Barbara thought he meant Erasmus Darwin who was killed; not a bit of it; he also talked about Cardinal Mazarin; and the works of Synge. But my tender heart was distressed to hear that Bunny has infected you all with his disease [influenza]. Barbara was rather vague, and thought that Duncan and Julian and possibly you were all ill in some way. Please send a line to say if this is so. She had just seen Bunny, looking very ill, and saying that he had been ill off and on since the day I was there.

This has so dashed my spirits that I think I will end here, and keep Lady Strachey and one or two other small fragments for another time, so that I can send this off, and you may let me have a line, whichever of you is able to write. The only interesting incident, however, with Lady S: was my terrible faux pas: "Have you yet been to Tidmarsh, Lady S.?"

She became perfectly glum and stony: and said at length, to L: "Well, what d'you think of it all?"

L: thinking she meant the relationship between Lytton and Carrington

1. Where Mary Hutchinson was living.

was beginning a long account of his views on buggery, when we realised
that she was changing the conversation to the food famine!

Yr B.

Do you want the white paint sent, or shall I keep it until you come?

Berg

904: To Lady Ottoline Morrell　*Hogarth House, Richmond*

[24 January 1918]

My dear Ottoline
　Of course every horror seems to settle itself upon Thursday, but we hope
to come, if not tonight, next time.
　I should like to come to tea, if I can find my way—perhaps Tuesday
might suit you—but here I am writing with a pen point in circumstances
which rasp and desiccate the soul—One does pray that there *is* some
difference between us and them[1]—(or rather me and them—you don't fit in
at all).

Yr.
V.W.

Texas

905: To Vanessa Bell　　*Hogarth [House, Richmond]*

Tuesday [29 January 1918]

Dearest,
　I now begin another letter, partly that should I die tonight you may
know that my last thoughts were of you. Not that you care—but think of all
the gossip you'd miss—yes, that touches the one sensitive spot. My chief
item—Barbara—is stale by this time. I daresay you've written her an ex-
pressive letter in your best style. She burst in this morning saying she was
going to be married on Friday. With consummate presence of mind I
exclaimed "Then you've chosen the right man!" I hadn't the least notion
which. She said "Yes, its Nick." So I said "Of course Nick's the right man",
and she said, "Yes, he's the right man to marry, but Saxon is very wonderful
as a friend. And its not going to make the least difference to any of us. We've
all discussed it, and we're all agreed, and we're going to Tidmarsh for the
honeymoon, and Carrington and Lytton'll be there—which makes it all the
nicer." I cant say I altogether understand the young; I'm not sure, I mean,

1. Virginia was writing this letter from the 1917 Club.

213

that I dont see a reversion to the devoted submission of our grandmothers. Do you think she's in love? Isn't she merely doing what will make him happy? However the sober sense of it all is sublime; in many ways this method of abolishing private property in love has its exaltation. Perhaps it doesn't imply the highest mental gifts; one might hint at physical deficiencies; or do you think that absolute sublimity in emotion is reserved for eunuchs? Think of the three of them discussing the question over the stove in her studio, and Nick saying "No, Saxon: you must marry her;" and Saxon refusing to be happy save in their happiness, and Barbara suggesting copulation with each on alternate nights, but at once realising her own selfishness and saying she'd marry either—only it must be the one she didn't most want to—Or how did they settle it? I'm told Saxon has written a full account to you.

Thursday. Well, you almost lost me. Nine bombs on Kew; 7 people killed in one house, a hotel crushed—but not a hair of Wattie's [Walter Lamb] head was touched. I know raids dont interest you when no one you know is killed, so I won't describe our night in the kitchen. Barbara was with us and we all slept on the floor—We have mattresses laid there every night. Talking to the servants from 8 to 1.15 (as we did the first time) is so boring—"but not so boring as a description" as you justly remark—so I pass rapidly to Ottoline.

She is up for a few days, and sent for me, I rather thought with a view to extracting something.

Friday.

To continue. Imagine Ottoline in a small triangular bedroom, at the top of a Bloomsbury hotel; dressed in black velvet which was dusty, and looking much like a shop walker in Marshall and Snellgroves. I suppose the light was bad for painting; it was amazingly visible; and a piece of cotton wool had got stuck in her hair; but she wore a great enamelled plate with pearls attached, round her neck. We sat on bedroom chairs and had tea out of a pewter pot, and there was practically no room for anything but a po-cupboard and a large double bed.

I didn't find any particular reason why she should want to see me—her only anxiety seemed to be that Leonard might stand as a Cooperative member which is apparently her ambition for Philip—Or he may become a writer—I suppose the truth is she must provide him with something to keep him from home. She is coming to town for 3 weeks. I think Fredegond's desertion has alarmed her slightly, and she wants to spread her net over another shoal of fish. But she's got Murry back again, so that's forgiven me.

15 *lines omitted*

. . . .

. . . .

After Ottoline, what on Earth's surface am I to tell you about? You see I go round pocketing small eatables for you. (This week we are without meat and butter; are you too?) Well, old Desmond [MacCarthy] turned up the other day, and I have scented a minute romance for you—I'm afraid only a figment, but still better than nothing. Did you ever meet a woman called Enid Bagnold[1]—would be clever, and also smart? who went to Ottoline's parties, and now lives at Woolwich and nurses soldiers? "That disagreeable chit?" Yes, that is my opinion too. But she has evidently enmeshed poor old Desmond. She has written a book, called, as you can imagine, "A diary without dates", all to prove that she's the most attractive, and popular and exquisite of creatures—all her patients fall in love with her—her feet are the smallest in Middlesex—one night she missed her Bus and a soldier was rude to her in the dark—that sort of thing. Desmond insists that I shall review it in the Times. First he writes a letter; then he comes and dines; then he gives me the book; then he invites me to lunch with a Prince Bibesco,[2] who is apparently one of Bagnolds lovers; then he writes again—and every visit and letter ends with the same command—For God's sake review this book!

So far I have resisted; but I don't know that Desmond's charms won't overcome me in time. The Roumanian Prince too has the most exquisite voice. To charm me further, Desmond rang him up, and I listened—but the appalling thing is that Desmond is now, whether from drink, Bagnold or bankruptcy in such a state of dissolution that one has to be very careful what one says. In the middle of a silence, he suddenly starts up and cries out, "O dear! O dear! O dear!" something father used to do. I guess that Molly's novel has been refused. I suspect that he has finally lost or burnt his proof

1. The novelist and playwright, who was then 28. *A Diary Without Dates* was her first book.
2. Prince Antoine Bibesco, the grandson of the reigning Prince of Roumania. His career was in diplomacy, but he was also a playwright and edited the letters of Marcel Proust. In 1919 he married Elizabeth Asquith, the daughter of the former Prime Minister.

sheets; and then, as he says, he feels it incumbent on him to eat and drink as much as he can when he dines out, so that his digestion is ruined.

Bagnold has said to him "Now I won't kiss you" (or whatever it is they do) "until you've got my book reviewed in the Times." Bagnold has him in her toils.

The question is, am I a match for Bagnold? You would be, of course, but then I'm so susceptible. Bagnold paints too.

I must bring this to an end, which will be most gracefully done on the subject of kindness to sisters. I took your watch, to the wrong man. But how can there be two watchmakers on Poland St one called Pilfduck, and the other Pfalmer? Pilfduck is my discovery; and according to Pilfduck the balance wheel of your watch is worn out, and no one in England can mend it until the war is over. So I brought it back, and Barbara, enchanted to be of the least service to you who are her moon of women and phoenix of desire, has now taken it to Pfalmer, who is quite different, she says, from Pilfduck, though I should prefer Pilfduck if it were a question of my watch which by the way it now is. Still there's Duncan's watch ticking away in my room—which is not what a watch should do, and if he likes I'll take it to Pilfduck and we'll—but this sort of thing doesn't really amuse you, as you say.

The general sentiment is always to the effect that you are the most beautiful and gifted of our friends. Your withdrawal has only veiled you with mystery. I am sometimes welcomed as the Toad who has heard the nightingale's song. Several people have told me that your picture of the enormous women was a revelation to them. Thank God, I say, that she doesn't write. Ask Julian why we should be glad that cows dont fly:[1] and tell him that I am going to send him a birthday present—only what?

How are you? Influenza, [Dr] Craig told me, poisons the nervous system, and nourishment is the only way to get rid of it. Do take milk and ovaltine. I have 2 glasses a day.

Yr

B.

Berg

1. "Birdie, birdie in the sky,
   Dropped some doo-doo in my eye.
   Gosh, I'm glad that cows don't fly!"
   (*Traditional children's rhyme.*)

Hogarth House, Paradise Road,
Richmond, Surrey

Tuesday [19 February 1918]

My dear Clive,

I haven't seen such a splendid bunch of grapes since the early nineties
when such gifts were not uncommon in our circles. The pink paper brought
it all back. The grapes were delicious.

We are off to Asheham this afternoon. We have spent the last 3 nights
more or less in the cellar, though there wasn't much need, but when the
servants take cover I can't help thinking what an irony if they should escape
and we be killed.

I hear Molly's novel is taken; the Shoves have broken loose, and it is
rumoured that you have bought the Egoist,[1] and engaged Bob T. [Trevelyan]
permanently as your poet.

Yr. V.W.

Quentin Bell

907: To Margaret Llewelyn Davies

Hogarth House, Paradise Road,
Richmond, Surrey

Tuesday [19 February 1918]

Dearest Margaret,

It was a great delight to get your letter, though tantalising to be told
that you would come and see me, when I couldn't get the dr. to allow it. Of
course I said you didn't count—were hardly visible and spiritually insignificant—No good. And now I hear you've collapsed and gone off to an Inn[2]
where Leonard and I had tea one January afternoon, and saw a trout farm.

We are off to Asheham today. Its as cold as—what is the opposite of
Hell? We had a very distant raid last night; the third running, so that we
merely go to bed in the kitchen and wait till its over. Even the servants are
getting used to it and play patience on a wooden box dressed in macintoshes,
in the midst of the coal.

Its a great nuisance having to go away just as we were at last getting
ahead with our printing. Our next effort will be a book of woodcuts by
Carrington and fables by Lytton Strachey. That I'm sure you'll like. I agree
with you about Clive. Most people are mixed, but I've never seen anyone
quite so jumbled as he is. One of the poems [in *Ad Familiares*] I thought
really good—the last one. And now he writes to the Cambridge Review to
say that he adores the ladies! I dont expect you make enough allowance for

1. See p. 215, note 1.
2. The Abinger Hatch Hotel, Dorking, Surrey.

the complexity of the literary temperament, though. Social workers have their particular vanity—hah! you can't contradict me! but then they huddle it up in a general cloud of benevolence to their kind.

I could go on upon this theme, but here's L: to make me get ready.

We both send our love. Get well.

Yr. V.W.

Sussex

908: TO VANESSA BELL

Asheham, [Rodmell, Sussex]

Saturday [23 February 1918]

Dearest,

Dont bother about the milk as we've now persuaded the Dairy at Southease to let us have a quart a day. I am shocked to think that it was only what you call your monthlies that prevented you from bicycling here and back with a can round your neck. I wish I could impress on you some of the remarks about influenza and the nervous system which I had to hear every day from [Dr] Fergusson.[1] You certainly mustn't come unless you can spend the night. I doubt whether Leonard is going to London; if he does it will be either Monday or Tuesday; but couldn't you come any day next week, and spend the night, and then we could gossip together all the morning in my room?

I think we shall go back next Friday or Saturday. I would offer to come to you for a night, but I'm expecting my affairs; they're already overdue, and I've had to promise to spend 2 days recumbent in future. You see, I'm rapidly becoming like poor Mrs Litchfield, whose doctor called every morning, but it isn't altogether my fault. In fact I've been grumbling a good deal—I'm not allowed even to work yet, which is the pit of Hell as you'll agree.

I had a mysterious letter from Fredegond yesterday; there is a wonderful piece of gossip abroad, she says, too risky to send in a letter. The only possible victim this time seems to me to be Norton; perhaps he's engaged to Pernel Strachey; or there's Ka; or perhaps Alix may have taken a turn—Do you know the facts? Gerald has been offered 2 jobs in London—and I hear from Karin that Adrian's tribunal want him to go back to work on the land.

We had a very melancholy letter from Saxon. He says that the sight of married happiness is at present too much for him,[2] and so he hadn't been to see us, but he does not mean to go on being unhappy—poor old wretch.

However I mustn't part with all my crumbs, or I shall never tempt my gilded dolphin to the surface.

1. Virginia had just been in bed for a week with influenza.
2. Barbara Hiles had married Nicholas Bagenal on 1 February.

You must teach Julian Greek. I find my chief consolation now in making out Greek plays, and even with what I know its quite worth while. Besides, it would be something to break his teeth against.

He wrote me a very charming letter. I think he has the Stephen gift of language (not that its much to boast of—) by the way I've been in communication with Mrs [Reginald] Smith about some of father's manuscripts— I'm also in touch both with Gerald Duckworth and with Waller.[1] These crumbs are artfully scattered on the rim of the deep lake, and I have already counted 3 bubbles which show that the spangled monster is meditating whether to rise—or not.

We hope Bunny will come over to any meal tomorrow. We're well supplied with food. As Duncan knows—but I expect he wants to paint.

V.W.

Berg

909: TO VANESSA BELL   *Asheham, [Rodmell, Sussex]*

Monday [25 February 1918]

Dearest,

It will be enchanting to see you on Thursday. We shall expect you for tea. I'm sorry we didn't let you know about the milk before; I thought my letter would reach you on Sunday morning. Trissie [Vanessa's cook] says you've kept some for us—which doesn't mean, I hope, that you've stinted yourselves—so Leonard may come over tomorrow and fetch it.

We are going on Friday, I think, but we are seriously considering whether we shant come back here for good, or anyhow for the moons, as its so delicious. We might possibly bring our little press down. But we can certainly let you have the blankets. I forget how many you want. As long as you could send them back in case we came you could have all we've got.

I suppose the country can't always be so nice—but at present it seems to me like a perpetual dance of the nymphs—which is exactly to my taste. But thats partly because of my sense of the presence behind the hill of the great mother of all the familiars—Didn't we have one once called Quince? There was Pert and Wilson and Peter Wombat who went to earth at Ely of course; and poor Mango, who died, and a red-haired one; delightful creatures! Happily they're all well and fairly randy at present, owing to the season of the year—but what can one expect?—

1. John Waller Hills, the widower of Stella, Virginia's half-sister. He was a solicitor. Virginia consulted him and her half-brother Gerald Duckworth (the publisher) about the sale through Sotheby's of the Thackeray and Meredith letters written to her father, as well as some of Leslie Stephen's own manuscripts.

219

It seems to me that Comedy has never been quite so bold in her advances as when she planted you and your establishment down at Charleston. Think of the arrival of Fossdyke,[1] or whatever his name is, tomorrow! Fate having touched his wits is such a fine conception too—but I must stop.

We can give you enough blankets for *one* bed to take back on Friday.

Yr

B

Berg

910: TO SAXON SYDNEY-TURNER

Asheham, [*Rodmell,*
Sussex]

Feb. 25th [1918]

Dearest Saxon,

Neither of us (I speak for myself at least) was 'hurt' by the silence between us, in the sense, that is, of thinking that it implied any change of affection; I'm afraid whatever you do or don't do you'll never shake my absolute trust in *that*; but a sense of your being possibly unhappy did hang about us and make us wish in spite of knowing that you did not know what we felt, to see you, or hear of you or have you in the room. I don't think that being happy makes one want ones friends less—Is this partly selfish? Perhaps it is; but not all your craft shall persuade me that my feeling for you has more than a thread of vice in it; the rest is heavenly true.

Perhaps you dont realise that those are Shakespeare's words.[2] I'm thinking of reading Measure for Measure this afternoon, and I wish you could be here, and then we'd ramble on about all sorts of things. I daresay you share my feeling that Asheham is the best place in the world for reading Shakespeare. Asheham is very lovely at this moment. I started upon Sophocles the day after we came—the Electra, which has made me plan to read all Greek straight through. Why doesn't one? why shouldn't we combine? I suppose life's too short or too merciless for such felicity—what with the trains going so early, and human nature being so imperfect: (this refers to myself, I need hardly say.) Still, the classics *are* very pleasant, and even, I must confess, the mortals. I found great consolation during the influenza in the works of Leonard Merrick,[3] a poor unappreciated second rate pot-boiling writer of stories about the stage, whom I deduce to be a negro, mulatto or quadroon; at any rate he has a grudge against the world, and might have done much better if he hadn't at the age of 20 married a chorus girl, had by

1. The tutor whose arrival Virginia had forecast in her letter of 2 January. His real name was Henry Moss.
2. "Oh she was heavenly true" (*Othello*).
3. Review of *While Paris Laughed* and *Conrad in Quest of his Youth*, by Leonard Merrick (*TLS*, 4 July 1918).

her 15 coffee coloured brats and lived for the rest of the time in a villa in Brixton, where he ekes out his living by giving lessons in elocution to the natives—Now if this were about a Greek writer, it would be what is called constructive criticism, wouldn't it? I'm not at all pleased with Jebb[1] by the way, he never risks anything in his guesses: his sense of language seems to me stiff, safe, prosaic and utterly impossible for any Greek to understand. Now surely they launched out into flowering phrases not strictly related, much as Shakespeare did. Jebb splits them up into separate and uncongenial accuracies. But I'm too lazy to look up the particular one I mean: something about an old man's hair. I can remember Jebb coming to dinner with us, and sitting at the far end of the room with Nessa and Thoby. I there and then saw and perhaps said that he had the soul and innumerable legs of a black beetle. I am appalled at the number of things I can remember. Meredith, Henry James; a great many others too, if I could think of their names; Lowell, Mrs Humphry Ward; Herbert Spencer, once; John Addington Symonds, and any number of Watts', Burne Jones' and Leightons.

Its so nice writing to you that I just run on, and it strikes me that this may seem to you not only foolish, which I don't mind, but lacking in understanding, which I should mind—I've been sitting in the garden all the afternoon, reading Measure for Measure, looking at the trees, and thinking as much of you as of anything. I suppose it would be merely silly to try to say *what* one thinks of you—moreover I hope that by this time you know.

Nessa is coming over on Thursday for the night. The new tutor arrives [at Charleston] tomorrow. I gather that he is recovering from a nervous breakdown, which is supposed to give him a chance of suiting the general atmosphere. I think we come back either on Friday or Saturday—If you want to come, do; but if you don't want to we shall take it for granted that you'll say whenever you do.

Yrs.
V.W.

Sussex

911: To Vanessa Bell   *Asheham, [Rodmell, Sussex]*

Tuesday [26 February 1918]

Dearest,

If you liked I could come back with you on Friday and spend the night, as Leonard has just heard that he must go back to London early on Friday morning. I could then help you to cart the blankets too. However, there's no

1. R. C. Jebb's edition of Sophocles appeared in seven volumes (1883-96).

need to let me know until you come—The servants were just starting for Charleston—but they now find they can't get Mrs Hammonds bicycle, so I must send this by post. You must tell me what you spent on the milk.

Yr

Berg   B.

912: TO KATHERINE COX   *Asheham, [Rodmell.*
Sussex]

27th Feb. [1918]

Dearest Ka,

I think it would have been the part of a good Bruin to write to me. Rumour has it that you've been decorated with an order of the British Empire,[1] and that after having this attached by King George's own hand, you ascend to a higher stool in an upper storey of a larger building in Whitehall. People are said to be jealous of you, and £500 a year is the least you earn. I've had to live on nothing but rumour the last fortnight, having spent 8 days in bed with influenza and come down here to recover. Thats another reason why you should have written. I believe though you're in the country; I hope you may be. Its very much better than the Strand at this moment. We sat through three raids on three nights running; and seriously think of moving down here for the rest of the war. Its not the noise I mind, but the infernal boredom of kitchen conversation.

Since we've been here I've read perhaps 20 books and not exchanged a rational word with any human being (I dont count Leonard, or servants, or cat). I can't say that I should mind the tap of a claw upon the drawing room window, followed by the soft bulk of the brute's body. Nessa comes tomorrow having now acquired a male teacher called Fossdyke [Moss] to supplement Mrs Brereton. He is touched in the head, which is said to be no disqualification and may even make him feel more readily at home. Then there's all poor Saxon's sorrow to be discussed; are you one of those who implored Barbara at the last moment to hold? Nessa put the case against marriage very forcibly, I'm told, her letter arriving on the wedding morning, and she still predicts the worst—openly, to all three of them. I've no room to give my opinions; which are subtle, searching and comprehensive; but there's not an atom of doubt but that poor old Saxon is as unhappy as he can be. Having said he didn't mind of course makes it all the worse. I'm in perfect health again and we come back on Saturday, hoping one day soon to see our glorious and be-ribboned Bear.

Yrs
V.W.

Mark Arnold-Forster

1. Ka was offered the O.B.E. in the Birthday Honours for her services in Corsica among the refugees, but she declined it.

March 8th [1918]

Dearest,

I've just had this letter from Fergusson. I'm afraid it isn't very helpful. How would it be, by the way, to try Lytton's dr, Dr Brinton, who lives in Kensington and is said to be very good? I believe the Vaughans have a very good doctor; and also there was Dr Venning, [Dr Edward] Horts partner, who came to Adrian once, and attended Barbara Vaughan.[1] But I'm afraid this is rather vague. I could find out more if you liked.

Life in London seems to me slightly tepid. We had a raid last night, though there's no moon. It sounded as if something blew up, but there are only the wildest rumours about at present. It lasted about 2 hours and went round and round us—

Nick came and gave his lecture the other night,[2] and seemed very much in love, very proud of the fact that Barbara made a conquest of an auctioneer in Gloucestershire; and I can't see that he differs from any other newly married husband. I've talked with Saxon on the telephone, and couldn't detect any signs of despair, but it was mostly details about health—you've heard, I suppose, that he's setting up with Alix in Faiths house? I met her at the 17 Club, more sunk than ever; and I think a little suspicious that the world would laugh at two rejected lovers[3] keeping house—Imagine how they'll compare notes! Saxon was only afraid, she said, that he'd depress her, but I think the race is nearly equal; in fact, I'd back Alix. I did my best to be very liberal, low in tone, and dismal myself; I find its my good spirits that makes her and Fredegond so melancholy. Barbara and Nick are giving a party and were set upon having you—even Nick's voice is now that of the true Charlestonian; reverent, awestruck, grateful for trifles— even a smart rap on the snout is better than nothing. Shall you go? My husband is a good deal against my going, and the trains make it rather hopeless of course. But his tone about Charleston is distinctly modified. He was very amiable about you when I came back. An invitation would completely convert him I believe—though he's so odd in this mood that one can never tell.

I wish my life promised many mornings alone with you and Duncan. But I'm not a Charlestonian of course; my devotion is founded upon reason,

1. The third child of Madge and William Wyamar Vaughan, who died as a child.
2. Nicholas Bagenal had lectured on his war experiences to the Richmond Branch of the Women's Co-operative Guild.
3. Saxon had been rejected by Barbara, and Alix Sargant-Florence, temporarily, by James Strachey.

and you both know what a solid diamond that is. Consider what it'll be too when I've been Pelmanized.

Love to Moss and B. They are a perpetual delight to me.[1]

Yr

Berg   B.

914: To Lytton Strachey   *Hogarth House, Paradise Road,*
                                          Richmond, Surrey

15th March [1918]

Couldn't it be arranged that you should come to Asheham on Thursday 28th, stay over Monday and go on to Charleston? We have felt bound to ask Barbara who has been rejected by Vanessa, but she is half engaged to Tidmarsh [Lytton] apparently, and if Carrington exerted a little pressure I think she would yield.

I've been having faint doubts, by the way, about reviewing your book. In the first place, if I review yours, then why not Clive's, Desmond's, Molly's and Fredegond's,[2] which would be more than I could stand. In the second, I was rather snubbed by Bruce Richmond[3] the other day, who thought, wrongly, that I was trying to get a friend's book reviewed, and told me it wasn't considered the thing to do—so I don't much like asking him. But these reasons aren't serious if you think it would be a real advantage. My feeling is that no review counts either way as far as making money is concerned. But I suppose you're certain of a long and flattering review anyhow. Mine would be highly flattering, of course. It's quite possible, though, that he'll send it me of his own accord.

I hope you got off safely today. We had an appalling Sunday—incessant chatter, or rather incessant gloom, and such spots on Saxon's face, such morose stupidity on Gerald Duckworth's—the only person with a spark of spunk was poor Nick, who pretended, I suppose. Katherine Mansfield has been dangerously ill,[4] and is still pretty bad, so that [Middleton] Murry was sunk in the depths, what with that and overwork, poor wretch.

Yr.
V.W.

With or without Barbara we hope you'll come.

Frances Hooper

1. Henry Moss and Mrs Brereton, whom Virginia suspected of having an affair.
2. The books Virginia mentions are: Lytton Strachey, *Eminent Victorians;* Clive Bell, *Pot-Boilers;* Desmond MacCarthy, *Remnants;* Mary ('Molly') MacCarthy, *A Pier and a Band;* and Fredegond Shove, *Dreams and Journeys.*
3. Editor of *The Times Literary Supplement.*
4. In France, with a haemorrhage of the lung.

Hogarth House, Paradise Road,
                                          Richmond, Surrey

Tuesday [19 March 1918]

Dearest

Do you want to sell the Meredith letter to you on father's death, which was printed?[1] I didn't put it up with the others, and now it strikes me you might think it better to sell it too—If so, would you let me have a line *at once*? I'm taking the Thackeray Ms. and the 1st edition of Modern Love [Meredith] and the letters to Sotheby today. L. wrote to them and they advise us to sell now, as they say that people are giving very high prices. In fact, I see that a Thackeray letter sold for £84 the other day.

I thought we might rake up a few more letters and books and send them later. But I'd better send your letter with the others I expect.

I shall ask their advice as to what reserve to put—also whether they think its any good selling father's mss. wh. L. doubts.

I cant think what happened to our telephone—it was working all right this end. However I could hardly have come, as we've been working at a book of Cecil Woolf's poems[2] and only just got them done.

I was never told that the day of the party was changed, so we went to the opera, but I don't suppose I should have gone anyhow. Lytton says that you and Fredegond were the success of the evening—incredibly brilliant—I wish I'd been there to see Dolphin balancing on her nose. We had an incredible visit from Gerald: also Saxon, Nick, Barbara and Murry—but I must tell you later—

I must rush off. We are hoping to get milk at Southease.

                                          Yr
                                            B.

I'll try to bring the clothes.

Berg

Asheham, [Rodmell,
                                          Sussex]

Friday [22 March 1918]

We now find it impossible to get any milk at all. We should be very grateful if you could help us. If your man could leave some at Glynde every other day we could go and fetch it—the more the better. It would be very

1. In the Sotheby sale, there was one letter from Meredith to Vanessa, which fetched £1.10.0. All the Leslie Stephen MSS fetched only £1.8.0. See p. 258.
2. A small posthumous volume of Leonard's brother's poems, which the Woolfs printed on the Hogarth Press for private distribution.

kind of you if you would explain to Nelly any way of getting some;[1] and could you be so angelic as to give her a drop (if you can spare any) to bring back. The man at Southease promised to let us have more this time, so we thought ourselves safe. He says its the lambs, however, and I'm afraid you may have run dry too.

I suppose our best way of meeting would be to walk to Firle and have a picnic there some afternoon, but I don't know what your circumstances are.

Lytton is coming here next Thursday for Easter and wants to stay on if you cant have him, which he's not certain of. As we have James [Strachey] and Noel [Olivier] coming the Tuesday after Easter, I rather hope you may be able to take him in—however, we can manage if you cant. Barbara may be coming, but I think there's a chance she'll go to Tidmarsh.

I got your letter in time and sent the Meredith letter with the rest. I saw Sotheby, who seemed to think highly of our chances with the Thackeray ms; he also advised us strongly to sell fathers' mss. and said they were of distinct value, so I sent him the Hours in a Library and Playground of Europe ones. The sale won't be till May, so I could send him some books when I go back. I sent Modern Love. He said that one couldn't say what things are worth, as they never know what people will give.

Yr
B.

Gunn has just been and says he can supply us [milk] at Glynde—but if you could let us have any today we shd. be very grateful. You must tell Nelly what it costs.

Berg

917: To James Strachey   *Asheham House, Rodmell,*
                                            Lewes

March 24th 1918

Dear James,

I think you had better find out what the trains are in April. They haven't changed so far. If you want a taxi to meet you at Lewes, you had better order one from

the County Garage
High St. Lewes,

if a fly, from

Slaughter,
Friars Walk,
Lewes.

1. In the original this first part of the letter has been crossed out.

I'm afraid you'll have to bring whatever cards for meat, sugar, butter you possess as we are strictly rationed here. Also could you let me know whether you'll be staying on after Thursday or Friday, so that I can arrange with a woman to do for you? Our present female believes, on what authority I don't know, that she is going to have a baby, but there is another I could get, if you'd tell me.

It is more than usually divine here.

Your
V.W.

Strachey Trust

918: To Lytton Strachey   *Asheham, [Rodmell,*
                                                        Sussex]

Sunday [24 March 1918]

We look forward with great pleasure to seeing you on Thursday: any time. As far as I know the trains are unchanged, we came by a very good one, 5.20 from Victoria, which connects almost exactly with another to Glynde, so that you get here for dinner. If you want to drive, you can order a fly from

Slaughter,
Friar's Walk,
Lewes

or a taxi from

County Garage,
High St,
Lewes

Perhaps you wouldn't mind handing this on to Barbara who seems to be staying with you. Our only difficulty is that we are strictly rationed—thus, I think if you want meat, sugar or butter you must bring your cards. According to Leonard, it is easy to make these available at Lewes. The question of food is the only drawback to your staying on, which we should like you to do. With Noel and James in the house you might find yourself starved—But by the time you come we may have made better arrangements.

It's all very well to come to the country in order to write, but the animals are carrying on so frantically and indecently that I can't hear myself speak. Lambs, thrushes, ewes, rooks—their conduct too is distracting. I find that scarcely anything but impassioned meditation stands up against it, and the passion tends to run much in a groove. D'you find that too? It's true, [J.S.] Mill on Liberty mayn't be the proper channel. But what divine days life holds, to be sure. Duncan has just been in, in corduroy breeches and gaiters, mumbling in his inspired way, like the first born of the human race, not yet entirely conscious.

Do bring some manuscript to read.

Yrs.
V.W.

Frances Hooper

919: To James Strachey   *Asheham House, Rodmell, Lewes*

March 27th [1918]

Dear James,

There need be no difficulty about the cards—anyhow in your case—All you have to do is to get your cook at Belsize [Park] to get you a week's rations of butter, sugar and meat which you pack in your bag and bring with you. The alternative is to get the meat from our butcher in Lewes, but to do this you'd have to go to the Food Control Office, West St, Lewes, and get yourself transferred for a week—which is perfectly easy to do, and then we'd pay for your meat with ours, which justice requires. Our Butcher is Marsh in the High St. But I believe you'd find it simpler to get your rations from your usual source and bring them. You cant get either butter or sugar in Lewes, so my cook says, so those anyhow you had better bring. We can supply all the other things, save meat, but don't fling out of your house in a temper if you find our diet dull. I'll write to Noel [Olivier] and try to explain some scheme for her—though I dont see why a dr. differs from the rest[1]—It will be quite easy for you to stay on till Monday 8th—grave doubt is now cast upon the pregnancy [of the daily woman]—in fact her health is better than ever—Noel might examine into the matter.

I suppose nothing would induce you to bring a few Rupert [Brooke] letters?

Yrs
V.W.

I've now read your letter properly and see you say teatime.

Strachey Trust

920: To Vanessa Bell   *Asheham, [Rodmell, Sussex]*

Wednesday [27 March 1918]

Dearest,

Its odd we didn't meet yesterday. I was in Lewes too. I went from Glynde.

1. Noel Olivier had qualified as a doctor in 1917.

228

It would, I needn't say, be enchanting to see you, but I really dont think its worth your coming all that way—and the weather seems broken too—only for tea. Couldn't you come for lunch and go back after tea or dinner? We have a bed free in spite of Lytton and Barbara, and the best thing of all would be for you to stay the night—Surely Mrs B[rereton]: can run the house? Otherwise I was going to have suggested first that I should come for the night—which, I leave to you; second, that we should have a picnic at Firle on Sunday if fine. Barbara stays till Tuesday, and wd. of course grasp at any chance of the Charleston heights. I hope to God Nick isn't already killed.

I've told all my visitors that they must either bring meat, sugar and butter, or their cards. James says this is very difficult, but I dont see why. One can get an emergency card at Lewes quite easily. Lytton hasn't got any cards I believe, but I'm hoping he'll bring his own supplies. I told him he must, and if you like I'll explain that you're rationed just as we are. They could get what they liked at Tidmarsh.

It'll suit us quite well if you have him on Wednesday. Noel and James come on Tuesday and stay on after we go. My affairs were too damnable on Sunday; they've taken to being punctual to the hour, and invariably upset something I particularly want to do.   Yr.

                                                                            B.

We shall be in both Thursday and Friday, but do consider staying the night, if not lunch. I hear that Adrian's got off [military service]. Lytton and Bar [bara]. come tomorrow. We made Nelly believe that the aeroplanes were German.

Berg

921: To Vanessa Bell   [*Hogarth House, Richmond*]

[9? April 1918]

Dearest,

Nelly has just heard that her niece has taken a permanent place, thinking that you only wanted her temporarily. What a nuisance— But there is a chance that Liz, the other sister may know of some one. Nelly has written to ask her. Shall I take any steps? I could go to registry offices easily.

I saw Barbara on Sunday, who had heard from Nick.[1] He seems to be out of immediate danger.

Great haste,

                                                                            B.

Berg

1. Nicholas Bagenal had been seriously wounded in the back and kidneys on 30 March.

I   229

April 15th 1918

Dear Nick,

I was immensely pleased to get your letter this morning, and to see that you are really much the same as ever. I'm told that a kidney more or less is a matter of no importance. And now you'll be back in the midst of us all again, but you'll never hear to your face all the fine flattering things your friends have been saying about you. The other day for example at the 17 Club there was Goldie [G. Lowes Dickinson], Leonard and myself—Well, I wont repeat what might still make you blush and possibly raise your temperature. The upshot of it was that you're proposed by Leonard (who's going to write to you) and seconded by Goldie, and its generally felt by the Club that you're badly wanted there. We must arrange a tea party.

We went and had tea with Barbara, and found her curled up asleep in an arm chair. One of her eyes remained shut for quite a long time. She had had your letter the night before and was feeling fairly elated. Saxon had just washed his head in an inner room, and was stepping about among the crockery in a brown vest like a Siamese cat. We had a splendid tea— two kinds of cake and a loaf specially baked by the char womans husband. We laughed a great deal at Barbara for missing all the trains to Asheham. It proves beyond doubt that her next visit must be made in company with her husband.

Since beginning this letter I've spent a night at Guildford with Roger, and read his translation of the Lysistrata, and talked about every kind of thing, and finally this morning I went to Gordon Sqre with him, and there we met Nessa and Maynard and Shepherd.[1] Nessa left the room and re-appeared with a small parcel about the size of a large slab of chocolate. On one side are painted 6 apples by Cezanne.[2] Roger very nearly lost his senses. I've never seen such a sight of intoxication He was like a bee on a sunflower. Imagine snow falling outside, a wind like there is in the Tube, an atmosphere of yellow grains of dust, and us all gloating upon these apples. They really are very superb. The longer one looks the larger and heavier and greener and redder they become. The artists amused me very much, discussing whether he'd used veridian or emerald green, and Roger knowing the day, practically the hour, they were done by some brush mark in the background.

I cant say much for the beauty of Richmond at this moment. We're so

1. J. T. Sheppard, the classical scholar, was sharing 46 Gordon Square with Maynard Keynes.
2. Maynard, on Duncan's advice, had just gone to Paris and bought the picture from the Degas sale.

busy printing that we hardly notice. And Leonard has Americans[1] to lunch who begin at once "We place you, Mr Woolf, at the very top of the men who are doing the constructive thinking of our time—at the very top." After 2 1/2 hours of this, they tear themselves away saying "Well well, we're due at Mr Balfour's[2] now, but we've only scratched your surface so far, Mr Woolf —and we have to thank you, Mrs Woolf, for showing us the interior of an English home."

They're on their way to the front; but you wont meet them—

Then a compatriot of yours, called James Joyce, wants us to print his new novel.[3] I should hesitate to put it into the hand of Barbara, even though she is a married woman. The directness of the language, and the choice of incidents, if there *is* any choice, but as far as I can see there's a certain sameness—have raised a blush even upon such a cheek as mine. Is this an Irish quality?

Well, I must immediately wash, for I'm all over printers ink, and the Mothers [Co-operative Guild] arrive in 20 minutes. I hardly like to have Joyce even in the next room to them.

There'll be great competition to come and see you in the hospital, and Leonard and I take up a position which is firm, obstinate, and patient. We want to see you very much.

Yr

Virginia Woolf

Berg

923: To Vanessa Bell   *Hogarth [House, Richmond]*

Monday [22 April 1918]

Dearest,

I'm very glad the operation is over.[4] It sounds rather horrid. I daresay you'd be surprised to know how often I thought of you and the Brats on Saturday.

1. Judge Wadhams and Hamilton Holt, who were members of 'The Committee of the American League to Enforce Peace'. Holt was the more distinguished. He was liaison officer between the League to Enforce Peace and the American delegation at the Paris Peace Conference. In 1925 he became President of Rollins College.
2. Arthur Balfour, Foreign Secretary in the Lloyd George Government.
3. On 14 April Harriet Weaver, editor of the *Egoist*, encouraged by T. S. Eliot, brought to Hogarth House the manuscript of *Ulysses*, and suggested that the Hogarth Press might publish it. Virginia read it, and was shocked by its language, while Leonard tried in vain to find a printer who would print it for them.
4. Julian and Quentin had gone to stay with Roger Fry at Durbins, Guildford, in order to have their tonsils and adenoids removed at the same time as Roger's daughter Pamela.

The whole of the Stores would only produce one box of chocolates; its a most desolate sight. I hope Julian may be sufficiently well to eat them. I'm also sending [Enid] Bagnold and Nevinson,[1] though it strikes me that even you can't be hard up for books at Durbins.

I wish I had any gossip to tell you. I've just come in from tea at the [1917] Club, where I talked to Ermengard Maitland. She is a stout handsome woman of about thirty, motherly and yet virginal, to me rather a consoling type, after our cropheads and their dauntless ways. She keeps a farm, and breeds prize oxen, which she says is far the most interesting of country pursuits. You never know what sort of calf you're going to get, and you go round the markets and try to judge the best sire to mate with your cow.

"Well then, what do you do in the evenings?" I said.

"I play the double bass. It is an enormous instrument, the largest of all, and it plays an octave below the cello, so that its the foundation of the whole orchestra—I also write children's stories—improper ones."

"But, my dear Ermengard, you've just become a Quaker—

"Well, I know that. But I told them I meant to write improper stories— and they're not improper in your sense." However she wouldn't tell me in what sense they were improper. I think it rather a masterly conception, to breed bulls and write improper stories and be a Quaker.

The Shoves are off tomorrow to try and get work on a farm in Hertford- shire.

But I can't describe to you what an agony this afternoon was to me. You know the horror of buying clothes, especially for one forced as I am to keep my underclothes pinned together by brooches. However things have come to a pass; so I flung myself into a shop in Holborn. I should certainly always paint shops with lots of looking glasses and boxes bursting with white frills, and all the young ladies powdered and painted, and their hair scraped tight back, and one enormous Jewess in black satin issuing solemnly from a wardrobe. The impropriety seemed to me beyond anything we know. So it went on: I tried shop after shop; and then in a perfectly random way went and bought a wine-coloured black striped coat or dress, for £6.10! in Leicester Sqre. Good Heavens! What a world we live in! The pressure of solid matter never seems sufficient to keep one altogether straight.

I've been writing about you all the morning,[2] and have made you wear a blue dress; you've got to be immensely mysterious and romantic, which of course you are; yes, but its the combination that's so enthralling; to crack through the paving stone and be enveloped in the mist. You must admit

1. C. R. W. Nevinson, the painter, who had exhibited at the Friday Club.
2. This is the first reference in the letters to *Night and Day*, which Virginia had begun to write early in 1917, and was to finish before the end of 1918. By 12 March she had written over 100,000 words. Vanessa was the model for Katharine Hilbery, the heroine of the novel.

that that puts the matter in a nutshell. However I must stop, though I believe I like writing to you better than seeing you—I mean, when we meet at Gordon Sqre, the lyric mood has to be suppressed. But have you got a servant? Nelly says Drewet in the High St is very good indeed. And Aunt Minna has suddenly emerged, asking us to lunch, and wishing *particularly* for news of Vanessa, and is she in London? She asks us to meet "the Orchard-leigh Children" Who on earth can they be? The days of childbearing for Edith and Amy must be over, and without result, so I've always thought.

Please send me another line about the children. If a word of love for the Apes were thrown in—They were enraptured the other day to find themselves one rung higher on the ladder than Roger. You did say so; you cant deny it. *Dont get overtired.*

Yr
B.

I've just had Sotheby's Catalogue. They want to know what reserve to put, if any. I'm telling them to put a reserve of £100 on the Vanity Fair. Do you agree? but none on the Meredith mss.

Berg

924: To Lytton Strachey   *Hogarth [House, Richmond]*

23rd April [1918]

I wrote to ask [Bruce] Richmond to let me do your book. He answers that though willing and anxious that I should, he has to make it a rule that reviewers don't review their friends—not that he's afraid I should be partial, but that people would guess, and *say* I was partial, which he admits to be base on his part, but he's afraid he must stick to it. I'm very sorry. Of course you will get enough praise to sell your book as much as reviews do sell books. I rubbed it well into Richmond that it was a work of surpassing merit. But I had a great many things I wanted to say, and felt already an affection for my masterpiece, as well as yours. Leonard suggests that I should write a short review for War and Peace.[1] But I shouldn't be able to take a purely literary line there, of course, and the circulation isn't such that it will be worth the sale of even half a copy. Do you think there's any use doing it? Anyhow you needn't bother about getting an advance copy. But I'm very anxious to see it.

We are sitting in the same fog that began 21 days ago. Sometimes we dimly discern snow falling—we have electric light for meals, but they talk of

1. Leonard had now become the acting editor of this journal, during the illness of Harold Wright.

cutting that off. I was at Guildford the other day and there it was worse, so don't talk to me about the country.

We've been asked to print Mr Joyce's new novel, every printer in London and most in the provinces having refused. First there's a dog that p's—then there's a man that forths, and one can be monotonous even on that subject—moreover, I don't believe that his method, which is highly developed, means much more than cutting out the explanations and putting in the thoughts between dashes. So I don't think we shall do it.

By the way, you've got my copy of the other one.

Yr.
V.W.

Frances Hooper

925: To Roger Fry   *Hogarth [House, Richmond]*

Wednesday [24 April 1918]

My dear Roger,

I haven't forgotten the cigarettes. In fact I went directly I got back, but owing to the approach of the Budget the man hadn't got them. He will have them in a day or two and I will send them at once.

It sounds as if you had all had a horrid time with these operations [Julian's, Quentin's and Pamela's]. Give Pamela[1] my love, and tell her she has roused my ancient passion for books, and I've been wasting hours, and finally bought the Poems of Collins[2] for 6d—a most charming little book, as nice as hers, but 5d dearer.

I enclose Murry's review of Et Cie.[3] It isn't a very good one—at least I think there was more to be said. The book diminishes in goodness rather as it goes on, I think, and gets rather clogged and costive. The truth is these Jews have such terrifically clear sight, and never know what to leave out and ram it all in with such emphasis. Still, he's far better than anyone we have, unless everything sounds better in French, as I rather think it does.

I've been reading Joyce's novel. Its interesting as an experiment; he leaves out the narrative, and tries to give the thoughts, but I dont know that he's got anything very interesting to say, and after all the p - ing of a dog isn't very different from the p - ing of a man. Three hundred pages of it might be boring. Anyhow its too long for us to attempt, though I think someone ought to bring out a piece of it.

I wish I had the chance of being thoroughly enkindled by you rather oftener. I suppose you dont know your own powers in that line, which I

1. Roger's daughter, now aged 16.
2. William Collins (1721-59).
3. A novel by Jean Richard Bloch, published in 1913.

hesitate to call divine, but still the amount of spirit that radiates from you may, for all I know, come straight from a holy source. It may be a variety of Quakerism. In fact I rather expect it is. Anyhow it gives me great pleasure, so don't get blown up or trodden underfoot, or made someone so important that it will be necessary to take you seriously

Have you been invited to the opening of [William] Rothenstein's show?

Yrs. V.W.

Sussex

926: To Vanessa Bell   *Hogarth* [*House, Richmond*]
Sunday [28 April 1918]

Dearest,

I'm afraid Liz [Nelly Boxall's sister] is no good. She heard of a woman, but she didn't want to be so far from home. Shan't I go and see Mrs Hunt, or try some other registry office—I know there's supposed to be a good one in Chelsea. I forget what wages you give. It would be perfectly easy for me to go, as I'm always rambling about London—and my well known talents might find you a woman who would die in your service, not directly, I mean, but after some 40 years service. You would then put a notice about her in the Times.

I see that you are very prominent in the Nation this week.[1] I suppose £100 isn't asking too much?—or does it work out at that? I saw some private school asked that, and I suppose ordinary people might think they gave more for the money there.

We are expecting Desmond for the night, and he assures me that he is going to tell me a great deal of news, so I hope I may have some for you. I went to the Hippodrome the other night by myself; we had a visit from Walter Lamb; all our guns went off in the middle of Friday night and we had just got the beds made in the kitchen when the bugles sounded and there wasn't any raid. The Academicians are trying to get rid of Poynter,[2] and wrote him a letter to say the work was too much for him, but he says it isn't. They mean to elect Sargent. Owing to Wattie's [Walter Lamb] influence the R. A will be smaller than usual this year. There is nothing of startling merit. Eighteen pictures from the Diploma Gallery have been put in one of the

1. Vanessa had advertised in the *Nation* for pupils for her projected school at Charleston. The advertisement ran: "Mrs Clive Bell proposes to educate in the country her two boys (aged 8 and 10) and hopes to find three or four other children to educate with them. She has already engaged a governess and tutor. The cost of education, board and lodging she estimates at about £100 a year for each child. Charleston, Firle, Sussex."

2. Sir Edward Poynter had been President of The Royal Academy since 1896. He resigned in the autumn of 1918, and died the following year.

Tubes (for safety). Lord Canterbury[1] is a nephew of the Duke of Rutland. He is a bugger. I can't think of anything else, except that the Whithams[2] have asked us to stay with them in Devonshire, and Jan finds agricultural work very good for his writing. On second thoughts, I put a reserve of £70. on the Thackeray, as I thought we should take that on the whole. I hope you agree.

Yr.
B.

Let me know about the servant. How many do you say there are in the house?

Berg

927: To Desmond MacCarthy   [*Hogarth House, Richmond*]

[early May 1918]

My dear Desmond,

This card arrived for you this morning. I send it on, though I see its no good, discreetly enclosed in an envelope.

I suppose you can't leave your mother, as you haven't rung up—I'm very sorry chiefly for my own disappointment, I admit. About the Princes [Bibesco] luncheon (how romantic that sounds) I don't know whether it was a real invitation for Thursday, or only a hint of possibilities. Anyhow, I don't think I can manage this Thursday but I have hopes that he may ask me, if he did ask me, for another.

Did you like the Times review? It wasn't half as good as mine.

Yr affate
V.W.

Mrs Michael MacCarthy

928: To Vanessa Bell   [*Hogarth House, Richmond*]

[4 May 1918]

Dearest,

I went to the Registry Office yesterday and heard of a servant [Ellen Walker] who wants to be in the country and is free on the 15th May. She

1. Henry, 5th Viscount Canterbury, who died in October 1918.
2. Sylvia and John Mills Whitham. She was a member of the 1917 Club, and he had written at least one novel, *Wolfgang*. Together they did translations from French.

wants from £26 to 28. She is 26 years old. She is leaving because her mistress is giving up the house. She has a very good character, and the woman at the registry knows her and says she is very nice and quiet. I am going to see her on Wednesday. Do you give me a free hand to take her if she seems all right? Shall I offer £28 if she seems wavering? Mrs Lucas, (the registry woman—a friend of Aunt Annies and most refined) said that owing to the size of the family she might want more—Do you want her on the 15th? Shall I advance her her fare?

Mrs Lucas *has a* perfect parlourmaid wanting to be near Lewes!—but thats no good of course.

Could you let me know before Wednesday.

Yr.
B.

Berg

929: TO VANESSA BELL   *Hogarth [House, Richmond]*

Tuesday [7 May 1918]

Dearest,

I heard from the woman this morning who says she could not take a situation where there is such a large family. I suppose it would have been better not to tell her what the family was until I saw her.

I've written to say that the place is really an easy one, and that you do your waiting yourselves and so on, and I've asked her to meet me at the Registry Office on Wednesday at 3.30. I shall go there anyhow, because Mrs Lucas told me that now is the best time for getting servants, and that she has never had so many wanting country places as this year, though of course they get snapped up at once.

I dont much think Ellen Walker will think it worth her while to come, so that if I were you I shouldn't bother about coming all that way. The address is 222A Kings Road, about 10 minutes from Sloane Sqre Station.

It might be a good thing for you to see Mrs Lucas yourself however.

If you do come I could meet you at 3.20 at Sloane Sqre Station, as the office is rather difficult to find.

Would you ring up tomorrow morning and say what you want to do.

I could come on to tea anyhow.

Nelly is going home for Whitsun, and holds out hope that she might find someone among her friends.

We are coming to Asheham for 10 days or so.

Yr
B.

Berg

[12 May 1918]

Dear Nick,

We met Barbara at the Club the other day, and asked whether we might pay you a visit.[1] We should very much like to.

Would next Tuesday about 4 suit you? I don't think you will have time to let us know, so we will come then. If it won't do, I have written our telephone number, and perhaps some one could ring us up.

A vote of sympathy, congratulation and anticipation of further favours was passed by my Mothers [the Guild]. I said I would hand it on. A great deal of emotion was displayed; you are called "The Lieutenant;"—we are having an address on Sex Education next week, and you'll be surprised to hear that after thinking over the paper on Syphilis for six months or so,[2] they have come to the conclusion that it is all true and "most valuable." So although it takes some time, one need never give up hope of something or other. I expect they still brood upon what you said.

I've been submerged in the waters of family life. I've had to go to tea with Aunts of 92;[3] to dinner with cousins who retired from the Calcutta bench 10 years ago;[4] and only by the skin of my teeth did I avoid lunching with a Roumanian Prince [Antoine Bibesco] whose mistress has written a book, which I did *not* review; but all the same they cherish hopes that we may print her play. At least, this is the only reason I can see for a grand party with Lady Cunard,[5] Mr. Birrell,[6] the Prince, and a wretched, illdressed, inkstained Suburban such as I am.

Of course in my own mind I don't think them worth a damn;—still flattery is flattery.

I see that none of us is really proof against that libidinous Ape Mrs [Margot] Asquith, if she chooses to reach a paw for us. The only hope for the preservation of our society is that people like you and Barbara, still comparatively young and uncontaminated, should make an enclosed space of virtuous life where we can be out of temptation. Saxon shall be the guardian. Nothing could corrupt Saxon. Imagine his bright sword descending

1. Nick was recuperating at Fishmongers Hall, London Bridge, which had been turned into a temporary hospital for wounded officers.
2. She was forgetting that it had been over a year since the lecture described in letters 818 and 819.
3. Aunt Minna (Sarah Emily Duckworth), who died in June, aged 90.
4. Harry Stephen, Virginia's first cousin, who was a Judge of the High Court, Calcutta, 1901-14.
5. Maud Emerald Cunard, the American hostess who lived most of her life in London, and was an intimate friend of George Moore.
6. Augustine Birrell (1850-1933), the liberal statesman and man of letters.

upon Lady Diana Manners,[1] and leaving nothing but a corpulent trunk! I can see him wiping the blade upon silk and coming in to tea as calm as a seraph.

But this is for you to develop. I am running on because I am waiting for my tea, and Leonard won't come in. The church bells and the trumpets are fairly distracting.

Have you seen Clives book [*Pot-Boilers*]? If not, please dont believe that Virginia Woolf wishes to be called next to Hardy and Conrad, the best living novelist; or that Duncan thinks himself the greatest European painter, or that Vanessa is—I forget what—equal to Duncan perhaps.

Here is Leonard.

Yours
Virginia Woolf

Berg

931: TO VANESSA BELL   *Hogarth* [*House, Richmond*]
Wednesday [15 May 1918]

Dearest,

I've just been to the Registry Office without success, I'm afraid.

She has a Cook who wants to be near Lewes, and is very good—but I suppose thats useless. However, she said this was the worst week for them to come in, owing to Whitsun, and she expects more next week. I said she was to write to you if she heard of anyone, and I would let her know—or it would be simpler if you wrote straight, Mrs Lucas, 222A Kings Rd Chelsea—to say if you want her to get a temporary, which she thinks she could do without much difficulty.

Perhaps it would be worth waiting to see if Nelly can get anyone.

We come down tomorrow. I hope we may meet.

Yr
B.

Berg

932: TO DUNCAN GRANT   [*Hogarth House, Richmond*]
Wednesday [15 May 1918]

My dear Duncan,

I wonder whether Nessa when she got back gave any account of a vow she made in Fitzroy Square, which was sealed with a sisters kiss. She promised

1. One of the most beautiful women of her times. She married Duff Cooper in 1919.

239

to drink 2 glasses of milk a day, until the end of the war. I think she made it a condition that you did too. I feel convinced its the only way in which either of you will pull through without some temporary absence, in one of those secluded houses where I'm such a brilliant success.

Now, my dear Duncan, I appeal to you to carry this out, with immense confidence in your fund of masterly common sense. Milk is at your door; it is cheap; it is the only pure food left; there is nothing but a queer superstition in Nessa's mind, derived I believe, from Aunt [Mary] Fisher, against drinking it. You haven't this in your blood; I entreat you therefore drink milk twice a day, and each time think of me with tenderness. Its remarkable to see how all our friends are shedding their flesh until in some cases only an arrangement of bones, loosely covered with skin, and I suppose, an intestine or two, remain. I've just been seeing Fredegond, Aunt Minna, and Sir Harry Stephen. Aunt Minna is shrunk to a small wizened brown kernel, and as she still wears her black velvet dress, you can almost see her shaking from side to side. I'm full of gossip for you. Sir Harry told us the life history of Great Uncle William, who was, in the 18th Century the illegitimate son of the first James Stephen [c.1733-79]. "I shall call the lady whom he seduced Lucy Waters, though that was not her name," he said. This chivalry, considering she died 150 years ago struck me very much. He is an amiable old creature, and I believe secretly wishes to live apart from Barbara [his wife] and become a pacifist, and our greatest friend—but I must own he did'nt say so.

I had a very cool reception from Sophie.[1] She was knitting bed socks, and I think she has turned entirely Duckworth, and might indeed be their illegitimate sister. I've always thought them likely to cohabit with stout kitchen maids. Aunt Minna said she heard that Clive was doing good work in Paris, and an irreproachable black female today asked me whether, as a reviewer, I considered that the Morning Post was fair to novels of the occult. She had just written one; but a gentleman friend, who also writes novels of the occult, had told her that the Morning Post disliked the occult "which makes it rather hard on us, as all our friends go by the Morning Post of course"—

I have seen Nick who lies on a terrace looking at the river and watching an old gentleman, whom Carrington says is Pissarro,[2] painting on a pier. Nick was apparently nearly well, and only slightly irritable. Saxon I hear moans aloud and says that he envies Bertie in prison[3] because life outside is so unendurable. All Nessa's predictions are coming true.

I had a romantic moonlight walk with Desmond in Richmond Park.

1. Sophie Farrell, previously with the Stephens, and now Aunt Minna Duckworth's cook.
2. Lucien Pissarro (1863-1944), son of Camille Pissarro. He made his home in England.
3. Bertrand Russell had been sentenced to six months' imprisonment for an anti-war article he had written in *The Tribunal*.

The Bibesco [-Bagnold] mystery is still unsolved, but Desmond was at some pains to explain that his relations with Molly are of the very best, and he considers her far more intellectual than most women who pass for such— Bonham Carter[1] for instance.

I had a most satisfactory and fascinating renewal of my friendship with Katherine Mansfield. She is extremely ill, but is going to Cornwall with Estelle Rhys [Rice], a woman painter, whom I'm sure is the worst of woman painters. But all the same Katherine is the very best of women writers— always of course passing over one fine but very modest example.

Please see about the *milk*. I am bringing you 2 small packets of chocolate, which are best eaten with milk.

Yrs.,
V.W.

Duncan Grant

1. Violet Asquith had married Sir Maurice Bonham Carter in 1915.

Letters 933-987 (mid-May–mid-November 1918)

The Hogarth Press turned down Ulysses *with the excuse that it was too long for them to print, and published Katherine Mansfield's* Prelude *in July. The closing months of the war were active ones for the Woolfs. Virginia finished* Night and Day *soon after the Armistice, stimulated by the success of Lytton Strachey's* Eminent Victorians, *which appeared in May, and was also writing her short-story* Kew Gardens. *They spent several weekends away, with the Waterlows in Wiltshire, with Lytton Strachey and Carrington at Tidmarsh, and again with Lady Ottoline at Garsington, while many visitors came to Asheham in spite of increasing food-shortages, among them the Webbs and Roger Fry. It was also the period when Virginia's servant-juggling between Asheham and Charleston began to reach its tedious climax, complicated by Vanessa's expected child. The Armistice came when the Woolfs were back in Richmond. Leonard had now accepted the editorship of the* International Review, *and was writing* Empire and Commerce in Africa.*

933: To Miss Harriet Weaver   *Asheham House, Rodmell, Lewes, Sussex*

Typewritten
17 May 1918

Dear Miss Weaver,

Thank you very much for your letter. We are down in the country for a fortnight, so I am afraid that I cannot come and see you as I should have liked to have done.

We have read the chapters of Mr Joyce's novel [*Ulysses*] with great interest, and we wish that we could offer to print it. But the length is an insuperable difficulty to us at present. We can get no one to help us, and at our rate of progress a book of 300 pages would take at least two years to produce—which is, of course, out of the question for you or Mr Joyce.

We very much regret this as it is our aim to produce writing of merit which the ordinary publisher refuses. Our equipment is so small, however, that we are finding it difficult to bring out a book of less [more] than 100 pages. We have tried to buy a larger press but without success, and therefore we are afraid that it is useless to attempt anything more ambitious. I have

242

told my servants to send the MS back to you, by registered post next Tuesday or Wednesday.

With many thanks for letting us see the manuscript,[1]

Yours sincerely,
Virginia Woolf

British Museum

934: To Lady Ottoline Morrell   *Asheham House, Rodmell, Lewes, [Sussex]*

May 24th [1918]

My dear Ottoline

We should very much like to come down, but might it be one week end in July?

June seems already rather crowded, partly because we have to finish and send out Katherine Mansfields story.

But that must be finished in a few weeks now.

We are down here, and have been arguing for the last 24 hours with Roger on every possible subject without ceasing. He hadnt been 10 minutes in the house before he began to discuss the immortality of the soul, in spite of having had a tooth out a few hours before. We are now moping over a fire, all traces of summer having disappeared.

I will send you a packet of my Belgian cigarettes. The address is on the cover. I think they're still nicer than any others, though they vary in goodness. But they only cost 11d for 20.

It would be very nice to see not only Garsington but you too. But can it possibly be more romantic than it was in the autumn?

Do you mind being looked upon rather as a mermaid in a divine aquarium?

But perhaps the image must be changed for another.

I saw Katherine Middleton Murry the other day—very ill, I thought, but very inscrutable and fascinating. After a good deal of worrying by me, she confessed that she was immensely happy married to Murry, though for some reason she makes out that marriage is of no more importance than engaging a charwoman. Part of her fascination lies in the obligation she is under to say absurd things. I wish she and Murry didn't think [J. D.] Ferguson a great

---

1. Leonard had consulted two leading printers, and was told by both of them that the publication of the novel would lead to prosecution. This was the main reason for rejecting *Ulysses*. But Virginia had also reacted with marked distaste to her first reading of it, an opinion which she later qualified.

artist. He has done a design for her story which makes our gorges rise, to such an extent that we can hardly bring ourselves to print it.[1]

We hope you will let us come some time in July.

Yours affate
Virginia Woolf

Texas

935: TO LYTTON STRACHEY   *Asheham House, [Rodmell, Sussex]*

[*Leonard's contribution typewritten*]
24 May, 1918

I think your suggestion of "Patriotism and History" on Marriott's book sounds very good. I will write for the book and have it sent to you. I haven't altered your article on Peace Traps, as [A. J.] Balfour's speech was really negligible and the point seemed rather niggling.[2]

We've been here a week in almost perfect weather and what is almost more perfect solitude. Except for Roger who came last night and left this morning. Why is it that we are all valetudinarians? Roger lies on his back before and after meals and even so is afflicted with perpetual gripes, a swollen jaw, a diseased tooth, an incipient cold in the head, a decaying brain, and melancholia amatoria. Saxon's head has sunk permanently upon his chest from rheumatoid arthritis. And even you suffer from green vomit. I am unfit for any kind of military service and Virginia's record is not of the cleanest. I don't understand this early valetudinarianism which seems to descend upon us.

V. wants me to thank you for your book [*Eminent Victorians*]. It seemed to me most imposing when one could read them all between the same black cover. I started on Arnold the evening it came, and could not stop reading it while V.'s co-operative women sang hymns in the dining room.

Leonard

The sun has completely dried the ink on my pen, or I would have written. And then L., by way of being a practical man went and packed for me, and left out your book, which I meant to read here. So I can't write that delightful letter which I'd meant to. Besides to tell the truth, rumours of your success have poisoned my peace even here.[3] Do write and tell me how complete it's

---

1. The first few copies of *Prelude* contained a lino-cut of a woman's head designed by J. D. Fergusson, a friend of the Murrys. It was dropped from all later copies.
2. Lytton was contributing articles to *War and Peace*, the journal which Leonard was editing. In 1918 John Marriott, the historian, published *English History in Shakespeare*.
3. *Eminent Victorians* had just been published, and Lytton found himself famous.

been—how many copies you've sold, how many guineas, how many Countesses, how many adorations and whether at heart you're still the same.

V.W.

Frances Hooper

936: To Vanessa Bell   1917 *Club, 4 Gerrard Street, W.*1.

[30? May 1918]

Dearest,

I have just bought you a present which may be slightly better than Rebecca West[1]—at anyrate the subject is more in your line. However, I'm writing chiefly to avoid joining in the general conversation with Nick and Alix. Nick seems to be going to Hampshire—not Eastbourne. I had a typical letter from Saxon saying that Barbara had an instinct that I was annoyed with them, and as Barbara's instincts are always right, he must apologise, and so on—

Let me know when Duncans and Bunny's plans are settled.[2] When Leonard asked me the question which Lytton may ask I said I was completely ignorant, and quite convinced him, so I think it'll be perfectly safe. Nelly remarked today that she thought being a nurse was as nice as being a cook. And she told me she liked taking a baby from the month [old], and had managed 3. However, do be discreet. They would never forgive me if Trissie heard anything.[3]

Do take care.

Yr
B.

Berg

937: To Vanessa Bell   [*Hogarth House, Richmond*]

[early June? 1918]

Dearest,

I have been to a new agency and have heard of two quite likely house-

1. 30 May was Vanessa's birthday. Virginia had offered her as a present Rebecca West's new novel, *The Return of the Soldier*.
2. It had several times been proposed that Duncan should go to France as an Official War Artist, but he refused because he would have been obliged to wear a uniform. David Garnett was considering an offer to join the Quakers as a relief worker in Russia after the Revolution.
3. Vanessa was expecting another child, and Virginia had suggested that Nelly be sent to help Trissie at Charleston. Leonard's 'question' was about the paternity of the child.

parlourmaids who want to be in the country (permanent). The man says that he thinks he can be fairly certain of suiting you before July 1st. Shall I do the whole business? He has also a housemaid and a houseparlourmaid, but I suppose you only want the one.

I shall probably see her tomorrow or the day after, I am writing in a p. o to catch post.

Mrs Lucas and Mrs Hunt were pretty hopeless—Write any directions at once.

Yr B

If its *necessary* to take her tomorrow I shall risk it—but I dont suppose it will be.

Berg

938: To Clive Bell

Hogarth [House], Richmond

Thursday [6 June 1918]

My dear Clive,

I wish I could dine with you on Monday, but unfortunately I have let myself in for I don't know how many engagements. Is it possible that I might be asked on another occasion? It would be great fun.

I had a long moonlit walk with Desmond the other night through the grove in which Miss Hickman's body was found,[1] but he was brimming with good will—in fact quite tipsy—and said not a word against you.

I've not seen or heard from Molly for ages. It seems an unreasonable accusation on her part, considering that the gossip came from so many sources.

I take it for granted that you would prefer K. M. [Katherine Mansfield] without the bold black woodcuts of Mr [J. D.] Fergusson. We are printing some plain.[2]

Yrs ever,

Quentin Bell

Virginia Woolf

939: To Molly MacCarthy

Hogarth House, Paradise Road, Richmond

June 7th [1918]

Dearest Molly,

Dont you think its time that you remembered my existence? Am I to be

1. See letter 99 (30 August 1903).
2. In fact, nearly all were plain. See p. 244, note 1.

for ever shouting out in tubes "Dont you think me the nicest person you ever saw?" Isn't it time that you wrote, off your own bat, and said so?

I came in contact with Miss [Helen] Dudley one day at the Club, and she said you were off for the rest of the summer. But what are you doing? How dare you wash your hands of us all in this perfectly irresponsible way? Dont you *want* us? I believe the truth is that you dont. There is an element of bluntness about you which has to be reckoned with. The vague softness is only half an inch deep, and beneath is rock or marble. Please go in to the matter fully when you answer this letter. It is being written, I may say, in the greatest difficulties, for I'm keeping up a lively discussion with Leonard about life in general. Is he happy? Are we successful? Do people like us? What shall we do when the war's over?

I saw a great many people yesterday, and I heard that Jos Wedgwood is marrying a deaf governess, and Lytton's book is going into a 2nd edition, and Katherine Mansfield has married Middleton Murry, and Maynard Keynes has refused to argue about the war and Barbara Bagenal is going to have a baby! They feel very strongly about Maynard; they say he must be talked to.[1] Our standard of honesty is frightfully high—high, but peculiar. (I add this thinking of some incidents in my own past)

We are going to stay with the Waterlows next Sunday. And then we are going to stay with Ottoline, and then, thank God, about August we shall withdraw to Asheham.

I am now going to read Rebecca West's new novel. Please spend 1½d on me, as I do on you, and let me find a letter, an enormous long letter, to read at breakfast. Next time I will tell you all about the books I am reading. But I must first feel in touch with you—I mean, do you really like me, Molly?

Yr. V.W.

L sends his love—

Mrs Michael MacCarthy

940: To Vanessa Bell   [*Hogarth House, Richmond*]

Monday [10 June 1918]

Dearest,
    I didn't speak to Nelly at once, as Leonard was rather doubtful about

1. A month earlier, Vanessa, Sheppard and Norton were discussing conscientious objectors at 46 Gordon Square, and Maynard declared that he did not believe that anyone could be a genuine C.O. When they expostulated with him, he told them to go to bed, and Sheppard retorted, "Maynard, you will find it is a mistake to despise your old friends" (Garnett, *The Flowers of the Forest*. pp. 148-9).

it—However, I've just spoken to her, and suggested that she and Lottie should go to you on the 1st July and stay till October.

They were on the point of offering to go themselves, and are very much excited and pleased, so I dont think there'll be any difficulty about that. I told her you were going to have a baby; I *didnt* say anything about staying on and becoming your nurse, as Leonard is doubtful of the experiment from our point of view, and thinks that we should at any rate see how it answers temporarily before we give them up entirely.

Would you therefore agree to say nothing to them or to anyone else about staying on permanently and treat it as a purely temporary arrangement?

We should know how it worked from our point of view by July and we could discuss it when we come down in August. But until we are more decided we think it most important not to unsettle them by suggesting something which we may never seriously think of doing.

Nelly seems quite ready to do house work or cook or anything, or run the whole house. Perhaps you'd better write to her.

We made £68 by the sale, but I don't know whether we sold the Thackeray or not. I hope not. If so, its pretty bad—

This is written in haste.

Yr.
V.W.

We also think we ought to make it understood that we can have them back in case of illness or emergency—You'd better burn this.

Berg

941: To Violet Dickinson   *Hogarth House, Paradise Road, Richmond*

10th June [1918]

My Violet,

It was very noble of you to buy two copies of Katherine Mansfield's book.[1] I hope you'll like it—and I think you will. She is a woman from New Zealand, with a passion for writing, and she's had every sort of experience, wandering about with traveling circuses over the moors of Scotland, and has kept herself by writing stories in the New Age; but this is much the best thing she's yet done.

We've been at Asheham, and come back again. I saw Nessa while I was there, in the midst of a whole colony of hares, rabbits, chickens and pigs.

1. Copies of *Prelude* were sent out on 11 July. Violet's was an advance order.

She has also a tutor and a governess, 2 children besides her own as boarders, and two others as day boys. She runs it all with small girls from the village to help and a cook who calls everyone by their Christian names—in fact I never saw such a jumble.

Leonard is working tremendously hard, and he spends all his spare time printing, which becomes more and more fascinating. We are just bargaining for a new press, which we shall put in the basement. We both think its high time you came and saw us, but I suppose we probably shan't meet till the course of nature has opened either your grave or mine. But you will bring a small bunch of flowers to drop upon the coffin; won't you? I went to see Aunt Minna the other day; and her grave still seems fairly far off. In fact she's just taken on her house for another 5 years.[1]

Yr
Sp:

Leonard sends his love.

Berg

942: TO LADY OTTOLINE MORRELL

Hogarth House, Paradise Road,
Richmond

10th June [1918]

My dear Ottoline

We're back here more or less until August, and so if you're in London we might manage to meet. The reasons against asking you here are that I dont like my chair covers, (I lost my head one day at the Omega) and the sordidity of our life might deprive you of breath. However as an experiment it would certainly possess a fearful interest.

I'm curious to hear about Lady Margaret Sackville;[2] but I dont see why you should write to your cowboy[3] and not to me. I suppose the truth of it is that the extremes of society are more picturesque than the upper middle class—which Dora Sanger accused me of being last night. How wretched she always makes me feel! If one has anything tender, morbid, uneasy about one she always comes down with her heel and gives it a good squirming.

Murry was here too, and such a suicidal conversation I've never listened to in my life. According to Murry we must choose between suicide

1. Aunt Minna Duckworth died a fortnight later.
2. A daughter of 7th Earl de la Warr. She had published many volumes of poems.
3. Possibly John Wain, a farm labourer at Garsington.

and indifference, and he vacillates between them. Dora agreed rapturously.

Leonard says that we should like very much to come one day in July.

Yrs
V.W.

Texas

943: To Vanessa Bell   [*Hogarth House, Richmond*]
Tuesday [11 June 1918]

Dearest,

I've just come in and found your telegram. I can't think why you haven't already had my letter, as I posted it myself yesterday afternoon. I suppose you'll have had it by the time you get this, so I needn't repeat all I said.

I put off speaking to the servants because after we came back I got a bad throat and Leonard said it was out of the question to do without servants, and in fact I thought it was hopeless to persuade *him*. However, he gradually came round to the idea, and I have now, I think, got a daily woman to do for us. I hope you don't mind having them in July, but that will give us a month in which to see how it works here.

I haven't said anything to Nelly about our not being able to afford to keep them, as Leonard thought it would be better to wait, though I dont really agree. I find today that they're both rather suspicious that we do mean to get rid of them permanently and Nelly told me that they counted upon coming back in October. I think she'll want rather careful handling, and I think you'd better say nothing to her about staying on at first. But she's so changeable that one doesn't know what she does want to do, and I've no doubt that she would stay if we decided against having them.

Of course you may think it would be better policy to secure Mr Ford's daughter—[1]

Personally I'm very anxious to try another way of living, and our books have been so high lately that I think we must try some change.

I've just been meeting Lytton, who is like a newly wedded Bride. He pretends to be made rather uncomfortable by his fame, but he's obviously in a state of rapture, and so sought after already that he's no time for anything. Clive's giving a party in his honour tonight, but unfortunately I cant go.

I've got any amount of things to write to you about, but I've no time now, and these blessed servants want such a lot of discussing, dont they—

Nelly said she was very fond of you, and they were both much excited at the prospect of a baby, so I expect you could seduce them in your usual way, and I feel pretty sure I can make my old woman a success.

Yr B.

Berg

1. Ford was head-cowman at Charleston farm.

Thursday [13 June 1918]

Dearest,

Nelly asked me this morning whether I would say for certain that we would have them back in October. I therefore thought it best to tell her that I didn't think you would want them if they had decided that they couldn't stay more than 3 months. We've had a terrific discussion. Finally they said that they couldn't make up their minds until they had been with you for some time. They say that they might want to stay on or they might not. I thought the only thing to do was to wire and tell you, and leave it to you to decide whether you think the risk is worth running. At the present moment I think they want to stay on with us, but once they were settled I expect they would get attached. From our point of view the position is that we can't in the least tell how our scheme will work. Therefore we feel we must have the right to take them back in October; and in fact they insist that they shall be asked in October what they want to do. Both Leonard and I want to try the experiment, but as you will realise we don't want to feel that we've cut ourselves off for good.

Personally I think they're such good servants that some risk is worth running on your part—but its all very complicated, and you're not in the least bound to have them in July. You need only write to me when you've made up your mind. (as soon as you can)

I must now rush off to see about my daily but I've not taken her. I've been careful not to say a word to N & L. [Nellie and Lottie] about our wishing them to go. I've said it was entirely your suggestion—directly they thought I wanted them to to go, they said they wouldn't go to you. So its important to keep up the idea that its done to oblige you and that Nelly herself suggested it—and that I'm not involved at all—

B.

Berg

Tuesday [18 June 1918]

Dearest,

I wrote in such a hurry the other day to catch the post that I expect I didn't explain myself very clearly. I quite realise that you don't expect N. and L to bind themselves to stay with you. I only thought that as you had a chance of a permanent servant it was absurd for them to go if they'd decided not to stay beyond October. But I made it perfectly clear that the chance of getting Miss Ford was what had changed the situation, and they agreed that it was perfectly reasonable that you should wish to know if there was a chance, and not in the least insincere.

As a matter of fact, ever since I first spoke about it they've said that they knew you would want them to stay because you'd be no better off in October. Nelly told me she meant to pack all her clothes, as she was sure you would persuade her to stay on—and this was before your letter came. What they seem to fear is that you will be very charming, and that I shall give them no choice of coming back here—so now I've promised that I will ask them in October, but they are to be perfectly free to stay with you.

The reason why they are ready to go to you if they think that I want them is that if they were certain that I didn't want them they would prefer to take a place at once either in London or near Guildford—at least this is what they say. But I agree its impossible to go into details, Also they change their minds every day, so I'm now going to refuse to discuss it any more with them.

I think Nelly would prefer that Trissie should have a holiday as her fear seems to be that there won't be enough for her to do, and also that she won't get on with Trissie—but I assure her that Trissie will be perfectly easy and friendly.

I believe myself that there would be more chance of her staying on if you made her a definite offer of a place as your nurse than if she stayed in a half and half place with you, neither cook nor housemaid. But it certainly wouldn't do to suggest this for some time. However, when you've got them you'll probably see how the land lies for yourself. Its frightfully difficult to describe, and I always feel I'm writing gibberish when I begin upon their condition. They make my head whirl.

But next time I write perhaps I shall be able to discuss something more interesting. Do tell me about your letters—or send them. [Mark] Gertler has suddenly asked to dine with us tonight—God knows why.

Yr

B.

We spent the week end with the Waterlows—their brats are inconceivably ugly and we discussed S's past with Margery [his wife]. He met Mrs Finberg in the park. She has married another man and he has been divorced; and Finberg[1] has married another woman and Jos Wedgwood is marrying his deaf governess.

Berg

1. Alexander Finberg, art historian, who married his second wife in 1914.

Friday afternoon [21 June 1918]

Dearest,

Trissie will have told you of our adventures. As far as one can tell, I think we've been very lucky. I thought Mrs Paton was rather particularly nice—very quiet and unpretending, and evidently delighted to be in a farm in the country. Mrs Bridger whom I saw about her character said she'd only been there for about 3 months, but she was a very good worker, and certainly came with a good character, though she couldn't remember much about it. The only fault she had to find with her was that she was apt to be untidy—but I said you would excuse that. As a matter of fact she's rather beautiful—something in the style of Bobo [Beatrice Mayor], with large dark eyes and a very sallow face. I suppose Trissie told you that she has a sister of 18 who has been in service and would like a place in the country. It struck me that you might turn Mrs Paton into your nurse, as she has her own child, and have the sister as well. But that can wait. I've just rung up the Registry Office who wanted to know the result of our visit, and the woman there says she knows that Mrs Paton is very respectable, although she was only a short time in her place.

She lives just behind the 17 Club; so I could easily go and see her one day next week, if you want any final arrangements made.

What on earth's happening with N. and L. I dont know. They seem to have spent most of the morning while I was out sobbing in Leonard's room—but they were so incoherent that he has told them to calm down and talk to me this evening. If the worst comes to the worst, we can always go down to Asheham and get Mrs Gell [Geall] to do for us. I think you're much better off without them, as they'd have made endless difficulties, and probably upset Trissie too.

I enclose the Agents card. Will you let them know as soon as you've taken Mrs P[aton].

I suppose you'll have to pay them at the same time.

Yr B.

Berg

Tuesday [25 June 1918]

Dearest,

I needn't say that I'm fearfully sorry that the affair has turned out in this way. I dont think I've ever spent a more miserable three weeks, and of course its been much worse for you.

I didn't mean to discuss it any more in writing, but as you've written I think I'd better say that I dont think you quite understand what happened. I gather that you feel that Leonard was always against their coming. This is not so. He only wished it to be clear that we had the right of asking them back in October. He himself was the first to suggest that they should go to you on July 1st, and he has never changed his mind that it was best that they should do so. He spent an afternoon in the kitchen trying to persuade them to.

He never produced a document for them to sign. I suggested to them, without telling him, that we should write a statement promising to ask them to return in October, as it seemed at the moment, the only thing needed to persuade them to go. In the end they said this was unnecessary, and I only told Leonard of my suggestion, afterwards, and he never spoke a word to them about it. In fact he can't remember that I ever told him.

The only point L. and I disagreed upon was as to whether it was best to tell them of our need for economy at first. He was against this, and I for it. Except for this, on which I gave way, he has agreed with me about everything, and never interfered with what I said, or tried to make the servants decide in any way against going. I think he's writing to you himself; but I wanted to make it clear that he never put the least pressure on me, and we've never confused the servants by giving them two points of view.

Since I wrote, N. and L. have told me the real reason why they did not want to go—at least they now say it is the real reason. They particularly ask me not to write about it, but to tell you when I see you. If they'd only told me at first we should have saved all this bother—and I cant think why they didn't. But it is nothing to do with the question of your wishing them to stay on (I read them of course the letter in which you made this perfectly clear) or of my wishing to get rid of them. Of course this doesn't alter the fact that they've treated you disgracefully. I think they're thoroughly ashamed of themselves.

However badly they've behaved, I rather wish Trissie had consulted me before she told them that we could not afford to keep them, but were unwilling to tell them so.

When I came down to tell them about the difficulty, I found she had already told them, and being apparently very angry with me, had added all kinds of things about my dishonourable conduct. I suppose you must have told her, and of course it doesn't matter, though, as she met Mrs Langston, one of my cooperative women [at Richmond], and told her also that my behaviour was not that of a lady, I've had to spend a good deal of time in these idiotic conversations, and I wish to goodness she had charged me with all my sins to my face.

The servants want to stay on with us, but I've told them that we must discuss it later when we know for certain whether Leonard is going to get this editorship, or not.[1] We may hear next month.

I shan't hear from Sotheby's till July 4th. They sold the Meredith poems separately, and only got £2 which is wretched. The story[2] seems to me very bad now, and not worth printing, but I'll send it you if you like—I thought perhaps I could rewrite it. I mean to write a good many short things at Asheham and I wish you would consider illustrating them all. We want to bring out a series of short pamphlets in the autumn. Gertler admired your pictures greatly the other night. We talked mostly about his views of art; I didn't much like him, but I suppose he is what they call 'powerful'. I'm going to see Jacques Raverat's pictures at the New English [Art Club].

Dont let Trissie in her anger with me persuade you that I was cross at going to Registry offices—its always a divine pleasure to do anything for you, and I trust to you and Duncan to tell me if I can do anything, though God knows, I shan't try another experiment as long as I live. I'm always in London, and I've heard of several new offices.

But I hope the new woman [Mrs Paton] may do. I thought she looked much nicer than they usually do.

Yr
B.

Berg

948: TO CLIVE BELL   *Hogarth House, [Richmond]*

Sunday [30 June 1918]

My dear Clive,

We shall be in on Wednesday, so do come in after the pictures, and anyhow stay to supper.

I'm a little alarmed at the ugliness of my chair covers, thrust upon me by the Omega, remembering Mary Hutchinsons house—however—she must excuse.

Lytton has come to such a stage that he affects positive disgust at the thought of admiration—How elderly we grow!

Yr.
V.W.

Quentin Bell

1. Leonard had been acting editor of *War and Peace*. Its financial backer, Arnold Rowntree, now suggested that Leonard might become the permanent editor of a more ambitious international review. The scheme at first came to nothing because Ramsay MacDonald, who first promised Leonard his support, later withdrew it. But later Leonard did edit for Rowntree the *International Review*, without Labour backing.
2. *Kew Gardens*, which the Hogarth Press published in May 1919.

Monday [1 July 1918]

Dearest,

Nelly has just been in to me to suggest that she should come to you for a fortnight when Trissie has her holiday. This is entirely her own suggestion, and she is writing to you herself. I dont know if you have made other arrangements; but we can manage all right, as Lottie has offered to do for us, so do have her if its any use. Only neither Leonard or I take any responsibility!

Would the last 2 weeks in July suit you; Then she could come on straight to Asheham—

I wash my hands of the whole horror, (I believe my character was damaged by Trissie, but nothing else suffered)—Poor old Leonard never for an instance tried to prevent them from going on July 1st; he always encouraged it—and I had only one moment of panic after Trissie had gone, when I thought she'd persuaded them to leave us anyhow, and didn't know if I could get anyone. But 4 daily women turned up the day after, without any effort on my part.

However, this is my swan song; I am now mute for ever. The only disaster that I still have to face is that my letters are evidently read by Trissie. She quoted a sentence from one of them, which makes me shiver slightly—I could of course write a truthful and highly unpleasant account of her soul as it was revealed to me in flashes of lightning the other day; but then there are other things to talk about. I dont want to devote my entire life to Trissie. What am I to do?

I try to get away from the servants but I cant—Karins couple have given notice, on the ground that they once had to wash Ann's tea cup, so Adrian has appealed to Sophie; they hope to get her for ever and ever. That was in my head for you—not that you should pension her. I've had a letter from Gerald, which I enclose. Isn't it superb to see how the Duckworths settle down like blue bottles directly any one's dead [Aunt Minna] upon the will?

I had a most interesting talk with Waller [Hills], at Rays [Strachey] party, which I should like to describe, but the small leaden eyes of Trissie are fixed upon this page. Isn't it wretched? However he was inconceivably like my memory of him—holding forth upon education; and very nice and affectionate, and I laughed at him all the time, and he told me how he'd had a row with George [Duckworth] at the Munition's office, and George was incredibly stupid, and then Margaret [George's wife] sent for him and told him he mustn't hurt dear George's feelings—"You say Vanessa has decided against the public school for her boys. Well, my dear, its a gamble, yes, its a gamble. The public school is far from perfect. But its the intellectual stimulus of companionship that one gets there. Yes, Eton did more for me than Balliol; but I suffered all my life from having no sisters. I never knew the woman's side of life until I met your family. All boys ought to know that. Now, take the case of my nephews; both of them killed now.[1] They changed at Harrow; they changed for the worse. But you and Nessa are both of you confirmed gamblers. Well, so am I. I've never been able to conform, my dear Ginia; that whats the matter with me. I'm not in the hierarchy. I shall never be in the government. No, I've gambled, and I've thrown away the game. Still, I find life gets more and more interesting—and I'm horrified at my age. Why, I'm 51; yes, I want you and Nessa to laugh at me, but I still find one or two people who don't take me seriously, Thank God."

He was extraordinarily nice; he seems to have lost a great many teeth; he is coming to dine with us.

The parrokeets [Clive Bell and Mary Hutchinson] have invited themselves for Wednesday, which makes me rather nervous. Gravé has made me 2 dresses. She's infinitely better than anyone save Mrs Young, I think.

I'm sending my story [*Kew Gardens*]; you will see that's its a case of atmosphere, and I dont think I've got it quite. Don't you think you might design a title page? Tell me what you think of the story. I'm going to write an account of my emotions towards one of your pictures, which gives me infinite pleasure, and has changed my views upon aesthetics; and I'm now so lacerated by my chair covers and the carpet that I've got to take steps—I can hardly sit in the drawing room—but all this is very complicated, and I must write a special letter about it. Its a question of half developed aesthetic emotions, constantly checked by others of a literary nature—in fact its all very interesting and intense. Jacques Raverat has revived the art of Ary Sheffer.[2] Dr May used to like his picture of Christ so much. Stone coloured smooth literary and yet falsely artistic pictures, pictures ashamed of being literary and yet crammed with suggestions of character and sublimity in every line. But what a show![3] The drowsy stupidity of the painter's point of view appalled me. There was a picture of a theatre that I liked; but I thought a John drawing knocked everything else out. There was a robust and uncompromising Rothenstein—protesting his fine simple emotions. I'm writing in a hurry, and I mustn't do injustice to my aesthetic philosophy.

How are you?

B.

Abbey Agency have rung up to know if you've taken Mrs Paton. Will you write straight to them? Someone else wants her. How is the baby?

Berg

1. See p. 116, note 3.
2. Ary Scheffer, the Dutch painter (1795-1858) who practised and died in Paris. He was known mainly as an artist of religious subjects, but was also a portraitist, and drawing-master to the children of Louis Philippe.
3. At the New English Art Club.

Monday [8 July 1918]

Dearest,

I've now heard from Sotheby. They sold the Thackeray for £45—the reserve I put on it—the Meredith letter for £21—the one to you for £1-10. fathers mss. for £1-8. They charge £8-12-6 commission, so that your share comes to £21-0-9. I enclose a cheque.

It's not very good, but as we couldn't get a private buyer I suppose we must be content. But I don't think its worth selling any more books there; I believe we should get as much from a bookseller like Quaritch, and we shouldn't have to pay a commission.

I fully intend to write my aesthetics for your derision, but I can't do anything just now except fold and staple 300 copies of K. M.'s story. It takes a good deal of time by hand, but we hope to send out some copies on Thursday. The parrokeets brought Borenius;[1] and we all chattered away at a great rate, except Mary [Hutchinson], who scarcely spoke. However we agreed to advance to Christian names, and we're probably going to print a story of her's.

If you do any woodcuts for my story, they'd better be about the size of Carrington's in our first book, I should think—anything that you like—I don't see that it matters whether it's about the story or not. My only doubt is whether we shall print it after all; I don't myself think its altogether good; and I've an idea for another, which might be better. Still, it might be worse.

There was an awful hymn of praise to you and Duncan from the art critics the other day; thank God, you don't write.

Yr
B.

Do say how you are. Are you still feeling sick—I do wish it would stop—Still I've no doubt the baby will be something miraculous. *You ought to burn my letters always.*

Berg

Monday [15 July 1918]

Dearest,

I've been and bought this lovely sheet of paper—a dozen for 1/6 about—solely to write to you on; such is love; but I wish I hadn't talked about aesthetics. I was merely extremely interested in my own sensations about

1. Tancred Borenius, the Finnish art historian.

your picture. First, however, I think your drawing [for *Kew Gardens*] is a most successful piece; and just in the mood I wanted. As a piece of black and white it is extremely decorative—you see my language is already tainted. Then second or perhaps its third, many thanks for the cheque; if you still want a copy of Prelude, will you remit 3/6—otherwise our accounts get wrong. But I daresay your appetite is satiated. Anyhow tell me what you think of it; and should you say that you *dont* like it as much as Kew Gardens, I shant think less highly of you; but my jealousy, I repeat, is only a film on the surface beneath which is nothing but pure generosity.

As for my aesthetic views, I can't do them justice, because I'm writing waiting for dinner, and in the suburbs an open window lets in passionate male and female voices all the time. We have a music teacher opposite; and also the Richmond mortuary, which accounts for the extraordinary number of coffins one sees about. Coffins at luncheon, coffins as I come back from London; and the gentleman next door is dead of the influenza.

However, the thing that happened was this. For some weeks I have been coming to dislike a chair covered in bright yellow check, bought at the Omega. It became like a small raw spot which I touched each time I came into the room. I brought your picture of the vase and the long flower in from the dining room, and used to sit upon the yellow check looking at it. It gave me exquisite pleasure—so cool, so harmonious, so exquisitely tinted; then I began to conceive the room as a whole, in relation to your picture. Now the yellow cover made me nearly frantic, and to cut a long story short, I went to Burnets. But there I was paralysed, for though I dislike things after a time I find it very difficult to combine them in my mind. I refrained from buying. I went to the National Gallery. It was shut, save to soldiers and nurses in uniform; I went to the National Portrait Gallery; it was shut, save to the widows of officers. You'll hardly believe my disconsolate state, with this picture tempting me to excursions in building up rooms harmonious with it, and no sort of power to fulfil my wishes. Finally, I went to Souhamis. The first time I brought back 2 18th century pieces of embroidery. At the sight of 18th century embroidery my confidence in my own taste completely returned. I flung them upon the yellow chair—for which I now felt little short of physical rage. No. Something again was wrong. Back I went to Souhamis', and now I have a blue and green Persian cover, on a yellow-white background. But you see what prospects are opened up. I came to the conclusion that there is a quality in your picture which though perceptible is at present much beyond me, but that in the main my aesthetic feelings are so undeveloped that I had better begin at the very beginning. But do you think that this semi-conscious process of coming to dislike one colour very much and liking a picture better and better points to some sort of live instinct trying to come to existence? I humbly hope so.

At any rate, there is no doubt that your painting gives me more pleasure than any painting in the National Gallery. I got in there this afternoon.

This letter is already so long and rather incoherent too I'm afraid, that I'd better perhaps draw to an end. But I must tell you of my melancholy at the National Gallery. How, I ask, can you expect English people to like art when they are treated thus? There is a room devoted to battle pictures; there is Millais' Gladstone, and Furses Return from the ride (the black in the hind quarters of the horse is all sunk in and dead—still the silk dress stands out quite stiffly); there are some large dull Italians; any number of the polished Dutch; and the rest I suppose, put away in the cellars. A herd of poor children was being swept from picture to picture by a wretched little servant girl, with a face like the inside of a penny bun; and her lecture always began "Now, children, dont stand too near or you cant see; and dont shuffle your feet so. D'you think they polish the floors for you to slide on? This is the Descent of our Lord from the Cross. etc etc" Now I wish you'd tell me what is the point of Veronese: a picture, I mean of a Goddess asleep and a man in armour approaching her: I see the nice warm ripe colours; but they dont much excite me; Delacroix I saw no point in: Botticelli, the round one of the Madonna may I daresay be beautiful, but to me it looks like a very perfect passage of pure style; but when I draw near the French I am at once amused and very much pleased. I refer in particular to Berthe Morrisot; her picture of 2 women in a boat is the kind of picture I like;[1] it gives me great pleasure, and I seem able to understand it. Also the Renoir umbrellas; also a picture of still life on a mantelpiece by Vuillard; also a beach by Boudin (?); but I dont much care for Corot.

The English I think are far best at landscape; they have a feeling for that; I like Cox and Constable; I like pictures of Norfolk heaths with windmills against the sky; I found a Turner which I thought very beautiful—a sketch, I suppose, since the iridescent haze had been left out. Then there were a great many Rubens drawings, or said to be by Rubens, which convey nothing to me. Mancini I see no point in. I liked a picture of men round a table by Legros;[2] and a very dark amber coloured landscape with one red cow in it, by an 18th [17th] century Frenchman called perhaps Bourdon;[3] that, again, is the sort of picture I should like to have.

What I am driving at is this; could you see your way to lend me any more pictures? Could I have any from Gordon Square?—(I like Fantin Latour's apples on a plate) would it be possible to get any lent me at the Omega on payment of a small sum? I want to change such as I have about; and we are badly in want of some at Asheham.

1. Berthe Morisot, *Summer's Day*.
2. *Le Repas des Pauvres*, now in the Tate Gallery.
3. Sebastien Bourdon, *The Return of the Ark*.

I'm now thinking of going to the Allied Artists;[1] and I will give you an account of them; since I suppose that there may be the same curious interest in a writer's account of pictures as the other way round. And yet the queer thing is that I accept your or Duncan's view of writing absolutely seriously.

I dont think your drawing, by the way is too big; the difficulty is, suppose we decide not to print that story after all?

In the world of letters Lytton is still predominant. I think his fame has changed him, as love might; he is immensely appreciative, even tender; jumps up and seizes withered virgins like Vernon Lee,[2] and leaves them gibbering with ecstasy. He spent last week end with the Duchess of Marlborough. Mrs Asquith, poor woman, does for herself by talking about books, and as her method is to say startling things and she can't settle down to discuss them, she becomes a fearful bore, and as wrong as she can be. Still, he admits that its all very pleasant; though agitating, because he fears it will soon die down. We are going to Tidmarsh on Saturday. Gumbo [Marjorie Strachey] is going to be there. She has renounced Josh[Wedgwood] and is as sprightly as can be— You heard, I suppose, that Mrs H[umphry] Ward accuses Lytton in the Lit. Suppt. of being a pro-German on account of the brutality of his methods?

Adrian has become a violent politician; and delivered an address on Peace to my Guild with the greatest success. He and Karin talk of finding rooms near us in August; possibly at Southease. I wish he hadn't married her (you put this straight in the locked drawer, if not the w.c. dont you?) A good cob of a woman; but so hearty and so without shade or softness. Age too will harden her; as it is she takes a businesslike view of life and duty and death too I daresay; and her family will coarsen her. I think its absurd to call Adrian a bore; he has great distinction; not that I could ever live with him tolerably.

Shall we get up a pageant of the 90ties? Waller [Hills] and Pippa [Strachey] are dining with us I think. Thank God for old Snow [Margery Snowden]; I hope I may see her, though I really prefer thinking of her since she dislikes me, I fear. I hope you'll bring the unborn baby up to appreciate me; I'm already half in love with her/him. It will have lovely great eyes; soft hair; a divine mouth; and then only think what a gifted lovable sprite it will be so understanding from its earliest years, and as wise as an idol, and as witty as a humming bird.

Yr

B.

Berg

1. The Allied Artists Association was founded before the war to exhibit the work of a wide variety of artists, including occasionally the 'Bloomsbury' artists, but the latter preferred to exhibit with the London Group and the Omega Workshops.
2. The novelist and critic (1856-1935).

Tuesday [16 July 1918]

My dear Clive,

We aren't coming to Garsington this week end as we're staying at Tidmarsh [Lytton Strachey]. Ottoline, I believe, has done her best to insist that the whole party shall remove to Garsington,—but so far without success. I'm afraid you're away the week end after when I suppose we do come.

I'm amused to hear of the Murry affair; I read his review[1] without recognising it. The tone seems a little superior for I think there's some merit in the war poems anyhow—still Ott's methods are monstrous, and I'm glad Murry didn't bow down.

I only maintain that K. M.'s story has a certain quality as a work of art besides the obvious cleverness, which made it worth printing, and a good deal better than most stories anyhow.

I'm sorry I was gracious to Mary: I didn't mean to have that effect, but I daresay its inevitable from one of my age to one of hers. Anyhow I hope you'll keep her to her story.[2]

Yours,
V.W.

Quentin Bell

Friday [26 July 1918]

Dearest,

Here is the picture. I hope you will do as many more as you can both for that story [*Kew Gardens*], and for the one about the party.[3] We could easily make the books a little bigger for the sake of the pictures.

Here it is pouring hard, and I am going in my devotion, to Gordon Sqre to fetch my pictures. No confirmation of the Ka rumour[4] has been had, and I am half hoping that it mayn't be true.

We are committed not only to give Adrian and Karin meals, but to have

1. A review by John Middleton Murry of Siegfried Sassoon's *Counter-Attack* in the *Nation*. Ottoline had brought pressure to bear upon Murry to review the book favourably, and Philip Morrell wrote an angry letter of protest when he didn't.
2. Which Mary Hutchinson had promised to write for the Hogarth Press. Mary was then aged 29, and Virginia 36.
3. Unpublished and unidentified.
4. Ka Cox was engaged to Will Arnold-Forster, the painter and publicist.

Ann[1] in the house! I don't mind Ann, but the thought of Mabel [Karin's maid] rather alarms me. I'm going to take to sealing my letters for reasons which I will give you when we meet.

Sotheby's has sent me £1-16 for the Meredith poems;[2] I will send you your miserable share.

Leonard has been asked to stand for Parliament.[3] By the way, I find that Carrington cross examined him about my new nephew. I rather think it would be best to tell him what I know. He would then be able to put dust in their eyes. As it is he has his doubts and rather increases theirs perhaps. But I wont say anything unless you tell me I can. I suppose Lytton put her up to it, and they probably think we know.[4] I enjoyed my vision of Dolphin in her majestic glory.

B.

But do you really mean that I dont know anything about human nature?

Berg

954: To Lady Ottoline Morrell   *Asheham, Rodmell,*
                                       Lewes, [Sussex]
[1? August 1918]

My dear Ottoline,

This letter is belated, owing to the difficulty of writing even a letter when one is moving. Moreover to describe my pleasure [at Garsington] during the week end is very difficult. I liked it all so much, from the comfort of my bed to the beauty of the view—and that is saying nothing about the human beings, who were all wonderfully interesting I thought. It is the loveliest of places.

This is lovely too, but very different—Entirely overgrown with weeds for one thing, and suffering from a plague of small frogs and black beetles, who come in through the windows. However one of these days we hope you will come and see it for yourself, though I should feel alarmed—not that I suspect you of travelling with six maids, but you carry your standards with you.

We expect the Murry's tomorrow, if they manage the journey, which is so horrid now that I shant be surprised if they dont.

1. Their daughter, born in 1916.
2. The first edition of *Modern Love*.
3. Leonard had received a letter from M. M. Green inviting him to stand as a parliamentary candidate for a newly formed group, The Seven Universities Democratic Association. It was the same group which nominated him in 1920, with Labour backing.
4. Carrington and Lytton were inquisitive about the paternity of Vanessa's expected child.

We met Koteliansky in London, who wanted us to come and meet [D. H.] Lawrence. I'm in two minds—tempted, but alarmed. I sometimes wonder why the intelligent people are so made that one can't see them without quarrelling—but it seems a law. I'm thinking of the Murry's and Lawrence, not of you and me!

I brought your flowers here—they were too lovely to leave, and the carnations are on the table as bright as ever.

We shall look anxiously for Philip's [Morrell] speech—

Leonard wishes to be remembered.

Yr aff

V.W.

Texas

955: TO KATHERINE COX

Asheham, Rodmell

Lewes, [Sussex]

Aug. 3rd [1918]

Dearest Ka,

I had heard from Bob [Trevelyan], but he was so muddled that I wasn't certain, and then we came here, and I was on the point of writing to you. Of course, as you know very well, no one seems to me more superbly fitted for every kind of blessing than my dear Bruin Cox. The only trouble is that I admired her so profoundly in her single state that I dont see how even marriage can improve her. Nor can I believe that any one loves her better or has more reason to bless her than I have. No, I don't think that even Will [Arnold-Forster] will ever know as many good things about you as Leonard and I do.

It's odd how little I know him (why shan't I like him?) My chief impression is that I'm immensely old and that he's extremely young; and we are sitting at Fitzroy Sqre on a Thursday evening hundreds of years ago discussing art.

But the point is now will you both come here next Friday to Monday? Please do. Ask him from us. Its our only free weekend for some time; and make it be Friday to Monday—The other is so short. If Will can't come, come alone, but we very much want to see him too. We shall be by ourselves.

Yrs

V.W.

I am *immensely* pleased.

Mark Arnold-Forster

956: To Vanessa Bell

Thursday [8 August 1918]

Dearest,

The servants want me to send you a note, so as to give them an excuse for going to Charleston and making it up with Trissie, if she's willing.

I wish we could meet, but I dont know what to suggest—the weather is so vile. Perhaps I might come over to lunch one day next week if it suited you— I rather think we have Ka and Arnold Forster here for the week end, but I'm not certain. If so, I expect they'll want to see you. If it were fine, perhaps we could have a picnic, otherwise I might suggest they're walking over on Sunday, if you dont object—unless Duncan and Bunny would come here, which would be charming. There may be a very dull man called Bonwick[1] who is coming to talk about starting the new [international] review.

Adrian and Karin are coming next week—for a fortnight, as their lodgings fell through. Ann has gone to Mabel's home.

I went to Gordon Sqre to fetch the pictures, but after searching everywhere could only find the one in the frame. Blanche [maid] thought that Clive had taken them to Charleston. If so, would you give them to the servants to bring back, or any others, as I'm in fearful straits, and have even had to unearth the Sargent portrait of Henry James[2]—Did I tell you about our week end at Garsington? This is one of the crumbs I keep to tempt my Dolphin out of her pool with.

Yr
B.

Berg

957: To Vanessa Bell

Friday [9 August 1918]

Dearest,

What a devil you were about the pictures! But as you've promised to give me 3 large ones, I'll let you off this time—still, your craft was scandalous.

I've heard from Ka that she and Will (as she calls him) have to work in their offices this Sunday, and they want to come later. Bonwick is coming— and probably (but we're in a great mess with our visitors) either Margery

1. Arnold Rowntree's business manager.
2. The original of this portrait, done in 1913 in commemoration of James' 70th birthday, was bequeathed by him to the National Portrait Gallery. James had given photographs of the portrait to many of his friends, including Leslie Stephen.

Strachey, Mrs [Molly] Hamilton, both, or neither. Its too vague to make any plans, so you'd better not expect us for lunch. If we came we would bring our own food.

Didn't you know that Ka was engaged? I had a letter from her. She says he's a "wild creature", and that I probably shan't like him, and that she's in love with him. They don't mean to be married till after the war—as I suppose the country must come first.

Do you think you could ask the Stephens [Karin and Adrian] for the 31st weekend? They go back on the Monday following, and we shall have Ka and Will and Pernel I think, so it would be a great convenience to us, and save them going to rooms in Lewes.

They arrive next Friday, and go to the Pelham Arms, and come to us on Monday. We are going to be strictly independent, and only to meet at meals, and only to speak when we wish, so that perhaps we shant altogether come to grief, as you think likely.

If we don't meet on Sunday, shall I come to lunch and spend the afternoon next Wednesday?

Katherine and Murry never came, as she is ill again. I'm a little disturbed by a story of hers in the English Review.[1] Its—well I wont say; and anyhow, please tell Maynard, its a great deal better than Margot's Love Letters. I live to a large extent upon her literary criticisms which Lytton hands on.[2]

Yr

B.

Give my love to my nephews; and say I should like to have a visit from them. Perhaps we might manage a treat for Quentin's birthday [19 August]—Tell me what he'd like for a present.

Berg

958: To Dora Carrington   *Asheham House, Rodmell, Lewes, [Sussex]*

Sunday [11 August 1918]

My dear Carrington

Will you come and stay with us next week end—17th? Now please do. I've asked Norton but even without him there are attractions enough, animal and spiritual. Also, I promise you shan't be tormented; you shall be

1. *Bliss*, by Katherine Mansfield, which Virginia found superficial and hard.
2. Lytton was constantly meeting Margot Asquith at Garsington, and her 'Love Letters' were not her own, but those of other people, which she had discussed with him.

treated like a real young lady on a visit, and given flowers in your bedroom and a lid upon your po.

Its terrifically hot. Imagine the corn all turning different shades of yellow over the downs; and then theres a green patch, and a red one, and so on— Even you might be tempted to—I will not say what. Its odd that painting should appeal to your modesty as personal chastity appealed to our mothers'. It must be a kind of inversion, I think. You young things are not to escape the curse of Eve as easily as all that. Nature will have her rights. (this is part of a lecture I'm going to deliver next Saturday—)

Leonard has taken our new friend Mr Bonwick of Purley over to Charleston, which he won't enjoy, but still it breaks up the afternoon. Mr Bonwick has the facial twitch, he is infinitely beneath us in social standing, dressed all in black, with great black boots, but morally so exalted that we only recover our balance by boasting of people like Lytton—and even so, moral height wins the day. Moral height without much in the way of intellect, so there's a chance for poor old Nick still. Still, Lytton's range will never include Mr Bonwick of Purley—oh no!

Would you have the great goodness to let me know about the week end as soon as you can?

Yr
V.W.

Robert H. Taylor

959: To Katherine Cox   *Asheham, Rodmell,*
                                         Lewes, [Sussex]

Aug 13th [1918]

Dearest Ka,

Our letters have crossed, I suppose: Are you to be married at once? I thought you said something about waiting till after the war—but this is much more satisfactory.

Anyhow, shall you be able to come on the 31st? It would suit us perfectly. Adrian and Karin will have withdrawn by then. As for Asheham now, with the corn ripe in a blazing sun I feel inclined to think all human arrangements a little insignificant compared with it.

I wrote the article on Rupert in the Times.[1] Bruce Richmond sent the book to me; but when I came to do it I felt that to say out loud what even I knew of Rupert was utterly repulsive, so I merely trod out my 2 columns as decorously as possible. It seemed useless to pitch into Eddy [Marsh]. James [Strachey] meant to try, but gave it up. I think it was one of the most

1. Review of *The Collected Poems of Rupert Brooke, with a Memoir,* by Edward Marsh (*TLS,* 8 August 1918).

repulsive biographies I've ever read (this, of course, is a little overstated!). He contrived to make the [Brooke] letters as superficial and affected as his own account of Rupert. We're now suggesting that James should write something for us to print. He's sending us the letters to look at. But if you tell Mrs Brooke would you ask her not to tell anyone else, as Richmond is always anxious it shouldn't get out who has done reviews.

I must now go and feed my white cat, and bicycle over to Charleston to spend the night. Leonard is up at York, interviewing Mr Rowntree about his new review.

Let me know whether you and Will will come here; and do come unless you are too tired and worried and cross and snarly or happy and engrossed etc. I've just seen the notice in the Court Circular, and realise with dismay that you'll be a niece of Mrs Humphrey Wards!

Yr V.W.

I suppose you couldn't tell Mrs Brooke, if you wish, that I remember her with the greatest clearness, at St Ives, when Rupert was 5 and I was 10 and Dick [his brother] played cricket with us, and we all went fishing. I can see her wrinkles at this moment—and feel a great respect for her, partly from hearing Rupert read aloud her letters—wh. were superb.

Mark Arnold-Forster

960: To Katherine Cox   *Asheham, [Rodmell, Sussex]*

Thursday [15 August 1918]

Dearest Ka,

How utterly damnable! I'm very sorry too that you've been bothered in this way. I suppose there's no use in trying to seduce you to come here by yourself, though I may point out that marriage is a lifelong affair, and I expect a short stay with us would do you an immense amount of good. I hear that you look worn owing to the burden of love and Empire and the heat and the general horror. Anyhow, if you should change your mind your room is waiting.

There are thousands of things I want to say to you: and I don't much expect we shall ever meet once youre married—One question is, what would you like for a wedding present? We all want to know—(Adrian and Karin too) and why do you say you are going to live in Lancaster Place? Surely only the widows of judges live there—and what's going to happen to Cliffords Inn—But whats the use of beginning, when I wanted merely to have you about the place, saying your wise things, and creating an atmosphere of sagacious peace—snuffing at the doors before you come in, and rolling in the long grass.

Please tell Will how sorry we are.   Yrs
                                                            V.W.

I heard from Mrs Brooke, who wants me to come and see her.

Shall I come and wait at the corner to see you married?

Mark Arnold-Forster

961: To Dora Carrington   *Asheham, [Rodmell, Sussex]*

Postcard
[16 August 1918]

Very glad you can come. Will you bring your butter, as we're rather badly off.

                                                            V.W.
Robert H. Taylor

962: To Vanessa Bell   *[Asheham, Rodmell, Sussex]*

[17? August 1918]

Dearest

I got the best toys I could for Quentin, but there wasn't much choice. The gun was 2/6 and the boat was 2/6—the writing book 4d. If you and Duncan like to give these, will you give him the other things as my present.

Carrington is coming, but Norton can't.

If its weather like this tomorrow, there won't be much use in having a picnic, I'm afraid.

The Stephen's come up this afternoon—so our trial will begin.

How delightful it was for you to have me the other day!

Is Barbara staying with you?

I'm writing to ask Duncan if he'll spend the night tomorrow. It would not only enchant us (this he knows too well) but Carrington, so I hope he'll come.   Yr
                                                            B.

If we can't come tomorrow, we will send the cake.

I've been hanging the pictures. They have given me several new ideas on art.

Berg

269

Asheham, Rodmell,
Lewes, [Sussex]

Sunday 18th Aug. [1918]

My dear Ottoline

I think you must be the only hostess who actually thanks her guests for having enjoyed themselves! As I always believe you have a conception of life which is far more magnificent than any that can be realised with the sort of material available. But it is superb that you should go on trying to make us out more beautiful and brilliant and humane than we can ever possibly be.

I can't think whats happened since we were at Garsington. The time passes, with proper nights and days, I suppose, but one seems to float through them in a disembodied kind of way here. For one thing we've been practically alone, which has a very spiritual effect upon the mind. No gossip, no malevolence, no support from one's fellow creatures.

I can't think why one doesn't spend the whole year in this way. I see— though I dont expect you to agree—that after 6 months I should be a kind of Saint, and Leonard an undoubted prophet. We should shed virtue on people as we walked along the roads. To prevent this transformation, Carrington and Adrian and Karin arrived last night, and I had such a bath of the flesh that I am far from unspotted this morning. We gossipped for 5 hours.

Carrington is a most useful guest, so broken into unselfishness by the Stracheys that she insists either upon cutting the grass or pumping the water. Lytton is staying with the Asquiths and wearing a whole wardrobe of new clothes. Katherine and Murry never came after all, so we couldn't go on discussing the review[1]—but I believe Sassoon has got far more praise because of it in all the other papers. The Statesman is full of him. Katherine was too ill to travel. She wrote me a line, only to say that her mother had died, and she was very unhappy.

Please write again; and do set aside an hour from your house, and begin your book.[2]

Your aff

Texas   V.W.

Asheham, [Rodmell,
Sussex]

Wednesday [21 August 1918]

My dear Duncan,

I confess it cut me to the heart to see that you preferred Barbara to me.

1. See p. 262, note 1.
2. Ottoline's memoirs. Although she kept a regular journal, she did not begin to write her memoirs until the early 1930's, and after her death in 1938, they were edited for publication by Robert Gathorne-Hardy.

However, there's now the attraction of Karin to offer you—so won't you come over and spend Saturday night? Then perhaps we could have a picnic on Sunday, and so take you home again. Barbara and Saxon threatened to spend a fortnight here—they still haunt my dreams. I won't say any more because I know my letter will lie about on the mantelpiece at Charleston. I *might* say a great deal of infinite interest. O what thousands of compliments rained over me the other day for you and Nessa, I mean. Carrington came back in a tipsy condition from seeing your pictures.

I have just written to the Pelman Institute[1] for a series of Grey Books. I want to hear about Trissie.[2]

Your V.W.

Duncan Grant

965: To Mrs M. R. Brooke   *Asheham House, Rodmell,*
                 Lewes, Sussex

21st Aug. 1918

Dear Mrs Brooke,

It was a great pleasure to get your letter this morning. I had rather hoped that you would *not* see my review, as I felt that I had not been able to say what I wanted to say about Rupert. Also I am afraid that I gave the impression that I disliked Mr Marsh's memoir much more than I meant to. If I was at all disappointed it was that he gave of course rather his impression of Rupert than the impression which one had always had of him partly from the Stracheys and other friends of his own age. But then Mr Marsh could not have done otherwise, and one is very glad to have the Memoir as it is. Rupert was so great a figure in his friends eyes that no memoir could possibly be good enough. Indeed, I felt it to be useless to try to write about him. One couldn't get near to his extraordinary charm and goodness. I was 5 years older than he was, and I saw him very little compared with most people, but perhaps because of the St Ives days I always felt that I knew him as one knows one's own family. I stayed a week with him at Grantchester [1911] and then he came down here, and we met sometimes in London. He was a wonderful friend. I married in 1912, and was ill for a long time afterwards, and never saw him after he went to America.

It would be a great pleasure to me if I might come and see you when you are in London. We go back to Hogarth House, Paradise Road, Richmond, S. W. in October.

1. For the training of memory.
2. Trissie Selwood, a maid who stayed eighteen months at Charleston, and then married the son of Mr Stacey, who leased several farms, including Charleston itself.

Perhaps you would write and tell me if you ever cared to see me.
Thank you again for your letter, and believe me

Yours sincerely,
Virginia Woolf

King's

966: To Vanessa Bell
Asheham, [Rodmell, Sussex]

Thursday [5? September 1918]

Dearest,

Liz says that she thinks she had better not take the place, on account of her baby, as she thinks it would be impossible to look after him and do the work.

Mrs Hammond is willing to come to you on the 16th for a fortnight; if that would suit you. She says she does not want to take a permanent place.

Liz would have liked to come apparently, if it hadn't been for the baby.

Mrs Hammond would like to see you. I will come over tomorrow, Friday, after lunch, about 2.30. and perhaps we could make arrangements then.

Of course the servants are going home soon and might hear of one of their friends. However, we can discuss this tomorrow.

Yr.

B.

Berg

967: To Vanessa Bell
[Asheham, Rodmell, Sussex]

[8 September 1918]

Dearest,

Mrs Hammond will come on the 16th for 2 weeks certainly, probably longer if you want her. At first she said she must have 20/—but I said this was absurd, and she seems quite glad to come for 15/—

Nelly says the pay has gone up. They all went to the picnic place to meet you yesterday. Nelly rode to Charleston twice but did not dare go in lest T[rissie]. should see her.

Apparently Liz had made up her mind that she would go to you, if you asked her to. I think there's no doubt she would come later as nurse if you wanted her.

I've said that you dont want to settle anything yet, and anyhow you wont want her as cook.

They quite enjoyed their picnic, so it didn't matter. Leonard would like to come and see you one afternoon this week if its agreeable to you.

The reason he was so silent with Duncan was that he went out into the garden and was sick, and felt sick all the evening, without saying so. We heard this morning that he is now made Editor of the New Review[1]—also that we can take Asheham on by the year—though they see no prospect at present of turning us out.

I'd like to come over again more than anything—in hopes of grading [apples]—but I must give this to Bunny, who has been very charming.

Yr
B.

Berg

968: To Dora Carrington

Asheham, [Rodmell,
Sussex]

Sept. 9th [1918]

Dear Carrington

We have just finished tea with your butter, and we dont know how to thank you. It seems to me that one can only compare you to one of the heroes of history or to the Pelican. We had dwindled to miserable dabs, the size of a finger nail, half dissolved, and spotted with flies. Then there's the shortbread. I have made enquiries and find that it only costs the incredibly low sum of 1/- a round. Our winter prospects are immensely brightened. You must come to tea. I've just bought 8 combs of honey, from poor Bunny, who develops distinct signs of humanity—if you dig long enough. He forced me to give him 2 photographs of Alix, and went off mumbling over them in a most touching way.

I dont know that there's any other news. Duncan came round in a passion and tore down the picture over the fireplace, which he says, he particularly dislikes. Nessa did the same by one of hers. Its mere vanity, and at their age absurd. Ka was married at 11 this morning, at which hour a cloud passed over the sun, and I seemed to hear the tolling of a bell.

We expect the Sidney Webbs and a maniac called George Young,[2] brother of Hilton, on Saturday. This maniac believes that he and the Webbs together can end the war—so if you read of a sudden peace, armies disbanded, terms settled, you'll know where it comes from. Anyhow it will be a most

---

1. Rowntree's *International Review*. See p. 255, note 1.
2. Formerly a diplomat, and now an officer in the Marines.

painful weekend for me. Leonard is now a proper editor with offices in Fleet Street; he is conducting his operations at my ear, so I must stop, but he says I am to thank you again for his tea, and give his love to Lytton to whom he is writing.

Yr
V.W.

We never meant that Wooler[1] itself was good, but only that it was the only place to stay in the neighbourhood.

Robert H. Taylor

969: To Vanessa Bell   *Asheham, [Rodmell,
                                                   Sussex]*

Tuesday [10 September 1918]

Dearest,

I haven't heard from Clive, so I don't know what he wants to do. As a matter of fact it would as it turns out suit us best to have them for the night of the 16th, as the servants will still be here. Wouldn't it be possible for them to bring the children here, and for Nelly to take them on to Charleston?

Mrs Hammond doesn't know the way, so that Nelly was anyhow going to take her on Monday, and I'm sure she'd take the children if they could get here fairly early.

I've asked Gertler to come for the 21st-23rd week end, and I thought perhaps you'd ask him over to you on Sunday. We may have a Jewish week end with my family in law. Leonard will come over the first fairly fine afternoon.

I'll come anyhow one day—but I think he'd like a little conversation with you alone.

Now that your domestic troubles are over, mine are beginning. I spent the whole morning in the usual horrors—but I don't think they amount to much.

If I don't hear from Clive I shall take it for granted they're not coming.

Your B.

We have settled to stay on here till Oct. 6th
It would give me infinite pleasure to see you.

Berg

1. In Northumberland, where the Woolfs had stayed at the Cottage Hotel in August and September 1914.

[*Asheham, Rodmell,*
Thursday [12 September 1918]   *Sussex*]

Dearest,

Leonard means to try and come in spite of the weather. I've not heard from Clive. We can have them later for the night if they dont mind putting up with our solitary char.

I don't quite know what arrangements to make about coming over, as I shall have my affairs next week. I'd like to come tomorrow, but I don't know if I shall be able to in this weather.

I suppose it wd. be all right if I turned up. Gertler is coming on Saturday week.

Both the servants have now given notice! Its the most idiotic story I ever heard, but Leonard will tell you. I don't think they will go in the end, as Nelly is very anxious to stay—still, I'm not going to press them this time.

Barbara [Bagenal] seems to have been too silly, and started all kinds of gossip about them down here, which adds to the difficulties. It's a lesson against lending one's house.

Do you think you have any small Chinese coat or wrapper which I could wear in the evening while the Webbs are here? My evening clothes are so thin they seem rather foolish. Also, have you any lace fronts that I could wear inside my little blue jacket instead of my yellow handkerchief. I seem to have got fearfully shabby and G. Young is coming too. Anything you could spare I should be glad of—and I would send them back on Monday— by Nelly. Do you want Mrs Hammond to bring all her ration cards? I suppose so.

I've lost the woollen cap you made me. This is a hint.

                                                        Yr
                                                          B.

Perhaps the best plan wd. be for me to come tomorrow for the night, if that suits you.

Dont tell Trissie anything about N. and L: as she of course seems to have been doing her best to get them to leave, and made some impression on Lottie, though none on N.

Berg

Asheham, [*Rodmell*
[September ? 1918]   *Sussex*]

Dearest Molly,

I know you detest getting letters, so this will only be the shortest possible line to say how greatly and sincerely I've enjoyed your book [*A Pier and a Band*] and only wished at the end that there was another volume to begin again.

For goodness sake write another entirely made of letters. I liked them best. I didn't care for the building disputes, or for Mr Tippits, or Sir John or Mr Villiers; I didn't want to be told about the German Empire; all the rest I thought purely delightful, and how I envied you your beautiful malicious phrases which look so simple to begin with and then give a flick of their tails and sum up an entire character or situation—Perdita's power, of course, which makes her so uncompromising, in spite of the fact that her manners are exquisite—indeed, one of the few ladies in modern fiction.

Fitzgerald is one of the most delightful characters in real life—But I assure you that you must at once begin another book entirely of letters.

Now, that's over! Aren't you glad!

Yrs
V.W.

Mrs Michael MacCarthy

972: To Clive Bell
Asheham [Rodmell,
Sussex]

Postcard
Saturday [14 September 1918]

Tuesday next would suit as well as any other night, if you and Mary [Hutchinson] liked to stop here on your way to Charleston.

The week end is no good for us—Would you let me have a line?
V.W.

Quentin Bell

973: To Vanessa Bell
[Asheham, Rodmell,
Sussex]

Monday [16 September 1918]

Dearest

There seems a fate against my coming. I've had to lend Nelly my bicycle today, and also I've got to interview Mrs Geall [daily help], so I cant get over. I daresay its just as well, and your brats will be coming, and I should be jealous.

I will try and come tomorrow, Early, about 11. or 11.30. and come back here for tea. Clive wrote, and I suggested they should come here for Tuesday night so I should have to get back; but it seems the only chance of seeing you.

God! What a week end we had! Incessant talk for 46 hours, and the Webbs up at 5.30 chattering in their rooms, and George Young, just like Hilton, holding forth in the most serious and romantic way, very slow and stiff and incredibly honourable.

It was really rather fun—anyhow now that it's over. But I must tell you—

Yr

Berg   B.

975: To Roger Fry   *Asheham House, Rodmell,*
                                                              Lewes, [Sussex]
17th Sept. [1918]

My dear Roger,

Is there any chance that you would come to us on Saturday next, 21st: for the week end? I've just seen Clive and Mary and they say they're not going to you till later, and are staying at Charleston over the week end. Gertler is coming to us; so it would be very suitable if you would come, and very delightful too, and then you could take Nessa back to Guildford with you (you see I am making out an unanswerable case).

I'm telling Gertler to catch the 1.55 at Victoria, and then catch the 3.58 on to Glynde and walk out, as I don't suppose he'll be able to afford a fly, and the trains connect, for a wonder.

Would you bring your butter, as we are kept very short of what we're allowed even. I cant promise much in the way of cooking, as the servants are on their holidays, but if you'll tell me what you're ordered, I will do my best to get it.

Its very lovely here. Even the barren heart of Mrs Webb kindled slightly at the view, and she has instructed me to find her a house near where she can die in—that being her mania, apparently. We had a wonderful week end, and I feel the whole world, and all its population, flattened out for myriads of miles in consequence of our argument.

Yr. V.W.

Sussex

975: To Barbara Bagenal   *Asheham, Rodmell,*
                                                              Lewes, [Sussex]
20th Sept. [1918]

Dear Barbara,

We can't thank you at all adequately for your pat of butter. Butter is far the most precious thing in the world here, because the Co-ops can only give us 2 ozs. a week, which merely greases the top of one's toast at breakfast, and leaves one to dry bread at tea. Now we look forward to 7 good teas; at each one you and Nick shall be blessed by name. But how on earth do you manage to spare it? It seems to me the height of generosity.

I had never missed the Hardy, I confess, but I am very glad to have it back again. It is infinite ages since we met—the last time is connected in my mind chiefly, but not entirely, with your very handsome brindled cat. I feel that your house will always be comfortable and distinguished with such a cat. But where is your house going to be, and is it true that Nick is becoming a farmer?[1] Well, I don't suppose any woman in Hampstead has lived through so many things in a year as you have. Printing at Hogarth must look like something seen through opera glasses upside down. I am so domestic as to think that nothing can be quite so important as child bearing, and I'm so envious that I dont think I shall speak to you; and yet they tell me you pretend to dismiss it all with a shrug, and the brat is to be looked after by a committee of matrons!

I have been entirely sunk in the pitchy and indeed stinking waters of domestic strife—in which by the way you are remotely concerned. After suffering for a long time, I told Lottie she must clean our jugs and basins. This, as I expected, produced first a torrent of abuse; then she gave notice; then she accused me of lending my house to strangers, who left it very dirty, and gave her a bad name with the cottagers, and used up all the coal. This refers to Mrs Mason [servant] of course. Do you think there's any truth in it?—I dont for a moment suppose that she left the house dirtier than she found it, but I wonder if she complained to Mrs Attfield, and also whether there *was* some mystery about the coal? Lottie now, as usual, wants to stay on; but we are assured that our coal has been stolen. Can you remember if there was much when you came, and any left when you went? It really doesn't matter, as we cant do anything more than buy a new padlock, which we have already done; and leaving the house as we do, one must expect a good deal of dirt and some stealing I suppose.

Charleston is full of Clive and Mary and Mrs B[rereton] come back, and the children home again. Clive and Mary should be here at this moment, but she took ill, as they say; and as we've only a charwoman, and Mary can't help being a lady, I'm a little relieved. We've been having the Sidney Webbs, and tomorrow Gertler comes, and then, thank God, absolute silence and sloth for 10 days. But shall you be in London on the 7th October? Are you going to take to vegetables too? I'll try to write to Saxon, but I feel unable to conceive him in a Homburg hat, on the Parade or in the Wall before breakfast.

We're sending you some mushrooms that we picked in the hollow this afternoon in thanksgiving for the butter.

Yr V.W.

Berg

1. Nicholas Bagenal became a horticulturist after the war, and worked at the East Malling Research Station in Kent.

976: To Clive Bell   *Asheham, [Rodmell,*
                                        Sussex]

Friday [20 September 1918]

My dear Clive,

We were very sorry that you couldn't come yesterday, especially as it seems impossible to suggest any feasible plan for meeting. I can't come over today, not only because of the weather and my puncture (I smashed the pump too, trying to blow the tyre up and so had to walk home) but also I have to squeeze out suddenly a long review.

We will try to manage something on Sunday. Roger can't come, so Gertler will be here alone.

I hope Mary is better. I can't help suspecting that she was overcome, on setting out, by her fear of meeting my just curiosity about that story [for the Hogarth Press].

Would she have the kindness to send me Eliots[1] address once more. I lost it the first time.

                                        Your
                                        V.W.

If anyone comes to lunch on Sunday they will bring their own food.

Quentin Bell

977: To Vanessa Bell   *Asheham, [Rodmell,*
                                        Sussex]

Saturday [5 October 1918]

Dearest,

What a fearful bore about your attempted miscarriage! For Gods sake be careful, and remember your responsibilities. The only 7 months child known to me was Hugo Montgomerie [*unidentified*], and I dont want my pick and cream of creation to go giving young women in hansom cabs khaki bibles.

I am immensely interested by the servant developments. I rather suspected something of the kind though Nelly said nothing about it when she wrote except that she had seen you. I dont think there's any good attempting to forecast what they will wish to do. Only 2 days before the row Nelly told me that they had never felt so settled—But if they say that they want to go to you I shall certainly not attempt to persuade them to stay. I'm un-

1. T. S. Eliot and Virginia do not seem to have met before 15 November 1918, when he came to Hogarth House, but they corresponded before then.

selfish enough to be rather anxious that they should go to you, as I believe they'd be on their honour to behave well, and you'd find them a great comfort compared with Emily—(God! what horrors you do have!) Anyhow, I'm not going to say anything, but I shall let them broach the whole matter to me. Of course, I don't altogether want them to go, from our point of view as they have great merits, and Nelly has been extremely nice all this time. On the other hand, I don't believe Lottie will ever swallow all her grievances (I wonder what she said that they were?) and of course I'm a good deal tempted by the idea of running Asheham and Hogarth on quite a different system. I will come to tea on Wednesday, and then I suppose I shall have discussed the whole thing about 20 times over with them, and may be able to throw some light on it. My own impression from what Nelly told me is that Lottie wants to go because she thinks we don't appreciate her, and she herself wants to stay.

Except for Gertler's visit we've been quite alone here, and there's a great deal to be said for living in the country. I wanted to ask the children over for the day, but I didn't know whether Mrs B. would like it— I suppose you have been in the heart of civilisation—I wish I knew whether you are really better. I don't believe you realise what a frightful grind you've had, what with rabbits, house moving, agriculture, governesses, for the last two years. Never have another child, and eat every bone in Gordon Sqre. I had a doleful letter from Barbara, who seemed to think that her life would be lightened if we asked her here, but I sent her some mushrooms instead—I had Mrs Sturgeon, Mr Sturgeon and Flora Woolf [Leonard's sister] who's now Mrs George Sturgeon over, and they told us all sorts of gossip about the country side. They want us to go and play tennis next summer. There's a house to let at Kingston.

B.

I think it would be wise to burn this letter at once.

Berg

978: To Lytton Strachey *Hogarth House, Paradise Road, Richmond*

Oct. 12th [1918]

Dearest Lytton,

I'm extremely sorry to hear distressing accounts of your diseases. Goldie [G. Lowes Dickinson] has been having the shingles too, and goes to a marvellous doctor, a quack, I suppose, who is curing him quickly and completely. He lays his fingers upon the tips of the nerves, and you can see the poison withdrawing as you watch. Would it be worth while to find out something more strictly accurate?

However, you must consider that boils, blisters, rashes, green and blue vomits are all appointed by God himself to those whose books go into 4 editions within 6 months. Shingles, I can assure you, is only a first instalment; don't complain if the mange visits you, and the scurvy, and your feet swell and the dropsy distends and the scab itches—I mean you won't get any sympathy from *me*. Did I tell you that Violet Dickinson encountered Mrs H. Ward who was raging publicly against the defamation of her grandfather,[1] and thereby giving the liveliest joy to Lady Horner,[2] who feels that you have worked off several old scores beyond her reach, and therefore blesses you every night as a benefactor? I'm now going to discover the Cromer attitude to Gordon in private.[3]

Here we are back in Richmond again, and even plunged into a mild form of society, mild to you that is—to me the climax of dissipation. What with the approach of peace and the Russian dancers [Diaghilev], the gallant Sitwells, and the poetical Edith,[4] Ottoline utterly abandoned and nefarious, Duncan covered with paint from head to foot, Nessa abounding in babies, Saxon wrung with rheumatics, Robbie Ross[5] found dead in his shirtsleeves, Roger going to lay him out, Oscar Wilde's widow bursting in dead drunk—and so forth—all the things that invariably happen in London in October—it's a pleasant change. We went to hear Lord Grey's speech[6] to begin with, and I had the pleasure of sitting exactly behind Mrs Asquith and Elizabeth [her daughter]. I felt, at that distance, fairly secure against their fascination, and when [Reginald] McKenna and Lord Harcourt came in and sat down beside them I felt it would be a very great condescension on my part to drink tea out of the same cup—which I suspect to be one of their domestic habits. However I was impressed and exalted by Lord Grey. What an Englishman! What a gentleman! As for accusing him of dishonesty, one might as well accuse a pair of brown boots—of which indeed he constantly reminded me. His speech was nothing to get excited over, but on the other hand it was obviously impossible for him to manage any kind of peroration, which I thought much to his credit.

Then there was the Sitwells' party, at which it was proposed to read

1. Thomas Arnold, whom Lytton had castigated in *Eminent Victorians*.
2. She lived at Mells, Somerset, and her house was a centre of cultural and political society in late Victorian and Edwardian times.
3. Virginia's friend Katie Cromer was the second wife of the first Earl of Cromer, the virtual ruler of Egypt when General Gordon was murdered at Khartoum in 1885.
4. The two brothers Osbert and Sacheverell Sitwell, and their sister Edith, whose book of poems, *Clowns' Houses*, Virginia had just reviewed in the *TLS* (10 October 1918).
5. Robert Ross, the writer on art, literature and drama, who had died on 5 October.
6. Lord Grey, Foreign Secretary under Asquith, spoke at a public meeting about the League of Nations.

aloud a sentence of banishment upon Ottoline (whose conduct seems to have surpassed itself—and yet even in vice what a magnificence she has!)—but this of course meant no more than that we withdrew to somebody's bedroom in great numbers and left Ottoline, got up to look precisely like the Spanish Armada in full sail, in possession of the drawing room. Perhaps more happened after I left. But how fearfully old one's getting! There I left her, with equanimity, to have her feathers pulled out by the vicious old Roger, who has a febrile senility coming on, as I told him in the cab, quite unlike our elderly benignity—It's an attempt at youth perhaps—Do you feel this tolerance creeping into your veins too? Literature remains of course—however there's no room to begin upon that. I read the Greeks [Sophocles], but I am extremely doubtful whether I understand anything they say; also I have read the whole of Milton, without throwing any light upon my own soul, but that I rather like. Don't you think it very queer though that he entirely neglects the human heart? Is that the result of writing one's master-piece at the age of 50? What about your masterpiece? And when are you coming to London? Please tell Carrington that we are waiting for her wood-cuts.[1] Leonard sends his love.

Yr.
V.W.

Frances Hooper

979: TO ROGER FRY   *Hogarth House, Paradise Road,*
15th Oct. [1918]   *Richmond, S.W.*

My dear Roger,

I am sending you a spare copy of our pamphlet [*Two Stories*]—rather damaged, but I daresay you won't see much to choose between it and the perfect copies. You never told me what you thought of Prelude. We are asking Eliot to let us print a poem, and I've done a new short story [*Kew Gardens*], illustrated by Nessa, and we've some [projected] woodcuts by Carrington, but we labour as usual under the difficulty of getting our [new] press delivered—it withdraws further and further.

Did you pick out any of Ottoline's fine tail feathers the other night? I heard of her early morning raid upon Gordon Sqre, and how Nessa de-molished her, and how the angularity of her body appeared like that of a foundered cab horse in the morning light. But with such a fund of dishonesty and vitality how is any arrow of ours to strike her heart?—it is a movable target—that, I believe, is what we find so disconcerting.

I had two hours alone with Herbert Fisher[2] last night, and found him

1. See Carrington's reply to this letter (in *Carrington*, ed. David Garnett, pp. 105-6): "You mustn't bully me." The project came to nothing.
2. Virginia's first cousin, H. A. L. Fisher, the historian and Fellow of New College, Oxford. Since December 1916 he had been President of the Board of Education.

though sedate and even aged infinitely improved from what he used to be at Oxford. Even Parliament, I suppose, is an improvement upon that. But what humbugs they all are!—or rather hypnotised by the incantation of some siren quite invisible to the outside world, as I tried to explain to him, without much success.

Yr. V.W.

Sussex

980: To Vanessa Bell   *Hogarth* [*House, Richmond*]

Saturday [19 October 1918]

Dearest,

I am sure you would like a little gossip from me this morning; and perhaps take to your old dried pen in response. Suppose I gave you a new one?

What I really want to know is how your domestic affairs are turning out? I suppose the cook has now come. I'm sure that I could find you not only a cook but a nurse, if she doesn't do; so please tell me and let me set my wits to work.

I expect the tide is already setting back to service again, and few things give me a greater sense of being like other mature women, which as you know is the ambition of my life, than going to registry offices, and talking about "my sister has a governess and two small boys." I feel at once on the road to reality or whatever one may call it. As for my domestics, they are now unfortunately, grovelling at our feet; Lottie and Leonard twit each other about their bad tempers, and of course its all very expensive and not really to my taste so nice as being with Mrs Geall at Asheham, except for the comfort.

Did I tell you how I had a visit from Herbert Fisher last Sunday? I was sitting alone at tea, very shabby, and the servants out when the bell rang, and I opened the door thinking to find the milk man and found Herbert and Olive and Michael Heseltine! Happily the Heseltines disappeared, and I had about 2 hours tête a tête with Herbert. He has become rather like one of those wise old sheep dogs whose eyes have become slightly pale; but he is much less supercilious than he was at Oxford. He had just seen Lord Milner [Secretary of State for War] who said that we had won the war that day and we shall have peace by Christmas; Apparently the French are sticking out for the evacuation of Alsace-Lorraine before they will agree to an armistice; but according to Lord Milner the Germans are so sensible that they see that it is best now to accept any terms and mean to fight no more. But I suppose you have heard all this from Maynard.

Herbert was surprisingly sensible—perhaps because he knew our opinions—about war in general: however, he believes in public schools, and said you'd better send Julian and Quentin to Winchester, where they get the best education in the world.

Then we had old Ka to dinner. Will is once more in hospital—this time with water on the knee—from what you and Duncan will doubtless draw your own conclusions. Clive and Mary whom I floundered in upon at Gordon Sqre are of opinion that some enlargement of his parts is necessary, though I dont believe they'd consent to undertake that at a naval hospital, and anyhow Ka doesn't mean to have a family until they're settled in the country. They are going to live on the top of one of the Wiltshire downs, so that Will can see nothing but the sky, which is the only thing he likes to paint though a certain amount of green is admitted very low down on the edge of the canvas. She said that his pictures—which are the passion of his life—are very old fashioned, but very remarkable.

It sounds to me about as bad as it can be, which is of course very satis-factory, and she also has to make out that he is very wild and mad—He is heir to an estate and a large income; but he has given it all up to his younger brother—so you can judge exactly the sort of pictures he must paint and in fact all about him. We're going to dine with them, so I'll let you know more, if the subject interests you. Unfortunately I've got my affairs and can't go to a large family tea party which Ka's sister is giving in Harley St. today—though it would give me infinite pleasure.

Then we had Saxon. Everybody, of course, has entirely failed to see what I saw at the first glance; he is happier than he has ever been in his life. After a short conversation I saw that Mrs Stagg[1] is far more to him than Barbara; and then he has got a complete or almost complete set of gold teeth. This is one of the great interests of his life. He takes them out and hands them round, and explains exactly which of the teeth are useful, which ornamental, and at what points others will probably—not certainly—have to be added next year. He has got through love, and has got down to the solid foundations—Stagg and false teeth. He is already talking of Bayreuth, and whether we shall have an opera next year—if so, will [Arthur] Nikish or [Richard] Strauss conduct—then the singers—and so on—Barbara was merely an interlude owing to there being no opera.

I have begun my artistic education again. I went to see the Rodins at the Albert Museum [posthumous exhibition]. I didn't think at all highly of them, except from the literary point of view, and even so they're not as good as Epsteins. But I see I shall have to write a novel entirely about carpets, old silver, cut glass and furniture. The desire to describe becomes almost a torment; and also the covetousness to possess. I dont think this has much to do with their artistic value though. Please tell me what picture shows there are.

1. Saxon's landlady in Great Ormond Street.

How are you, and the remarkable baby upon whom all my future hopes
for the world may be said to rest?

Yr

B

Have you cut the wood blocks? Would you send them? We hope to begin
next week.[1] We have a chance of another press.

Did you find out anything about twilight sleep.[2]

Berg

981: TO ROGER FRY   *Hogarth House, Paradise Road,*
                                     Richmond, S.W.

Monday [21 October 1918]

My dear Roger,

   I saw your father's death[3] in the paper—it must have been a great
mercy, after all these months. I'm afraid though all the surroundings must
be half gloomy and horrible perhaps and how strange for you to be there
arranging things.

   I can't come this Thursday, as I'm going out—but could you ask me the
week after—any night but Monday or Tuesday would suit me. I'm immensely pleased, of course, with what you say about the Mark [on the Wall],
and would like to believe it true, since the quality you speak of is one I
recognise certainly in others. I'm not sure that a perverted plastic sense
doesn't somehow work itself out in words for me.

   I spent an hour looking at pots and carpets in the museums the other day,
until the desire to describe them became like the desire for the lusts of the
flesh.

   However, I'm rushing to catch a train, and I must hope to see you and
have an enormous talk.

Yours ever,

Sussex   Virginia Woolf

982: TO VANESSA BELL   1917 *Club, 4 Gerrard Street,*
                                     *W.*1.

Friday [25 October 1918]

Dearest,

   I've just been to the Omega show, and had the great pleasure of seeing

1. The printing of *Kew Gardens*.
2. A method of easing childbirth by the use of anaesthetics.
3. Sir Edward Fry, the judge, died on 18 October, aged 91.

your picture sold for £15 to Mr Jowett,[1] so Roger said—however I'm not writing to say that but to have some occupation which shall save me from Jack Squire, in the midst of the most appalling uproar, of the most degraded looking C. O's who are all met here to croak like so many dull raucous vociferating and disgorging cormorants. This being so, I can't give you my extreme and intense impressions of the show, as I mean to. I have to wait for Leonard to come out to dinner. There is Mrs Manus, and Langdon Davies, and Old Hobson and Commander Grenfell[2]—but I fail to convey the horror of their joint attack. We've just had tea with Roger and discussed the Burial Service [of Roger's father]; and Lytton has wired to us in "extreme desolation" to go there for the week end; which L. is going to do—at least for Saturday only. Oliver [Strachey] says the twilight of Carrington approaches. I feel more and more convinced that advanced views are purely a matter of physiognomy. For instance the lady in green, with check trimmings in her hat and a face like a ruddy but diseased apple—one cleft asunder by a brown growth—had nother [sic] excuse for existence. The noise is terrific.

Perhaps I can pull an evening paper towards me. The show was a great success—according to Roger—drawings selling like potatoes. Bobo [Mayor] was there, sumptuous and prolific: Sitwell: Irene [Noel-Baker] is going to have a baby.

Berg

983: TO VANESSA BELL   *Hogarth* [*House, Richmond*]

Sunday [27 October 1918]

Dearest,
    I dont know whether to laugh or hold up my hands in amazement at the charges made against me in the Mary [Hutchinson]—Gertler affair, and at the general state of affairs revealed by your letter and Lytton's account, both of which were sprung upon me yesterday. However, I'd better tell you what happened at Asheham. We both remember quite well the only conversation with Gertler about Mary, and agree as to what was said. Gertler told us how extremely interesting Mary was, how easy he found her, and how they discussed every subject together. I said that I'd no doubt this was true, but that she was always very silent with me, and that I scarcely knew her.

1. William Jowitt, the barrister and politician, who later became Trustee of the National Gallery and the Tate Gallery.
2. Three of these members of the 1917 Club were: Mrs Manus, Leonard's assistant on the *International Review*; Bernard Langdon-Davies, the manager of the Labour Publishing Company; and J. A. Hobson, the economist and writer of several books on politics and international relations. Commander Grenfell is unidentified.

There was no question as to whether I liked her or not. Gertler then said how strange it was that she was silent with us and asked whether I had ever seen her at Charleston and whether she was silent there too. I said that I'd only seen her there once, but that I thought she was just as silent with you as with me. There was absolutely no discussion as to what you thought of Mary. Gertler did not ask me; and was much more interested in discussing his own relations with her than anyone elses.

In fact, I'm prepared to write to Mary or to swear in a court of law that nothing was said or insinuated which could have led Gertler to suppose that you were bored by Mary, criticised her, or in any sort of way found fault with her.

After all, why should I have made out that you dislike Mary? You've certainly always said you liked her to me, and I've always maintained that the whole of your relationship is a triumph of sense and civilisation for every one concerned. As Shearman[1] and Hutchinson[2] have a motive for making mischief I should have thought it was more reasonable to impute it entirely to them. I don't think Gertler was in the least malicious or even inquisitive, but entirely absorbed in himself and his own relations as usual.

At the same time I cant conceive why, even had I said that you disliked Mary, it should have 'nearly had disastrous results' for you, as you say, or upset Mary for more than a moment. She had only to go to you and ask you the truth, and spend an hour or two in abusing me, which she is quite welcome to do. The exaggeration seems to me terrific and absurd.

However, thats none of my business. What I object to, naturally I think, is being made the victim of this infernal spy system. It's quite plain that it's hopeless for us to try and know each other's friends, and in future I shall try and steer clear of Gertler, Shearman, Mary, Jack, Clive and all the rest of that set. I suppose I should have been wise if I had done so in the beginning. But shall I wind up my relations with Mary by writing her an exact copy of what I have said to you?

Now I've wasted all my time writing this, and I cant go on to tell you about Edith Sichel's life,[3] or Saxon or Lady Mary Murray[4]—After all, how am I to know that Mrs Stagg mayn't have committed suicide already on hearing through Barbara through Trissie through Blanche that I said he preferred his gold teeth to her?

Yr

Berg   B.

1. Montague Shearman, a barrister who was interested in the arts.
2. St John ('Jack') Hutchinson, Mary's husband.
3. Virginia had been reading Edith Sichel's *Letters, verses and other writings*, edited by Emily Ritchie. Privately printed, 1918.
4. Lady Mary Howard, eldest daughter of the Earl of Carlisle, had married Gilbert Murray, the classical scholar, in 1889. The Woolfs had been to tea with the Murrays that afternoon.

Hogarth House, Paradise Road, Richmond

Nov. 4th [1918]

Dear Nelly,

How delightful to hear from you again! I wanted to write to you the other day at Asheham, but not knowing your address seemed to make it perfectly useless.

I'm afraid luncheon on Sunday is impossible, but would it suit you if we came about 4 that afternoon instead? We should very much like to.

With all respect for your neighbours the Sidney Webbs, Mrs Green, and the Herbert Fishers, I dont think they're a good exchange for Grove End Road.[1] Still, I remember finding the river very pleasant to look at when I've been sitting in the Webbs drawing room feeling more than usually convinced of my own ignorance. In future (that is if I'm ever asked again) I shall fix my mind upon you.

Your aff.

Hatfield   Virginia Woolf

985: To Vanessa Bell   *Hogarth [House, Richmond]*

Thursday [7 November 1918]

Dearest,

There are so many different matters to go into that I think I'd better address you in the form of a newspaper. In the first place,

Domestic Quarrels.

The situation is much calmer. I daresay Lytton's account of Mary was rather highly coloured. I got the impression that she was conveyed about London in taxi cabs in a fainting condition, only recovering to execrate me and then burst into tears, fling herself into Clives arms, grovel on the floor at your feet, denounce us all for traitors and vipers, so that finally Lytton himself had to be invoked to assure her that she was universally (with the insignificant exception of V. W.) adored. Naturally, I contrasted this with my own unflinching courage under far worse persecution; and you enduring spites and malevolences innumerable with the scorn of Cleopatra's needle. I said to myself (everything in future is to be said to myself) that if Mary plays games she oughtn't to mind burning candles; the truth is that these young people rush into situations which they can't carry out. The only solution for Mary seems to me divorce; otherwise she must spend the rest of her life in the swamp with these stinging but semi animate reptiles.

1. The Cecils' London house in St. John's Wood, from which they had moved to Grosvenor Road on the Westminster Embankment.

But I must also clear my reputation for common sense. Carrington had warned me about Gertler as well as you; so that my position was guarded in the extreme. If you could have heard my fulsome praises of Ottoline—and how I picked my way whenever Mary was mentioned with the foresight of an elephant—moreover, except to you I never find fault with Mary and the utmost I've ever said about her was that she was sleeping in a forest with the cockatoo's singing their sweetest in the moonlight—purely visionary remarks, since to me she is little more (at present, and I suppose forever) than a highly sympathetic shade. Molly [MacCarthy] seems to have struck up a friendship with her.

Practical Affairs.

I have sent you a parcel of eatables, which, they say, will be at Glynde station on Saturday morning without fail. They wouldn't go by post, so they had to go by train. I chose them rather at random, so please tell me which turns out best, and please eat some of them yourself.

Woodcuts

I enclose a proof—not nearly black enough, but we only had our hand machine. If you can't see the details, I will get a better one done on the printers machine.[1] We should be very glad of another, if you would do one; but it ought to be small—about half the size of this. I think the book will be a great success—owing to you: and my vision comes out much as I had it, so I suppose, in spite of everything, God made our brains upon the same lines, only leaving out 2 or 3 pieces in mine.

Art. Gossip. Friendship etc. etc. etc.

I've got any amount to say, having been to the Omega twice, the National Gallery once; having gone to tea with Katherine Murry, and dined with Ka and Will, and promised to go to tea with Nelly Cecil, and having some compliments for you, as well as a profoundly interesting theory about Duncan's painting: and theres Miss Sichel too—I could write pages about her—but I've been seized by toothache, and I must now rush off to the dentist, and I couldn't do my ideas justice. Please tell me how you are.

Embrace Duncan.

Yr
B.

Am I to write to Mary?

Berg

1. The Woolfs had found it too laborious to print *Prelude* on their small press, and having set the type, took it to McDermott, a jobbing printer in Richmond. Leonard himself worked McDermott's machine, and this is the one on which Virginia now proposes to run off a new proof of Vanessa's woodcut for *Kew Gardens*.

11.30, Nov. 11th [Armistice Day, 1918]

Dearest,

The guns have been going off for half an hour, and the sirens whistling; so I suppose we are at peace, and I cant help being glad that your precious imp will be born into a moderately reasonable world. I see we're not going to be allowed any quiet all day, as people seem to be whistling and giving catcalls and stirring up the dogs to bark, though its all done in such an intermittent kind of way that its not in the least impressive—only unsettling. Besides its very grey and smoky,—oh dear, now drunken soldiers are beginning to cheer.

How am I to write my last chapter[1] with all this shindy, and Nelly and Lottie bursting in to ask—here is Nelly with 4 different flags which she is putting in all the front rooms. Lottie says we ought to do something, and I see she is going to burst into tears. She insists upon polishing the door knocker, and shouting out across the road to the old fireman who lives opposite. O God! What a noise they make—and I, on the whole though rather emotional (would you be, I wonder?) feel also immensely melancholy; yes, you're well out of it, because every taxi is now hooting, and the school children I know will form up round the flag in a moment. There is certainly an atmosphere of the death bed too. At this moment a harmonium is playing a hymn, and a large Union Jack has been hoisted onto a pole. But this must be fearfully dull to read about.

As to gossip, we went to tea with Nelly [Cecil] yesterday, and afterwards to a concert given at Shelley House;[2] but first imagine poor Nelly more shrivelled and sunken than ever, wearing the most piteous expression, like an imprisoned monkey; I've never seen anyone who seemed to ask one more to put her out of her misery. They've moved to a horrid little house on the Embankment, which she has done up in the old Kitty [Maxse], chinz curtains, white walls, green boards style. I rather liked her though. She agreed that Leo and Lord Northcliffe[3] ought to be banished as well as the Kaiser, and said she thought the English in many ways worse than the Germans. And then we went on to this appalling [Shelley] house, where I'd been asked by Bruce Richmond, and there I saw our entire past, alive, incredibly the

1. Virginia finished *Night and Day* on 21 November.
2. The Chelsea house belonging to St John Hornby, where he had installed his Ashendene Press in 1902, and gave frequent concerts. Bruce Richmond was presiding there that evening.
3. Leopold Maxse had been editor of the *National Review* since 1893. He consistently argued against a League of Nations and in favour of maintaining Britain's imperial position. Lord Northcliffe, proprietor of the *Daily Mail*, was urging Lloyd George to 'Hang the Kaiser' and make Germany pay for the war.

same as ever—Mrs Rathbone, Mrs Muir MacKenzie, Enid M. M., precisely as she was at Hyde Park Gate, Hervey Vaughan Williams,[1] any number of people who weren't exactly George [Duckworth] but might have been; all dressed up so irreproachably so nice, kind, respectable—so insufferable—. You remember the kind of politeness, and the little jokes, and all the deference, and opening doors for one, and looking as if the mention of the w.c. even would convey nothing whatever to them. I enjoyed it immensely; but I couldn't help seeing us in white satin Mrs Young's[2] being taken down to supper. The house itself is incredible—an enormous, cultivated, sham 18th century house, with vast portraits of young girls holding bunches of roses, and looking into the future, while a small white path meanders away under apple trees in the distance. And then, painted on the panels, were those sort of geographical pictures which are meant to be not quite serious but very charming; maps of Chelsea hospital, with decorative clouds, all very flat, and brightly coloured. And pale green Morris curtains; and china pots standing on little wooden stools; Italy represented too, by casts of the Virgin and child; scrolls of Japanese figures; but all infinitely pale, watery, and ugly, far worse than any plush lodging house.

This, by the way, applies also to the decorations of Wills and Ka's flat, which impressed me very disagreeably; acid lemon colours against black curtains, and one white rose against a wall the colour of skim milk. There's no doubt that you have done a great work in rolling up the shams; at least I dislike a great many things now with an intensity which owing to my punishment in the case of Mary [Hutchinson], I daresay I should be wise to hide.

What one instinctively says about Will is "What a Whippersnapper!" but I implore you, don't give this out as my considered opinion. Its the effect of his little mongrel cur's body; his face which appears powdered and painted like a very refined old suburban harlots; and his ridiculous little voice. I saw Ka get nervous when my eyes rested too long upon him. She was much relieved when he began to use slang and talk manly; and I daresay he has his parts, (I dont mean only in the physical sense) but I'm as convinced as I am that the church bells have now begun to ring that he'll never be a painter. I saw one worried and fretful work of his—the downs by moonlight; but he said it was a sketch, and hinted very modestly that he didn't belong to the Omega school. He expressed great admiration for you and Duncan, as painters; and you'd be amused to hear what an impression you as a human being made on him. You had only to come into the Friday

1. Mrs William Rathbone was the mother of Mrs Bruce Richmond; Mrs Muir MacKenzie, a daughter of Lord Aberdare, had married Montague Muir MacKenzie, a barrister, in 1888, and Enid was their only child; Hervey Vaughan Williams was the elder brother of Ralph, the composer.
2. Sally Young, who had been the Stephen girls' dressmaker in their youth.

Club[1] he said to change the feeling completely; I gathered you made things real, and large, and infinitely composed and profound.

"Yes, I'll always maintain, said old Ka, who sat on the hearthrug stitching at one of her usual cushions, that Vanessa is one of the few great people I've ever known."

"Ah but my dear Ka, try and explain how she does it!" I cried.

Then we set to and analysed the famous remark of mine about your reality, which they both said that they felt strongly, and thought most remarkable, so I'm not alone.

You will have heard of Barbara's brat.[2] Saxon seems fairly composed, and means to call it Judith. According to Oliver [Strachey] he assumes that he is the spiritual begetter at any rate, and Nick scarcely counts even for that act; Oliver agrees with me that Saxon is happier than usual.

Then we had [H. T. J.] Norton to dinner, and I felt a kind of reverence for him, as the representative of old Cambridge, as we knew it, in the days of "personal emotions"; I must say I think it probably the highest type in the world, and it solves all my religious feelings. We've now had marriage bells, one hymn, God save the King twice over, about a dozen separate cheers, and the old gentleman opposite has climbed to the top of a tree with an immense Union Jack.

Yr
VW

Berg

987: To Vanessa Bell   *Hogarth [House, Richmond]*
Wednesday [13 November 1918]

Dearest,

Modesty requires me to say that you will be sick of the sight of my handwriting—So now thats said. The truth is that its still very difficult to settle to anything. Peace seems to make much more difference than one could have thought possible, though I think the rejoicing, so far as I've seen it, has been very sordid and depressing. I expect it was much better in the country, and I wish we'd been at Asheham, and come over and had a civilised debauch with you and the brats.

I had to go to the dentist in Wigmore St. on Monday, at 3, and by 4 the streets were in such a state that if I hadn't met L: and buffeted through the crowd with him I dont think I should have got home. As it was a small boy was almost crushed in the tube at my feet; we were so packed we could

1. The club founded chiefly by Vanessa in 1905 for the discussion of the fine arts.
2. Barbara Bagenal's first child, Judith, born 8 November 1918.

hardly pick him out; everyone seemed half drunk—beer bottles were passed round—every wounded soldier was kissed, by women; nobody had any notion where to go or what to do; it poured steadily; crowds drifted up and down the pavements waving flags and jumping into omnibuses, but in such a disorganised, half hearted, sordid state that I felt more and more melancholy and hopeless of the human race. The London poor, half drunk and very sentimental or completely stolid with their hideous voices and clothes and bad teeth, make one doubt whether any decent life will ever be possible, or whether it matters if we're at war or at peace. But I suppose the poor wretches haven't much notion how to express their feelings. At present it seems to be a mixture of Bank Holiday and Sunday. The clocks strike incessantly, in a very disordered way. So far the only change I've noticed is that we get no newspapers because the boys won't deliver them, and the buses are lit up, but our lamps are as dark as ever, and the telephones have practically broken down.

I'm going up to see Katherine Mansfield today, and I shall ask Fortnum and Masons about your parcel. It contained only delicacies like paté de foie gras and short bread which won't go bad; and I think its most likely that the trains were too disorganised to deliver it. But I'll add a note at the end of this to say what the people at the shop think.

Did Bunny ever get a letter from me containing a £1 note for honey, I must have sent it more than a week ago; I hope it wasn't stolen; we've had to take to making our own butter by shaking milk in a bottle, as our allowance is very scanty. Jam also is rather scarce, so I hope we may get our honey in time.

Poor Katherine Mansfield seems very bad, though I dont like to ask her how bad, and she says she's going to Switzerland with Murry and will be cured. I can't help finding her very interesting, in spite of her story [*Bliss*] in the English Review; at least she cares about writing, which as I'm coming to think, is about the rarest and most desirable of gifts. I had a fearfully depressing talk with old Janet Case the other day; at the end of which I came to the conclusion that when nice educated people who've spent their lives in teaching Greek and ought to know something about it, have less feeling for modern fiction, including my own which she advised me to give up and take to biography instead since that was 'useful', than a stranded jelly fish on which the flies have already settled, its high time for us writers to retire to the South Seas.

There's practically no one in London now whom I can talk to either about my own writing or Shakespeares. I'm beginning to think that I'd better stop writing novels, since no one cares a damn whether one writes them or not. Do you ever feel that your entire life is useless—passed in a dream, into which now and then these brutal buffaloes come butting? or are you always certain that you matter, and matter more than other people? I believe having children must make a lot of difference; and yet perhaps its no good making them responsible for one's own inefficiency—but I mean rather transparency—nonentity—unreality.

Here I am now at the 17 Club. London seems quieted down—only one drunken soldier abusing an officer—only one old lady making a speech in the train about "what we owe you boys."

I've been to Fortnum's and Masons, who say that the parcel was probably not sent last week owing to the rush they were in. If it hasn't come in the next day or two, would you send me a line, as they will find out about it.

I've sent the woodcut. I'm very pleased you're doing another. We are getting along with the printing so send them as soon as you can—at least the big one. The other wd. do later.

What are Duncan and Bunny going to do? Adrian seems to be staying on at present—so does Norton—Gerald [Shove] asked L. to lunch today, I suppose to discuss how he's to get work.

Now I must go—but I feel as if I could write you sheets every day. For example, I want to express my views as to your and Duncan's duty to civilisation in future—but as I say, that must wait. I ran into Mrs Flower [*unidentified*] in the London Library. We merely spat at each other. Here is Oliver's jolly lady. And Oliver [Strachey] too!

B.

Oliver's young lady has a thin, disagreeable face (O here's Oliver coming over)

Berg

Letters 988-1001 (mid-November–December 1918)

Soon after the Armistice Virginia finished Night and Day, *finding it, as she wrote in her diary, "a much more mature and finished and satisfactory book than* The Voyage Out. . . . *I don't suppose I've ever enjoyed any writing so much as I did the last half of* Night and Day." *The Hogarth Press began printing her* Kew Gardens, *which Vanessa illustrated with wood-cuts. T. S. Eliot, whom Virginia now met for the first time, came to dine at Hogarth House, and the Press accepted his Poems for publication. Virginia was also seeing much of Katherine Mansfield and her husband Middleton Murry, whose* The Critic in Judgment *they agreed to publish. Leonard was mainly occupied with editing the* International Review, *and did not stand at the General Election of December 1918. On Christmas Day Vanessa's third child, a girl, was born, while Julian and Quentin came to stay with their aunt at Asheham and Richmond.*

988: TO ROGER FRY   Hogarth [House, Richmond]

Monday [18 November 1918]

My dear Roger,

I was just writing to insist upon being asked to dine with you, but was prevented by the fear that you might think it a bore. (I imagine you, quite honestly, having all sorts of people always about you, and rather liking to settle down alone occasionally). But there's nothing I should like better, and I only wish it happened oftener. What about next Friday, about 7.30, I suppose.

I think you *are* enviable, in spite of what you say, I dont mean so much in circumstances as in being yourself. I envy you for being that, but my envy is only skin deep, partly a measure of self-protection, and it doesn't interfere in the least with my profound affection. I'd much rather dine alone with you, and talk of innumerable things.

We've been having that strange young man Eliot[1] to dinner. His sentences take such an enormous time to spread themselves out that we didn't

1. In 1918 T. S. Eliot was 30. He had settled in England in 1915, and became Assistant Editor of *The Egoist* in 1917. His first volume of poems, *Prufrock*, was published the same year. At this dinner in Hogarth House, Eliot read to the Woolfs some of the poems which they published in May 1919.

get very far; but we did reach Ezra Pound and Wyndham Lewis, and how they were great geniuses, and so is Mr James Joyce—which I'm more prepared to agree to, but why has Eliot stuck in this mud? Can't his culture carry him through, or does culture land one there? Not that I've read more than 10 words by Ezra Pound by [*sic*] my conviction of his humbug is unalterable.

Yes, Roger, the more I think of it—and I often do—the more I am convinced that you are of immense importance in the world.

Yours ever

V.W.

Sussex

989: TO VANESSA BELL   *Hogarth* [*House, Richmond*]

Tuesday [19 November 1918]

Dearest,

I hope I shall be praised for taking up the pen so soon again. But you know the form of thanks I like—a few reflections, however bald; not but what you possess a natural style of considerable eloquence and vigour, as I have told you more than once.

As to business—in the first place about Asheham. I think it can be managed all right if you would let me know fairly soon which weekend you want to have it. We had some thoughts of going down ourselves one weekend before long—Would it do if the children had our bedroom, and Mrs B[rereton, the governess]. my study, and do you think they could manage with one sitting room—either Leonard's or the drawing room?

I don't expect they'd use much coal, but the rooms would have to be aired first, and we've got to make our coal last over Christmas—but I think we've got plenty. There's a certain amount of wood cut up in the little room out of Leonard's room. We always use this in the sitting room; and I think there's enough for a week end. I'm sure Mrs B. is most economical; implore her not to say anything about the filthy condition of the house; nor to be shocked at the number of my old skirts.

Let me know when they want it, and I'll write to Mrs Geall [caretaker]. She's very good if they should want her to do anything.

We're getting on with the printing [*Kew Gardens*]. Have you any idea how many copies we ought to sell—what price we could ask? I saw a dummy copy of the Omega book,[1] which is very magnificent but fearfully

1. *Original Woodcuts by Various Artists* (1918), published by the Omega Workshops. It contained work by Duncan Grant, Vanessa Bell, Roger Fry, McKnight Kauffer, Edward Wolfe and Roald Kristian.

expensive; I don't see how one's to buy it; and the sands are running out; soon it will be 15/-.

Possibly you know some names of artists whom I might send notices to; we think of getting 2 or 3 little books ready before we send out, so as to give people something at once.[1]

By the way, is there any paper thats specially good for wood cuts? I rather think we shall print the big one on a separate sheet and paste it in, so we could get the right paper for it—What about the cover? I dont think Roger's prices have gone down, but I'm dining with him tonight, and I'll ask. Suppose I dashed off another little story, would you do some pictures for that, or is the priceless specimen, my nephew, too near to make it possible? Talking of babies, [G. E.] Moore has got a son today; and Gladys Holman Hunt[2] is married to a captain of some kind—a bold kind I should think to wipe up that appalling mid Victorian mess. When did it happen? In the early nineties of last Century? I know I was mad at Welwyn at the time [1904]. And as for gossip, you'll be amused and delighted to hear how Ottoline spent the first day of peace. She wrote an account of it to Katherine [Mansfield]. She has reached the depths of disillusionment. Siegfried Sassoon was there and "terribly, terribly *Spoilt*. I *never* want to see him again—so coarse, so ordinary, so just like any other conceited young guardsman—I felt he had been seeing *odious* people, who had changed him *completely*." That was more or less her account of it; and she said how she was tired of doing kindnesses, and having her hand bitten in return; and how though on peace day she put a candle in every window, she didn't feel happy in the least.

I'm pretty certain that Gertler has made mischief there too; she's been in London for a week or so and never asked me to see her. The malice of that man must be considerable. Did he really make out I'd had several conversations with him about Mary? I expect that was his purpose in coming to Asheham.

The question of peace is an extremely interesting one. We literary people have been comparing our feelings a good deal. Desmond heard the news early in the morning, and went straight to Buckingham Palace. He says the crowd was very good there, and they had bands, and climbed all over the Victoria memorial, pulling themselves up by her nose and breasts; then the King and Queen came out; like two little dolls. Afterwards he wandered into a restaurant and found two men fighting, and tried to separate them and was knocked on the head, and then they apologised, and he led one of them off,

1. They intended to canvass their friends for subscriptions to the Hogarth Press. One group of subscribers would receive a copy of each publication as it came out; another group would receive only those which they chose from an advance list.
2. Gladys Mulock, the daughter of William Holman Hunt, the painter.

whose nose was bleeding, and they spent some time in a lavatory; and he became rather depressed, and wandered off, and found things a little flat, and gave a great shout by himself on the Kings Road, and nobody took any notice of it. But he is writing an account of his feeling. I think I shall too. The dazed discontented aimless feeling was so queer; starting with such emotions and high passions, and getting gradually more and more sodden and depressed, and wanting to do something very exciting and not knowing what. [Middleton] Murry was at the War Office. He said he tried to feel but couldn't feel anything except horror and misery. Old war office officials began saying the most extraordinary things; but he remained completely cold and disgusted. Harrison, the dentist, said that peace was much worse than war; nobody kept their appointments. Harry Stephen said that Mafeking night was far better; James Strachey didn't seem to have noticed much difference; Oliver thought the spectacle slightly sad, but rather amusing; we've been trying to get up a peace party, but Ray has influenza, and no one will lend a room. Everybody walks about the streets, and looks very happy.

B.

Berg

990: TO VANESSA BELL   *Hogarth [House, Richmond]*

Tuesday [26 November 1918]

Dearest,

Nothing would please me better than a letter every day in your roughly eloquent style. Even the handwriting has the quality of a great sheep dogs paw—a sheep dog which has been trotting sagaciously through the mud after its lambs all day long—

But to business. I haven't been able to take a proof of the caterpillar yet [for *Kew Gardens*]; but I will in a day or two, and send you one. Here is another of the women, which I think comes out much more clearly. What we want to suggest is that you should now do a full page wood cut for the cover—anything of course that you like, without reference to the story. Would it be possible to cut the words Kew Gardens. Virginia Woolf. somewhere in the design? We had a notion that if you would do this we could get a wood cutter later to cut out the writing, and use the design, with another title, for further stories. If you did this, would you remember to cut the letters as clearly as possible. I enclose a sheet of paper to show you the exact size of the cover. Rogers coloured papers are very nice, but so thin that one would have to fold them over something else; and I'd much rather have a design by you—believing that your designs will be a tremendous draw. There now remains the question of what it is fair to do about payment. We think of printing 150 copies, and don't want to charge more than 1/- each; if all are sold that makes, I think, £7-10. Would you rather have a commission on the sale, or a sum down; and have you any idea how to arrange it?

I suppose the blocks themselves are rather expensive. Then we thought of putting on our notice that copies of the wood cuts are to be had separately —say at 6d each; by which means we might sell some more. One shilling is very little, considering the pictures, but the story is so short that we can easily reprint, and we want to keep our prices as low as we can.

Eliot has sent us some of his poems, which we are going to print as soon as Kew Gardens is done. Then I suppose we shall do Carrington, and perhaps a thing by Murry; and issue them all at the same time.[1] I've just started another story,[2] which may never be finished, or may go wrong; so I dont think its worth your while to do a design, though if it comes off, I hope you might do a picture for it—in fact I mean to retain your services for *all* my works. The story begins with two young men sitting on a beach under the skeleton of an old pilchard boat. One young man is throwing stones into the sea; the other is burrowing a hole in the sand. The beach is a long semi circular one, and they are quite near the sea (as of course they must be to throw stones into it.)

I dont see much force in Mrs B[rereton]'s. arguments against Asheham. If you would let me know in time, Mrs Geall, who is to be depended on, would have fires burning in readiness, and there's absolutely no reason, from our point of view, why they shouldn't stay a week.[3]

They could have hot baths when they arrived if they got wet. I should prefer the variety of a daughter—how I should adore her!—but why talk of it?—the abundance of Judiths[4] makes another boy inevitable; and I own so far you've produced nothing unseemly; its the possibilities of womanhood derived from you that I dream of.

Nick has just rung up to say how lonely Barbara is, and will I go and see her—upon some desolate promontory near Primrose Hill; which I suppose I must do; and also have Nick himself to dinner. Two nights ago we had Saxon. He told us he did not wish to live, and had decided the exact day on which he knew he would die; but when the day came, though he remembered in the morning, he forgot all about it afterwards, and so supposes that his foreboding meant nothing. He rang me up later to say that it was chiefly the rheumatism that made him dismal, but he had no absolute *desire* for death since the pain in his head went; and rheumatism was to be expected in November. I still think there's some truth in my diagnosis; the gold teeth

1. They issued three books together, in May 1919; *Kew Gardens*, Eliot's *Poems*, and John Middleton Murry's *The Critic in Judgment*.
2. *Solid Objects*, first published in *Athenaeum*, 22 October 1920.
3. The plan was that Julian and Quentin should stay at Asheham during the period when Vanessa's baby was expected.
4. The recently born daughters of Barbara Bagenal and Karin Stephen were both named Judith.

and Mrs Stagg do count for a good deal; also the opera's coming in February. Roger and I had a frogs chorus such as you might have heard at Charleston; but you'd only have asked Duncan to shut the window if you had.

"Yes she's the most remarkable human being I've ever known in my life" was the theme of it. You can imagine the dismal croaks—how we loved and sang and despaired.[1] I rather suspect that a very grave miscarriage of emotion, portending terrific developments of a sensational kind, has happened. I got a letter from Roger this morning, no doubt continuing our rhapsody and despair; but when I opened it, it began "My dear Marie, Do come to lunch on Wednesday etc etc." Marie must have got mine. I rang up the Omega, and the Omega says it is Marie Beerbohm [the actress]; I have written to Marie Beerbohm; begging her to read no further if her letter begins "My dear Virginia—As we said last night, my whole happiness depends upon Vanessa etc etc etc" But Marie will read further. What a set! What a set! We had Eliot, I may tell you, one of Mary's friends; and when it came to mentioning Hammersmith I said Ealing on purpose, sacrificing veracity, even sense, upon the altar of Mary's susceptibilities; Mary, you see, lives, or once lived at Hammersmith; and I suppose I had led Eliot to think and therefore repeat that I loathed Hammersmith? (This is now one of my favourite jokes.)

Eliot, I may add, said that he greatly admired your painting, and thought it superior even to Duncans! And yesterday I went to the London Group;[2] couldn't bear Allinson,[3] or the lady whose name I cant remember, I like the witty Mdlle Lessore;[4] and Ethel Sands[5] has two commendable pieces, until you see that she can do nothing different; [C. R. W.] Nevinson has a piece of wall paper representing the seasons—each different, like eggs out of a hat— to me very depressing; purely conjuring tricks; Nina Hamnet does roofs; why are you artists so repetitious; does the eye for months together see nothing but roofs? Gertler certainly dominates his wall; and rather impresses me; I believe Roger *has* taken a turn. Who d'you think I met at Charing X? George Booth![6] We had an affectionate conversation. Mrs Booth has 22 grandchildren, she prefers on the whole to live alone—"but we are all near her."

Yr
B.

Berg

1. Roger Fry was at this time still in love with Vanessa.
2. Founded in 1913, it included Walter Sickert and Wyndham Lewis.
3. Adrian Allinson (1890-1959), the landscape and still-life painter, who had been influenced by the Post-Impressionists.
4. Thérèse Lessore, the third wife of Walter Sickert.
5. Born an American, but naturalised a British subject, she became a friend of Virginia.
6. Son of Charles Booth. Charles had died in 1916.

991: To Lady Ottoline Morrell   *Hogarth House, Richmond*

[early December 1918?]

My dear Ottoline

Leonard has to be out all Thursday, and feels that it would be better, if we might come in after dinner, the Thursday following, the 12th. We will keep that free, and then, we shall enjoy it enormously.

I heard a fascinating account from Mary Hutchinson of the delight of real conversation in a chair. It sounded too good.

> Your affate
> Virginia Woolf

Texas

992: To Vanessa Bell   *Hogarth [House, Richmond]*

Monday [9 December 1918]

Dearest,

I am very much concerned to hear that you are diseased. For Gods sake be careful. Is there anything I could get for you—either food or medicine? Would you dose yourself with malt extract, if I sent you a bottle? I take it twice daily; I have also an excellent tonic the only one that really improves the spirits perceptibly; if I got that would you take it?

But I know your unscrupulous disposition. You read all that sort of thing with a buzzing sound like a large Bee; it's only when you come to the gossip that you pay attention, more or less like a human being. Chiefly for your sake, I went to another concert at Shelley House yesterday, and there I saw Miss [Ethel] Sands, Morty Sands,[1] Katie Cromer, John Bailey[2] and daughters, Elena Richmond, Logan [Pearsall Smith]; Bowyer Nicholls.[3] Ethel Sands, sitting behind me, touched me with one of her bony claws and said "Now, I know you don't remember me, Mrs Woolf—" I replied without hesitation "I've just been admiring your pictures at Heals."

"O those were things I did a long time ago. I've been nursing in France for four years . . *so* interesting—the French soldiers *so* grateful—like my own children. Yes, it's been a great sacrifice not to paint all this time, but I've owed so much happiness to France—I felt I *must* do something for them. . . . What a lovely picture Vanessa has at the Omega! I do admire her things so much . . . Where is she now?"

1. Ethel's younger brother, Morton Harcourt Sands (1884-1959). He was a bachelor, a collector of Eastern art and John drawings, and for several years before the First War a secretary to Lloyd George.
2. John Cann Bailey, the critic and essayist.
3. The writer on art.

So I said very loud "Vanessa has a farm for Conscientious Objectors."
"Doesn't she find them very troublesome?" "O no. They're her friends—
Duncan and Bunny Garnett." Poor old Ethel didn't much like this, but had
to pretend that it was monstrous that Duncan should be made to dig fields
instead of painting pictures. You can't conceive the atmosphere of opulent
respectability and refinement of mind in that room. Then I saw old Katie
[Cromer] bobbing her head at me. She is still rather a superb figure, slightly
afflicted with a twitch of the lower jaw, but well shaped especially in the
upper part of the head. Unfortunately she tends to be too much of an
aristocratic matron. However I went up and spoke to her, and she was very
amiable, though we had nothing whatever to say, and then Elena [Richmond]
came across and I was, as usual, overcome by feminine charm. She hasn't
much changed. I suppose she's as stupid as a stone, but her manner is
adorable. She made me promise to go and see her, which I shall do, and tell
you about it. What does one talk about to Elena? I cant conceive how she
spends her day; or attempt to imagine her and Bruce performing any of the
operations of nature. I'm very curious to discover exactly when and how
they become so different from, shall we say, Carrington or Gertler, or Roger.
Its all a great mystery. I suppose you know for a fact that they're damned?

But then, after all, so is Barbara. I went to tea with her at her Home—a
dismal affair, as she shared a room with a widow, in order to cheer the widow
up. The sight of Nick was supposed to reconcile her to her own loss—not
that I said anything of the sort to Barbara; but it made conversation difficult.
She seemed slightly depressed, I thought, for one thing because her doctor
had told her that she must feed her baby for 9 months; which she said would
entirely cut her off from society, and also ruin her health, which is already
giving way from the demands of nature, and she has now gone to stay with
George de Vesci for a fortnight. You see how our past finds us out. I
shouldn't be surprised to hear that the Viscountess[1] wishes to renew her
acquaintance with us. She takes in soldiers wives after childbirth as a
charity in her house at Englefield Green. Of course Barbara is as open as a
summers day, but I'm not sure that thats not a duller form of damnation
than the Philistines; because it's so transparent. However, I admit we could
neither of us show at our best under the widows eye. Judith is exactly like
Nick—small featured, brown eyed, snub nosed. Adrian's Judith, according
to him, is a very lively, swarthy, vigorous baby, but I haven't been there.
Then we had Sydney Waterlow to dinner, who told us a most dismal story
of Saxon's condition. "I am bored when I am with other people, and lonely
when I'm by myself" he said. He agreed that the only remedy was to find
some one to marry, but he said that he had now no opportunities of meeting
young women, and was inclined to think that he had better emigrate. He

1. Widow of the 4th Viscount de Vesci, whom Virginia and Vanessa had known
   in their youth.

302

was not actively unhappy, according to Sydney, but completely hopeless. Of course I can't help thinking that this is a judgment upon Cambridge generally; its what happens if you go on telling the truth. You lose all generosity and all power of imagination. Moreover, you inevitably become a complete egoist. Please impress this upon Julian and Quentin, to say nothing of the nameless one, whom I dreamt of last night, and of course it was a boy.

Roger has now told me the story about our birth. His latest discovery is Mrs McColl,[1] as you probably know. He told her to read The Voyage Out. She asked Mr Cox,[2] the elderly gentleman at the London Library, for it. "Thats by Virginia Woolf isnt it?" he said. "She's a sister of Mrs Clive Bell. Strange whats come to those two girls. Such a nice home they had. Sir Leslie our President. But of course they weren't baptised!" So you see, how even in the London Library they follow us up; its thought you're slightly worse than I am; but Mrs McColl said there wasn't much to choose between us. Your life's pretty bad, but my writing is considered coarse.

Now, to the business of the wood cuts. Wouldn't the simplest plan be to share the profits? first deducting our expenses of paper and postage and possible advertisements, and your expense, for wood blocks? We don't count our printing time; and I expect the artists time and the writers time were about equal in this case. We now think of charging 1/6 anyhow; so we ought each to get a certain amount.

The other way would be to pay you something for each block. I wonder what your arrangement with Roger for the Omega book is? We might go by that.

The idea of the marbled covers is very attractive, if it wouldn't use up all our profits. If Duncan would explain the method to Wolfe[3] I could go and see him one day this week, and perhaps he'd give me an estimate.

If its too expensive, I should be inclined to have a plain white paper cover, with the title merely.

I see we shan't print the wood cuts nearly as well as Roger's man; but apparently one ought to use a special ink, so we may get them a good deal better than those first proofs.

The printing is almost done, but as usual we have to wait for the printers [McDermott's] press to be free.

I've a good many schemes on hand for future works which I should like to explain to you.

We shall probably come to Asheham on the 20th or 21st, and I think the Shoves are coming either for Christmas or after it. I should be very grateful

1. The wife of Douglas MacColl, the writer and painter, and at this time the Keeper of the Wallace Collection.
2. Frederick Cox, who from 1882 to 1952 worked at the book-issue counter of the London Library, and had an encyclopaedic knowledge of its books.
3. Edward Wolfe, the young South African painter, who was then working at the Omega Workshops.

for a line to say how you are. You might remember to say whether I can send you anything; also what are your plans for the future?—Have you got a nurse and a doctor? But I meant by the future the future of your whole establishment; which I suppose may be practically anything. At any rate its certain to be a source of acute delight to me.

I'm sending you Desmond's account of peace day. It sometimes fills me with depression to think of all the things you must have let fall upon public occasions and life in general without me to hear them. Just consider that immortal evening last summer when you summed up the situation over a bottle of wine—the cinema and the submarine. Does Duncan see what a joke you are? I trust Sebastian [Vanessa's unborn child] will.

Your

B.

We make out, roughly, that *our* expenses will come to between £2 and £3.

Berg

993: To Vanessa Bell   *Hogarth House, Paradise Road, Richmond, Surrey*

Thursday [12 December 1918]

Dearest,

Of course we will have the children [Julian and Quentin]—there is nothing I should like better, and I will do my best not to let them come to grief in any way. Our plans are to go to Asheham on the 20th, and to come back here on Jan. 3rd. Duncan or Bunny could bring them over at any time while we were there, as I will have the room ready for them. If the baby doesn't arrive till after the 3rd you could send me a telegram and I would meet them at Victoria, and bring them here. But there's no hurry about that. Suggest whatever suits you about the time of their coming—whether before the baby arrives or after.

The only difficulties I can think of are the difficulties about milk at Asheham, which I suppose we shall find it very hard to get—Do they want a great deal?—Also, can they safely be left to amuse themselves with occasional visits most of the morning? Some mornings I have to write in order to get reviews finished. Otherwise everything would be perfectly easy, and I should enjoy it immensely. Perhaps you could let me have a sketch of their hours and meals—what time they go to bed, and whether they sleep in the afternoon—in fact any hints so that I mayn't get them into bad habits. Dont bother to settle how long they're to stay—I shall expect them for a fortnight, and longer if its better for you not to have them back. Its *most* important that you shouldn't hurry back to ordinary life. Even

Barbara, in the lap of luxury, said 3 weeks was too short. As for payment, I never heard such nonsense.

I'd somehow thought the baby wasn't due till the middle of January. I hope I may see you before it comes—anyhow I adore every hair on your head, which is also true of Duncans—many though they are.

Yr.
B.

The Shoves are only coming for the week end after Christmas.

Berg

994: To Vanessa Bell   *Hogarth House, Paradise Road,*
                                         Richmond, Surrey

Tuesday [17 December 1918]

Dearest,

We can easily have the children on the 28th—in fact it is more convenient to know exactly when they will come. We can settle whatever suits you best about they're going to you and coming back here. Nelly and Lottie are overjoyed at the thought of having them—in fact I see you will have great difficulty in getting them back again. I'm going to take them to the pantomime, and I've a great many plans for enjoying myself with them. I know I shall be more envious of you than ever when I get to know all their attractive ways—and of course they are the most adorable creatures. I find myself constantly thinking about them.

As for Trissie—Nelly and Lottie would much rather she did not come here, and I don't think there'll be the least need of help. But if she very much wants to come, of course I don't want to prevent her. She's never communicated with the servants since she's been in London; so they thought she meant to drop them after the row. I will ask Mabel [Trissie's sister] to come.

N. and L: are going home for Christmas; I will tell them to look out for your needs; several of their friends have already gone back to service, so there may be a chance. Mrs Lucas is not in the telephone book; I *believe* her address is 122A Kings Rd., Chelsea, because I've got it down 222A, and I know that was wrong.

This is only about the children, so I will write again, if I can get any gossip; you having no need of affection ha! ha!

B

I go to Asheham on Friday.

Berg

Asheham, [Rodmell, Sussex]

Saturday [21 December 1918]

Dearest,

The servants are coming here on the 27th—so its quite all right about the children. I've no intention whatever of letting them wear me out—on the contrary I expect to lead a more healthy life than usual, as I shall take them for regular walks, and spend my afternoons in the open air instead of gadding up to London. However, we shall have a few dissipations—such as the British Museum and the Pantomime—perhaps they would like a Cinema? You see how craftily I shall work in my favorite expeditions. I rather think of teaching Julian the Greek alphabet, and making them both write me essays.

I will get Quentin his boots in Richmond.

I don't suppose Mabel has much time off, but I'll tell her to come whenever she can. I shall leave N. and L: to do what they like about Trissie; they seem to have all sorts of feelings about her—but I daresay they'll strike up another violent friendship in the end.

I came down by myself yesterday, as Leonard had to stay till today about the [International] Review. I should like to come over for the day one of these days, if the baby doesn't interfere. Perhaps I'd better keep my gossip such as it is until I see you; it only amounts to my tea with Elena and Bruce [Richmond] in South Kensington. I despair of conveying to you, either in writing or speech, the utter and immense horror of that visit. Of course, Barbara and even Nick are as Princes of Light compared with them— the banality, the frigidity, the sterility, the respectability of that couple; and underneath perfect callousness, and, I suspect, even brutality—at anyrate a stupidity so crass that they would trample you to death without seeing it. I was there for an hour; and we began by talking of country cottages, and we were still talking of country cottages when I left. Elena is a buxom matron, with white hair, but no longer more than comely. She is almost inanimate with stupidity. She sits looking at the fire like a spaniel. And my God! What a room! She told me that her only ideas of decoration were that she liked brown carpets and blue curtains; so she had blue of the colour of bad ink, and brown of the colour of musty chocolate; walls glistening and cold as wedding cake; a few chill water colours of Pompeii; and sham Sheraton bookcases, filled with shiny books under glass. Not a chair or cup out of place; a silver table; all so polished you could see your face. There were terrible pauses, when she clearly was slightly afraid of me, and he disapproved. Thats the man I write for! Good God! And they wanted to know if you'd ever let them Charleston; upon which I said "Well, Vanessa's ideas of decoration—" but I couldn't go on. "Yes?" said Elena. "She's done most of it herself—stuck up bits of paper, you know—" Here came one of the horrid pauses. "I'm sure she must have made it look very nice" Elena said kindly; but Bruce, who's got some sort of wits about him, was *not* sure. "I suppose the eldest boy is at school now," Elena continued. I couldn't go into that, so I said that the difficulties of education in the country were very great; and then we got back to country cottages again; and how Elena had been to a delightful party at the [Ralph] Vaughan Williamses and met Susan Lushington.[1] All my illusions are gone.

B.

I asked Murry to send you the Mrs Ward;[2] it seemed to me a masterpiece without rival—Have you reached the account of Tottie and Clara?[3] Would you say if you wd. like me to come before, or wd. rather wait till afterwards.

Berg

996: To Vanessa Bell

[*Asheham, Rodmell, Sussex*]

Postcard
[24 December 1918]

Necklace just arrived—exquisite and my only remaining jewels[4]—a thousand thanks. May I come to lunch on Boxing Day, if fine, 1. P. M. and go back after tea.

V.W.

Berg

997: To Vanessa Bell

Asheham, [*Rodmell, Sussex*]

Saturday [28 December 1918]

Dearest,
     Owing to this beastly weather I have had to yield to Leonard and not come this morning, much against my will. I'm fearfully cross and disappointed, especially as the wind seems to be going down now—but I shall try to come tomorrow anyhow, about 12.30. and stay to luncheon. You cant imagine how excited I was to hear of my niece[5]—in fact I think even

1. A friend from Virginia's childhood, and the sister of Kitty Maxse.
2. Mrs Humphry Ward's autobiography, *A Writer's Recollections*, 1918.
3. Charlotte and Clara Pater, the sisters of Walter Pater. Clara had taught Virginia Latin in 1900.
4. Virginia had sold most of her jewels to pay the expenses of her illnesses.
5. Angelica Bell was born on Christmas Day.

you would have been touched to know how completely my pleasure here was spoilt until I heard it was over. I see I'm going to become a perfectly sentimental old Aunt (I'm dropping into Aunt Marys language already) about her. She must be the most adorable little creature.

But I want most to know how you are—whether sensible, ruminative, tender, peaceful and sublime.

Perhaps Leonard will bring me some news. I should only bore you if I went on saying be careful.

Ka and Will are not coming, so its easier than ever to have the children, and the servants are enraptured. It is just possible that Nelly is in touch with two friends who might come to you—but I'll tell you all about it tomorrow.

Clarissa.
Miriam.
Rachel.
Venetia.
Sabina.
Clara.
Sarah.
Sara.
Euphrosyne.

I think on the whole I prefer Clarissa but I know there's a better one on the verge of my brain which I cant remember.

O damn! how I wish I were with you and had disregarded my husband flatly. It's not going to rain after all, and I said it wasn't.

A thousand embraces in all the tenderest parts from your Apes. Has Clarissa got a lovely little down at the back of her neck. Shall we all be allowed to kiss her?

Yr.
B.

Berg

998: TO DUNCAN GRANT   *Asheham, [Rodmell, Sussex]*

Sunday [29 December 1918]

My dear Duncan,

What a nuisance about the milk. I hope it is better today, but I feel sure that it is best not to see anyone for the first week, as the Gamp always says: and I could very likely bring the children back at the end of the time and stay a night, when Nessa would enjoy it more. However, let me know what you think. Also would you say whether I'm to bring the children over on Thursday. We can quite easily take them to Richmond on Friday if that is what is wanted.

They haven't got any pocket handkerchiefs. Perhaps you would send me the book Adrian gave Julian. We tried a Waverley novel last night, but found it too dull, and I'm afraid we haven't any good ones. They are perfectly well, and angelic in behaviour. Julian says he slept all night long—he was fast asleep at 8, and I uncovered his head without waking him. It was rather marvellous, considering that we were roused at 12.20 by Nelly with the news that Lottie thought she was dying. We found her in a state of hysterics for no reason that we could discover except that she felt very cold, and thought she had influenza. However she made a great noise which happily did not wake the children, and this morning seems all right though very lugubrious. This is the fourth time apparently she has woken Nelly and said she was dying and had to be given brandy. The wonders of the domestic world will never cease. The thing which really settled her was when we took her temperature with a broken thermometer and told her it was normal.

Give my love to the old creature.

Yr V.W.

Duncan Grant

999: To Katherine Arnold-Forster   *Asheham, [Rodmell,*
Sussex]

Dec. 30th [1918]

Dearest Ka,

It's a great pity, but we go back to Richmond on Friday, taking the children with us, so that I'm afraid we can't even offer you a week end of a sort there.

Have you heard of Nessa's daughter? She was born on Christmas Day, very successfully, and they both seem to be doing well. Nessa sounds very happy, and says the baby is already perfectly beautiful—with large blue eyes, Greek nose, lovely mouth, and adorable character. She was very pleased it was a daughter, and so am I—As you politely say beauty and talents seem inevitable, considering her Aunt.

But what a nuisance not to see you and Will here. It's the only place for seeing people. However, do ring us up after Friday and suggest something. I'm longing to hear about Cousin Mary Augusta.[1] Her book was the last Nessa read before the birth—the first she asked for afterwards. She and Duncan can talk of nothing else. They knew several passages by heart—the Memoirs, I mean, not the last novel. In its way it seems to me only comparable with Hamlet—for the insight it gives one into the recesses of the human heart. And what a heart! And you know her in the flesh.

---

1. Mrs Humphry Ward (Mary Augusta), granddaughter of Thomas Arnold of Rugby, and an aunt of Will Arnold-Forster.

What part of Cornwall are you going to? Is this the beginning of complete retirement? Shall you see no one but Sydney Waterlow for the rest of your lives, and the old woman who does for you? But read carefully this last sentence contains a hint—a hint and a grievance too—the poor Wolves were never asked to Aldbourne, and they took it a good deal to heart.

Your V.W.

Mark Arnold-Forster

1000: To Vanessa Bell   *Asheham, [Rodmell,*
                                         Sussex]
Tuesday [31 December 1918]

Dearest,

Its most disappointing that I shan't see you and Anonyma [Angelica] before we go, but we've now settled to go tomorrow, and I'm afraid I shan't be able to come over today. The children are both perfectly well, and more angelic than words can say. Lottie however has surpassed herself; she has got into such a state about her own health that she makes life here impossible and it seems best to go back where at any rate we are near doctors and chemists. If it weren't so irritating it would really be very amusing. After waking us up to say she was dying, she said next day that she felt perfectly well. However, when night came she again got into a panic, though her only symptoms were that her feet were very cold and her head was very hot. She said of course that she was in a raging fever; we could not take her temperature as the tube was broken. Happily I had an old sleeping draught which we gave her, and she went to sleep at once. Next day she said she was certain she was very ill indeed, and must see a doctor. It was Sunday, and finally she agreed that if we got a temperature tube and found that she was normal she would be content. So we sent Will off to Lewes: to ring up a chemist, but the chemist was sold out of temperature tubes. Then I gave her a talking to, and said there was nothing whatever the matter with her, and she ought to be ashamed of herself. This had some effect, and we got through the night without being called. Yesterday morning she was worse than ever, and accused me of being heartless, and insisted upon seeing a doctor at once. Just as she and Nelly were starting, it came on to rain, and she decided to stay at home, and let Nelly go and find another chemist and bring back a thermometer. Nelly came back saying that there was not such a thing in Lewes. Leonard finally went to the Killicks and borrowed one. We took her temperature and found it to be normal; we took it at night and found it to be normal. She then said that although she hadn't any fever, she was very ill internally. Her symptoms were impossible to describe, but such that she only wished she could die. Nelly, who has been having this for the

310

last fortnight began to get rather hysterical, alternately scolding Lottie and abusing me, and finally the only chance of peace seemed to be to say that we would return to Richmond and have [Dr] Fergusson. Lottie refuses to go to bed, and makes Nelly do most of her work, and altogether I expect we shall be better off at Hogarth.

However, as I say, the children are perfectly well, and no trouble at all. They play in the drawing room most of the morning, and we go for a walk after luncheon, and they seem to be full of their own games and ideas, which fit in extremely well with mine. They are amazingly interesting as well as attractive. Julian of course, knows infinitely more about science and history and geography than I do. He and Leonard had an argument yesterday about what would happen if you put a barometer into deep water. Leonard was very much impressed by his intelligence, and is, I see, getting to be very fond of them. Quentin's mind is very like mine, I expect. I hear him telling himself stories about Lady Suffolk, and how she will only eat chickens, which she breeds in enormous numbers, and she's the richest woman in the world and a Peeress in her own right. How they get hold of all their language I don't know; it seems to me very superior—in fact their minds altogether seem much quicker and more intelligent than ours. Mrs B. must have trained them very well, to do what they are told. Their great delight is to pretend to be dolphins in the bath, but they get out the moment I tell them to seriously, and their table manners are perfect. They seem to have most economical minds. Quentin told me the first night "I think it is an unneces- sary expense for you to have bolsters in your beds", and Julian said "You seem to me to be very extragavant [sic] with your coal." Quentin would only put a scraping of strawberry jam on his bread, because he said that it was very precious in war time. However, their appetites are very good,—They have just been in to say will I ask you to send them King Solomon's Mines [H. Rider Haggard], and Quentin's black book, as he wants to do some writing. You are not to send Adrian's book as Julian has finished it.

Lord! What a mercy they are to talk to after the servants!

Leonard has gone up to London today, and it makes all the difference having the children to play with, so that I needn't discuss Lotties health with her. As to your servants, I will find out more when things have quieted down a little. What Nelly said was that she had seen Lil (her niece, I think) who is either leaving or has left a place; and asked her whether she would come to you as nurse. Lil has not been a nurse, but is very fond of children. She said she did not want to live in the country; but perhaps this could be overcome, if you thought she'd do. But Budge sounded more hopeful. She is Nelly's sister, and has been a general [cook-general] for years. She is now in munition works, but thinks they will soon be dismissed, and then wants a place, and would go as houseparlourmaid. She wants to stay until they have to go, as she is forewoman. But she is a first rate servant according to Nelly, and very nice. It might be worth while to write and explain about your place, so that she could think it over before she heard of anything else. I know she was seven years in her last place before the war. Emily [Vanessa's current maid] sounds appalling—but in a different way I expect Lottie is just as bad. In fact I am once more seriously considering whether it is worth while to go on like this. This is the third time she has completely spoilt Asheham for us. It was perfect with Mrs Hammond [daily] alone. If she has everything her own way at Richmond she is all right, but even so she is very bad at most of her work, and I do get more and more to detest having servants living in the house. However, I shall see what happens—the difficulty is that Nelly is very good and very nice, and it mayn't be feasible to run a house with dailies. At the same time, I'm sure it could be worked now, and I always believe that it would be a perfect arrangement if you had them both, as the source of Lottie's temper is I'm certain that she hasn't enough to do, and you could start being severe with her, as I ought to have done. This is only a vague idea on my part, of course.

The children are now having a very polite conversation with Mr Gunn. It is said that he has broken off his engagement. Here is a list of the things we are going to do.

> Zoo.
> Movies.
> Tea at the Omega (Quentin says if we do this he needn't write and thank Roger)
> Pantomime.
> Russian dancers.
> Richmond Park.
> Sliding staircase on the Tube.
> British Museum.
> Tea at Buzzards.

But the thing Julian wants to do *almost* most of all is to learn the Greek alphabet! So I shall teach him that, and they are also very anxious to write essays and stories for me to judge, so we shall be very literary, and I hope to persuade Quentin to be a writer and not a painter when he grows up.

What an enormous long letter!—and now I must answer Aunt Anny. I daresay its better for you not to see me, but I'm very cross and disappointed —I'd meant to come tomorrow—its another reason for cursing Lottie. Please ask Duncan to write as often as he can and tell me how you are, and describe the ways of the adorable little creature. It is an enormous pleasure to me that she is a daughter. Think what an interest all her ways will be— much more than a boys—though I admit there's a good deal to be said for the firstborn (by which I mean of course, darling B.[1]).

You'd better destroy this, in case of Emily.

Berg

1. Virginia is thinking of herself ('Billy goat') as Vanessa's first-born.

Tuesday [31 December 1918]

Dearest Margaret,

We save as many of your sweets as we can from Julian and Quentin and enjoy them immensely. The children say they are 'gorgeous'. Thank you very much indeed, and also Lilian [Harris], and remind her that she is expected to come to luncheon, the first fine day.

Have you heard of my new niece—Vanessa's daughter—born on Christmas Day? They are both very well, and Vanessa says the baby is already perfectly beautiful, and an adorable character. I haven't been able to get over, but I can quite believe anything in the way of beauty and gifts in my niece—it seems inevitable. We both very much wanted a daughter this time—the difficulty is what to call her? They incline to Allegra—I prefer Sabina—I dont suppose we shall dare either.

I'm coming up with the children, who are going to stay a week or two, tomorrow. Leonard has gone today in order to correct proofs with his industrious sub-editor [Mrs Manus], but I doubt whether, even between them, the Review will be out on the first.

We had a perfect week here, quite alone, with only a cottage woman to do for us. Directly the servants came Lottie announced, in the middle of the night, that she was dying, and she is in such a panic about her health that we are coming back partly in order to see a doctor. Her temperature is normal; apparently there is nothing the matter; but she keeps Nelly awake every night with her fears, so I think we had better put an end to it.

The children are heavenly creatures, really it depresses me to see how much more intelligent and how much nicer they are than grown ups. I suppose the chief harm to human character comes from taking an interest in politics—but I dont expect you to see the profound truth of that remark.

We paid a man 6d on Saturday to bring us the news of the Elections[1], and Leonard has been plunged in gloom ever since. Maynard Keynes came over the other day and said that Lloyd George is all in favour of a League of Nations, and it is going to come right in the end, as [President Woodrow] Wilson has been privately assured. Publicly they have to pretend to agree with France and Italy: but Maynard being behind the scenes is almost invariably wrong.

I've not read any books, so I cant talk to you about them. As to Saxon, I hope you will persevere, in spite of discouragement. He is in a tepid state far worse than despair, and to rouse him in any way is a blessing—poor man. It seems melancholy that any attempt to improve the ordinary way of

1. Polling Day was on 14 December, and the result, an overwhelming victory for Lloyd George, was declared on 28 December.

falling in love should end disastrously, but I'm afraid his experiment has, at least as far as he is concerned.

Now I must go and fetch the milk.

Please come and see us soon. We shall have the children for a fortnight I think.

Your
V.W.

Sussex

314

Letters 1002-1065 (January-June 1919)

In May the Hogarth Press published three books on the same day: Virginia's Kew Gardens, *T. S. Eliot's* Poems, *and Middleton Murry's* The Critic in Judgment, *of which the first two were printed and bound by the Woolfs themselves, who were again without an assistant since Barbara's marriage.* Kew Gardens *at first sold at a disappointing rate, but its sales picked up after a favourable* TLS *review, and a second edition, which they had printed for them by an outside firm, was soon called for.* Night and Day, *far too long a novel for them to undertake publishing themselves, was accepted by Gerald Duckworth. Virginia's work on the Press and her reviews was interrupted by a fortnight's illness in January, and by recurrent servant troubles which are recorded in numerous and very detailed letters to Vanessa. Angelica, finally so-named three months after her birth, had a severe infantile illness which further complicated their domestic lives. A more permanent blow was a notice from their landlord that the Woolfs must leave Asheham. They at first considered re-renting Little Talland House at Firle, where Virginia had lived before her marriage, but on impulse, in June, she bought the Round House, a converted windmill in the centre of Lewes, and at about the same period rented three contiguous cottages at Zennor in Cornwall. There is no evidence that they occupied either the Round House or the Cornish cottages for a single night, since a more attractive alternative to both suddenly appeared. They discovered Monk's House, at Rodmell, a mile across the Ouse from Asheham.*

1002: To Vanessa Bell   *Hogarth House, Paradise Road,*
                                         Richmond, Surrey
[2 January 1919]

Dearest,

I wired to Lily this morning, and have just had an answer to say she will come as cook. She has been both cook and houseparlourmaid and left because the work was too hard and is Nellys niece. I will write to the other one [Budge Boxall] in the munitions works, but she is not yet looking for a place, and may stay on there.

Children perfectly well. I've just had a tooth out so excuse scrawl. I will write again.   Yr
                                                                      B.

I wrote to Lily today and said you wd. give £35 and were only in the country for spring and summer, liberal outings, no waiting very free—

Berg

315

1003: To Vanessa Bell   *Hogarth House, Paradise Road,*
                               Richmond, Surrey
Typewritten
6 Jan. 1919

Dear Vanessa,

Virginia has asked me to write this letter for her. She is in bed with a head ache of the old kind. It was brought on by having a tooth out last Thursday. The bleeding would not stop, and we had to have the doctor twice on Thursday night before he succeeded in stopping it. The loss of blood and pain seem to have brought on the headache, and of course she had rather bad nights before the tooth was taken out. It was in no way connected with having the children here. The doctor insists upon her being in bed for at least a week which will mean until Friday. She is rather better the last two days.

The children are extraordinarily good and no trouble at all. They have been very well, and have slept splendidly. Friday and Saturday the servants took them out, and yesterday we went to the South Kensington Museum which they seemed to like. I am taking them to Hampton Court this afternoon, and Maynard is taking them to the Coliseum to-morrow. Wednesday Ka will probably take them out, and Thursday Mabel.

Both Nelly and I wrote to Budge [Boxall] yesterday, and Nelly seems to think that there is a good chance of her coming to you, now that Lily is coming.

                                                          Leonard
[*in Virginia's handwriting*]
This is only a line to say that my headache wasn't caused *in the least* by the children—They have been angelic and I'm only very cross that I cant go out with them. Would you send *all* the money they've got, except coppers. I'm really better today—Let me know how you are—

[*in Leonard's handwriting*]
I enclose Boxall's letter which probably ought to be answered by you.

Berg

1004: To Vanessa Bell   *Hogarth [House, Richmond]*
Typewritten
14 Jan. 1919

Dear Vanessa,

I am writing for V. She is better than she was, but it is rather a slow process and there are always ups and downs. Yesterday she was rather tired again, but to-day that has gone. She will not get up until Thursday, and will then take it very quietly for a bit. She has been very sensible. The doctor will not let her have the children back next week, as he thinks she ought to be very quiet still. We are very sorry not to be able to have them again, but perhaps they might come later on in the spring?

Your letter was a great entertainment to her, and she would like another with news of yourself and the servant problem. We have heard nothing from Lil, nor has Nelly. It is thought she is ashamed of herself. Nelly heard from Budge: she is on the point of marriage, otherwise it is though [*sic*] she might have come to you, but she has several times before been on the point of marriage and shied off at the last moment (once actually on her wedding day), so that she may do it again.

Leonard

[*in Virginia's handwriting:*]
Your letter was a great delight. Do tell me if you've got a nurse and any domestic details. I dont like Claudia—pompous and aristocratic—I like Susan—Suzannah suggests an old Negress on a Savannah—Thank Roger for writing—I enjoyed it very much.

Berg

1005: TO SAXON SYDNEY-TURNER *Hogarth* [*House, Richmond*]

Tuesday [21 January 1919]

My dear Saxon,
    This is not the first instalment of my projected work on friendship, as my head is aching slightly (only very slightly—nothing to count). But I shall want all my faculties to deal with Clive, shall we say, whose letters I've been reading this morning. I'd no notion what numbers he wrote at one time. So careful, literary, affectionate—full of compliments. But as I say, I won't go into all that now, tempting though it is, and much as it would delight me to trace the ascent or descent of his taste from me to his present flame—but I, at any rate, was the one he learnt to write upon. Then there's Walter Lamb, got by accident into the same box, but without any of Clive's saving qualities, and nothing to recommend him at all, poor wretch, that I can see. Saxon's account of hearing Parsifal for the first time has an inimitable charm, —not that he would altogether see where it lies—but I do. And there's a letter in French from him too, and a scrap of Greek. But as I say, I am *not* writing a letter; what I am writing is an invitation to dine on Sunday night— come before dinner if you can. Alix and James [Strachey] may be here for dinner or not, and Leonard may be out till dinner or not; anyhow I shall be here, and if I've had a long letter from No. 37[1] to go upon, we might enlarge

1. Saxon's flat in Great Ormond Street.

with infinite subtlety and abandon in converse over the fire. Would you bring *Antigone?* (by Sophocles).

Sussex

1006: TO VANESSA BELL   *Hogarth [House, Richmond]*
Wednesday [22 January 1919]
Dearest,

Domestic affairs

Anny Boyce came to see the servants yesterday, so I had her up to see me. She would like to come to you as h. parlourmaid if you can wait for her. The difficulty is that she doesn't know how long it will be. Her present people may want her to stay till the end of June.

She is paid by the week, so she might go at any moment.

The people are Americans and are waiting to get a house in America. The man has gone to get one, and will be back in 6 weeks; so they may go then but its quite likely that they'll stay on anyhow till the end of June.

Anny has a friend, who is cook with her, and they want to be together; and she would also like to come to you. Anny said that she has several friends and could perhaps find two who would go to you until she and the cook are free. I arranged that she should try to find two, and let me know directly she is free. Meanwhile I said I would ask you whether you would wait for them. Anny B. is one of Nelly's oldest friends, and seemed very nice; Nelly also knows the cook who is said to be very nice. She is married and has a child of 10, but the child is away. Anny told Nelly that she thought she would like to go to you, and would certainly take the place if you wanted her. I enlarged upon the freedom and pleasure of it. She seemed rather independent, and not much like a servant. She is 27.

So would you write and say what you want. I heard from Mrs Geal, but she knows of no one. This is my first day of writing, and I'm limited to one hour, so I musn't enlarge too much. I wish you'd write, or aged Duncan would write, and say how you are. I'm better, though my affairs gave me rather a headache again, and I had to stay in bed for two days. I'm going out today I hope, and I think I've quite recovered, though I mean to have the discretion of an elephant. Please imitate me; but I live like a sultana among pillows and fowls and you are a lean old drudge and mother of millions. I've such a mass of things to say that I dont know where to begin. First I want a sketch of Sidonia, Griselda, Leslie, Vashti [Angelica]; a line on an envelope wd. be better than nothing. Then I meant to write a long account of J and Q [Julian and Quentin]. I was immensely impressed. Moreover I have now read part of your riddle; yes, I made several discoveries about you. Then I

318

suppose you've heard all about Norton and Alix? I had the story from her. I never heard such a farce. Copulation every 10 days in order to free his suppressed instincts! I rather think she'll marry him in the end. She asked my advice—but nobody ever takes my advice. I told her on no account to copulate from a sense of duty, but to advise him to invest his capital either in a new theatre or picture gallery or string quartet and his instincts would be liberated spontaneously. Norton is the pure flower of Cambridge isn't he? But I can't go into it. And then I saw Fredegond [Shove], who is writing to you, so I wont spoil her story of Aunt Anny [Ritchie] and Cordelia [Fisher] and Ivy Tennyson (who was Pretious).[1] Aunt Anny, on hearing that your daughter was beautiful, wrote to Ivy in an ecstasy saying that the lovely little girl had brought you and Clive together, and all the Fishers now know for a fact that it is undoubtedly the child of Clive, though having heard of your admirers they had once suspected[2]—However, F [redegond]'s account of Cordelia was so repulsive, and the Fisher atmosphere is so infinitely penetrating and degrading that I had to tell her to stop. Aren't I a good Ape to get gossip even when I can't go to London? And then you tell me that I'm only 5th on the list!

Yr

B.

Berg

1007: To Vanessa Bell   Hogarth [*House, Richmond*]

Friday [24 January 1919]

Dearest,

I am appalled at your crises. I suppose it means that you have to be nursemaid and get no food or looking after from that wretched couple E. J. [Emily and Jenny]. I have written to Budge, whose name is H. Boxall, 23 North Street, Farncombe, Surrey.

Nelly thinks there's not much chance of her coming, as she's still at her [munitions] works; but I've asked her to write straight to you.

I'm sure I could get you temporary people in London, if these fail. Liz has written to say that the reason why Lil didn't go to you was merely that she found she could make so much more money by going as temporary. I'm afraid you're very worried too about the Baby, as I know how anxious they are when small. However, J. and Q. do you credit.

I suppose you've had my letter about Annie Boyce, and will let me know. I'm confronted this morning by a demand for a rise from N. and L: or they'll

1. Ivy Gladys Pretious, who married Charles Tennyson, the grandson of the Poet Laureate.
2. Angelica was the daughter of Vanessa and Duncan Grant.

go! I'm inclined to say go to the Devil— Also we're warned by Hoper[1] that he will probably want Asheham after Sept.—so I don't know what we shall do. Are you going to get your nurse back? I'm really better. Do send a line and say how you both are. and let me do anything I can. I shall be able to go to London next week, I expect.

In haste

VW.

Berg

1008: To Vanessa Bell   *Hogarth* [*House, Richmond*]

Saturday night [25 January 1919]

Dearest,

To my great surprise, I have just had a visit from Budge [Boxall], who started off on getting my letter in order to explain the situation. She cannot come herself, but she has two friends who want a place together, as cook and h. parlourmaid, at once, and permanently, and think yours would suit them. They are 22 and 23, have been in a place together before, and according to Budge are perfectly respectable and very good workers. They have always been in the country, and like children. Budge promised to tell them definitely on Monday morning whether you would take them, so I have taken it upon myself to say that you will, and also that you will have them as soon as they wish to come. Of course I have only her word to go upon, but they have been working under her in the factory, and she says they are very good characters, and were in service before the war, at a school in Sunningdale.

She is going to tell them to write straight to you, so you will hear from them on Tuesday, I expect. Their names are Marks and Osgood (I think.) I said that you would want characters, and she said you could get them both from their former mistress, and from the manager at the works. She has told them all about your place, and they liked the idea of it. She had told them that you would give them wages from £25—and she said she thought they would be content if the cook had £25, the other £27, with a rise if satisfactory. She thought £35 was much too much at their age. I couldn't quite make out whether they wanted to leave and go to you at once, or wait a week; the factory is closing in a week or 10 days anyhow, and as they can leave with an hours notice, they might want to come on straight. However I have said it would be perfectly all right if they came at once.

I hope to goodness something will come of this; I think they must mean it seriously, or Budge wouldn't have come all the way up to see me about it.

---

1. A solicitor from Rugby, the owner of Asheham, who now gave warning that he needed the house for his farm-bailiff.

I hope you wont think me very precipitate in engaging them, but if I didn't say something definite, I think they might slip away.

Yr

B.

Berg

1009: To Vanessa Bell   [*Hogarth House, Richmond*]

Sunday [26 January 1919]

Dearest

I have just had another talk with Budge who is going back.

She says Beatrice Marks is the name of the h. parlourmaid, and Alice Osgood is the cook, 22, and 23 or 4, are their ages. They have been in places together for some years, and she has known them and their families all her life, and they are very respectable. She is sure that they will take the place, as it is just what they want.

I scrawl this, as you may like further details. They will write tomorrow without fail. They would either come at once or wait a week she thinks as you like.

Yr

B.

Berg

1010: To Lady Robert Cecil   *Hogarth House, Richmond*

Sunday [26 January? 1919]

My dear Nelly,

I wrote you a very long letter the other day, sitting in my window looking at the downs, and comparing them very favourably with the view from your window—but I never sent it. This was not modesty but having my nephews to stay, and a niece born to me, —and after all, the whole purpose of the letter was to fish for an invitation to come to tea with you again. You can't count last time, owing to your concealing your position on the [Chelsea] embankment. Perhaps, though, you're in Paris, or even Washington. Even so, you could answer a letter.

I am reading through the whole of George Eliot, in order to sum her up, once and for all, upon her anniversary, which happily is still months ahead. So far, I have only made way with her life, which is a book of the greatest fascination, and I can see already that no one else has ever known her as I know her.[1] However, I always think this whatever I read—don't you? I think she is a highly feminine and attractive character—most impulsive

1. George Eliot was born on 22 November 1819. Her *Life* (3 vols. 1885-7), was written by J. W. Cross whom she married in 1880, the year of her death.

321

and ill-balanced (Mrs Prothero[1] once told me that she—George Eliot that is
—had a child by a Professor in Edinburgh—she knew it for a fact—indeed
the child is a well known Professor somewhere else—[2]) and I only wish she
had lived nowadays, and so been saved all that nonsense. I mean, being so
serious, and digging up fossils, and all the rest of it. Perhaps, too, she would
have written, not exactly better, but less facetiously. It was an unfortunate
thing to be the first woman of the age. But she comes very well out of it so
far, better anyhow than Herbert Spencer, and George Frederick Watts,—
but I haven't begun her novels.

Are you ever going to write something for us to print? That was what
I meant to write about, and not George Eliot, and here I have finished my
paper and dare not begin a new sheet. What I want you to write is an
account of your childhood. Don't you think that opens up infinite possibilities? You need not be intimate or indiscreet. Think of the description of
the garden and the house, and so on. Please do.

We are just bringing out some little books.

Yours aff.

Hatfield   V.W.

1011: TO VANESSA BELL   [*Hogarth House, Richmond*]

Postcard
[29 January 1919]

Karin has not got diptheria. It came from her ears, and is better.
James has got influenza. Ka has narrowly escaped bronchitis.
Peter Studd[3] is dead.
I have put on 2 ½ lbs:
Julian Huxley is engaged to Juliette (?)[4]

V.W.

Berg

1. Wife of George Walter Prothero, the historian and Fellow of King's College,
   Cambridge.
2. This piece of gossip was quite unfounded. The child was Thornton Lewes,
   the legitimate offspring of Agnes and G. H. Lewes. When George Eliot started
   to live with Lewes in 1854, the boy often spent his holidays with them. This
   gave rise to the rumour that Thornton was George Eliot's son by John Chapman. He did not become 'a Professor', but emigrated to Natal, whence he
   returned to London to die in 1869, aged 25.
3. Arthur Studd (1863-1919), the artist and collector. Virginia had known him
   since Hyde Park Gate days.
4. Juliette Baillot, a Swiss girl who had been living at Garsington while she was a
   part-time student at Oxford and governess to the Morrells' daughter. Julian
   Huxley and Juliette were married in March 1919.

1012: To Lytton Strachey   *Hogarth [House, Richmond]*

Thursday [30 January 1919]

Desolated, but acquiescent.[1] Will you ask Carrington whether she is going to produce her wood-cuts—if so, when; and will you see that she does it.[2]

V.W.

Frances Hooper

1013: To Vanessa Bell   *[Hogarth House, Richmond]*

[late January 1919]

Dearest,

Will you give me your opinion as to which of these papers to have, if either, for our book [*Kew Gardens*]. Could you let me know as soon as possible, as I have kept them waiting. Also would you send them back before Sunday, as I want to show them to Eliot.

I'm appalled at your disasters,[3] which I learn from Duncan's letter. Thank him very much for writing, and I say I should be grateful for further news. also about Budge's friends.

I'm in a hurry now, but I will write later.

B.

Berg

1014: To Vanessa Bell   *Hogarth [House, Richmond]*

Saturday [1 February 1919]

Dearest,

I'm writing before getting an answer to my telegram, as if I dont I shall miss the post. Nelly herself suggested going to you, and we can manage quite well for a week or 10 days with Lottie, as we have done before.

I've made vain attempts to get a temporary this morning. I telephoned to Mrs Hunt, and Nelly went to the registry here, but there seems no one to be had. I've just heard from Faith [Henderson] that she can hear of no one either.

But if Nelly is with you for a week, I daresay I could find one meanwhile. She seems to think she could get one at Brighton or Eastbourne by going herself. Any how its quite impossible for you to go on like this. My other suggestion, which is Leonards also, is this. If, after Nelly's been with you

1. Lytton had cancelled a dinner with the Woolfs.
2. See p. 282, note 1.
3. Angelica Bell was seriously ill when she was only a month old.

323

for 10 days, you can't get anyone and the baby's better, why don't you, Duncan, and the baby go over to Asheham, where Mrs Geall could do for you; and surely Mrs B: and the children could manage with the cook at Charleston. Mrs Geall is rather a good cook, and a very nice woman. You could stay as long as you wanted. There is plenty of coal, and Mrs Hammond, Mrs Attfield, and the Woolers all able to come in by the day if wanted. I would go down a day or two beforehand, as I've been meaning to, and see that everything was warm and ready for you; and order in supplies. Do think of this. Or is there any chance that you and the baby would come here? Nelly and Lottie would love helping to look after it, Fergusson is round the corner, and far the best dr. I've ever had, and we could promise you a certain amount of comfort anyhow. The room is there empty; and if Duncan came to London at the same time the more he was here the better.

I suppose it all depends how the baby is. Of course you could interview Anny Boyce and others for yourself if you were here, which would be more satisfactory.

I can throw no light upon Budge and her doings. She was so positive to me that I thought there could be no doubt this time. According to her, the girls actually asked her to get them the place. But its no good going into that. Anny Boyce is the name; Coombe Brook, Coombe Lane, Kingston Hill, Surrey. I am writing to her to ask her to let me know if she knows of any temporaries whom I could see; she said she knew a good many girls around here. I feel very strongly that it is perfect madness for you to be embroiled in all this when you're just out of bed; but there's no good saying that. I hope to goodness the baby is better—but my God, what a time you've had!

Nelly's been extraordinarily nice, and says she would do anything to help you, so do make any use of her you can. I've just raised their wages, and they're both overflowing with good will.

Yr
B.

I am quite well again, and went to London without being tired yesterday. I only got your letter this morning, or I could have gone to Mrs Lucas.

Berg

1015: To Vanessa Bell   1917 *Club, 4 Gerrard Street, W.*1.
[3 February 1919]

Dearest,

I have got a temporary h. parlourmaid who will come on Wednesday. Her name is Phoebe Crane, and she wants £1 a week, and her railway fares.

Can you manage that some one should meet her at Glynde on Wednesday at 12.8 She seemed amiable, though rather foolish looking. I saw 3 characters; all said she was perfectly honest, clean, sober, and two said she was very obliging—the third that she would not go to Church. Anyhow I suppose she will do for a time. though the expense seems fearful. Abbey charged 12/6 also for his fee; She said she liked the country; I told her she would have no waiting. She was anxious not to have to look after children. I am seeing Liz tomorrow, and may find out some more about Budge and her doings from her. You must have 2 proper people, and I shall go on till I get them. Do think of coming to Hogarth.

V.W.

She said she could not possibly find her way up, so I promised some one wd. be at Glynde. Age about 35 prominent brown eyes: one front tooth missing.

Berg

1016: To Katherine Arnold-Forster

Hogarth House, Richmond

5th Feb. [1919]

Dearest Ka,

I should have written to you before, but being limited to one hour's writing a day, and having to use that to polish off an old gentleman [George Meredith] whose life I've promised to write for the Times, I put off good Bruin Cox. I hope she's in no need of having her life written. Is the brute better? bathing, walking, shouldering her way unperturbed through the thickest of the gorse bushes? However to be ill at the Lizard seems to me better than to be well here. You can't conceive what existence is like without trains or tubes,[1] a heavy snow falling, no coal in the cellar, a leak in the roof which has already filled every possible receptacle, and probably no electric light tomorrow. We in Richmond can still get to Waterloo; but Hampstead is entirely cut off. Leonard's staff of course live upon the northern heights, and hardly get to the office at all, so the poor man has to go up himself, and here I sit waiting, and God knows, what with the snow and the fog, when he'll be back. Then the experts say that the working classes have behaved with such incredible stupidity that the Government will beat them; and this strike is only the beginning of others far worse to follow. They say we are in for such a year as has never been known. Sensible people like you go and live in Cornwall. I wish you'd go to Gurnards Head and see if there's a

---

1. The inflation which followed the Armistice led to a series of strikes, particularly in the mining and transport industries.

cottage there to let, as I've been told. We are faced with the appalling prospect of having to give up Asheham. It's wanted for the farm probably; there's still a ray of hope, but I'm afraid not much. If we have to go, we're rather inclined to pitch somewhere by the sea, though Sydney and Dawks [Waterlow] have found us a house near Oare, where they're collecting a colony round them—MacCarthy's, Pophams [Hugh and Brynhild],—but not the Wolves—not if I know it. There are lodgings at Zennor, I believe, kept by cultivated ladies, who advertise in one of Leonard's sheets, which I've always meant to try.

I'm quite well again, though slightly restricted in my jaunts to London, so I haven't a great deal of gossip. I suppose, though, you've heard that Alix thinks of taking a large house in Gordon Sqre and running it on the Brunswick system,[1] with James for an idol in the best pair of rooms, and poor old Harry Norton up at the top. Poor old Harry has dropped into one of his queer states of mind, and wishes either to marry her, or have the rights of marriage, but she seems still set with the ferocity of a vulture—it quite alarms me—upon her usual victim [James Strachey]. Thats a fine piece of gossip isn't it?

Have you heard of the catastrophes at Charleston? I cant go into them in any detail, since they would fill volumes. But imagine a country doctor ordering some medicine for the baby which made it ill by day and by night— Nessa commands him to stop—he refuses—he wont say what it is—the gamp has to obey him—child loses more and more pounds—Duncan goes over to Brighton and interviews Saxon's father about the quality of Nessa's milk—without result—Noel[2] telegraphed for—lady doctor[3] arrives secretly —finds the doctor is ordering some form of poison—Mrs Brereton thinks it her duty to inform the Dr of his rival's presence—scenes, explosions, dismissal—triumph of Nessa and the lady doctor and partial recovery of the Baby. Just as this was over, the servants took to drink or worse, and had to be got rid of; frantic efforts of course to get others; none to be had; telegrams sent, interviews arranged, cook discovered, fails at the last moment—whole thing begins over again; more cooks discovered; just about to start when their father falls dead in the street, upon which both Nessa and I rush about in a fury, with the result that we each engage cooks without telling the other, and one has to be dismissed at enormous expense and terrific cost of energy. You cant think what a lot of time this has all taken up, or how sick I am of beginning my letters, "Jane Beale, I am writing for my sister—" For one thing I detest that style of sentence, and then the bold abrupt handwriting is what I can't compass.

1. i.e., sharing it between friends, as Virginia had done in Brunswick Square before her marriage.
2. Noel Olivier, who had qualified as a doctor.
3. She was Dr Marie Moralt, a friend of Noel Olivier.

Thank God! here is my husband back. We have just had an enormous tea over the fire of hot toast and honey, and things look a little brighter. It is possible that he has done a masterly deal and bought a satire off Mr [H. G.] Wells, which will appear in the In' [International] Review, and brighten it up for the degenerates who cant fix their minds steadily upon Poland. But the strikes are bad as ever, and the snow worse, and we cling desperately to the thought of April when we've been asked by the Arnold-Forsters to stay at Aldbourne. Our only engagement is on April fools day when Leonard is addressing the Ethical Society upon the Rights of Democracy.

He wants me to thank you very much for the subscription, and would have written, but his labours have been severe, and he considers me "considerably better, but still in need of care." "I hope that Will will read the Jan and Feb numbers of the I.R.[1] and let me have any criticisms. Love to Ka".

Yrs
V.W.

Mark Arnold-Forster

1017: To Vanessa Bell   [*Hogarth House, Richmond*]

Saturday [8 February 1919]

Dearest

I got your letter last night. Faith rang up and said both her women had fallen through. So I telegraphed to Phoebe Crane this morning, to ask her to go to you this evening and telephoned at the same time to the Registry. They said she was disengaged yesterday, and thought she could certainly go, but might be out for the day.

I've had no wire from her, and its now 6.30, so I suppose she was out (I sent her a reply paid) I left orders (I had to be out) that Nelly was to wire to you; but apparently she hasn't done so.

I expect I shall hear from Crane on Monday. Anyhow I will wire then and say whats happening, and try to provide some one on Monday. I didn't mean that I didn't think much of Crane; she seemed rather nice, and wrote me a very polite letter. Also, Emily's character wasn't Abbey's fault as they said they knew nothing, but gave me the woman's name she's worked for; whom we saw—I've seen 3 characters of Crane—and all good. The strike cuts us off from everywhere except Waterloo, so I couldn't go to Mrs Lucas, who's not on the telephone.

I'm fearfully sorry not to have got Crane to go today, I'll write again— very hurried to get the post now.

VW.

Berg

1. The first two numbers of the *International Review*, which Leonard was editing.

Sunday [9 February 1919]

Dearest,

Things were in such a muddle yesterday that I'm afraid I wrote rather an incoherent letter. The difficulty was that having waited for an answer to the telegram it became too late to telegraph to you—I would have arranged that Nelly was to catch the 5.20 anyhow, but she had a bad cold and was very anxious not to go till Monday. Also it seemed absurd to send her late on Saturday if Crane were coming on Monday. She has shown some signs too of getting into one of her usual states—thinking that you would want her to stay over the week and that she could not resist you—so I was alarmed lest she might in the end refuse—as Leonard thought and still thinks likely—to go at all. However, I've just spoken to her, and she is quite decided to go tomorrow if Crane fails. Her cold is much better and she appears very cheerful. I'm now writing to Crane, and telling her to ring me up tomorrow morning, so as to allow time for wiring to you. I'm fearfully sorry that you've had no one this week end, but anyhow you will have one or the other tomorrow—before you get this, I suppose.

Faith was anxious for me to explain that though she got into touch with two possibilities, both failed. I dont think she much wants to send Flossy, as there seem to be difficulties with the other servant. If I have a week, however, I'm sure I could get someone, should Crane fail. Nelly heard of someone from the Registry here, who sounded promising; and if the strike is over, it will be easy to go to places in London. All last week we were practically cut off—we could get to Waterloo, but the buses are so crammed in London that it means walking everywhere.

Mr Abbey, by the way, was emphatic that C. is a most respectable woman; and to do him justice I can't remember that either Trissie or I enquired much as to Emily's character in our anxiety to get someone that day. Crane's expression did not seem to me intelligent, though amiable, and temporaries get a battered look—that was all I meant.

We are now faced with a shattered boiler, which has to be replaced, and will take some days, so we may possibly come to Asheham this week—as the prospect of no kitchen fire is depressing in this weather.

I'm afraid its almost certain we shall be turned out of Asheham. But if we should come to Asheham, and Nelly is with you, would you like to have Lottie as well, for a few days? But this can wait. She'd probably prefer being with you at Charleston to being alone at Asheham, and Mrs Geall does all right for us. The ramifications of the servant question are such that there's no time for gossip—even if I'd seen anyone, but of course no one could get here. Alix is taking a house in Gordon Sqre. "so that I can live with James", she told us quite openly. It is to be on the Brunswick system. But I daresay its fallen through; it may represent the poor woman's death agony. In death she may become the bride of Norton, a terrible bridal it will be. I feel convinced myself that it'll be all right about Nelly. Lottie was rather upset last week, which made the difficulty.

Yr
B.

Berg

1019: To Vanessa Bell   *[Hogarth House, Richmond]*

Monday [10 February 1919]

Dearest,

Here is Nelly at last. She was perfectly ready to come, as I thought; and only wishes me to ask you not to try and persuade her to stay longer than next Monday; I've said you certainly won't.

Crane is ill. I only heard this morning. I'm going to Mrs Lucas, and hope to get some one in a few days. If there were a chance of a permanent, I should take it. Nelly will explain how Budge's friend's father died, and all else.

If you want to alter plans in any way, let me know as early as you can. Letters take a fearful time. I suppose I'd better send anyone off at once, if I find one.

I don't think Faith's much good—so I shouldn't count on getting Flossie

Yr
B.

Berg

1020: To Vanessa Bell   Hogarth *[House, Richmond]*

Wednesday [12 February 1919]

Dearest,

I have just been rung up by Abbey to say that Crane is recovered and ready to go to you tomorrow. I have told her to catch the 5.20, and that you will send to meet her at Berwick. I suggested that she should wait till Monday, but he says she is quite all right, and wants to take a place at once, so I had to decide at once.

If you'd like Nelly to stay till Saturday we're quite ready that she should, and she might help to settle Crane in; but I must confess that we should be rather glad to have her back then. Leonard is getting rather restive, and it would be a relief if I could count on getting her on Saturday. I went to Mrs Lucas, who was hopeless, and said she hadn't had a h. p. for weeks, even for London. Then I went to Mrs Stuarts agency and got the names of two, but of course neither has answered. I have also been to the Registry here, but the one Nelly heard of had been taken. There were various possibilities, however; there were 2 friends, cook and h. p. wanting to go together; also an h. p. with 5 years of character wanting the country; Would you tell me what you'd like me to do supposing I hear of someone, or two permanents

329

or one permanent, in the next few days—or supposing I do get answers? I shant tell any of the registries that I'm suited until I hear from you. Abbey says they have no one else in prospect at all. Faith seems to have worked the West End without success. They say the only chance is to be there at the moment, and take someone straight off. Still, now theres a breathing space, something permanent might turn up.

They all ask either 18/6 or 20/-

I hope to hear how you are, but I suppose owing to the strikes, all the posts seem erratic—and I think I'd better not count on your getting this in time, but send you a wire.

7 lines omitted

. . . .
. . . .
. . . .
. . . .
. . . .
. . . .
. . . .

I haven't much gossip, as we have been so cut off. But I shall now put my bag on my back and pick up crumbs for you in London. O dear, when shall I ever see you, and my adorable Niece? Paula is a name of character, and so is Susanna; and I see one must consider Bell as part of the colour scheme, though, if she marries a man called Tristram or McCawney it will be sad to have sacrificed Sidonia, Esther, Vashti and the others. I like a name that has the look of a clear green wave; there's distinct emerald in Sidonia, just as there's the splash of the sea in Vanessa; and a chandelier or lustre in Miriam, with all its eyes. By the way, Leonard wants you to call her Fuchsia; that is his favourite name, and he long ago decided to call his daughter that. I wonder if you've told Nelly about Asheham. I meant to tell you not to—but it doesn't really matter.

Yr

B.

Let me know as soon as you can about the servants, so as not to miss a chance. By the way, I've had another letter from Crane, explaining why she couldn't go, and very polite, so I think she must be quite decent.

Berg

1021: To Vanessa Bell   *Hogarth* [*House, Richmond*]
Sunday [16 February 1919]

Dearest,

Nelly has come back in the highest spirits having enjoyed herself immensely. In fact I see that I ought to have made a condition that you shouldn't seduce her by your charms. I fully expect a week of the most odious comparisons between you and us—and I daresay she'll end by giving notice—or at anyrate make herself and Lottie miserable by wondering whether they wouldn't be happier with you. Anyhow, you need have no fear that she won't be ready to go to you next time. She makes out that you don't like Crane, or that Crane won't do any thing outside her work. If Crane is intolerable, I believe I could get you some one here. The Registry seems the most reputable of all I've seen, and being so near I can bombard her, and have people sent round directly. So let me know. The things I paid were £1.10. for the children's boots; £1. to Crane, for the week when she was engaged and put off; and 12/6 fee to Abbeys for engaging her. Together they come to £3.2.6. Let me know if I can do anything about the Nurse. From Nelly's account you don't have a moment to yourself, which I'm sure is the most exhausting life under the sun.

Duncan gave us a delicious meal at Verreys—a most distinguished place. I never saw a more remarkable figure than that adorable man—dressed in a nonconformist minister's coat; but under that an astonishing mixture of red waistcoats and jerseys, all so loose that they had to be hitched together by a woollen belt, and braces looping down somewhere quite useless. He is more and more like a white owl perched upon a branch and blinking at the light, and shuffling his soft furry feet in the snow—a wonderful creature, you must admit, though how he ever gets through life—but as a matter of fact he gets through it better than any of us. Did I tell you how Sickert is a great painter? In fact he's now my ideal painter; I should like to possess his works, for the purpose of describing them.

Duncan will have stripped London bare of gossip. I cant think of any— save that Clive and I had a long and intimate conversation chiefly about my writings at Verreys, while Mary paid a visit to Hutch [St John Hutchinson] in a home; and I thought him delightful and got some compliments, and some raps on the snout; and then Mary appeared, and I asked him which of us he liked best; and she was extremely modest and sympathetic, and we walked all through Soho in a state of semi-intoxication, recalling the past, and chattering like a cage full of parrokeets. I'm afraid I've quarrelled with Katherine Mansfield,[1] and Mirrlees[2]; which makes me think that these young women with all their charm are as brittle as barley sugar. Saxon has not that drawback anyhow. He is persistent and loyal but rather in the manner of an undertaker; at least he makes me slightly dismal, especially when he insists upon my inviting him and Barbara to dinner. They're coming tonight—B.

1. There was no actual breach between them, but their relationship was always slightly uneasy, compounded by Katherine's illness. In this case, the 'quarrel' was that Virginia had not heard from her for several weeks.
2. Virginia had met Hope Mirrlees, the author, who was then 32, in the beginning of this year. This 'quarrel' too was mostly imaginary.

gets 2 hours off from feeding the Baby; she already has the voice, on the telephone, of the Madonna. There's an indescribable goodness about it. Old Mother Bell never went in much for that; no, her maternity is of the tigress kind—splendid, devouring, unscrupulous. Murry has been made Editor of the Athenaeum.

Yr

B.

The Snowdrops are lovely; I daresay I shall come to Asheham in a week or so, and might then see you. How near you may we settle—and is there any house possible?

Berg

1022: To Vanessa Bell   *Hogarth* [*House, Richmond*]

Tuesday [18 February 1919]

Dearest,

I'm afraid it sounds as if Crane had done little or nothing to solve the difficulty. But its the absence of a nurse that distresses me. Wouldn't it be as well for me to get into touch with [Dr] Moralt or Noel, and shan't I go to some registry or institute devoted to Nurses? *Nothing could be easier for me.*

Do let me try if you are still without a prospect—or interview and pursue any possibility.

I believe, too, I could replace Crane by a spryer bird if you liked. The worst is the charge these Registries now make—Mrs Stuart asks £1. for anyone.

I had great compunctions about having Nelly back, and so had she about coming. She has offered to go down whenever we can spare her. My difficulty, as you can probably guess, is that I don't much like upsetting Leonard, and of course it is rather upsetting—not that Lottie didn't manage perfectly this time, but she isn't very dependable, and may at any moment rush into one of her tempers.

You've made a complete conquest of Nelly; "such a taking way with her", she says; and we're the nicest pair of ladies she's ever known. The drawback though to devoted domestics is the expense. I find our books have jumped to £5 a week—for no perceptible reason.

We thus spend our entire income and more on house keeping; and there seems no reason for it. According to Nelly we have about twice as much to eat as you do—indeed her account of your meagre meals desolated me; but I suppose La B. [Mrs Brereton] (do tell me all her eccentricities) is trying to economise.

Nelly, by the way, formed a very high opinion of Jenny, and thought her highly moral clean and with the makings of a good cook.

But I'm only writing to offer my services about the nurse: they are seriously intended. I'm now very well, and as we take our temperatures on the least pretence I don't think we shall get the flu this time. I hope Duncan is better; and say how you and Susanna are. She has hair like mine, Nelly says. I'm longing to examine her points.

Alix is coming to tea, and I will extract some gossip and let you have it. I rather expect some dramatic development; and suspect that she may wish to confide in me. I think there must have been a crisis with James. He is alone at Tidmarsh, and will be away for some time. She has taken the Gordon Sq house and is as sepulchral as a toad in a hole.

Yr

B.

Berg

1023: To Vanessa Bell   *Hogarth [House, Richmond]*

Monday [24 February 1919]

Dearest,

Nelly showed me your letter to her this morning, and it led to considerable talk. Indeed, ever since she returned she's been thinking she ought to have stayed with you, as I knew she would. Some days ago I suggested that she should go back to you, until you got a nurse. However, Lottie then said she felt too lonely by herself here, and the work was too hard. They have been quarrelling together the whole week about it.

Nelly laid the whole thing before me this morning. She feels that she ought to go to you because you want her so much and she likes you so much; but if so Lottie must come too, and as this would be unfair to us, they would have to leave us and go to you permanently. They dont know whether they want to do this—in short, its the old story over again. I have taken up the position that I refuse either to persuade them to stay or to persuade them to go.

Mean while, Budge's young man never turned up on the wedding day and it is thought he has gone for ever. Budge is in a great taking, so that it wouldn't be wise to approach her now, but I suppose later she'll take a place. Anny Boyce has written to me to say that she knows of no temporary people at the moment. Leonard saw Mrs [J. C.] Squire yesterday, who says that Mrs Hunt has several temp. nurses on her books, but they ask 25/ a week, which Mrs Squire can't afford. Shant I try and see what can be done? The position with N. and L. is so obscure that I don't in the least know what to make of it. When your letter came with all its thanks and compliments Nelly felt that she must make up her mind to go to you—but then, next minute she turns round and wants me to say that I find her indispensable. However, as they couldn't go for a month, I suppose, its not much help to you at present; and I see you say that you *are* getting very tired. I'm sure its a desperate thing to attempt both feeding and nursing—All those ounces are sucked off you, though I'm very glad they go to Susanna—still—What a hellish business it all is!

We are coming to Asheham on Friday till Monday. I'll come over for the day anyhow one of the days—We might then decide on some plan.

But I'm pretty sure nurses can be got easier than other maids.

I've collected a good deal of gossip, but domestic details swallow up my juice like sand. Chiefly for your benefit I went to a concert and a tea party yesterday, and sat between Sir Valentine Chirrol[1], Katie [Cromer], and Sir Henry Newbolt.[2] I walked with Sir Henry to the concert, and with Katie back again.

Then there's the house[3] to describe to you. But the pen falters. It faces the Stuffed Beasts. Inside they have a complete collection of autotypes of the Dutch school—old women in white bonnets—Rembrandt heads—all chocolate brown in gilt frames. This is on the staircase. The drawing room has gilt mirrors, triangular shaped, several important oil sea scapes, and heads of horses, to the shoulder, in water colour on little easels. There are photographs of soldiers and babies on every prominence. Sir Henry smelt me very suspiciously at first. He has the appearance of a grey weasel, tapering to a point at both ends.

"I never listen to music, but I think my own thoughts", he said. "I see things. I find it very difficult to write poetry without hearing music—yes, Mrs Woolf, probably something will come of this—something almost always does come of a concert—"

"Surely you ought to keep a quartet", I said—which I thought a very pretty compliment; and I see I could shine in South Kensington, which I don't believe either you or Duncan could do. They have a simplicity which is very engaging—they dont hunch up in corners, like Murry, and say nothing. Bruce and Elena [Richmond] are infinitely polite. And yet, I wonder how far one could go—I feel like a rabbit, who's really a hare, on a lawn with other rabbits, who are really rabbits. Or is this my conceit? Anyhow, Sir Valentine and Katie are full of doubts about the future.

"For myself, I'm a fatalist", said Katie. "We may be shot at any moment —any how we shall all be shot together." "But why?" I asked. "Who's going to shoot you?" "O the Jews—the Russian Jews," she replied. "Yes, said Sir Val; Nobody can accuse me of being a pacifist, but after 4 years of war the people are not the same people they were. We shall never see 1914

1. Traveller, journalist and author (1852-1929).
2. The poet (1862-1938) and a friend of Leslie Stephen.
3. In the Cromwell Road facing the Natural History Museum, and belonging to Mrs Samuel Bruce.

again: They're strung up—they're unreasonable—they want higher wages—
and, as Lady Cromer says, there are the Jews, the Russian Jews. There are
Jews in every town—colonies of them. They will supply the motive power,
and—once the shooting begins—well, I'm a fatalist too, like Lady Cromer."
I almost proclaimed myself a Russian Jew, but I'm keeping this for the next
concert. And tonight I dine with Ottoline—God knows why she's sent for
me. We dine in a hotel in Pall Mall. I could go to a Registry on Thursday
if you let me know.

Yr
B.

Murrys address is, 2 Portland Villas, East Heath Rd. Hampstead. I think
you'd better not say anything to Nelly about my writing, if you should be
writing to her—not that it much matters. Only I want to keep out of it.
I think its useless for either you or me to say anything.

Berg

1024: TO VANESSA BELL   *Hogarth [House, Richmond]*

Thursday [27 February 1919]

Dearest,

To revert for one moment to the domestic business—I didn't in the least
wish to hint that you had influenced Nelly unfairly—I was only a little
bewildered as to what *had* happened. Apparently nothing whatever—At
least she's now back again where she was.

I'm only writing to say that I very much want to see you and the small
white owl (wasn't that a good phrase of mine about Duncan?) but I find
that Leonard thinks the walk too far; and therefore would it be possible to
take me a bed for Tuesday night at Bo Peep?[1]

Let me have a line at Asheham to say the name of the farmer and proper
address and I will write to him. Dont attempt putting me up.

I should come over to lunch on Tuesday.

You may be surprised to hear that I want to see Owlina [Angelica]
almost as much as you—she hasn't of course your demonstrative ways, or
flood of eloquence, but I'm told her silence is profoundly mysterious, and
she looks at one so as to melt the marrow. Besides I want to set on foot a
scheme of mine which I may tell you is to confuse her mind from the first
as to her maternity; she is going to think me something more than an Aunt
—not quite a father perhaps, but with a hand (to put it delicately) in her
birth. I warn you I shall drop hints at every opportunity. I have a great

1. A farm two miles from Charleston.

feeling for my nephews too. You have promised to send them here again, remember.

Gossip is what you want, though; and I liked my little compliment, though it comes much easier to me to write letters than to find Cranes. Lord! Lord! what a lot we could say about servants still! An inexhaustible subject! Why, this very morning your picture of St Ives bay fell off the wall onto Lotties head and she went off into a dead faint, and was only recovered by making me and Leonard both feel her bump.

My dinner with Ottoline was a frigid success. The poor woman has broken out into eruptions which she tries to make dramatic by pasting pieces of black plaster on them—but they exude at the edges. It's a terrific business whipping her into life now. One has to bow and scrape and do all sorts of antics, and implore her to tell one the history of her life from the beginning before she will get up steam at all. She fishes for compliments worse than I do—I mean without that airy certainty which is so adorable in me that there is no limit to one's store and one has merely to shake the tree for them to fall thick as apple blossom in May. She shakes the tree—oh yes,—However, I did my best; and when she said that I dressed so beautifully that I made her feel older and uglier than ever, I said, "My dear Ottoline, like the Lombardy poplar you have only to stand up naked to put us all to shame!" She liked that. But still she is fundamentally suspicious of us all, I'm afraid, and goes ravening like a dog about Bloomsbury. She insisted upon walking from the Strand to Gordon Square in a bitter wind merely to see your wretched cockatoo [Clive] and get a little of the strong wine of the male, when she felt me flagging. She now walks exactly as Queen Alexandra is said to do; and her mind vapours off about friendship and love and literature—"I could never love anyone who does not care for literature—that is my cross—my refuge, Virginia—when people are cruel—and they are *so* cruel sometimes —And I suffer so terribly—my back gives me agonies—my feet are swollen with chillblains, and I am *always*, *always* tired. What would I not give to be able to work as you do—to create—to be an artist—" imagine crossing Holborn with this dribbling out, as painfully as two old witches on crutches.

Of course, her character has an element of the superb; there's no denying it. She has swooped down upon Rose Allatini, the authoress of despised and Rejected,[1] had her to tea that afternoon, and sucked from her the history of her illicit amour, so that at last Rosa Allatini put up her hands, turned a deathly white and said "I'm afraid I'm about to faint—I've eaten nothing all day—" upon which Ott: burst a bag of bath buns which she happened to have by her and fed her with them until she was recovered. But Allatini

1. *Despised and Rejected*, a book about Conscientious Objectors, was published in 1918 under the pseudonym 'A. T. Fitzroy'. Rose Allatini published under her own name *Payment* (1915), *Root and Branch* (1917) and *Requiem* (1919).

won't do—she is a disagreeable creature. On the other hand, the wife of Lord Henry's[1] agent in Westmorland is a "wonderful, sympathetic, *very* literary and most cultivated woman" married to a husband who's sole interest lies in tapping drain pipes; and Ott: is going to bring her to see me; and hopes I will give her advice about her novel, which is full of exquisite touches, but terribly, terribly sad.

Now all this seems to me to be a cut above the Barbara's, and in particular the Faiths, who sit in Hampstead doing nothing but pick little holes in all our characters like so many magpies. I don't see any point in being a magpie if you haven't got a brain. Still this doesn't apply to our Barbara, who is nicer than ever; and really Ottoline hit her off rather exactly as the image of a respectable barmaid; pulling handles behind a counter, as fresh as a rose. She still frisks into the room, but she is fundamentally sedate.

I can't think why I'm writing you this enormous letter. By the way, Henry Lamb is on our tracks, without success so far, and has sent a message to Ott: through Anrep,[2] to say that he does not mean to renew his acquaintance with her, or with any of his old friends—why he excepts us, I dont know.

I rather like Griselda[3]—light and fantastic.

      Nerissa

      Lesley—but I must stop having worn my pen to a tremulous thread of wire. Let me know about Bo Peep, as soon as you can.

Yr
B.

Berg

1025: TO CLIVE BELL   *[Hogarth House, Richmond]*

[5? March 1919]

My dear Clive,

I've sent off your money[4] to Bruce R[ichmond] and here is the half crown over.

I shall be delighted to dine after the concert, and rub off a little of Shelley House, though it has an unspeakable fascination, as you'll see.

Yours
V.W.

Quentin Bell

1. Lord Henry Cavendish Bentinck, Ottoline's brother.
2. Boris Anrep, the mosaicist, born in Russia, and settled in England.
3. Vanessa's baby, now two months old, was still unnamed.
4. For tickets for the concert at Shelley House.

1026: To Vanessa Bell   *Hogarth [House, Richmond]*

Postcard
[11 March 1919]

Do you by any chance want to let Charleston for April and May? The Bruce Richmonds want to know.

If so, would you send me a line *at once*, saying rent; but I don't suppose you do.

V.W.

We've now been given notice by Hoper,[1] and he can't let us The Farm so do enquire for houses if you ever have a chance. How is Griselda, Theresa, Bridget [Angelica]?

Berg

1027: To Robert Mayor   *Hogarth House, Paradise Road,*
                                          Richmond, S.W.
March 11th 1919

Dear Mr Mayor,[2]
    I wonder if there is any chance that you are wishing to let the cottage at Firle, unfurnished, at any time?

We have just heard that we must leave Asheham at the end of September, and we are looking for some place in the neighbourhood. If there is a chance of your wishing to give up Firle it would be very good of you if you would let me know.

                                    Yours sincerely,
                                    Virginia Woolf

Executors of Andreas Mayor

1028: To Clive Bell   *Hogarth [House, Richmond]*
Friday [14 March 1919]

My dear Clive,
    The Carbis Bay address is,
                        Miss Nicholson,
                        Gwêl Martin,
                        Carbis Bay.

1. See p. 320, note 1.
2. Robert (Robin) Mayor had known Leonard at Cambridge and married Virginia's friend Beatrice ('Bobo') Meinertzhagen in 1912. When Virginia took Asheham House at the end of 1911, she leased Little Talland House, her cottage at Firle, to him. He retained the lease throughout the war.

I'm not sure about the accent on the e, but I don't suppose it is essential—I should write at once, and possibly name Mr and Mrs Woolf, if you want rooms soon as she is apt to be taken. We were just discussing the question of a subscription to the Press when your card came. I think something of the kind must be devised. The difficulty is whether people wont want some security as to the nature of the bargain—names of writers who have promised —and when they *do* promise they don't always fulfil. This is a hit at Mary, who also refuses to dine with me. Still we had Mr and Mrs Bruce Richmond to dinner last night, which was a greater feat than having Mary. He apologised profusely for the politics in the [Times Literary] Supt.—but no other books are coming out. However I meant to insinuate in the proper place higher up the page the request that Mr Clive Bell should do what Mary won't do, write for the Press—no room for compliments is left me.

V.W.

Quentin Bell

1029: To Vanessa Bell   Hogarth [*House, Richmond*]

Sunday [23 March 1919]

Dearest,

I was on the point of wiring to you to call your child Angelica. Helen's beautiful, and so's Vanessa,[1] but then there's the difficulty of young Nessa and old Nessa, and Nelly seems to me for ever appropriate to Boxall; whereas Angelica has liquidity and music, a hint of green in it, and memories of no one except [Angelica] Kaufmann, who was no doubt a charming character. Can't you still write in Angelica on the Registry Card? I have a feeling that unless people are registered they are all like Aunt Minna and Emphie Case, and Pensa Filly[2]—playing at real names.

You don't say how you are, which I think you might have done; for I scarcely like to ask for fear of being called Aunt Mary again. I am much tempted to come and stay, but in the first place I am now inseparable from my typewriter. I was on the point of taking my novel [*Night and Day*] to Gerald when I discovered that about half was illegible; my typewriting is not my strong point; I am picking out the worst bits and doing them again, and I've promised to lunch with him at the Savoy on Friday—

Then, though you won't see the strength of this, I dont much like leaving Leonard with Lottie. She is all right so far, and Lil is excellent in

1. The baby had at first been registered as Helen Vanessa. Shortly afterwards, her mother added Angelica.

2. Pensa Filly appears in *A Memoir* by Vanessa Bell (ed. Richard J. Shaubeck Jr. Published by Frank Hallman. New York, 1974), as a fellow-student of the Stephen girls at Miss Mills's music classes. Pensa's piety had made Virginia "shriek with laughter".

every way, but Lotties temper shows signs of being unstable, and probably Leonard would dismiss her if I went away; anyhow I should feel slightly guilty. But don't breathe a word of this to Nelly.[1] The vagaries of domestics are quite unintelligible; however so long as my extraordinarily sweet nature is in the house to keep the peace it will be all right.

Couldn't I transfer my invitation till you've got your nurse, and Nelly is back here again?

I believe the [Adrian] Stephen's go down to Asheham tomorrow— damn their souls! and they stay a fortnight at least, and I don't much like the thought of those great pillar like legs in my bed; and all that breezy good heartedness, and immense munching, and public spirit about the house. We almost let it to the Richmonds, but I think thats fallen through for the present. I'm rather in despair about getting a house. I've written to several agents; most of them don't even answer; one did, but said that there was nothing to be had anywhere for £50. Meanwhile we're greatly tempted to take [D. H.] Lawrences cottages at Zennor.[2] He had two on the Cliff with a superb view and a garden for £27—and of course Cornwall is almost irresistible; so I've written to find out, and we rather think, if we take them, of moving all our furniture and books down there from Asheham, and taking a tiny cottage in Firle or thereabouts as a week end place. But I fully expect to find that they're already taken. Katherine [Murry] says its the most divine place in the world—3½ miles from St Ives, so its sure to be taken, and I suppose we shall be on the Streets. Yes, and of course Adrian and Karin will step into some old farm near you, which Karin will proceed to decorate with her needle, which is her rage—she does her own designs too—and every evening you'll have a jolly talk about the cistern or the kitchen boiler. You dont know enough about the League of Nations and democracy to keep your end up there, and as for poor dear old Duncan I dont suppose he could keep the League distinct from the boiler for long. Does he realise, by

1. Nelly Boxall was helping Vanessa at Charleston for three weeks.
2. These were the cottages at Tregerthen which D. H. and Frieda Lawrence had rented in 1916-17, and where he wrote *Women in Love*. For a short time Katherine Mansfield and Middleton Murry had occupied one of them, and Katherine had told Virginia about them. In January 1919, Lawrence had written to Koteliansky: "About the cottage in Cornwall, I think the Woolfs might have it. . . . And do they have a house in Richmond? I wonder if they would care to change houses?" (*Collected Letters of D. H. Lawrence*. Ed. Harry T. Moore. 1962). In an unpublished letter to Leonard, Lawrence describes Higher Tregerthen as two cottages, in one of which he had lived with Frieda ("with a downstairs sitting-room, a rather lovely bedroom upstairs, and a back scullery—no more"), while the other was the landlord's summer-cottage, usually shut up, in which the Lawrences had lodged their guests. "The houses are planked on the hill side, slap above the sea, which is about ten minutes, down the fields. It is beauti-ful, I think, and as lonely as necessary."

the way, that he is now, in a sort of way, my brother in law, and all that implies?

Our chief amusement now is Murry and the Athenaeum.[1] He is in a state of high exaltation, something like a Prime Minister, for everyone buzzes about asking for appointments, and needless to say, *though please dont repeat this*, the Stracheys have induced him much against his better judgment, to adopt James as Dramatic critic. They are a masterly race—at least the male Stracheys are, in asking and getting; poor old Gumbo [Marjorie Strachey], on the other hand, has just been dismissed from her school on account of short sight, and seemed to me in the depths of despair. She has no bounce left any longer. She only just manages to live on her pay in a room in Kensington. James, of course, has an allowance from Lady S[trachey]: and by pulling the right wires has now got a comfortable income out of Murry.

Perhaps I am unduly severe upon him though. Has he given up being a doctor, do you know?

It is rather fun about the Athenaeum, as every one is to write what they like, and Mrs [Humphry] Ward is to be exposed, and in time they hope to print imaginative prose by me—Murry has got a man called John Gordon, a very bad painter he says, to do art criticism; but I suggested that he'd much better get Duncan to do the important things at any rate—not that Duncan is exactly fluent in composition, but I don't see why he and I and you shouldn't maunder about in picture galleries, and what with his genius and your sublimity and my perfectly amazing gift of writing English we might turn out articles between us. Do consider this.

I dined with the Yellow Cockatoo [Clive] the other night, and he said how you are the greatest decorator of large spaces in England; and we sang a musical duet in your praise, until a prostitute who was dining at the next table suddenly threw her glass on the floor and upset the mustard and walked out, leaving her poor young man to look most uncomfortable. It was a very remarkable scene; and altogether I enjoyed myself very much. But its useless to pretend that I have any real connection with the Bohemian world any longer; I see that its my fate to be sucked under by the Bourgeois and made a sacrifice of to old family friends. I've just had a long letter from Meg Ritchie,[2] imploring me to go and see Mrs [Charles] Booth, while there is still time, (though Mrs Booth is perfectly well) and saying that she and Billy and the children are coming to live at Wimbledon, and hope to see a great deal of us. You would be brutal; I am at once touched almost to tears. And then you tell Clive that I'm perhaps the most dangerous, unscrupulous, impossible, undependable character you know!

1. At the age of 30, John Middleton Murry had just become editor of the *Athenaeum*, the journal of literature and the arts which was founded in 1828.
2. Margaret Ritchie, *née* Booth, the wife of William Ritchie. He was the son of Aunt Anny Ritchie, whose sister was Leslie Stephen's first wife.

We had Bruce and Elena to dine the other night. I own that I was slightly moved once more by Elena. It is true that she is very stupid, but then dressed all in black with one jade ornament, and her now white hair, and her almond blossom complexion, and her air of melancholy she is undoubtedly very distinguished; and, though we did not mention the subject, I feel certain that the reason of her sterility and her melancholy is her hopeless passion for Stephen Massingberd[1] which still persists; and that on every anniversary of Margaret's death she steals down secretly to Gunby and puts white flowers on her grave. Don't you think its all quite possible? Its a case of one of these hopeless, canine affections of which you and I are, according to Clive, so incapable. Do you ever think of poor old Waller now, except to laugh at him?—and what do I feel, after all, for Walter Headlam, except that one of these days I shall put him into a novel?[2] I wish Duncan would write me a long letter, all about your character, and say what he's discovered in those labyrinthine catacombs, where the bones are piled so high, and innumerable jackals laugh in the light of the moon.

I suppose, if I could come for a week end, and sent a telegram, it would be all right? Give Nelly my love, and tell her that we are both longing to have her back, but Lil seems to be quite happy.

Yr
B.

Berg

1030: TO CLIVE BELL   [*Hogarth House, Richmond*]

Postcard
[29 March 1919]

Any day next week, which begins on Monday; choose; communicate. Your wishes were observed last night, which was, I thought, particularly charming; and Desmond very affable; but the star of the night was Mrs B[ell]: really, like a bud slipping its sheath; virginal; auroral; but yet with all the sorrows of all the ages. This does not refer to Mrs Brereton or Mrs Briggs, for the matter of that. Choose any day, but let it be before Friday. I am off to secure a charwoman's character in the back streets.

V.W.

Quentin Bell

1. Widower of Margaret Massingberd, who had known Virginia in her youth, and was the sister of Kitty Lushington (Maxse). They lived at Gunby Hall in Lincolnshire.
2. John Waller Hills, after the death of his wife, Stella Duckworth, had loved Vanessa; and Walter Headlam, the Greek scholar, had flirted with Virginia in 1907.

1031: To Vanessa Bell   [*Hogarth House, Richmond*]

[2 April 1919]

Dearest,

"Man and wife seek situation in any place of trust: man with life-long experience as coachman and 10 years as chauffeur: wife a hospital trained nurse; family grown up and out; highest references . . J. Burgess, Orchard-leigh, Frome, Somerset."

They must be with the Duckworths[1]—This is from the Times—today. The Agency here is

Clare Carlisle

The Green

Richmond.

Yr

V.W.

Berg

1032: To Vanessa Bell   Hogarth [*House, Richmond*]

Friday [4 April 1919]

Dearest,

It's perfectly all right that you should keep Nelly, as Lil seems willing to stay more or less indefinitely. As she came on a Wednesday, an extra week would bring us to Wednesday 16th. One would have to take her for a full week, so you had better have Nelly till then anyhow. I shall take it for granted that you want this, and tell Lil definitely.

I went to the Registry here today, and was told of a lady nurse asking £40, but would probably take less. I went to see her, but found she was out, but I'm going to see her tomorrow. She is about 37 and seemed nice and had great experience was all the Registry knew: the servant said she had not yet got a place. I dont for a moment suppose she will do, but it might be a good thing if you told me what wages you would give etc. in case the registry sent me round someone. There is also a young girl, now h. p., who wants to become nurse, but has no experience. I'm to hear about her on Tuesday. The lady nurse is Miss Pruden, 1 Gloucester Gardens, Richmond. The registry, Clare Carlisle, the Green, held out hopes, as I suppose they always do. I told her to write straight to you. She said it was much better she should ring me up in case someone came in and wanted to see me at once. So I have told her to do this. They all seem to live in Richmond so that one has a

1. Captain and Mrs Campbell Duckworth. He was George Duckworth's first cousin.

chance of seeing them instead of merely writing; but I see one becomes quite hopeless.

But if any chance appeared on the horizon it would be worth seducing Nelly to stay on a little at Charleston to avoid coming up with the baby.

We have now settled to come to Asheham for Easter—that is on the 17th. If Nelly would stay on till then, I would send Lottie down to you on the 17th till the 22nd, if that hope would keep Nelly pacified.

I should like to hear about the party, which was I suppose, the most brilliant there's ever been, though the chief jewel shone at Richmond.

I might telephone all this, if only Gordon Sqre were civilized; as it is I must send it to Charleston.

O God! What a horror of desolation your life seems to be—only through domestic troubles, I mean. If adoration, sympathy and all the rest of it are any balm—By the way, Mary rang me up yesterday in great agitation about Eliot, imploring me to say nothing, denying the whole story, and insisting that he only abused Bloomsbury in general, and not me, and that Clive had completely misunderstood!

Yr

B.

Berg

1033: To S. S. Koteliansky

Hogarth House, 285 Paradise Road, Richmond

April 4th [1919]

Dear Mr Koteliansky,

We quite understand your feeling, which we rather share ourselves— at least we would generally rather not dine with people. If you would come in after dinner on Sunday we should like it very much. We have Mr and Mrs Eliot coming—perhaps you have met him, or have read his poetry. He wrote a book called Prufrock. If this doesn't suit you, perhaps you would ring us up and suggest some evening or afternoon. The evenings are generally best, as Leonard is then more likely to be in. We are engaged on Tuesday.

Yours sincerely,

Virginia Woolf

Our number is 496 Richmond.

British Museum

1034: TO VANESSA BELL

The International Review, 10 *Adelphi Terrace,*
*London, W.C.*2

Typewritten
5 April 1919

My dear Vanessa,

I am writing for V. to explain a crisis which has arisen and which will
come to you through a letter from her to Nelly. What exactly it all means,
we do not know; but the facts are as follows. This morning Lottie came up
in a terrific state with the following story: a letter, posted in London, had
come addressed outside to her and inside to Lil, saying that she Lil was
trying to get Nelly's place, that Nelly was being made to stay on in Charleston
and would not, that as she was not wanted by us she was going to leave
Charleston at once and go back home, etc., etc. The letter was not signed.
Lil appears to have got into a state, and to have put the letter and envelope
into the fire, so that we never saw it. Lottie said that Lil had immediately
posted a letter to Nelly, and so we thought we had better write to Nelly at
once. Apparently Lil's letter was not posted. Things have quieted down here,
but V. has written to Nelly saying that of course we have always meant her to
come back here, and that if she prefers to come on Tuesday, she certainly
must do so.

V. got the name of a nurse from a Registry Office here, and is going to
see the woman this afternoon.

Yours
Leonard Woolf

[*in Virginia's handwriting*]
I am perfectly sure that the letter has nothing to do with Nelly, as she would
have written to me herself. I think it possible that my letter to you was
opened at Gordon Square and they [Blanche and Jessie] wrote for a joke to
upset Lottie.

If Nelly is willing to stay on with you, there's no reason why she shouldnt;
I only wanted to make it clear to her that I have never dreamt of taking Lil
in her stead, or that she should stay with you indefinitely.

Berg

1035: TO VANESSA BELL   [*Hogarth House, Richmond*]

Saturday [5 April 1919]

Dearest,

I've just sent you a wire about Nelly Feulkner. I went to see Miss Pruden,
and saw the lady of the house, Mrs Parry, who told me that she was extremely

severe and strict and over 50, and didn't think she would be any good with a baby. I said that you would really prefer a young girl whom you could teach, upon which she said "I think my housemaid would suit her—she is an extremely nice girl of 27 who wants to be be a nurse, and has already had a good deal to do with children." So Nelly Faulkner was sent for, and turned out to be a charming, pink faced Scotch girl, with a slight accent, very clean and healthy looking. I told her she would have complete charge of a baby of 3 months. She said this was just what she would like. She had had to do with children—I dont think as nurse but as help—in her last place, and is devoted to them, and would like nothing better than to be taught by you. I asked Mrs Parry about her character. She has only been 5 weeks there, but Mrs P. said she is perfectly honest, clean, and most considerate, and doesn't mind what she's asked to do, and that she would never have parted with her except that her husband is getting a valet, and does not like having housemaids. You can get a character for $2\frac{1}{2}$ years from the place before that; she was with a doctor in Scotland. She wants £36 wages. She likes the country very much. Her only anxiety was that you might want her to wear uniform.

She is leaving on Monday, but wants a few days to get things, and would be ready to go to you on Thursday. I said I would wire to you, and you would write to her on Monday. She will then come and see me and hear how to get to you.

If you would rather see her yourself, of course come and stay here. It's only 5 minutes off—Mrs Parry seemed very nice, and respectable.

Of course, like all the others this may come to nothing, or I may have thought her nicer than she is; but certainly she seemed to me particularly nice—rather humorous and simple, and ready to fit in with ones ways. Also she's so near that I can keep an eye upon her. If you've any directions for me, perhaps you'd better wire them, and I could go and settle with her in person.

Yr
B.

I believe Trissie must have sent the anonymous letter—

Berg

1036: To Vanessa Bell   *[Hogarth House, Richmond]*
[8 April 1919]

Dearest,

I've just been round to see N. F. [Nellie Faulkner], as I thought it best to arrange that she should see you here, and find that she has already left 1 Gloucester Gdns and Mrs Parry tells me that she decided not to go as nurse, and also that she wanted to stay in Richmond. It seems hopeless therefore. Three other people have been after her, as parlourmaid and Mrs Parry said it was useless.

I have the address of her rooms, and will try to see her tomorrow, but she was out today.

I don't suppose its any good though—

Great haste

V.W.

Let me know what you decide as soon as you can about Nelly and coming up.

I'll write tomorrow.

Berg

1037: TO VANESSA BELL   *Hogarth* [*House, Richmond*]

Wednesday [9 April 1919]

Dearest,

I enclose a letter from Faulkner. I dont know what your plans are now, but I suppose you will let me know. I am only keeping Lil on by the day, as you seem to think Nelly may come back on Friday or Saturday. If you want to keep N. till Monday do; only let me know, and make it quite clear to her that she is to do what she likes. Lil has turned out to know nothing of cooking; and is unable to do housework, so, as you may suppose, she and Lottie have almost daily quarrels, and I don't think Lottie will hold out much longer. Of course Nelly's letter made things much worse, and the usual scenes and warnings have taken place almost daily—

However, I don't much look forward to having Nelly back, as I can guess what a fuss there'll be. They are intolerable I think whether one has them or fails to have them—But I'm only grumbling because my whole morning has again been ruined over the question as to who broke the mincing machine—

The Eliots dined here and were overcome by the charms of Walter Lamb! I think that places him in the scale of humanity. They confided to Gumbo [Marjorie Strachey] on the way home that they had never met a more charming and beautiful young man—so witty too. Gumbo was superb, and insisted upon talking about purges and bottoms and the w.c. in the most dramatic way.

Oliver has just rung up to ask to bring Inez[1] to dine here. But I've no time for gossip.

1. Inez Ferguson, who was then 23, and General Secretary of the National Federation of Women's Institutes. In 1923 she married Frederick Jenkins, and became national organiser of the Women's Land Army during the Second War.

I'm very sorry about Faulkner. I thought her exceptionally good. God, what a time you have!

Yr
B.

Berg

1038: TO VANESSA BELL   *Hogarth [House, Richmond]*
Wednesday [16 April 1919]

Dearest,

We have settled not to come down for Easter after all, but next week instead. I hope I may see you then and tell you the fascinating story of Lil. I still spend a large part of every morning in going over all these matters with Nelly, but peace is restored. She never ceases to praise you and to boast of her pendant, which I have to admire profusely, though I think it must have been a present from George.

I seem never to have a moment for writing to you, owing partly to domestics and partly to having to get a long article done, and then I'm now in the toils of Gravé [dressmaker] again, and Herbert Fisher came and wasted the whole of Sunday, and then we had Oliver and Inez [Ferguson], and I'm now off to tea with Katherine Murry—But I take it for granted that the Yellow Bird of Bloomsbury [Clive] keeps you aware of all the cackle of life such as it is. Another interruption just as I was writing to you, was Desmond; who stays with the Bretts[1] in Belgrave Square; but they've [Desmond and Molly MacCarthy] taken a house at Oare, next the Waterlows, and Molly is now getting in, so I should send her letters there. Herbert was more like poor old Marny [Vaughan] than anyone—pale and ascetic and mild, speaking in a kind of whisper, and never committing himself to any statement. But he has the intolerable Fisher superciliousness; and makes my spine curl—no longer with despair at my own insignificance though. I feel worth ten of him, and in fact we made ourselves rather disagreeable, and abused George Duckworth, and the Cunards and Lady Manners, with whom he seemed to be impressed. And he abused Lytton's book, with which I rather agreed of course. It's said that he's a government spy (Herbert I mean) for he pounces upon the Oliver Stracheys too, and stays for hours, and makes them disclose their views. But Lord! What watery and wobbly minds these politicians have—and always afraid to say what they mean, and such an air of being behind the scenes.

Inez is a pert young professional, by no means of the seductive kind, I should have thought; and ill spaced, indeed rather vulgar looking and splotchy in the face. However, she has more wits than Barbara, and may have floated

1. Oliver Brett, later 3rd Viscount Esher, and Chairman of the National Trust.

in on that tide. Oliver was very testy because the [Bernard] Berenson's won't endow him so that he needn't work—O the Stracheys—the Stracheys! If it weren't for their grace of mind, which you must admit to be considerable, how I should detest them. But I'm inclined to think Marjorie the best at this moment. [E. M.] Forster is back again [from Alexandria]; and I find him very sympathetic.—but all this gossip is to entice you into telling me about that house you said you heard of. We have practically abandoned the idea of Cornwall, owing to the distance. We mean to get something, however possible, near Lewes, and put our things there and hang on until we can get something better; or perhaps Gunn may leave Asheham. Could you tell me whether Mr Stacey [the Charleston farmer] told you, and what his address is, and whereabouts the house is. I would then write to him, and we could arrange to see it when we come.

Angelica is a lovely name; I wish it had been possible to include Moll Flanders though; or Roxana. If ever anyone reminded me of you it is Moll Flanders. But I think you read that work and probably know it by heart; don't you think its quite superb?

Yr
B.

I will tell you the whole story of Elizabeth Asquith's engagement to [Antoine] Bibesco, and how Hugh Gibson rejected her, and why, and what happened to Mrs Asquith in Bond Street, and whether Bibesco played the Knave, and what Elizabeths real feelings are, and how she sent a love letter through Desmond, with permission to read it, which he did, and what Asquith said when he was told of the engagement, together with various other lewd and diverting details when we meet. Desmond gave us a superb account.

Berg

1039: To Duncan Grant   *Hogarth [House, Richmond]*

Thursday [17 April 1919]

My dear Duncan,

I am sending you this book, which I bought in the year '5 at Florence, in case it may do for you or Nessa (old Nessa) to draw in. I also want to ask whether it would be possible for either of you to do some coloured papers for Kew Gardens—We have bought 25/- worth off Roger, but they only cover 80 copies, and there are 150: the price seems to me extortionate—at anyrate impossible, so I have told him to do no more. The size is 12 inches across and 9½ the other way. We should want enough for 70 copies. Perhaps you could send me a sample if you would do it, and could do it cheaper than Roger. It ought to be on as stiff and thick paper as possible. We are only waiting now for the covers: and there need be no likeness between one cover and another.

All my gossip was skimmed for Nessa: I went to tea with the Murry's and the mystery of Eliot was further thickened by hearing how he'd praised me to the skies to them; and now we have a letter asking us to dinner, and I'm determined, in spite of Mary [Hutchinson], to draw the rat from his hole (I beg to remind you that rabies is now prevalent). Murry was very cadaverous, and I told him he would sink the Athenaeum with his bad philosophy, and how bad I thought Lytton[1]: but 3 publishers have already written on the strength of one article to ask to publish his next book, and all the clerks in the office are wild about it. So you see what we may expect—and don't you think it very odd how exactly all our friends are fitted out by Fate! There's Sydney governor of the left bank of the Rhine,[2] or practically; poor old Desmond still doing pot boilers, and sending stories about Bears who have swallowed rubber balls to papers for prizes: and me obscure; and Nessa and Duncan with all the bloom on, like great purple plums half hidden beneath their leaves.

By the way, the great story of Vanessa has had another chapter added to it. By two separate people—Fredegond and [Dorothy] Brett—not in collusion, have I been told how she turned Mary off the sofa at Roger's party— Mary decked like a butterfly in May—and said "Its time you got off that sofa, Mary". This is thought to symbolise all kinds of things, and is being acted by Fredegond, and will figure in her repertory. Katherine acted it too yesterday. "Its time you got off the sofa Mary": Vanessa is represented like a tawny old Goddess, all crusted with brine and barnacles shouldering her way out of the sea—But there! How could there be a sofa in the sea, Nessa will ask?

I must take this out; I was so thankful the Stephen's weren't a success.

Would you tell me about the house you heard of? We think we might take 2: and always have one let; one in Cornwall, the other in Sussex, and make the rent of both. I have written a very frivolous (but clever) article for Murry,[3] in which you figure under the disguise of Adolphus Blatt. Nessa is Caroline Mew.

Yr V.W.

Duncan Grant

1. *Lady Hester Stanhope*, which Lytton had published in the early April issue of the *Athenaeum*.
2. Sydney Waterlow had been re-employed by the Foreign Office at the Paris Peace Conference.
3. *The Eccentrics* (*Athenaeum*, 25 April 1919).

1040: To Vanessa Bell   *Asheham House, Rodmell,*
                                         Lewes, [Sussex]
April 28th [1919]

Dearest,

If I can come tomorrow or one day soon I will. This, however, is to ask, with a sense of contrition, whether you would pack and send my green wool coat, left in my bedroom. I only brought summer things, and the snow lies thick on the ground.

Has the nurse come?

How is Angelica?

Anyone would be welcome here, I need not say, at any time.

                                                                      Yr
Berg   B.

1041: To Lady Ottoline Morrell
                                         Asheham House, Rodmell,
                                         Lewes, [Sussex]
April 29th [1919]

My dear Ottoline,

Your letter was sent on here, where we have come for a week's holiday to find snow on the ground, and such wind and rain that we cant face the downs.

We very much want to come to you. But we can't settle upon any week ends at this moment, owing to the horrible need we are under of finding another house to go to in September. We are being turned out of Asheham—and we are spending Leonard's spare time in house hunting. You probably want to settle your week ends now; so that I'm afraid we ought to say we can't come, and ask you to have us later. Or if Leonard finds he can't get away, might I come alone?—But he would like to come—

We are tempted to take Lawrence's cottage in Cornwall, but it means a tremendous journey to see it; and the owner refuses to answer letters.

What is happening to you? Are you ever in London—and will you come and dine with me this time, perhaps at the 17 Club—only that is too earnest and right-minded and altogether respectable. I've been seeing Katherine and Murry, and find great fascination in both of them, though the difficulty of conversation, especially when the brother and the Rhodesian lady are there,[1]

1. Richard Murry, who was 13 years younger than his brother, and Lesley (Ida) Moore, Katherine's lifelong friend, who published *Katherine Mansfield: The Memoirs of L. M.* in 1971. She was not a Rhodesian, but her father settled there in 1910. She had known Katherine Mansfield since they were school-children together in London, and remained her devoted companion until Katherine's death in 1923.

351

is very great. The Athenaeum seems to have cheered Murry; it is at least a channel for some of his miseries; but I do my best to rout out his philosophy, which will sink the paper to the bottom if it goes on.

The Coles,[1] (the social reforming Cole) dined with us the other night, and he said he had stayed at Garsington; but I couldn't imagine Margaret Postgate, his wife, at your table; nor Cole himself, though he's a clever, pugnacious young man. Social reform however is not seductive; I hate always taking sides, dont you?—and being right or wrong, and so ugly into the bargain.

I have been reading Yeats new poems[2] with great pleasure. I think—for the first time—that he really is a poet.

But how much pleasanter it would be to discuss all this wandering through the streets of London together!

Your affate
Virginia Woolf

Texas

1042: To Vanessa Bell   *Asheham*, [*Rodmell, Sussex*]

Sunday [4 May 1919]

Dearest,
Curse this weather. There is at present a white fog and a gale of wind; we've had to give up coming. But we shall be here in a fortnight again, and I might then spend a night if convenient.

Would you let me know about the paper [for *Kew Garden* covers] as soon as you can: how much it would cost, and how long it would take to do, if you are able to do it.

As the notices are sent out, I want to get the books ready as soon as possible; so that if its likely to take more than 10 days, I think I'd better get ordinary coloured paper, dull though it is. I could send you down white paper from London. But perhaps Roger has done his black and blue; in which case I could cover 80 copies in that, and you might finish off the edition, which is only 150, with yours.

What do you think it would cost to build a 6 or 7 roomed house in this neighbourhood? Perhaps Roger would know. Apparently we should have to buy whatever we find, and it might come cheaper, any how in a year or two to build: besides you might design and decorate and plant us near Charleston, but not too near.

1. G. D. H. Cole and his wife Margaret (*née* Postgate). Jointly and separately, they published a series of books on social and political questions.
2. *The Wild Swans at Coole* (1917), a book which marked a major change in Yeats' style.

352

Here is a letter from Murry which may amuse you. Do you think that his version of Mary is correct? I think they're a little hard on her, but they owe her a grudge of some kind. Would you send the letter back.

Gerald has read my novel with the greatest interest, and is delighted to publish it, which is convenient, but rather disappointing, as I should have liked to try the other way.[1]

I'm sending you a loaf and a cake of my making, with the request that you will keep them for a 2nd course at dinner. I never sit down to my spread without a sigh, thinking of you. Still the ducks eggs are delicious; we enjoyed ours immensely. Did you have an explanation with Mabel? How is Nelly settling down?

Yr

B.

I wrote a very tactful letter to Adrian, and I will tell you what he says—I don't think he gets his share of Waller until October.[2] I made it clear that you had not asked me to write, and did not count upon it.

Berg

1043: TO JANET CASE   *Asheham, [Rodmell, Sussex]*

Sunday [4 May 1919]

My dear Janet,

I meant to enclose some words of friendship with the notice[3] which I sent off yesterday but fastened it up and forgot.

I'm not in the least surprised by the way, nor is Leonard, that the Ceylon Editor is not up to what you sent him. We've just read the letter about the League of Nations. We don't see how he could feel your charity either for the Germans or the C.O.'s. Why you should feel humiliated, we can't conceive; if you'd seen those little timid coffee coloured men you would realise that they are neither advanced nor philanthropic; and at present all their effort is to keep in with the [British] Government in order to get their

1. Gerald Duckworth, her half-brother, had published Virginia's first novel, *The Voyage Out*, and now accepted *Night and Day*. But it was already the Woolfs' hope to publish Virginia's future novels themselves, and they began to do so with *Jacob's Room* in 1922.
2. When his wife, Stella Duckworth, died in 1897, John Waller Hills had generously made over her marriage settlement from the Duckworths to the Stephen children, until he remarried in 1931.
3. Of the three Hogarth Press books which were published on 12 May: Virginia's *Kew Gardens*, Eliot's *Poems*, and Murry's *The Critic in Judgment*.

own reforms pushed through. The late correspondent, who believed in British honour and King George, was much more in their line. But I admit its horrible to be rejected even by the coffee coloured; I was even a little pleased this morning to be accepted by Gerald Duckworth—who doesn't know a book from a beehive—but Leonard soon put that right. Here he is, in from the garden; and having read the first page of this letter, he says that it does not quite express his opinion. He says that he doesn't think it quite fair to say that the poor wretches aren't advanced, but they may feel that as they're going strong for self government in India and Ceylon and therefore are liable to be called disloyal by foolish people out there they shouldn't run the risk of being also called disloyal by other silly people from another point of view. When you wrote to Leonard at first this possibility did not strike him, particularly as he hasn't himself written about European affairs for the paper but always about Ceylon affairs. This I have taken down from his dictation, and used up almost all my paper.

We are in the midst of packing to go home tomorrow; and there is a great shortage of paper; save of printed paper, which seems to be the chief perquisite of Editors. All the cranks and crack brains in Europe send him [Leonard] their sheets, which they seem to have faith in to reform the world —I can't think why.

We saved up this last week for a holiday, rejecting Easter, and we've only had one fine day. We've had snow, wind, rain, and at present a thick sea mist, so that the railing which used to please you so much along the field opposite is hidden. Nevertheless, we have enjoyed ourselves immensely; partly because we have no servants; only a woman to clean up.

What are your conditions? I'm not going to propose a visit, so don't be afraid to confess how comfortable you are. But did you manage to shake off everyone, as you hoped—and did you take Chaucer with you—what have you been doing, Miss Case, in short? I strongly advise Sir Thomas Browne.

By the way, we've taken three cottages on the Cliff in Cornwall, between St Ives and the Gurnards head,[1] for £15 a year; which will admit of another cottage somewhere here. But my dear Janet you *must* come and stay with us. When Violet Dickinson got into her house, she had a clergyman to read a service; I prefer to have mine hallowed by Janet Case. She need merely lie on a sofa and look at the Atlantic, while her pupil puts a few intelligent questions to her—which reminds me that Vanessa was asking whether you'd teach her little boys next autumn. They are outgrowing the Governess.

Your affate
V.W.

Sussex

1. D. H. Lawrence's cottages. See p. 340, note 2.

[8? May 1919]

My Violet,

It is very good of you to throw a pound into our jaws, when you know nothing of what you may get out of them.

Mr Eliot is an American of the highest culture, so that his writing is almost unintelligible; Middleton Murry edits the Athenaeum, and is also very obscure. I mean you'll have to shut your door and give yourself a quiet few days—not for Kew Gardens, though; that is as simple as can be. Roger Fry has done covers for Eliot's and mine.

But all the same, virtuous and philanthropic as you are and a forgotten benefactor, (I'm hoping one day to write your obituary) I dont see why you dont ask me to tea. I would, of course, bring my own butter and sugar. Katie [Cromer] was quite benevolent in her imperious way the other day when I saw her; Nelly [Cecil] still writes an affectionate letter. I'm not such an outcast as you suppose.

But I see that the only tea party that I shall be asked to is the one with the black icing on the cake and the crystallised violets daintily arranged in the form of a heart.

I saw my new niece, Angelica, the other day; very lovely with vast blue eyes, and long fingers. Nessa presides over the most astonishing ménage; Belgian hares, governesses, children, gardeners, hens, ducks, and painting all the time, till every inch of the house is a different colour. We have just been turned out of Asheham—isn't it damnable? and have taken 3 cottages near the Gurnards Head, 4 miles from St Ives.

Leonard sends his love; he is an editor.

> Yr.
> V.W.

Berg

Thursday [15 May 1919]

Here is a copy of the [Eliot] poems—very dirty, but I only made it worse by trying to clean it. This is a bribe to make you come and dine with us.

Telephone 496 Richmond.

I very much enjoyed my afternoon in Manchester St.

> V.W.

Berg

Thursday [15 May 1919]

My dear Roger,

I find that Mr Osborne, secretary of the I.L.P. [Independent Labour Party], is delivering an address to the Branch of the W.C.G. [Women's Co-operative Guild] of which, till lately, I was president, on Tuesday, and I must be there, to represent the middle classes, so may I come to you on *Monday* instead of Tuesday?

I would come to tea—but where? which is your new Studio?—and then perhaps, if you could have me to dinner at your house we could continue our discussion there. But I know you'll be entertaining Piccasso and Lady Cunard, or something of the kind; for I never heard such outrageous nonsense as you were talking down the telephone yesterday. The comment which the instrument made seemed to me extremely appropriate—*I* to have deserted you! *I* to be taken up with new friends! When the truth is that like the wistaria and the lilac I droop in my remote suburb, chaste and unviolated save by the bees of Heaven—

We dined under the apple blossom last night with Ottoline, and though fairly garish in the moonlight, which was not so discreet as it might have been, and showed up the powder like snow on the higher reaches of the Alps, she was extremely charming; her soul seemed to be shedding its husks; she was frank and with Leonard on one side and me on the other kept strictly to the path of truth. She loped along it like a large white hare; and in fact we were convinced of her *fundamental integrity*. Of course, it is not in the Cambridge style. She spoke of you with enthusiasm. But then as everybody does that, such little tributes as I have to make pass unnoticed. For instance, the other day Murry said "Roger Fry is far the nicest of all your friends"— to which I replied "My dear Murry, have you only just discovered that Roger is not only the most charming but also the most spiritually gifted of mankind? Where we have a rag, he has the whole cloak—" "His sweetness, his largeness, his magnanimity"—went on Murry—"and then the random fire of genius" I interrupted, "The most beautiful house in London" said Murry, "and his portrait of Edith Sitwell I think the best he ever painted". I interposed, "Of his art I cant speak, but of his temperament, his generosity—" "O if we could all be like Roger!" I wound up, and plunged the whole party into gloom. This is strictly according to fact I assure you, but as Nessa would say, coals to Newcastle.

Yours ever,
V.W.

Sussex

Sunday [18 May 1919]

Dearest,

I am so fuddled with conversation that I can hardly write an articulate letter—but I daresay you won't notice. All the people have come out of their holes and there is a general swarm. We've had Ottoline and Lytton, and Roger, and Logan and Ray and Oliver, and Danes and Armenians—and I dont know who; and we've just been lunching with the Webbs. I think your method of seeing people in the country is really better. Yesterday we talked from 1.30 to 7 without stopping. Roger appeared with Pamela and a Russian lady. Roger is a miracle. And I need not expatiate upon his powers, though on a hot afternoon, after talking to Derain[1] and seeing pictures all the morning, his incessant activities surprised me. But you want gossip.

I put my foot into it by asking Logan to meet Ottoline; and then by asking Oliver to dine here with Ray. Logan considers Ottoline the seducer of Bertie[2]; she, of course, longed for a reconciliation scene, in the moonlight, under the appleblossoms; but he refused. We had her alone. We dined in the garden; and she was simple and frank; I assure you this is true. No one will believe it. Anyhow she was trying to be so; like an old snake wriggling out of its skin. For example, she said her hands were red; when I looked, I saw they were not only red but very clumsy, with thick joints into the bargain. But why did she say so unless in a sudden spasm of honesty? And so with the rest. She lamented her quarrels, and praised everybody, and finally went off without her hat, which I have to send after her: very queer she looked on the platform with her short red hair standing on end, wrapped in a Spanish cloak, and striped blue and green like the Cornish sea.

But Oliver and Ray was a worse business altogether. Oliver wanted us to take him to a party at the Squires to meet Inez; indeed it was hinted that I might invite Inez here. Losing my head, however, I asked Ray instead; and though I have only my own senses to go by, I can't help thinking that the situation between them is now considerably strained. Ray is becoming more and more the public woman[3]—floppy, fat, untidy, clumsy, and making fewer concessions than ever to brilliancy, charm, politeness, wit, art, manners, literature and so forth; full of news upon women's future of course; but, my God, if *thats* the future whats the point in it? To make matters worse, two semi-literate and very earnest Danes arrived on the same evening; refused to go to the Squires, and so did Ray; so Oliver went alone; and altogether I

1. André Derain, the French painter.
2. Bertrand Russell had married Logan Pearsall Smith's sister Alys, and left her. Logan blamed Ottoline for the collapse of the marriage.
3. Ray Strachey (*née* Rachel Costelloe), a niece of Logan Pearsall Smith, and Oliver's wife, was becoming a leader in the women's movement. She wrote several books on the subject.

think the case of husband and wife who have no love for each other, but still live together is an embittering spectacle. I rather think Ray is becoming tart under the perpetual presence of Inez.

But, for Gods sake, don't quote me—As I say, I'm so fuddled I can't write; then there was Logan, who is a very spruce man—He has a collection of the finest prose sentences in a little notebook; and he chanted these aloud, and we had to guess the writers. But his real object in coming was to ask us to print some of his works.[1] Indeed we are now besieged with manuscripts.

But Logan says we shall never make a success on our present system; because no one buys privately printed books but collectors; and they will only buy expensive books; but if we charge 5/ or 10/—we shall have a large sale, and be able to pay writers and painters; so we've got to go a round of the bookshops next week carrying our wares.

It sounds a little too American to be altogether to one's liking; but I suppose we must. Then Lytton came; he's doing a grand season, with Cunards, Asquiths, and all the rest; completely happy; still, he assures us his soul is untouched; and I think it probably is. The food he says is wonderful; and there is gold and silver plate; but the great ladies are very discontented, and never know whats the right thing to admire next.

Then there was Violet [Dickinson]—she hasn't turned a hair; her dresses are exactly the same, and all the chains and bangles. She was very charming and asked after you of course innumerable questions; did you get on with Clive, was the baby like you, was Quentin as charming as ever, how was Duncan—but as she never listens, it doesn't matter what one says; and her jumps are as wild as ever. She had got lots of odds and ends of Japanese embroidery, and coloured papers as usual. But she has great merit I think. We are coming to Asheham about the 27th, I think, for a week—Shall I come for a night? The agents wont even answer, either in Sussex or Dorsetshire, so I daresay its as well we took Tregerthen.

Yr
B.

Will you remember to send me the name of the powder that Mary H[utchinson]. recommends.

Berg

1048: TO LADY OTTOLINE MORRELL
Hogarth [House, Richmond]
Wednesday [21 May 1919]
Dearest Ottoline,
I had sent off the hat before your letter came. The only hat box we could

1. In 1920 the Hogarth Press published Logan Pearsall Smith's *Stories from the Old Testament*.

come by was one of Leonards; I pray that it may have kept the exquisite creation—which gave such distinction to the drawing room that I left it out on purpose—safe. I think the box was stiffer than most.

There's been such a chaos of conversation these last days that I've not sat down to write a letter to anyone. This is very unfortunate for you, as I meant to record the outburst of appreciation which fell from Leonard when you left us. As his praise is written in letters of gold, I rate it very high; but it was to the effect that Ottoline was not only charming, distinguished, rare, and remarkable, but also 'very nice'—According to him this is the least common gift among my friends; so that I repeat it, and hope you will see how permanent and sterling it is among your other tributes. I always imagine you heaped like an altar every morning with the offerings of your friends. Very well; here is a small brown acorn.

We had our visit from Logan—I think there is a good deal of the priest, it may be of the eunuch, in him. Partly his shaven face perhaps; but then Roger, who came too, is also shaven, without share in the other attributes. I mean, I think, that Logan is celibate; and has had time to bring his virtues to a chaste perfection which one might find a trifle chill. He was infinitely kind, and infinitely agreeable; but I couldn't help seeing his perfect sentences of English prose served up in a muffin dish, over a bright fire, with the parrot on a perch. He begged us to reprint Elia[1]; and thought it very delightful to extract the flower of Urn Burial,[2] 6 words long, and print it by itself in an exquisite little volume, to carry in the breast pocket, like a scent bottle. He has several of these sentences always on his person, and read them aloud in a high nasal chant, which again suggested the priest, and the eunuch.

Not a word was said of you; though I almost burst out, and shattered his recitations, by demanding what business he had to be such a frost-bitten old prude in real life, while so free and expansive in literature. After 6 hours of Roger's conversation, however, one's energy is exhausted. Anyhow, Logan is a wonderfully trim old bird.

I have been going through the calendar, in search of a week end. As far as I can see, June 21st, is the only possible one for me. And no doubt you've chosen that for someone who would make me feel completely dumb, dowdy, and derelict. That last sentence is offered in trembling, remembering your strictures upon poor Hopes [Mirrlees] efforts in the way of alliteration. Indeed I scarcely like to read this letter over in case too great signs of what you and Leonard condemn appear—for I shall never have the patience to write it over again.

Lytton lunched here, and we examined his soul under the apple trees, and

1. *Essays of Elia* (1823 and 1833), by Charles Lamb.
2. By Thomas Browne (1658). Perhaps Logan quoted the famous line, "But the iniquity of oblivion blindly scattereth her poppy". In 1919 Logan published *A Treasury of English Prose*, which contained many excerpts from Thomas Browne.

gave it back to him without serious criticism. His imitations of Winston, Lord Ribblesdale, and Lady Cunard would pay for all Maynards crimes in the matter of worldliness; but the truth is of course, that no one humbugs Lytton for the wink of an eyelid. In fact, I'm ready to risk his soul once a year, on condition he bring us down such rare fruits from the poison tree. He is much struck by the unhappiness of the great; this, I feel, is as it should be. He says they are perpetually bored.

I've seen Carrington, and Mr and Mrs Sidney Webb, and Bob Trevelyan, and an Armenian, called Altounyan,[1] who wants us to print his novel. The poor man's mouth is fixed open, like that of some large fish, in hope of praise; it is positively alarming. Compared with him, I merely flicker a long thin tongue. But the attitude is not graceful; and God knows what we're to say to his novel; and how can we advise him, as he wishes, to throw up his career, desert his father on the edge of the grave, and devote himself to fiction? It's a case for Garsington. Shall I send you his address? Would you forward this to the Bishop of Oxford?[2]—or what does one call him? I will leave the envelope for you to fill up. He is said to admire Eliots poetry.

You aff

Texas   V.W.

1049: TO CLIVE BELL   *Hogarth [House, Richmond]*

Friday [23 May 1919]

My dear Clive,

Possibly, I see on looking at a calendar, the usual indisposition of my sex may make me unable to come on Monday. If you'd like to come to tea with me here instead, you'd find me alone; then you might stay to dinner, and meet my husband.

But dates are movable in my case. The only solution seems to be for you to ring me up on Monday morning. I'm sorry to be such a trouble, and so illegible into the bargain, but we are rushing off to wild dissipation—an evening party at the [J. C.] Squires!

Your

Quentin Bell   V.W.

1050: TO CLIVE BELL   *Hogarth [House, Richmond]*

Monday morning [26 May 1919]

My dear Clive,

I suppose you did not get the letter I wrote saying that circumstances

---

1. Ernest Altounyan. He was the author of a book of poems *Ornament of Honour*, 1937, and became a surgeon in Aleppo, Syria.
2. Charles Gore, a friend of Ottoline.

might make it impossible for me to come today—so they have—damn them. We'd be very glad if you came to dinner, and I shall be alone here all day; I suppose, though, you'll be back too late for tea. But come or not as you like. There'll be enough dinner anyhow.

Your
V.W.

Quentin Bell

1051: TO LYTTON STRACHEY   *Hogarth [House, Richmond]*

Monday [26 May 1919]

I forgot to ask you about the meeting with the Webbs: Saturday, 7th June, appears to be the day, and that is the Saturday before Whit Sunday. As far as I know it does for the Webbs. Will you let me know about you, and then I will write to them.

We go to Asheham tomorrow. Ottoline seems to have caught Picasso [for Garsington] after all. But we shall be away from these gaieties—and Murry wants me to review Belshazzar—his poem—in the Athenaeum.[1] For God's sake, say you'll do it instead. I shall try to wriggle out on the ground of my connection, and pecuniary interest. Addison[2] improves a little —if one likes that sort of thing. I mean he's very much better than Robert Lynd[3] or Jack Squire—O what a party! I may tell you that your illegitimate sister-in-law [Inez] would have been a beacon of light, an oasis of green, in that assembly. "Yes, I give these parties because they're cheap" said Mrs Squire, and continued in that style on a sofa in a draught and without respite for ¾ of an hour: the last quarter was occupied by old decayed Cobden Sanderson,[4] wearing a red ribbon round his neck, and a workman's blue shirt—but not very inspiring all the same. Moreover, Jack Squire himself was more repulsive than words can express, and malignant into the bargain. As for the conduct and appearance of the rest, it was deplorable to conceive oneself of the same shape, more or less—not altogether thank God! Please assure me that we are rather different—some of us at least.

How did Katherine Asquith[5] impress you? I have sheets from Ottoline this morning calling her "statuesque" and lamenting her lack of passion; so that I suppose she failed to respond to pressure—But what's the use of

1. *Belshazzar of Baronscourt* was the sub-title of Murry's *The Critic in Judgment*.
2. *Joseph Addison* (*TLS*, 19 June 1919).
3. The essayist (1879-1949). He wrote an essay almost weekly, first in the *Nation*, and then from 1913 to 1945 in the *New Statesman*, under the pseudonym 'Y. Y.'.
4. Thomas Cobden-Sanderson (1840-1922), the printer and publisher.
5. Widow of Raymond Asquith, the son of the former Prime Minister. Katherine was formerly Katherine Horner of Mells, Somerset, and her husband was killed on the Somme in 1916.

asking questions, eh?—Since the telephone rings, and Lady Cunard, or Princess Arthur of Connaught requests the pleasure—but no! it's Mrs Saxton Noble to meet Mr Walter Lamb this time, so you can spare a moment. Clive assures me that he lunches out every day.

"Where?"

"Ah, with beautiful creatures!" Still, if you can't put a name to them—

Yr.

V.W.

Frances Hooper

1052: TO SAXON SYDNEY-TURNER   *Asheham, Rodmell,*
                                                [Sussex]

May 30th [1919]

My dear Saxon,

I suppose that you may be back again in London by this time—though I hope not. Anyhow, it's no good looking for a letter from you, and were it not for a deep principle of devotion in me, conquering an extreme disinclination to write, you would never, never, never see my hand again. I've no excuse, but I'm perpetually dropping off to sleep, or rather I'm in the state of a dog in front of a large fire. I sit at the window and go off into a drowse. It's partly the yellow of the field—and the heat—and the pigeons crooning— and the long grass swishing up and down. I thought I'd read so many books, and I've scarcely opened one.

So you see this all leads up to a tribute to your virtues—since no one else can make me write a letter, and as I say, I've no hopes of an answer. But did you go to the New Forest? Was it nice? Did Mrs Primmer[1] do well for you? Did Barbara come? How is Barbara? What did you do all day? Did you read aloud? Did you go to Fritham, or where? Did you see the ghost of Aunt Minna, or visit her grave? I suppose you took a book and sat in a glade, and pretended to read, and then watched insects or made one of those rare observations which like the flower of the aloe, justify 100 years of silence— something very sudden and penetrating and summing it all up. I wish I'd kept a note book labelled 'Saxon'; a small one would have done, but it would have been very choice. But then one can't always be thinking of posterity.

We came down last Tuesday, unable to resist the weather any longer. Duncan came over the other night, driven out, so he said, by the prospect of an evening alone with Mrs Brereton, who has got on his nerves. But then the poor woman was abruptly told by Vanessa 10 days ago that her presence in the house was extremely disagreeable to them all. As Vanessa said, there was no denying it and therefore there was no reason for Mrs Brereton to go

1. The landlady at Beech Shade, Bank, New Forest, where Rupert Brooke had taken lodgings.

off in a huff and complain to Roger that she was ill used. "She is a bore, said Nessa; and its a great nuisance having her there at meals; which she might have known, and naturally I thought she did know it". Anyhow, she does now. But what is one to do with Nessa and Duncan? We all wear clothes; why should they be allowed to go about naked? Thats how it strikes me, but they on the contrary insist that decency and drapery are carried to the utmost limits at Charleston—what with the bath, and Mr and Mrs Pitcher,[1] and Duncan having bought a new grey summer suit. We're going for a picnic today, as it's Nessa's birthday—I'm terrified to think which,[2] but it doesn't seem to matter much.

And now, Saxon, what is your opinion of Addison's writings? That is the problem of my life. But owing to my lethargy, I can't endure to open the Spectator; in a sort of coma I've glided through Sir Roger de Coverley, who seems a very pleasant old gentleman, but not the sort who much interests me. The propriety is so fearful, and the kindliness; and his death leaves me—well I'm ashamed to say I began my great task of weeding the terrace, and then Duncan came—however I know its one of the masterpieces of English prose—Can I say, on your authority, that he's a complete humbug? The worst of it is that he's not.

I saw Lytton the other day; very agreeable and flitting from house to house, and settling upon the great, as if he were an ordinary house fly; he dines with Lady Cunard, and meets Princess Arthur of Connaught; but his sting is in perfect order, it seemed to me. He is writing a whole volume about Queen Victoria. He says Cambridge is very nice now, though the undergraduates are very stupid, and have never heard of him.

We come back on Tuesday. Ring us up and suggest a night for dinner.

Yr. V.W.

Sussex

1053: To Clive Bell
Asheham, Rodmell,
[Sussex]

Friday [30 May 1919]

Dearest Clive,

I'd almost forgotten your indiscretion, and some relic of caution or perhaps mere forgetfulness had made me say nothing even to Leonard. It doesn't seem to me very interesting anyhow.

Here we are basking, drowsing, feeling infinitely wise and stupendously philosophic—though its true that I must now bicycle off to a picnic at

1. The gardener at Charleston and his wife.
2. She was 40.

Firle. Was the Murrys' party a success I wonder? and what happened to Ott? I had a letter bidding me not come. "Piccasso party prevented!" Why?

Yr.
V.W.

Quentin Bell

1054: To Lady Ottoline Morrell

Asheham, Rodmell
[Sussex]

Sunday [1 June? 1919]

My dear Ottoline,

I was so glad to find the Picasso party given up, as we were down here; and now have hopes it may take place another time.

Nothing however, no number of Picassos, quite come up to the trees and the rest of it down here. We go back on Tuesday—

I'm so glad the hat survived. So many interruptions take place in the country; now its a murder in the chalk pit—the rag and bone man killed by a Canadian soldier:

Yr
V.W.

Texas

1055: To Clive Bell and Vanessa Bell

Hogarth [House, Richmond]

Wednesday [4 June 1919]

Clive

Would you give this to Nessa? I don't know whether she's staying at Gordon Sq., or when she arrives, but I should be very grateful if you could convey it to her somehow as early as you can.

V.W.

Dearest

We came back to find ourselves flooded with orders for Kew.[1] It is sold out, and orders are still coming in for more, so we must reprint at once. We think of having an edition of 300 printed for us; but it is rather difficult to know how to do it. Would you like to undertake the whole thing?—not only woodcuts, but title page and text.[2]

1. *Kew Gardens* had been enthusiastically reviewed in the *Times Literary Supplement*.
2. Vanessa had been upset by the poor reproduction of her woodcuts in the first edition.

I am going this afternoon to the printer [Richard Madley] you spoke of out of Soho Sqre to ask whether he could print it, in a week if possible.

You would perhaps be able to see him and give him full directions while you are in London.

The alternative is that we should employ Macdermott the printer here. We should have to direct him about the text; as I suppose you wouldn't be able to come and see him. But in that case could you get some printer of your own to print your woodcuts as you liked, at our expense, and we could get Macdermott to bind them up with the text?

I think personally that it would be better if you could get the Soho man to do the whole book from your instructions; but I don't know whether you would have time to do this. Also it is very important to get it done quickly.

I don't think either that we could afford to pay you for supervising the printing, so that you mayn't think it worth your while. Almost all the orders are from book shops, and we have to give them the trade discount, which means that we shall make very little profit on the second edition. Would you ring me up tomorrow afternoon, as early as you can?

I enclose a cheque for £3, which is your share of the first edition.

Yr
B.

Berg

1056: To Vanessa Bell   *Hogarth [House, Richmond]*

Friday [6 June 1919]

Dearest,

Perhaps Clive has forwarded my letter, but I had better repeat it. There has been a great rush for Kew Gardens and we have sold out the first edition and have orders for a great many more.[1] I wrote to ask whether you would direct the printing of the new edition, which must be got ready at once. After writing to you, I went to Madley, Rogers printer, and asked him for an estimate for 500 copies. We have settled that he is to start printing at once— that is tomorrow. The question is, who is to instruct him? I showed him a copy of our book, and rather to my pleasure, I admit, he said that in his opinion I had been quite right to place the first woodcut where I did, and that he would have done so himself. He also advised us not to change the spacing between Kew Gardens and the first paragraph, as he thought it was right. He thought he could improve the title page; but he said he didn't know whether the caterpillar woodcut wants moving up or down. Therefore, if it is to be improved, I think someone must advise him. I told him, thinking

1. They had only printed 150 copies of the first edition.

you were coming, that you would instruct him both about the text and the woodcuts. I suppose Roger or Woolf[1] would be ready to do this, and you would feel safe with them, so I have asked Roger to ring me up, when he comes back, but he hasn't yet done so.

We had 15 new orders this morning, and several letters asking why copies had not been sent, so we must get Madley to work at once. I suppose, however, you've put off coming altogether. I will either get Roger or Wolfe, or leave it entirely to Madley. He hasn't got our type exactly, but a smaller one, so that there would, he thought, be room to allow a whole page for the caterpillar. Possibly you could mark the position of the print and woodcuts on your copy and send straight to Madley. His address is, Richard Madley, 151 Whitfield Street, Tottenham Court Rd. W. 1. As we're having such a large edition, it would be a good thing to get it done properly according to your ideas.

There's going to be a review in the Athenaeum, which may sell more copies, I suppose; we have to spend all day binding copies and sending out.

Yr

B.

I saw a house in Lewes on Monday and we've offered to buy it freehold for £300—very old, small, but rather charming—however some one else is after it and has probably got it.

Berg

1057: To Saxon Sydney-Turner *Hogarth [House, Richmond]*

Wednesday [11 June 1919]

My dear Saxon,

We will send you one of Roger's edition when its out.[2] I had the proofs today, and I don't think they compare well[3]—still, I believe he means to alter them. The printer rang us up in some distress at his orders; to our pleasure. I believe Nessa's in London today, and will see about it herself.

I don't mind how thickly I flatter old gentlemen if they will give me peonies—I suppose I might be wandering by, see them over the garden wall, and ask to be allowed to look closer—Would that be a good opening? Or will you take me to tea there, and pretend that I want to buy a house in Mortlake—then accidentally, I might look out of the window, and exclaim Peonies! etc etc. It lends itself to many variations.

1. She means Edward Wolfe, the young Omega artist.
2. Richard Madley, who was reprinting *Kew Gardens*, was the printer of Roger Fry's Omega books.
3. With the first edition, printed on the Hogarth Press.

I dont know who wrote your quotations: but then that's the kind of thing I never do know. Why do all quotations look so much better than any whole poems? I could swear that both these were of the highest merit.

I must now rush up to the Alhambra [Diaghilev's ballet].

Come and dine again.

Yr V.W.

We'll deduct the copy of K.G. [*Kew Gardens*] from your deposit, I suppose.

Sussex

1058: To Dora Carrington   *Hogarth* [*House, Richmond*]

Sunday [15 June 1919]

My dear Carrington,

I saw Lytton yesterday, and got his consent, on your behalf, to the following plan. We are having 500 copies of the Mark on the Wall reprinted with your woodcuts.[1] [E. M.] Forster is going to write about it in the Daily News, and it is thus necessary to get the printing started at once in order to have some copies by the time his review appears. So I'm taking it for granted that you don't mind, and that you will allow the Pelican Press or any other to print the woodcuts as they think best, and will abide by their decision, since there's no time for you to direct them how to do it. (Nessa disliked the way we did hers in Kew Gardens—that is why I'm so particular—) We shall give you 25 per-cent of the profits, and in time I hope we may each make a few shillings out of it—which you ought to spend in coming to have tea with me, since the 1917 [Club] atmosphere is not favourable to the subleties and intimacies of refined female intercourse.

We've bought a house in Lewes[2]—on the spur of the moment. Its the butt end of an old windmill, so that all the rooms are either completely round or semi-circular.

One of the chief decorations is going to be a large showpiece by Carrington, found in an attic at Asheham; doesn't that make you blush all over—upset the tea—and scald the cat? But I suppose there's no cat at Tidmarsh.

What about the hens this year? Have they grown tail feathers? What a sight it was—when we rounded them up and drove them into the river!

Your

V.W.

What about your book of woodcuts?

Robert H. Taylor

1. Actually they reprinted 1,000 copies.
2. The Round House, on the Castle hill in the centre of Lewes.

1059: To CLIVE BELL 1917 *Club, [Gerrard St.,*
Soho, W.1.]
Monday [16 June 1919]

Please excuse this sheet—I'm in the Club, cheek by jowl with Marjorie and others. *Tomorrow Tuesday* would suit me very well. I will be here, 1917 Club, at 3.30. Would you add to your load of obligations Duncan's hat— said to be waiting me at Gordon Sqre. (the hat he painted for me, I mean). If you could bring it, I should make a more gallant show at Gunters [tea-shop]—God! What solace an ice!—the arguments of the virtuous but alas, so repulsive, hurtle round my head.

Quentin Bell

1060: To DORA CARRINGTON [*Hogarth House, Richmond*]
Wednesday [18 June 1919]

My dear Carrington,

Alas—we took the woodcuts [from *The Mark on the Wall*] to the Pelican press yesterday and they put so many difficulties in the way that we had to consent to print the story without them. The printer said they'd have to be cut down and stereotyped, and he couldn't answer for their being done in time, and it would cost a good deal. I'm very sorry, as they added greatly to the charm of the work which will look very blank without them.

We're thinking of getting an office and a secretary—all our time goes in doing up parcels and writing notes—and now we expect another rush of orders for Eliot and Murry. I believe a poor man could make his fortune out of this trade—but combined with editing, reviews and writing novels it's a little overwhelming.

O dear—my turn at Garsington comes next—a whip to remind me from her Ladyship this morning.

I suppose, indeed insist, that the fruit of Alix's labour shall be printed by us. Give her my love, and tell her—but there's no room.

Yr
V.W.

O these blots!

Robert H. Taylor

1061: To VANESSA BELL Hogarth [*House, Richmond*]
Wednesday [18 June 1919]

Dearest,

Roger is a cussed old devil; he must have gone off and forgotten all

368

about us. We took the law into our own hands, and told Madley to print off, since he said he would have to charge extra for the delay. He will send some copies tomorrow, and I will send you one. But O dear!—he's gone and cut *all* the covers crooked, some too large and some too small, and to add to my melancholy troubles I've had to pare down the books edges with a pen knife to fit them. But we complained, and perhaps the new lot will be better. All I mean is, a professional printer isn't necessarily infallible as you seem to think. Did you realise that it was your severity that plunged me into the recklessness of buying a house that day? Something I must do to redress the balance, to give myself value in my eyes, I said; and so I bought a house; the blood will therefore be upon your head.

Did anyone ever suffer as I did? You might have seen my soul shrivelling like a—I cannot remember the image exactly, but its something one does by rubbing a piece of sealing wax and then everything curls up—as if in agony. Not that there was any imagery about it in my case. But the immanent sweetness of my soul formed, as it were, a cream upon the surface. I survived.

Now I suppose I must rapidly deliver myself of gossip. Well, I dropped in on Adrian and Karin the other night, to find them scrubbing their sauce-pans in the kitchen in rather a surly mood; but having done, they explained that they are now both about to become medical students at University Hospital. They've given up philosophy, social reform, law, and all the rest of it; they're going into practice together as Psycho-analysts.

This wont be of course for 5 years, but they think they stand great chance of success, as man and woman in combination ought to be invincible. I suppose one'll whisper one's symptoms to Adrian, and he'll bellow them to Karin; and then they'll lay their heads together. Isn't it a surprising prospect? I see in it another of Karin's gallant attempts to roll her huge stone up the hill. But she is brighter than ever. Her hat is now of the shape of a Welshwomans hat, only scarlet, then her dress is sage green; and her decorations many-coloured beads; and the whole effect like that of some debauched parrot who has been maltreated by the street boys, but doesn't know it, or only half suspects it, poor fowl. Still, who am I to talk about matters of taste? who indeed?

My other piece of gossip was from Fredegond so it may be discounted a little, about Alix and James.

James came to Fredegond in an appalling state of fright. He said that Alix was on the point of killing herself. They had quarrelled over something quite unimportant. Alix had lost her temper, said she would no longer live with him, that the strain was intolerable, and dismissed him for ever. He went to fetch Fredegond. Fredegond found her sitting on the edge of her bed, which had not been made, in a room strewn with old food and litter, sobbing. She was completely broken down. She could explain nothing. They got her to Chelsea, where she announced that the breach was final, and the Shoves persuaded her to go abroad. Carrington was sent for. Just before Carrington arrived, James made his way in; there was a reconciliation scene; then, so far as I could gather, the same passions on Alix's part started again. Finally she was packed off to Tidmarsh, where she still is, writing reams of poetry, alone with Carrington. Fredegond cross-examined James to some extent but without great success. He won't admit he's in love; in fact he denies that there's such a thing as being in love. Meanwhile, as Alix provides food and shelter, I suppose he'll keep his grip on her, in a muddled kind of way, though she has come to such a pass, according to Fredegond, that either she'll break down, or succumb entirely and for ever. For my part, I think that if there was a breach, James ought to have done his utmost to widen it. Still how is one to know the truth about anything? For the present James is master of Gordon Square, and is thinking of setting up a gas oven.

We shall be coming down for a week about the 26th or 27th., so I may see you. I'm a little nervous, not only of seeing you, but of showing Leonard the Round House; I've rather forgotten what its like. I still remember the features of Mrs Dolphin [Vanessa] though—O dear; I must write a story about it. Kew goes on selling at the rate of about 10 copies a day. We are flooded with manuscripts, and a young man has offered to help us in printing them. I think we shall have to set up a shop.

On Saturday I go to Garsington; God knows why. Eliot is to be there. He and Murry were much abused in the Times for their works, and Murry a good deal depressed.

By the way, would you like to let Charleston to Murry for the months you don't want it? Katherine is going abroad for a year, and Murry wants to live in the country near Lewes if possible. I said I'd look for a house, but of course there aren't any.

What a nice long letter! Its affection partly, but also to remind you of the necklace—though I'm not worthy of necklaces, or of hats, and you'll find in future that I never mention aesthetic subjects, or ask for more than mute toleration. I haven't yet got the hat; but would you let me know what I owe dear, doddering, divine, Duncan.

I'm sorry that you're sending Julian to school; he will have his hair cut and wear a collar I suppose, and of course he'll enjoy it immensely—besides its only a day school. But I see my influence will be required not so much to keep my nephews straight as to crookify them.

Yr

Berg
B.

Thursday [26 June? 1919]

My dear Roger,

This[1] is a very small return for all your goodness—but I'm becoming sick of your goodness. You should hear poor old Ottoline be-praising you, with some muddled idea of pleasing the deity I suppose since there's nothing else to be gained by it. Goldie[2] encouraged her to attempt one more grand scene of reconciliation[3]; I was not optimistic—though if you'd arrange it so that I could attend, behind a curtain or in a chamber pot—I'd have no objection whatever. Please give this your serious consideration. Ott: of course, would be magnificent, merely as a matter of art—

Your
V.W.

Sussex

1063: To Lady Ottoline Morrell   *Asheham, Rodmell, Lewes, [Sussex]*

27th June [1919]

Dearest Ottoline,

Philip must be wrong about my heart—that arrow you see is deep driven into me—because here I am, doing what of all things I detest doing, sitting down to write a letter. Letters in general aren't so bad, but when one has to sum up one's feelings, to give thanks, to make Ottoline understand how happy she made one, and how the time seemed to lapse, like the Magic Flute, from one air to another—this is what I call, or Clive calls, a problem in art. But, to return to Philip, I must be practically all heart, for at intervals of half an hour since Monday I've wondered where you were, how you were, whether the operation was over, how you felt after it, whether you've gone back, how hateful the Home must be, what your nurses thought of you, how odious doctors are, matrons in nursing homes even worse, Welbeck Street detestable, Garsington divine, books intolerable within range of a medicine glass— and so on. Doesn't it seem to prove some rudiment of an organ—not like yours I admit, or Philips [Morrell], or Goldies, or Gertlers, or Lord de la Warr's,[4] but a literary heart of some capacity? You seem to think that all that's wanted is a practical heart, but isn't there some place for the theoretical heart, which is my kind—the heart which imagines what people feel, and

1. Perhaps a copy of the second edition of *Kew Gardens*, which Roger had helped to arrange.
2. G. Lowes Dickinson had spent the past weekend with Virginia at Garsington.
3. See p. 91, note 6.
4. The 9th Earl De La Warr ('Buck'), who succeeded his father in 1915, aged 15.

takes an interest in it, but never conceives how to do anything. Perhaps you have both, you are, of course, a very gifted woman, but then that's no merit of yours. But you see, this is a sore point—no heart indeed! I meant to make this a letter of thanks; and its turned to the opposite.

We are down here involved in so many dealings with houses that we may well find ourselves bankrupt; and then the first person I shall come to for refuge will be you, of course. But why, when we've just bought a house, should another[1] appear much more desirable,—and how can one resist buying and chance selling?

Anyhow this letter must end with thanks. You would have been wise to secrete yourself in the rack of the third class carriage in which Goldie and I travelled up on Monday. You would have heard much to your advantage.

Your affate

Texas   V.W.

1064: To Vanessa Bell   [*Asheham, Rodmell, Sussex*]

Sunday [29 June 1919]

Dearest,

It looks too bad to come for a picnic, so I'm sending this by Nelly. I might be able to come over for the night on Tuesday—if that suited you.

We have just seen rather a good house at Rodmell, which is being sold on Tuesday. We are going to bid for it and if we get it we shall sell the house in Lewes. Do you think Roger would like to be told about it? If so, we would give him the first offer; some one else is said to want to buy it. As the sale is on Tuesday afternoon in Lewes, I may be too late to catch the train, in which case I'm afraid I shant see you, as we go back on Wednesday.

I believe that Duncan, when he thought of buying the huts, got Powell or someone to bid for him. I should be very grateful if you would send a line by Nelly to say if he thought this a good plan, and whom he employed. There is great competition apparently for the Rodmell house, and we thought of asking Wycherley [Lewes agent] to bid for us—but perhaps it's better to bid oneself.

Needless to say we should be very glad if you or Duncan or Maynard or the children or anyone would come over anytime—and we've plenty of spare rooms. But I'll try to come on Tuesday—Now it seems clearing up—but its this damned wind that makes sitting out so unpleasant. I must tell you about Garsington—What do I owe for my hat? The necklace broke last night. Could you put 2 strings? It would be angelic of you.

B.

Berg

1. Monk's House, Rodmell.

Asheham, [Rodmell, Sussex]

30th June [1919]

My dear Philip

What a budget of psychology I might discharge upon you in answer to your letter! If you feel this about me, what don't I feel about you, and why do I feel it, and what does it prove about both of us—and so on, and so on, —But first, I was very glad to hear of Ottoline. I was amazed at her high, and I suppose aristocratic, bearing in the face of the operation, and forgave the peerage many sins on the spot. I'm very glad its over; please give her my love (for what its worth, of course).

But as to the problem between us, it would be worth investigating; but writing it out takes, I'm afraid too long. Still, if I frighten you, you, invariably, produce in me sensations I've not had since I was 18, and dragged by my half brother to a ball, where I knew nobody, couldn't dance, and as for dress, and hair, and conversation—Perhaps its that you're so well dressed—a gentleman—a man of the world—accustomed to society? I don't know. But I'm certain that I contract once more to the condition of a miserable schoolgirl; I become rigid; I say priggish things; I fancy that you smile; I'm certain that I detect a sort of well-bred amusement at the angularities and barbarities of Bloomsbury. And yet, of course, you're *not* Mayfair; no, its partly the old complex which the misery of youth stamped on one—the sense of being with people who laugh at the things one cares about. But there's no time to get it all straight—George Duckworth's at the bottom of it, in my case, and you don't know him.

You are partly right and partly wrong about the article.[1] The truth is that Murry asked me to do it, and I refused; then he insisted, and with the greatest labour in the world I began an article, but broke down. Leonard went on with it; and then we cobbled the two parts together hoping that no one would recognise either of us. It's rather important both for the Hogarth Press and for the Athenaeum that nobody should know this; so please keep the secret. It's such a mixture of Leonard and me both trying not to give ourselves away that we're surprised that you should have suspected either of us. I thought of telling you, but had promised not to, and hoped you'd forget. On the whole, its more Leonards work, I think than mine; but I never owned up to Murry that I had to call in help, and would rather he didn't know.

Leonard's theory about Daisy Ashford,[2] by the way, is that it is certainly not pure child; but touched up by Daisy at a mature age upon re-reading, and then sent to Barrie, who can thus say truthfully that its none of his doing.

1. Virginia had been asked to review Hogarth's own publication, T. S. Eliot's *Poems*. See letter 1138.
2. Author of *The Young Visiters*, written at the age of 9. The short novel was published in 1919, with an introduction by J. M. Barrie.

He suspects the same passages that we suspect without suggestion from me, so that I think there must be a reason for it.

We're feverish with excitement tonight—tomorrow we go in to Lewes to bid for a house that has taken our fancy, so much that we are determined to sell the one I bought the other day. Thirty people it is said, will bid against us—heaven knows where we shan't land ourselves—and I'm distracted from writing a clear and critical account of this very interesting question—our extreme embarrassment at being in the same room together— which doesn't prevent me from hoping that you'll come and see us at Richmond.

Love to Ottoline,

Yours Ever
Virginia Woolf

From my own experience, I think you'd like Philip Woolf.[1] He's very modest, sensitive, and friendly.

Texas

1. Leonard's younger brother.

Letters 1066-1106 (July–December 1919)

On 1 July the Woolfs bought Monk's House at a Lewes auction, and sold the Round House a fortnight later. Monk's House was to be their country home for the rest of their lives. They moved there from Asheham on 1 September, two farm-waggons carrying their furniture and belongings, and lived at first in considerable discomfort, which did not deter them from inviting immediate guests, of whom the first were Altounyan and Nick and Barbara Bagenal. Night and Day was published on 20 October, and Virginia received adulatory reviews and letters (except from Katherine Mansfield, who thought it snobbish, and E. M. Forster, who preferred The Voyage Out). She replied self-analytically, never having mentioned the book to her friends while she was writing it, and boasted of the first two offers she received from American publishers. In early October the Woolfs returned to Hogarth House, and in December bought it, together with its Siamese twin, Suffield House, next door, having rented Hogarth House since 1915. At this moment, therefore, when their income was no more than £700 a year, they owned, part-owned, or rented five properties (Hogarth, Suffield, Monk's, 22 Hyde Park Gate, and the three Cornish cottages). Leonard's International Review ceased publication for financial reasons at the end of the year, and simultaneously he went down with malaria. Virginia herself was in bed with influenza on Christmas Day.

1066: To Clive Bell   Asheham, [Rodmell,
                                             Sussex]
Tuesday [1 July 1919]

My dear Clive,

I got your letter here this morning, so I'm not able to go to Molly's party. But if one night next week you would ask me to some humble restaurant, and then go on to the Ballet I should be enchanted—I've never seen Petrouska, and was meaning to go. Could you get me a ticket—7/- I think they are; ordering on the telephone, they put me off with the worst in the house. I think I'm free most nights next week.

We come back to Hogarth tomorrow. Did you hear I'd bought a house in Lewes? Well, the first thing we saw on getting out of the train the other day was the advertisement of another, highly superior, at Rodmell. So we're off now, in this flood of rain, to bid at an auction[1]; and then we shall sell the

1. That afternoon the Woolfs bought Monk's House for £700.

375

other—but the process is so exciting and charming that I rather hope we may go on like this until, I suppose, we're forced to live in a tower on the top of a hill which will be known as Woolf's Folly. Still I shall have enough cash about me to pay my dinner and seat: I bid you mark this.

I'm much encouraged by your praise of Addison.[1] I thought it rather good myself—considering all things—

Yr.
V.W.

Quentin Bell

1067: TO VANESSA BELL   [*Hogarth House, Richmond*]

[July 1919]

Dear Dolphin,

Here is 3/- for my lunch; I daresay it cost more, but if so, I will allow you to pay it.

If you could send the picture, my gratitude would be unbounded, and I would pay the carriage, or any other expenses.

Let me know what you settled to do about Mr Cholmondeley[2]— Leonard was under him at St Pauls, and says he was very popular and had much the best house there, though L. thought him rather a muscular Xtian. But this must have been ages ago.

Yr
B.

Berg

1068: TO VANESSA BELL   Hogarth [*House, Richmond*]

Thursday [17 July 1919]

Dearest,

I wish you'd write and say what happened to Julian at his examination. I've a secret hope that he did so abominably in everything that Mr Chol-mondeley took you aside afterwards and said "Mrs Bell, I am sorry to have to tell you that your son will never repay education—in fact he's next door to a natural". But being my nephew, I see little chance of this. Poor brat! What a melancholy thing—he'll begin to be ashamed of going on the po in public. It's melancholy, too, about London, and only getting away for holidays—

1. Her article on Joseph Addison had appeared in the *TLS* on 19 June 1919.
2. Vanessa was thinking of sending Julian to Owen's School, Islington, of which R. F. Cholmeley was headmaster 1909-27.

We sold the Round House, for £320, so we shan't lose anything over it; and I believe if we'd risked waiting we could have got £400. There's not much gossip, I imagine, that you haven't already had, since you've been in touch with Clive who is the fountain and well. I wish you'd explain to me the truth about Lopokhova.[1] Did she run away—and with whom—and why—and where is she? Mrs Hamilton pretended to know for certain that she was ill in a villa in St John's Wood. But then dear old Molly Hamilton has a tempermental lust for the commonplace. She brought her younger sister [Margot] here the other night, and seldom have I seen such a prodigy; as white as an egg—a large ducks egg; bound about the brow with a fillet of silver; with the manners of a professor and the speech of an elderly and pompous Prime Minister. She writes poems—but no relation of Mrs Hamilton's could write anything save leading articles. She has another sister who paints stained glass; in fact it is generally understood that genius has once more come to earth; which I cannot allow. Altounyan and his sister [Norah] have been dining here. I'm afraid he is a great bore—Why will people talk so much nonsense about their writing? After having made me read his manuscript, he told me that he didn't care what I thought of it, but only wished to see how much I was capable of understanding. There's the cloven hoof of Cambridge in this,—rather like Hom [Meredith] I mean; the honest sort. How I detest them!

The whole of Richmond is already ringing with Anthems,[2] and I was almost thrown into the river this afternoon by a man letting off a Squib under my feet for a joke. I don't believe anybody wants it, but we have to go through with it I suppose—even the servants are completely cynical.

There is little gossip—except a morsel about Fanny Cornford,[3] which I got from Fredegond. The poor woman has a delusion that she must never be tired, and has now spent 2 years in going from rest cure to rest cure. She refuses to see either her husband or children. The doctors have at last sent her home, but think she may be incurable. Of course its all the result of Mrs Litchfield, and old Joseph [error for Richard]—was he called?—who used to have the chemist calling with the butcher. All Darwins incline that way. The number of one's undeluded friends is now very small. I spend a good deal of my time at the Royal Academy. It is a very amusing and spirited place. I get an immense deal of pleasure from working out the pictures. But I mustn't tell you, or you wont read my article.[4] I can't settle down to write

1. Lydia Lopokova, the Russian ballet dancer, who came to England with Diaghilev during the war. In 1919 she was performing in London with Leonide Massine in *La Boutique Fantasque.*
2. The Treaty of Versailles was signed on 19 July 1919.
3. Frances Cornford, the poet, and granddaughter of Charles Darwin. She suffered from depression on several occasions, but each time recovered, and continued writing until her death in 1960. Mrs Litchfield was her aunt.
4. *The Royal Academy (Athenaeum,* 22 August 1919).

it, though, because I always remember pictures that I haven't quite worked out, and I have to go back again. The crowd is such that it is often difficult to get a clear view of a picture. I think Cocaine is one of the best, but there is a marine piece which is also very good.[1]

The Bussys[2] are going to set up a private printing press in France and are, naturally, coming to us for advice. Did I tell you of my visit to Bain the bookseller? I went with a bag of our books. "Mrs Woolf, he said, so long as you print things yourself I can guarantee you an immediate sale and high prices; but when you have books printed for you, its a very different matter." "But you see, Mr Bain" I said, "my taste is very bad." "Its not a question of taste, Madam," he replied; "Its the personal touch." Still, what a mercy it is being rid of one's taste! It's not unlike the riddance of God. And I saw the most lovely piece of glass today—all volutes and spirals, gold-sprinkled and iridescent. Monk's House will be perhaps the ugliest house in Sussex—not plain ugliness, either, but cultured ugliness, which is worse. By the way, when is [E. M.] Forster coming to you? He wants to combine it with a visit to us— but seemed vague as to the date you'd settled. We come down on the 29th— thank God.

I hear you're having Adrian—not Karin? Don't dissuade him from being a doctor. Leonard played Bridge there last night and saw something of such girth and grossness on a chair that he cried out in horror: it was Karin's leg.

Your

Berg   B.

1069: TO JANET CASE   *Hogarth House, Richmond*

Wednesday [23 July 1919]

My dear Janet,

I was dreaming about you so vividly last night, that I must write and find out whether this means that you were thinking with kindness of me. I'm afraid not. In my dream you were entertaining a Princess, and you wouldn't look at me—whereupon I flew into a rage, and turned to Emphie [Janet's sister] for comfort, and she was immensely grand, and made me feel myself so much in the way that I marched down the garden and out into the road, and left you bowing over the hand of your Princess. What can it all mean?

1. 'Cocaine' was a painting by Alfred Priest of a young man, drugged, with his head on a woman's knee. The 'marine piece' was 'The Wonders of the Deep' by John R. Reid.
2. Simon Bussy, the painter, and his wife Dorothy, a sister of Lytton Strachey, and author of *Olivia* (1949). They lived only half the year in France.

Anyhow, it is time I heard something about you. I suppose you've now made a good many friends in the neighbourhood. Small children come and see you in the evening. There is an old lady who brings her sewing. In the intervals I daresay you read Meredith or somebody. Still this is rather a fancy scene on my part, for I don't know anything about the Old Cot. Did Leonard tell you how we bought a house in Lewes, and then saw one we liked better at Rodmell, and so bought that, and have now sold the first house, and have only 3 cottages in Cornwall, and Asheham, and the house at Rodmell and Hogarth House to live in? We shall move in September; and then our address will be Monk's House, Rodmell: rather a good address; and the house is an ancient Monk's House, with niches for the holy water, and a great fireplace; but the point of it is the garden. I shan't tell you though, for you must come and sit there on the lawn with me, or stroll in the apple orchard, or pick—there are cherries, plums, pears, figs, together with all the vegetables. This is going to be the pride of our hearts; I warn you; and I see already we talk a great deal too much for our friends.

I spent a weekend at Garsington the other day. Its an unfortunate thing that the habit of lying should so dissolve the soul. What Ottoline feels, why she says what she does say, its no good asking oneself now; and after two days of it, the discomfort is considerably worse than mere boredom. There are, of course, visits by night to one's bedroom; and then if one can't come up to the scratch, the poor old creature gets more and more harassed and desperate; her paint runs too, and her powder blows off—I'm afraid the spirit of the Cavendishes[1] won't see her through.

Katherine Murry is going abroad soon, to San Remo I think. I have tea with her, and she looks very ill, though she says she's better. She has written several stories, which we think of printing. Everyone is setting up private presses now. In fact I ought to be dressing at this moment in order to be ready for a French couple [the Bussys] who want to set up a press in France. It's a great bore; I can't speak a word of French; and how to describe printing when one cant even talk about the weather I don't know.

Have you read the poems of a man, who is dead, called Gerard Hopkins?[2] I liked them better than any poetry for ever so long; partly because they're so difficult, but also because instead of writing mere rhythms and sense as most poets do, he makes a very strange jumble; so that what is apparently pure nonsense is at the same time very beautiful, and not nonsense at all. Now this carries out a theory of mine; but the poor man became a Jesuit, and they discouraged him, and he became melancholy and died. I couldn't explain this without quoting however, and now I must go and wash. But you, my

1. Ottoline was the daughter of Arthur Cavendish-Bentinck. Her half-brother succeeded in 1879 to the Dukedom of Portland.
2. Gerard Manley Hopkins (1844-89) never published his poetry during his lifetime. The first edition of the poems, edited by his friend Robert Bridges, appeared in 1918.

dear Janet, needn't wash, and so you might write to me, at Asheham. We go
there on Tuesday. Please say how you are.

Your affate

Sussex V.W.

1070: To Vanessa Bell *Hogarth Hosue, Paradise Road,*
Richmond, Surrey

Tuesday [29 July 1919]

Dearest,

Your catastrophes are appalling; still, if you wish me to believe that a
hair of your infants heads isn't worth chicken poxes innumerable—I dont.
In fact I spend my nights in envy of you. The terrible thing is that I see
Quentin will inspire me with an illicit passion—which he won't return. He
wrote me a most charming letter. Still, I wish you ever had a holiday—poor
old dolphin—whose young peep out from every crevice. I daresay somehow
or other you may be up for Maynards party today. I was amused to hear
from Katherine Murry that Ott: has taken the opportunity to come to town.
It's thought she's going to force her way in, if uninvited. I hope you'll be
there to face her down.

If Julian's school doesn't turn out well, would it be worth while to ask
George Young[1] about his plan? He said he wished you would join. They have
a tutor, and spend 6 months in London, the rest in the country. He said it
worked splendidly, and the boys learnt much more than at school. They
wanted others to join. I could get his address. The eldest boy was 15 I think;
but there was one younger and 2 little girls.

I ought to be packing at the moment. The agent wrote to us about
[farmer] Staceys meadow; but we have already more land than we want. I'm
afraid we shall have to give up the Cornish Cottages, much against my will.
James and Alix are going there for August, on condition they furnish them
with beds. I suppose they'll go there; but I dont feel sanguine about the beds.

That affair is once more composed, and Alix by taking our cottages, has
persuaded James to give up going to Italy. She deserves to win. It's piteous to
see her ladling out silver to him for dinners and operas.

The Bussy's dined here, and Simon said he thought you the most gifted
painter of your set; but then he also said he thought our production of Kew
perfect. So you must choose between them.[2] An American publisher has
asked to bring it out in America. Forster is coming to us on the 22nd
August.

Perhaps we shall meet some time. Do tell me how the parting with

1. Hilton Young's older brother.
2. This refers to Vanessa's criticism of the first edition of *Kew Gardens*.

Mrs B[rereton]. went off, and what fate the poor woman is going to—not that I feel required to take her on as my printer's devil.

Yr
B.

Berg

1071: To Hope Mirrlees

Asheham House, Rodmell,
Lewes, Sussex

July 30th [1919]

Dear Hope,

Would it be possible for you to come here from Friday 8th August till Monday?

Please do if you can. Lewes is our station; but I will send directions later.

I can't promise comfort, since we are done for at present by a village woman; but then theres the downs and books, and—modesty forbids me to go on; but anyhow we shall be very glad to see you. Besides we must discuss the bringing out of your poems.[1]

An early answer would be very kind.

Yours,
Virginia Woolf

Hope Mirrlees

1072: To Violet Dickinson

Asheham, Rodmell,
Lewes, [Sussex]

[11? August 1919]

My Violet

You were black-hearted not to come to dinner; but perhaps in the winter—

We've gone and bought a house down here, with a garden full of cabbages and roses, and we have to move in next week, or the week after. And we still have 3 cottages in Cornwall. Perhaps one of these days you might step out of your motor at our door. Leonard's passion will be such for his garden that I foresee that even the Hogarth Press may be neglected. We are blossoming out as printers, and manuscripts shower upon us. In fact we think of starting an agent to do the business for us.

We had a picnic with Nessa and her family yesterday. She is coming to London in September to live in a flat and send Julian to school. The governess failed to manage him, and the difficulty of a winter in the country is beyond belief.

1. The Hogarth Press published Mirrlees' *Paris* in 1920, although it carries a 1919 imprint.

If you should be writing a poem, or something very choice in prose, please remember us—which indeed you might do anyway.

Leonard sends his love

Yr

Sp.

Berg

1073: To Katherine Arnold-Forster   *Asheham, Rodmell,*
Lewes, [Sussex]

Aug. 12th [1919]

Dearest Ka,

It was pleasant and encouraging to see your hand again—though if you think I shall forget you, I can never forget the tea at Buzzard, the ice, the cakes, and the young lady who suddenly rose and began making polite conversation. Now however I must very rapidly put you on the track of our fortunes. You are much behind the times.

We came down last month to look at the Round House; on the way up from the station saw a notice of an old house to sell at Rodmell; went and bought it at auction for £700; sold the Round House for £20 more than we gave for it, and now in 10 days or so Mr Gunn is going to move us in the farm waggons across the Bridge to Monk's House. That will be our address for ever and ever; Indeed I've already marked out our graves in the yard which joins our meadow. But one's friends can't be asked to imagine any more houses; so I dont go into the question of Monks House. Meanwhile we have our three cottages in Cornwall inhabited now by Alix and James on condition they leave us a bed or two, which the cynical say they won't do. The brilliant, if wild, idea has come into my head, that we might arrange to share the three with you and Will. One of them has a tower and great windows. There are 7 rooms in all: and in the best country in all Cornwall to my thinking, between St Ives and Gurnards Head, a mile from Zennor. Rent is £15 a year, £16 with rates. Monk's House makes it a little difficult to keep them, and yet I should feel desolated to let them go again.

Of course, literature is the only spiritual and humane career. Even painting tends to dumbness, and music turns people erotic, whereas the more you write the nicer you become. Do write the Life of somebody—a vast fat book, running over into the margins with reflections and cogitations of all kinds. Do my dear Bruin—I assure you your style is perfectly fitted to some rich thick compound, infinitely humane and judicious, not of course to be run off in a hurry. But in the long winter evenings you might fill page upon page.

Katherine Murry is, poor woman, very ill; she has been all the winter, and gets no better. Probably she will go to San Remo; but I feel rather dismal about her. You thought her too painted and posed for your more spartan taste I think. But she is all kinds of interesting things underneath, and has a passion for writing, so that we hold religious meetings together praising Shakespeare. I dont much care for Murry's poems though. As for Sydney [Waterlow] his good opinion is much in his favour; but alas—his literary judgement has always reminded me of an elephant in a tea cup—His blunders are monstrous there as I suppose they are in office. He's taking Nessa's flat, at once, I think, until he can get a house, Dawks [Margery Waterlow] remaining for ever interred.

Clive, Duncan, Maynard are all over the place, Nessa presiding over the usual hurly burly, and on Sunday we had Hope Mirrlees, a capricious young woman, but rather an exquisite apparition, scented, powdered, dressing for dinner, and very highly cultivated. My cheeks are burning with the sun; they burn all night. You say you're going to be in London for a day or two—couldn't you come here for a night? Saturday 23rd? Sunday? Let me know.

Yr
V.W.

Mark Arnold-Forster

1074: To Vanessa Bell   *Asheham, [Rodmell, Sussex]*

Sunday [17 August 1919]

Dearest,

Here is Quentins present. Would you give it him on his birthday.[1] Wont they come and spend a day with us before they go? We should like it very much—Would they come to lunch, and go back after tea? Of course it would be very nice if you'd come too, but if you can't, I daresay we could arrange for Nelly to meet them and take them part of the way back. Tuesday and Friday this week don't do—but any other days.

[E. M.] Forster and Pernel[2] come next week end. We get possession of Monks House tomorrow. I bought 3 pictures![3]

Yr
B.

Berg

1. Quentin was 9 on 19 August. Julian was now 11.
2. Pernel Strachey, Lytton's older sister, a tutor in modern languages at Newnham College, Cambridge, and afterwards Principal (1923-41).
3. All three are still in Monk's House.

1075: To Margaret Llewelyn Davies   *Asheham, Rodmell,*
                                       Lewes, [Sussex]

Aug. 17th [1919]

Dearest Margaret,

The difficulty of getting writing paper is such, as you will perhaps see, that it is only upon occasions of great stress that I can manage to write a letter. However, if you send such lovely things, one really must. At first I thought that it was a tribute to Leonard from some native whom he had freed from the British rule: but it seems to have a much odder history. How did it come to Walberswick? Don't tell me that its the product of one of those little artistic cottages which used to annoy us so[1]—I dont want to credit the artists of Walberswick with any decent feelings. You will gather that I've insisted upon taking it for myself—in fact its on the back of my chair as I write.

I wish I had your generous impulses. Then I might give you in return one of the three pictures which I bought at the sale of the Monk's House furniture the other day. They're the work of an early Victorian blacksmith, and sold for 4/- the three. For myself, I dont ask anything more of pictures. They are family groups, and he began the heads very large, and hadn't got room for the hands and legs, so these dwindle off till they're about the size of sparrows claws, but the effect is superb—the character overwhelming.[2] You must come and see them. Indeed, there's a very great scope for you at Monks House. A lawn, an orchard, an old granary, and two outhouses. My idea is to sit at my window and have my friends dotted about on the estate. I should like to see you and Beatrice and Sidney [Webb] and Mrs [G. D. H.] Cole and Janet [Case] and Lilian [Harris] and others of a more frivolous variety dissolving and combining in patterns in the distance. But you must really come alone and sit in the middle of the fireplace, with Leonard in one inglenook, and me in the other; its time we had a good gossip. The summer is rather cut up by our move. We actually possess Monks House tomorrow, but we have to wait for the farm carts to take us over, and it may be next week, or the week after.

Last weekend, however, we had a young lady [Hope Mirrlees] who changed her dress every night for dinner—which Leonard and I cooked, the servants being on holiday. Her stockings matched a wreath in her hair; every night they were differently coloured; powder fell about in flakes; and the scent was such we had to sit in the garden. Moreover, she knows Greek and

1. Virginia and Leonard had stayed at the Bell Hotel, Walberswick, Suffolk, during their engagement, in June 1912.
2. Monk's House had been owned by the Glazebrook family 1796-1877. They were millers, and the most interesting of the three pictures was of four Glazebrook children in about 1850.

Russian better than I do French; is Jane Harrison's[1] favourite pupil, and has written a very obscure, indecent, and brilliant poem [*Paris*], which we are going to print. Its a shame that all this should be possible to the younger generation; still I feel that *something* must be lacking, don't you? We had Maynard Keynes to entertain her, since we could offer little in the way of comfort. He is thoroughly disillusioned about Governments and bigwigs, and only goes to the Asquiths because he wins £40 in a weekend, and Margot flings her arms round his neck and sobs. The poor woman had lost £80 at Bridge; so she has her troubles like the rest of us.

We have both just finished correcting the proofs of our books[2]; and we both feel (this is a little in the style of the Webbs) so old and conceited and indifferent that neither praise nor blame nor anything seems to matter. I suppose it does, when it comes to the point; I suppose this is only a refinement of vanity. Still, nobodies books seem to matter very much. I've got to read the whole of George Eliot, the whole of Hardy, and a good deal of Henry James in order to write articles about them.[3] Its rather humiliating, reading other peoples novels. George Eliot fascinates me. Did your father know her? or was she too much under a cloud? Nobody called on her, so she says; and yet her virtue seems to me excessive—but there's no room left. Love to Lilian.

Yr.
V.W.

Sussex

1076: TO ROGER FRY

Asheham, Lewes,
[*Sussex*]

Aug. 17th [1919]

My dear Roger,

I enjoyed immensely finding my name in your article.[4] Also I thought your translation, what you call a parody, most charming. Why don't you do some more? Do, and let us print them—or, for I know that prospect doesn't entice you as much as it ought—let Madley print them. If it didn't

1. Lecturer in classical archaeology at Newnham College, Cambridge, until 1922. Harrison and Mirrlees shared a flat in Paris, and collaborated on two scholarly books. She died in 1928 at the age of 77.
2. Virginia's *Night and Day*, and Leonard's *Empire and Commerce in Africa.* Leonard's book was written for the Fabian Society, and made him one of the leading Fabian authorities on international affairs.
3. The article on George Eliot appeared in the *TLS* on 20 November 1919, but she did not write on Hardy and James until later.
4. In the *Athenaeum* of 8 August Roger Fry had reviewed an exhibition of modern French art at the Mansard Gallery, and claimed that the pictures by Survage were a parody in paint of Virginia's prose style.

look like soliciting more compliments, I would go on to say how much I enjoy reading your articles. Are you getting on with your book?[1] But when I think of Portsmouth[2] (I am on Christian names terms with him) and the baptismal rite, I see your first duty is to commemorate the Frys.

Shall we ever see you? I hear vaguely that you're at Cambridge, leading all the old mammies a fair dance I suppose. We are hovering on the verge of our move to Rodmell, so that I don't know how long we shall be here. Its all a great bore, and very melancholy to give up this place. Nothing will ever be like it; and Gunn is going to have every room painted, damn his soul! I shall haunt his wife and no doubt blast his first born.

Its very nice here this August—I hope you'll come to Charleston anyhow, and set everyone chattering with your discoveries. I have just bought 3 pictures. The work of an early Victorian blacksmith who painted against the discouragement of his family. I think them all one wants in the way of painting, but Nessa has left me no illusions about taste. And I must say I like knowing that for a fact!

Yr V.W.

Sussex

1077: To Vanessa Bell   *Asheham, [Rodmell, Sussex]*

Friday [29 August 1919]

Dearest,
Many thanks for the cheque. Leonard quite agrees with you that I shall be merely in the way during the move.[3] I, on the other hand, think myself indispensable. I don't see how they could manage without me. But I am very grateful for the offer. Perhaps I might come over one day later in my shay, if you have any horse accomodation at Charleston.

The move begins on Monday; we are already strewn with old boxes full of the most interesting letters—yours and Madges [Vaughan] and Walter Lambs, and I see a very tart one from Maynard about my arrangements at Brunswick Square. We shall be in by Wednesday; but I'm afraid I shant be able to ask Lytton to stay, as the servants will be distracted, and I suppose, giving notice. Tell him I'm much disappointed.

When will you come over and see Monks? If you took train to Lewes my shay would meet you and bring you out; and then take you back. I shall be doing a good deal of brush work on the house, but without any false shame.

1. *Vision and Design* (1920), a collection of his articles published previously in the *Burlington Magazine* and other journals.
2. After a brilliant youth, Portsmouth Fry, Roger's brother, contracted an illness which made him a life-long invalid.
3. From Asheham to Monk's House on 1 September.

Every one felt that Mrs Dolphin [Vanessa] was the soul of the party the other night. Morgan said he was going to tell you that he thought you beautiful and charming, but he might be too shy. What struck me most was the farewell—every one feeling a little sentimental about Asheham—old mother Bell hurrying about the Terrace looking for her Badmington set. "Its no good being sentimental on these occasions. Now Leonard, wasn't there a bit of old carpet—?" Immortal woman!

Yr

B

Berg

1078: To Vanessa Bell   *Monk's House, Rodmell,*
                                         [Sussex]
Sunday [7 September 1919]

Dearest,
        We are now more or less settled. Of course, my necklace broke the first thing, but I think necklaces always do on getting into a new house.
        When do you go to London? I will try and come over one day before; unless you and Duncan or Clive would come here.
        I've not yet found out about a shay, but there seem to be several. However it is extremely easy to get into Lewes.
        There's great scope for distemper here, and a niche in the wall where I want to stand a statue. My great family piece looks very handsome. We spend all our time picking apples and pears which we sell in the village. It is a great squeeze after Asheham and we have to use the loft as an E. C. [earth closet].
        How are the children getting on in Scotland?[1]

Yr

B.

We have 2 spare rooms so do come for the night if you can.

Berg

1079: To Vanessa Bell   *Monk's House, Rodmell,*
                                         [Sussex]
Tuesday [9 September 1919]

Dearest,
        If I can I will come over to lunch on Friday and spend the afternoon. I shall take the train to Glynde.
        We have had one domestic crisis after another (Nelly asked me not to

1. Julian and Quentin were staying with their Bell grandparents, at Invergarry near Inverness.

387

tell you, but she says she told you herself) however, they have now gone to the extreme of good spirits, which I suppose may last a day or two. Otherwise, we begin before breakfast with lamentations, boxes are packed about eleven o'clock, and the general reconciliation takes place at 12 precisely.

Nelly however has been angelic—its only that wild ass Lotty. But I sometimes think domestic life is hardly worth while.

I wish you could have come here. This place has great charms—

Yr

Berg   B.

1080: To Leonard Woolf   [*Monk's House, Rodmell, Sussex*]

Thursday afternoon [11 September 1919]

Dearest M[ongoose],

So far everything has gone very well. I had Dean [builder] down to to see the kitchen and he said he was certain that the damp comes from nothing but the tank and the gutters and can easily be stopped. He is coming first thing tomorrow to do it—and it wont take long. A new gutter is going to be put across; the tube from the tank lengthened, and the grating scraped. Mr Verrall[1] did his own jobs, and never had things properly seen to. The servants are laughing and joking in spite of a thick sea mist. I'm going now to look for mushrooms.

The papers came 5 minutes after you'd left. Dedman[2] has been picking pears. Dean said he had never heard of the kitchen or any other room being damp. Nelly is sure that it will now be all right. Dean said the cupboards could all be moved into the kitchen, but I said I would let him know later. I worked very well this morning, and in spite of everything I think this place is divine. It will be a joy to see Master tomorrow. The furry little beasts send their love.

M[andril].

Sussex

1081: To Saxon Sydney-Turner   *Monk's House, Rodmell, Lewes, [Sussex]*

Sept. 12th [1919]

My dear Saxon,

It is high time you wrote to me, but I know your perverse and secretive nature too well to expect any such thing. You see the move's accomplished, but what you can not see is the extreme horror of the whole process. One

1. Jacob Verrall had owned Monk's House from 1877 until his death in 1918.
2. Mr and Mrs Dedman lived in the neighbouring cottage, and occasionally worked for the Woolfs.

gets one's furniture in, but as for living in it—Then the kitchen was flooded the first night; the servants had hysterics; they packed their boxes. Leonard dismissed them both. I pacified them. Peace was restored. The rain came down again. So we went on the first week. Meanwhile to have left Asheham was bad enough. I can't altogether get over that, though Leonard infinitely prefers this, chiefly on account of the garden, which pours pears and plums and apples and vegetables upon us. I can't ask you to come and stay; and you certainly would refuse to; because the kitchen is in process of being disembowelled. What I like best is the water meadow onto which our garden opens. You see every down all the way round you. Then there's a nice walk to a deserted farm in the Telscombe downs, where the rats collect round you, and merely sit and think about you. But one of these days we will take a walk together.

Nessa and Duncan came over yesterday, and I'm bicycling to Charleston today. When its fine like this, I can't believe its ever going to change, can you? There seems no reason why weather shouldn't be fine weather. I have almost forgotten how to read; of course, I can spell words out, but I can't remember how one goes on page after page. The mechanism of the brain is very amazing to my mind; a move like this is utter destruction. Even having a different shaped room to sit in almost destroys me. But I've rambled very painfully over the diaries of Wilfrid Blunt, and through some of George Eliot, and a little bit of Sir Thomas Browne, and I see that I want to read some Plato. But this sounds very industrious, which is a complete lie. I dont like aristocrats when they write. I have a great prejudice against Blunt, though he hates the British Empire; but then he reads his poems to Mrs Asquith, and they have parties where they make speeches, and they're all so rich and distinguished, and their writing is so much admired, and it is so pretty and smart compared with middle class writing. But I have no room to develop this very important argument. All I want is a long letter from you. I don't even know where you are—Hampstead or Ormond Street. Is there any good music to hear? About this time of the year I become ravenous for music.

Your affate

Sussex   V.W.

1082: To Lytton Strachey   *Monk's House, Rodmell,*
                                          Lewes, [Sussex]
Sunday 14th [September 1919]

Dearest Lytton,

I wish we had been able to see you; but we were in our agony when you were at Charleston. Things aren't much better yet, owing to domestic horrors, it now looks as if the kitchen would have to be rebuilt. What can one do with a sweating floor? However, there are charms in this place, though very humble and unromantic compared with Asheham. I like the morning sun in one's window, though, and the youth of the village nightly play cricket outside the garden wall, which would recommend itself to you.

What are you doing? Polishing Old Victoria?[1] Legends of your high flyings pass across our horizon now and then. I'm not really anxious. Maynard seems much the same as ever only more and more genial, and, superficially, kind! I suppose the danger lies in becoming too kind. I think you're a little inclined that way already—take the case of Ottoline. It seems to me a dark one. Still, kindness don't flourish in our corner of Sussex. I spent the day at Charleston yesterday, and came away feeling purged, bruised, scraped and raw, but morally regenerated. I've no news whatever to give you. About 10 days ago I had a letter from Nick Bagenal. They seem all right. I rather hope I may get one from Saxon. The effect of a move upon the intellects and morals is utterly destructive. Moreover Leonard has become what I daresay is called garden proud. We can't resist going out to look at pears, and then the potatoes have to be weighed. I suppose you couldn't guess what they weigh. We are very charitable too, and when they want sprays for funerals they come and ask us. Altogether, I find it very hard to settle to my book, which is, at this moment, the complete works of George Eliot. But you have never read them. I wish you had, because then perhaps you would explain the whole puzzle. At anyrate you might write me a letter, which is the sole object of this one. I read Wilfrid Blunt (diaries) at breakfast; I don't like aristocratic writing, do you? I don't like the Souls[2]; I don't like George Wyndham; Heaven knows what one does like, though, on the whole, what I like is first going a walk; then having tea; then sitting and imagining all the pleasant things that might happen to one. I should like to be asked to Tidmarsh for a week end in October. But you will be in Spain, perhaps.

Leonard sends his love—in all sincerity.

Frances Hooper

Yr.
V.W.

1083: TO CLIVE BELL   *Monk's House, [Rodmell, Sussex]*

Wednesday [24 September 1919]

My dear Clive,

Will you come on Sunday or Monday for the night? Come over for

1. *Queen Victoria* (1921).
2. The 'Souls' were young aristocrats with intellectual interests, who formed a group of friends in the 1890's and 1900's. They included the Tennant sisters, George Curzon, A. J. Balfour, Alfred Lyttelton, the poet Wilfrid Blunt and George Wyndham, the statesman and man of letters.

tea, and seek us at the very bottom of the village street. At this moment Leonard is tortured with eczema, but I hope by then the disease may have gone, and I have to review Hope Mirrlees,[1] which is even worse, as every word will be picked over. It's all sapphism so far as I've got—Jane [Harrison] and herself.

Yr.
V.W.

Quentin Bell

1084: To Katherine Arnold-Forster
Hogarth [*House, Richmond*]

Thursday [9 October 1919]

My dear Bruin,

It was charming to hear from you. After many wanderings, your letter dropped into the box as we got home. We did our best to keep the [railway] strike going in our neighbourhood, and doled out potatoes to the signalman at dusk, but it was all very heroic of us. One's household doesn't like a strike; the servants' point of view is that the lower classes should be kept down.

But this is all moonshine compared with your news. Haven't I always said that I could practically see the shapes of little Bruins[2] attached to your neck? It will be a superb nursery—the old mother bear occasionally rolling over to give her cubs a lick, and everything smelling so nice of milk and straw. But I can't pretend that I'm not envious. Well, well—I think all good mothers ought to consider me half their child, which is what I really like best.

London is, so they say, in an intellectual ferment. Maynard was speaking last night, but instead of going to hear him, we snuggled over a fire and read our books. I've got to write articles without end. I'm very highly thought of —as a reviewer. Did you ever read George Eliot? Whatever one may say about the Victorians, there's no doubt they had twice our—not exactly brains—perhaps hearts. I don't know quite what it is; but I'm a good deal impressed.

Turning, however, to the immediate present, I see that *Night and Day* will be out shortly. Gerald Duckworth lost the last chapter, so I daresay it will be November instead of October. I don't feel nervous; nobody cares a hang what one writes, and novels are such clumsy and half extinct monsters at the best; but, oh dear, what a bore it will be! All one's friends thinking they've got to say something; old Bob Trevelyan hustling up, and saying, of course, the wrong thing; and when people praise me, I never know how to

1. Review of *Madeleine, One of Love's Jansenists* (*TLS*, 9 October 1919).
2. Mark Arnold-Forster was born in April 1920.

answer; and if they don't praise me, that's not exhilarating either. Leonard is completely callous. His book may be out any day too.[1]

But I hope we shall meet before any of the books are out. I want to discuss Cornwall. I should be very glad if we could make some arrangement, for though Monk's House has its charms, it has also a great many drawbacks. We shall have to alter it considerably, I'm afraid. Still, I find that a sunny house is incredibly cheering. Asheham was gradually rotting all our books, and I never realised how little one got either sun or air (you see I'm very cleverly making the best of things).

I don't suppose this will reach you.

Ring me up; it's my turn to give Bruin an *enormous* tea.

Yrs.
V.W.

Mark Arnold-Forster

1085: TO VIOLET DICKINSON   *Hogarth House, Paradise Road,*
                              Richmond, Surrey

Tuesday [21 October 1919]

My Violet,

How delightful of you *not* to want to be reviewed—I'm so pestered by people who *do* want it.

As a matter of fact, I'd just written to Bruce Richmond to ask him to let me do it. I daresay he won't,[2] as he knows I'm a friend. But I do want to do it, and I shall be honest, candid, brutal, unpleasant as possible. I've always admired your literary gifts, though. (If you'd rather I didn't review the book, I'll send it back, of course)

Do come and see us. Would you dine one night—but I'll write and settle a day later, as this week seems full.

I'm asking Gerald to send you a copy of my new novel; but its sent solely as a token of ancient affection and gratitude and you needn't mention it. The matter may drop.

L. sends his love. We're in the middle of taking proofs of a poem [Hope Mirrlees' *Paris*] in the very latest style. By the way, would you send me Bob Nichols[3] address? I'm told he might like to send us something.

Yr
V.W.

Berg

1. *Empire and Commerce in Africa: A Study in Economic Imperialism* was published early in 1920.
2. Virginia did review Violet's book, *Miss Eden's Letters* (*TLS*, 6 November 1919).
3. Robert Malise Bowyer Nichols, whose books of poems included *Invocation* (1915) and *Ardours and Endurances* (1917).

Monday [27 October 1919]

Dearest,

Of course you always know more about writing than anyone else.[1] I was immensely pleased by your letter, and I think I'd rather please you than anyone, if only because I feel that its all your doing if I have any wits at all. Where should I have been if it hadn't been for you, when Hyde Park Gate was at its worst? You must admit the Apes were a fair handful in those days. I'm longing to hear what else you think, when you come to the end—if you ever do. I'm a little surprised that it gives you the horrors. When I was writing it, I didn't think it was much like our particular Hell—but one never knows.

Yours and Clives are the only letters I've had, so I suppose most of my friends find it rather tough. But I'm amazingly callous, and I'm quite content with my dear Dolphin's good opinion—Especially as she says it will take a practical form. Of course, I should like a picture above all things: but, as a matter of fact, I was thinking of asking you to do a small job for me—to paint the Greek vase I brought from Corinth (in 1906). Could you? Its a kind of terra cotta.

How infernal about Budge [Nelly Boxall's sister]! Its all Bert's doing apparently; he seems to be most disagreeable; and after advising her to go, turned round and refused to keep the baby. I'm afraid its useless to suggest anything else to her—at least Nelly seems to think so.

Shall I go to the Registry here? I feel, though, that I have a fatal effect upon your domestics.

Shall I come and see you on Friday? I might be able to come to tea or supper. I suppose you weren't thinking of going to the Russian dancers? I want to, but they're so expensive.

We're threatened with a visit from Sydney [Waterlow], who now thinks himself the greatest man in England, and I want to be out.

Ka came here the other day—very model and maternal, and tremendously well pleased with herself. She will go on saying how mad and wild Will is, and I feel he must really be as mild as a Guinea pig—a neurotic Guinea pig. He is painting hard—I wish Ka wasn't always so damned condescending. She couldn't write Night and Day if she tried.

Shall I get a notice of the London Group [of painters]? I want to go very much, and perhaps I might write an account of it, but I understand that you'd rather I didn't. I meant to send you my stories,[2] but I've had such a rush of reviews to do, I've had no time to copy them.

1. On 21 October Virginia had sent Vanessa an advance copy of *Night and Day*.
2. Some of the stories which were published in *Monday or Tuesday* (1921) by the Hogarth Press. Besides the title story, these included: *A Haunted House; A Society; An Unwritten Novel; The String Quartet; Blue and Green; Kew Gardens;* and a revised version of *The Mark on the Wall*.

I'll ring you up and ask about Friday later.

O how I adore you!

B.

The dedication [to *Night and Day*]¹ was, you know perfectly well if you weren't so deceitful, meant every word—in fact there would have been a good many more if I hadn't been afraid of being thought sentimental; and I meant to write my dear Duncan's name with yours (in ink) but again said he wd. prefer not. however my sentiments are such

Berg

1087: To LYTTON STRACHEY   Hogarth [House], Richmond

Oct. 28th [1919]

Ah, how delightful to be praised by you! I tell myself that of course you're always too generous about me, and one ought to discount it, but I can't bring myself to. I enjoy every word. I don't suppose there's anything in the way of praise that means more to me than yours. There are myriads of things I want to ask you; about the male characters for instance. Do they convince? Then was Rodney's change of heart sufficiently prepared for to be credible? It came into my head on the spur of the moment that he was in love with Cassandra, and afterwards it seemed a little violent. I take your point about the tupping² and had meant to introduce a little in that line, but somehow it seemed out of the picture—still, I regret it. Never mind; I've an idea for a story where all the characters do nothing else—but they're all quadrupeds! However, as I'm afflicted with rheumatism, this had better wait, I only wanted to say how happy your letter had made me,—dialogue was what I was after in this book—so I'm very glad you hit on that; I mean it was one of the things—there are so many million others!—but I can't help thinking it's the problem, if one is to write novels at all, which is a moot point.

Tell Carrington I went into the question of the roses with some care, and will write to her on the subject. It's not as simple as it sounds. Was it stated in the book [*Night and Day*] that Elizabeth Datchet took a first prize for them the year before? She did however and so—but I can't go into all this at length.

1. "To Vanessa Bell
   but, looking for a phrase,
   I found none to stand beside your name."
2. "An old black ram
   Is tupping your white ewe" (*Othello*, I, i, 88).

394

We should like immensely to come on the 8th—and why ask anyone? Don't for our sakes. We shall be quite content with the two natives.

Your
Virginia

There's an amusing book just come out—Miss Eden's letters, Edited by Violet Dickinson.

Frances Hooper

1088: To Clive Bell   *Hogarth [House, Richmond]*

Thursday [30 October 1919]

My dear Clive,

It was a great pleasure to get your letter. I'm sure you're too enthusiastic; at the same time I dont think its ever been easy to take you in. I think I may enjoy about half your praises; of course, if I gave my mind to it, I could pick any number of holes in Night and Day. For instance—but lots of people are sure to do it for me.

Besides I've no time to write this evening, expecting Ka to dine any moment; but I said to myself I must write and thank my brother in law, who after all, always did believe in me, and made a great deal more difference than perhaps he thinks to that exacting and troublesome, but not cold-hearted woman Virginia.

Quentin Bell

1089: To Roger Fry   *Hogarth [House], Richmond*

Nov. 2nd [1919]

My dear Roger,

It was delightful to see your writing. Once you got to France, I looked upon you as lost—inapproachable and certainly not making the approach. So when my book came out (this great event happened 2 weeks ago) I sent it to Dalmeny,[1] not daring to send a large, old fashioned, high minded English novel to Roger in the South of France. If it ever reaches you, please tell me what you think of it; if not, you can think of a tribute of sincere devotion lying upon the hall table in Camden town. O how I want now to write

1. 7 Dalmeny Avenue, Camden Town, where Roger now lived with his sister Margery.

nothing longer than 10 pages for ever! Does Proust[1] come out of it well? Ah, but then he writes French. Please bring him back for me to read.

Perhaps you never will come back though. There is not much to offer you in the way of entertainment. I have my private sources of pleasure of course—an afternoon concert at Shelley House (the St John Hornby's), a meeting of the Women's Cooperative Guild, a tea at the 1917 Club. But you never enter entirely into the romance and splendour of middle class life. It may be fancy, but the whole neighbourhood of Fitzroy Square sounds a little dull and hollow, when that enormous vibration—your presence—is removed.[2] You know one can hear it a mile off. I was conscious of this when I went to the private view at Heals the other day. I will say nothing of the pictures which were almost obscured by Jack Hutchinson and cut in slices by Ethel Sands[3]; but the atmosphere seemed to me detestable. Imagine a November fog, and everyone got up to a certain point of eccentricity, and not knowing what to say, and probably feeling nothing, and trailing round in the semi-dusk. I went on to tea with Vanessa; which is always an adventure, even if she spends the whole time with an electrician in the passage. The earth has got into the main at Regents Square: all light therefore cut off. So there we sat with one candle for which I've no doubt you could have improvised a candlestick, but we're not much good at that. Then, Madame Champcommunal[4] came in, and in ten minutes we had arranged to share my Cornish cottages together. Is this rash? I was so struck by her mastery over furniture that I have given it all into her hands. But God knows what she's like—handsome, unhappy, hard and discontented? Anyhow, we shall never meet, and I have a kind of hunger for someone not Carrington, Barbara, or Alix, so far as looks are concerned at any rate.

Mrs Colefax[5]—this is the first fruits of Night and Day—has intimated through Logan her willingness to receive me; to which I have replied that I have no clothes. It is now her part to provide them; but so far she continues to think the matter over.

I've been reading one book you'd like—George Moore, Avowals[6]— partly memories, partly criticism and very amusing though when I said in a review that I felt strong affection for him, the Times went and cut it out. Otherwise, I'm sunk in George Eliot, who was born a hundred years ago—

1. By this time two volumes of Marcel Proust's *A la Recherche du Temps Perdu* had been published, the first in 1913. The second, *A l'Ombre des Jeunes Filles en Fleurs*, was published in 1918, and received the Prix Goncourt in 1919.
2. In June Roger Fry had closed down the Omega Workshops.
3. St John Hutchinson was a very large man; Ethel Sands, rake-thin.
4. Elspeth Champcommunal, the widow of the French painter who was killed in the war, and a friend of Roger Fry.
5. Sybil Colefax, later Lady Colefax, had already made her house, Argyll House, a centre for political and cultural society.
6. Review of *Avowals* (*TLS*, 30 October 1919).

I daresay a very ugly baby. But you see how I'm giving you the feel of England? which I must at once stop doing in order to catch a train, in a drizzle, to go to the London Library.

Do write again. I think you owe it to us.

Yr.
V.W.

Sussex

1090: TO VIOLET DICKINSON   *Hogarth* [*House, Richmond*]

Tuesday [4 November 1919]

My Violet,

I've just read your Aunt's letters [Emily Eden] with great joy. I think its one of the best collections for ever so long. But why not more from your own pen? Surely, the style is identical with hers. I was kept happy for hours with them, and only wished they'd go on and on and on. Are there no more? I've written a review, but had to keep it so short that I couldn't say half I wanted to.

Lytton Strachey has just written to me to say that he's reading them too, and finds them far superior to anything of the present day. He had read some years ago in Lord Clarendon's life, and always hoped for more. Also, he finds that he's your cousin—through the Colviles.[1] But this is to ask whether you will dine here next Wednesday, 12th, at 7.30? I think Nessa is coming.

Please do—in your natural coat. Train from Baker St to Hammersmith and there change; or from Baker St to Waterloo; the trains from Waterloo go at all the 8s—7.8—7.18—7.28—etc. every 10 minutes.

Yr
V.W.

Berg

1091: TO VIOLET DICKINSON   *Hogarth* [*House, Richmond*]

[11 November 1919]

My Violet,

Nessa has just put me off; and wants me to try and get you to come on Wednesday week, 19th, instead of this Wednesday.

That would suit us equally well; but if it doesn't suit you, please come next Wednesday as we had arranged; and we will get Nessa another time.

We shall be alone, but all the same, we will try to make up by our

1. Lytton's mother was a sister of Lady Colvile, who was a niece, by marriage, of Miss Eden.

pleasure in seeing you—Would you send me a line. Nessa is a d—d old wretch.

Yr
V.W.

Berg

1092: To Janet Case   [*Hogarth House, Richmond*]

Tuesday [11 November 1919]

My dear Janet,

Thank you very much for your letter. I should like to come and see you, but I don't know when to suggest—this week being full, and next destroyed, I'm afraid, by going away for two nights in the middle—But I expect, as usual, you have too many visitors. I will write later, in case you have a free day.

I rather hope you won't take the cottage in Suffolk—its an awful way off, though the country has a peculiar charm I think. I detest most of Surrey, but this may be prejudice. The difficulty is, I suppose, to get anything anywhere—unless you follow our plan of buying at sight. We now have to decide whether to buy this house and the next door house or be turned out.[1]

I don't know anything about Miss Stella Benson[2]—A.B. is, I'm fairly sure, Augustine Birrell—articles about books in the Nation, aren't they—Violet Dickinson has brought out a book of Miss Eden's letters which I think very amusing.

Yours aff.
V.W.

Sussex

1093: To Lady Ottoline Morrell

[*Hogarth House, Richmond*]

[mid-November 1919]

Dearest Ottoline

It was very good of you to write, and a great pleasure to me to think of your liking my book. I hoped you would; but one never knows. I tried to get a little more 'beauty' into this one, and risked spoiling the 'originality'. Indeed, Jack Hutchinson, Mary's large red husband, says its an old fashioned domestic work, too dull for words. Now I shall quote Lady Ottoline. But

1. The owner of Suffield and Hogarth House, of which the Woolfs only occupied the left half, gave them notice that the lease would not be renewed. They decided to buy both halves, and did so in December 1919 for £1950.
2. The novelist and traveller. In 1919 she published *Living Alone*.

O dear—what a lot of work goes into a long solid book!—I feel as if I should never write more than three pages again.

We were staying with Lytton last week, all very charming and domestic in the midst of bitter cold; and he says you're coming to London, but I begin to doubt that you ever will, and it is at the moment more repulsive than I can remember. People have grown much more numerous and much uglier. Each time the door at the 1917 Club opens, a fresh deformity enters. I sit in a corner and stare in a kind of trance, as though one had fallen to the bottom of some awful pit in a nightmare. And they're all quite young—the coming generation—which makes it seem worse. In my youth, though crude, we were invariably lovely—and then what passion we threw into existence! Poor Alix sits like a paralysed cat. But I must stop, or I shall forfeit my newly won right to a heart. It was charming of you to write to me.

Your affate.

Texas
V.W.

1094: To Margaret Llewelyn Davies
Sunday [16 November 1919]
Hogarth [*House, Richmond*]

Dearest Margaret,

I was extremely sorry not to see you yesterday, having braced myself for the deed. I managed to miss my train and spent a long time with Lilian, and enjoyed myself very much. She is an exalted character. Then Emphie [Case] came in, and I cant help feeling that though she's as brave as can be, this departure[1] is very melancholy. I hope you'll see your way to make some suggestion about what we all wish. If it was for Janet's sake, surely she would consider it. She talked of living very simply, which sounded ominous.

I dont really feel much difficulty in bearding you, all the same. You have an atmosphere; no doubt about that; but then all incorruptible and dominating characters have; and they suffer for their insight with one eye by being blind with t'other. I think thats the case with me too. We are imperfect human beings, but that's no obstacle to friendship, (on my side) in fact rather an incentive. You'll never like my books, but then shall I ever understand your Guild? Probably not.

As to Night and Day, and our argument, I was pleased to find on the hall table this testimony to my sympathy. I dont know that I agree, or with the other man who says I'm chiefly remarkable for common human wisdom? Massingham[2] in the Nation this week is annoyed and abusive in a way that

1. Janet and Emphie Case were leaving Hampstead in order to economise, and were searching for a place outside London.
2. H. J. Massingham (1888-1952) editor of the *Nation*, regularly contributed articles on literary topics to the *Nation* and the *Athenaeum*.

makes me feel I've done some good. Then there's the man who says I'm Jane Austen (but I'd much rather write about tea parties and snails than be Jane Austen). And a Bishop's wife detects undoubted Xtianity, and an elderly lady writes to tell me that the love scenes make her 'jumpy', but she feels that its, "the forerunner of a new species of book" (very intelligent). You see, its a question of the human heart, and cutting out the rotten parts according to ones convictions. Thats what I want to do, and thats where we differ, and thats why you'll dislike N. and D; and I shan't mind much if you do; but I should mind quite enormously if you didn't like me.

O yes, my dear Margaret, I think we've got a great deal in common; and you might ask me to dinner.

Your affate
Virginia

Sussex

1095: To Janet Case   *Hogarth [House, Richmond]*

[19 November 1919]

My dear Janet,

It seems a long way off, but I think Saturday the 6th, tea, is the best for me.

I shall like very much to discuss my [*Night and Day*] people with you— save that I'm beginning to feel that they're not mine at all. I'm told so many different things about them. But try thinking of Katharine [Hilbery] as Vanessa, not me; and suppose her concealing a passion for painting and forced to go into society by George [Duckworth]—that was the beginning of her; *but* as one goes on, all sorts of things happen. Its the conflict that turns the half of her so chilly; but I daresay this was overdone; and then there's the whole question, which interested me, again too much for the books sake, I daresay, of the things one doesn't say; what effect does that have? and how far do our feelings take their colour from the dive underground? I mean, what is the reality of any feeling?—and all this is further complicated by the form, which must sit tight, and perhaps in Night and Day, sits too tight; as it was too loose in The Voyage Out. And then there's the question of things happening, normally, all the time. But Leonard is typewriting at this table; and someone's coming into dinner, and my niece Angelica who is staying with us has pulled my hair down; so I must stop.

We have not yet bought our house; we're trying, to fill up time, to sell Hyde Park Gate.

Yr.
V.W.

Sussex

1096: To Lady Robert Cecil *Hogarth House, Paradise Road,*
Richmond, Surrey

[late November 1919]

My dear Nelly,
    We shall like very much to lunch with you next Tuesday.
    I dont know what to say about Christianity—perhaps one has it inborn
in one. I expect so. I didn't write on G. E. [George Eliot] in the Times;
but in the Suppt, and I was so much struck by her goodness that I hope it
wasn't my article that you thought hard. She is as easy to read as Tit Bits:
and it was a surprise to me; and magnificent in many ways.

Your affate.

Hatfield   Virginia Woolf

1097: To Lytton Strachey   *Hogarth* [*House, Richmond*]

Wednesday [26 November 1919]

    An American publisher wants to bring out Night and Day and the Voyage
Out—indeed, I can't resist telling you that I've had offers from two[1]—
asked to write for an American paper (don't ask which), asked to write for
the London Mercury, invited to meet Miss Elizabeth Asquith, Lady Russell
['Elizabeth']; and Miss Constance Miles—Still I've not time to go into this
with any fulness.
    But would you be so angelic as to tell me if any special misprints,
obscurities or vulgarities in either occur to you. I have to send the books off
on Monday and they say the more alterations the better—because of copyright. I've just glanced between the boards and see that the whole thing must
be re-written from the beginning—and only 2 days to do it in!
    I never wrote a Collins to say how much I enjoyed Tidmarsh, but I did.[2]

Yr.

V.W.

If you can send any corrections, could you let me have them by Saturday?

Frances Hooper

1098: To Violet Dickinson   *Hogarth* [*House, Richmond*]

Thursday [27 November 1919]

My Violet,
    What a strange miracle! I was wetting my pen to write to you—the

1. Macmillan and George H. Doran.
2. The Woolfs had stayed with Lytton Strachey 8 to 10 November.

postman knocks—servants out—I go to the door—and there's your self in person. One of these days, when the feast with the black cake and Violet in white comfits has taken place, I shall collect your notes! Please see to it at once. "To my dearly beloved niece and intimate Sp:—all my papers without exception" What a book! What a book! It makes my mouth water.

What can I have said to make you believe that praise from anyone, of anything, is other than the breath of life in my nostrils? And who would I rather have praise from than Violet? Wasn't it she who first said that though afflicted with every conceivable vice, crooked in spirit and deformed in nature, still when it came to writing—It was certainly your doing that I ever survived to write at all[1]; and I suppose nothing I could say would give you an idea of what your praise was one night [in 1902]—I can see it—sitting in a long room at Fritham [New Forest], after a walk on the Common: O how excited I was and what a difference you made to me! But I dont suppose you realise how often I think of it, or how grateful I am—not only for praise, gluttonous though I am. Oh no—for being all you were to us. And Greece—and Thoby. Life has had its wonders—

But I wasn't writing to tell you how I put you among them. I was writing to ask you about roses. The Times reviewer says that I can't have roses at Christmas—anyhow not in Lincolnshire. The book is now being published in America, and they want me to alter any mistakes at once. At Kew there are certainly roses at Christmas—the long pink ones. Even on the East Coast wouldn't it be possible for a careful gardener to have enough to fill a small basket?—thats all I said.

Someone else has written to protest; but I'm anxious to keep them, and intend to go by what you say. Only could you let me know at once.

And if at the same time you would write out your views upon Night and Day I should be enchanted; somehow I thought you didn't like my writing, and being so modest, I was anxious not to be told so; and thus shot the book at you, and then ran away.

Leonard sends his love, and we hope to have you to dinner again. You have a fur coat, so you've no excuse for not setting off to the remotest suburbs in a blizzard.

I saw Katie [Cromer] yesterday at a Concert, in the 5/6 seats, wearing a new blue hat, so she survives still; but I hope to live to see her mount the scaffold—after all the only end for that type of beauty. As for Lady Dorothy Nevill,[2] she made me laugh so with her pigeons, guinea pigs, funguses and the rest that I couldn't hurt a hair of her head.

Yr,
V.W.

Berg

1. Violet had looked after Virginia during her madness in 1904.
2. The daughter of Lord Orford, and the friend of Thomas Hardy and Charles Darwin. Virginia reviewed *The Life and Letters of Lady Dorothy Nevill* by Ralph Nevill (*Athenaeum*, 12 December 1919).

27th November 1919

My dear Clive,

I hasten to say that the books were sent off the day after your card arrived.[1] Various forms had to be got and filled in, which may have kept them back another day; but you certainly should have received them by now—indeed days ago (they were sent on the 13th)—and we wish you'd make enquiries. The postage was paid at this end.

However, as this has brought me the pleasure of your letter [about *Night and Day*], how can I complain? Fortunately it arrived on a blue and brilliant morning together with one or two communications of a flattering kind or I should have been outraged. I hope you laid on your colours a little thick. It sounds too good to be true; yet I know you wouldn't deceive your sister in law. Paris a nest of popinjays, and you the brightest of the lot. That, of course, is quite credible; the translators I have learnt to tolerate. But conceive our English society—literary circles are agitated by the news that Thomas Hardy has invited the Mills Whithams to stay with him. She, you know, was Sylvia Milman; he has just produced his 21st imitation of Tess of the D'Urbervilles. Then Ottoline will soon be with us, but she has ransacked Ireland and finds nothing big enough to stick in the teeth of her comb.

But you ask of Night and Day—and even if you hadn't asked—Still its nothing compared with you and Lytton—But did *two* American publishers offer to bring out *both* your books—suggest that you should write for their magazines—and insist upon publishing your portrait? I suppose so, I'm afraid so. But I'm greatly flattered, and have made terms with Messrs. Doran, and I'm now engaged in trying to get [Bruce] Richmond to let me print my articles over there. It's said he won't. The reviews have drawn the Americans I suppose. They've praised me highly for the most part, and wrongly too; in fact, as criticism, they're worthless so far. But the serious sixpennies have still to speak. I couldn't grasp what Katherine meant but thought she disliked the book and wouldn't say so, and so muffed her points.[2] Murry, however, tells me that she admires it, but thinks my 'aloofness' morally wrong. (She's practically cured, by the way, and they think will be completely so). But every day I get letters and they all pick out different points, and no two people seem to agree, and Molly Hamilton says one thing and Molly MacCarthy another—and some say the first chapters are the best, and others say the last, and some say its in the tradition, and others say its not, but the great battle, so Murry tells me, is between those who think it unreal and those who think it real. (What do they mean?) The only person who thinks what I think is, oddly enough, James Strachey.

1. Clive was staying in Paris.
2. Katherine Mansfield had reviewed *Night and Day* in the *Athenaeum*, 21 November 1919.

All this ought to make it sell, but Gerald [Duckworth] remarks that that's out of the question with a 9/- book. Anyhow I'm to meet the Bibesco's, by command, and the Bishop of Exeter's wife wants to know if I'm a Christian—she thinks I am; and Squire begs me to contribute to his slop pail of stale tea [the *London Mercury*]—and as for Ottoline—she's made the plunge this time, and gone in out of her depth, poor woman. I thought she would.

Still, enough of Night and Day. Unfortunately what with the sympathy of my correspondent and the gigantic importance of my theme, there's no paper left. And I wanted to tell you about Idialus Odsfish [*inexplicable*] and heaps of things. I'm in the midst of domestic crisis—both servants leaving; Nessa, however, has surmounted hers, and I see, as at the end of a telescope, a glimpse of an enchanted world, where I turn a handle and hot mutton chops are shot out on a plate—human agencies entirely ignored. This can mean less than nothing to a popinjay.

Gerald Ritchie[1] has gone mad. He races round presenting ladies with melons and abuses his wife. She has had him certified on these grounds. This I had from Molly [MacCarthy] who flaunted in the other day, sleek in sealskins, brave but bankrupt. Desmond expected daily.

Our weekend at Tidmarsh was charming, though a little chastened by the presence of Saxon, who spent 24 hours in looking out trains from Banbury to Bude, and communicating his discoveries at intervals. Barbara was lost at Bath without a Bradshaw, so it's thought. I leave you to make the necessary connections. O yes—I liked your articles on France: and entirely agreed, so far as I am able. Did I say that a reviewer has just written to express gratitude and admiration. What for? Night and Day, of course.

Yr.
V.W.

Quentin Bell

1100: To Lytton Strachey   *Hogarth [House, Richmond]*

Sunday [30 November 1919]

Many thanks for the correction; I have put it in; undoubtedly there are hundreds more, but it can't be helped.

Philip's address is

Greenmoor Hill Farm
Woodcot
Oxon.

Leonard was there yesterday, and found him fearfully dark and dismal,

1. Brother of Sir Richmond Ritchie, who married Thackeray's elder daughter.

and apparently breaking down in health into the bargain.[1] No cook, no food, and half his house pulled down.

O no, I shall never reach your heights. Elizabeth Asquith will be at once the beginning and the end; but I'll write and tell you what passes between us. Gerald Duckworth has entire control of my arrangements [royalties] so I expect nothing. Did you see Massingham's onslaught in the Nation? I wonder why. But I feel it's to my credit, whereas when the Bishop of Exeter's wife says she feels certain I'm a Christian, I'm a good deal depressed. Squire has been put in his place.

I'm in the 2nd vol. of Ethel Smyth.[2] I think she shows up triumphantly, through sheer force of honesty. It's a pity she can't write; for I don't suppose one could read it again. But it fascinates me all the same. I saw her at a concert two days ago—striding up the gangway in coat and skirt and spats and talking at the top of her voice. Near at hand one sees that she's all wrinkled and fallen in, and eyes running blue on to the cheeks; but she keeps up the figure of the nineties to perfection. Of course the book is the soul of the nineties. Did you ever know Sue Lushington? Much the same type. Then Ethel's passion for the W. C. (it occurs in every chapter) is of the highest merit.

We've got to buy 2 more houses [Hogarth and Suffield]; both servants are leaving; and the Int. Review is coming to an end.[3]

Yr.
V.W.

Frances Hooper

1101: To Lady Robert Cecil   *Hogarth House, Richmond*

[1 December 1919]

My dear Nelly,

Leonard has a touch of malaria, and the doctor forbids him to go out for two or three days. He is very much disappointed at not being able to lunch with you tomorrow, but it is, of course, out of the question. He would particularly like to see you and Lord Robert, and hopes that you may ask him another time.

If it would not be inconvenient to you to have me without him, I will

1. Philip Woolf, Leonard's younger brother, who was wounded in the war and remained deeply affected by the death of his brother Cecil. Lytton wished to send him Stephen Graham's *A Private in the Guards*.
2. The composer, author and feminist (1858-1944), who was to become an intimate friend of Virginia in the 1930's. Her autobiography was called *Impressions that Remain* (1919). She later wrote five additional volumes of autobiography.
3. The *International Review*, which Leonard edited, ceased publication for financial reasons after a life of only one year.

come. But perhaps you wouldn't mind ringing me up tomorrow morning to say whether you expect me or not.

Our telephone number is 496 Richmond.

Yours affate,
Virginia Woolf

Hatfield

1102: To Violet Dickinson   *Hogarth House, Richmond*

Postcard
[1 December 1919]

A thousand thanks. I have left the roses in [*Night and Day*], and shall tell my critics what you say. Nothing could be better—not that I think it matters either way, except that old gentlemen get so angry.

V.W.

Berg

1103: To C. P. Sanger   *Hogarth [House, Richmond]*

Tuesday [2? December 1919]

Dear Mr Sanger,

It was very good of you to write to me about my book. It is a great pleasure to me that you should like it, for there are few people I would rather please.

I think one's readers tend to identify one's characters more than one does oneself. Of course there are touches of Lady Ritchie in Mrs Hilbery; but in writing one gets more and more away from the reality, and Mrs Hilbery became to me quite different from any one in the flesh.

We should very much like to see you and Mrs Sanger. At present we are going through a domestic crisis, but when that is over I hope you will come and dine with us.

Yours very sincerely,
Virginia Woolf

Daphne Sanger

1104: To Molly MacCarthy   *Hogarth [House, Richmond]*

Thursday [4 December 1919]

Dearest Molly,

I seem to be fated not to be able to come to you. Last week I had a domestic crisis to overcome; this week I thought perfectly safe, and was about to write, when Leonard began his malaria—a mild attack, but it settles on him every night, and I don't like to go away. This comes of a visit to Oxford.

If Desmond's back, there would be no point in my visit; but let me postpone it.—Perhaps after Christmas.

You dont, I suppose, want to let your country house? There are two oldish but most desirable ladies [Janet and Emphie Case], seeking everywhere in your neighbourhood—Or Wilson's folly?[1] But I have asked Margery [Waterlow]; and I dont think that you can hold a finger to Margery in practical affairs.

London is at its worst—a drunk charwoman with child by the pauper lunatic—that's my feeling, something lewd about it, as well as indecent and detestable. I've been meeting your friends, the Bibesco's: Elizabeth [formerly Asquith] seemed to be an admirable but almost timorous matron. Is this a conceivable account of her? A child is within her, of course. I said all the most impossible things in a very loud voice; abused Lady Glenconner,[2] and then attacked Rupert Brooke: but at my age and with my habits, how conform to the way of the world? Hair pins dropped steadily into my soup plate: I gave them a lick, and put them in again. [Prince Antoine] Bibesco talked about Ruskin and religion. This was at the Cecil's, and she [Nelly] as deaf as a stone.

Yr V.W.

Mrs Michael MacCarthy

1105: To Vanessa Bell   *Hogarth [House, Richmond]*

Wednesday [24 December 1919]

Dearest,

Here are some handkerchiefs for Dolphin's snout. They are really gent's size, so you might cut them in half.

Do write me an account of Xmas at Seend[3]—do they still have the carols after dinner? You know how every detail consumes me. I'm afraid we shan't get away on Friday after all. [Dr] Fergusson won't let me get up so long as I have this little temperature. It's an infernal nuisance Still it may go down today.

If you come back on Saturday and we're still here, of course I should much enjoy a visit, but you'll have the brats I suppose, and no cook as usual.

1. Mona Wilson, the writer, who lived at Old Oxyard, Oare, Wiltshire, with G. M. Young, the historian.
2. Who married Lord Grey of Fallodon after her husband's death in 1920. She was the sister of George Wyndham.
3. The home of Clive Bell's parents in Wiltshire.

I hope Gordon Sqre is settled. Adrian and Karin seem very hard up. We hear from the agents that we shall have no difficulty in selling H P G.[1]
Do write

Yr

B.

Berg

1106: To J. T. Sheppard

Monk's House, Rodmell.
Lewes, Surrey

31st Dec. [1919]

Dear Sheppard,

(which you said I might call you—I becoming Virginia—but perhaps I always was).

Do you remember saying that you, Miss Joshua, Mr Doggatt, and Mr Taylor[2] would dine with us on Jan. 7th? Owing to influenza, we shan't be back till Jan 8th.—Would you arrange to come (the same party) any day after that? Please do. If you cant get them all, come with some, or come alone. I leave it to you—only let me know, which and when.

Yours

Virginia Woolf

King's

1. 22 Hyde Park Gate, where the Stephens had spent their childhood, was now on the market.
2. Cecil Taylor, a master at Clifton College until 1948; James H. Doggart, then an undergraduate at King's College, Cambridge, and later the distinguished eye specialist; Miss Joshua unidentified.

Letters 1107-1160 (January–December 1920)

Virginia was elated by the compliments she received for Night and Day, *and wrote (besides reviews) a series of short stories, to be published in* 1921 *under the title of one of them,* Monday or Tuesday. *In the spring she began* Jacob's Room, *her first truly experimental novel, but only her diary recorded what hopes and occasional despair she experienced when writing it. Virginia's letters give an impression of unquenchable zest, and it is well to remember her concurrent melancholy. In October, for instance, she wrote in her diary:*

> "Here I sit at Richmond, and like a lantern stood in the middle of a field my light goes up in darkness. Melancholy diminishes as I write. Why then don't I write it down oftener? Well, one's vanity forbids. I want to appear a success even to myself. Yet I don't get to the bottom of it. It's having no children, living away from friends, failing to write well, spending too much on food, growing old. I think too much of whys and wherefores; too much of myself."

But she was very active. Bloomsbury, which was now beginning to concentrate on Gordon Square, acquired a post-war, post-Omega, vitality with the first meetings of the Memoir Club, and there were many visitors to Monk's House, including Lytton and T. S. Eliot. There was also the Hogarth Press, now expanding rapidly with the publication of books by Logan Pearsall Smith, E. M. Forster and Hope Mirrlees, and Ralph Partridge, the lover of both Carrington and Lytton, was brought in as a part-time assistant in October. Leonard's career was leaping upwards. He became Editor of the international supplement of the Contemporary Review, *and leader-writer for the* Nation *on foreign affairs, published* Empire and Commerce in Africa (*January*), *wrote* Socialism and Co-operation, *and in May was adopted as Labour candidate for the Combined English Universities.*

1107: TO KATHERINE ARNOLD-FORSTER

Monk's House, Rodmell,
Lewes, [Sussex]

1st Jan. 1920

Dearest Ka,

Here we are recovering from our diseases[1] over a superb fire, after a large tea, during a violent storm (the ink's turned purple of a sudden). These are

1. Leonard had had malaria; Virginia, flu.

the pinnacles of human existence (thank God, we've got no servants) and I ought to write you a very sublime letter. In fact I did write one, ten minutes ago, looking at the fire. Now it comes to pen and ink of course—and then I've got to accept your invitation at once—I mean the one to stay with us. Do come on the 10th. We go back on the 8th. Ring me up and say so. By these means you will avert Bob [Trevelyan] who has returned from Madrid, and threatens to read his last composition aloud. Oh dear—I didn't even buy the Death of Man[1]; though I asked for it. One can't ask twice for Bob. That leads me to say how relieved I am that you like Night and Day. I should have thought the worse of you if you hadn't; but I want to know *why* you like it. Its foolish of me to ask. I'm already pestered and blinded and be-wildered by my friends opinions. They give them with and without being asked and they're all different; some old creatures have crept from what I supposed to be their graves to hiss at me. My characters seem to exacerbate even the moribund. (I seem to be dropping into Latin—I daresay the sublime letter was to have been in Latin—) On the other hand, my dear Ka, I've had my compliments—and when you stay with us you'll find that the conversation imperceptibly glides towards America. Well, to have done with it—two publishers have proposed publishing both N. and D and the Voyage Out: of course I was very proud, until I met Nessa, and she like the Matter-horn, made me see human glory in the light of the universal: I crept home a good deal abashed, and only managed, under the shelter of Leonard, to fan a subdued glow. Anyhow I may make a little money, which I shan't here: but I'd like to have Bruin's opinion of the whole business.

One of the curiosities of the past week has been the resurrection of Jacques[2] at the Ballet—apparently not only in health, but also well disposed; cordial, friendly, sympathetic, charming, so Nessa said. But then Gwen was in childbed, which may explain the lapse of the severer moral sense. I wish he would come back to us. I always had a deep affection for him—until he got talking about red and green and reality. To return (while there's room) to my works. My George Eliot was more on her legs, I thought, than Sydney. But then if alone one supports the Foreign Office—if the Oranges of Nigeria depend on one—if Lord Hardinge[3] can't be trusted to sign a telegram, without one—George Eliot, poor woman, hasn't much of a chance. That, I was informed, was what happened to her. "Overworked, my dear Virginia: still I feel that its a duty for anyone with more or less decent ideas, for any man of parts" etc., here I looked anxious and blushed. The allusion referred elsewhere. I mean I thought of poor Dawks [Sydney's wife Margery]

1. *The Death of Man and Other Poems*, by R. C. Trevelyan, 1919.
2. Jacques Raverat, who was married to Gwen Darwin. Both were painters, and lived in France.
3. Permanent Under-Secretary of State for Foreign Affairs. Sydney Waterlow was one of his Foreign Office subordinates. In 1918 he persuaded the Government to buy the entire orange crop of Sicily, to prevent it being sold to the Germans.

conscientiously breeding his product among the downs, while poor old Sydney expanded and bubbled in front of our fire. But surely he's as innocent and amiable as—well, I always come back to the same image of a hollow pig —the kind you blow out through a hole in the tail.

My next work will be on Henry James' letters,[1] I think—unless someone else has done it for me during the influenza. I shan't be sorry, since I'm stuck in the Ambassadors.

I hope you have time for reading letters, since this one has run on so far, but still I've thousands of things to say—one being that I highly commend you for living in the country. Everything seems a hundred times nicer there. The whole of London is now concentrated into Gordon Square; Vanessa and Adrian: [No.] 46: Alix: the Stracheys. This being so, we've gone and bought Hogarth and the house next door [Suffield]. I saw myself being swept into the vortex, and there whirled like a drowning leaf, till I was stuck in the mud and decayed.

Leonard sends his love to you and Will and hopes to see *him*. We can't offer him a bed, I'm afraid; but couldn't he join us at meals?

Yr V.W.

Mark Arnold-Forster

1108: TO VANESSA BELL   *Monk's House, Rodmell,*
                                         [Sussex]

Friday [2 January 1920]

Dearest,

I suppose the necklace is bewitched, but it must be a very forcible devil, as the string is jerked apart. I'll bring it to show you. I chose the handkerchiefs at night, and next morning was amazed at the colours. Did you know that they change? Perhaps you did.

We have had storms, gales, thunder, rain—mud to our knees, every conceivable horror until today when it might be June, except that its freezing.

I feel much better—though attacked with heart disease, you'll be sorry to hear, the day before we left. I thought I was probably dying, but Fergusson says its only the nerves of the heart go wrong after influenza, and get all right, and he's given me some medicine, and I'm practically recovered. But I'm afraid I shant get much pity from you; though thats what I'm after. I wonder why anything with one's heart makes one think one's dying.

I heard from Margaret Davies that she's been seeing Kitty Maxse, who asked after us, and said she'd read Night and Day and thought it very bad,

1. Review of *The Letters of Henry James*, ed. Percy Lubbock (*TLS*, 8 April 1920).

the characters bloodless, the writing dull, the love insipid; so Margaret said that Katharine was meant for you, upon which Kitty exclaimed that she couldn't have guessed it and that she always felt, and apparently still feels, the greatest admiration for you. Why don't you ask her to dinner? To couple my lacerated feelings, [Sir George] Savage thinks N. and D. one of the great novels of the world. Life is queer—But I see the solution of it is to live down here without servants. Mrs Dedman cooks our food in her cottage and brings it over piping hot; a girl [Elsie] does the house in about 2 hours. I suppose we save £3 a week. The peace is infinite. I dread going back to the complications of Hogarth, but we must on Thursday.

Then Ka is coming to stay with us. Bob T[revelyan]: has reached England, but I don't suppose France will have made him either younger or handsomer. Give my love to Roger. I hope his influenza is better. When shall you get in to Gordon Sqre.—and when can I invite my guests to ham and roll? Have you a cook? The girl here I believe wants a place in a town; she's very nice so far; aged 18; has been housemaid—I dont think she can cook. Barbara [Bagenal] tried for Budge [Nelly Boxall's sister] without success, and seems half paralysed with desperation, poor wretch; so that perhaps I ought to tell her of this girl.

Love to Angelica—I'm delighted to hear that her taste is already infallible.

Yr

B.

Berg

[*Monk's House, Rodmell, Sussex*]

[3? January 1920]

[*in Leonard's handwriting*]

Our first 3 days here were a hurricane of wind and rain, but despite that it has, I think, already done V. good. Today is perfect bright sun and still. Your visit did not at all tire V. and she takes Night and Day with philosophic calm. I imagine Kitty Maxse's unfavourable opinion is a great compliment. It means that the book has at any rate moved on to something beyond Kipling, Sir Henry Newbolt, and possibly Stanley Weyman.

Leonard

[*in Virginia's handwriting*]

I think L. is a little hard upon poor old Kitty—I used to hate her friends and her views, so its quite right that she should find mine dull—We always did quarrel about what constitutes 'blood' and 'narrowness'—In fact, we parted, when I went to Fitzroy Sqre, on those grounds—so did Nessa, who knew her much better than I did. Its perfect here; I'd like to come down and find you sitting by the fire. We live in luxury; dinner brought over piping hot from the next cottage by an old woman who has borne 11 children and has the sagacity of the whole world since the Flood in her. Lord! how useless they make one feel! (but this is not true, only put in for the sake of Mary Datchet.[1]) Leonard's book [*Empire and Commerce in Africa*] comes out next week—what will the Maxses say to that! How she used to implore Nessa and me not to know people like Leonard!—I'm reading it for the 2nd time—to me it seems superb.

Sussex

1110: To Violet Dickinson   *Monk's House, Rodmell,*
                                                Lewes, [Sussex]

4th Jan 1920

My Violet,
    (Excuse this paper) I will certainly write to Middleton Murry about Mr Freeman.[2] But I think he would have a much better chance of getting books to review if I could say that he has a subject; I think editors prefer that. Also has he written articles that Murry could look at—in some paper? The Athenaeum ought to suit him; Murry got into trouble at Oxford himself and lived for years on bread and water.
    We're down here recovering from influenza. Leonard prunes apple trees all day with a knife you gave him. But we have to be back on Thursday though its nicer than all London rolled in one here.
    I hope you'll come and see us again. Bring Mr Freeman to dinner, won't you? Lunch is rather hopeless for Leonard.
    Seven hundred copies of your book [*Miss Eden's Letters*] seems to me quite good, considering the price; and it ought to go on, considering the value of it. Of course, its too good to be snapped up.
    I have to be photographed for America, in order to appear in person when the novels come out. Shall I borrow Beatrice's [Thynne] pearls? or look as dissolute as I am? I've just been told that Kitty Maxse thinks N. and D. the dullest book she's ever read; but then you know—my opinion of Kitty Maxse—I never succeeded with Kitty. I never put on her clothes right. She gave me an entire outfit, all black, when Thoby died—But you neglected your duties in that line:

1. A main character in *Night and Day*.
2. Possibly Harold Freeman (b. 1899), who later wrote on religious subjects.

Is Crum ever coming to the surface again? not Ella—Walter.[1] I should like immensely to see him.

Yr
Sp:

Editions vary I think; Gerald Duckworth must print about 2,000 in one—but it may be different with memoirs.

Berg

1111: To J. T. Sheppard   *Monk's House, [Rodmell,*
                                 Sussex]
[Jan. 5th 1920]   (We go to Hogarth House, Richmond,
                              on Thursday)

My dear Sheppard,

The 14th (Wednesday) will suit perfectly, and we look forward with great pleasure. We dine at 7.30. I think your best way is from Waterloo; and when you get to Richmond, ask for Eton Street. Paradise Road runs across the top; our house is the 2nd on the left at the join. Sometimes on a dark night people can't see the name; but we're only 5 minutes from the station.

Whatever I said down the telephone to Fredegond, shivering with the influenza, wasn't to the discredit of Jimmy [Doggart]. I thought him a resolute, defiant young man, which is what I like, when young men are too much in awe of their elders to talk. I very much wanted him to talk, and I hope he will. I liked Miss Joshua when she said in answer to my question 'What d'you do?' 'Wales'. What absurd trifles one does make liking and disliking from!

It gives me immense pleasure that you should like my book—a man who reads Sophocles. If there was a dash of anybody in Rodney, I think it must have been Walter Headlam—not you—Oh no, one of the most fixed obsessions of my life has been that I should never, never, never call you Sheppard—in fact that you disliked me. But let us not trench upon this dangerous ground. And then that you should like anything I've written! Perfectly amazing. I daresay I am hard on the men compared with the women. But you see men are at their worst with women—perhaps their best, but certainly their worst. Isn't that so the other way round too? And then early impressions—but here we begin my autobiography, and that's a little too long.

I don't suppose that Jimmy *was* in awe of us, by the way. Heaven knows with these defiant young men. One knows nothing, which is part of the

1. Walter and Ella Crum were Violet's neighbours at Welwyn.

fascination I suppose; and I feel, too, he might at any moment come out with something to slice one from head to heel. His truth might be terrific. So you see how exciting it is to think that you're coming to dinner. Leonard's sympathies of course are with Miss Joshua. Considering what a flare and a glare Gordon Square is, I thought she showed up very well; at her age I should have been quite ridiculous, frantic, hectic, as hard as—well, the thing I have in mind is a wood louse, when it rolls up in a ball. Miss Joshua— I mean she seemed quite natural.

Yours ever,
Virginia Woolf

King's

1112: To Janet Case

Monk's House, Rodmell,
Lewes, [Sussex]

5th Jan. 1920

My dear Janet,

Here is Hopkins, whom I said I'd send. Might I have him back in time, since I spent 12/6 upon him and also haven't yet made him out. But I don't think you need this caution. Some are very lovely and quite plain; others such a mix of beauty and horror that it takes hours to sort them—for instance the long one on the wreck [*The Wreck of the Deutschland*]. But how I love—

> I have desired to go
> Where springs not fail
> To fields where flies no sharp and sided hail
> And a few lilies blow—[1]

Yes, I should like to have written that myself.

We have recovered from our influenza, though I don't like influenza; and in the end I thought I had heart disease, but it was only the nerves of the heart; nothing to matter, but incredibly unpleasant as I daresay you know, while it lasted. But thats all right too.

Did you find a house? Did you see the Waterlows? Molly MacCarthy wrote to say that you must come—for quite selfish reasons, of course; to get Emphie to teach Dermot [Molly's son]. It seems to me that all the virtues and all the humanities can only flourish in a country village. Don't you think human beings improve very much spaced out with fields between them? And then nature—no, I shall never say how much I adore and respect nature. We crept on to the Downs yesterday and saw the sea over Telscombe, and a Hawk kill a partridge, and a white owl. By the way, there are all sorts of small brightly coloured birds hopping in our hedge and waiting for Janet

1. Gerard Manley Hopkins, *Heaven-Haven*.

to turn her eye upon them—which she could do without leaving the drawing room, and to reach the drawing room she need not step up from her bedroom, and the dining room's adjacent and out of that will be one day the bathroom; and then the garden gate admits to the water meadows, where all nature is to be had in five minutes.

I am reading, not only my husband's masterpiece, (I think that a masterly and brilliant work) but also a book called the Education of Henry Adams. I find it absorbing so far, but autobiographies always begin well and to my mind never can be dull, so I don't know if you should at once order it or not. Night and Day continues its chequered career. "The dullest book in the world", Kitty Maxse. "A great novel—particularly in its psychology", Sir George Savage: and then this morning I had 2 others equally contradictory; but I don't know whether I think Kitty Maxse, or Sir George Savage the worse judge of literature (and here are 4 pages from Roger Fry). But of course, I don't deny that I'm immensely flattered and pleased, and if the post came in without a scratch or a purr I should inflict my malice on Leonard. But he [his book] will be out next week, and then I shall retire. Will there be a little preserve of praise for me in Hampstead—something moderately encouraging for poor denuded Mrs Woolf, when the world's talking about Mr.? He sends his love.

Yr.
V.W.

Sussex

1113: To Roger Fry   *Monk's House, Rodmell,*
                                      Lewes, [Sussex]

6th Jan. 1920

My dear Roger,

What a pleasure to think you're back again [from France]—London no longer altogether dumb. Of course you deserve your jaundice (I hope its better) but I didn't deserve my influenza. No one has been more faithfully patriotic. It's been the very devil of a winter, and the worst still to come.

I'm tremendously relieved that you got through my book without disaster. There are some rather swampy places, particularly in the first part, which I had to write for 10 minutes at a time, with only half my brain working. Later I think I got at something interesting—but I want to discuss it with you, if you'll ask me to come; and I've thousands of things that I want your opinion of—You can't imagine what the critics are like—or rather I suppose you can—but it was a shock to me after all my talk about the English sense of literature to find how little they know or care—what idiotic things they say—the praise if anything worse than the blame.

I was highly flattered to hear that you and Vildrac are translating me.[1] Did you have a copy of the 2nd Edition to do it from? I made some slight changes, I thought for the better. Is it to appear somewhere? I think its a little absurd though that you should spend your time translating me—Won't you let me look out your old articles in return? Please do. That would be something worth doing.

Of course my heart leaps up, as the poet says, at the thought of Portsmouth.[2] Not that the thought of Portsmouth is long from my mind. O if only one could merge more freely in these miraculous spheres—third class smoking carriages—Brighton Parade—of course that's not Portsmouth—and so on. But can one get in without bursting the whole thing to pieces? Wouldn't he suspect me? I managed the other day to set foot in the Rectory here. Old Miss Eve[3] was cutting out calico drawers and said it was all very very sad—her mother's death at Torquay she meant, and then something about a Princess walking through the drawing room window and the Great Exhibition and the Tottenham Court Road, and Roehampton being so pretty. But this is pale beside Portsmouth. I promise I won't dish him up raw. He shall be entirely renovated on the outside, tell your sister—only the innards remaining. My dear Roger it must be done—with the Pier and the Porticoes as a background. Why did he choose Weston? and then what about his marriage night—and the evenings—what do they do then? For God's sake let us spend the spring with Portsmouth!

We come up on Thursday: O if it were only to Weston!

Yr V.W.

Sussex

1114: TO KATHERINE ARNOLD-FORSTER
Hogarth House, [Richmond]
Jan. 25th [1920]

Dearest Bruin,

We are, as they say, looking forward (on my part not with great confidence) to coming on the 8th—I know we've been asked; still I don't altogether believe in Aldbourne, though Wotten Bassett is now one of the chief features of my life[4]—the yellow room, the pink room, the lawn room. Nessa agreed with me that to give it up when we could all have lived there

1. Roger Fry and his friend Charles Vildrac, the French poet and dramatist, intended to translate *The Mark on the Wall*, but the project was never completed.
2. Roger's brother Portsmouth was living at Weston-super-Mare.
3. Mary Eve, maid to Mrs Hawkesford, the Rector's wife.
4. Aldbourne, where the Arnold-Forsters lived, and Wootton Bassett, are small neighbouring towns in Wiltshire.

417

so happily was a great mistake. She said all you had to do was to give old women porridge and blankets twice a year, and she was prepared to do it herself.

I see you ask us a day earlier, but then Friday is one of the worst of days—Committee breaks into Committee like a melody by Mozart. I am waiting for Leonard to have done digging a flower bed in the back garden. Perhaps I'd better tell you how there's such a demand for my words that the Voyage Out is being reprinted, and Night and Day is going into a second edition. Now Bruin, you're a talented censorious beast: would you tell me if there's anything in Night and Day that I'd better alter—bad sentences—bad grammar—mistakes of names? I wish you would let me know. I see I shall have to re-write them both if I pluck up courage to read them: but I cant possibly read them: I rely on you.

Oh God! such a party at Moll Hamiltons. The cattle market at Lewes was nothing to it for uproar: Moll herself like a frantic cow entangled in a net—plunging and stamping—the poetess [Molly's sister Margot]—well, when it comes to roaring I'm no match for them: and she followed me down till all I could do was to stand on tiptoe against the wall and shout "I think you're *disgusting*", quite true too; but not at all in my usual vein of suave mendacity.

Yr
V.W.

Mark Arnold-Forster

1115: To Saxon Sydney-Turner *Hogarth [House, Richmond]*
Sunday [25th January 1920]

My dear Saxon,

I wonder if you would once more tell me the number of the Beethoven sonata that Rachel plays in the Voyage Out—I sent the copy I marked to America, and now they're bringing out a new edition here—I can't remember what you told me—I say op. 112—It can't be that. Night and Day is also being reprinted, and I'm putting in your correction of my grammar, and if you have any remarks of any kind to make, they would be gratefully received and promptly attended to—I feel I ought to re-write both from start to finish.

Desmond sent me a letter for you, which I forwarded—I think to implore you to write for him.[1] I hope you will. Indeed, Saxon, I think its your duty to unpack the bonded warehouse of your knowledge. That is Jorrocks [Surtees], though, as Thoby used to say, it might well be Shakespeare.

Well goodbye Saxon—if we meet on t'other side of the grave, I shall be

1. Desmond MacCarthy had just succeeded J. C. Squire as literary editor of the *New Statesman*.

wearing a white rose; so don't forget. I make assignations with you there, under any tree you like to name, since its out of the question here.

Yr. old spirit

Sussex
V.W.

1116: To R. C. Trevelyan *Hogarth House, Paradise Road, Richmond*

Jan. 25th [1920]

Dear Bob,

You told me the other day of a bad or difficult sentence at the end of Night and Day. There is going to be a new edition; and I should like to correct it if possible. It would be very good of you to send me a line with the page if it's not too much trouble. I am very grateful for the misprints, and for any other corrections.

I suppose you did not mark any special howlers in the Voyage Out? Gerald Duckworth is reprinting that and wants me to correct it.[1] I remember your saying something should be altered—short of re-writing the whole which I've no doubt it wants.

I have got Charlotte Mews book,[2] and I think her very good and interesting and unlike anyone else. I forgot to tell you that I asked twice at the Bomb shop in Charing Cross Road for the Death of Man and was not given it. I must try again, but one can scarcely feel encouraged in the study of modern poetry when this is what always happens. They had the Ajax[3]; and said they would get the other [*The Death of Man*] in 2 days, and never did. I lost Unwin's form of course.

Your ever,

Sussex
Virginia Woolf

1117: To R. C. Trevelyan *Hogarth House, Richmond*

Friday [30 January 1920]

Dear Bob,

Thank you very much for the correction in N & D. I think you are quite right and I will alter it. I am altering op. 112, to 111 [Beethoven]. The goats certainly are mysterious.—I fancy something must have dropped out; but I dont see what to do with them now—

1. Duckworth never 'reprinted' *The Voyage Out*. They bought sheets of Doran's American edition, and issued them under the Duckworth imprint in 1920.
2. Charlotte Mew (1869-1928), the poet. Her book was called *The Farmer's Bride* (1915).
3. Trevelyan's translation of the *Ajax* of Sophocles, 1919.

Leonard happened yesterday to be passing Unwin's shop, and went in and bought The Death of Man: which I shall now be able to read. It looks very well printed and bound.

I hope you will take to prose—but prose doesn't, I suppose mean the death of poetry; in which case I shouldn't begin my sentence I hope, since I like very much 'Wind' the only poem I have yet read in the death of Man. Also, if you can keep Desmond supplied you may keep his spirits up. He is already a little burdened, I think, Jack Squire having now left the whole thing to him.

Please remember me to Mrs Trevelyan, whom I dare not call by her Christian name.

Yours
Virginia Woolf

Sussex

1118: To JANET CASE   *Hogarth House, Richmond*

Sunday [1 February 1920]

My dear Janet,

Winchelsea—Cottage Residence. Immediate possession. 2 rec. 4-5 bath, Lav. (h. and c.) etc. etc. £850 freehold.

Reeve and Finn,
Estate Agents,
Rye, Sussex.

The farm I told Lilian about is in our village—Rodmell. You had better, perhaps, write to the owner, Mr Botten, Rodmell Place, Rodmell, Lewes, mentioning us. I was told last summer that he wanted to let half the house, which is said to be easily divided and very up to date; and looks from the outside substantial, old fashioned, with large windows, some view, not much of a garden, a dwelling place, not a farm. Mrs Botten is an invalid— and would want to be downstairs—thats all I remember.

(My quotation is from the Observer today)

God knows when I can come and see you—I feel as if I could never make another engagement as long as I live—what with Ottoline and Eily Darwin[1] and the dressmaker, and staying away, and coming back and going away again, and printing a poem [*Paris*] and re-writing the Voyage Out— (did I make it plain to you and Margaret who say I'm no novelist, and only write for the parish of Bloomsbury that such is the demand among the lower

---

1. Virginia's old friend Elinor Monsell, who in 1906 had married Bernard Darwin, the writer on golf.

middle classes for my work that new editions of the V.O. and N. and D. have to be prepared at once?) Still, perhaps, Saturday 14th?

I think you had better make it clear to Mr Botten that you have only heard from us a rumour that he may wish to let—since it came to us indirectly.

Yr V.W.

Sussex

1119: To Janet Case   *Aldbourne, Wilts.*

[8 February 1920]

My dear Janet,

I find we are having people to dine on Saturday—(I think it was Saturday you asked me to tea) so Leonard says—but you know what Leonard says. Might I come another day the following week?

I can't write this letter, owing to the abomination of Ka's pen—which distorts, not merely the letters, but the language—Here we are spending the weekend [with the Arnold-Forsters]—and you can't think what a letter I would write you if it weren't for the pen. Wherever I see a house I ask if its to let to the most charming lady I know. Have you heard from Mr Botten?

But oh this pen!

Yr V.W.

Sussex

1120: To Duncan Grant   *Hogarth [House, Richmond]*

Wednesday [11 February 1920]

My dear Duncan,

I know I oughtn't to accept—at the same time I can't resist it. Nothing in the world would give me greater joy than a water colour of yours—though I shan't tell you why, or what I think of your pictures. But I think anyhow you're sublimely generous. I chose what seemed to me a lovely one, and I had 5 most exciting minutes, when I thought an old fur bearing dowager was after it—and I didn't know how to buy a picture, never having bought one—and this old woman looked as if she bought them every day of her life. So I dashed up to Mr Clifton and he produced a little red seal out of his waistcoat pocket. But as I say I won't tell you what I think of your pictures. This is the more vexatious, as I should immensely like to describe them— Its the sort of thing I do rather well—I should begin with the naked Venus and go all the way round, keeping my crescendo for the right place, descending thence in curves and spirals like an alighting swan—But I won't do it— dont be nervous—my masterpiece shall give way to yours—and when I've got 2 of your pictures hanging on the wall, I daresay I shall have the right to indulge in soliloquies. But my dear Duncan—I do feel its wrong to take anything of the kind, only as I say I cant resist it.

What a charmer your mother is! And the noble Colonel Young[1]—I was introduced, and given another 5 minutes I should have been invited to Wilmington, which is the goal of my desire. To see them in the flesh was at once strange and rhapsodic—suppose one saw Miss Elwes and the white dogs—but this might be too much.

Ottoline yesterday was in fine feather about your show. The poor old thing undulated and eulogised till really it was like talking to some poor fowl in delirium—her neck became longer and longer and you know how she always hangs to 'wonderful' as if it were a rope dangling in her vacuum—but as Nessa says, this is nonsense—. Poor Tony Birrell[2] was there, said to be underdeveloped, but to me most sympathetic and in fact I wish we'd married. He sat on a low stool eating sugar cakes and laughing—God knows about what—but I saw nothing lamentable in his state. However, we shall meet. This is an endeavour to thank you without allowing myself to describe your pictures.

V.W.

Duncan Grant

1121: To Lady Robert Cecil   *Hogarth House, Richmond*

[19 February 1920]

My dear Nelly,

Of course it now turns out that we shall be away next Sunday—and the Sunday after—(you see I still hope that you may ask us again)

I regretted every minute of my lunch with the Webbs, which was of the most drastic description, and left one in a state where human life seemed scarcely worth while. Never, never, never do I go there again. I can't think how two small old people like that manage to destroy everything one likes and believes in. She attacked me for not sending Leonard into Parliament, which according to her wants redeeming so badly that she is sacrificing Sidney for that purpose.[3]

1. An old friend of Duncan Grant's parents, whose portrait Duncan painted. Miss Elwes was Mrs Grant's companion.
2. Younger son of Augustine Birrell. He suffered from arrested development, which he may have inherited from his mother, and his mental age remained that of a child of 10.
3. Sidney Webb, who had fought the 1918 Election unsuccessfully, was adopted in 1920 as Labour candidate for the Seaham division of Durham, which he won in 1922. Leonard was adopted for the Combined English Universities in May 1920, standing as the candidate of 'Seven Universities Democratic Association', affiliated to the Labour Party.

But this [1917] Club's pens are as bad as the Webbs—scratchy—hard, and as sharp as a pin.

Please ask us again (but I have said this already)

Yrs.

V.W.

We are going down to Sussex to plant flowers.

Hatfield

1122: To Lytton Strachey

Monk's House, Rodmell,
Lewes, [Sussex]

21st Feb. Saturday [1920]

As you see, we are already here. The difficulty about coming next Saturday, which is I admit the most attractive prospect that life has to offer, is that we have to attend two auctions, buy 2 army huts, get them carted over here, put into position and transformed into a kitchen if possible by Saturday—As the huts are connected with Colonel Young who is connected with Mrs Grant, who is connected with Duncan whose new studio depends on them, you will see how complicated it is, and how unlikely to end well. Also Leonard is entirely re-making the garden.

But couldn't we induce Tidmarsh to come to Rodmell? Please convey a warm invitation on our part to Mr Partridge[1]; press Carrington's hand—stroke your own beard. Beds abound; our cook turns out excellent—and they say there's a peculiar virtue in spending the 40th birthday between strange sheets: that is if you want to beget sons, and keep your hair. An uncle of mine—but I'll tell you his story if you'll come. If you won't surely we might meet somehow? Leonard suggests that you should stay on and deal with Vic[toria]. here: he very much wishes to see Mr Partridge.

Yr. V.W.

Frances Hooper

1123: To Lady Robert Cecil

Monk's House, Rodmell,
Lewes, [Sussex]

[end February 1920]

My dear Nelly,

May we lunch with you on Sunday the 14th? Unless you stop us, we will come then with great pleasure, at 1.30 I suppose—and what joy it

1. Ralph Partridge had first met Lytton in 1918 when he visited Tidmarsh. After the war, he often went to Tidmarsh from Oxford, and fell in love with Carrington, while at the same time Lytton fell in love with him.

will be to turn t'other way and leave no 41 to scowl upon the river un-affeared!¹

Please forgive this old sheet, which I have retrieved from a kind of avalanche, the fact being that I'm in the midst of painting my dining room pomegranate colour, and have speckled everything within reach, red and yellow.

Yr affate
V.W.

Hatfield

1124: To Vanessa Bell   *Hogarth House, Paradise Road,*
Richmond, Surrey

Monday [March 1920]

Dearest,

Infinitely though I should like to have your picture, I feel compunctions at taking it. Its too much—you must lend it to me and have it back for a show. I think it's one of the loveliest and I had meant to buy it, but I thought you would certainly tear up the cheque. So let this be arranged—I've a passion at this moment for owning pictures, especially yours.

What a mercy Sophie is with you!²

Please give her my love, and say that I am greatly relieved to think she is once more in control of the family. I feel much more respectable myself.

Yr B.

Berg

1125: To Violet Dickinson   *Monk's House, Rodmell,*
Lewes, [Sussex]

[29 March 1920]

My Violet

Here we are for Easter, so that I'm afraid luncheon on Tuesday is im-possible—but mightn't I come later—to tea? when we come back.

Nessa is in Italy, having got old Sophie back, who manages children, lessons, flat, food, everything. She has been with Lady Victoria Herbert, but doesn't find the great to her liking, I think.

I have never had the courage to get myself photographed—you know you said I'd better conceal my face and pose as the virgin of 20—but Margaret

---

1. Beatrice and Sidney Webb lived at 41 Grosvenor Road, Westminster Embank-ment. The Cecils lived at 100 Grosvenor Road.
2. After the death of Aunt Minna Duckworth in 1918, Sophie Farrell, the Stephen family cook, went into service with Lady Victoria Herbert, George Duckworth's sister-in-law, and, temporarily, with Vanessa.

Duckworth has just sent me about 50 old copies of the picture of father and me—would you like one? However, if you know of a photographer I must face him, I suppose.

Now, let me come in to tea one day,—and tell me how Emily Eden goes on.

Berg

Your
V.W.

1126: To Vanessa Bell   *Monk's House, [Rodmell,*
                                          Sussex]
Good Friday [2 April 1920]
Dearest,

I was very glad to get your post card [from Italy], though some passages were obliterated, I suppose by the channel spray.

Here we are with the bells ringing for church—daffodils out—apple trees in blossom—cows mooing—cocks crowing—thrushes chirping—this is to move your compassion. I suppose you're sitting in a Roman street sucking iced soda through a straw while Duncan, having made friends with the waiter—and there are goats, and large spotted dogs—and nice brown and yellow pots—donkeys—mules—beautiful girls for me—and etc—I wont describe it all, as I daresay you can see it for yourself. Still I do shoot forth a pang of odious envy. England is a little soft and sappy after all. I haven't much news, as we've been here for a week, and our only prospect is a visit from the Sturgeon[1] family tomorrow and the possible advent of Saxon, Nick, and Barbara.

10 lines omitted

. . . .
. . . .
. . . .
. . . .
. . . .
. . . .
. . . .
. . . .
. . . .

Then I went and had tea with the children; it's an illusion to think they wanted me—nothing of the kind. Julian was lying on his elbow reading a book, and Quentin carving a bit of firewood—the table strewn with sweets. I could hardly tear them off to tea. Then we played cards, and Angelica came in, and sat on the table as good as gold and pulled Julian's hair, and said 'pretty' and 'tick-tock' and was altogether lovely and adorable. They all looked flourishing, and as I say had need of no one, though we chattered

1. Leonard's sister Flora and her husband George Sturgeon.

away and Quentin said something extraordinarily witty and profound, in my style, but I've forgotten what. They had a great story of throwing parcels out of the window, and how the policeman had been in to tell them not to, and they had dropped a letter—a very rude letter—to Quentin's mistress into the Square and seen it picked up and delivered and she had been very cross to him that morning—though they had got a friend to write it for them. Sophie was in complete charge of every thing, and seemed to make herself responsible not only for the children but for the lift and the carpet and Henry and Charleston and life death immortality in her usual way. I don't think you need feel any compunction in staying away. I'm asking Clive whether I shan't put Charleston in the hands of Wycherley [Lewes estate agent]—so far I've had no news from Hampton [London agent], and I think W. would be far more likely to produce a tenant.

We had a great splash of people before coming away—dear old Roger and Murry—and a very rich composition of Mrs Clifford,[1] Sydney W[aterlow]. and Goldie—who came in by chance. Mere brilliancy is not in it with richness, ripeness and a touch of rottenness. I assure you you must have an element of decaying South Kensington in your parties—which by the way—light up the horizon for me.

Isn't it exciting to start a new epoch as you're doing?—not A. D. I wouldn't say that, oh no—but an entirely new Pagan Era, with dear old Dolphin in her many coloured multiplicity presiding and ladling out scents and spices from the steaming obscenity—what a sentence! but I've been reading Henry James' letters till my brain rings and swings—do pictures affect you like that? He stayed in your hotel, by the way, and no doubt wore out some rich leather seat with his rotundity. This, however, you skip; and want to know about Mrs Clifford—who was, indeed, all that you've ever imagined her to be—wattled all down her neck like some oriental Turkey, and with a mouth opening like an old leather bag, or the private parts of a large cow. Her stories were magnificent—about Ruddy Kiplings wedding—and how [William] Heinemann came too late with a bouquet—and picture Sundays[2]—and how Professor Sylvester[3] suddenly sank on his knees on the black hearth rug and recited his sonnets to her, with Ethel [her daughter] at her breast—and then 'yes, a great many young men have come to me in their troubles, for a lone woman who has once been married and considers herself married still, is a great help to young men—and they all know that Lucy Clifford never gives away a secret and never thinks harm of a friend"—upon which we all fell silent and almost sobbed—

1. Lucy Clifford, the novelist and playwright, wife of W. K. Clifford, a friend of Leslie Stephen.
2. On the Sunday before sending-in day at the Royal Academy, artists were in the habit of inviting their friends to their studios to view their work.
3. Professor James Sylvester (1814-97), a brilliant mathematician, who also wrote verse and *The Laws of Verse* (1870).

This was to explain why she wouldn't write her memoirs. Moreover, she moves about all in black, lurching like a beetle thats lost a front leg, so I suppose I shall have to review her novel [*Miss Fingal*] after all—her courage and fertility move my heart to tears. Mrs Ward[1] is dead; less notice has been taken of it than you would think. She was escorted by constables to the grave, and old Lucy Clifford was there, too, of course.

It's too tempting, if you can get me objects to be sent with yours—A small table is what I most want—crockery of any kind—plates—bowls—cups—only I mustn't spend since we're plunging wildly—still I cant resist any small thing sanctified by your taste.

The post said they could insure your coat, but couldn't warrant its reaching you for some time. Nelly hadn't done it. I'll let you know if she sends it.

I must now bicycle in to Lewes.

Love to Duncan and Maynard.

Yr
B.

We go back on Wednesday.
Please write.

Berg

1127: To Vanessa Bell   *Hogarth [House, Richmond]*
Sunday, April 11th [1920]

Dearest,

Our letters seem to take a long time—*my* letters—*your* postcards. Still, I'm very grateful for postcards, though its tantalising to hear only the names of Susan [Lushington] and Mrs Holman Hunt and Packard—I thought Packard was dead too, which makes it the more exciting to hear that she's in Rome. I daresay you'll meet Miss Bulley[2] next,—and Jack Nicholls. It's a little obscene—this scratching up of bones by you and Duncan. G. T. Worsley[3] is dead; 10 minutes before seeing it in the Times I'd been thinking of him. How d'you account for that?

10 lines omitted

. . . .
. . . .
. . . .
. . . .

1. Mrs Humphry Ward died on 24 March 1920.
2. Margaret Bulley, the art-historian, later Mrs G. W. Armitage. Packard and Nicholls are unidentified.
3. Headmaster of Colham House, a private school, and previously a master at Clifton College, where Thoby Stephen had been educated.

We only came back on Wednesday, so that I've not much news. James [Strachey] is setting up a theatre. He's going to start with Rosmersholm [Ibsen], and has offered Leonard a part—which I think he ought to take, and thus change his life, since he's bent on changing his life. It—the new theatre—is quite a serious affair—its to be the most perfect of all theatres,— and already all the actors are engaged. Meanwhile Alix is setting up a photographic studio, the point of which is that a million candles flash in your face, and thus absolute truth is obtained—no sentimental evasions— what they call facing facts. She told me that she is now very happy. Frede-gond, on the other hand, is not happy; at least I expect she is really, but you know what it is to have remorse on the death of a parent.[1] She had a reconciliation with Florence however, shortly before, and is now going through the family papers—masses of letters from Granny [Maria Jackson] to Aubrey de Vere.[2] By the way, I had a letter from Margaret Duckworth the other day, who has also been going through family papers and found about 50 Beresford photographs of father, which she sends me, and says I'm to share them with you, and George [Duckworth] is fearfully busy, and the spring has been so wonderful this year, and she hopes we are all well— So I said you were in Rome with Duncan. Nelly has finished your coat, but has not sent it, and will keep it for you. It is the pride of her life; a very fine foxlike work, picked out with some old buttons of mine. Oh I must tell you how much I admire your picture—I think it one of your finest—such a solid, entirely impersonal, and—I see my command over artistic language is still too poor to let me launch out. What I mean is "starry"; do you understand? Do buy me grey gloves; but I know buying is much harder than it sounds, so don't think that you *must* bring me back something—but if you saw a small bright piece of china, cheap but vivid, that's what I want for Monk's House. I daresay they do the heads of celebrities in earthenware. I have a sort of feeling that poor Moll MacCarthy is very unhappy; Desmond has asked me to act as dramatic critic, and I'm going to a play tonight for the first time for 15 years; but I don't suppose Moll is in the least unhappy, only, poor woman, with her ears cut off, more like a squirrel in the dark than ever. Talking of squirrels, we were kept awake till 4 this morning by mice in our bedroom. At last Leonard started to make his bed, and a mouse sprang out from his blankets, whereupon he had a wet dream—you can't

1. Florence Maitland, who was Fredegond's mother and Virginia's cousin, had just died.
2. The 19th-century Irish poet.

428

think what his sheets are like this morning. And what can Lotty think of it? You, who know so much about the minds of the lower classes, can perhaps say. When are the children coming back? Its no good pretending that they want to see me: its awful to find that I'm beginning to want to see them, and to want them to want to see me. Thats how it begins, and we all know how it ends. Still, Angelica—then theres Quentin—and I find Julian very interesting—so like a brother with Angelica. "Now I'll get you a chair, and then you cant drop your silver paper on the floor" so then she pulled his hair, which didn't prevent him from going on reading; much like the day nursery at H.P.G. [Hyde Park Gate].

Why doesn't the dissipated old Owl—I shall never forget the sight of him hitching his trousers in the long black overcoat—Duncan, I mean, write to me?

Which Henry James did you read?

Give Duncan my love; in fact kiss him, and then write to your adorable singe,

B.

Berg

1128: To Vanessa Bell   *Hogarth House, [Richmond]*

April 15th [1920]

Dearest,

You are well advised not to be in this dreary country. It rains and blows and the sky is black as dirty water. Then our only Duchess is dead—do you see that in the paper? Cousin Adeline,[1] I mean; and never again shall we have a cousin in the dukeries. It will be a great blow to George [Duckworth]. I like to think of his appearance at the funeral, which is at Chenies.[2]

There is a good deal doing in the art world. A show of Negro carvings at the book club—the X group—pictures in Shaftesbury Avenue, and the entire works of Bach played; Beethoven next week. I went to see the carvings and I found them dismal and impressive, but Heaven knows what real feeling I have about anything after hearing Roger discourse. I dimly see that something in their style might be written, and also that if I had one on the mantelpiece I should be a different sort of character—less adorable, as far as I can make out, but somebody you wouldn't forget in a hurry. But then an unknown young man wrung me by the hand—Hannay[3] he said he was—and Desmond came in with a highly respectable male aristocrat, of

1. Adeline, daughter of the 3rd Earl Somers, and wife of the 10th Duke of Bedford. Virginia's grandmother and the Duchess' mother were sisters.
2. In Buckinghamshire. The church contains the Russell family tombs in the Bedford Chapel.
3. Alexander Hannay, the art critic of the *London Mercury*, 1920-34.

429

whom I could see he was slightly ashamed.—as I should be ashamed if you passed me by when I was walking with Elena Richmond. How much simpler life is for painters! How can I possibly afford not to know South Kensington? You cant think how much this problem puzzles me—the humanity of South Kensington, I mean. You see, to go to the grave with that problem unsolved would be a bitter failure in my eyes. If you see me kick and stir in my death bed, that'll be it.

Adrian and Karin have sent out cards for a large evening party on the 28th, I think; so you wont be back; and I daresay its a kind of assertion of independence on their part. I shall try to go, but not in the same spirit that I bound up your flight,—still always expecting a romance at the top; whereas, in the case of the Stephen's, I feel that I'm the romance. Its really very dismal now that you're away. I didn't think I should miss you so much. There's no conversation to [be] had in my style, and I have to have my tea at the 17 Club, and altogether there's something about Dolphin [Vanessa] and her ménage that can't be matched. For sheer ridiculous comedy partly, of course, for you're not altogether in the high classic style—and poor old Duncan, well—there's a good deal to be said about him. The Athenaeum has ceased to talk about Wyndham Lewis. On the other hand, they've adopted Katherine [Mansfield] as their writer of genius, which means, I'm afraid, that poor Mrs Woolf—but we writers are never jealous. Thank Heaven, I say to myself that genius has arisen, though not in my particular headpiece. Whereas, what you painters say is,—but I'd much rather hear about Susan Lushington. Do tell me, not on a postcard, the whole history of your liaison, and what your future relations are to be; and whether she had to swallow scruples to have tea with you; I'm sure she got over them in fine style; what I remember chiefly about her is that she had to move on after 5 minutes because her head piece gave out; then she took to giving high shrieks. Is this still true?

We came in to find Nick [Bagenal] and a young Mr Wright, son of a Dorsetshire clergyman, here the other day. Nick is a fearful surly brute now; like a rheumatic labourer; I can't conceive any fate I should like less than to be his wife.

By the way, shaking my dirty clothes basket the other morning, a dead mouse dropped out—starved to death. Nelly believes that I brought him home from Monk's House in my petticoats. Lottie says if she had shaken him out of her petticoats she would have died. This is about all the news there is.

We are sending out Logan's book, Hopes poem, and printing Morgan's story,[1] so we're rather busy, plenty of time though to read letters from Rome.

Yr

Berg B.

1. Logan Pearsall Smith, *Stories from the Old Testament;* Hope Mirrlees, *Paris;* and E. M. Forster, *Story of the Siren.*

May 1st [1920]

Dearest,

Need I say that your letter has entirely changed the face of nature to me? The cock has thrown itself upon the hen, and the bee burst the blossom. We are here for the week end, expecting Desmond, whom we've tried to put off, so I suppose he is certain to come. You will be glad to hear that London has been very dismal the whole of April; wet, black, sodden, sinful; Walter Lamb my only adventure,[1] and Clive will tell you all about him. Poor Prince Albert is backward—that is all he had to tell me, save a little gossip about one of the Gerrards, who has married a farmer, and Walter has taken rooms for them at Hounslow—no, that was Miss Saxton Noble,[2] I think.

We dined with Clive the other night; old Lytton was there, and his eyes have turned blue and his beard red and virile; I heard him whispering secrets to Mary, and I think something happened on the Spanish passes though what I don't guess. If I felt sure that you wouldn't breathe a word of it to Clive and Mary I'd tell you about Gertler, and his revelations. You remember the little affair 2 years ago, when my character was blackened?[3] Gertler has another another [*sic*] version which throws all the blackness elsewhere; but I can say no more; and I don't think I can face a meeting with Gertler which would be necessary to get it all straight. He wishes to clear himself.

Do you want a man and wife at Charleston? A couple here want a place as house keeper and gardener; the man an old sailor; woman seemed respectable; and they only want enough pay to live on.

I've heard nothing from Hampton.[4] Ka has had a son [Mark Arnold-Forster]; the doctor couldn't be got; and she was very bad, but is now better—but this interests you not at all; and yet the mere mention of Susan [Lushington] suffuses me with crimson. The lily of valley from her bosom was a superb touch; but what colour is she? Does it turn a blackish purple, that particular red in age? and her hair? and does she still wear green sequins at night? There was a dreadful party at Adrian's the other night—entirely composed of different versions of Mrs [Bernard] Berenson and Aunt Lou,[5]

1. Virginia had met Walter Lamb at the Bach concert. He told her that he was writing a speech for Prince Albert (later George VI) to deliver at the banquet of the Royal Academy, of which Walter was Secretary.
2. Cynthia, daughter of Sir Saxton William Noble Bt., the industrialist. In 1929 she married Gladwyn Jebb (Lord Gladwyn).
3. See letter 983.
4. About leasing Charleston.
5. Alys Russell (*née* Pearsall Smith), who married Bertrand Russell in 1894, and was divorced from him in 1921. She was a sister of Mrs Berenson, and an aunt of Karin Stephen.

in full evening dress, hale and buxom and breezy, but not really answering to those names. Heaven knows who they were; and then Hope [Mirrlees] came in, but the affectations of that young woman! Why, I've written novels, I've been a beauty, I know Greek, and yet—I thought the difference very marked. She improved later, I'm told. Karin, as I see, has made up her mind to show her spots—if thats the expression—I mean not to go in for art; so there was no nonsense, and Adrian in evening dress, but it is much better like that; and I am going to tea with her to see the children, and one of these days you will be surprised to find how much nicer Karin is than any one else.

I must now go and paint the house bright yellow. As you'll never come here, I can give my taste full rein. The curtains at Hogarth are an immense success, and convey the illusion that we are grasshoppers sitting on a vine leaf, which was what I wanted. If neuritis has to do with the nerves, Florence will be fatal to it; at least the climate always drives me to thoughts of suicide; but I hope Paris may be good for it—and I don't know what it is except that my dentist suffers from it owing to using his arm—But please come home anyhow, and kiss me all over.

What a master of the post card Duncan is!—his style, I mean: I mean himself. Kiss him where the—but I must stop.

Yr

Berg   B.

1130: To Lady Robert Cecil   *Hogarth House, Richmond*

[*Both parts in Virginia's handwriting*]
[June 1920]

Your Ladyship:—

The Manager of the Hogarth Press presents his compliments to your Ladyship and humbly thanks you for the favour of yours received and solicits further patronage, which he has the honour to inform you he is shortly bringing out works by E. M. Forster and The Table Talk of Tolstoy[1] containing much likely to interest your ladyship whose literary moral and social interests it will ever be his privilege to serve, to the best of his ability, and taking the liberty of remaining your ladyship's obliged, obedient, humble servant.

H.P. [Hogarth Press]
per V.W.

Dear Nelly,

You see this is what the wretch writes when I am not there to look after

1. *Story of the Siren*, by E. M. Forster; and *Reminiscences of Tolstoi*, by Maxim Gorky. The Tolstoy book, which Leonard and Koteliansky translated, was the third book (after *Stories from the Old Testament*, by Logan Pearsall Smith, and Murry's *Critic in Judgment*) to be printed for the Hogarth Press by a commercial printer. They continued to print shorter works themselves.

him. To tell you a secret, we don't altogether think Stories from the O.T. up to the very very highest standards of prose composition—but then, What is one to do? Three poets, one female, which made it worse, have been rejected; its all very well talking of young writers of genius, but my belief is they died out about a year after I was born, and modesty forbids me to draw the inference from that.

When you come to see the Royal Horse Show at Richmond, please come in to tea with us.

Yrs
V.W.

Hatfield

1131: TO LADY OTTOLINE MORRELL

Hogarth House, Richmond

[June 1920]

Dearest Ottoline,

I am ashamed not to have written before, but I spend most of my time addressing envelopes, and get to hate holding a pen.

I suppose you won't be coming to London? The difficulty about getting to Garsington is that we spend every week end Leonard can get away at Monk's House, where we are having to alter the house. Unless we go there, nothing is done. But it was very nice last year when you dined here—Might it not happen again? Or perhaps we might come later? The workmen should be done early in July—they wont, I suppose.

I didn't see much of you when I came to tea with you, but I remember Tony Birrell with great pleasure. Our society would be much improved by a few half-wits.[1]—Whereas, we all grow cleverer and cleverer. Richmond alone seems to me to keep its purity. Have you discovered anyone new? I still have illusions that people are extremely nice and interesting—but now that Mr Asquith is at 44 Bedford Square, I don't suppose one will ever meet them.

Your affate
Virginia Woolf

We are bringing out a story by Forster, and a very good thing of Gorkis about Tolstoy, so I hope you will get something worth having next time. Thank you for subscribing.

Texas

1. See p. 422, note 2.

433

1132: To Vanessa Bell   *Monk's House, Rodmell,*
                                         [Sussex]
[24 June 1920]

Dearest,

I rang up to ask whether the servants may apply to you in case of emergency while we're away. We had to go before the dr. had been to say whether Nelly may travel today. I think its possible he wont let her, in which case it's *conceivably* possible that there might be one of the usual panics, which would be calmed if they heard your voice.

But Nelly is practically all right, and has had no panics for 2 days. She seems to be having exactly what we had at Christmas—nothing wrong except a slight temperature. The panel doctor is fearfully strict however, and will neither let her eat nor get up.

I never asked you after your arm the other night—not lack of affection, but scatterness of brain: How is it?

Madge is reviewed in the Times,[1] by John Bailey I think, all lies, very polite, and as dull as ditchwater; poor Richmond rang me up to say that he understood why I would not review it—'she takes offence very easily I know.'

We've been having strawberries for tea, and there'll be raspberries for dinner—don't this tempt you down! Besides, I'm asking Saxon over.

I hope Julian's all right. Tell him he must be well for the Sticklebacks next week.

                                                        Yr
                                                         B

Perhaps I'll come in to tea on Monday on my way home.

Berg

1133: To Violet Dickinson   *Hogarth House, Paradise Road,*
                                 Richmond, Surrey
[13? July 1920]

My Violet,

I ought weeks ago to have thanked you for your handsome and encouraging cheque, but I seem to spend my life in addressing envelopes. The Hogarth Press is growing like a beanstalk, and we think we must set up a shop and keep a clerk. The Tolstoy, in spite of being the publisher, seems to me splendid; and we've just sold it to America, which of course tempts us to set forth on fresh enterprises. Why has Miss Laura Forster

---

1. *A Child of the Alps,* by Margaret Vaughan.

attacked you? I have never seen her, but at one time she took to writing me letters—twenty pages about her relations. She's an aunt, I think of E. M. Forsters. Are you going to Edit her remains?[1]

Leonard is standing for Parliament with the sole object of annoying Herbert Fisher.[2] Thank goodness, he's got no chance of getting in.

We're going down to Rodmell at the end of the month, and there we shall dig and weed until October. Should you be going to Dieppe or spending a week end in a hotel at Brighton, we trust you will look in on us.

Leonard sends his love.

Yr
Sp

I was much interested to meet Bowyer Nicols [Nichols] again. He seemed exactly the same.

Berg

1134: To Margaret Llewelyn Davies

[Hogarth House, Richmond]

[mid-July 1920]

Dearest Margaret,

I have read Mrs Layton with the greatest interest. I don't know how far I'm always biassed in favour of autobiographies, but I enjoyed it all. My only criticism would be that sometimes she writes too like a book. When she is natural she is very good. Now and then she drags in something rather shop-made. I'm keeping it, as Leonard wants to read it, but I'll send it back next week. You must make her go on, and go into every sort of detail, and try to make her say *everything*, but of course thats the difficulty. I feel she hushes things up a little. The description of the women sitting in front of the big house is so good—in fact I keep thinking of different scenes.

We have settled to go off to Rodmell next Thursday. Leonard is really tired out with all his work on our books added to the rest of the usual grind,

1. Laura Forster was an aunt of E. M. Forster, and he used her unpublished *Recollections* in writing the life of his great-aunt, *Marianne Thornton: A Domestic Biography* (1956). Laura was the daughter of Charles and Laura (*née* Thornton) Forster, who were married in 1833.

2. H. A. L. Fisher, Virginia's first cousin, had been President of the Board of Education in the Lloyd George Government. He was one of the two sitting members for the Combined English Universities. Leonard contested the seat because, as he wrote of Fisher in *Downhill All the Way* (p. 34): "I thought it to be almost a public duty to oppose [him] in public life. For he was the kind of respectable Liberal who made respectable liberalism stink in the nostrils of so many of my generation."

and must get a holiday before he starts the Nation[1]—which I must say I grudge his doing—but Massingham is so pressing that he feels he must.

Are you off? Write and tell us what happens, at the Baths.

Your V.W.

What a disgraceful review of the Child of the Alps [by Madge Vaughan]—unless I'm quite wrong, and read it in the light of her letters. Have you got it?

Sussex

1135: TO LADY OTTOLINE MORRELL *Hogarth House, Richmond*

18th July [1920]

My dear Ottoline

It is very good of you to ask us again, and we wish we could come—but if you could see us! Orders are pouring in for Gorky, and there are 200 copies of Morgans story to be stitched, bound and covered. We must get through it all before we go away on the 28th, and there is only next week end—I'm afraid we must spend next Sunday as we are spending this—hot and cross,—almost hoping that there won't be any more orders tomorrow.

It does seem wretched not to have seen you this summer, and I hear from Lytton that the statues are divinely beautiful. I wonder how you manage to find them. Still, I would rather see you than the statues.

I must now get my scissors and paste and start again upon the Siren [by E. M. Forster]. Did you like her? I can't judge any of our productions when I've done with them; in fact they cease to be literature in an early stage of the process.

Shan't you ever come up again?

Your affate
Virginia Woolf

Texas

1136: TO VIVIENNE ELIOT   *Hogarth House, Richmond*

July 20th [1920]

Dear Mrs Eliot,

I am very sorry that you can't come, and so is my sister. She hopes to meet you in the autumn.

1. Leonard had been invited by H. W. Massingham, editor of the *Nation*, to take the place of H. N. Brailsford temporarily as leader writer on foreign affairs.

Unfortunately we are going to the country on Thursday, or we should have liked very much to dine with you.

I hope Mr Eliot's book[1] will have poems in it. I have been wanting to say how much I enjoy his poems—but I never know whether it is better to say so or not.

Yours sincerely,
Virginia Woolf

Houghton Library, Harvard University

1137: TO DAVID GARNETT   [*Hogarth House, Richmond*]

[21 July 1920]

Would you send Tchekov's plays to me at Monks House, Rodmell, Lewes, as we go there tomorrow.

Would you send also a good, cheap, Greek grammar, containing the verbs fully—The sort of thing they have in the lower forms of public schools. I should be very grateful if you could find one. L[eonard]. thinks Rutherford's grammar, Macmillan, is, or was, the best.[2]

V. Woolf.

Berg

1138: TO T. S. ELIOT   *Monk's House, Rodmell, Lewes, [Sussex]*

28th July [1920]

Dear Mr Eliot,

I have to confess that it was not I who reviewed your poems[3] in the Athenaeum, but my husband. (I don't think I told Murry this). We felt awkward at reviewing our own publications, and agreed to share the guilt: he reviewed you, and I reviewed Murry.[4] He wants me to say that he would very much like to do your new book [*The Sacred Wood*], and will ask Murry for it, if you wish it.

I very much look forward to reading it, though with some trepidation, as if my lot as a reviewer would be certainly the heavier afterwards. (I mean this in a highly complimentary sense, but have not time to explain) I read Prufrock the other day again, with great pleasure.

We would like to ask you and Mrs Eliot down here for a week end. The

1. Eliot's new book was his collection of critical essays, *The Sacred Wood*.
2. After the war, David Garnett and Francis Birrell, the son of Augustine Birrell, had opened a bookshop in Bloomsbury.
3. Those published by the Hogarth Press in May 1919.
4. *The Critic in Judgment*, also published by Hogarth.

only thing is that the discomfort is so great and arrangements so primitive that I dont think she would find it possible.

Yours sincerely,
Virginia Woolf

[in Leonard's handwriting]
P. S. and N. B.

I never do review literature or literary criticism except on the rarest occasions as with your Poems. I doubt whether I'm the proper person to do your new book.

Houghton Library, Harvard University

1139: TO ROGER FRY   *Monk's House, Rodmell,*
                                      Lewes, [Sussex]

Sunday [1 August 1920]

My dear Roger,

I am cursing myself for having missed seeing you twice. Is there any chance that you'll come down here?—not just now, because we are cooked for by a cottage woman, but later Nelly will be here and we could manage, if you explained what you want. Our orchard is the very place to sit and talk for hours in—though we haven't anything like Asheham to show you.

I enjoyed the party [Vanessa's] very much, chiefly because parties always —well, not always, but sometimes have the effect of making one do what one would in no other circumstances do—for instance, catch Mary Hutch by the neck, and embrace her passionately, with Clive there to explain how it was he fell in love with her. Only its so soon over.

I'm coming up tomorrow to say goodbye to Katherine Murry. She goes away for 2 years. Have you at all come round to her stories? I suppose I'm too jealous to wish you to, yet I'm sure they have merit all the same. It's awful to be afflicted with jealousy. I think the only thing is to confess it. And its really irrational for there's room for everyone, unlike love. (This is not clearly expressed.)

I'm just starting Goa le Simple,[1] on your advice—But of course if I don't like it, I shall stick it out that you know nothing about Literature. If that were true, however, I shouldn't follow your advice—When's your book coming out?—I don't see any chance of being allowed to review it. Leonard says that the Nouvelle Revue [Française] would know all about the Mallarmé copyrights. We should certainly have to get permission before printing 40

1. *Le Livre de Goha le Simple*, by two Egyptians, Albert Adès and Albert Josipovici (1916).

of them—But probably it would be much better worth while than anything else we've done.[1] Did you like Morgan's story.

But whats the use of beginning a conversation in a letter, with Lottie in and out all the time too, in a transparent white petticoat up to her knees, and a head like a dahlia in disarray.

Do get perfectly well, and ask me to come again, or better still, come down here.

Yours ever
V.W.

Sussex

1140: To T. S. Eliot   *Monk's House, Rodmell,*
Lewes, [Sussex]
Sunday [8 August 1920]

We shall be so glad if you and Mrs Eliot will come one weekend in September. Will you suggest one, and I will see whether it does for us.

Leonard says he will review your book, if you will ask Murry to send it to him.

Yours sincerely,
Virginia Woolf

Houghton Library, Harvard University

1141: To Roger Fry   *Monk's House, Rodmell,*
Lewes, [Sussex]
Friday August 13th [1920]

My dear Roger,

I think the translations are extremely interesting—also very difficult. The difficulty may be partly that I've left my Mallarmé in London, and thus can't compare them with the French. But I've no doubt at all that they're very good, and give one the same strange feeling as he does. We are inclined to think notes essential, and also that a few pages by you on Mallarmé would make all the difference, and be of the greatest interest.

We are in rather a turmoil about the press—The bookshop idea seems to be too difficult, and we now think of setting up a proper printing plant and doing all the production ourselves—that is with a manager.[2] Of course this may fall through, in which case there will be nothing for it but to bring the

1. The proposal to publish Roger Fry's translations of Mallarmé was postponed from year to year, and they were not published until 1936, after Fry's death.
2. Leonard had conceived the idea of inviting Ralph Partridge to assist them with the Hogarth Press, and to start a small bookshop at Hogarth House in association with it.

Press to an end, as we can't go on with it as we've been doing. Therefore, as you see, we can make no arrangements for doing anything for certain, and you must of course, be free to make any use of the translations you like, without considering us. But if we can bring off our scheme, we should very much like to have them—We shall decide anyhow this winter.

At last—a hot day—What does moss on a roof prove? I see it has some mystic meaning—I have such a prejudice against the Welsh that I've never read Caradoc Evans.[1] Must I? I suppose so. I think you're probably right about Goha [le Simple]; anyhow its a very remarkable book; though I trace in it also all those vices and limitations which are inherent in French literature. What a pinch of snuff it is compared with the Mayor of Casterbridge [Hardy]! very pungent, I grant you but—there! and Nessa says every woman falls in with your views! of course my perversity may be a tribute, wrong way round, to your dominion. I'm reading a lot of French in a highly critical spirit, and wish, as usual, that conversation could continue incessantly towards every point of the compass. So you might write another letter, as a makeshift. Eliot is coming here, a little to our alarm, and wants us to publish something of his, so what with you, Clive,[2] and him we should start well.

Yours ever,
V.W.

1142: To Vanessa Bell   Monk's House, [Rodmell, Sussex]

Sunday [15 August 1920]

Dearest

I went to see Mrs Hawkins, and find that she drove over to Charleston the other day, and thought the loneliness of the house would cause her to think too much of her dead son, so she has decided to take a place in Surrey. Her teeth are horrible, and from the way in which she spoke about the air raids, and memory coming over her if she sat alone, I'm sure she would soon become frantic. However, she told me that you would easily get a married couple to suit if you wrote to the address I enclose. They are supplying the man who has fits with a couple to take the Hawkins' place. He will certainly have a fit tomorrow, she said, when the news is broken to him. The scene in the garden was indescribable, as he hurried out to talk to us—upon which 2 bees got into my hair, and with great presence of mind, I put a finger into each ear while Leonard searched my head. Neither of us could therefore answer him—but his conversation continued. The bees swarmed round us—Mrs Hawkins told the story of her sons death and cried a little—and as I say Mr Fears was evidently on the verge of an attack.

1. The Welsh fiction writer (1878-1945).
2. Clive Bell's Poems were published by the Hogarth Press in 1921.

But I dont see why you shouldn't come over all the same: Nelly Cecil, for some extraordinary reason, proposes to come to lunch on Tuesday—Won't you come too? I wish you would.

I greatly enjoyed my visit. I left my nightgown and my spectacles behind, but Lottie will bring them.

Nelly Boxall seems to think she's coming on Thursday, so if anyone will come for a night we can house them with ease.

Yr

B.

Berg

1143: To Vanessa Bell   *Monk's [House, Rodmell, Sussex]*

Tuesday [24 August 1920]

Dearest,

Do let us meet in Lewes—I also have to go there—Thursday or Friday —Only, if it's to be Thursday you must send a card at once. I wish you'd come back and spend the night; but it's no good asking. Our Zinnia's are at their best.......

I had one more farewell visit to Katherine [Mansfield] yesterday, as she got ill, and had to put off coming here. Another magazine is being started by Michael Sadler,[1] with pictures; you ought to contribute; I've not been asked to; Katherine has. But there's still hope, as it doesn't begin till January. Of course I'm going to review her book.[2] Otherwise I didn't get much gossip.

I hear from Molly [MacCarthy] that Michael [her son] lives with a family on the Loire to learn French, which sounds rather a good idea. Leonard is writing to [H. G.] Wells about the school at Hunstanton—which is in existence, though the master may be dead. We had Nelly Cecil here from 12 to 5, and had to talk incessantly through the ear trumpet, except for one break when I shut her up in a bed room alone with a large po and forgot that the [door] handle only turns from outside—so there she was battering in vain. But she did her duty, which was the important thing. She is losing her faith. As I think its the only thing that keeps her from despair I did my best to revive it—without much success.

Incredible they are—the elderly aristocracy—the shabbiness, dirt, and disorder of the house surrounded her like a deserted battlefield. I can't think how they manage to affect one so. Kitty Maxse has a house in Kent, and is as lovely as ever. I heard a good deal about Irene Noel, whose husband

1. Michael Sadleir, publisher (Constable's) and author.
2. *Bliss and Other Stories* (1920).

is Lord Bobs secretary[1]—but let us have ices and sugar cakes and go into all this libidinously.

I think Clive might come for the night.

Duncan I suppose is on the high horse. I shall have to write to him. I should like to be asked again.

Yr

B.

We've got Carrington and Partridge for the weekend. Dont you think it would be a good thing to bring about a legitimate union?

Thursday would suit me slightly better than Friday, if its the same to you; but in that case you'll have to write by return without fail, and I think you might come back for the night.

Berg

1144: TO MARGARET LLEWELYN DAVIES

[Monk's House, Rodmell,
Sussex]

[6 September 1920]

Dearest Margaret,

I am so fearfully sorry about Rosalind Nash.[2] What a terrible thing to have happened. I've often wondered how she was.

I'm afraid you are having a very bad time, and we are both very sorry for it, and not to see you here.

Yours

Sussex
V.W.

1145: TO VANESSA BELL

Monk's House, [*Rodmell,
Sussex*]

Sunday [12 September 1920]

Dearest,

I'll come over one day the week after this—and spend the night, but I can't be quite sure which. I'll let you know—perhaps Tuesday or Wednesday.

---

1. Philip Noel-Baker was the assistant to Lord Robert Cecil, who played a leading part in the Commission which established the League of Nations.

2. A cousin of Florence Nightingale, of whom she wrote a brief life in 1937. She was also active in the Women's Co-operative Guild, and edited the Women's Corner in *Co-operative News*. The nature of her disaster is not now known.

I dont think Wells is coming, but L: says he can easily find the address if you can wait till we're in London. It's probably in Whittaker.

(Your Nelly has just arrived; and finds us in the greatest mess, Lottie having scalded her arm and so on)

Nelly has been examined at the hospital and they say there's nothing whatever wrong except her teeth, so she's going to have them done, and I suppose she may believe it for a time.

Lytton and I went to Kingston yesterday and saw the beautiful Ruth Humphries, now Bigge[1]—to me a little disappointing—but then she was running along the road carrying her baby.

I'll give you my version of the visit when I come—

We shall go back the week after you—It seems a great pity; and I do hope (as our great Aunts say) that your arm is better. Lytton thought you looked tired. Do my dearest lovely dolphin take care of yourself, and dont start all the rush of London overtired and get ill. All the burdens fall on you, I feel.

My only burden is an approaching visit from Robin and Bobo [Robert and Beatrice Mayor]. Mixed with Eliot I expect it will be pretty bad though.

Love to Duncan

Yr

B.

Berg

1146: To T. S. Eliot   *Monk's House, Rodmell,*
                              Lewes, [Sussex]

15th Sept. [1920]

Dear Mr Eliot,

We are hoping to see you on Saturday.

If you can catch a morning train the best thing is to take the 11.55 from Victoria to Southease halt. You change at Lewes, and we would send a trap to the halt (a mile off). It arrives 1.28—The best afternoon train is the 3.20 from Victoria; but this does not connect with the halt. It arrives at 4.47 and we would send a trap to Lewes,—if you will let me know which you will come by.

Please bring no clothes: we live in a state of the greatest simplicity.

Yours sincerely,

Virginia Woolf

Houghton Library, Harvard University

1. The daughter-in-law of Sir Amherst Selby-Bigge, who was Permanent Secretary at the Board of Education, and lived at Kingston Manor near Lewes.

1147: To Vanessa Bell   [*Monk's House*], *Rodmell*
                                         [*Sussex*]

[15? September 1920]

A trap, or fly, very shabby, will be at the station on Saturday to meet the 4.47.

I expect Tom will come by that—but he may come by an earlier one, so if he doesn't appear, will you get in and drive off.

Would you give the enclosed to Blanche [maid]—with many thanks. I forgot it—but I dont think I forgot anything else, which is remarkable.

How I did enjoy myself—thanks to a loving heart, and a head full of maggots. It strikes me that this house is tiny compared with yours, like a nut shell.

Berg

1148: To T. S. Eliot   *Monk's House, Rodmell,*
                                         Lewes, [*Sussex*]

24th Sept. [1920]

Dear Mr Eliot,

It is very good of you to send me your poems, though I feel that it is the wrong principle, when I was about to become a genuine purchaser.

I am glad to see that there are several I don't know. They will probably take me some time to read (as I explained to you) so I write to thank you now. I have been away.

We very much enjoyed having you, and hope you won't find Richmond too far off to come and see us. We go back next week.

                              Yours sincerely,
                              Virginia Woolf

Houghton Library, Harvard University

1149: To Vanessa Bell   *Hogarth* [*House, Richmond*]

Sunday [31 October 1920]

Dearest,

Here is £15-6-6. with a thousand thanks.

I suppose you wouldn't like to dine on Wednesday to meet Nelly Cecil? —no, of course you wouldn't.

Could I have the table some time, *and the bill?*

Just off to my concert in my neat nigger brown costume and parrot hat.

Yr
B.

I hope Angelica is all right.

I'm getting doubtful whether I shall have time to write the story called Monday or Tuesday—if not, I dont know what to call the book.[1]

Berg

1150: To Janet Case   *Hogarth House, [Richmond]*
Nov. 4th [1920]

My dear Janet,

You see how long I've waited to collect gossip for you. Well, last night Lady Robert Cecil stayed here; on Sunday I take tea with Countess [Katherine] Cromer; on Monday I dine with Roger Fry, and on Friday— a very shady party in Chelsea. Doesn't it look grand? The truth is nothing is like what its written like. I mean, Lady Robert is the most modest and humble of women. I penetrated to her bedroom, and examined her night-clothes—pink muslin with a pink lace cap, and a prayer book by the bed. Indeed, when I thought to give her a second quilt, and dashed into her room at midnight (she cant hear) I think I surprised her on her knees, which gave the house the most unusual flavour, as I crept down again. It's a great lack—never to have had a religious element; even the servants believe nothing. I try to bring back some belief in Hell at least as I order dinner, thinking it essential to the proper ordering of a household—but what's the use? All their savings they spend on dancing lessons. I must in a minute cook our dinner for that very reason.

I like Nelly Cecil very much, and hear about the Duke of Devonshire and what's said at Buckingham Palace about the Prince [of Wales] and his love of married women. The amazing thing is that Nelly harbours a profound reverence not so much for me as for the class to which I belong—the intellectual cream, that is, of Europe. A man called Mark Rutherford,[2] my father, and old Lord Salisbury[3] are her three heroes. Lady Cromer is an old battered beauty wearing such a hat as you see on Bank holiday in the gutter. We talk about the revolution, and how it's high time that the daughters of Longleat (her father's house) stepped onto the scaffold. She buys herrings

1. It was called *Monday or Tuesday*, and was published in March 1921.
2. Pseudonym of William Hale White (1831-1913), the philosophical writer, novelist and critic.
3. 3rd Marquess of Salisbury (1830-1903), the Prime Minister, and Nelly Cecil's father-in-law.

for her dinner, and as we walked along Cromwell Road in the moonlight, she had out her purse and turned the coppers, with which it was bursting, to bring her luck. Seeing an apple stall, where the apples were a penny less than in St John's Wood, she darted off, and there I left her, cheapening apples, while from her neck swung a dozen large cupboard keys, attached to a bootlace, for as she told me, one can't trust charwomen. Now all this, though written quickly, is quite true. Oh dear! I've been writing an article and getting all my dates wrong, and a furious old gentleman has written to wring my neck. Never will I write another article.

We are hard at work publishing with a partner called Partridge.[1] Several books will come out in the spring. I don't know where its going to stop. I fancy next time I see you I shall live over a shop, called Woolf and Partridge, in the Strand. Leonard has been once more dismissed by Mr Rowntree from the International supt., and it was the rumour of that that forced us to deny ourselves your sideboard last summer. Just as we had settled to a self-denying life of virtuous industry, Rowntree changed his mind, but it is still uncertain whether he will stick to it. How damnably inconsiderate employers are! Three hardworking people, two of them women with less than the usual feminine charm, are kept dangling while old Rowntree, I suppose, rolls out infinite slabs of chocolate.[2]

I am reading the Symposium [Plato]—ah, if I could write like that! Poor Goldie Dickinson tries, and that doesn't encourage me to experiment. Then I finished Sophocles. This I say to show you how your seeds bear fruit after 20 years—anyhow 17—(for one must be accurate). Miss Matthaei was telling Leonard the other day how you taught her, and how inspiring it was—

We are sitting in a brown vapour, hearing fog signals from time to time, while your moon, I suppose, is stuck among the apple trees and Emphie, having grown very weatherwise, foretells a fine day. Is that what happens? Janet meanwhile reads Greek with one hand, while she slices potatoes with the other.

Love from both.

Yr V.W.

Sussex

1. Ralph Partridge spent most weekends at Tidmarsh with Lytton and Carrington, and from the beginning of October came three days a week to Richmond to help Leonard and Virginia with the printing and machining of their books at a salary of £100 a year and 50 per cent of the net profits.
2. Leonard was editing the international supplement to the *Contemporary Review*, which was owned by Arnold Rowntree, the philanthropist, chocolate manu-facturer of York. Leonard had two women on his staff: Miss Mattaei, Assistant Editor; and Miss Green, Secretary.

Nov. 24th [1920]

My Violet,

Who is Miss Chad?[1]—and why is Gerald marrying her, and is she an heiress, and elderly; or the daughter of a stockbroker, and virginal? I dream of her every night, and Gerald says she has made a good impression at Dalingridge, which seems to me sufficient. I wish you'd call and find out.

When are you coming to dine with us again? Its high time you did. Nelly was charming, but I'm never sure how much one exhausts her with talk.

Yr
V.W.

Berg

Nov 24th [1920]

Dear Mr Eliot,

Would you dine with us next Sunday 28th, 7-30? I think we shall be alone. We have a spare room, and I should like it very much if you would stay the night—we breakfast early.

Leonard wants me to say that he has been reading your book with great pleasure.[2]

Yours sincerely,
Virginia Woolf

Houghton Library, Harvard University

[late November 1920]

Dearest Molly,

I was on the point of coming to tea with you. But will you dine here next Friday, 7.30—3rd Dec, no evening clothes. Do you know the way up from the station? We were to have been honoured by a visit from Mr Sidney Webb yesterday, and he spent an hour wandering in the dark, and finally

1. She was Cecil Scott-Chad of Pynkney Hall, Norfolk. Gerald Duckworth, Virginia's half-brother, was 50 years old.
2. T. S. Eliot's *Ara Vus Prec*, which was published in December 1919 in a limited edition, contained among other poems, *Sunday Morning Service; Sweeney among the Nightingales;* and *Gerontion.*

went home without finding us—just as I'd primed myself with intellectual talk, too.

Please come

Yrs
V.W.

Mrs Michael MacCarthy

1154: To KATHERINE ARNOLD-FORSTER

Hogarth House, Paradise Road,
Richmond, Surrey

Nov. 30th [1920]

Dearest Bruin,

Miss Hobhouse has sent her MS[1]: which I will read as soon as I can. It looks long—but of course might be the very thing.

There's no need to tempt us to Cornwall with Marquises[2]: the mere rocks, let alone the Cox, are enough for me.

At the moment we are so overpowered by the Press that we cannot move. But after Xmas, a new arrangement is going to be made, and then we shall be freer.

Of course I will come to the Home. But I never knew people so surgically disposed as you and Will. What an awful bore it must be! I take Will's point about L. S. Woolf. But mine is that these rare Wolves scarcely scratch the [George] Lloyds and the [Bonar] Laws and get broken themselves in the process. There's Herbert Fisher for example—a good man, or don at least, become an old tin can for platitudes. But I cannot write my opinions, as I am in a hurry to get tea, and then must review a book, and spend the night talking to Molly MacCarthy, who is now isolated at Oare, and comes up to breathe now and then, but is horribly deaf. Leonard is dining with Clive Bell to meet Mr and Mrs B. Russell.[3]

But, however I may boast, I dont think our entertainments are worth the view from the drawing room window, at which you are now looking, and feeling very sublime, and not in the least envious of anyone. Is that your state of mind? I shall go into it when you are in bed and unable to escape.

Yr
V.W.

Mark Arnold-Forster

1. The Hogarth Press never published it.
2. The 'marquise' was an engagingly wayward English woman who had got rid of a titled French husband and lived happily in a tin-mine shack near Bosigran. The Arnold-Forsters were now living at Eagle's Nest, Zennor, about four miles away.
3. Bertrand Russell and Dora Black were now living together as man and wife, and were married in September 1921, as soon as he was divorced from Alys.

1155: To Clive Bell   [*Hogarth House, Richmond*]

Postcard
[7 December 1920]

Leonard will like to dine with you tomorrow. I'm afraid I can't, as I'm dining with Morgan.

Who is going to read then?¹ Nobody?

V.W.

Quentin Bell

1156: To Katherine Mansfield²   *Hogarth House, Richmond*

Dec. 19th [1920]

My dear Katherine,

I wish you were here to enjoy your triumph—still more that we might talk about your book [*Bliss*]—For what's the use of telling you how glad and indeed proud I am? However, I must to please myself send a line to say just that.

Yours ever
V.W.

The Alexander Turnbull Library, Wellington, New Zealand

1157: To Vanessa Bell   *Hogarth House, Paradise Road,*
                              Richmond, Surrey

[21? December 1920]

Our sister-in-law!³
How old is she?
Merry Xmas.
A thousand thanks for table.

V.W.

Berg

1. Probably a reference to the Memoir Club, which had met for the first time on 4 March 1920, and continued for many years. Various members of the Blooms-bury group read papers to each other, some of which were subsequently published.
2. Only one other letter from Virginia to Katherine Mansfield is thought to survive. It is dated 13 February 1921 and is in the ownership of Frances Hooper, Kenilworth, Illinois, but it is not yet available for publication.
3. With this letter Virginia enclosed a newspaper photograph of Miss Scott-Chad.

449

1158: To Roger Fry   *Hogarth [House, Richmond]*

Tuesday [21 December 1920]

My dear Roger,

This is just to say that the things arrived,[1] but with all the glass smashed. In fact there's a large gash in one of the designs. (I'm acquitting myself in case you want them back.) The book case is splendid.

We go to Rodmell tomorrow,—and hope to meet you sometime.

I'm in the middle of your book and fascinated. 200 envelopes have been despatched.[2]

                                                              Yrs V.W.

Are there any knobs for resting the shelves on?

Sussex

1159: To Desmond MacCarthy   *Hogarth [House, Richmond]*

Friday [1920?]

My dear Desmond,

I just want to add to my telephone conversation (for my own satisfaction —Leonard thinks it funny, foolish, and altogether out of proportion of me) that I did not mean to give the impression that I thought L: merely grumpy and ill-tempered in writing to you as he did. I saw his letter and agreed with it and advised him to send it. I did think it unfair of you (as an editor) to send him worthless books and expect a review at a moments notice.[3] That is still my feeling. Overcome by friendship at the sound of your voice, I did not stick to my guns, as I should have done. Hence this letter, which of course ends with an expression of everlasting affection and admiration for D.M. (the man).

                                                        Yrs affect. V.W.

Mrs Michael MacCarthy

1. A bed, a bookcase, and some stained glass windows, presumably from the now defunct Omega Workshops.
2. In return for addressing some envelopes for Roger, Virginia had been given a copy of his *Vision and Design*.
3. Desmond MacCarthy was Literary Editor of the *New Statesman* from 1920 to 1927.

Monks House, Rodmell, Lewes, [Sussex]

Dec. 23rd [1920]

My dear Barbara

I cannot think why you never write to me. Saxon says you live on the bank of the Severn. Perhaps looking into the water destroys the memory; and you are a wise old witch, much happier than any of us. Well, I hope so.

We have just come down here for Christmas, and the sun on the cabbages is a sight. Indeed, I think this place has great points over Asheham. Do you find that wherever you live is the best place in the world? Is the Severn better than the Wye? Have you a perfect cottage? Do you do all the work yourself? I hope not. But then when are you coming to see us? I must tell you we've turned the dining room at Hogarth into our printing room, so we have a proper spare room; fit for a proper matronly woman—Come soon, or the press will have swamped us. I can't tell you how hard we work. Partridge is immensely energetic, but I regret to say that his hands get very cold, and then, taking a whole box of type, he drops it on the floor. You can imagine the scene—printing to get 8 pages finished—fog—cold—4 in the afternoon —then this disaster. We shall produce about 6 books in the spring.

I spent a night with Saxon not long ago, at Great Ormond Street—I only mean I went in after dinner. I was immensely impressed by his bachelor apparatus. I think he is the most masterly man I know. He has complete control over his tea, his coffee, his chess, his books, his cat (if he has a cat), Mrs Stagg, the full moon—when he takes a walk—and friendship. He sees nobody, and his affections are entirely pure. I sat there like an old dirty clothes basket. Does he give you that feeling? Carrington has been in London; Gordon Square is like nothing so much as the lions house at the Zoo. One goes from cage to cage. All the animals are dangerous, rather suspicious of each other, and full of fascination and mystery. I'm sometimes too timid to go in, and trail along the pavement, looking in at the windows.

Nessa has been painting her rooms flesh colour and orange (that's my impression.) Angelica has the charm of a beauty, already. She always takes off your hat and tries it on herself. Julian is getting up an intrigue at school— It seems to me very elderly to be writing about children's gossip; but I can't think of anything middleaged. What a bore it is that we're all married— except old Marjorie Strachey who teaches shop assistants, and fell down the stairs at Debenhams the other day and cracked her behind. Noel Olivier is marrying a Welshman called Jones[1]; and will live in Wales; and as I think you're in the next county, perhaps you'll meet—Oliver and Ray [Strachey] dined with us the other night—and I must say I think its high time—I will not be so indiscreet as to say what I mean. Only, she becomes more and more

1. In fact she married a fellow doctor, Arthur Richards. He was a Welshman, but did not live in Wales.

like that very handsome cat of yours that I admired so, the day we came to tea and Nick was wounded. With this hint, I leave the subject.

Do you think you would send me a picture postcard of your neighbourhood? My private vision of you is so wildly romantic that it can't be true. I suppose you do do something besides sit on a high bank under a willow tree braiding your hair while the Severn rushes past in the moonlight? Barbara, who hasn't time what with scrubbing and washing and attending to Judith to read this long aimless letter, is filled with scorn. But if you wont write to me, how am I to know better?

Your affate

V.W.

Love to Nick; and thank him for his letter, 3 months ago.
I'm going to try liquid manure.
Please write an account of your entire day from dawn to sunset.

Berg

5 Virginia Woolf in the 1920's

6a Dora Carrington and Lytton Strachey

b Barbara Bagenal at Charleston

Letters *1161-1179* (*January–May 1921*)

Virginia's main literary activity in 1921 continued to be Jacob's Room, *and she also learnt enough rudimentary Russian to help Koteliansky with his translations. With Leonard she went to Manchester in March to attend his adoption meeting, and afterwards they spent a happy holiday near the Arnold-Forsters in Cornwall, from where she wrote ecstatic letters. Among other books published by the Hogarth Press was Virginia's* Monday or Tuesday (*March*). *It won less acclaim than Lytton's* Queen Victoria (*April*) *which he dedicated to her, and she barely troubled to conceal her jealousy of his success, nor of Katherine Mansfield's. But she was very fond of both of them, and encouraged the marriage of Ralph Partridge to Carrington in May, mainly for the sake of keeping them with Lytton at Tidmarsh.*

1161: To Vanessa Bell   *Hogarth House, Paradise Road, Richmond, Surrey*

Friday [7 Jan 1921]

Dearest,

How you must be wanting to hear from me! Perhaps you're back though.

We came back [from Rodmell] last Saturday. Poor Barbara is up in London, and we went to a party at Bunny's, and danced,—poor B. didn't dance. I expect she is very unhappy, and likes being unhappy—but perhaps I am quite wrong. Saxon was there; and it was frightfully dull really, but at any moment it might have become amusing—

By the way, we're in treaty for a house in Gordon Square, so you may have me for your neighbour after all. Still, we needn't see each other. Ralph's just been telling me of a wonderful tea party at Clives—all Spanish, all prostitutes, all musicians, all talking French. Ralph's father is threatening to commit suicide, and it is thought that he ought to join the firm, in order to prevent him. He is 56 and his wife won't copulate with him—that seems to be the trouble. By mistake Ralph has left a revolver in the house—which is miles in the country.

Yesterday we lunched with the Webbs; I cant tell you how this excited me, seeing that I got onto terms of humanity with her; but how it will bore you! Besides you don't believe in other people's humanity—I wish I didn't.

Here we've got Richard Hughes[1] and Don Claudio de la Torre dining with us; a detestable bore, I expect. Hughes an Oxford undergraduate; and wants us to print his works; on the telephone I couldn't help asking him to dinner. And we've never seen either of them—and how shall we know which is which?

Will you ask me to tea when you get back? Well, says Nessa, I daresay I shall *have* to. A thousand thanks for the table. As we shall be next door you needn't send it very far—I didn't think Gwen's woodcuts[2] up to much, did you? Are you jealous of her? I'm not in the least jealous of Katherine [Mansfield], though every review praises her.

Desmond is coming to stay because they've lost their cook—thats all the gossip I can remember.

Yr.

Berg

B.

1162: To Vanessa Bell   *H.[ogarth] H.[ouse, Richmond]*

[January 1921]

Dearest

Many thanks for the cheque—what an amazing surprise!

It's been impossible to attempt seeing you owing to printing and various horrors—however you seem to have been invisible. Then Old Snow [Margery Snowden]—I'm longing to hear about her.

If I can, I'll come to tea tomorrow, but don't wait anyhow. Ah, I've lost my heart to an undergraduate [Richard Hughes] myself—aged 18, with a stammer.

I have just kissed Ralph on the nape of the neck—Its these elderly passions that are so dangerous. I'm longing to hear your memoirs.

V.W.

The woodcut came safe—I hope to have a proof of the first one soon—
By the way, I have a cold (not bad) in the head—Would you rather I didn't come for fear of giving it the children?

Berg

1. The author (b. 1900) of *A High Wind in Jamaica* (1929). He had written a long short-story called *Martha* about life in the East End of London, and submitted it to the Woolfs, who turned it down. Richard Hughes does not now (1976) remember Don Claudio de la Torre. He thinks that he was alone at the dinner, which he found extremely alarming.
2. Until 1933 Gwen Raverat did not publish a book of her own woodcuts, but single prints, and in 1915 she illustrated Frances Cornford's *Spring Morning*.

Hogarth House, Richmond,
                                              Surrey
Typewritten
Jan. 18 1921

Dear Mr Turner,[1]
    I shall be glad to do the article on George Eliot, and will let you have it
some time next week.
    My husband asks me to say that he will do the article on Mill.
                                              Yours sincerely,
                                              Virginia Woolf

George Spater

Hogarth House, Richmond
[19 January 1921]

My dear Sydney,
    We shall see you on Friday, but I don't want to let your letter go
unanswered. I believe I do understand more than you think. Anyhow,
you've made it clearer to me than it ever has been before. I think, too, that
your explanation is the right one. Where I think you exaggerate (I don't
accuse you of falsity—thats absurd) is in your estimate of your external
position. You say people drop you, and don't want to see you. I don't agree.
Of course I understand that when one feels, as you feel, without a core—it
used to be a very familiar feeling to me—then all one's external relations
become febrile and unreal. Only they aren't to other people. I mean, your
existence is to us, for example, a real and very important fact. If I treat you
as a joke (and my manners are far too haphazard) thats only a method. Of
course, one of the things about you that I like, admire, and find interesting
is this sensibility—this introspection—this sense of the importance of things.
    I know this seems to you off the point. But you admit that a wider social
life would make it possible to rub along. This seems to me easily within
your reach. Why not tackle that part of the problem at once? Let's discuss
it when you come. We are branching out a little in that direction, as it
happens.
    I am not trying to pretend that this touches more than the surface. I
feel that your explanation is the true one. The only way to meet that seems to
me to be to realise it as you have done. Indeed, I had guessed what you say.
    I do, however, return to the aspect which I believe you can't possibly
see as clearly as I do—I mean your own powers, and the effect which, if

1. W. J. Turner was simultaneously dramatic critic of the *London Mercury*,
literary editor of the *Daily Herald* and music critic of the *New Statesman*.
Virginia's article was for the *Herald*.

you believed in them, they could have upon the whole position. No; if I've ever accused you of pretending unhappiness it was because your sensibilities and capacities are so obvious to me that I can't understand how you don't find pleasure in them.

This is hastily, and I know confusedly written. But I've read your letter with a sort of pleasure (that you should trust me sufficiently to write it) and with a good deal of distress. This scribble is only meant to say that I believe I understand, and don't try to minimise the meaning of it.

Also I've a wish to sign myself yours affectionately—is that sentimental? —but perhaps you don't know how fond I am of my friends.

V.W.

John Waterlow

1165: To Lytton Strachey *Hogarth [House, Richmond]*

Jan 25th [1921]

Ah—but this is what I may have dreamed of, but never hoped for. What could I like better? Only my inordinate vanity whispers might it not be Virginia Woolf in full?[1] Some Victoria Worms or Vincent Woodlouse is certain to say it's them, and I want all the glory to be mine for ever. But it's better than a glory and comes on my birthday too.

We look forward to Saturday, and shall we have Vic[toria]?

Dearest Lytton,   Your V.W.

Frances Hooper

1166: To Maynard Keynes *Hogarth House, Paradise Road,*
Richmond, Surrey

Thursday [3 February 1921]

Dear Maynard,

Would you let us have your manuscript in order that we may read what we missed last night?[2] It will be kept private and returned instantly.

We thought it quite magnificent, and I cant say how much I envy you for describing characters in the way you do.

Yours ever
Virginia Woolf

King's

1. Lytton's *Queen Victoria* was dedicated to 'Virginia Woolf', not 'V.W.'
2. Virginia and Leonard had had to leave the meeting of the Memoir Club before Keynes had finished reading his paper.

1167: To Violet Dickinson   [*Hogarth House, Richmond*]

[5 February 1921]

My Violet

What a pleasure to hear from you—and what queer company you keep!

I think it will be very good for your morals to visit the simplicities and refinements of Richmond.

What about next Thursday, 10th,? 4.30. We should be in, and like it very much.

If you don't answer, I shall expect you.

Berg

Yours
Sp:

1168: To Vanessa Bell   [*Hogarth House, Richmond*]

[March? 1921]

Dearest

I wonder if you'd like this ticket for the Magic Flute at the Old Vic tomorrow night. I'm threatened with headache and suppose I mustn't go, damn it. If you cant use it, would you give it to anyone else—Gumbo [Marjorie Strachey], perhaps.

I think you had better not repeat what I said about Norton being frightened of people at Gordon Sqre—I think this was one of the things Bob [Trevelyan] told us in confidence—but he was so muddled I can't remember.

Berg

Yr
B.

1169: To Vanessa Bell   *The Queen's Hotel, Manchester*

Thursday, March 17th, 1921

Dearest,

I am reminded of you at every turn in this hotel—How you would love it! in fact, why you and Duncan don't do a series of hotel scenes I cant conceive. A vast green plush room—pillars—candelabra—silver trays—urns—coffee pots—large British family groups reading newspapers—drinking—the clergy—mothers and daughters—all grey tidy skimpy incredibly respectable—save for one or two hippotamus females basking in corners all stuck about with diamonds—and old gentlemen bursting through their waistcoats—indeed they never stop eating fried fish, tea, and meringues. But I can give you no idea; and then just outside the window are trams, Queen Victoria, the Duke of Wellington, and the man who invented the

Spinning Jenny—now who was he?—all black as soot, noble,—pointing at the opposite houses—I say I can't finish this sentence, and then there's Mrs Snowden clearly writing to Lily (was that her name?) about airing the curtains.

Last night Leonard made a speech in a chemistry theatre, and I talked to Mrs Unwin[1] about the beauties of Derbyshire, which are indeed surprising, but too melodramatic for your taste. This was at the University, where Watties [Walter Lamb] father is professor, and they're all somehow like Wattie, provincial, smug, destitute of any character, hopelessly suburban, yet trying to live up to the metropolitan intellect (me, I mean) which they can't do. Somehow, we have got off the rails for real middleclass intellectual political life. Does that ever strike you? Tonight we're dining at what they call the Refectory with Professor Weiss and Professor—I forget; and I've prepared 2 things to say. The first is "I am Herbert Fisher's cousin" the 2nd is "I am Leslie Stephen's daughter." But supposing nothing whatever happens? And why did you bring me into the world to go through these ordeals?

I spent the morning at the Art gallery. There's Work by Ford Madox Brown, the Hireling Shepherd by Holman Hunt, Love and death by Watts; and I assure you the number of incidents one can pick out is amazing. If Leonard hadn't got impatient I could have found grasshoppers copulating in the very background of Holman Hunt. The shepherds hair is done one by one. Then there's a lamb with 8 separate whiskers. Theres Aunt Susie by Dodd[2]—and Mr Beccles by Aunt Susie, and Nymphs by Waterfield and —God knows what all—Your art is far more of a joke than mine. But dont think that I am unaware how dull this letter is—We spent the afternoon at the Zoo. Imagine (oh God, says poor old Dolphin, how much longer is this going on? Why should I imagine the Manchester Zoo) well, but you must admit it was exciting to find a dromedary and an Indian buffaloe, with ingrowing toe nails, poor beast, in a grotto of pale grey stone, totally forgotten, there being only 2 charwomen about the place, which is the size of Regents Park, and almost entirely given over to the scaffolding of a panorama, and a lake. But how I love these places! The whole expedition is one long rapture of romance—and if I could live in hotel lounges I think I should be—Yes, here are more people come in. Mrs Snowden has settled down beside me after a very tiring day, she says—When you know a waiter by name, in fact shake him by the hand, what does it mean? Its the clergy who do it. However, I will say no more. When I'm old, when Julian and Quentin and Angelica are out in the world, do let us become travelling

1. The wife of a professor at the University of Manchester, where Leonard had gone to be adopted as Labour candidate for the Combined Universities.
2. 'Aunt Susie' was Isabel Dacre (1844-1933), a member of the Manchester Academy of Fine Arts, and a close associate of Francis Dodd, who had himself done several drawings of Virginia in 1907-8.

matrons, and go round the provinces together, in handsome style, having buried our husbands, for I think its best to be a widow (I mean in an hotel—)

Did you hear that Lytton has thrown us over on what must be a pretext about Lady S.?[1]

So Leonard and I are going alone; but there's more in it than meets the eye. Ralph [Partridge] has a fixed and gloomy look which reminds me of his father the suicidal Colonel. I imagine (but for Gods sake dont shout this about Gordon Square) that there's been a crisis. Anyhow I hope so. I hope they're all at daggers drawn. I think Carrington is losing Lytton and spurning poor Ralph—but here is Leonard—I must wash and rehearse my 2 speeches. I am Leslie Stephen's Cousin—thats what it will be.

Of course my only wish is to know how you are; and that I shant know.

To lecture you is equally useless. But for God's sake be careful, and go away, and love your dear grey ape. May I come to tea, Monday, perhaps? We go away on Wednesday

Yr
B.

We come back tomorrow.

Berg

1170: To S. S. Koteliansky   [*Hogarth House, Richmond*]

[March 1921]

Dear Mr Koteliansky,
    (I wish there were some less formal name I could call you).
    Leonard asks me to say that our address will be c/o Mrs Hosking
                    PONION,[2]
                    ZENNOR,
                    St. IVES,
                    CORNWALL
    I hope that is clear.
    We are taking our Russian.[3] The aspects seem to me very interesting—that is not to say that I understand them at all.
    I shall like very much to read the letters you are sending.[4]
                            Yours very sincerely,
                                Virginia Woolf

British Museum

1. Lytton had cancelled his plans to go to Cornwall with the Woolfs, saying that his mother was ill.
2. The name of the hamlet was actually Peniou, according to the O.S. map.
3. Virginia and Leonard had begun to study Russian with Koteliansky in February.
4. He was translating the letters of Anton Chekhov with Katherine Mansfield.

Ponion, Zennor,
                                                            St. Ives
Sunday [27 March 1921]

Dearest,

The only small printer we know is MacDermott, Duke Street, Richmond. I think he would probably do your catalogue in time, and much cheaper than you could get it done in London. You would have to instruct him rather carefully about type and so on. He is on the telephone, and would give you an estimate anyhow. We found Madley as expensive as the Pelican. Partridge comes back on Thursday, and will be going down to Richmond. He might superintend MacDermott.

It is pitiable to think that you are bothering about pictures and no doubt losing your umbrella on Haverstock Hill while I am watching two seals barking in the sea at Gurnards Head. This is no poetic licence. There they were, with their beautifully split tails, and dog shaped heads, rolling over and diving like two naked dark brown old gentlemen. Two minutes before a viper started up under my feet. The smell of the gorse which is all in bloom and precisely like a Cornish picture against a purple sea is like— I dont really know what. Then there are deep rivers running down with all those plants that used to grow in Halsetown bog.

We are on the cliff, quite by ourselves, nothing but gorse between us and the sea, and when I have done this letter we are going to take our books and roll up in a hollow over the sea, and there watch the spray and the ships and the bees, peacock butterflies (tell Julian). However I admit its rather windy today. Also Ka may at any moment turn up with Henry Lamb who's staying with the Kennedy's,[1] who married Millie Dow's daughter,[2] and they have a cottage somewhere, as indeed most of the cottages are inhabited by the riff raff of Chelsea.

Ka and Will are the great people of the neighbourhood, with a large solid house [Eagle's Nest], views from every window, water closets, bath rooms, studios, divine gardens, all scattered with Logan rocks.[3] Ka is a very nice woman, to my mind, and everyone stops and talks to her on the road, and she is already a country lady with a cupboard full of medicines and bandages. Will improves, I think (you see, I don't like to be too appreciative, knowing your scepticism). He is shedding the Youngs and the Trevelyans a little. He paints pictures of the Campagna in Mrs Westlakes [former owner of Eagle's Nest] Studio. On the floor he has a photograph: then there are about 6 studies in monochrome of the photograph on different easels—I think probably he's under the influence of Ruskin: anyhow, they take a lot

1. George Kennedy, the architect.
2. Thomas Millie Dow (d. 1919), the painter, had lived at Talland House, St Ives, where the Stephens spent their summer holidays in their childhood.
3. Rocks precariously balanced, so that they moved when touched.

of time, and he works all day, and I rather believe (but this is malicious gossip) that Henry Lamb has persuaded him that they ought to exhibit at the Royal Academy, which, as Henry says, is only bad because people like him and Will don't show there. Henry doesn't see anything in modern French painting. Now if Lytton had been here, we should have had an interesting combination. Ka is very ill at ease about Henry. It is incredible that she ever had an amorous youth. But I assure you she is a broad-bottomed, sensible, maternal woman, and I've just borrowed some sanitary towels off her—not that it's likely I shall give them back. By the way—I got a piece of gossip for you. Olive Heseltine has annulled her marriage with Michael, with a view to his marrying a young woman in an office, the plea being that he is impotent; and Olive has gone to Vienna to feed the starving, having scarcely sixpence a year herself, and will, I doubt not, once more proceed to the quest of Hilton.[1] Then Bunny is engaged[2]; but this I daresay is known in Gordon Square. I'm going to Treveal this afternoon to look for cowries. Yesterday we went to Bosigran. Doesn't this make your mouth water? Nobody comes here. There is no agriculture. There are a few hobbled donkeys, but not a thing has been done since we were here. Its the only place to stay at—and there is a cottage to be had on the top of Tregerthen Hill. Now if you had the spunk of a caterpillar you would telegraph to me to buy this for you for ever. Have you heard about Charleston?[3] How is Ann?[4] We shall be back on Thursday.

I am going to send you some butter. They've almost given up making cream, owing to having bought separators. Miss Eddy lives next door, Mrs Berriman is at the farm, and our landlady is Mrs Hosken. Ka wants me to lunch with the Millie Dows at Talland—he is dead; but she is very nice, and fears that the associations may be too painful for me. L. met Dr Nicholls yesterday, who said that he should never forget Miss [Stella] Duckworth coming to tell him that we were giving up Talland; and he almost bought the house, and has always been sorry he didn't.

B.

Berg

1. Olive Heseltine, *née* Ilbert, had pursued Hilton Young in 1909 when he was in love with Virginia.
2. To Rachel Marshall, whom Virginia and Vanessa had known as a girl.
3. Vanessa had received notice to leave Charleston, but the notice was later withdrawn.
4. Adrian and Karin's daughter was having an operation on her ear.

1172: To Saxon Sydney-Turner   *C/o Mrs Hosking, Ponion,*
                                    Zennor, St Ives,
                                    Cornwall

Bank Holiday [28] March 1921

My dear Saxon,

Why do I always connect you with Zennor? Did we walk over here
from Carbis Bay [in 1905]? I rather think you were carried off by Thoby to
look for a raven on the cliff—which raven I saw yesterday, and two seals
walloping on their backs off the Gurnards Head so near in that I could have
swum out to them. Next holiday you must come here. Mrs Hosking is quite
adequate, though suffering from the death of her husband, which has
affected her eyes, and thus a little irresponsive to my endearments, but
speaking—as they all do—a faultless and colourless English. But the country
—my dear Saxon. We are between Gurnards Head and Zennor: I see the
nose of the Gurnard from my window. We step out into the June sunshine,
past mounds of newly sprung gorse, bright yellow and smelling of nuts, over
a grey stone wall, so along a cart track scattered with granite to a cliff,
beneath which is the sea, of the consistency of innumerable plovers eggs
where they turn grey green semi transparent. However when the waves
curl over they are more like emeralds, and then the spray at the top is blown
back like a mane—an old simile doubtless, but rather a good one. Here we
lie roasting, though L. pretends to write an article for the Encyclopaedia
upon Cooperation. The truth is we can't do anything but watch the sea—
especially as the seals may bob up, first looking like logs, then like naked old
men, with tridents for tails. I'm not sure though that the beauty of the
country isn't its granite hills, and walls, and houses, and not its sea. What do
you say? Of course its very pleasant to come upon the sea spread out at the
bottom, blue, with purple stains on it, and here a sailing ship, there a red
steamer. But last night walking through Zennor the granite was—amazing,
is the only thing to say I suppose, half transparent, with the green hill
behind it, and the granite road curving up and up. All the village dogs were
waiting outside the church, and the strange Cornish singing inside, so unlike
the English.

I think a good deal about the Phoenicians and the Druids, and how I was
a nice little girl here, and ran along the top of the stone walls, and told Mr
Gibbs[1] after tea that I was full to the chin. Do you like yourself as a child?
I like myself, before the age of 10, that is—before consciousness sets in.
Still I expect I muddle it all up with Cornwall.

Certainly this is the place to come to, as no one has built here since
about the year 1840, when everything seems to have been built at the same
moment, why, God knows. If you will send me a wire, before Thursday,
I will buy you a cottage and 4 acres of moor on the top of Tregerthen Hill.

1. F. W. Gibbs was a friend of Leslie Stephen.

You could probably keep a cow, and sell peat: your firing would be gorse, and the sublimity of your thoughts, reading Greek in the morning, and Latin in the evening would in time to come invest your lodging with radiance.

Unfortunately for my romance, the [Tregerthen] cottages (not yours, but the ones we had) are inhabited—you know the sort of people—tremendous thick boots, blue cloaks, orange ties and squash hats. How I hate them! Ka and Will sit among the rocks in Mrs Westlakes stone mansion, rather windblown, but sublime, observing hail storms miles out to sea, and the descent of the sun; the difficulty being I should think to keep together any identity in such circumstances. However Will retires to an outhouse, and paints, and Ka has a very lively rosy baby, whom I can't help envying. What illusions, my dear Saxon, one would have if one lived in Cornwall and was eleven months old.

I have just done my Russian lesson, and can read one page of Aksakov[1] in 45 minutes. There were 3 clusters of words which I knew, and these bear me on in hope. Otherwise I have to look out each one, and, what is worse, forget them by the time I reach the end of the sentence. But we say we have broken the back of the language. Then I am reading Candide, and Ethel Smyth's Streaks of Life [autobiography]. And tomorrow if this sea mist stops (for the sunshine was an illusion which I wished to produce for poetic reasons—it is the first bad day though, and even so we're going to the top of Bosigran Castle this afternoon) tomorrow we go to St Ives, where I shall buy you a little compass set in serpentine such as I used to give my father very ugly, but perhaps when you're walking it may save your life. Home on Thursday alas. But we've nothing to complain of.

Ring us up and come out and then you shall have your serpentine compass.

Yours,
V.W.

Ponion is not the name of the house, but the name of the village, or rather the 3 houses. I think you will like to know this.

Sussex

1173: To Lytton Strachey   *Ponion, Zennor,*
                                            St Ives, [Cornwall]
Wednesday [30] March [1921]

The enclosed card[2] gives you no idea of the place, which is indescribable —far better than the Lizard or the Land's End, or St Ives, or indeed anywhere. (I have just had to move my chair out of the blazing sun). One

1. Sergei Aksakov (1791-1850), the novelist.
2. A picture postcard of Gurnard's Head.

walks out of the window on to the cliff. There are 2 seals bathing in the bay. Two adders curling round my ankles. Gorse, cowries, Cliffs, Choughs, Ravens, Cream, solitude, sublimity and all the rest of it. It's true that Ka is perched on the hill a mile and a half away, with the oddest collection of good little grey men who spend their time scrambling up chimneys and funnels and are hardly articulate in consequence. But there is Henry Lamb for you— not for me. I've not seen him. We take our books out and lie in the sun; occasionally I say, why aren't you here?—but even so, a general benignity pervades us. I like Will better, and have looked through portfolios of grey-blue rock-scapes—not of Cornwall; of Italy as it was before the war. I met a man yesterday by appointment to discuss literature—"which is my whole life, Mrs Woolf." But I can give you no idea—He lives with a half perished dumb wife on a headland in a cottage with Everyman's Library entire. "I read no moderns. Life is not long enough for anything save the best. Hardy has taught me to look into my heart. I have enjoyed this conversation, Mrs Woolf. It has confirmed me in my own opinions." This stunted animal was a clerk in the post office, became infected with books, and is now like the oldest kernel of a monkey's nut in the Gray's Inn Road. However—why is it that human beings are so terribly pathetic? God knows. Or am I becoming rotten with middle age? I did refrain from asking him to correspond; but left with tears in my eyes—almost. I can't help thinking that we are hope-lessly muddled. Then there was the theosophist, Mr Watt in the cottage which I once hired; and he lives on nuts from Selfridges, and a few vegetables, and has visions, and wears boots with soles like slabs of beef and an orange tie; and then his wife crept out of her hole, all blue, with orange hair,and cryptic ornaments, serpents, you know, swallowing their tails in token of eternity, round her neck. The rain, they said, often comes through the walls on a wet day, so I'm glad I didn't settle there. But can you explain the human race at all—I mean these queer fragments of it which are so terribly like ourselves, and so like Chimpanzees at the same time, and so lofty and high minded, with their little shelves of classics and clean china and nice check curtains and purity that I can't see why its all wrong. We tried to imagine you there, snipping their heads off with something very witty.

Well, I shall read Queen Victoria and try to see how its done. I see the New Republic is publishing it, and it's an incredible gem, and a masterpiece of prose. I quite believe it, though my jealousy is twinged—and I thought I had no vices left in me after this week. I thought I was going to read the whole of Shakespeare and I haven't; but I come back longing to get my teeth into your book—Is it quite magnificent? And why weren't you here? And now I must take a last look at the country: which will dissolve me in tears.

Give my love to your mother.

Yr.

V.W.

Sunday April 17th [1921]

Well, I feel I must write to you either in your own style or in Victoria's. There's no escaping you after reading the book. Indeed, it is quite magnificent, better as a whole, I should say, than the other. I've seldom enjoyed anything more. I suppose the chief marvel is the way you spin the story perfectly straightforwardly, never a line slack, and yet contrive those wonderful little portraits, one after another, each exactly in its place, illuminating, without interruption or fuss or for a moment stopping, it seems, to go on talking simply. The effect is not merely satiric by any means. You seem to have reduced it to the last possible ounce, and yet to have kept all the meat and bone and guts. The great moments seem to me really moving. And the Queen herself comes out somehow surprising, solid and angular, and touching, though not exactly sympathetic. Amazing woman! My only criticism (and I'm not sure of its truth) is that occasionally I think one is a little conscious of being entertained. It's a little too luxurious reading—I mean, one is willing perhaps to take more pains than you allow. I couldn't bear to sacrifice any of the amusements (the boy Jones is superb, and there are a million others) but now and again perhaps, where the space is so limited, the jokes are a little on the surface—But I don't know. I must read it through. The first time one races. Literally I snatched it up, put it down, snatched it up, till it was all done. One of the things I thought particularly magnificent and original was the description of the possessions. It was so massive, and summed it all up, and opened up, I thought, infinite vistas of new forms. But we must talk about it when you come.

Yr.
V.W.

Oh, and I must say how I enjoyed your Batesian[1] version of the Queen on the Great Exhibition. "Sir George Grey in tears, and everybody astonished and delighted."

Frances Hooper

1175: To Violet Dickinson   *Hogarth House, Richmond*

[April 1921]

My Violet,

We are fearfully ashamed of ourselves—but somehow the card with your name got overlooked. You have a large balance to your credit—

1. The enthusiastic Miss Bates in Jane Austen's *Emma*.

£1.13.6.—of course you ought to have been one of the first to get our list. Here it is. All 3 books are now out.[1] If you want the others, they shall be sent directly we hear, and we will deduct from your deposit.

We are much ashamed of the printing of my one. We were persuaded to let a little printer [McDermott] here try his hand at it, and he has produced an odious object, which leaves black stains wherever it touches. Leonards we did ourselves.

We are selling much better this time, in fact we have beaten all records, which is very encouraging but keeps us on the run. I must now go and boil some glue.

I will tell Lytton that you like his book. He is a little nervous what the old courtiers will say. By the way, he shares my admiration for Miss Eden. Won't you do another volume? I wish you would. They are the best letters there have been for a long time.

Nelly (my cook) is hoarding a pot of marmalade for you.

Will you come and eat it here? Do.

I hope you are better, and feeling affectionately disposed towards us.

Sp:

Berg

1176: To Sydney Waterlow   *Hogarth House, Richmond*

May 3rd [1921]

Dear Sydney,

We were just going to ask you to dine, and now Saxon says you are ill. Of course, he knew nothing more, and this seemed hearsay. But we should like to be informed of the truth.

He came to play the great [chess] tournament with Leonard, and beat him, I am sorry to say, owing to a mistake, I think. Who have you been seeing and what have you been reading? These are the sort of questions that Ottoline used to ask one, and one was expected to say something very high minded. I am reading Miss Romer Wilson's new novel,[2] which Jack Squire says is the greatest work of genius ever written by a woman (or words to that effect). Naturally one doesn't like that. And I am hopeless at judging novels. I keep thinking that I should write them better. Now you are saved all these horrible spites and vanities owing to being in the Foreign Office—at least that is my romance about the Foreign Office.

And I have just looked into Eliot on Prose in the Chap book,[3] and am shocked as usual, when I read Eliot, to find how wrong I am, and how right

1. Virginia's *Monday or Tuesday*; Leonard's *Stories of the East;* and Tchekov's *Notebooks*.
2. *The Death of Society*, for which she won the Hawthornden Prize in 1921.
3. An article entitled *Prose and Verse* in *Chapbook* (April 1921).

he is. The nuisance is that one must go into the matter: he doesn't like Sir Thomas Browne, and he does like Poe. I'm sure he's wrong; and I shall perk up again, but what a shock it is. I think he is a Puritan, as well as an American. Then Wyndham Lewis has been abusing everyone I'm told, in his paper,[1] and Roger and Nessa read him in shops, and won't buy him—which, as I say, proves that they fear him. But this is all great nonsense—Do write and say how you are.

I can't remember that I have seen anyone in particular. Clive gave a great party to which all his ladies went in different colours of the rainbow, and were utterly outshone by Vanessa in old lace. The Spanish lady[2] is very stupid, but so incredibly beautiful that one forgives it all: and she orders dinner for 10 when there are only 3 to eat it, and loads of plovers eggs, ices, and salmon are wheeled off to the servants hall; which gives one a great sense of luxury. Also we were in Manchester and I met a Mr and Mrs Weiss who knew you, and asked a great deal about you, and what had become of Alice [Sydney's first wife].

Yours ever,
Virginia Woolf

John Waterlow

1177: To Lady Robert Cecil   *Hogarth House, Paradise Road, Richmond*

Monday [9 May 1921]

Dear Nelly,

(I never can remember to buy notepaper—so you must forgive this sheet, upon which I ought to be making notes about Mr Coventry Patmore).[3] I hope our books will make you cheerful, but I doubt it. I think you must come and see us. Why not spend another night here on your way to your committee? Its a long time since you came—the day Mrs Asquith's autobiography came out, do you remember. You would have a proper bedroom; one not shared by the Hogarth press I mean. That is now eating us out of our dining room.

I went to tea with Lady Cromer yesterday—and *she* doesn't find things dismal. Then we went to lunch with Mr Herbert Fisher, and he made me despair—of everything. Poor man! Is it inevitable that politics should eat out your inside and leave you but a shell? Perhaps its being in the Cabinet; I felt that if the window was open, poor Herbert would be blown down Victoria Street—yet so good and well meaning.

1. *The Tyro*, which only survived for two issues in 1921 and 1922.
2. Juana Ganderillas.
3. Review of *Courage in Politics and other Essays*, by Coventry Patmore (*TLS*, 26 May 1921).

Now I have to go with Miss Fry to lecture the Women of Richmond upon prison reform[1]—According to her—if this cheers you at all—the criminals are the good people invariably; grandmothers are murdered from the highest motives, she says, generally to shield someone else. And there they are, the murderers, shut up for life, perfect martyrs. The drunkards especially are always most tender hearted and generous. However, I see this is pretty dismal too. Leonard is rather pleased though—no, he's not; he says everything is as bad as it can be—except that our books are selling.

But do come here.

Yr. aff.

Hatfield   V.W.

1178: To Vanessa Bell   *Hogarth [House, Richmond]*

Friday, May 13th [1921]

Dearest,

I feel inclined to quote you some of your own letters about the imbecility and criminality of not taking care of one's health. Oh, how idiotic I think you! And you won't take an extra glass of milk for anything I say; or go away for anything the whole world says; its Aunt Mary in the blood. You are very interesting psychologically: in some ways so reasonable; in others—. Well, the family strain must be ineradicable. There'll be Angelica one of these days saying she *will* sit up till one; and *won't* drink her milk; and *will* be amused by the young men. For as I write this, waiting for my dinner, in the innocence of Richmond, I can see you bundling off in a taxi to a restaurant to sit chattering with that little man who always had a fly on his head—was his name Maurice? I daresay he's drunk himself to death. And you wont live long either. Still, never say I didn't tell you of it—We've had the influenza in this house, in the usual form: I mean Lottie suddenly dropping the fish and bursting into tears. Then we put her to bed. Then Nelly has pains in her leg. Then they both go cold up the spine. However, thank God, its now over.

Then I went to tea—solely on your account—with Lady Cromer: all the way to St John's Wood. They die very beautifully, the aristocracy; there's that to be said for them. But I stirred my breast for any cinder of romance—I stirred among the cinders, it should be; and found nothing but benevolence and boredom.

The baby[2] we once saw, if you remember, is now a great fat bumpkin, with a little Greek head, only the Greeks didn't have blubber lips: anyhow his

1. Roger Fry's sister Margery was Secretary and later Chairman of the Howard League for Penal Reform. In 1926 she became Principal of Somerville College, Oxford.
2. Evelyn Baring (later Lord Howick) was born in 1903.

manners were perfect and his thighs so shapely that if I had passions any-
more, I should have seized Evelyn by the neck. Far from that, there we sat
in a room the identical copy of Kittys [Maxse] drawing room on a larger and
more aristocratic scale: chintzes, green paint, white walls, Lady Bath [Lady
Cromer's mother] by Watts; Lady Alice [Thynne, her sister] by Cope;
Lord Cromer by Sargent.

I made this profound observation that the aristocracy is hopelessly
amateurish. In youth this has a certain charm; in age it is a little banal.

"Now do tell me—whats Vanessa doing?—And I was so interested to
hear that your sister in law had taken poor Mary Maggs for her cook—poor
girl, I used to visit her before the baby came, and she kept her room so
clean . . . I do so like the Bruce Richmonds—both of them. But how does he
manage to get up to the office now?—You know Mr Keynes don't you?—
He wrote that very clever book."—

I don't say that she's not a superb piece of flesh, but why say these
things? And she's too much in the later style of Du Maurier[1] for my mature
taste.

You have heard I suppose of George's [Duckworth] descent upon
Gordon Square?—first having tea with Julian and Quentin, then going on
to Adrian. He said they were nice jolly boys, you'll be glad to hear. Adrian
said that he is now harmless, a little shabby, quite whiteheaded, and talks to
the dog a good deal in baby language—you remember how he used to do it?
Adrian thinks him practically witless: for instance when he heard that they
were becoming psychoanalysts he said "Oh but does that mean you'll be
able to cure poor Laura?"[2] I daresay you've had the account, though. He'd
come to see you, so you are in favour—He always calls me "the poor goat"
—which I suppose means that I'm permanently mad—never mind—I'm
very crusty, because you've got the influenza; and I haven't enjoyed my day
at all; and I thought I was going to, and its all your fault. However, I admit
I rather admire your pictures. As for Duncan's new style—did you know he
had completely changed?—I see it is of the utmost importance. I rather suspect the influence of Van Goch [sic]. I refer to the technique of Haverstock
hill—The agitation of the trees—and the angle of the tea cups. But you
won't follow me. I liked your snow scene best of all. Then I liked one called
the Farm by Porter very much; and a landscape by Seabrooke.

But, I said to myself, why leave out poor old Carrington and put in
this marmoreal chocolate box nymph?—and behold it was Rogers! I'm in
training for the Unknown Show,[3] and rather plume myself, as I got you,

1. George Du Maurier (1834-96), the writer and artist who drew fashionable women
   for *Punch*.
2. Laura (b. 1870) was the only child of Leslie Stephen's first marriage, to Harriet
   Thackeray. As a young child she was seen to be mentally deficient, and spent
   most of her life in asylums. She died in 1945.
3. The 'Nameless Exhibition', organised by Roger Fry at the Alpine Art Gallery.

Duncan, Roger, Seabrooke, and Ethel Sands right every time. I confused Keith Baynes watercolour with you once. I don't like Lessore. Not one was sold, at least there were no red tickets, so that I think we must start the tea room gallery.[1] Roger was seeing Champco: [Elspeth Champcommunal]; L is seeing [W. J.] Turner, and I've wheedled Bobo [Mayor] out of £200— if we want it, and I see that the udders of our friends are full of gold and only need gentle manipulation. The question is—will anyone keep up their enthusiasm after the first quarter?—when the cups are cracked, and one of the waitresses has been seduced, and somebody has quarrelled with me—which reminds me, Inez[2] *loathes* me; and I'm universally hated by women, they say, for being such a domineering character, so crafty, dishonest and insinuating. Yet I adore them—all except Inez: Mary and I are respectable enemies.

I must now stop this charming letter; though I've just begun to talk about myself. The Daily Mail says that Leonard has written one of the greatest stories of the world [*Pearls and Swine*]. In consequence we are flooded with orders, and were photographed this morning for the Sphere— as an advertisement merely. My feelings as an artist were ravaged;

Please send if only one line to say how you are.

Its hopeless to impress wisdom on you.

Yr

Berg   B.

1179: To Vanessa Bell   *Monk's House, Rodmell,*
                                                                        [Sussex]
Sunday, May 22nd [1921]

Dearest,

I was very glad to hear from you, the account of Miss Lloyd[3] delighting me. What a nuisance about Versailles! All my party must be removed from the terrace to a back street. I don't think your proverbial wisdom meets my arguments about the influenza. But your blood be on your own head: My poor husband has been ill for 10 days with some disease of the inside. However he's better now, and here we are, like a sensible couple, recuperating.

Haven't I been wonderfully discreet? Theres Carrington and Ralph [Partridge] gone and got married yesterday and I said nothing about it. Yet I was in the thick of it and gave motherly advice. Poor Carrington is a little uneasy, as indeed I should be in the circumstances, and they've left for Italy. She had to break the news to her mother, who endeavoured to

1. The Woolfs proposed to open a combined tea shop, book shop and gallery in Bond Street, but the idea was a fleeting one.
2. Inez Ferguson. See p. 347, note 1.
3. Probably Constance Lloyd, the painter, who lived in Paris.

470

explain that there is a certain thing the man does on the first night, by pointing to a bee copulating on a flower—but she broke down—and Carrington couldn't get her to proceed. "I think that lump on the back is a gentleman bee" was as far as she got.

Then there's been a tragedy as usual—Michael Davies has been drowned bathing at Oxford—Arthur Davies' son.[1] How amazing it is the way fate pursues them!—He was extraordinarily nice, I believe—I've just had a letter from Madge [Vaughan], asking to come and stay with us at Hogarth, because Lytton dedicated his book to me, which she thinks a work of genius, and therefore there must be *so much* in common between us, and "I have *never* been able to reconcile myself to the *drabness* of my part in life—I am scarcely grey at all. My hair is almost *wholly black* still" and so on. I'm afraid there's no way out of it. But I have arranged with Roger that we are going to put her through her paces. "Now Madge, whats all this nonsense about Chastity?" I'm going to begin, and then I shall bring in the loves of the schoolboys.[2]

Still it will be a very harrowing visit—think of all the questions and exclamations.

We had a party the other night to tap Desmond—that is we had him and Molly, made him drink 2 bottles of wine, and then set Miss Green [Leonard's secretary] to take down his talk in shorthand. It worked perfectly, as he talked for 2 hours, but Miss Green says it is the dullest thing you can imagine to read. Molly has had her hair dyed, not very successfully I think. At least the dye is too much like the yolk of an egg on the top, leaving black beneath. She looks much younger, but rather shady and like someone at the seaside—We didn't tell Desmond what we were doing, so don't write and tell him, will you, in one of your strange moods of expansive hilarity. Then Karin gave a great tea party to have the honour of meeting Lady Colefax. I didn't go, on principle, being rather on the high horse about London society, and daily refusing invitations which other people would give their eyes to accept. A splendid tea was spread, and Colefax never came. Poor old Karin is very open and humble, I must say, and takes this sort of thing like a nice mongrel dog—which you and I wouldn't stand. Now I have no more news that I can think of—except that Gerald Ritchie[3] is dead and buried, poor man, after rushing about London for six months buying melons and grand pianos and ordering the police to shadow his wife. In short, he was not altogether compos, and everyone is very glad to have him safe at Kensal Green [the London cemetery].

1. Michael Davies, the son of Margaret Llewelyn Davies' brother Arthur, had been adopted at his father's death by J. M. Barrie. Margaret's brother Theodore was also drowned.
2. Madge's husband, William Wyamar Vaughan, became Headmaster of Rugby in 1921.
3. See p. 404, note 8.

Affection I know you don't care for; so I will give you none. Art criticism, as you observe, is not my strong point; so I wont tell you what I thought of the Unknown Show. There was a large picture of a tea party in one room. Roger stands out quite unmistakable. Clutton Brock[1] pounced upon him in the Times and made him very miserable.

Now, my lovely Dolphin, with the spangled tail, the sea-blue eyes, and the heart of a fish, please rummage about for the old pen which Duncan saw somewhere or other a few days ago and write and tell me how you have seduced from me my solitary non-admirer—for Eliot never admired me, damn him.

6 lines omitted

. . . .

. . . .

We go back tomorrow, so tell Duncan to address his letter there. And do describe a dinner at a café and how you artists talk. Please do. Just scribble down about pictures and so on. Who are the young artists nowadays?

Your

B.

Berg

1. Arthur Clutton-Brock (1868-1924), art critic of *The Times*. His essay *Simpson's Choice* had been the first publication (1915) of the Omega Workshops.

Letters 1180-1208 (June–December 1921)

In June and July Virginia was often bedridden by fluctuating illnesses—headaches, sleeplessness, pains and frets—and she did not properly recover until September, spending most of the intervening time at Monk's House. Her illness did not prevent her from reading nor from writing letters, but she was unable to receive guests, and made little progress with Jacob's Room. *"No one in the whole of Sussex", she wrote in her diary of 18 August, "is so miserable as I am; or so conscious of an infinite capacity of enjoyment hoarded in me, could I use it." She finished her novel at Hogarth House on 4 November, and once again began dipping into London life, boldly defying her cousin Dorothea Stephen when she dared to criticise Vanessa's morals. The Woolfs were now sufficiently confident about the future of the Press to buy a larger printing machine, which they installed in the basement of Hogarth House, once their refuge from the air-raids. Ralph Partridge came every day to work at the Press, mainly on a book of Roger Fry's wood-cuts which rapidly went into three editions.*

1180: To EMMA VAUGHAN   *Hogarth House, Richmond*

June 2nd [1921]

Dearest Toad,

 I should think that everything depends upon the merit of the Count's pictures [*unidentified*]. The usual arrangement is, I think, for the owner of the gallery to ask an artist to exhibit, hoping to recoup himself by a commission on the sales. If his work is good, it would be quite easy, I imagine, to get Roger Fry or someone to give him an introduction to one of the usual galleries. There is a new gallery just started in Grafton Street, called the Independent Gallery which is by way of taking modern work. Vanessa knows the owner well; but without any of his pictures to show, it is difficult to see how to make arrangements. If you have them sent over, I'm sure Nessa would look at them and give you her advice. Her address is 50 Gordon Square. I will tell her about it when I see her.

 Its ages since we've seen you. How are you both; and is it true that Marny's halo is now visible on dark nights from Kensington to Hammersmith? I hear from Madge [Vaughan] about her novel [*A Child of the Alps*].

Your

V.W.

Sussex

Monk's House, Rodmell,
                                          Lewes, [Sussex]

[20 June 1921]

My dear Molly,

What a pity it was that I couldn't see you!—but my head was so fuddled with sleeping draughts that rational conversation was impossible. Are you still unhappy? And why? and won't you write to me here—and explain everything. We are here for another week and there's nothing I should like better than a long letter from you.

I am reading the Bride of Lammermoor—by that great man Scott: and Women in Love by D. H. Lawrence, lured on by the portrait of Ottoline which appears from time to time.[1] She has just smashed Lawrence's head open with a ball of lapis lazuli—but then balls are smashed on every other page—cats—cattle—even the fish and the water lilies are at it all day long. There is no suspense or mystery: water is all semen: I get a little bored, and make out the riddles too easily. Only this puzzles me: what does it mean when a woman does eurythmics in front of a herd of Highland cattle? But I must stop.

Please write.

Your

V.W.

Mrs Michael MacCarthy

1182: TO VANESSA BELL   *Monk's House, Rodmell,*
                             [Sussex]

[June 1921]

Dearest,

Your account of Dodder[2] filled me with delight. I rather expect your letter will have exterminated the beast, as I have never heard a word from her since our Dreadnought affair.[3] I wrote and told her what I thought of her then. But what a pullulating monster she is! I wish you could see her again and trounce her—or that I could. One forgets that these horrors still exist. My only triumph is that the Ritchies are furious with me for Mrs Hilbery[4]; and Hester is writing a life of Aunt Anny to prove she was a shrewd, and silent woman of business. But this is nothing to compare with Madge [Vaughan] and Dodder.

1. Lawrence drew an unpleasant portrait of Ottoline in the character of Hermione Roddice.
2. Dorothea Stephen (1871-1965), Virginia's cousin.
3. See Vol. I of Virginia's letters, pp. 422-3.
4. Mrs Hilbery in *Night and Day* is based upon Lady Ritchie.

I'm practically all right, and slept without a sleeping draught last night. I wish you'd ever undergo my horrors—bed for a week—no writing for 3 weeks—and milk and all the rest of it. We come back on Monday, and I'll come to tea one day next week.

My great excitement is that we're making a beautiful garden room out of a toolhouse with a large windows and a view of the downs—you will never see it, so I will say no more. But do you think we could spout [sell] the Lawrence drawing of Thackeray?[1] Having bought the Porter[2] picture, I'm rather hard up, and yet improvements here are a great seduction. Or did we sell it? I suppose this is the season for Americans.

Do please write another letter. I get immense pleasure out of them.

Of course, I should find Mary considerably more trying than Dorothea. In fact I think you must be a miracle of broad minded magnanimity—I mean what I should dislike would be finding her there as a matter of course, at 46 [Gordon Square]. I would rather find Virginia Woolf. By the way, Eliot was so desolated at not dining that night, and meeting you I suppose, that we must set up another party.

Tell me about Mary's party. Don't go on the char a bang. They always upset. Here are a few flowers. The garden is burnt up but we get peas strawberries beans and lettus [sic]. I sit out most of the day reading the Waverley novels which are superb and all last night I dreamt of Julian. We were buying eclaires together.

Yr
B.

I've been lent Lawrence's novel about Ottoline [*Women in Love*]. Shall I ask if you can have it? It's fearfully long, but Ott: is there to the life, and Pipsy [Philip Morrell] too.

The country is amazingly beautiful. I can't think why one doesn't live here.

Berg

1183: To S. S. Koteliansky   *Monk's House, Rodmell,*
                                     Lewes, Sussex

June 25th [1921]

Dear Samuel,

Do you think you would be so very kind as to send me 100 cigarette papers? I did not bring enough, so that if you could send them at once, I should be more than grateful.

1. Samuel Laurence did two chalk drawings of Thackeray in about 1853, one of which was already in the National Portrait Gallery.
2. Frederick J. Porter (1883-1944), later Vice-President of the London Group.

I am reading Women in Love. It is much better than the Lost Girl I think, and I wish I had reviewed it in the Times instead of the man who did— for I thought him stupid and unfair. I can't help thinking that there's something wrong with Lawrence, which makes him brood over sex, but he is trying to say something, and he is honest, and therefore he is 100 times better than most of us.

I am practically all right, but we are staying till Friday to make sure. Then I hope we shall see you: but you will not find that I have learnt Russian.

Yours ever,
Virginia Woolf

Our house is shut, or I would not bother you about the cigarette papers.

British Museum

1184: To J. C. Squire   *Monk's House, Rodmell,*
Lewes, [Sussex]

Aug 14th [1921]

Dear Mr Squire,

In reading your article in todays Observer, which I did with great pleasure, I was interested to find you quoting the lines beginning
He did but float a little way.
Years ago I saw them quoted in a book of letters as if they came from an old poem. Later I found them in one of [James Russell] Lowells poems. I have often wondered how he came to write them—whether he was imitating or perhaps adapting an older poem, as they are not much in his style. I haven't got his poems down here, but I am pretty sure that the poem they come from is one of his earliest.

Yours sincerely
Virginia Woolf

George Lazarus

1185: To J. C. Squire   *Monk's House, Rodmell,*
Lewes, [Sussex]

[August 1921]

Dear Mr Squire,

To return for the last time to Lowell—I am not a profound student of his works, but the lines quoted seemed to me a great deal above his usual standard,—certainly in the manner of some older writer—though overlaid with the 19th century. What I should like to prove is that he imitated them consciously. He was my Godfather. I dont like to accuse him of plagiarism.

Would it be possible for you to come and spend a week end here? Saturday the 27th would suit us: Leonard agrees that it is a very long time since he has seen you.

I have not been allowed to do any work for the last three months, as I have been ill, and am only just recovering. But one of these days I should like to send you something.

Yours sincerely
Virginia Woolf

George Lazarus

1186: TO ROGER FRY

Monk's House, Rodmell,
Lewes, [Sussex]

[Aug. 29th 1921]

My dear Roger,

KT —— KT 3

That is Leonard's cryptic message [chess]. Nor have I anything remotely resembling the intellectual to add. I have been plagued with all sorts of minor ailments since we came down, and thus led a dull, dreary, scarcely human life—until last week, when I recovered, and thank God, took to writing again. But why did they invent a nervous system?

Then, having become very ambitious about our garden, we hear that the Squire [J. M. Allison] is going to build a villa overlooking it. He is only a sham Squire too; and altogether the prospect of having Ted Hunter[1] in the orchard is so distressing that we are off to look at a farm in the meadows near Ripe [Sussex]. There's nothing I enjoy more than looking for houses, and imagining that I am going to find the very thing, so I don't much mind. But the truth is this bit of the country is becoming picturesque. Old gentlemen sit sketching—I watch them through field glasses. You know how they do it—a grassy road—a few cows—a child in pink—perhaps a goose in the foreground. Now a dead horse has just gone by in a cart. You know my passion for sensation. I try to make Leonard come and look at it—but he won't—He is writing a review. What he longs to do is to find some excuse for exposing Murry publicly. Every week there is an article in the Nation which sends the blood to his head. Last week it was about you—the architecture pamphlet[2]—too futile, I thought; all about the greatness of Professor Lethaby,[3] which you don't realise. (Now another horse has gone by—this

1. The solicitor, a partner in Hunter & Haynes, Lincoln's Inn.
2. *Architectural Heresies of a Painter.*
3. William Richard Lethaby (1857-1931), Surveyor to Westminster Abbey and a writer on architectural subjects.

time a brown one, alive). I think Murry is profoundly perverted: I mean all his criticism, and his fury, and his righteousness, and his deep, manly, honest, sturdy, stammering, stuttering, endeavour to get at the truth seem to be a desire to stick pins—but he doesn't get them very far into you.

I have been reading Henry James—the Wings of a Dove—for the first time. I have never read his great works; but merely pretended. Certainly this is very remarkable—I am very much impressed. At the same time I am vaguely annoyed by the feeling that—well, that I am in a museum. It is all deserted. Only you and I and Melian Stawell[1] and some wretched little pimpled spectacled undergraduate, and say Gilbert Murray, are to be seen. It is vast and silent and infinitely orderly and profoundly gloomy and every knob shines and so on. But—I am too feeble minded to finish—besides, little though you believe it—they are actually burying the white horse in the field; a man has arrived with two pick axes.

Please write again. It was really delightful to hear from you; I bubble with chatter—I mean I should, if only you were here. Leonard and I spent part of our honeymoon at Vauclure—We went to a village play. We also saw Mistral.[2] I'm trying to impress you—but its not a bit of good—

Yours ever

V.W.

Sussex

1187: To Lytton Strachey   *Monk's House, Rodmell, Lewes, [Sussex]*

Aug. 29 1921

What a devil you are not to write oftener—considering your command of the language.

When are you coming? That is the purpose of this letter. We want to avoid an encounter between you and Jack Squire. Yes: it is quite true; he has been asked.

I've seen nobody; I have done nothing. All sorts of plagues descended upon me, very wearisome, but, thank God, suddenly disappeared. I'm now recovered, gained 6 lbs; and we're off to look at a farmhouse. Ted Hunter is going to build a cottage overlooking the orchard; I believe him to be a partner of Haynes.[3] And one hears Mrs Shanks, over the wall, asking Shanks[4]

1. Florence Melian Stawell (1869-1936), the classical scholar.
2. Frédéric Mistral (1830-1914), the poet, who was awarded the Nobel Prize in 1904.
3. Edmund Haynes, the solicitor.
4. Edward Shanks (1892-1953), the poet, novelist and critic. He was awarded the first Hawthornden Prize (1919), and from 1919 to 1922 he was assistant editor of the *London Mercury*.

whether he'd like his cocktail mixed. The worst of it is that the country is lovelier and lovelier. We have put brick edges to the flower beds. We have a garden room. Tell Ralph that every flower that grows blows here. We have pears for breakfast. I have taken out a subscription to Lewes free library, which exactly suits my case. But even there Lytton Strachey predominates. I want to turn an honest penny; and behold, when I come to write about old Mrs Gilbert [*unidentified*], it runs of its own accord into two semi-colons, dash, note of exclamation, full stop. Do you recognise your style?

I've not seen Charleston; but L. has. Mary, Sprott,[1] Duncan, Clive, Maynard (very argumentative), Nessa, refusing like all Stephen women to lie down and drink milk, or go to bed before 2 a.m.; Clive writing an article upon the obscure, which can't be done without consulting Virginia. Virginia rather testy; says she's *not* obscure; Duncan offers to come over—bicycle broken; Mr Botten's horse drops dead in the field of strangled guts—but this probably belongs to Rodmell news, and is indeed all I can think of— The Literary Supt. by the way, says that Prewett[2] *is* a poet; perhaps a great one.

So do come, and let us know, and we'll keep off the Squires and the Shanks.

Yr. V.W.

I am reading Evan Morgan's novel[3]: "Je suis vaincue,' and she sobbed on his breast, clinging to him. Both were exhausted, the emotions of the soul had overpowered them, they fell half fainting against the cool grey stone, and there . . . they leant in the twilight against the protecting buttress of the House of God, the God of Love and of Life."

Frances Hooper

1188: To J. C. Squire   *Monk's House, Rodmell,*
                               Lewes, [Sussex]
Aug 30th [1921]

Dear Mr Squire
    We shall be delighted if you will suggest a time—either a week end or two nights in the week—after next week—that is after the 12th.

1. W. T. J. ('Sebastian') Sprott, the social psychologist, whom Maynard Keynes had introduced to Bloomsbury as an undergraduate at Cambridge, where he was an Apostle.
2. Frank Prewett, a Canadian, whose *Poems* the Hogarth Press had published.
3. Evan Morgan, later 2nd Viscount Tredegar, had submitted a manuscript to the Hogarth Press, but it was not accepted. Lytton and Virginia had met Morgan at Garsington.

I think you know how to get here. Indeed I saw you being bowled out not so very long ago, in the meadow. By coming in the morning one can catch the train to Southease.

Yours sincerely
Virginia Woolf

George Lazarus

1189: To David Garnett and Francis Birrell

Monk's House, Rodmell,
Lewes, [Sussex]

Postcard
[31 August 1921]

Please send to the above address
Anthology of Modern Poets by J. C. Squire.

V. Woolf

Berg

1190: To Saxon Sydney-Turner

Monk's House, Rodmell,
Lewes, [Sussex]

[Sept. 1 1921]

My dear Saxon,

I was about to write to you: if I had written, our letters might have crossed. How pervasive and persuasive your style is. That sentence, is, I think, unmistakable Saxon.

I have absolutely no news. My disease seemed to get better, and then got worse—not very bad, but incapacitating, so that I lay in the garden room and watched the cows, and read every book in the Lewes library—which is a very good one—all the old memoirs. However, I've now jumped up again, and can walk, and I think it is all done with, which is a mercy.

I enjoyed hearing from you immensely—but I was mystified by your ceaseless progress through the fogs and shades and summer nights and winter darks, which seemed to continue endlessly and bring you nowhere. It was so characteristic. I could see you tapering away in a crepuscular haze towards the North Pole—an exalted figure, bound on some quest—but what?[1]

Did you reach it? Was there nothing there? And then, of course, you turn up still in a fog (this you admit is true) and drink old Brandy at Hull. Oh what a pleasure you are to me! But this is beside the point. If you want a compass, I expect Ka, Eagles Nest, Tregerthen, St Ives, would get you one.

1. Saxon was travelling in Finland.

They are much scarcer than they used to be: but tell her to go to a shop, almost next to Curnows, the bakers. I dont remember the name.

Next week Lytton comes: and then James and Alix and so on. Won't you come? Then I would take you on the marshes, where I walk every evening: and now all the ditches are dry, so that I can explore without falling in. As I say, we have a very nice room, looking over to Caburn. There is no news really—but a succession of small excitements. All the Rectors plums were stolen, which he was very proud of; then our eggs disappeared. Do you think the same man took both? Do you think it was one of the school-children? Or do you think that our hens have taken to laying in the long grass as they sometimes do when the old hen goes broody? We have bought Mrs Dedman's chickens; and also 2 fine geese. Geese live on nothing but grass; yet they are very fine birds; and we are killing one on the Gooses day—24th Sept. I saw Barbara in London: and we discussed names for boys. Which did she choose?[1] Give her my love: and say that Leonard wants to read L's Victoria. Will she send it back *here:* I do trust the child hasn't in some way gnawn the cover. Another letter at your leisure.

Your aff.
V.W.

Sussex

1191: To Janet Case

*Monk's House, Rodmell,
Lewes, [Sussex]*

[Sept. 2nd 1921]

Dearest Janet,

I am fearfully sorry to hear such bad news of you. I have been thinking of you picking your apples and watering your plants—quite falsely and envying you for I was in bed, and I thought you were up. I think the hot weather must have done for us both. However, my old horrors have given way to the usual cure of lying in bed and seeing no one and not writing a line. But oh how sick I am of wasting time like this! I expect you are much more patient—But I hope you'll get quite well, and not keep all the china bright and polish all the beautiful chairs and tables—which I never ceased to envy—until you are. I have precious little news to give you—here is L: V. "What is Harry Johnston[2] like?" L. "A very curious person: and Janet's conjecture is probably correct. He is infinitely better than 99 out of 100 Imperialists, and I think fundamentally must be a very decent man indeed. He is a very sensible man, as he breeds peacocks for the table, somewhere in Sussex. He is of course slightly tainted with Imperialistic fallacy, but he is

1. Barbara Bagenal's son, Michael, was born in July 1921.
2. Sir Harry Johnston (1858-1927) was an explorer and colonial administrator chiefly in Africa, where he did much to abolish slavery.

obviously naturally—an extremely fair-minded man, for instance his letter in the Times a week ago with regard to the Indians in E. Africa. I have only met him once, when I asked an awkward question at a meeting of the Anti Slavery Society and he immediately afterwards came round to me not knowing me at all and entered into an animated conversation with regard to it. He is a small man with a very large round face, and is I believe perpetually dying."

Leonard adds that he thanks you very much for your review of his book [*Stories of the East*]; which he liked.

The last people I saw were James and Alix, fresh from Freud[1]—Alix grown gaunt and vigorous—James puny and languid—such is the effect of 10 months psycho-analysis. I read nothing but old memoirs which I take out from the Lewes free library and find entrancing. I am now going for my evening stroll in the water meadows and wish I could turn in at Windmill House.[2]

Love to Emphie. Please let me know how you are.

Yr. V.W.

Sussex

1192: TO VANESSA BELL

[September 1921]

[*Monk's House, Rodmell, Sussex*]

Dearest,

I hear from Duncan that you're expecting Mary [Hutchinson] tomorrow —in which case I think it would really be better if I didn't come, but came on Monday to dinner instead. Would that suit you? If anything it suits me rather better. I'll come then unless I hear.

I know I should either sulk or chatter, and then M. wd sulk—besides I've got several matters to discuss with you in private (which doesn't mean anything exciting—only business etc—

Yr
B.

Berg

1193: TO CLIVE BELL

Tuesday [13 Sept 1921]

Monk's House, [*Rodmell, Sussex*]

My dear Clive,

We are very much pleased that you enjoyed seeing us—as we did you. I suppose that 'atmosphere' is what one never, never realises for oneself.

1. In June 1920 Alix and James Strachey had gone to Vienna, where they studied psychoanalysis under Sigmund Freud.
2. Janet Case's house at Rowledge, Surrey.

But alas, we can't go into the matter on Friday, as we should like, as that is Leonard's day in London.

Perhaps you would come over one day next week—Monday or Tuesday. Perhaps Mary would come too? I have heard so many versions of our quarrel, that I should like to decide with her which is the one we ought to believe.

I will say nothing to Jack Squire—after reading his little book of poets, I doubt whether there is anything to be said. Still, for the honour of English Literature perhaps I ought to.

Forgive this writing. Age and imbecility and a walk to Rat farm have undone me.

Yr
V.W.

Quentin Bell

1194: TO VANESSA BELL   [*Monk's House, Rodmell,*

[mid-September 1921]   *Sussex*]

Dearest,

Hester has written as you see. I have no letters—but perhaps you have? —or have you any of father's?[1]

God knows when I am to see you. Perhaps I might come over and spend a night Thursday or Friday next week? Only I can't be certain of the day, as I have now taken a turn in the opposite direction and wait for events which never happen—But, of course, they will.

How are you? And is it true (I have it on good authority) that (but I mustn't be indiscreet) I mean have you forgotten me? Well, I dont mind if you have. So there. You'll miss my letters though in France. Leonard says you wont. I have a bet on with Lytton about it.

Here is Nelly, so I must stop.

Yr
B.

I suppose you wdn't come for the 24th? When Eliot will be here?

Berg

1195: TO VANESSA BELL   [*Monk's House, Rodmell,*

[early October 1921]   *Sussex*]

Dearest Dolph:

We think you had better choose what size you like—Our Tolstoy was

1. The *Letters of Anne Thackeray Ritchie* were edited by her daughter, Hester Ritchie, in 1924.

Crown 8vo: Kew Gardens was Demy 8vo: Roger is having a square size which is being cut for him.[1] We can really do any size you like.

I should like of course to see you, but the difficulties seem great. The pedals of my bicycle spin round and round without moving the wheels. But if you would let me know any day that suits you (we leave on Thursday) I would drive in and meet you, and drive you to the train again.

Has Duncan let his Fitzroy studio? Would the person like to let to me for our dinners now and then?—I should like the name anyhow.

Please explain to Quentin that the flotilla which he wanted has, of course, gone out of fashion; so I got the nearest thing, but I hear they catch large live—or almost live—fish, so my magnets will be very dull. However, I should like them, if he doesn't.

The Clergyman is coming to tea—What an excitement!

Yr

B.

Berg

1196: To Roger Fry   *Hogarth House, Richmond*

Oct. 17th 1921

My dear Roger,

Your letter arrived precisely one hour ago, and here I am sitting down to answer it. Whether the answer will be sent is, of course, another matter. Your last—slightly tipsy, very brilliant, sympathetic, inspiring and the best you ever wrote,—sent me flying to the inkpot, but when I read my production and compared it with yours my vanity as an author refused to be pacified. I can't endure that you should write so well. If you want answers let your letters be like bread poultices: anyhow I tore up what was, I now think, the best letter I ever wrote. Would you like it if I dashed off a little sketch of the eclipse of the moon last night, which entirely surpassed your great oil painting of the Rape of Euridyce—or whatever it is?

You will say that you don't have eclipses of the moon on the shores of the Mediterranean.[2] Well, its true we have been having the devil of a time— the influenza. Leonard refusing to go to bed; Nelly like a hen run over, but unhurt, by a motor car; Lottie something after the pattern of an intoxicated Jay: the house ringing with laughter and tears. Do other people go on like this, I sometimes wonder, or have we somehow (this includes you, by the way) slipped the coil of civilisation? I mean, we've jumped the lines. There you are bathing naked with 50 prostitutes; yesterday we had Goldie [G.

1. Roger Fry's *Twelve Original Woodcuts* was published by the Hogarth Press in December 1921. Hogarth did not publish this proposed book by Vanessa.
2. Roger was in St Tropez with Vanessa, Duncan and the children.

7a (left to right) Nelly Boxall, Lottie Hope, Nelly Brittain. Angelica Bell in foreground

b Duncan Grant and Maynard Keynes

c Charleston, Firle, Sussex

8a Molly MacCarthy

b E. M. Forster

c T. S. Eliot at
    Monk's House

Lowes Dickinson] to tea. I do my best to make him jump the rails. He has written a dialogue upon homosexuality which he won't publish, for fear of the effect upon parents who might send their sons to Kings: and he is writing his autobiography which he won't publish for the same reason.[1] So you see what dominates English literature is the parents of the young men who might be sent to Kings. But Goldie won't see this—having a mystic sense, in which I am deficient. He was as merry as a grig, though; and had forgotten whatever it was—the ruin of civilisation I suppose—that used to distress him.

Tonight we go to Weybridge to dine with Mrs Forster and read an address upon article 22 of the Covenant. Wells has asked us to a party. George Booth has asked us to another. Life, as you see, whizzes by with incredible rapidity, and its all I can do to cling to my arm chair in Richmond, and add page upon page to a story which you wont like but will have to say you do.[2] That reminds me of the Nation; of Murry; of Sydney; of a thousand things which I long to say but can't see how to get in on this sheet of paper. Murry has bred in me a vein of Grub Street spite which I never thought to feel in the flesh. He has brought out a little book of those clay-cold castrated costive comatose poems[3] which he has the impertinence to dedicate to Hardy in terms which suggest that Hardy has adopted him as his spiritual son. Thank God, he is soundly drubbed in the newspapers. But his article on you has drawn his fangs for ever; he has no sting: all one hopes is that he may bite each one of us in turn before he is finally discredited and shuffled off to some 10th rate Parisian Café, where you'll find him, 20 years hence, laying down the law to the illegitimate children of Alaister Crawley, Wyndham Lewis, and James Joyce. Eliot says that Joyce's novel [*Ulysses*] is the greatest work of the age—Lytton says he doesn't mean to read it. Clive says—well, Clive says that Mary Hutchinson has a dressmaker who would make me look like other people. Clive has cut his hair, drinks wine only once a day, says eggs and sausages is his favourite dish, and comes to Richmond to confess his sins—after which, I suppose, he sins them worse than ever. But he is trying to reform.

Love to Nessa—I don't write to her on principle. Nor do I read over what I have written to you: but now, send me another.

V.W.

King's

1. His autobiography was not published until 1973.
2. Virginia had been writing *Jacob's Room* since April 1920.
3. *Poems: 1916-20.*

Hogarth House, Richmond

Oct 24th, 1921

Dearest,

Well, so you have arrived [at St Tropez]. The vision of large hats against a translucent sea and the white legs of prostitutes is I admit very attractive; oh and the butterflies: how they make my mouth water—the apollos, the white admirals, the Sulphurs, the purple emperors; and Dolphin sitting on a terrace in flowered muslin drinking coffee out of a glass, and first dipping an oblong piece of sugar in the coffee and nibbling the brown bit.

Still I dont see why I should write you a letter about yourself. But tell me—are there great spear shaped bunches of cactus? Oleanders? Perhaps Oleanders are too romantic. I have enough without them.

Ottoline has been in London—in fact she has had another seizure in the grand style, racing up to the Thackeray hotel Bloomsbury, with her troupe, which now consists of Sydney Waterlow, Gertler, Brett and Countess Russell ['Elizabeth'] in order to catch Charlie Chaplin. Ott: says that Charlie Chaplin is the greatest, most *genuine* artist who has ever lived. She heard that he was to be at a party given by Wells. She does not know Wells. She telephoned to Wells. She bought herself an early Victorian umbrella; put white feathers in her hair, and dressed herself in a sealing wax green silk crinoline; set off with Gertler, Sydney, Brett and Countess Russell; reached Wells'; demanded Charlie Chaplin;

But he had not come. Whereupon she took up a commanding position in the middle of the room; Her influence is said to have struck people dumb even on the balcony: Countess Russell was sent scavenging to collect notabilities. And the Wells' utterly disappeared.

She is said to wield her umbrella with astonishing aplomb. Alas!—we were asked, and could not go, and this comes through Koteliansky, who was on the balcony, and was dragged half across the room by Countess Russell; then broke free, which created a very bad impression. At least Ottoline meeting him in the hall, opened her umbrella in his face. It is white silk, with tassels.

Do you know that when the Booths, Macnaghtens, Gore Brownes and Ritchies are alone in the family circle on Sunday night the talk often turns upon poor Vanessa and poor Virginia? What is so remarkable, according to Betty Meinertzhagen, (who came to tea to discuss her approaching suicide—she's an actress—too large a nose, the managers say; in desperation;) is that the Booths never argue about us or discuss us but merely state the facts, which are accepted with sweetness and resignation. "Clive Bell brought them into touch with people of bad character. It is untrue that Maynard Keynes is a friend of Clive Bell's. We have the greatest respect for Maynard Keynes. Roger Fry is, of course, a charlatan. You have only to see Vanessa and Virginia now to realise how unhappy they are. Could we have done more for them? No, dearest Dodd, we could not." It only remains to be said that Dodd goes through severe operations constantly without a murmur, and has dedicated her eldest daughter, who wished to go to Newnham, to the care of old Mrs. [Charles] Booth who is 78, and lives alone at Gracedieu [Manor, Whitwick, Leicestershire]. "The greatest pleasure in my life, she said to Betty, was to amuse my brothers in their holidays." But George is apt to be sentimental about you, and remembers how lovely you were long ago.[1]

We have just bought a press for £70,[2] and are turning the basement into a printing shop. Ralph comes every day. I walk through the woods of Richmond which are yellow, but the weather is like early May, and think of you: oh and of lots of other things: don't suppose I'm not completely disillusioned about you, and ready to throw myself into a life where you and Duncan are merely shadows upon doors—feathers—films—I dont know what all.

Laura's [Stephen] expenses [for her asylum] are now £100 a year above her income. The trustees therefore say that we must somehow make this good. We owe her £2,000. There is however a sinking fund; in which they have invested some of her money every year, with a view to realising a capital sum in the year 1940. They propose that we should either mortgage this, or find £100 a year between us. I am seeing Adrian, who is making investigations, on Friday, and will let you know. The trustees are affable, and do not wish to press us.[3]

If it were not that my hair is falling I think I could still pick your husbands soul out of the flames. At least he dined here on his own asking; was friendly in the extreme; made out that he has given up drinking; advised me to go to Mary's new dressmaker; and hopes that we shall meet constantly this winter. I'm afraid he uses us as a hair shirt though. A severe intellectual dinner with the Woolves—and then a debauch on the sofa at River House [Mary Hutchinson's house].

Yr

Tell Duncan to write. B.

Berg

1. The identifiable family connections were these: Antonia ('Dodo' or 'Dodd') Booth, eldest daughter of Charles Booth, married Malcolm Macnaghten; Imogen, another daughter, married Eric Gore-Brown; a son, George Booth, married Margaret Meinertzhagen, Betty Potter's sister.
2. The press was a second-hand Minerva platen machine, worked by a treadle, and similar to McDermott's press on which Leonard had printed *Prelude*. This press was given by Virginia to Vita Sackville-West in 1930, and is still at Sissinghurst Castle, Kent.
3. In 1906 the four Stephen children had mortgaged their childhood home, 22 Hyde Park Gate for £489, to provide for Laura's expenses. By 1919 this sum had increased, with interest, to £1,883.

1198: To Alice Clara Forster

Hogarth House, Paradise Road,
Richmond

Oct. 25th [1921?]

Dear Mrs Forster,[1]

We have spent a most delightful evening reading Morgan's letters, which I return. How vivid and amusing he makes things! They give one an extremely queer and interesting view of his life. It was very good of you to let us see them, and if ever we might read any others, we should be so glad.

I feel we didn't half thank you for having us that night, owing to the hurry, but we enjoyed it all, and caught our train easily. Thank you, too, for sending the newspaper. The horrid lady at the lecture was so good looking—which seemed to make it worse.

It is good news that Morgan thinks of coming so soon.[2] I find that one misses him a great deal.

Yours Very Sincerely
Virginia Woolf

Berg

1199: To Katharine Stephen   [*Hogarth House, Richmond*]

[26? October 1921]

My dear Katharine[3];

I was just writing to ask you to come etc etc.

I shall be very glad to see you on Wednesday; but to be frank, I feel slightly awkward about seeing Dorothea; owing to her attitude to Vanessa.[4] I dont want to exaggerate; but I am sure both you and Dorothea will understand my feeling.

Your affect V.W.

Berg

1200: To Dorothea Stephen   [*Hogarth House, Richmond*]

[28? October 1921]

My dear Dorothea;

I didn't mean this Wednesday; I meant next.

Your view that one cannot ask a friend who has put aside the recognised

1. Morgan Forster's mother, with whom Virginia and Leonard had been dining.
2. He had been in India since early in 1921, as temporary private secretary to the Maharajah of Dewas Senior, and in 1912 for a longer period. On these experiences he based his novel *A Passage to India* (1924).
3. Katharine Stephen, Virginia's cousin, was the eldest (65) of the four daughters of Sir James Fitzjames Stephen; Dorothea (50) was the youngest.
4. See the following letter.

conventions about marriage to one's house because of outsiders and servants seems to me incomprehensible. You, for example, accept a religion which I and my servants, who are both agnostics, think wrong and indeed pernicious. Am I therefore to forbid you to come here for my servants sake? Yet I am sure you agree with me that religious beliefs are of far greater importance than social conventions. I am quite willing to suppose that all you said to Vanessa was dictated by kindness and good will, though I do not think it struck her quite in the same way. Anyhow my point is different—it is simply that I could not let you come here without saying first that I entirely sympathise with Vanessa's views and conduct—since, for your own reasons, you have drawn attention to them. If after this you like to come with Katharine, by all means do; and I will risk not only my own morals but my cook's.[1]

Yours affly. V.W.

Berg

1201: TO ROGER FRY

Hogarth House, Paradise Road,
Richmond

Nov. 2nd [1921]

My dear Roger,

I feel impelled to write to you, by the fog; (three o'clock and lights lit): by the rain; by the fact that Dr Gardiner's[2] funeral has just passed the house, with 10 mourning coaches stuffed with chrysanthemums; and a detachment of police and postmen in long black coats. Everyone came to the window and they are even now burying him at East Sheen. Perhaps you didn't hear, though, how he dropped dead last Saturday on the surgery steps. Richmond rang with it. And then Dorothea and Katharine are coming to tea. Tell Nessa that if she'll write to me I will send her a dossier of letters passed on the question of her (V's) morality between Dorothea and me: short, but very fine; ending, alas, with protestations of eternal affection on her side.

I had meant to apologise, however for—well, I think I must have sent you a silly vain egotistical letter: I think you cannot judge how intoxicating words are; how I get run away with: how I plume and preen and can't sit still on my perch. At least I think I detect a tone of reproof in your letter; perhaps its only some fundamental difference between us: perhaps I ought to be a nicer woman: perhaps I am still inhibited by some strange quality

1. To this letter, Dorothea responded, "Very well then. I will come with Kate on Wednesday." For a description of their meeting see Letter 1204.
2. Dr Matthew Henry Gardiner, a Scotsman, who for 37 years had been in general practice in Richmond, as a partner of Dr Fergusson, and police and Post Office surgeon in the borough. He died of a heart attack on 28 October, aged 65.

in you—some queer light cast on you by number 46 Gordon Square. I can't tell: and at this distance it is worse than useless to spin words, as I cannot give them the precise shade of levity mixed with concern which I require. I merely throw this out, in case you have my passion for taking feelings to the window and looking at them. But you have your fun; and I have my Dorothea: and who shall say that I don't deserve my fate? By the way, I see that you're all being a great success at the London Group. I see it in newspapers; you are taken seriously; but I feel it in the atmosphere. I think Nessa will boom very shortly. Clive says so too. I'm in touch with that little hop o'my thumb. But I must take Nessa's opinion on the state of the case. Why drag in Gandarilla by the hair of the head in a letter from Paris asking me to resume more frequent intercourse?—and then there's a lot about Elizabeth Asquith [Bibesco] and how she interrupted their tête à tête "not that we had anything much to say to each other"—Its all very queer; and to me would be intoxicatingly romantic, were it not that my hair is falling: my dress stained with paint (I am doing stencils all day long): and my temper now too crusty and cranky to be easily set aswim. I have been reading Anatole France too: and Hardy at the same time: I feel a profound distrust of the Gallic genius in literature; so light, so slight, so pointed, and the point always snapping at the least pressure: but oh how delicious—

It pours, it pours, it pours; all the roofs from my window are like policemens waterproofs. Yesterday the Thames overflowed; and one poor old gentleman, being caught asleep on a seat, was marooned in midstream; lost his head; ran up and down like a polar bear at the Zoo, while the crowd collected on the Bridge and hooted.

Please write. I shall never see you. We think of going to Rome in February and staying there.

Yr V.W.

Sussex

1202: To Clive Bell   *Hogarth* [*House, Richmond*]

Tuesday [8 November 1921]

My dear Clive,

I'm frightfully sorry not to have written before. First I thought you were abroad, then I made sure you were drowned, and finally we were away, marooned from postcards.

But we shall be delighted to come on Friday. Only I must forewarn you, knowing your susceptibilities, that I shall have been tramping the streets; in large boots; shabbier than ever—I've had an accident with my only dress. Still, I think you make too much of these things. I rather believe I am commissioned by God to wean you.

I'm glad you warned me about Betsies' book.[1] I shall now be on my guard if [Bruce] Richmond should propose it.

Yr. V.W.

Quentin Bell

1203: To Lady Ottoline Morrell

Hogarth House, Paradise Road,
Richmond

Nov. 8th [1921]

My dear Ottoline,

Alas!—we have people dining here on Saturday night, so that I am afraid it is impossible. Shan't you ever come to London—or rather, since London is useless, to Richmond? I heard of you at Wells' party, but I was sitting toasting my toes.

Far from being brilliant, I spent most of the summer in bed or on the verge of it, completely comatose.

But then life is so pleasant when one gets up again.

However, as you insist upon my catching the post, I must stop writing this very moment.

Your affate
Virginia Woolf

Texas

1204: To Vanessa Bell   *Hogarth House, [Richmond]*

Sunday, Nov. 13th 1921

Dearest,

You say, perhaps untruly, that you wrote your letter on Friday, 5th Nov. (Guy Fawkes day). Well, I got it last night—Saturday, 12th.—I mention this to show how prompt I am. With Duncan in the house, though, I suppose one can't count upon getting letters posted. Why don't you turn out his pockets on Fridays? Why don't he write to me? He reminds me rather of the Lemur ape, who as you know gets all the other apes to feed it because it is too lazy to feed itself, and also too beautiful.

I think your plan about Keats is a very brilliant one. There would be no difficulty about printing some lines on every page; but don't ask *me* this sort of question, because I always get the answers wrong. However Leonard corroborates this. By the way, Rogers cover paper was not designed by Carrington; I get it from a little man in Holborn; it is clearly an imitation of the Kew Gardens cover.

1. Elizabeth Bibesco's novel *Balloons*.

But you want to hear about Dorothea [Stephen]. I enclose a copy of the letters. I don't see that I was indiscreet; and I am sure I triumphed; but only with the mind. She came to tea, of course, with Kate; devoured huge quantities of muffin and cake; and so oppressed me with her moral depravity— her sheer repulsiveness and obtuseness and stodge—that I was practically fainting. Really, she makes one dizzy with dislike. It all came over me at the first sight of her—She said how d'y do in her condescending way, and began to eat like a poor woman at a charity tea, fast, stealthily, every crumb, thanking me with insincere sweetness; but happily Leonard had her. He loathed her. They talked about Ceylon. Meanwhile poor dear old Kate half blind, all blurred and worn and misty, kept eating butter by mistake for bread and putting her cup down on the tea pot, crunched up in her chair, with her hat over her eyes, and those good leather gloves that she always wears, and shoes like some old statues. She told me about Laura; who is the same as ever, and never stops talking, and occasionally says, "I told him to go away" or "Put it down, then", quite sensibly; but the rest is unintelligible. Then I was accosted by Dorothea. "Virginia, do you like having that book about the Queen [Lytton's *Queen Victoria*] dedicated to you? I should. It seems to me a very intimate kind of book. But I do not know that I should like the Brahmans to read it, or the Americans. You see, we can laugh in the right places, because we understand; they would laugh in the wrong, because they do not understand. I should not like that." Does that bring her back to you?—her odious selfcomplacency; her extreme brutality—I felt as if she had a thick stick as well as a thick leg; and if I did anything unseemly she would kick and beat. She lives in a village; can't talk a word of the language, which is Candarese; learns sanskrit with a pundit, and intends to expound the fallacies of Buddha. I pretended that I had not heard of her book.[1] Being excessively vain, she was furious. "Then you do not read your Literary Supplement. There was a very long review of me there—by an exceedingly ignorant man. I also had one in the Indian Observer. That was slightly more intelligent." As she stumped out of the house she drew herself up, pressed her hands to her forehead and muttered some gibberish which she said was the Eastern form of farewell upon leaving a dear friend for some time. "How long will it be?" I asked. "Five years" she replied.—Thank God!

I have got led away in my fervour. There were various other things I had to tell you, but my hands are so cold I can scarcely write. Winter is upon us; fog, frost, every horror. One creeps about the house longing only for bed. Even without a cold, one's nose drips perpetually. The influenza is rampant, and it is the fossy influenza, in which all one's teeth drop out. Ralph is very obstinate and crude. He and Leonard argue incessantly; and then appeal to me, and I have been thinking about something else.

1. Dorothea Stephen, *Indian Thought* (1918).

Oh but I must tell you! I am getting into mischief. At least I think there is every probability that I shall be in mischief within a day or two. It is all your husband. I told you how I had a second letter from him, regretting our separation—And so we dined at 46 two nights ago, and there was Mary and Maynard and Aldous Huxley; and as I was going Mary took my hand and pressed it and said "I don't at all like this plan of quarrelling with you. Will you come and see me—will you come next week?—Will you come anytime you like? Please do." Of course I pressed her hand—it is an exquisite claw and she has a new coral bracelet—and said, "yes"; and I am going. Well?——

Lord! I've just remembered another bit of gossip—but this, on your honour as a Dolphin, you must only whisper to the waves of the Mediterranean, if to them. You will see that indiscretion would have very serious results. I should be ostracised—a long word—Ask Roger what it means. You remember our friends the Waterlows. Well, Sydney has been getting more and more intolerable. He goes down to Oare for the week end and complains that the flowers have come up red when they ought to have been blue. He complains of the eggs, and the beds, and the beef, and the pudding. Nothing that Dawks [Margery Waterlow] can do, nothing that she can wear, say, or insinuate, pleases him for a second. Yet her oven is the best in Wiltshire, her Buff Orpingtons [chickens] the admiration of the village, and her brats, though the ugliest, the furthest on for their age, and the healthiest. This went on all the summer—Sydney coming down, grumbling, going away again. At last Dawks could stand it no longer. She determined to separate. She refused to allow him to come. He sat in London and considered what to do. He sent for Desmond. Dawks sent for Molly. After long deliberation and envoys going to and fro—Dawks still refusing to see him—the MacCarthy's persuaded them to go to Germany for six weeks alone together. They have just returned. No one knows yet what the result is: but why trailing Dawks unter den linden for 6 weeks should reconcile one to spending the rest of one's days with her, I know not; or for that matter watching Sydney eating sausages in a beer garden.

Molly's sympathies are all with Dawks. But the animals ought to be in the Zoo—that is my feeling.

Please let none of this get to Gordon Square.

There was another piece of gossip much better than this one, on the tip of my pen; but I've entirely lost it, as I wrote. What could it have been? Anyhow I've no room—We've been asked to Garsington—but that wasn't it; Lord Tennyson's[1] second marriage has turned out unhappily, and he finds his chief comfort in marching slowly with Hester [Ritchie] on his arm down

1. Hallam Tennyson, the son of the Poet Laureate. His first wife had died in 1916, and two years later he married the widow of Andrew Hichens. They lived at Farringford, Freshwater, in the Isle of Wight.

the Poets walk at Freshwater; Hester finds it very comforting too—but that wasn't it; the [Adrian] Stephens are going to the Baltic in their yatcht [*sic*]; the Woolves are going to Rome; no; I've entirely forgotten what it was; and so you shan't have it until you have written me another letter; which you must post, for letters really aren't much good unless they are posted, remember. Dear old Saxon has broken our telephone. He rang me up every day for three weeks, without getting on once, with the result that our telephone sometimes rings all night, and when you go to answer it, there is no one there. How like Saxon. Barbara has been at Gordon Square. Poor Bob Trevelyan—poor Bob Trevelyan—Well, if one meets Bessy [his wife] at the 1917 Club on a cold afternoon with her handbag and her great boots and her nice red Dutch nose, and her liberal sympathies—one does fall in love with the Duchess of Marlborough. I did at once. She is taking Bob to the doctor. The alarming thing is that he can't write. And Norton comes out of his Retreat this week; so I shall retire to mine; and you'll never hear from me again, and how you'll survive that I can't think, though you must admit I've wasted a whole morning writing this letter, when I ought to have been stitching Roger's woodcuts.

Yr
B.

Thanks for the cheque; and the photograph. Do send me a sketch of the place—La Tropez.

Berg

1205: To Katherine Arnold-Forster

Dec. 2nd [1921]   *Hogarth House, Richmond*

Dearest Ka,

Well, I thought it was high time you wrote. But after all there's not much use in writing once a year, because there are then so many important facts to state that one can't say anything interesting. There will be no room for my essay upon Mr Percy Lubbock,[1] but I agree he has his merits—only he is the colour of putty and wears spectacles, or did so 20 years ago when I last saw him.

I spent the summer chiefly in bed—Oh what a damned bore! It was all very dull, and dreary and stupid—sleeping draughts and that sort of thing. But I am now arisen, and scribbling away to make up for lost time. Leonard is rushing in an express from Manchester to Durham, from Durham to Newcastle at this moment. Whenever the train stops he gets out and makes

1. Percy Lubbock (1879-1965), the critic, whose *Craft of Fiction* appeared in this year.

a speech on International politics, or the Cooperative Movement. He will drop into my arms at 6 tomorrow morning in a state of coma I imagine, having travelled all night. Then we are in the frenzy of our Xmas publishing season—the first edition of Roger's woodcuts sold out in 2 days, and another to be printed, folded, stitched and bound instantly. Our partner [Ralph Partridge] sleeps in the house, and lives in the basement, where we have our fine new press. Did I ever tell you about Mrs Manning Sanders, your friend? She sent us a long poem, which seems to have a good deal of merit, and we are going to bring it out this Spring.[1] Do you know her? Its rather exciting and altogether most unexpected.

How your description of the Provencal dancing by night in the public square made me see my old neo-pagans[2] once more! You will think this sarcastic; it is really affectionate. Why doesn't Gwen [Raverat] ask us to stay? I should like to have a fine set to with her once again before I die. Send my love when you write.

But when am I going to see Bruin's brindled pelt? For God's sake don't let them take you for a seal and shoot you on the beach one of these days. We think we are going to Italy in February: or possibly to Greece. I don't know, and can't therefore make any plans. But there can be no doubt I shall be seen coming along your road one of these days. Shall I ever forget Austin Phillips [*unidentified*]?

Now I have answered and asked and got it all in; but rather untidily I fear. Literature has been left out. There's nothing interesting, or very improper about it. Just life, my dear Bruin. Leonard told me to say that he had made a note of your letter—whatever that means.

Your
V.W.

I liked the photograph very much. He's an interesting little boy [Ka's son Mark].

Mark Arnold-Forster

1206: To Violet Dickinson   *Hogarth House, Richmond*

Dec. 6th [1921]

My Violet,
    The Hogarth Press at least has the merit of making you write to me. I'm always afraid that the mongrels will oust your original bantling. Your

1. Ruth Manning-Sanders' *Karn*, printed and published by the Hogarth Press in 1922.
2. A term invented by Bloomsbury in 1911 to describe the intellectual group which included Rupert Brooke, Ka Cox [Arnold-Forster], Gwen and Jacques Raverat, Frances Cornford and David Garnett.

marmalade awaits you,—but I suppose there's no chance of seeing you before Xmas. Why not ask me to tea one day? We shall go away for that horrible festival. At this moment all my time is spent in stitching Roger Fry's woodcuts. We sold our first edition in 2 days, and now have to provide a second in a hurry. Its very encouraging, but I wish we had a capable woman on the premises. (This is a hint that you might become our second devil).

Who admires John Bailey? I dont; and I gather that Lytton Strachey feels quite safe against John's version of old Victoria. Still poor John is thin; he must be protected; you are his old friend and yet you laugh at him.

I wish you'd disinter my [Walter] Crum (male) for me. He's worth 20 Johns.

Leonard sends his love and invitation.

Yr
VW.

Berg

1207: To Violet Dickinson   *Hogarth [House, Richmond]*

[10? December 1921]

My Violet,
   Alas! we're in the midst, or rather beginning, of a domestic crisis—both maids down with German measles, and no char will come for fear of infection, so Leonard carries the trays and I do the beds. I think anyhow I'd better not come, as at any moment we may break into rashes ourselves. What a d—d bore! Ask me again sometime, and give my love to Walter Crum.

Yr
VW.

Berg

1208: To Barbara Bagenal   *Monks House, Rodmell,*
Lewes

Dec. 30th [1921]

My dear Barbara,
   I have just stuck your photograph in my book. Many thanks for sending it. Your son is exactly like his father. But one always annoys people by finding likenesses, so I will say no more.

   I would send you a photograph in exchange—but mine all got the foggy dew this summer. I don't know how yours are so good—There is Saxon to the life.

   We are just returning to Richmond; where we shall immediately be

496

engrossed in printing. Roger's woodcuts have gone into 3 editions;—I like to rub this in, to show you how bad a bargain you made when you deserted us for marriage and the hills of Wales and the waters of the Wye. I don't know what news to send you—for why should you be excited by the immense excitements of this village? Mr [Edward] Shanks has pneumonia; the Squire [Allison] is selling all his land; we hope to buy a field, in which case Leonard will have the finest potatoes in the Kingdom. You must come and see our new garden room.

Saxon has completely vanished from my life. He broke our telephone early in the autumn, which he took amiss, and refuses to ring us up, or pretends that we don't answer if he does.

However, when he came in person he seemed younger, stronger, sprightlier than ever, after travelling to the heart of Finland, and finding no one to receive him.

Nessa is as usual uncertain what to do—whether to plant the children at Gordon Square and stay on with Duncan in France, or to face family life in London. She seems more than ever contemptuous of England—What a bore it must be to be a painter, and need light and landscape, instead of a f.re and a book!

I never thanked you for the wonderful condition you kept the Queen in.[1] She came back considerably more purple and spruce than she went out.

Are you making a fortune? Couldn't you do a scoop in apple trees—or discover a caustic?—something to make apples grow in December? I say caustic because L. is spraying our trees all day long with it.

Love to Nick and your family.

Your aff. V.W

I am ashamed to send this letter which got stuck in a book, and has thus lost any interest it may have had. But now I can wish you a happy new year. Jan. 3rd 1922

Berg

1. Barbara had borrowed Virginia's copy of *Queen Victoria*. In 1970 this copy was sold at Sotheby's for £620.

Letters 1209–1261 (January–June 1922)

In January Virginia reached the age of 40. To the general public her name was still unknown. She had published only two novels and some short stories, and a mass of literary criticism, most of it anonymously in The Times Literary Supplement. *Leonard was advised that she might not have long to live, and a series of illnesses in January, February and March (flu, followed by a murmuring of the heart and a high temperature) kept her in bed at Hogarth House for most of that time, although she was sometimes able to work with Koteliansky on translations from Dostoevsky, and in April on her story* Mrs Dalloway in Bond Street. *The extraction of three teeth in May helped her recovery, and she was able to complete her revision of* Jacob's Room, *and even attended with pleasure the Women's Co-operative Conference in Brighton. She was reading Joyce and Proust, the latter with admiration. Leonard carried on the Hogarth Press with Ralph Partridge, in spite of growing friction between them, and in June T. S. Eliot came to Hogarth House to read them the manuscript of* The Waste Land, *which they were to publish in 1923.*

1209: TO VANESSA BELL   [*Hogarth House, Richmond*]

3rd Jan. [1922]

    This is the best I can find. They say the needles are as good as can be had; and more money would only be spent on case. This cost 3/- so I owe you 2/-.

    No time for more. I'll write tomorrow.

Berg

1210: TO E. M. FORSTER   *Hogarth House, Richmond*

21st Jan: 1922

My dear Morgan,

    It was a great pleasure to get your letter. I meet Goldie at dinner and I say "I've just had a letter from Morgan" "Ah, what wonderful letters he writes!" says Goldie. Clive and Maynard, who are the other guests at table, feel jealous, as I intended they should.

    Does this present Bloomsbury with sufficient force? Two days later I was stricken with the influenza, and here I am, a fortnight later, still in bed, though privileged to take a stroll in the sun, for half an hour—after lunch.

But its not going to be sunny today.

Writing is still like heaving bricks over a wall; so you must interpret with your usual sympathy. I should like to growl to you about all this damned lying in bed and doing nothing, and getting up and writing half a page and going to bed again. I've wasted 5 whole years (I count) doing it; so you must call me 35—not 40—and expect rather less from me. Not that I haven't picked up something from my insanities and all the rest. Indeed, I suspect they've done instead of religion. But this is a difficult point.

I've not much news. Lucas dined here with Topsy Jones, his wife,[1] and brought a play; and I peep between the edges, and see it won't do. Then Luce[2] dines here tomorrow; and we are to bring out a new edition of his poems—I don't know him, but feel like his grandmother twice removed. Bob [Trevelyan] dined here—oh—Bob was delicious! He has two white tufts above his ears like rabbit scuts; and his dear old mahogany face is alternately pig like—hungry greedy—growling—and divine. His love for the Duchess [of Marlborough] (this is Gordon Square gossip) has subdued and softened him, and he's having his arteries vivified in order to write more poetry, and out he pulls, as usual, manuscripts—in fact he was bustling off to see a new publisher. We praised you. (I'm ashamed to put in these little compliments; for you will only say to yourself how Virginia likes praise—but it can't be helped). As for our other friends, Sydney is attached, in a trailing sort of way, to an Irish man called Sullivan,[3] who is, this time, the authentic voice of God. I'm all for letting things be, and even bowed before Sullivan myself the other night, hypocritically, for I didn't think well of him—too black and hairy and singular for my taste; but I do want Sydney to settle down.

Every one is reading Proust. I sit silent and hear their reports. It seems to be a tremendous experience, but I'm shivering on the brink, and waiting to be submerged with a horrid sort of notion that I shall go down and down and down and perhaps never come up again.

Otherwise we are where we were.

I've now come to the point of this letter—which is this. Leonard and I are going to Italy about March 20th.[4] Would there be any chance of meeting you there? Where? you ask. Well, it might be practically anywhere—Rome, Sicily, Greece (thats not Italy I know)—Anyhow, do think it over, and inform us in time. We should like it very much. I liked your mother very

1. F. L. Lucas, the critic and poet, then a Fellow at King's College. His wife was born Emily Jones.
2. See p. 596, note 1.
3. John William Navin Sullivan (1886-1937), a frequent reviewer for *The Times*, and author of many works on popular science. He and Aldous Huxley were Murry's assistant editors on the *Athenaeum*.
4. They did not go because Virginia fell ill again.

much. But it was rather a tragedy. She had prepared, I should say for some days, a wonderful dinner; and all the family silver was out. The maid (who chased us across Monument Green in the dark crying Mr Woolf! Mr Woolf!) had a new apron on. There was coffee, and a box of dates. Well, all this had to be swallowed in 10 minutes. Perhaps though I am wrong about the silver and the apron. That may be your ordinary style. Please forgive me, if so. What fun it would be to go into the matter with you at this moment—or on the slopes of the Parthenon!

Here is Leonard: here is the Nation. "Too Late in India?" occurs on the front page in the largest letters. Yes, I think it must be you.[1] The neckties and the grammar I seem to recognise. Anyhow I've had a good laugh: I wish our Indian correspondent wrote more of the Nation. But I won't bother you about your writing.

Leonard wishes me to say that he knows no one of any interest in Egypt: (I know the widow of Lord Cromer). He says things are pretty black. He has to write a monthly article in the Contemporary; and he also writes for the Webbs, for the Nation, for the Herald, for the Statesman—in short he is becoming, not rapidly, but what alarms me more, solidly, one of our public men. God knows—he may be Member for 7 universities next month.

So good bye, and write to me again. I am feeling ever so much better since beginning this letter.

Yours ever
Virginia

Berg

1211: To J. T. Sheppard   *Hogarth House, Paradise Road,*
                                 Richmond, Surrey

Jan. 25th [1922]

My dear Sheppard,

I was in the middle of writing to you, asking, indeed imploring you to get us tickets when I was struck by the influenza, and have only just emerged. We shall be delighted to dine with you at 7. But I dont think 2/- and a great deal of pleasure (I like you much better and for good reasons too than [R. C.] Jebb) is adequate payment. We will fight it out when we meet. Are you positive it is Feb. 10th? Someone said Feb. 1st—but I suppose you know.

Vanessa says she stays in the rooms of a Mrs Bell at Cambridge— Maynard's Mrs Bell. Could we have a room there too? Would it be an awful bore to engage one with 2 beds for the week end?

1. Morgan Forster was still in India.

I'd like to keep the poem, secretly, if I may. Mr Sheppard has very brilliant gifts, hasn't he?[1]

Yours ever
Virginia Woolf

King's

1212: To Lytton Strachey   *Hogarth [House, Richmond]*

Wednesday [1 February 1922]

The one thing needed, so the doctor says, is a letter from the great master of biography. That would set me on my feet again. So please put down whoever it is—can't be still Voltaire?—and write a long long over-flowing letter.

No news here, except what I collect through Ralph—highly amusing and gratifying I must say. This refers to Maynard. The other news—how you're a sharper[2]—also gratifies. I guessed that long ago.

Couldn't you lend me the proofs of your new volume?[3]

That would be something to read. With all your faults—how is it that one enjoys reading you?

V.W.

Frances Hooper

1213: To Lady Robert Cecil   *Hogarth House, Paradise Road, Richmond*

6th Feb [1922]

My dear Nelly,

I have been in bed with influenza for 4 weeks, and I think it is high time you wrote to me.

You have been silent so long that I find it very difficult to think of you in any particular place. You may be in Westminster or Geneva or Sussex. Then, what are you doing? You have read the Memoirs of a Midget [Walter de la Mare] and thought them very good. Well, I couldn't get through them. You have just ordered Elizabeth Bibesco's stories from the library. I feel inclined to praise them, because all the lily livered journalists are afraid to praise the work of a Princess—even a sham Princess. My brother in law

1. J. T. Sheppard was a classical scholar, and became Provost of King's College, Cambridge. His published work included several verse translations of Greek plays.
2. Virginia had heard from Keynes that Lytton had paid no tax on his literary earnings.
3. *Books and Characters* (1922).

Clive, who drives about in motors with her and drinks cocktails and all the rest, says she is just as clever as any gutter snipe; and a very good hard-working woman.

I wish I ever saw you; but until they make telephones which look into peoples drawing rooms I shall very seldom do that. All the summer I couldn't sleep, and had to lie in an outhouse at Rodmell reading through the lives of forgotten worthies from the public library.

We are—Mr Partridge and Leonard are—busy printing a new long poem by a short fat poetess [Ruth Manning-Sanders], who came to correct her proofs the other day and stayed for 2 hours and a half, like a baby sucking a coral, discussing her genius. But she was very nice, and very modest. Poetry is not like prose. Clearly these poets feel themselves the mouthpiece of God in a way which I certainly dont.

This, you see, is merely a bait to make you write to me.

I still can't go out; and my great excitement is to open letters. When Lottie brings up my tray with only the Westminster Gazette on it, and I am reduced to reading Lord Robert upon Winston, which gives me the greatest pleasure—but does Lord Robert really read Dryden, or did you put him up to it?—when this happens, I say, I invariably curse Nelly Cecil. Surely one of her gifts is letter writing?

Your aff.

Hatfield   Virginia

1214: To Lady Robert Cecil   *Hogarth House, [Richmond]*

Saturday [11 February 1922]

My dear Nelly,

It was very nice to get your letter, which confirms me in my belief that you have inherited the letter writing gift, along with your castles, and makes me think twice before I demolish the Nellies and the Castles.

I'm now condemned to lie in bed for 2 or 3 weeks, until my heart gets right, which the influenza has put wrong. So letters are more than ever needed. I can't say that the disease is good for the brain.

I read two lines, and go off into a trance, quite pleasant, like an animal in a hot house.

I've been reading the life of Lord Salisbury.[1] I find it absorbing. What a queer character—I'm reminded, oddly, of my father. And Lady G. writes like twenty able men crushed into one. As hard as a paving stone. I mean this complimentarily. When will the 3rd Vol. come out?

Yr.

Hatfield   V.W.

1. *Life of Robert, Marquess of Salisbury*, by Lady Gwendolen Cecil, his daughter. She never completed it.

1215: To LYTTON STRACHEY   *Hogarth House, [Richmond]*
Saturday 8th? 9th? [11th] Feb. [1922]

Your correspondence is about the only bright spot in my day so please continue. My lethargy is that of the alligator at the Zoo. And the alligator doesn't have very clear ideas of Racine. A. B. W.[1] in the Times almost suffocated me by saying that Molière, Don Juan, is tedious twaddle. Surely it is the best of the lot—so I seem to remember. Then that Mule, Alice Meynell, says that Jane Austen is a frump, and that Mr Patmore is equal to Milton and that Tristram Shandy should be read in Prof. Morley's edition with every 10th page cut out. There can't be anything left to castrate of Meynell, or I should do it myself. Alligators can't endure the moderns— Peacock is what I like. You don't know how good he is—Crotchet Castle— surely nothing survives except the perfection of prose. And you read Miss Sinclair![2] So shall I perhaps. But I'd rather read Lytton Strachey.

Well, if you do come it will be something to look forward to. Clive is suspended above me, like a Cherub, all bottom and a little flaxen wig. Roger looms in the distance, so let me know which day.

The infirmity of this handwriting is *not* entirely heart disease: I am reduced to a fountain pen. And you make them work.

Princess B[ibesco] exactly suits my tank. Poinsettias, arum lilies, copulation in tepid water, spume, sperm, semen—that's my atmosphere. She doesn't shock me as Katherine [Mansfield] does, all the same.

Yr

V.

Frances Hooper

1216: To VIOLET DICKINSON   *Hogarth [House, Richmond]*
Sunday [12 February 1922]

My Violet,

Alas! I have been in bed with influenza for the past 5 weeks, and have to stay there at present as my heart is invalided temporarily. So I shan't be able to lunch with you; but thats no reason why you shouldn't come to tea with me. No infection is left; only this damnable organ, always in my case as you know, so warm and loving, jumps by night, and gives me a slight temperature.

Only two days ago Nelly the cook said why doesn't the tall lady whom we liked so much come and fetch her marmalade? There it is waiting for her!

1. A. B. Walkley, dramatic critic of *The Times*.
2. May Sinclair, *The Life and Death of Harriet Frean* (1922).

Leonard sends his love. We have just bought a new press and new type and keep our partner busy in the larder, which has been turned into a printing shop.

Your
Sp:

Berg

1217: To Clive Bell   *Hogarth [House, Richmond]*

Tuesday [14 February? 1922]

My dear Clive,

For God's sake send me some gossip. It's lacerating to pick up scraps from chance meetings in the London Library. Besides, there are masses of affairs passing through your brain every moment of which you've no cause to be ashamed. Here am I, apparently the favourite breeding ground of the influenza germ: but my head remains what it was;—and my heart too.

In short, devote a morning to your poor sister in law, and she will ever pray—for what?

Now what would you most like to happen?

Your
V.W.

Quentin Bell

1218: To Vanessa Bell   *Hogarth House, [Richmond]*

Monday, Feb. 20th, 1922

Dearest Dolphin,

Really you are getting too eccentric—to conduct your correspondence by addressing the envelope only and putting Clive's letters to you inside. I liked Clive's letter very much, but I should have liked your's better. And then Clive said nothing against me. Altogether he was perfectly discreet and amiable, save for one queer statement, which amused me very much, but which I've sworn not to reveal. There! That'll make your fins water. Come back and I'll explain all. But instinct tells me that you want to hear of nothing so much as the state of my health. Did you hear of my heart disease? Did you get your cheque? Did you think it a very small one? My heart is better; I'm still in bed though; and furious, speechless, beyond words indignant with this miserable puling existence which has now lasted over 6 weeks, and doesn't really pay. I've been having visitors this last week; but you know what frauds they are. They come in and sit down and produce a bunch of violets, and then say how nice it is to be in bed, and how they wish they could be in bed, and how well I look—which as you know always makes me furious. It's something like seeing the rabbits cross the heather in a shooting gallery.

504

Still, I have to amuse you—thats my mission in life—and so I must rake the ashes of memory. I have *not* seen Roger. Roger rings up and asks himself to dinner. When told that I cant see people at night he heaves a sigh and replies that, alas, every hour of daylight is sacred to art. So he sacrifices my society, which mayn't be long for this world, to some livid teapot. His blood be on his own head.

I have seen Adrian—perfectly charming, detached from Karin; and really a success in his own way: I've seen Lytton: very depressed because that dunderhead Ralph has been trying sharp practices with his publishers and, naturally, failed; Mollie Hamilton; oh and so on—too dull to write out. I had great fun with Elena [Richmond] the other day, however. I think she is quite the nicest human being I have ever met—solid—splendid—sedate— with the body of a matron and the mind of a child and the tastes of a school-boy; so maternal to me that I fell in love with her at once—Perhaps I always have been in love with her. Well this gigantic mass of purity sat down by my side and I told her the story of George.[1] It is only fair to say that she began it. Do you realise that she still dines with Elsie and Mrs Popham[2] in Bruton Street, and sees Lady Sligo and the ladies Browne, and lunches with George and Margaret [Duckworth]? "I am going to be perfectly frank about your brother—your half brother—and say that I have never liked him. Nor has Bruce [Richmond]. I never did like him even in the old days." This being so, I couldn't resist applauding her, and remarking that if she had known all she would have hated him. The queer thing with Elena is that one never knows what penetrates, what slips off. She was shocked at first; but very soon reflected that much more goes on than one realises. I rather think she was alluding to her father and Miss Lülling. Now she'll tell Bruce, who being a perfect gentleman will probably have to spit in Georges face in the Club. Dont you think this is a noble work for our old age—to let the light in upon the Duckworths—and I daresay George will be driven to shoot himself one day when he's shooting rabbits.

Until Elena married at the age of 35 she was never allowed to read a book that Mrs Rathbone [her mother] hadn't read first; and the improper pages were folded over, so that her knowledge of literature is naturally imperfect. She never unfolded the pages: they still remain folded. I think its the right way to bring up girls. Please do it with Angelica. There is nothing like the charm of a perfectly ignorant innocent woman of 40—But then I am in love.

Molly came and talked, as you said, about Michael [MacCarthy]; who is, she says, very unhappy. I sent Julian a present, but got no answer—little devil. However, I told him he neednt write. I wish next time you write, you would enclose Julian: not your dentists bill. I draw the line at menus, washing accounts, and household books.

1. Her recollections of George Duckworth's conduct towards her and Vanessa when they were girls.
2. Elizabeth, Dowager Countess of Carnarvon, and her sister, Mrs Popham.

Moxon is dead. Moxon is—or rather was—Saxon's father; and he died after long agony, leaving Saxon in control of two households of lively lunatics,[1] one of whom broke its leg; another had violent influenza, and Mrs Moxon was prostrated; so that Saxon, what with the burial, and condolences from public bodies, was never so happy in his life. Adrian met him, come up to buy a suit of blacks. He is probably going to set up house with his mother, and I am more than ever overcome by the supreme justice of fate—who else could have composed the life of Saxon with such mastery? Molly seemed to me rather spry; but she has grown very fat; and has curious lapses, when she looks like a seal at the Zoo.

I hear from Koteliansky that Gertler [his paintings] does not sell very well—and from Violet Dickinson that the Sitwells have been reciting what seemed to her sheer nonsense through megaphones[2]—so Clive and I overlap. I'm afraid the parrokeet is back at his old tricks with the beau monde: I'm seeing him tomorrow;

Shall I ask Mary Hutch. to come and see me? But then I can never hide my po successfully; and one ought to wear a lace cap in bed.

[Dr] Fergusson is coming in a minute, and I'm going to make him let me out. Then I shall get back to my writing; but I'm not a good writer. Violet said "And how is old Nessa looking? . . . How is Adrian looking? . . . Of course, I think you were quite right about Duncan Grant—he is a great painter . . . How's old Sophie? I shall never forget Fritham—and your father taking my cup of coffee. I loved your father." and so on, without any stops, or listening for a second.

I'm now getting dull, and as you don't like dulness, I must stop.

We think of going to Sicily on March 20th—but God knows.

Does Duncan ever say that he loves me?

Yr

B.

Yes, I was rather depressed when you saw me—What it comes to is this: you say "I do think you lead a dull respectable absurd life—lots of money, no children, everything so settled: and conventional. Look at me now—only sixpence a year—lovers—Paris—life—love—art—excitement—God! I must be off". This leaves me in tears.

Tuesday.

Your own letter just come.

I return Clive, to set your heart at rest, and I should like Norton back to

1. Saxon Sydney-Turner's father was a doctor who had cared for mentally deficient patients in his house at Hove.
2. Edith Sitwell had been reciting her poetry through a megaphone at private parties, to music by William Walton. In 1923 the performance was given publicly under the title *Façade*.

deposit in my catacombs. According to Lytton, he's worse than ever, sweats profusely under the armpits, and congeals if left silent a moment.

Ott is upon me—perhaps Philip too.

What is one to do? I'm sure I should shine in your society; and for Gods sake make friends with Joyce. I particularly want to know what he's like.

Also, do you know a Mr or Mrs Manning Sanders? The woman, whose poem we're printing, came to tea the other day, and jumped at the sound of your name, apparently admiring your works. She haunts Fitzroy Street. Her husband was a painter till he got struck in the legs and now can only write novels. I can't place her. She has a sister with business in Paris, rather sordid, squalid, and sympathetic—(Mrs M. S. I mean)

Berg

1219: To Lady Ottoline Morrell

Feb. 21st [1922]

Hogarth House, Paradise Road, Richmond, Surrey

My dear Ottoline,

It is most tempting to hear of you in London, and makes me curse my fate more than ever. I've been in bed with 2 attacks of influenza for the last 6 weeks, and my heart has gone wrong in consequence. I'm ever so much better, but not yet allowed out.

Of course, if you could come here to tea on Friday—but I expect your days in London are too full for that to be possible. If it is, ring us up. Lytton held out hopes that you were going to settle in London. It always seems to me your duty to do so— If only you saw what a wretched draggled puddle London has become for nice quiet women like myself who want to sit down and talk for 12 hours without stopping you would have pity. There are Mrs Asquiths windows aglow as I pass through Bedford Square; and I feel inclined to throw a dead cat in. Only she would not notice it.

Your affate

Texas   V.W.

1220: To Lytton Strachey   *Hogarth [House, Richmond]*

Thursday 23 Feb. 1922

I think you *must* now tell Clive the truth.[1] He is evidently making him-

1. Clive had criticized Shaw's *Back to Methuselah* in *The New Republic*, and Carrington, who felt that Clive's attack was unjustified, forged a letter of insulting protest from Shaw to Clive. (It is printed in *Carrington*, ed. David Garnett, 1970, p. 202). Clive was completely taken in, and replied to Shaw, who in his turn answered that he had never written the letter of which Clive complained.

self the laughing stock of London, and his accounts get wilder and wilder. I'm not sure he didn't say he was going to write to Shaw again. I had the whole story without any pressing (indeed the reverse) after he'd been in the room 10 minutes. It is evidently his favourite topic. He says he has shown the letters to several good judges who all agree that Shaw has been driven mad by Clive, which, says Clive, is what I've always foretold. "These vegetarians, my dear Virginia, always go at the top. He needs Bullocks blood" and so on and so on. I'm to see him again next week.

Well, what about Byron's letters?[1]

Yrs
V.W.

Clive also said that your behaviour at a party at 46 struck him as extremely queer.

Frances Hooper

1221: To Clive Bell   *Hogarth* [*House, Richmond*]
Saturday [25 February? 1922]

I am horrified to find that Leonard left you the Henry James' without my condition attached—that they be left at 41 G.S. [Gordon Square] on Wednesday morning at the latest. They are James' [Strachey]. I stole them, finding the door open. Last year I stole his George Eliot, in the same way: he was seized in the night with a passion to read Middlemarch; couldn't find it, accused me and our friendship has never recovered.

Your adroit flattery is I see, driving me to spend the half hour before tea in writing a letter. As you know, it should be the half hour after tea; and that is dedicated to L's brother [Philip] who is about to sail for India to improve the breed of cattle in the Punjaub [*sic*]. He is bringing a white mongrel and a hive of bees as parting gifts. I am taking to Apiary. I have asked Desmond to let me review the Beekeepers Vade Mecum.[2] Needless to say, he won't. Yet my mind is just fit to go in and out of cells and dwell upon the amours of the hive. What a charming book that would make to be sure—and what a charming evening I spent last night with Saxon! I have promised to find him a house here, in which to live with his mother.

V. But what about the lunatics?

S. Um—m. They might of course come too—at least the two old ladies

1. *Lord Byron's Correspondence chiefly with Lady Melbourne* was published by John Murray in 1922.
2. For the *New Statesman*.

might—but the eldest of them, who is 90 next May, is certified. I am not sure that we should be allowed to keep her. Besides . . .

V. Is she quite mad?

S. Um—m—She can't talk so that you can understand. Sometimes she shouts. She did at Christmas. Lady Young, who is getting old herself, and has some complaint, I don't know exactly what it is—she lives at Eastbourne now—Lady Young forgot to send her anything. This upset her a good deal. She would have had no presents if I hadn't bought her a box of chocolates . . .

V. But Saxon, how much money have you got—I mean by your father's will?—

S. I have a mortgage on a house at Portslade. . . . Um—I may foreclose. I'd better ask Niemeyer about that. . . . Peonies.

V. Peonies?

S. Niemeyer has purple peonies in his garden. They come from Copenhagen.

V. Shall you like living with your mother?

S. Um—m-m. I don't think Thersites is a good character altogether, do you?

V. Shakespeare?

S. Well, I believe there *is* a play by the Elder Nashe; but I *meant* Shakespeare.

Here is the mongrel and the hive, I must descend. But for Gods sake remember James: Henry James: no 41: Wednesday.

Yrs
V.W.

Quentin Bell

1222: To Violet Dickinson   *Hogarth House, Paradise Road, Richmond, Surrey*

[27 February 1922]

My Violet,

What a pleasure to get your too short, but not too sweet, half sheets of notepaper at breakfast. Do make a habit—as some people, pray.

We are now driving into London to see another doctor, as my heart and my temperature still annoy me; and the dr. here, wants to get it settled. I can't go on lying in bed.

Anyhow, you will have to come and see me if I do. I hope though that we shall get away and be all right

I was wanting to write to Nelly about her sister—but I see I have nothing to say, except that I feel more sorry for her than for most people who lose sisters.[1] Wasn't Lady Anne her favourite?—But one can never

1. Nelly Cecil's sister Anne, the youngest daughter of the 2nd Earl of Durham, died on 24 February 1922.

communicate with people in this world, and that is the great tragedy; I'm thinking of your burial feast with the black sugar cake, you see; and how we shall all be so jealous, Lady Horner of Ella Crum, Ella Crum of me, and me of the Chow dog, I daresay. I could go on writing for ever, but fate has cut this paper short—

Yr

Berg   VW.

1223: To MOLLY MACCARTHY [*Hogarth House, Paradise Road,*
                                                                   Richmond, Surrey]

[end February 1922]

Dearest Molly,

This is one of the finest letters in the world, so for God's sake dont spill the tea over it, but put it away carefully, for Michael's 21st birthday, and then sell it and buy a herd of cattle.

(it is going to be a great deal better than that—I am only tuning up; preluding with a few more or less simple chords in the bass.) Ahem!

I can't possibly answer your question till Leonard comes downstairs. Meanwhile, we will have a little conversation. I can't think what to say— We have just had tea. Partridge has killed 2 geese, and has given us one of them. Here is the post. A letter from Clive. Elizabeth Bibesco has given him her book. My temperature is 99 pt. 2. Lottie's womb—no, no, no—it makes me sick. Do you want to know about Miss Stanford's womb? She keeps the milk shop. Desmond had a story about a piece of beef and a spinster's womb. That's what I feel about the milk puddings now. To change the subject—I am reading Byron's letters—Thank God: here is Leonard.

Yes, by all means.

Next Wednesday.

Only understand that *nothing* can be provided; not drink, not eggs, or biscuits either.

Bring paper bags.

yrs

V.W.

Mrs Michael MacCarthy

1224: To VIOLET DICKINSON   *Hogarth House, Richmond*

[1 March 1922]

My Violet,

The dr. [Dr Sainsbury] was a very nice man, but rather severe—Wont let me out till next week, and we mustn't go to Italy in April as we had planned. What a Curse it is! He said that my old intermittent pulse had rather tired my heart, and the influenza has made this worse, and he wants me not to walk up hill until this has got normal. The temp. is influenza going on, but it is so low that it doesn't matter. Savage of course always made out that an intermittent pulse didn't matter—

What is a 'murmur'?—I dont know; but I gather it's not a thing that matters in the least.

I wish you would give a fuller account of the wedding.

I see I am writing nonsense, but that is the result of talking to a dress-maker.

Please tell me why Pr. Mary married Ld. Lascelles[1]: what is his character; and hers; do they share the same bed; did you believe in the ceremony; I wish you wd. write this out, and we will print it. The question is whether the Royal family can still be taken seriously—my maids were cynical.

Yr
V.W.

Berg

1225: To PHILIPPA STRACHEY   *Hogarth* [*House, Richmond*]

Sunday [5 March 1922]

My dear Pippa,

Is it true, as I seem to remember, that you once suffered from a temperature that wouldn't go down?

Part of my disease is that my temp. for the last 2 months has remained fixed at about 99 with a drop below normal at night. The dr. has tried quinine and the usual things without result. Its so little, that it doesn't matter, but I'm so anxious to finish off this business that if you did know of any remedy I would suggest it to him. It's nothing to do with my heart, he says, but rather keeps that back.

Forgive me for treating you like the family medicine book, but as you know, your place in my life is not that of the casual friend: no: you live in the medicine cupboard.

What day, now, will you come and see me?

The shadow of my mother-in-law hangs over this week, like that of a bird of prey—a very tattered old eagle, poor woman, but you know how they take things to heart. She has to start life again at the age of 71. Philip [Woolf] is going to the Punjaub. Clara is in New York. Bella in Ceylon.[2]

1. In February 1922 Princess Mary, the only daughter of George V, married Lord Lascelles, who succeeded his father as Earl of Harewood in 1929.
2. Bella Woolf, Leonard's sister, had married as her second husband W. Thomas Southorn, who was a member of the Colonial Civil Service.

Sylvia has had a miscarriage.[1] Freda[2]—so it goes on—you can imagine how. All our names end in a; but, speaking into the privacy of the medicine cupboard, I have always felt myself somehow exotic. This has to be concealed. Yet I get on with Mrs Woolf. She reads Rasselas [Samuel Johnson, 1759]. Isn't the world odd?

But how do I dare to dribble like the bathroom tap when you are all haste and energy and snatching moments to read speeches? ~~Ah, but~~ No: *this must cease.*

Your affec.
V.W.

But what day will you come?

Strachey Trust

1226: TO VIOLET DICKINSON   *Hogarth House, Richmond*

Thursday [9 March 1922]

My Violet,

(Please excuse what seems to be the last piece of paper in this room)

It fills me with compunction to think that it takes you an hour each way: and then you only get cold buttered bun: but you must count in the pleasure it gives your forlorn intimate. And then you leave gold-sprinkled glass on the mantelpiece. However, this is a letter of business. We want to know whether there is any chance that you would let us print the Miss Eden letters which were not included in your book—What we want is that you should write *notes and an introduction.* Surely this might be possible? We have never done anything of the kind. Besides, if they are as good as the others, we should sell them. Also we are probably entering into alliance with a real printer,[3] who prints beautifully.

I daresay this suggestion is foolish and wearisome to you. If so, don't bother to answer.

I should so much enjoy a long and intimate gossip with you; uninterrupted; hot buns;—but as I say, I'm afflicted to imagine that 2 hours are needed to bring you.

1. Sylvia Woolf, first wife of Edgar, Leonard's third brother.
2. Freda Major, who had married Herbert Woolf, the eldest brother.
3. William Maxwell, managing director of R. & R. Clark of Edinburgh, who printed *Jacob's Room* for the Hogarth Press, and many of their subsequent books. The Press never published any letters by Miss Eden.

There seems some hope that Lottie won't need an operation, but nothing is yet settled.

Yr
V.

(This side of the paper is even dirtier than the other)

Berg

1227: TO VANESSA BELL   *Hogarth [House, Richmond]*

Wednesday [15 March 1922]

Dearest,

It seems to me that circumstances which I don't control will make it impossible to come up on Friday.

Would you be able to come for certain on Friday? Bobo wants to come; and wants me to let her know tomorrow morning. So have the extreme goodness to ring me up tomorrow as early as you like. Its little use my ringing you up. Nothing happens.

Would you add to your kindness by at once delivering this message to Maynard?

Miss Green is extremely anxious to know whether Maynard thinks that there is any chance of his wanting her for the work on the Manchester Guardian.[1]

She has just rung up about it, and seems to be rather urgent, so I said I would try and get an answer.

She is penniless, toothless, and all the rest of it.

Your
B.

I think Julian's [Bell] letters about the best I have ever read. I shall correspond.

Berg

1228: TO JANET CASE   *Hogarth House, Richmond*

March 20th 1922

My dear Janet,

It is quite useless to write letters once a year, because there is too much

1. Miss Green had been Leonard's secretary on the international supplement to the *Contemporary Review*, and Leonard had handed over the editorship of it to George Glasgow at the end of 1921. Maynard Keynes was editing for the *Manchester Guardian* a series of supplements on European reconstruction. In April Virginia employed Miss Green to type *Jacob's Room*.

to say, and so one can't begin. I shall just have to go on telling you facts, and there's nothing that bores me more; and this huge sheet depresses my spirits, and I've been having influenza since Jan. 6th, and I had it twice over, and it affected my heart, and I had to see a specialist, and he said my heart must be broken of the habit of beating in the wrong rhythm, and that I must go to bed again; and I have a temperature of 99½ every day, and I take short walks, and come in and lie down, and see my friends, and read books and write stories, and don't feel very ill, but like sympathy and attention, and ladies to write to me, and gentlemen to bring me boxes of chocolates from Bond Street—

(Long pause)

We now begin again:

Lottie Hope my parlourmaid, a Miss Sichel's foundling,[1] went for a bicycle ride last September and got a pain in her back and thought it was rheumatics, and rubbed it with oil, but it came on worse in November, and worse in January, till she went to her panel doctor who says she must have an operation, and my doctor says she must not do anything of the kind, and so we don't know what to do, and Heaven help us!—I mean we are quite distracted and talk of nothing but the insides of women, and we can't go away till she settles, but how is she to settle? As I say, God knows.

Is that enough news for you? No: I must tell you that Leonard is working very hard, writing a book,[2] nursing his wife, advising his maids, digging his garden, and printing books. (Here he is with an apple tree in his hand: and sends love).

I know by instinct that none of this seems to you either interesting or important compared with building your own house in the New Forest. I quite agree theoretically. Nothing could be more exciting. How you keep up even your little pretence of interest in the Woolves I can't think. You don't do it very well. I mean I see through you. You wont get to the end of this letter without stopping to think about your doors and cupboards and hat racks. What fun it will be to see all your devices! I hope you've made provision for heating the linen cupboard: and then there's the blue china, which Emphie has left me in her will.

I see a great many people, but I don't take part in the ordinary Commerce of life, so I can't put you in touch with the League of Nations or the U.D.C. and the new Liberal party.

Literature still survives. I've not read K. Mansfield,[3] and don't mean to. I read Bliss; and it was so brilliant,—so hard, and so shallow, and so sentimental that I had to rush to the bookcase for something to drink. Shakespeare,

1. Edith Sichel was a leading figure in the Metropolitan Association for Befriending Young Servants.
2. Leonard did not publish his next book (*Essays on Literature*) until 1927.
3. Presumably *The Garden Party* (1922).

Conrad, even Virginia Woolf. But she takes in all the reviewers, and I daresay I'm wrong (don't be taken in by *that* display of modesty.) Middleton M[urry]. is a posturing Byronic little man; pale; penetrating: with bad teeth; histrionic; an egoist; not, I think, very honest; but a good journalist, and works like a horse, and writes the poetry a very old hack might write—but this is spiteful. Do not let my views reach the public. People say that we writers are jealous. I've left no room to tell you all my compliments—how I've been asked to copy out passages from my novels for the Queen's dolls house[1]; which has a real bath; and a library all bound in morocco; 3 inches high; but Leonard wouldn't allow—and as I say, I have no space to tell you my compliments—He has a good many too. [H. J.] Massingham says L. is the best writer on the Nation: But what did Massingham say of Night and Day?

So we go on: and the page is filled, just as its getting interesting.

Love to Emphie.

Yr V.W.

Sussex

1229: To Clive Bell   *Hogarth [House, Richmond]*

Monday [20 March 1922?]

I have pitched onto the sofa after a very exhausting, terribly trying performance of the Phoenix[2]—which I hope will turn to hard boiled egg again —and remain so. My mythology is inexact—All I have to say however, is that you're expected to dine (as well as tea) on Wednesday. Bring your spats and go to Bobo if you like: I refuse to stir. I draw up over the fire after dinner. I read Byron. I write diaries. Still, if Bobo isn't liquified and Robin fossilised and the fiddlers St Vitused, I daresay it will be pleasant enough. But all I can call to mind at the moment is an empty floor, and gentlemen spitting and [William] Rothenstein advancing with an ingratiating smirk. The fiddlers then begin: bang goes the piano lid: a woman shrieks. This is as good an end to a party as any other. A woman shrieks. Imagine it, if you like, though romantically; we stray out into the garden: it is May, June: there are apple blossoms. Even poor dutch-faced wooden-chopped Isabel (Robin's sister) looks like a gothic grotesque by moonlight; etc., etc., etc., (This is in imitation of Katherine Mansfield and rather better than the original)

But I am drivelling and dribbling, and can hardly hold my pen and only

1. Designed for Queen Mary by Sir Edwin Lutyens. Many leading authors were invited to contribute miniature volumes in manuscript for the library of the doll's house, which is now at Windsor Castle.
2. A performance of *All for Love* (Dryden) by the Phoenix Society, which was founded in 1919 for the revival of the early English dramatists.

agitate it in order to convey to my poor old fellow pilgrim that he must bring his spats as I say—and a white tie in a band box on Wednesday;

Do you think my handwriting is that of a child of 10? But then I am so tired, so palpitating, so affectionate and, to put the lid on it, adorable, that it don't matter how I write.

                                                                Yr V.W.

Quentin Bell

1230: To CLIVE BELL   [*Hogarth House, Richmond*]

Sunday [26 March? 1922]

My dear Clive,

No—I | I compute that I still owe you 7/- I can't possibly buy a P.O: so here is a
have got | cheque: $7 + 6 = 13$—which may have been the cost of my dinner. I paid you
the P.O. | 6/- so you see how it works out.

Life—life—life—what was I going to say?

Anyhow I can't go into that now.

                                                                Yrs
                                                                V.W.

Who d'you think has invited us to spend Easter with him? H. G. Wells!

Quentin Bell

1231: To VIOLET DICKINSON   Hogarth [*House, Richmond*]

Thursday [30 March 1922]

My Violet

(Please excuse notepaper)

We are now waiting for Lottie to go to the hospital, and we have a very voluble char, and everyone is rather distracted, and Partridge has gone to Spain, and we have a great deal of work to do. Countess Tolstoi has written an autobiography which Leonard is translating: Dostoevsky has written 2 new chapters to the Possessed which I am translating.[1]

If all goes well, we may retire to Rodmell next week for a time. I get about more, and don't feel so shaky, but can't get rid of this wretched temperature. The downs will cure me; I wish you were over the hill. You

1. Leonard was helping S. S. Koteliansky with his translation of *The Autobiography of Countess Sophie Tolstoi*, and Virginia with his translation of *Stavrogin's Confession*, by Dostoevsky. Virginia and Leonard only knew enough Russian to improve Koteliansky's ungrammatical English.

see, I don't wish you actually in my garden, but only over the hill. How you whirl about! and shall you have whirled to Welwyn by the time we're back?

Your ash tray mutely receives my ashes.

Now write again; and don't let the dust of Mayfair seal our ancient friendship.

Yr.
Sp.

What am I to do with this press cutting?
I do hate to be classed with Mrs Clifford[1]; at the same time, a little praise, being my father's daughter, pleases.

Berg

1232: To Clive Bell   [*Hogarth House, Richmond*]

Sunday [2 April 1922]

Yes, if God wills it, come on Wednesday, 4.30. This implies that I may have to put you off, owing to hospitals and charwomen: but I hope not.

My hand is cramped with cold. Saxon and Miss Green [Leonard's former secretary] are coming to tea—They have false teeth in common. But do you know what Miss Green is coming for—the entire manuscript of an entire novel—mine.[2]

Oh but I can't write, can't think, can't feel: and we dine at 7 with the MacCarthys.

V.W.

Ask me to show you Mr Blodgetts letter[3]—Mr Blodgett of Chigaco [*sic*].

Quentin Bell

1233: To Lady Ottoline Morrell
Hogarth House, Richmond

April 3rd [1922]

My dear Ottoline,

I need hardly say that we are going down to Rodmell on Friday—My only chance of seeing you is that we might somehow have tea together on

1. Mrs W. K. Clifford, the novelist.
2. *Jacob's Room.* She did not complete her revision until July, and it was published in October 1922.
3. See letter 1234.

Thursday, when I have to be in London. But you, I suppose, are engaged all the time.

I have discovered the secret of perfect health—to have a temperature of 99. I do this, and feel better than I have ever felt in my life. The doctors must have been mistaken when they made the temperature normal. Anyhow I can rush up to London and go to the play without any bad results.

Where have you got to in your astonishing progress—for so I always think of it—? Have you reached some new islands, found new inhabitants, and astonishing flowers and wild beasts? It's such an age since I was at Garsington, and it never seems to me a house on the ground like other houses, but a caravan, a floating palace—And who lives there now?

But isn't life awful—the way we never see each other, and only make these occasional remarks!

Your affate
V.W.

Texas

1234: To Mr Blodgett   *Hogarth House, Richmond*

April 5th 1922

Dear Mr Blodgett,[1]

I am glad to think that the spirit of Chaucer still lives in his descendants and am

Yours faithfully
Virginia Woolf

George Spater

1235: To Clive Bell   *Monks House, Rodmell,*
[*Sussex*]

April 9th, Sunday [1922]

Dearest Clive,

This is a letter purely on business, and therefore bound to be dull, though if you listen attentively the note of suppliancy may not be ungratifying—which is this: after you left the telephone rang. Bobo: "For God's sake Virginia, come and see Betty.[2] She's out of all bounds—desperate—if you *can't*—well, it'll be the river this time." So of course I could: sat in a horrid subterranean cell at the Club on Windsor chairs, parted by table and blotting paper, and laid down the law to poor Betty (who is, I may say, no longer dissolved by suffering but bitter).

1. An unknown American admirer.
2. Betty Potter (*née* Meinertzhagen), an actress and the sister of Beatrice ('Bobo') Mayor.

"If I could only get a play—a modern comedy—to act—that would be something to live for—No: I couldn't do Mr Strachey's tragedy.[1]

"Clive Bell has written a comedy!"[2]

"*Clive Bell*! But would he let me read it! With his name—a comedy—thats the very thing!—I could get my friends—But would he let me read it?"

All I have promised, on my word of honour, is to lay the matter before you. Would you communicate direct—Bedford Gardens—number in the telephone book—And for Gods sake, send it *at once*: (I have delayed). My view is that she wouldn't perhaps act it, but might tide over her predicaments, which are not merely ambitions, but of the heart. Didn't I leave her at a door in Greek Street where an actor lives, who loves no one? Bobo had two offers for the Street:[3] and Sybil Thorndike sees herself in the girl, so what about the future of the stage?

You don't care for lambs, so I will say nothing more. You don't care for [Edward] Shanks, church bells, daffodils, the unpublished novels of Dostoevsky, or cold beef and coffee—which things make my life at present, and so farewell.

Yours
V.W.

My boast:

2 invitations: one to stay with Cecils and meet Ly Gwendolen: the other to spend 5 days at Easter playing Badminton and discussing fiction with H. G. Wells. Yes—this sort of thing *does* give me pleasure.

Quentin Bell

1236: To DAVID GARNETT   *Monks House, Rodmell,*
                                          Lewes, [Sussex]

April 9th [1922]

Dear Bunny,

I see it is necessary to read Mr Joyce, so please send Ulysses to the above address; I'm afraid I shan't have the courage to sell it.

On the other hand, I do want to part with Astarte,[4] the first privately printed edition. Old Mr Bain told me it was worth about £20—that was before the new edition appeared. Would you sell this for me, and could you

1. *The Son of Heaven* (1913).
2. Clive had written *Love and Liberty*, a farcical comedy in three acts. It was unperformed and unpublished.
3. In March 1922 Beatrice Mayor's *Thirty Minutes in a Street*, 4 one-act plays, were performed at the Kingsway Theatre. They were published in 1923.
4. The story of Byron and his half-sister Augusta, by Ralph Milbanke, Lord Lovelace, privately printed in 1905, and for general sale in 1921.

give me any notion what I might expect to get? Then I shall be able to buy some more books.

I hope you'll come and see us one day with your wife.

Yours ever
Virginia Woolf

Berg

1237: To Vanessa Bell   [*Monk's House, Rodmell, Sussex*]

Thursday [13 April 1922]

Dearest,

Yes, I have been and got a box and cut the flowers,—and now must forage for string and paper all for love of you.

Shall I get a letter in reply? Well, the pen is lost. No it isn't. Duncan had one that night to write his cheque with.

You are wise not to come into the country, unless you are devoured with a passion for work—as I am. I write—read—write—read—from morning to night. For an hour I wet myself on the high road—back to tea— Shakespeare, Joyce—and so on. It is a very exciting life, entirely devoid of human beings. But, as you say, leads to damned dull letters. Well, can't you send me a little news? Do the cat and dog go out as much as ever?—or are they keeping the fire warm? Never did I read such an outburst of spite as Wyndham Lewis on Clive in the Herald. Why do you artists write like that? We dont. Even poor little squint eyed Murry wouldn't.

I must write to your husband. Why doesn't he say a word about his play? I asked him to send it to Betty. He replies with a full account of Lady Aberconway's[1] party and sends me some chocolates—nothing else. What is Mary up to?

We have got to spend the day at Gale [Chelwood Gate, Sussex] with the Cecils, all very old world; compared with your visit from Nina [Lamb], who according to Clive, wears an umbrella. We are also going to stay with H. G. Wells.[2] Why do we do such things? Just to catch a glimpse of life—it don't much matter what. All's milk that comes to my nest, as you would say. Must I for ever invent your sayings, or shall we ever drop into the old familiar gossip? Is the shade of death between us, and is this my valediction to one who played a part in youthful jaunts and jollitries? I *must* weed my path. Then toast our tea: then Joyce, Shakespeare and so on. Life is too quick;

1. Laura, wife of the 1st Lord Aberconway, of Bodnant, North Wales.
2. This weekend visit was cancelled at the last moment.

But still there's time to kiss Duncan on the neck; select a pen; brew a little ink out of lamp black—you painters use lamp black don't you? Should I like Cotman's[1] pictures?

V.W.

Berg

1238: To T. S. Eliot

Monks House, Rodmell, Lewes, [Sussex]

Good Friday [14 April 1922]

My dear Tom,

Leonard wants me to say that he could not send you any Russian translations at once,[2] but could be certain of sending something by Aug. 15th. He has in mind some interesting Tchekhov letters, which are hitherto untranslated. Koteliansky also writes to say that there are other materials, but his account is vague: Leonard will find out what he means when he sees him. (As you know, Koteliansky is a fanatic about Russian literature, and rather inarticulate). I'm now translating the newly found chapters of the Possessed, but [J. C.] Squire [of the *London Mercury*] has these under consideration.[3]

As for my own story, I won't anyhow send you anything now. I'm trying to finish off, and send to the printer, a long story[4]; and though I mean to do this in 3 weeks most likely it will take six. If I can, I will try and write something, less than 5,000 words, by Aug. 15th: I should very much like to be edited by you, but you know how ticklish these things are. When one wants to write, one cant. Anyhow, you will not only have to fix the length—you will have to be sincere, and severe. I can never tell whether I'm good or bad; and I promise that I shall respect you all the more for tearing me up and throwing me into the wastepaper basket. When are we to see your poem [*The Waste Land*]?—and then I can have a fling at you.

Did I tell you that I have laid out £4 upon Ulysses, and spent an hour or two yesterday cutting the pages. Leonard began to read last night. I mean to, if it goes on raining. And then, you know, your critical reputation will be at stake.[5]

1. John Cotman (1782-1842), the Norfolk landscape painter, whose pictures were being currently exhibited in London.
2. In 1922 Eliot founded the *Criterion*, the literary magazine which he was to edit until it ceased publication in 1939.
3. In fact the Hogarth Press published them in October 1922. One chapter was also published in the *Criterion* of this month.
4. *Mrs Dalloway in Bond Street*, which was published in the *Dial* (July 1923).
5. Because Eliot had warmly praised *Ulysses*.

So far I remain 99; in temperature, not age, but I feel astonishingly well.

Yours ever
Virginia Woolf

Houghton Library, Harvard University

1239: To Clive Bell   *Monks House, Rodmell,*
                                             Lewes, [Sussex]

Good Friday [14 April 1922]

Dearest Clive,

This is the sixth letter I have written this evening, my principle being, as you observe, to keep the treat for the last; only by the time one's ordered the coffee and politely bandied compliments with the aristocracies of birth and intellect—Cecil's and Wells—(see how proud I am!) and addressed a perhaps too familiar gossip to Tom Eliot, and also dashed off a kind of one syllable, one idea, one page epistle [to Lottie] to the Homeopathic Hospital in Great Ormond Street one has small control of pen, ink, grammar, or manner. Do you like very long sentences that cant be read in a breath? I do. It's part of my anti-naturalistic bias.

Now Mr Joyce. . . . yes, I have fallen; to the extent of four pounds too. I have him on the table. His pages are cut. Leonard is already 30 pages deep. I look, and sip, and shudder. But why do I not simply attend to business, which is to thank you for the chocolates—How I relish these old world observances! You shall have a skyblue valentine next 14th of February. Indeed, indeed, you are too good. It sends me back to the old days of Peter Studd[1] and sugar tongs: yes, in the old days there were sugar plums, and little tongses, and now there is Wyndham Lewises and Tonks[2]: Did you read the Herald? What is the psychology of the underworld? What scurvy of the soul are they afflicted with that they must scratch in public? These questions are mere rhetoric, addressed to miles of sodden downs and pouring rain, for I shan't get an answer; and did I ever wring a word from you about your play? True, I was stirred by the white bosoms of your actresses: Diana, Pamela, Olga, and the rest. I like to stitch a bright page to my sober one of Good Friday bells, and a child's funeral, now being despatched in the rain. Mr Deadman [Dedman] dug the grave—and oh God!—you said a bitch was on heat for 3 days: its a fortnight. We let ours loose; she was lined in the churchyard by the Vicar's pomeranian, Jimmy, who had lived chaste for 10 years as the Vicar's wife told Nelly; "and now he's lost" she said—

1. See p. 322, note 3.
2. Henry Tonks (1862-1937), the painter.

522

"running wild in the Brooks" and indeed they didn't catch him till eleven that night. The village rings with the scandal, in passion week too.

Yrs
V.W.

Quentin Bell

1240: To Vanessa Bell   *Monk's House, [Rodmell, Sussex]*

Sunday [16 April 1922]

Dearest,

I hope you won't mind Nelly coming to you for the night. She has got into a state about her health, and suddenly announces that the journey up and down to see Lottie is too much, so we are arranging for her to stay at Hogarth until we come back. She'll go there on Tuesday, if you can have her for the night.

We shall probably stay on a week or 10 days, if we can get some one here to do for us. Oh these domestics! What a worry and fidget they are!

I am coming up, I think, on Thursday next to see Lottie. Could you possibly give me lunch, either at the studio or Gordon Square? I'll let you know for certain, as other events may interfere. Or shall you be coming to Charleston?

At moments it is divinely lovely here—hot, birds, daffodils, blue sky: generally a moist mop of rain and mud and a cold east wind. Thank God we're not in Essex with the Wells', as we should be had I not told a lie.

I should like to see Julian, in order to see what difference school has made. I'll try and buy him a swimming duck, tell him, with my love.

Yr
VW.

Berg

1241: To Clive Bell   *Monks [House, Rodmell]*

Wednesday [26 April 1922]

Dearest Clive,

Here come this moment some remarks upon Princess Bibesco, not very profound, but in payment of 17/6 which I owed Ray [Strachey] for her damnable sheet.

Well, the hail is hissing like sausages in the fire: I'm packing up. We leave early tomorrow, thank God; after three weeks incessant physical discomfort.

I saw Bobo and Robin [Mayor], and hear that there was a violent scene

in the 1917 Club when Betty [Potter] attempted either murder or suicide—
I don't know which. They had a letter to say she was gone for ever. So she
has, up to the present moment; but is safe at Bristol. The rhyme or reason
I know not—

Writing impossible—the wash must be paid—

Yrs V.W.

Quentin Bell

1242: TO LADY OTTOLINE MORRELL

[*Hogarth House, Richmond*]

[April 1922]

My dear Ottoline,

May we come May 27th? Leonard wants to come, and hopes to come,
but says may he leave it open, and let you know later?—if this doesn't
suit you, please say so.

It will be very nice—and I would write more, but have just burnt my
3 fingers, picking up the kettle, so please excuse this horrid mess.

Yr. aff.

V.W.

Texas

1243: TO MOLLY MACCARTHY   *Hogarth House, Paradise Road,*
                            Richmond, Surrey

[early May 1922]

Dearest, adorable, darling Moll,

Yes, you shall have the pleasure on *Monday*, but not on *Wednesday*
because we are going to Roger's lecture on Wednesday, as you should be
doing, too.

But won't our old friends ask us again?—only I cannot pitch my tune
seductively because I am rushing to catch a train, in the rain, and so must
refrain.

But remain,

loving, devoted too, to you.

V.W.

After all, poetry's much easier than they make out.

Mrs Michael MacCarthy

Hogarth House, Paradise Road,
                                        Richmond, Surrey

Saturday [6 May 1922]

My dear Roger,

It is so enchanting to get a letter from you, that I'm inclined to write every day—can you tell me the address of your little man who cleans carpets? sells canaries? buys old false teeth?

Here I am sweating out streams of rheumish matter from eyes, mouth, ears, solely in order to attend your lecture. I have the most violent cold in the whole parish. Proust's fat volume comes in very handy. Last night I started on vol 2 [*Jeunes Filles en Fleurs*] of him (the novel) and propose to sink myself in it all day. Scott Moncreiff[1] wants me to say a few words in an album of admiration—will you collaborate? If so, I will: not otherwise.

But Proust so titillates my own desire for expression that I can hardly set out the sentence. Oh if I could write like that! I cry. And at the moment such is the astonishing vibration and saturation and intensification that he procures—theres something sexual in it—that I feel I *can* write like that, and seize my pen and then I *can't* write like that. Scarcely anyone so stimulates the nerves of language in me: it becomes an obsession. But I must return to Swann.

They threaten to put a knife to my throat, in which case I shall certainly insist upon your presence at the bedside.

Anyhow, it would be awfully and fearfully nice to see you. But I don't like to scramble for your time, among the flights and swoops of great ladies who must be screaming and gobbling—for you can't deny you are a d—d success. Passing down the Strand the other day I saw a most raucous version of your head in the Saturday Review. Being a snob, I stopped, and said to my companion, thats Roger Fry—whom I know.

Do you ever do these silly things? Suppose by any chance I can't get out on Wednesday, when do you do that lecture in the drawing rooms?

However, I shall.

                                        Ever your
Sussex   V.W.

[*Hogarth House, Richmond*]

[11? May 1922]

Dearest,

I'm afraid we shan't be able to come tomorrow, as my heart has gone rather queer. However I hope to be all right in a day or two.

1. The novel, *A le Recherche du Temps Perdu,* was published in an English translation by C. K. Scott-Moncrieff.

Perhaps I might come to tea on Friday? if that suited you.
Don't you think this is the letter of a prize prig?[1]

Yr
VW.

Berg

1246: To Lady Ottoline Morrell

Hogarth [House], Richmond

May 16 [1922]

My dear Ottoline,

I am very much afraid that we must ask you to let us come later, and not on the 27th—I've been having another attack of influenza, which has again made my heart wrong, and now the dr. insists upon pulling out 2 teeth, to see whether the germs have settled at the roots. This has to take place next week, and they can't promise that I shan't get another few days of fever. So it seems useless to think of coming. But please don't say you will have nothing more to do with me—annoying as these habits are. Perhaps you would ask us later at the end of June, or July.

I no longer much enjoy the height of my temperature, and very much hope to be normal again. Still there is little trust to be put in doctors—as I think you know.

What are you doing? Do you like Fredegond's poems—and what do you think of Karn?[2] I should very much like to know. Mrs Manning Sanders is a shabby shapeless quite simple woman, who lives in Cornwall. That is all I know. We have met a charming young man called [Gerald] Brenan— a friend of Lytton's, and I think we shall follow his example and buy a castle in Spain. They only cost £10 a year. Come too; and let us see what England does without us.

Your affate
Virginia Woolf

I do hope that I have not upset your plans—but probably I have.

Texas

1. Virginia enclosed a letter from Sylvia Mills Whitham of 10 May, in which she refused to subscribe to Hogarth Press publications.
2. *Daybreak*, by Fredegond Shove, and *Karn*, by Ruth Manning-Sanders, were both published by the Hogarth Press in 1922.

Wednesday [17 May 1922]

My dear Roger,

I was frightfully disappointed not to come to your lecture. Faintness overtook me on Sunday, and the dr. who unfortunately happened to come in, assured me that I should faint if I went up to hear you. The sight of my senseless body borne out would I thought so depress the audience that on that account alone I stayed away. I prayed all night that it might be a complete failure. Alas! I hear on all sides that it was a triumphant success. Never was anything so brilliant, so interesting, so subversive, so much appreciated: if I had fainted, no one would have minded. This is what I hear on all sides. You must admit that its pretty damnable. Now, when are you going to do it again, and when am I going to see you?

We have been in a welter of Hogarth Press affairs, and my fingers are like cauliflours [*sic*] from addressing envelopes. Also I may have to have all my teeth out.

But here I stop—I don't want to snuff out all chance of ever seeing you again.

If you don't mean to lecture again, might I read your manuscript? Seriously and honestly, it was the devil's own luck not to come.

Yours ever
V.W.

Sussex

Wednesday [17 May 1922]

Dearest,

At last here's the cheque—

Would it be possible for you to have me to tea or after tea, on *Friday*; then for me to have Oliver [Strachey], who was dining here alone with me, to dine at the Etoile; then to come round either to 50 or 46[1]; then would you come too; would Duncan come too; should we in short have a little party— Only I must let Oliver know, *so could you ring me up*.

I'll try to ring you, but can't ever get on.

Yr
B.

L. has to dine at the [Charles] Sangers, wh. thank G—d I got out of.

Berg

1. Adrian and Karin Stephen lived at No. 50 Gordon Square; and Maynard Keynes at No. 46. Vanessa had the top two floors of No. 50.

Hogarth House, [Richmond]

Thursday [18 May 1922]

My Violet,

I am indeed a wretch not to have answered you before. Your £ note came safely, and has been placed to your credit both in the books of Hogarth and in the books of God. We are becoming rather full blown and important. You will receive a circular to this effect before long. It is our 5th birthday this month, and we have published 19 books.

God knows what is happening to my influenza germs. I cant get rid of this miserable little temperature, and last week it flared up into another attack, and laid my heart flat again. So now they're going to pull out 2 teeth, and catch the escaping microbes which harbour at the roots, and vaccinate me with them afresh; the doctor thinks this may be the end of it. Well, I hope so. It keeps me hovering between bed and sofa, when I've a million things I want to do.

We hope to get to Rodmell for Whitsun. There Leonard is making a new flower bed, pulling down an out house, and building an earth closet. He particularly wants to know where he can buy old paving stones to make a path. Could you tell us? A place near here, if possible; because this garden too is being renovated. There's no end to his activities. All I pray to God is that he don't get into Parliament.

Lottie (the yellow legged) has had her operation and is recovering at home. We drag on with Chars. She writes me long letters, from friend to friend, not at all in the style of old Sophie.

I'm very sorry about Nelly's ears.[1] To sit all day and look at the view in complete solitude seems to me dismal. We were much amused by Lady Gwendolen [Cecil] who talked politics without ceasing.

When shall we see you again?

Berg

Yr
VW.

1250: To Janet Case *Hogarth [House, Richmond]*

Sunday [21 May 1922]

My dear Janet,

I am so sorry about the cost of the house. Not to be able to start building at once must be so damnable. There's Arthur Clough at Burley who pretends to be able to build cottages cheap. Why not let me ask him?—his wife was a Freshfield. Still, these ideas are too vague, I expect. My passion is set on houses, and I'm desolated to think of anyone held up in the pursuit.

1. Nelly Cecil was growing increasingly deaf.

If you're going to be at Hampstead, we must meet. I can't be sure about Monday, as we are away for the week end [at Tidmarsh], and I rather fancy I'm dining in London that night. Would Tuesday suit you? Of course I would come to you. That is the only chance: we go to Rodmell on Wednesday.

The dr. now thinks that my influenza germs may have collected at the roots of 3 teeth. So I'm having them out, and preparing for the escape of microbes by having 65 million dead ones injected into my arm daily. It sounds to me too vague to be very hopeful—but one must, I suppose, do as they say.

I feel much better again—in fact, it wouldn't matter at all except for the heart, which seems to object. Why isn't one made rather more simply? without a heart.

We've been sitting in the Park and listening to the Band and having a terrific argument about Shaw. Leonard says we owe a great deal to Shaw. I say that he only influenced the outer fringe of morality. Leonard says that the shop girls wouldn't be listening to the Band with their young men if it weren't for Shaw. I say the human heart is touched only by the poets. Leonard says rot, I say damn. Then we go home. Leonard says I'm narrow. I say he's stunted. But don't you agree with me that the Edwardians, from 1895 to 1914, made a pretty poor show. By the Edwardians, I mean Shaw, Wells, Galsworthy, the Webbs, Arnold Bennett. We Georgians have our work cut out for us, you see. There's not a single living writer (English) I respect: so you see, I have to read the Russians: but here I must stop. I just throw this out for you to think about, under the trees. How does one come by one's morality? Surely by reading the poets. And we've got no poets. Does that throw light upon anything? Consider the Webbs—That woman has the impertinence to say that I'm a-moral: the truth being that if Mrs Webb had been a good woman, Mrs Woolf would have been a better. Orphans is what I say we are—we Georgians—but I must stop.

Sussex

1251: TO LADY OTTOLINE MORRELL

Hogarth House, [Richmond]

Monday [29? May 1922]

My dear Ottoline,

I am ashamed not to have written before. I have been rather knocked up by these myriads of germs.

Might we come on the 15th July? We have to visit H. G. Wells—I make a boast of it, but only by way of disguising the horror. I think we must go there on the 1st.

What a week end this has been! When England brings it off [climate], she is really better than Spain—but we are thinking of January and making our plans.

Leonard, of course, what with Parliament, press and life in general, can't be certain of the 15th, but hopes, if it doesn't worry you to leave it open for him.

Your affte
Virginia Woolf

Texas

1252: To Lady Ottoline Morrell   *Monk's House, Rodmell,*
near Lewes, Sussex

June 1st 1922

My dear Ottoline,

You will think me far more nuisance than I'm worth.

I find that Leonard has to lecture early on Monday 17th July, so might we come on the 8th, instead.

If this suits you, dont bother to write. I can hardly form my letters, owing to the heat, which is splendid, but horrible.

Your aff
Virginia Woolf

Texas

1253: To Margaret Llewelyn Davies
Monk's House, Rodmell,
Lewes, Sussex

June 1st [1922]

Dearest Margaret,

Why do you want to cut me off one of the things I most look forward to?

Of course I'm coming,[1] however unworthy, and there I shall sit and take notes, in order to make a speech about you at the Guild. I admit, I don't make a word of sense of Co-operation; but when its a question of honouring the greatness of Margaret Ll. Davies—then no one beats me.

What an awful time you're having with Lilian [Harris]! I am so sorry, and hope it is now well over. May I come up and see her when we're back?

We had looked forward to your visit—but come later, and it will be better. Lottie is still rather invalidish.

This heat shakes my hand, and dissipates my sense—So goodbye—and how I shall admire you on Monday—merely as a human being, of course, which is as far as my wits stretch.

Your V.W.

Sussex

1. To the Co-operative conference at Brighton, over which Margaret presided.

Monk's House, Rodmell,
near Lewes, Sussex

June 1st [1922]

My dear Janet,

I was much disappointed at the upshot of Emphies' and Leonard's confabulations, but I agree that, as usual, our elders know best. But I wish you could have come. The drawback, apart from the fatigues of travelling, is that we couldn't have made you very comfortable, with Lottie invalidish still—But we want to pin you down now for a proper week end in August or September. Please let us settle one, after 14th August: any: now: immediately: take out your calendar and look. Surely we are somehow on the road to the New Forest.

My glimpse of you was only like a peep show—There was Janet under the tree in the garden: then gone. Just, too, as we were approaching the proper heights of unstinted self-praise.

It is blazing here: and here I am in my garden room, overlooking the meadows, waving in the heat. But when I have had my tea, I shall take my walk along the grass path, when among the multitude of my thoughts I shall think of your black tar house.

I'm so cross. Three teeth pulled out that might have lasted a lifetime, and temperature still up. Next they'll cut out my tonsils, and then I suppose adenoids, and then appendix, and then—what comes next?

However, I must settle down to think about Mr Percy Lubbock and the Craft of Fiction,[1] about which I have to write tomorrow, and every idea has gone under water. They were swarming last week, when I wanted to write a story.

Margaret will have a great triumph, and I shall feel very proud of my sex, and write and tell you all about it.

Yours
V.W.

Sussex

1255: To Katherine Arnold-Forster

Monk's House, Rodmell,
Lewes, [Sussex]

June 3rd [1922]

My dear Bruin,

I left your letter at Richmond, and I can't for the life of me remember whether you wanted me to answer any particular question. You said you loved me—which is very right and sensible, and also you abused all the

1. *TLS* (20 July 1922).

Hogarth Press books. But we can't manufacture genius. There they are, these particoloured creatures, and its God's fault, not ours. Anyhow Fredegond and Ruth Sanders are the pick of millions of baskets. Consider the stuff we *don't* print. A huge manuscript arrived today. Our autumn output will crack Bruin's brains into splinters—that I promise you.

We are down here for Whitsun; Leonard planting, Lottie recovering, and I taking the dog for walks. The influenza goes on like a very respectable grandfather's clock. I got it back again 3 weeks ago: then they said there must be germs at the roots of your teeth. So they pulled 3 out; 3 I could ill spare; and so far no result. But then I didn't expect any. I believe these temperatures are like winds and draughts—no one can say whither they come, or where they go, and they don't much matter.

I missed Will's [Arnold-Forster] exhibition to my great disappointment. So far as I saw any, the criticisms seemed to be good, but then the critics are such long ears that there is little use in that. I hope they sold. But as you both seem perfectly happy, and lead lives of pure bliss, and complete sense, what does it matter?

I'm afraid Cornwall is becoming a little too exalted—there is Bertie [Russell] at Penzance, and Roger painting him—the [Manning] Sanders colony at Sennen. However, as you know, nothing will shake my belief that Cornwall is heaven: but don't wait for me to die to ask me to come and see you. I don't want to be heard as a strain of music at dusk.

Forgive this scrawl, and see how fond I am of Bruin to write at all, when I've been writing all day.

L. sends love.
Yr V.W.

Mark Arnold-Forster

1256: To Lady Ottoline Morrell   *Monks House, Rodmell, [Sussex]*

Whit Monday [5 June 1922]

My dear Ottoline,

My handwriting must be on its last legs. I meant 8th July, not 18th.— If 8th suits you, then we will come without further trouble.

We are just in from hearing Margaret Davies address 1600 cooperators in George 4ths pagoda at Brighton—a great success.

The germs still live on, in spite of my sacrifice of 3 teeth.

Forgive the scrawl and the scrap of paper.

Yr
V.W.

Texas

Monk's House, Rodmell, near Lewes, Sussex

Monday [5 June 1922]

Dear Gerald,

Please tell Ralph with our love, that he is a donkey. Unless indeed more is hidden in his remarks than appears. Why should you get on our nerves at Hogarth and not here? Perhaps he meant that the Woolves are milder (he hopes) in Sussex. However, this is not an analysis, but a repetition of our statement—we expect you next Saturday for the weekend at Richmond.

The difficulty here was domestic—a maid recovering—an old friend threatening—and so on. The pound, as I said, was obviously and rightly our pound—still I'm too hot and muddle headed to argue.

We have been attending the Co-operative Congress at Brighton, perched on prominent seats behind the speakers, and there was the Mayor and Mayoress, and the organ, and addresses, sentiments of universal brotherhood, with illustrations from the animal world, which surprised me— but Miss Davies said it was a well known fact—animals love each other. Anyhow I wept and Leonard corrected proofs surreptitiously.

Oh what a bore about Joyce! just as I was devoting myself to Proust— Now I must put aside Proust—and what I suspect is that Joyce is one of these undelivered geniuses, whom one can't neglect, or silence their groans, but must help them out, at considerable pains to oneself.

Bring him [*Ulysses*] on Saturday. And is there anyone in the whole world you would like to meet on Sunday? Merely say and I will wire.

And excuse this dribbling garrulity, which is due to the fact that a little human intercourse would be so acceptable at this moment.

Yours
Virginia Woolf

George Lazarus

1258: To Dora Carrington *Monk's House, [Rodmell, Sussex]*

Wednesday [7 June 1922]

My dear Carrington,

I have a pathetic letter this morning from my old Greek teacher, saying that Carrington's mother has never come. In fact, nobody has come; so is there any chance that Carrington's mother could be induced to come? The address is, Miss Case, Windmill House, Rowledge, Hants. They are wildly building a black tar house in The New Forest, on the strength of Carrington's mother—so please produce her.

Now would you tell Gerald that we expect him between tea and dinner on Saturday: then that he might confirm this by a card to Hogarth House, which it should reach on Saturday.

Then your husband must be told that we have had Mr Dobree's[1] stories sent us. Further, Mr Holt, the agent,[2] has worked himself into such ecstasy over Leonard's stories, that he is motoring over tomorrow, and will undoubtedly put us in the way of £1000 p.a.

Then—its too hot to write, and really too lovely in this garden room to concentrate the mind, should I have one.

How I wish Gerald had come here, merely to take back a report of the flowers, vegs., lawn, and E.C.

Was Lytton favourably impressed by Murry's effusion last week?[3]

A little too much Uriah Heep for me—so very 'umble. Aldous in the Herald, however, poses as the simple man of feeling, but as I say, I cannot think, and find, alas, that I have lost 3 fine fangs for nothing: Cant eat my tea, and remain abnormal.

Make a plan to come here this summer.

Yr
V.W.

Really, if you could do anything for Miss Case, it would be a charity.

Robert H. Taylor

1259: To Janet Case   *Monk's House, [Rodmell,*
                                           Sussex]
Wednesday [7 June 1922]

My dear Janet,

Well, it was all the greatest success imaginable.[4] First imagine a vast crowd assembled in a gaudy kind of tea caddy all arabesques and horse shoes and chandeliers: but the crowd has nothing rococo about it. No: the coops are sturdy, square headed, and a little drab, considering the weather. Considering Miss Davies too, who, very cool and distinguished looking,

1. Bonamy Dobrée (1891-1974), the literary critic. The Hogarth Press published three of his books in 1925, 1926 and 1932.
2. Henry Holt, the literary agent. Leonard describes his visit in *Downhill All the Way*, pp. 88-90.
3. Murry's review of Lytton's *Books and Characters* in the *Nation and Athenaeum* of 3 June. He described the first essay, on Racine, as "one of the finest pieces of pure criticism ever written in English".
4. The meeting of the Women's Co-operative Guild at Brighton. Margaret Llewelyn Davies had retired from the Secretaryship of the Guild in 1921, but addressed the meeting as an honoured guest.

chiselled like a Goddess, and yet rather peremptory, enters, precisely at 10, all in grey, but with a dash of kingfisher blue about the bonnet. Cheers, a general standing up, sitting down etc: One of the worthys then says what an honour this is for Miss Davies: what a woman Miss D. is: how she has devoted her life: how she has changed the womens' lot: how she is known, respected, loved, and now she will speak, and they must remember Miss D. is a lady.

Whereupon up gets Margaret: and says that the honour is not hers, but ours: (so I feel it myself)—women's in general. At first, she was a little unyielding, and spoke rather statuesquely; but soon this utterly disappeared, and the address, which I do not propose to give verbatim, was superbly spoken—spoken as she might speak up at Hampstead, only with a mastery and fervour, never becoming shrill, and always on the right side of emotion, which took my breath away. The blessed address, which read in type, may sound too general and lofty, as she said it seemed on the contrary very stirring and particular. And far from spreading herself in mild and glorious retrospect, I thought she stood up to the Board and the movement and flicked them very energetically. One man, Leonard said, told another he thought it just what they wanted; and the other man said yes, it was a splendid speech, and the best they had ever heard. Besides, it was vivid and imaginative. And so I listened to every word; and she spoke till eleven exact, and then left off, without any peroration in the offensive sense, but as if, having spoken her mind, she meant to sit down. In short (and I am scribbling to catch post) it was as dignified and masterly as could be: and as a snob, liking birth and education, I thought to myself that I could see how she ruled them by virtue of these qualities, as well as her own particular genius, which came out, Leonard and I agreed, as we ate our lunch, quite unmistakably. Her vitality, her vigour, addressing this innumerable hardheaded drab middle class mass, completely conquered. Then came the Mayor; who chucked the Mayoress under the chin, and we all laughed. Then the Mayoress extracted 3 roses and gave them to Margaret. Then Mr Ray produced a cardboard case and took from it a vermilion gold stamped book, with an illuminated address, which he recited. Her name, he said, will always be remembered among the great. It seemed to me very true and right. Up got Margaret and said with great spirit, and some gratitude, but she was far from obsequious, "Not my name, but the names of Mrs Laurenson, Mrs Reddish etc., etc," "and now", she said, handing the gilt and crimson to a lackey, "Let's to business—the pleasant part of the Conference now begins. . . ." So she drank her water and sprang her bell.

There we left her, controlling perspiring men; and the only other thing I remember is that the Germans were cheered as if they had been our benefactors.

I am sorry to write such a confused scribble, but if I put it off, I should never do it. So you must excuse.

Directly we came here, I was of a mind to wire, and suggest your coming. If I had not been rushed, we could have arranged it; and anyhow, you might have spent the week end, even if the Conference was impossible. I am annoyed to think of it.

I have written to Carrington giving your address, so that she may inform her mother. Whitsun, anyhow, is a close time; but let me know if there is any plan I can further later.

Your
V.W.

Sussex

1260: To Lady Ottoline Morrell

Hogarth House, Richmond

Typewritten
June 9th [1922]

My dear Ottoline,

Our correspondence is now so voluminous that I must use the type-writer—with disastrous results, for I cannot think, or spell in print.

We like the Bussys[1]; we should like to meet them; but—we have to confess—we cannot speak French. An awful silence falls. Simon gets cross. He talks French—we answer in English. Somehow this makes both languages unintelligible. So we may ruin the party. So would you prefer it if we came as we said once upon a time, when the correspondence was still young, on the 15th July.

Leonard might have to go that night. But you have only to speak; and, though I should prefer a letter, really and truly you need only write a date on a post card.

Thank you for the dr's name. I am rather indisposed at present, having lost my three good teeth, to submit to doctors again. The germs dont worry, so long as they keep below 100. If they swarm again I shall have to take steps.

I hear from Morgan[2] this morning that he enjoyed himself with you. And as he never tells a lie this is a very good Collins to have.

[handwritten]

Here I have come to an end of all that can properly be said on a type-writer, and must finish

Your affte
Virginia Woolf

Texas

1. Simon and Dorothy Bussy. She was Lytton Strachey's sister and the author of *Olivia* (1949). He was a French painter.
2. Morgan Forster had returned from India in March.

Hogarth House, Paradise Road,
                                   Richmond, Surrey

Wednesday [14 June 1922]

Shall I come to tea on Thursday, that is tomorrow? Friday seems doubtful, so this is your only chance. Unless stopped I will come—but don't put yourself out, as I may even so be prevented.

4 *lines omitted*

. . . .
. . . .
. . . .

                                                                    B.
Berg

Letters 1262-1295 (July–early-October 1922)

Virginia, with Ottoline Morrell and Richard Aldington, and Ezra Pound abroad, attempted to raise for T. S. Eliot a sum of money which would liberate him from drudgery at Lloyds' Bank, and enable him to concentrate on his writing. The scheme miscarried. First, it soon became clear that few of their friends could afford to subsidise a fellow-writer—the total raised by December was only £77, with vague promises of more. Secondly, Eliot, when he became fully aware of what was afoot, objected that the target of the appeal, £300 a year for five years, was not enough to risk throwing up his job. He must be guaranteed at least £500, and any smaller sum must not place on him the moral obligation to leave the bank. Virginia persisted with the appeal, but it failed, the money being returned to the subscribers some five years later. In spite of recurrent illnesses (for a time, tuberculosis was suspected), Virginia continued writing, chiefly translations from Tolstoy and her story Mrs Dalloway in Bond Street. *The Woolfs entertained frequently at Monk's House: among their summer and autumn guests were Lytton, Waterlow, E. M. Forster and T. S. Eliot.*

1262: To Lady Ottoline Morrell

Hogarth House, Paradise Road,
Richmond, Surrey

Tuesday [18 July 1922]

My dear Ottoline,

I am going to carry out your orders to write a very dull letter—how can it be anything else, considering that I've just dropped The Things We Are,[1] half paralysed with disgust and boredom?

If Murry lives next door to you, I assure you the mildew will sprout in every room—Useless to instal hot water. But the subject is worn out, and I shall only drive Philip to another display of philanthropy.

I got into very good society on Oxford platform—Lady Isabel Margesson,[2] Sir Somebody, and Miss Margesson; and they took me, so they said, for Lady Muriel Talbot, but soon discovered their mistake. I don't

1. A novel (1922) by John Middleton Murry, who had been much discussed during the weekend which Virginia had just spent at Garsington.
2. Lady Isabel Hobart-Hampden, daughter of the Earl of Buckinghamshire, who married Sir Mortimer Margesson.

like the upper classes; though I like meeting them, for the pleasure of getting free.

Yes, this letter is dull, and will soon be duller. Leonard and I sat up gossiping about Garsington last night; and if Julian had been under the sofa in her blue dress she would have heard nothing to her disadvantage, tell her.[1] Nor would you. How I shall enjoy the combined funeral [*inexplicable*]! Don't you think you and I have now proved our fidelity, and ought to break a sixpence in half and wear it on our watch chains?

Anyhow, I enjoyed myself every minute, and go back in thought to the whole weekend, though I have my compunctions that I tired you with talking, in your green room. But was there ever anyone with your invincible spirit? When I write my great Garsington novel,[2] look out for a streak of white lightning, and that will be you. Yes; I must set about it soon, or the market will be spoilt.

No invitations from Lady Colefax or Lady Cunard. So you see, I have fallen out of the nest before I got in.

It was very nice of you to have me and be so good to me.

Your affate
Virginia Woolf

Texas

1263: To Roger Fry   [*Hogarth House, Richmond*]

[28 July 1922]

My dear Roger,
My handwriting must be dissolving. THURSDAY was our party[3]— yesterday. But I'll come to the Commercio [restaurant] on MONDAY 7.30 —if you don't mind no party. I'll ask Eliot; but doubt his being able. Anyhow it will be very nice seeing you—tho' I've been in your spiritual company, with great satisfaction, going round the Marchands'[4] that is, reading you aloud. What a critic to be sure!

And what about your lectures?
Frightful haste for post.

Yr V.W.

Sussex

1. Ottoline's daughter, aged 16.
2. See Letter 1268.
3. With Vanessa, Duncan, Hope Mirrlees and T. S. Eliot.
4. Jean Marchand (1883-1931), the French painter who was exhibiting in the Carfax Gallery. Roger Fry greatly admired his work.

1264: TO DORA CARRINGTON   *Hogarth [House, Richmond]*

[end July? 1922]

My dear Carrington—

Oh horror horror! I sent Gerald [Brenan] my copy of the Proust book in June, so I suppose it never reached him, and is now lost for ever, and I've not even read it myself. Would you tell him it was sent, with a copy of the Voyage Out, sometime in June, by parcel post, and ask him to make enquiry if possible. He got another book safely, so I took it for granted he had got these.

Roger is the only person likely to have a copy, I think. He was asked by the Nouvelle Revue to distribute them. Jegen, Ujigar, Granada is the address I put on parcels and letters alike.

Give Gerald my love.

George Lazarus   Yrs V.W.

1265: TO LADY OTTOLINE MORRELL

Hogarth House, Paradise Road,
Richmond, Surrey

Tuesday [1 August 1922]

My dear Ottoline,

You are the most generous of hostesses to send photographs—My own picture has a distorted interest for me.

Here is Murry's novel [*The Things We Are*]—I beg to say that the damp spots are not my doing. They come from within. He has a mania for confession. I suppose his instinct is to absolve himself in these bleatings and so get permission for more sins. But I am forgetting that he is by this time your next door neighbour.

I wish you or Philip would send a card to Tom Eliot stating on oath that Julian did say Prufrock through by heart. He refused to believe me.

I have been thinking about the subscription.[1] I find that the few people I have talked to would much prefer to give a lump sum down to Eliot himself, than to subscribe £10 yearly through the [Ezra] Pounds. One may so easily die, and still more easily go bankrupt; and where would poor Tom be then?

We are just off to Rodmell and I shall try to come to some decision, for I want to do something, and I think many people are in my state of mind. I wonder if you agree?

I enjoyed myself so much, and I don't see why you should talk of fading. Lightning is always lightning, oddly enough.

V.

Texas

1. For T. S. Eliot. See introductory note p. 538.

1266: To CLIVE BELL *Monk's House, Rodmell*
[Sussex]

Saturday [5 August 1922]

Dearest Clive,

I take it for granted that Duncan never got the book which I also take it for granted you never asked him to get.

I have to go up on Wednesday to see a doctor to decide whether my right lung is diseased as Dr Hamill says it is, and so might go to Gordon Square and forage for myself. But would Gordon Sq. be open? I am in want of something to relieve Ulysses. A card before Wednesday would be in keeping with the charity of your disposition.

Dedman, the gardener, says that there was a great deal of trouble when the [Edward] Shanks' came back from Germany. In fact, sir, Mrs Shanks did a bolt. But its all kept very quiet. But she did a bolt, sir, thats what she did. Thank God. They say too that Shanks is shortly leaving, but my peace of mind is greatly disturbed by a boy scouts camp beneath the window, and the village fête, for which I must now change. The rector has just made a speech. Guns are going off, Leweses arriving.

We went to the races yesterday, and as I climbed the hill, tell Nessa, a stout man stopped me and said he could not yet oblige me with two wicker arm chairs but hoped to shortly. I said "you are mistaken". He said "You are Mrs Bell." I said "In God's name I'm not," feeling, tell Nessa, divinely beautiful in every limb at once, but not so quick in the head as usual. How strange it is to be a painter! They scarcely think; feelings come only every other minute. But then they are profound and inexpressible, tell Nessa.

Leonard had a touch of the mumps in the middle of his neck yesterday. I hope everyone else is recovered. I will come over next week.

Your V.W.

Quentin Bell

1267: To LADY OTTOLINE MORRELL *Monks House, Rodmell,*
Lewes, [Sussex]

Aug. 6th [1922]

My dear Ottoline,

I return Aldington's letter. I should certainly like some copies of the [Eliot] appeal, but I don't myself believe that many of my friends will find it possible to guarantee £10 a year for ever. On the other hand, practically every one I have spoken to has been ready to give something down. One [Lytton], even, was willing to give £100 down, if it could be given direct to Eliot himself. It seems absurd to let this money be wasted; so do you think it would be a good plan if I tried to collect as much as I could, and we gave it to Eliot in a lump sum, for him to invest, or spend, as he liked?

Anyhow, he would be secure of the money, which I don't think would be the case under Ezra Pound's scheme.

Or do you think that a plan of this kind would draw people away from subscribing to the other? However, one really knows so few people, willing to give at all, that I don't think this is a serious objection.

I wonder if you know at all what Tom's own views are—has he agreed to accept the money, and for what amount will he give up his Bank?

I wish Aldington wouldn't give out that Tom is 'very ill', by the way. There he is going about, dining out, and so on, and I'm sure people will think this a trumped up excuse.

I've almost forgotten Murry's novel—it was writ in dirty water. My impression is that all his characters were embodiments of his own faults and his own entirely sentimental and unreal aspirations. Simplicity and truth were represented by the landlady, and in consequence she was nothing but humbug. However, I have forgotten it, except as a whine in a corner. Now I have some respect for Rebecca West, and I wish you would get to know her, and introduce me. She has written a stout, generous, lively voluminous novel[1]: I have only read 20 pages; there are some 600: but so far I think she is a brave clever woman, and sometimes she writes a few words very nicely.

I must break off, chiefly owing to the Boy Scouts who have camped in our field, and sing to keep their spirits up in the rain—Scout songs, I suppose. They have a Union Jack, and go to church. I wish one liked these things naturally.

Yr affate
V.W

Do you, by any chance, take in the Dial, an American paper, and keep back numbers?[2]

Texas

1268: To Lady Ottoline Morrell

[*Monk's House*], *Rodmell*,
[*Sussex*]

[10? August 1922]

My dear Ottoline,

I have sent the form to Lloyds. I shall be seeing Lytton next week, and, I think, Mary Hutchinson, and hope to squeeze something out of them. Mary offers to distribute forms, so please send me ample.

1. *The Judge* (1922).
2. Eliot's *The Waste Land* was published in the *Dial* this year, and won its $2000 poetry prize.

Of course your germs flourish if you go thinking about the sufferings of Russia and the income of Tom, and I suppose, country house week ends, Aldous Huxleys, Virginia Woolves, and all the rest.

I have written 2 chapters of my Garsington novel,[1] you'll be glad to hear. Three weeks ago a doctor told me I had consumption: now they say its pneumonia germs in the throat; but I'm perfectly all right.

It is lovely down here, and I read as a weevil, I suppose, eats cheese. Love to Julian.

Your aff
V.W.

Texas

1269: To Vanessa Bell
Monk's House, [Rodmell, Sussex]

Thursday, Aug. 10th [1922]

Dearest,

I am much distressed to hear of your miserable condition. I would have written, but I gathered from Clive that you were already at Charleston. Leonard says there is nothing such agony as the mumps; they entirely ruined his temper; and as you can't bite, you fall into the depths of exhaustion. I remember Stella describing them. Please be very careful. No—no one ever sympathises with one's diseases. They are only an opportunity for describing their own—still this doesn't apply to Duncan, Roger, and myself, whose hearts are always wrung for you, if for no one else. I often wake in the night and cry aloud Nessa! Nessa! Doesn't that comfort you? Well, not much, you say.

We think your design[2] lovely—Our only doubts are practical. L. thinks the lettering isn't plain enough, and the effect is rather too dazzling. Could you make the r of Room into a Capital? And could the lettering be picked out in some colour which would make it bolder?

These considerations may spoil the design though. Here it is, in case you could alter it.

But we could explain better by word of mouth. Let me know when you reach Charleston. I will come over—infection must be over by that time.

I dont think you have missed much pleasure, and certainly no society, by not coming. It has rained every day—thundered and lightened—Mrs Uppington has hid behind the door—Mrs Dedman is accused of stealing 5 face towels—Mrs Shanks has run away with a German—Mr Shanks sits on the banks flirting with a whore—but worse than all, the Boy Scouts are

1. Virginia was writing her long story, *Mrs Dalloway in Bond Street*. In referring to "my Garsington novel", she was teasing Ottoline, since the story, and the novel which developed out of it, *Mrs Dalloway* (conceived in the autumn of 1922), contained only faint echoes of Garsington life and conversation.
2. For the jacket of *Jacob's Room*.

camped under my window, and sing "Here we are" (that one line and no more) about a million times daily. Painters wouldn't mind; writers are driven crazy. Then you talk of the mumps. By the way, you must be alleviated by the thought that Mary has them. Clive sounded me as to a visit to Wittering—the famous party with Desmond, but I haven't been asked, whether on account of the mumps or of my female sex I don't know. I think her [Mary Hutchinson's] charm pales slightly in the distance. I find it difficult to believe I ever kissed her, or ever shall again. I wonder if the move to 50 is decided on.[1] What a hive, not of bees but of wasps, you will be in the autumn! I met that rakish bitch Margery in the Square—incredibly dirty, dowdy, and raffish. She has been advertising her school at 15 Gordon Sq. as well as 51.[2] Dark rumours have therefore spread abroad. What about subscribing for a toothbrush?—the pupils will contract the itch along with the grammar. I get long letters from Ottoline, deploring the tragedy of life, which is that she only sees me twice a year, and my affections are going to Julian and not to her 'fading mother.'

I'm afraid I shall have to start a subscription for poor Tom. No one will give to Ezra Pound, lest he should drink it all first; but then no one has any money. I lost my umbrella, and really see no prospect of buying another— Can you?—fifteen shillings is too much nowadays.

I have been employing myself in making coloured papers, with wild success. But that won't interest you. The important thing is that I think I've discovered the perfect ink for our purposes—made for marbling. Now if you designed a pattern for a stencil, and we had it cut (I have found the shop) then I could lay on the colours for ever. Here are a few samples—I have to produce 300 sheets by October.

All our visitors are coming in September. Meanwhile we have Mrs Uppington, shall have Nelly's niece. I dont like the children of the poor— On the other hand, when I saw Julian [Bell] the other day, with his gun, looking like a grown man, very handsome, in his trousers I was overcome with the emotions of an Aunt. He gave a complete history of the downs to the cook and Mrs Up. "Firle Beacon is the highest of them all. I should say it is the second highest. If you look out of the window you will see where the Newhaven downs etc etc"—all very positive and well informed. It reminded me of Thoby lecturing the nurses.

Would you be so angelic as to look in Clives room for The Heir,[3]

1. Clive proposed to move from 46 Gordon Square, where he had retained rooms, to No. 50, where Adrian and Karin Stephen were living, and Vanessa had the top two floors.
2. Marjorie Strachey lived with her mother at 51 Gordon Square and started a small school there, which several Bloomsbury children attended.
3. Virginia and Vita Sackville-West were not to meet until December 1922, but Vita already knew Clive. A collection of her short stories, of which *The Heir* was the longest, had been published in May 1922.

by V. Sackville West, and bring it with you? She admires me; therefore I must try to admire her, which, of course, I shan't find difficult.

Leonard, who is full of sympathy for you, sends you his love, and says it is the 10th anniversary of our wedding day.

V.W.

Berg

1270: TO GERALD BRENAN   *Monks House, Rodmell,*
                                         Lewes, [Sussex]

Aug. 12th [1922]

Dear Gerald,

Is there any chance that you would come here for the weekend of the 23rd August? We hope you will. I think we saw you flashing through Lewes in a car—and so perhaps you are still in England: but where, I dont know, and must trust to Lytton to forward this.

Yrs

George Lazarus   Virginia Woolf

1271: TO GERALD BRENAN   *Monks House, [Rodmell,*
                                         Sussex]

Aug. 12th [1922]

My dear Gerald,

I have been making a muddle—Leonard says the 23rd weekend is impossible for him, so would you suggest a night that suits you—in the week, perhaps, not weekend—I expect we can arrange whatever suits you—Forgive my stupidity and come and see us.

Yours in haste and illegibility

George Lazarus   V.W.

1272: TO ROGER FRY   *Monk's House, [Rodmell,*
                                         Sussex]

Sunday [13 August 1922]

My dear Roger,

Would you be so angelic as to send me Mr Whitalls[1] address? It sounds most promising—from our point of view; but there are so many things to

1. The Hogarth Press was expanding so rapidly that it was monopolising too much of Leonard's and Virginia's time, and Ralph Partridge was proving unsatisfactory as an assistant. James Whitall, an American, offered to take over the whole business management of the Press, but Leonard turned him down.

explain that we think we had better try to get him to come here and talk it over. Meanwhile, please don't breathe a word of it, as our present position is perfectly vague.

Are you off again for ever? But didn't you promise to lecture in London? When you are a success, then you're such a damned snob that you can't stand it—that's my theory. When you're offered the O.M., as I've no doubt you will be, you will retire to Japan for good.

I get frightfully depressed when I read Murry—and the creature pullulates everywhere. I dont think anything can stand up against the power of muddleheaded mediocrity when combined with the manners of the servants hall and the morality of a boarding school for officers widows—or is it a girls school I mean?—any place full of spite and backbiting and gush and highmindedness will do.

However the Press does show some signs of flourishing—We have got a lot of new subscribers lately, and if we could launch out boldly, with you to run a series of modern paintings, then we might let Murry rise to his heights in peace.

I don't suppose I shall come over: still I think Vanessa Bell might ask me, please tell her.

I'll send you my book [*Jacob's Room*] when its out—but it is too much of an experiment to be a success.

Yours ever

V.W.

What age is Whitall? Comparative youth is rather essential.

Sussex

1273: To Clive Bell   [*Monk's House*], Rodmell,
                                        [*Sussex*]
Monday [14 August 1922]

Dearest Clive,

Yes, do come over on Thursday—we shall expect you to lunch, about 1, that is, or before. And please discover details about the new buses, as we want to come over one day next week.

The doctor said he could find no tuberculosis, only one lung is different from the other, but not so different as to matter. Apparently it might well mislead a dr. He thought the disease was probably pneumonia germs or influenza, and should disappear of itself if I lead a healthy life, and take quinine, and burn my throat twice a day. These medical details are for Nessa—Leonard meant to write to her. But he would like to come and see her. How is the poor woman?

I wrote to Roger at Charleston. Would you forward it if he is not coming, as I want an answer.

What news have you of the burying of Mother Cornish,[1] and why did she die?

I'm afraid she won't cut up to the advantage of the MacCarthy's—though I'd willingly endow Desmond to continue his fight with Murry.

Your
V.W.

"Ah yes, poor Shanks had a great deal of trouble for some time with Mrs Shanks. A very flighty young woman—gone with a German they say" so old Hawkesford[2] told us. Leonard said "And I suppose that makes it all the worse" with a broad grin; but this was not well received.

Quentin Bell

1274: To Margaret Llewelyn Davies

Monk's House, Rodmell,
[Sussex]

[16 August 1922]

Virginia's note added at end of a letter from Leonard.

L. has cut me and my gossip down to the merest scrap. Why dont you come and drink at the fountain head? So you think I've not read the Princesse de Clèves![3] What a charming cover, though! I'm in the thick of inventing new covers for our autumn list. Our village is ravaged by the elopement of Mrs Shanks, the poets wife, with a German. L. has to play tennis at the Rectory. He has a record crop of potatoes. We are pickling beans. Mrs Webb has confessed to a niece that she loves L: *not* V. News bubbles up; must be stopped. Sydney Waterlow is coming on Saturday. His soul is once more troubled. Love to Lilian.   V.W.

Sussex

1275: To Lady Ottoline Morrell

Monk's House, Rodmell,
Lewes, [Sussex]

Aug. 18th [1922]

My dear Ottoline,

I send back the [Eliot appeal] notice, which I don't much like—but I

1. Molly MacCarthy's mother, Blanche Warre-Cornish, the novelist and widow of Francis Warre-Cornish, Vice-Provost of Eton.
2. The rector of Rodmell.
3. The story (1678) by Madame de La Fayette.

think that is immaterial. I have struck out my own name on the Committee. I think it is a mistake to have two out of the three names feminine. It gives an impression that poor Tom is our lap dog: and I can be just as effective anonymously.

I begin, of course, to fear that I shan't be effective in any capacity.

I am told that most people are as badly off as Tom; and as most people again have to earn their livings, they don't see why they should bind themselves for ever to earn £10 yearly for some one else.

Still, one can only try; and I propose to scrape together as many small sums as I can, and then, when the time comes, I will either send them direct to you, to add to your collection, or if the givers specially desire it, to Tom himself. I see that a footnote says that sums of £25 and *over* will be accepted; but I shan't pay any attention to that. Surely it is better to take the givers that are in the hand (rather grudgingly in the hand) and leave the twenty-fivers and over in the bush. Here is another case that has occurred. "I don't suppose I shall be able to pay my own bill this year, let alone Eliots. But next year I hope to be better off. Could I send my cheque then?" I suppose I have to encourage this unsatisfactory but well meaning friend also. One can always send a cheque to Mr Aldington, I am saying. I don't much like human nature, do you, in money matters.

Poor Rebecca Wests novel [*The Judge*] bursts like an over stuffed sausage. She pours it all in; and one is covered with flying particles; indeed I had hastily to tie the judge tight and send it back to Mudies half finished. But this irreticence does not make me think any the worse of her human qualities. I imagine she talks a great deal. Mary Hutchinson met her in a furniture shop and says she looked like a large wet dog, in a waterproof, very shaggy. I cannot write with this debauched pen, but I must stumble along and tell you that I do admire poor old Henry [James], and actually read through the Wings of a Dove last summer, and thought it such an amazing acrobatic feat, partly of his, partly of mine, that I now look upon myself and Henry James as partners in merit. I made it all out. But I felt very ill for some time afterwards. I am now reading Joyce, and my impression, after 200 out of 700 pages, is that the poor young man has only got the dregs of a mind compared even with George Meredith. I mean if you could weigh the meaning on Joyces page it would be about 10 times as light as on Henry James'.

They say it gets a little heavier. It is true that I prepared myself, owing to Tom, for a gigantic effort; and behold the bucket is almost empty.

I tremble as I write. I shall be struck down by the wrath of God. Next I go on to Proust; and then—I think something old.

I hope you are staying in bed. Really it is worth while pampering one's body; and then it gives one a free ride. So dont bother please to read or write or talk or pour out tea for 55 strange young men.

V.W.

Texas

1276 To: Katherine Arnold-Forster

Monk's House, Rodmell,
Lewes, [Sussex]

Aug. 23rd 1922

Dearest Ka,

What is the sense of coming to London in September? You must know that the Woolves aren't there then. How could we be? Why should we be?—and then you pretend to expect to see us.

As I have said before, letter writing at these intervals is utterly impossible. Please let the Boer woman send us her book, though we are rather overwhelmed at present. What to do with the Press we don't know. I have read 4 manuscripts in the past fortnight: Leonard writes 6 or 7 letters daily; and when we go back we have to tackle six books of the highest importance, all promised before Christmas; and authors are as exacting as mothers. But this is not a hit at you. I was thinking of Sydney Waterlow who has been here for the weekend, and wishes his children were bigger. He has mellowed. Oh if you could have seen him bathing in the river Ouse, which could hardly close above his immense soft pink stomach, belching and bellowing like a walrus. As I say, he has improved.

I don't think Cornwall beats this. I have a garden room which looks across the watermeadows to Mt Caburn. Do you remember it? I shall go and stay with Gwen and Jacques [Raverat] in January, I think. He wrote to me, and revived my ancient affection—you know how faithful hearted I am. Yes: I have got consumption and heart disease—and feel perfectly well. I assure you, Harley Street drs discovered both these diseases. I have ceased to take my temperature, and that is the main thing. Really, it is pneumonia in my throat—the germs copulating too vigorously. Nessa's house is decimated with mumps; and we can only meet in the open. I was to have been taken to see Mr Hudson[1] this winter by [Dorothy] Brett, who adored him,—I think her sister was in love with him?—no, I have got it wrong. Parts of his books are very good—only others are very bad; isn't that so? Anyhow, I wish I had seen him.

The Criterion only costs 12/6; so I think you must take it in. Besides it will have a story, I think, by me[2]; and Eliot will develop his critical theories —I suppose, but this is *highly and strictly* confidential. You don't know any admirers of his works who would help to give him £300 a year? He has broken down, and has to work all day in a Bank, being penniless, with an invalid wife, and if he could get £300, he would live in a cottage and write. I can't find anyone rich enough to promise 10 or even 5 pounds a year for ever. But I'm not hinting that you ought to give even sixpence. Times are—what is the expression? hard? bad? stoney?

1. W. H. Hudson, the novelist and naturalist, had died on 18 August 1922.
2. *In the Orchard*, Criterion (April 1923).

T

549

Charlie and Dora [Sanger] are soon to be our neighbours. Charlie is to me as much of London as a pillar box or a hansom cab: Dora, on the other hand, will romp bareheaded. Then we have dear Morgan Forster coming, as all the old ladies call him.

But I am running on—idiotically, sloppily, and I daresay illegibly. I have been standing talking to Leonard in the orchard which he prunes, and it being past seven on a cloudy night, my hands are stiff as carrots.

Well, but when are we going to see Brox?—Bruin Cox that is? Oh yes, I remember Vernon Lee,[1] in the dining room at Talland House [St Ives], in coat and skirt, much as she is now—but that was 30 years ago. She was a dashing authoress. She gave my father her books, which were in the dining room too. I saw her 10 years later, at Florence, when she fell in love with Nessa; and 2 years ago at the 1917 Club, when she talked so incredibly slowly, and looked so faded and battered and distinguished that I let her be. You see, I am going to write my memoirs. Molly MacCarthy is writing hers, but that is because they are very hard up and now live at Oare, and the winter evenings are so long.

So is this letter.

Leonard would send his love I am sure, but as I say he is pruning the pear trees.

Lady Young[2] is dead and old Mrs [Warre-] Cornish.

Your V.W.

Mark Arnold-Forster

1277: TO LYTTON STRACHEY   *Monks House, Rodmell,*
                                  [Sussex]
Aug. 24th 1922

Yes 8th to 11th, (but why not a little longer?) will suit us perfectly—so we will consider that fixed.

I don't know that one can call Sydney Waterlow news. He has been here; he has found God—only Mr Sullivan: he bathed; the Ouse was too shallow; he says Katherine Mansfield, completely recovered, is at Bretts. Mrs Shanks has done a bolt with the son of the poet [Gerhart] Hauptmann. Mr Shanks springs up from behind cornstacks with Boen, daughter of the Clergyman. Mrs Dedman says its 6 of one and half a dozen of the other. Clive has been—with a new poem. The Sangers are coming. So is great Tom Eliot—which brings me, my dear Lytton, to the question—only its no longer a question—to the so creditable fact of your contribution. One

1. Violet Paget (1856-1935), who wrote novels and criticism under the name of Vernon Lee.
2. Alice Young, widow of Sir George Young, an old friend of the Stephen family.

hundred pounds did you say? You shall have a receipt. Cheque payable to Richard Aldington or O. Morrell as you prefer. My own contribution, five and sixpence, is given on condition he puts publicly to their proper use the first 200 pages of Ulysses. Never did I read such tosh. As for the first 2 chapters we will let them pass, but the 3rd 4th 5th 6th—merely the scratching of pimples on the body of the bootboy at Claridges. Of course genius may blaze out on page 652 but I have my doubts. And this is what Eliot worships, and there's Lytton Strachey paying £100 p.a. to Eliot's upkeep.

Well, we've been eating ices at Brighton, too hot to stir—early tea today, and then a loiter through the cornfields. A record crop of pears; green peas for dinner; and after dinner we light the Tortoise stove, which I assure you burns whole books—which do instead of coal, and are ever so much hotter, did you know that?

Yr. V.W.

Love to C:[arrington] to whom I now write with the debauched remnants of the pen with which I have written a story for the Criterion, which (I use too many whiches) which the C. will reject. Alas, alas, it is clouding over.

Frances Hooper

1278: To Dora Carrington   *[Monk's House], Rodmell, [Sussex]*

Aug. 24th [1922]

My dear Carrington,

Your letter gave me great pleasure. There still seem to be a great many towns in England. Which to settle in, I know not. I rather hoped you would smash up somewhere—never mind—Lytton says it is freezing [in Manorbier, Pembrokeshire]; and here I daresay the air is blood heat. The wind is howling I admit. Leonard has let himself in to play tennis with the Rector's daughter, who walks out, even on Sundays, with the poet Shanks. That melancholy story rends us asunder. Mrs Dedman is going to say straight out—but I have told Lytton all the gossip.

Actually a spot of rain! How remarkable! But to turn to practical matters —what about a day in the first week of September? Would that suit you and Ralph—say 4th 5th 6th—I don't think it matters which.

The beds are frightfully rocky this year. Old Sydney committed some outrage on the mattresses. My God! What a sight he looked bathing! like Neptune, if Neptune was a Eunuch—without any hairs, and sky pink— fresh, virginal, soft—I sat on the bank and peered through the rushes, for he asked me not to look.

I want to see you, and this year, I have my fears, will be the last of privacy.

I'm sure Allison[1] means to build. He walks about in his leggings with another man, and they take bearings—damn his soul—otherwise the country is more and more and more divine—and I cannot endure the thought of going back. And at my age, my dear Carrington, life I may say melts in the hand. *You* think a day quite long enough. But I sit down, just arrange my thoughts, peep out of the window, turn over a page, and its bed time! Nothing is accomplished. Moreover, at my age one ought to be doing something violent. We went to Brighton it is true. There I bought a blue silk dress. I open the paper and find Michael Collins dead in a ditch.[2] But what a fool to go shooting—dear me, its all very foolish and perplexing. Was Barbara [Bagenal] firm on her feet? A great many chickens, I daresay. Clean as a pin, I suppose. A little fussy about sheets and boots? Saxon is walking in Northamptonshire —he's immensely struck by Bagfield Abbey—frescoes—or at least the part of one frescoe,—If he says "Bagfield"—be sure to say you think the frescoes overrated—save that when a man has only one joy, it is hard to deprive him. We will keep any day for discussing the business that you like; and I hope really you have enjoyed yourself.

V.W.

Captain Graves, the poet Graves, wants us to print a poem,[3] with a portrait by Eric Kennington[4]—who is he? The Brimley Johnsons,[5] brother and sister, have been rejected. Miss Mary Butts[6] has never answered. Torrents of rain.

Robert H. Taylor

1279: TO SYDNEY WATERLOW   *Monks House, Rodmell,*
                                    [Sussex]
24th Aug. [1922]

My dear Sydney,
   It was a great pleasure to get your letter, which says exactly what we also felt; and if we are all agreed that we enjoy each other's society, surely there

1. James Murray Allison (1877-1929), formerly advertisement manager of *The Times*. He owned a large house and land in Rodmell.
2. The Irish revolutionary leader, who was killed at the age of 32 in a skirmish near Macroom, County Cork, on 22 August 1922.
3. Robert Graves had published three volumes of poetry during the War, and in 1923 the Hogarth Press published *The Feather Bed*.
4. The painter and sculptor (1888-1960), who made his reputation as a war-artist.
5. R. Brimley Johnson (1867-1932), the author of many critical works, particularly on Jane Austen. His book of poems, *Out of my Keeping*, was published elsewhere in 1922.
6. The author of several works of fiction, including *Speed the Plough and other Stories* (1923). She married John Rodker.

need be no more talk of illusions and fragments of stale ashes and all the rest of it. Nor, I assure you, does Virginia think Sydney a perfect ass; nor does Virginia mind if Sydney thinks her a complete humbug. So now we can go straight ahead. The horrific pilgrimage has its moments of verdure, even you must admit. Anyhow we had a wonderful day at Brighton, hot, noisy, band, pier, ices, buns, prostitutes, old gentlemen, home over the downs, sunset etc etc.

What a joke that the Murry's have turned up again![1] I long to know further developments. I can't help thinking that Murry is to be the new editor of the Quarterly Review; and is over to prospect. However, no doubt you'll be feeling warmly in their favour, as I daresay I should too, if I saw them, for you must admit that though you have all the manly virtues, and I all the feminine foibles, we are united by a certain instability, which I prefer to call generosity of temperament, which leads us to extremes of passion and repulsion.

I've just heard from Lytton, and feel quite convinced that the whole of Hampstead boiled down, can't produce so much of the essence of literature as issues without effort from his little finger. But then his letters are masterpieces. And then his mind is sympathetic. I have not space to develop my theme. You must come one day and let me pour forth my views, and utterly demolish yours.

Ever yours
Virginia Woolf

John Waterlow

1280: To Jacques Raverat   *Monks House, Rodmell,*
Lewes, [Sussex]

Aug. 25th [1922]

Dear Jacques,

Anyhow you haven't forgotten one feature in your old friend's character —vanity. I enjoyed your praises [of *Monday or Tuesday*] immensely, and Gwen's, and felt quite set up for many days. I rather expect abuse for that book. Now you must give me your opinion of my novel which comes out soon—foreigner you may be, but you're a highly interesting character still.

Shall we really come out sometime next January? Could you find us rooms in your village [near Vence, in France]? We talk perpetually of going abroad, but I want to settle in where one can read and write, and if you were

1. Katherine Mansfield and Middleton Murry had returned from France, and she stayed for six weeks in Dorothy Brett's flat in Hampstead. It was the first time she had been in England since September 1920, and it was her last visit. She died at Fontainebleau on 9 January 1923.

there it would be great fun. Then perhaps we could talk off some of our arrears. I feel a little shy, do you? Not fundamentally, superficially. My impression is that we used to argue a great deal about the way we live. Now we have solved all that. You have a house in France, and we in Richmond. It's rather nice, shabby, ancient, very solid and incredibly untidy (I'm talking of Hogarth House) but then we print all over the place. One of Ka's gallant youths—I mean the sort of person Ka used to have about—is our partner. We meet at lunch and tea. We gossip. The poor young man tries to tell us what Lytton Strachey thinks about Proust (he lives with Lytton and has married Carrington). Then I go up to London: walk the streets, on the excuse of buying something—nothing so amazing; drop in to tea at the 1917 Club, where one generally falls into gloom at the extreme insignificance, dowdiness, of the intellectual race—darkies, actresses, cranks, Alix, James— that's the sort of creature one meets there. Well, I don't boast. I'm only one of them myself, but inwardly one still feels young and arrogant and fright- fully sharp set. I can't resist boasting still—can you? and trying to talk people down. Still, we have grown a little mellow. Everyone in Gordon Square is now famous.

Clive has taken to high society. I assure you, he's a raging success, and his bon mots are quoted by lovely but incredibly silly ladies. Really they give parties to meet Clive Bell. Maynard of course scarcely belongs to private life any more, save that he has fallen in love with Lydia Lopokhova, which is, to me, endearing. Nessa and Duncan potter along in extreme obscurity. That is all I can think of at the moment, and I am afraid that it may sound vague and dismal in your ears. The truth is you must write me a proper letter and expose yourself as I hereby expose myself.

I feel that in the great age of the world, before this present puling genera- tion had come along, you and I and that remarkable figure Gwen Darwin [Jacques' wife] were all congenial spirits. By the way you'll have to give up calling Woolf Woolf: Leonard, that is his name. I assure you, I couldn't have married anyone else—But when Ka praises Will the sound is unpleasant in my ears. So I refrain. I have nothing whatever to say against Ka and Will. At first sight he is a mere sandhopper; but later I think he has some sort of spine—indeed, he's a muscular little man, considering his size. Ka, of course, keeps a medicine chest and doses the village, and gets into a blue dress trimmed with fur for tea, when county motor cars arrive, and she is much in her element. Is this malicious? Slightly, perhaps, but you will under- stand.

I wish I could discuss the art of writing with you at the present moment. I am ashamed, or perhaps proud, to say how much of my time is spent in thinking, thinking, thinking about literature. It is a dangerous seed to plant in your children. Still, I doubt whether anything else in life is much worth having—so there is the philosophy of an old woman of 40. Do you maintain that one can think about painting? Is Gwen Raverat still so extreme? And what about Lady Darwin [Jacques' mother-in-law] and dear poor pin-cushion Eily?[1]

But I am drivelling. Tell me when you write if there are any good French books, and say if you would like me to send you anything from England.

Love to Gwen,
Yours ever,
Virginia Woolf

Sussex

1281: To Clive Bell   *Monk's House, [Rodmell, Sussex]*

[late August 1922]

Here is a letter from Hawk[2]—pleased I think—which I should like back —together with 2 or 3 pages from you—anything that comes into your head—melanism, if you like. How that pleased me!

Now, of course, I'm forced on to Tom's Committee, by the Bank; and so shall die bankrupt in the workhouse, aged 80, all for having a good heart, and loving poetry.

V.W.

Quentin Bell

1282: To Lady Ottoline Morrell *Monk's House, Rodmell [Sussex]*

Aug. 26th [1922]

My dear Ottoline,

I have written to Mr Aldington to say that he can use my name for the Committee, if he likes, though I still think a male name preferable. Leonard is very doubtful as to the wisdom of the whole scheme, so I can't thrust him on.

Whenever the forms are ready I should like some to send out.

Your affte
Virginia Woolf

Texas

1283: To Lady Ottoline Morrell

[Monk's House], Rodmell, [Sussex]

Friday [1 September? 1922]

A Post Script

Would you send me some forms [for the Eliot appeal] when you have them as soon as you can.

1. Elinor Monsell, who had married Gwen's cousin, Bernard Darwin.
2. Desmond MacCarthy, who had adopted the pen-name 'Affable Hawk' for his reviews in the *New Statesman*.

The people I am writing to are these, so that we may not overlap.

Logan Smith,
Roger Fry,
Maynard Keynes,
Lytton,
Clive, Mary Hutchinson,
Vanessa,
Mrs Berenson,
Charlie Sanger,
Hope Mirrlees,
Sydney Waterlow

I can think of no more at the moment.

I leave the rich ladies, like Lady Colefax, Cunard, Ethel Sands, for you or Mr Aldington.

Texas

1284: To Dora Carrington   *Monk's House, [Rodmell, Sussex]*

Saturday [2 September 1922]

My dear Carrington,

We've just had your wire to say you'll come on Tuesday.

Please come as early as you can, to lunch if possible, as Mrs Woolf, Leonard's mother is coming on Wednesday morning, and thus we shan't have much time for seeing you.

This, Leonard says I must explain, cancells his letter.

We both have a great relish for your letters, strangely enough, and I a great admiration for the handwriting.

Your aff
Virginia W.

Key of Hogarth enclosed—my own, so beware of losing it.

Robert H. Taylor

1285: To Katherine Arnold-Forster

Monks House, Rodmell, Lewes, [Sussex]

Sept 8th [1922]

Dearest Bruin

Nothing could have been more welcome than your buns, short of your bodily presence. It was an inspiration on your part. There were the 3 Sangers coming up, underfed and hungry. When I said I had buns from

Buzzard [teashop] from Ka (whom they then all remembered with love) their faces changed. Today I shall cram Lytton with them. Also the servants have a friend coming—So you see it was a stroke of genius.

Why choose Christmas? We shall be here then. Cant you ever come, like a decent woman, when London is properly going?

I see I have craftily made out that only guests and servants eat your buns. Leonard and I have our full share, and I feel the pneumonia germs perishing in front of them.

Did you see Sydney at Oare, and did you find him a changed character (once more)?

But, as you say, letters are useless.

I must jump up and rush over to Asheham to pick mushrooms before tea. We went in the other day. The house has been made into a suburban lodging, with draped mantelpieces, silver egg cups on little tables, and gigantic blue and brown vases with ferns in the windows,—dark, dreary, smug, respectable—no traces left of Bruin's pelt and soft wet paws.

Yours

Mark Arnold-Forster   V.W.

1286: To Vanessa Bell   *Monk's House, [Rodmell,*
                                          Sussex]
Tuesday [19 September 1922]

Dearest,

If it is fine, we will come on Friday, about 4. If it is not fine we will try to come with Tom and Morgan on Sunday (I'm not sure what time the Sunday buses arrive) for tea. I badly want some gossip with you, but I don't suppose I shall detach you from all your familiars. We had a day full of interest to me—but I cant go into details, in writing. The real plan, as Brunswick has fallen through temporarily, is that Lytton shall take Suffield—[1] this is quite serious.

I've just heard from Barbara, in wild joy, as Nick has got a place in Kent,[2] and thus will see more of you.

She is having a holiday in Wales with Saxon, who has brought an elderly cousin, the mother of 7 children, who shares B's bed, and prefers washing in cold water.

Julian is a most charming and witty character, and kept us all agog with his views upon life.   Yr

                                                        B.

Berg

1. A plan, which never materialised, to solve the domestic problems of Lytton, Carrington and Ralph by installing them in Suffield House, Richmond, the 'other half' of Hogarth House. 'Brunswick' was 38 Brunswick Square, which Virginia and Adrian had shared with Maynard, Duncan and Leonard in 1911-12.
2. As a horticulturalist at East Malling Research Station.

[21 September 1922]

My dear Barbara,

I am very much excited, and moved, and pleased by your letter. Maidstone is a great oyster and typhoid centre—that is all I know—But I shall never write to you now—Unhappiness was the condition I made, and you never fulfilled it. Now you will be rich; keep a motor I daresay. Anyhow, I shall come and inspect into the matter for myself.

Its you who should write letters. Leonard and I shouted with pleasure over yours—and the old gentleman Lytton, and then Saxon taking his chess board out. Are Saxon's Aunts 7 children also in the bedroom? Why has it been kept so dark? Please tell me whether they are the children of the icthyologist (which means fish something). If so, I have a niche for them in my memory.

Lytton has just gone, and Morgan Forster is just coming, and we go over to Charleston tomorrow, God willing. But oh the weather! One day of fine, then six of wet; rain spitting in the fire; pipes choked; birds found drowned; and my work cut out, merely raising the dahlias from the ground. Chickybiddiensis Bagenalia[1] is doing very well.

You'll be able to come over and see us from Maidstone. But what will Nick's work be, and does it lead on, and is it more suitable than what he had? I can't help regretting Garsington, slightly, on selfish grounds. Going to see Barbara would have been such a boon on Sunday morning.

The Partridges came too, for one night. Carrington rather bitter against the institution of marriage still; but she is going to paint it down.

Tell Saxon with my love, that I am reading the Odyssey. But as Barbara is never quite certain whether it is Early English or Norse, my very profound remarks shall wait. Its no good pluming oneself on scraps of learning with you matrons, however—who are rearing families and feeding hens. Will you be able to take part in the Hogarth Press? Violent crises are now taking place. I am starting a coloured paper manufactory this autumn. I enclose our circular—not for you, but for the Danish matron [Saxon's aunt], who might spread our fame among the Scand[inavian]s. I'm sure they don't like to be called Scands; so don't mention it.

We have entered village life. Leonard plays tennis at the Rectory, and has raised our reputation tremendously by beating them all. We had the poet Shanks to dinner to meet Lytton; but the poet Shanks only talks when drunk, so Lytton has now discovered—unluckily too late. Dora and Charlie and Daphne Sanger have been staying at Southease; Daphne is a stout

1. During one of her visits to Rodmell, Barbara had identified some yellow flowers as 'Tropaeolum Canaryensis'. Impressed by her knowledge, Virginia had nicknamed Barbara 'Chickybiddiensis'.

woman of 16: I thought she was still in the cradle: and I can't talk with ease before virgins. Then Sydney Waterlow came and bathed in the Ouse, which barely covered his shanks—it would have drowned the poet Shanks completely—unless he had been drunk.

I must pick apples, or raise asters, and as you see I am drivelling like an infant in arms.

Please write again, and tell me about Maidstone—what fun to have to find a house! I've just found one, but don't see how to manage to live in 3 at the same time.

Love to the old Reprobate [Saxon], who might have written to me.

Yr
V.W.

Berg

1288: To Janet Case   *Monk's House, Rodmell,*
                             [Sussex]
Sept 23rd [1922]

My dear Janet,

I was thinking of you and wondering about the house that very morning, before Lottie brought in the breakfast. I am immensely glad that you have £1100 in your pocket. Nor can I imagine any more enviable state than to be building ones own house—black tar and thatch in the heart of the forest [New Forest]—You will be in time to see the leaves falling, and for myself, I like winter there much best. Yes—this is a hint that I'm to be asked.

Here I am sitting in my garden room, with Morgan Forster beside me writing an article for the Nation upon the East—upon this new war,[1] I think: and I have to exercise great discretion in not sneezing or knocking things over. He has been staying with the great Thomas Hardy who is, alas, a very vain, quiet, conventional, uninteresting old gentleman, who complains bitterly that the Spectator cuts him up, and the Westminster Gazette finds him tedious, as if he were a penny a liner living in a garret in Soho. Its all very disillusioning—but perhaps at 82 one rots a little. His great pride is that the county families ask him to tea; and his chief topic of conversation the deaths of his cats—three were run over on the railway line, which is odd, as the railway is at some distance.

Now I will plunge into medical history—only it is so long and various that I must curtail. Only one dr says my right lung is wrong: upon which the other says it is perfectly all right: they compromise now upon pneumonia germs in my throat, which are said to cause slight fever. Last week however,

1. The Turks, under Mustapha Kemal, had defeated the Greek army in Anatolia, and on 9 September captured Smyrna.

559

getting wet, I had the flu again—but a slight attack, and I feel none the worse and in my view the whole thing is merely a mix up of influenza with my own remarkable nervous system, which, as everybody tells me, can't be beaten for extreme eccentricity, but works all right in the long run.

I apologise for this egotism, and might write a better letter if it weren't for the distinguished author, who is now scratching out every word he has written. Also Grizel, our dog, will sit not on my knee, but at my back; and her scratching, coinciding with Morgans, is enough to drive one frantic.

Love to Emphie. Please tell me how the house goes on. We return next week.

Yr V.W.

Sussex

1289: To T. S. Eliot

Monk's House, Rodmell,
Lewes, [Sussex]

Sept 25th 1922

Dear Tom,

I hope you will forgive me for what I feel to be an impertinence on my part, but circumstances compel me to risk annoying you.

I think it best to explain to you openly that Ottoline asked me some time ago to join Mr Aldington's Committee for what they call the Eliot Fellowship Fund. I did not altogether agree with their proposals, particularly as I could not make out that they knew what your views were. But I agreed to join. From what you said on Sunday I gathered that—as I had thought—the scheme was impracticable from your point of view. Today Ottoline has sent me a revised version of the scheme which is still less satisfactory than the first. I feel therefore that I must explain the position to her and must ask you therefore whether I am right in understanding you to say that

1) £500 a year is the least sum that would make it worth your while to leave the Bank.

2) that you do not consider that pledges to pay a yearly contribution are a sufficient security to warrant you in giving up your present work.

If you simply put "Yes" on a postcard I shall take it to mean that I am right on both points.

(Perhaps I may add that Leonard and I entirely agree with you, if these are your views).

Yours ever
Virginia Woolf

Mrs T. S. Eliot

560

Typewritten
Sept 25th. 1922

Dearest Ottoline,

I wired to you to day to stop sending out the circular because I cant agree to the scheme which is now proposed, and—what is far more important —I find that Tom himself, (who was here yesterday) is not ready to accept the original scheme, let alone this one. He told me definitely that he will not leave the Bank unless he has a sum of £500 a year assured him, by which he means that he must either have a capital sum to bring in £500 or securities for that amount in a bank. He does not think that pledges to contribute so much a year for life are good enough to warrant him in giving up his present position. Anything less than £500 would, he says, throw him into journalism, and he prefers the Bank.

But now I see from the revised circular that we are trying to get only £300 a year for a period of not less than five years, and this depends upon pledges to contribute yearly. In five years time therefore, having given up the Bank, Tom may very likely find himself in serious difficulties. I certainly will not ask people to contribute to such a proposal, even if Tom himself agreed to it—which he certainly does not.

The only thing we can do, so far as I can see, is to ascertain from Tom himself that I have understood him rightly, and then issue another appeal in accordance with his views. I am writing to him therefore by this post and asking him to say whether £500 a year is the least sum that would make it worth his while to leave the bank; and what securities he would think sufficient. When I have his answer I will write at once to you. I will then draft for your approval another scheme, keeping so far as I can to Philip's wording, which seems to me admirable.

In talk with Tom he said also that a sum down, if no condition were made that he should leave the Bank, would be a great relief, and leave him freer for writing. Therefore it seems to me very important not to limit sums subscribed, and possibly to hint at some such scheme should the original scheme prove impossible.

It is a thousand pities that Pound and Aldington didn't get Tom to explain his views before they launched the scheme. Let alone the worry to Tom himself—and I'm afraid he takes it all much to heart and feels his position most awkward—the scheme once muddled will be very hard to start again.

Privately I hear that the fate of the Literary Supplement [the *Criterion*] is very doubtful, so he may not have that to count on; and looking at it all round I think he is perfectly right to take up the line he does. But I will get it in writing before doing anything further.

Please excuse this hard faced typewriter—but my hand has given up making letters clearly.

[*handwritten*]

If you feel that it is better now to go on with the scheme, and re-arrange it with subscribers later, of course do as you think best—but I should like my name scratched out, as I couldn't be responsible for it.

Yr affate

V.W.

P. S.

On re-reading this document, I fear that my efforts to be clear and practical may lead you to think me dictatorial and faultfinding with *you*. I hope you won't do so, for my only grudge is against Pound and Aldington, who ought I think, to have got things clear at the start. Tom is so reticent about it, and also so much on edge that I've no doubt he made it very difficult to find out his wishes. Of course I may have got it all wrong myself—However I will do my best to find out, and will let you know without a moment's delay.

You have taken such an awful lot of trouble that it seems a shame to make difficulties—but I'm sure you'll see what I feel about it—and excuse asperities of language.

We are here till Oct 5th.

Ever Your affate

Virginia

Please make any further suggestions that occur to you—I only offer to draft another letter to save you trouble.

Texas

1291: To T. S. Eliot   *Monks House,* [*Rodmell,*
                                                 Sussex]

Monday [25 September 1922]

Dear Tom,

Since writing to you this morning I have been in to Lewes, and saw a house to let in rather a charming position. So I went in and found a flat of 4 rooms, the ground floor that is of a large old-fashioned house. It is in that crescent which you pass on the left as you drive out to us, standing back from the road, and quiet. There are 3 good big rooms, and one smaller, with a little kitchen opening out of it, a bathroom with hot and cold water, and a W. C. They ask £75 without rates, which haven't yet been assessed, but cant be very much, I expect they would take less. It is all new done up and clean. There is a very good garden which would belong to you, except for a flight of steps which the owners of the upper part have the right to cross. There is nothing at the back between you and Newhaven, and it is the best part of Lewes, near the downs, and only 5 minutes walk from the station. I think it would be worth your seeing, if you seriously think of a house in this part.

I enclose the owner's card. Let me know if you think of coming to look at it before Oct. 3rd, and we would meet you, and give you a bed.

Yours ever

V.W.

Mrs T. S. Eliot

1292: To T. S. Eliot   *Monks House, Rodmell,*
                                         [Sussex]
Typewritten
Saturday, 30 Sept. [1922]

My dear Tom,

Of course I understand how difficult your position is, and only regret that I was forced to open the question again, for it must be a torment to you.

I have had a very reasonable letter from Ottoline, and no harm has been done. She will wait until she hears from me again.

Please come and see us, for that will be much better than writing. We go back on Thursday. Will you dine on Sunday, (the 8th, I think.) Dinner is at seven thirty, but come earlier if you will, for we shall be in anyhow.

I am extremely sorry to hear such bad news of your wife.[1] Please give her my sympathy. I can't imagine any fate more odious. Indeed, you have had a frightful time of it.

Ever yours,

Virginia Woolf

Mrs T. S. Eliot

1293: To Lady Ottoline Morrell   *Monks House, Rodmell,*
                                         [Sussex]
Typewritten
Saturday [30 September 1922]

Dearest Ottoline,

I have just heard from Tom who writes—"I should like to be able to answer your questions as you ask them, but when I force myself to put my

1. Eliot's first wife, Vivienne, was chronically ill.

mind on it I know that the whole matter is or has become so very difficult and complicated that I cannot without going into it from top to bottom. I have had to keep my mind off this matter as much as possible and concentrate on what I must do from hour to hour. It has been an incessant strain, knowing that this business was going on, and yet not knowing exactly *what* was going on; I have been assailed from all sides, and the situation has been made in some quarters very difficult. When no definite offer has been made one cannot let ones imagination run on what one might do in one set of circumstances or another. I find the only way to live at all is to fix my attention on the particular work of the moment. If I may come and see you as soon as you get back to Richmond, I should like to discuss every aspect thoroughly with you, and I think I can make clear why it is so difficult. I am sure however that you will understand my present attitude; so do you mind waiting until I see you? I hope it will not put you into a difficult position."

So we have asked him to come next week, and I will let you know whatever I can make out from him. But I feel rather hopeless. It seems such a muddle; though I suspect it is all Tom's own fault, and if only he would have swallowed his shyness at the beginning, something might have been done.

I wonder if you know exactly what *has* been done? Is a certain sum secure? And on what conditions? I think Aldington gave some facts in a letter to you. I should like to be able to tell Tom exactly how the matter stands so that he may not be in the dark any longer. So could you let me hear before Sunday.

It was very good of you not to curse me for writing as I did. I have met with nothing but rebuffs from my friends, and should be delighted to let the whole matter slide—except that I'm sorry for him. And he says that Mrs Eliot has now been ordered to undergo treatment at some remote place for several months—another expense, I suppose.

Is anything known about the progress of the American fund?

We go back to Richmond on Thursday.

Ever affect

V.W.

Texas

1294: To Vanessa Bell   *Monks [House, Rodmell, Sussex]*

Tuesday [3 October 1922]

Dearest

Here are some photographs—I know you'll like the parrokeets at their parrokeeting. Will you hand them on to Clive.

I hear you've been infected with bugs and even Centipedes. Mrs Uppington cant tear herself away from the fray to clean Hogarth. You lift a piece of brown paper and out crawl creatures that have slept there for 20 years.

Tom was *very very* sorry not to see you, and wished to be particularly remembered. I'm now involved in a most ticklish business with him and Ottoline about his money. They've muddled the whole thing between them, and Tom will be lucky if he gets a 10 pound note. It all comes from having fine feelings; which leads, of course, to complete rupture.

We go back on Thursday. I want to go to a Promenade Concert on Friday. Could we meet? I don't mean that you're to give me dinner, but we might go in the same bus or something. But if you ring up on Thursday, we could arrange.

There are several matters I must consult you about immediately.

We've sold several [advance] copies of your book of drawings—yesterday one to Sir M[ichael]. Sadleir; so do for God's sake get on with it.

Here is the finished cover.

Yr

B.

Berg

1295: TO ROGER FRY

Monk's House, Rodmell,
[Sussex]

Oct. 3rd 1922

My dear Roger,

Long ago a slab of nougat arrived without any expression of affection attending it. The label was addressed in a curious forcible crabbed unknown hand. Clive says it is you. But you might have written. It was delicious while it lasted, and now is a memory. I suppose you are at St Tropez—perfectly happy, quite forgetful, painting all day—the sun perhaps too hot.

I haven't much news, except of the usual English kind—weekends; Clive, Mary; Eliot, Morgan; Lytton, the Sangers. We go back to Hogarth tomorrow, and have at once to beard a crisis with Ralph, which has been brewing some time. I expect he'll stay on, however; but possibly we shall combine in some way with Mr Whitall, who is coming to see us.[1] Several books are emerging; and I may point out that we've sold several copies of Mallarmé by Roger Fry.[2]

Our Murry is back in London: and Sydney who has sloughed his skin for the 20th time and is now a simple, deep, suffering man of the style of Koteliansky, repudiates him, but wobbles. This is all horrid gossip to send out to your purer skies. I write in the horror of packing—I ought to be rolling stockings into balls. My great adventure is really Proust. Well—

1. See p. 545, note 1.
2. See p. 439, note 1. This was a bait to urge Roger Fry to complete the work.

what remains to be written after that? I'm only in the first volume, and there are, I suppose, faults to be found, but I am in a state of amazement; as if a miracle were being done before my eyes. How, at last, has someone solidified what has always escaped—and made it too into this beautiful and perfectly enduring substance? One has to put the book down and gasp. The pleasure becomes physical—like sun and wine and grapes and perfect serenity and intense vitality combined. Far otherwise is it with Ulysses; to which I bind myself like a martyr to a stake, and have thank God, now finished— My martyrdom is over. I hope to sell it for £4.10. (I see my language is not as clear as it might be—)

But this is only a flourish to awaken your memory, which is I suppose, dissolved in sunshine. They are building up the churchyard wall here, and Mrs Dedman, has I regret to say, stolen 5 face towels.

Ever your
V.W.

Sussex

Letters 1296-1340 (October–December 1922)

The Woolfs returned from Rodmell to London, and on 27 October Jacob's Room was published (but not printed) by the Hogarth Press as their first full-length publication. Virginia began to receive letters from her friends, full of praise for it, among them, Eliot, Lytton, Desmond MacCarthy, Logan Pearsall Smith, E. M. Forster and David Garnett; and she did not much mind being called by the Daily News *"an elderly sensualist". Sales soon justified a second printing. As usual she was quite willing to discuss the book once it was public property, and her fullest analysis of what she had attempted was written to a new friend, Gerald Brenan, on Christmas Day. The novel, as Quentin Bell wrote in his biography of Virginia, "marks the beginning of her maturity and her fame". No sooner was the excitement about* Jacob *dying down than Leonard was involved in the General Election, at which he stood as a Labour candidate against Virginia's cousin, H. A. L. Fisher. He came fourth in the poll out of six candidates, and much to Virginia's relief was not elected. Virginia still busied herself with the Eliot Appeal, now floundering, and Leonard with offers to amalgamate the Hogarth Press with established firms, which he turned down. At the end of the year Virginia first met Vita Sackville-West, the most intimate friend of her middle years, and Virginia's first letter to her, one of many hundreds, is the penultimate letter in this volume.*

1296: TO GERALD BRENAN   Hogarth House, Paradise Road,
                                              Richmond

Oct. 5th 1922

Dear Gerald,

What is happening to you? And also what is happening to your writings? You promised to let me see some of them. But nothing has come my way, and I don't feel very sure that this letter will ever find you. I'm often sorry that we didn't see you again. But perhaps this spring we shall be taking a steamer down the coast of Spain. If so, may we look in on you?

We are just starting on our publishing season, going back to Richmond today after two months soaking down here [Rodmell]. I have been nibbling at village society. The Rector, his wife and daughter, tennis, tea parties— and much regret to find that we intellectuals not only have the brains but also the blood of the world. I dont see the point of stupidity and simplicity unless they serve as a counterpane to protect the grosser powers—lust, passion, virility, femininity and muscle. Nothing of the sort; they are anaemic, and spend their time in gossip and vain lamentations for West Kensington.

Lytton was here for a few days, and Carrington and Ralph, after their motor tour, which was frightfully expensive, Lytton said, but opened up the entire pageant of England.

I can't quite imagine how you spend your day. Scratching out sentences, and reading the classics? Please enlighten me on all this, and, particularly, let us know if there is a chance that you'll send us something for the Press. I shall send you my new novel, which we shall bring out at the end of the month. I should like criticism, if you can bring yourself to write it.

I am putting off, by writing this letter, the awful moment of dismissing our charwoman. She is a powerful old lady, much like a hippopotamus to look at, full of craft and guile, and may put her head down and gore me to death. So if you hear no more, understand that I have met my fate.

Leonard wishes to be remembered.

Yours ever
Virginia Woolf

George Lazarus

1297: To Clive Bell   [*Hogarth House, Richmond*]
Postcard
[7 October 1922]

I'll send the ballad¹ to Nessa to keep tomorrow—as I'm incapable, owing to conversation, of correcting it in time.

By all means publish in America—It makes no difference to us.

V.W.

Quentin Bell

1298: To Lytton Strachey   *Hogarth House, Paradise Road,*
                                                Richmond, Surrey

Oct. 9th [10th?] 1922

I breathe more freely now that I have your letter,² though I think your praise is extravagant—I can't believe you really like a work so utterly devoid of so many virtues; but it gives me immense pleasure to dream that you do. Of course you put your infallible finger upon the spot—romanticism. How

1. *The Legend of Monte della Sibilla*, which was published by the Hogarth Press in 1923.
2. Virginia had sent Lytton an advance copy of *Jacob's Room*.

do I catch it? Not from my father. I think it must have been my Great Aunts. But some of it, I think, comes from the effort of breaking with complete representation. One flies into the air. Next time, I mean to stick closer to facts. There are millions of things I want to get your opinion on—This is merely to heave a sigh of relief that you don't cast me off, for nobody else's praise ever gives me quite as much pleasure as yours.

Thursday lunch.

Your loving
Virginia

Frances Hooper

1299: To Lady Ottoline Morrell

*Hogarth House, Paradise Road,
Richmond, Surrey*

Typewritten
Oct 10th 1922

Dearest Ottoline,

We saw Tom yesterday, and I think he has now made his position quite clear. He is definitely of opinion that his circumstances are such at present that he could not undertake to leave the Bank unless he had a certain and guaranteed income of not less than £500 a year. By a guaranteed income he means that, if it were subscribed in any way, it would not depend upon a bare promise of people to contribute so much a year, but that the money should be in the form of a trust so that he should be assured of its continuance. We both feel that he is quite right in this, and I am sure you will agree.

It is clear—and he agrees with this—that under these circumstances any circular which asks for less or which does not contain these conditions ought to be stopped. We think that the circular which was proposed in England cannot now go out. Would you let me know whether you will communicate this to Mr Aldington, or would prefer that I did?

Tom suggests that the best way of dealing with the Ezra Pound Committee and the American Committee would be for us to have a circular printed which could be sent to subscribers. In it we should say what I have said above—that the present scheme is impracticable; but I shall add that subscribers are invited to continue their subscriptions without making it a condition that Tom should leave the Bank. He has had very heavy expenses, and an addition to his income would make it, as he owned, possible for him to give more time to writing. I will send you a proof of this circular as soon as it is ready. We could send copies to Mr Aldinton [*sic*] if he wished to distribute them to the English subscribers. I suppose you do not know who is managing the American fund?

Tom was most anxious that you should know how grateful he is to you, and how much troubled lest you should think him in any way inconsiderate. He says that the plan drifted on without his knowing what was happening. He is very much upset about it—especially at the position he is in of refusing what other people have been at great trouble to get.

But of course, you'll sympathise with all his miseries without my going into them. I thought it best to write, so as to run no risk of muddle.

Ever Your affate
Virginia Woolf

Texas

1300: To Clive Bell   [*Hogarth House, Richmond*]

Postcard
[11 Oct 1922]

Margery Fry is dining here Friday next, 7.30. Will you come and give her a taste of intellectual life?

Yrs. V.W.

Quentin Bell

1301: To Richard Aldington *Hogarth House, Paradise Road, Richmond, Surry*

Typewritten
19 October, 1922

Dear Mr Aldington,

I am writing to you about the T. S. Eliot Fellowship Fund. Mr Eliot was staying with us the other day in the country and I found in talk with him that he has decided that 1) he will not leave the Bank unless he is guaranteed £500 a year and 2) that he considers that securities at a bank or a capital sum which would bring in £500 are the only safe guarantee. I then received from Lady Ottoline the form which I enclose. As you will see, the proposals which are now made—to get a sum of £300 a year, for not less than five years—are useless in view of what Mr Eliot himself says. I do not myself think, and I find that Lady Ottoline agrees with me, that we have any chance of getting the very large sum of money required. Of course I do not know what success Mr Pound has had in France, or what has happened to the American Committee. Lady Ottoline's views are that we should either write a new circular or add the following postcript to the one which I enclose:

Postcript.
"Since the scheme in the accompanying circular was prepared it has come to the knowledge of the committee that circumstances have arisen which

make it necessary that Mr Eliot should be allowed to use his own discretion as to continuing or relinquishing his present work at the Bank. It is certain however that any addition to his income would not only remove from him considerable anxiety which the expense of illness has brought upon him but would make it possible for him to give more time to writing than he can now do. Under these circumstances the committee propose to continue the scheme in its present form, but without imposing or implying any condition that Mr Eliot should give up his work at the Bank."

It is a complicated matter to settle in writing. Is there any chance that you would be able to come and see me here, or if you are in London could we arrange to meet?

Tom Eliot was, as you can imagine, very anxious that no one should think him inconsiderate; and greatly worried about the whole thing. He wanted me to communicate with Mr Pound, but I don't feel I can do so without knowing what your views are first.

Yours sincerely,
Virginia Woolf

Texas

1302: TO DAVID GARNETT   *Hogarth House, Richmond*

Oct: 20th 1922

Dear Bunny

It was extraordinarily nice of you to write to me [about *Jacob's Room*]. One has so many doubts about one's books—about this one in particular I was doubtful whether it did keep together as a whole.

So I am very much relieved by your saying that it does. But how far can one convey character without realism? That is my problem—one of them at least. You're quite right that I can't do the realism, though I admire those who can.

Anyhow, I'm extremely pleased to think that you like it—and shall try to get on a step further in the next one, now that I've got rid of some of my old clothes. It is supposed to come out on the 27th; Leonard says he put a notice in to say so.

But what about your book?[1] Please remember to keep me a copy.

I'm much excited by the accounts I hear of it—from Vanessa even, and you must admit that it takes a good deal to make *her* interested in mere literature.

Unlike her, I become more and more absorbed; and wish you and your wife would come out one day and let us go on talking.

1. *Lady into Fox*, which won both the Hawthornden and Tait-Black prizes for 1923.

Will the [General] Election ruin both our chances of selling? It is a most damnable piece of luck.

I expect you're rather hard on Tom Eliots poem [*The Waste Land*].

I have only the sound of it in my ears, when he read it aloud; and have not yet tackled the sense. But I liked the sound.

Ever Yours
Virginia Woolf

Berg

1303: TO ROGER FRY   *Hogarth House, Paradise Road,*
                                      Richmond, Surrey

Sunday Oct. 22nd 1922

My dear Roger,

I am racking my brains to think of some gossip to send you but as I suppose this to mean something spicy—Dora Sanger for example, raping Goldie in Piccadilly, or Ottoline redeeming her soul by some act of unparalleled magnanimity—I wait and wait—sitting over the fire, Lottie chattering about the best way to toast muffins and how the woman next door has had half her toe cut off because of an ingrowing nail; rain, I suppose, falling; and the autumnal church bells beginning as usual, it being now 20 minutes to six, to summon the Christians—an outrage upon my peace which always makes my gorge rise with indignation.

I have been involved in an appalling shindy about poor Tom Eliot's annuity. Were you asked to subscribe £10 a year towards it? The story is long, and reflects credit upon no one save myself: but the upshot of it is that Tom remains in the Bank, and I am in correspondence with Ezra Pound. A complete muddle, as you may imagine. But Tom's psychology fascinates and astounds. There he has let us all go on writing and appealing for the past 6 months, and at last steps out and says he will take nothing less than £500 a year—very sensible, but why not say so at first; and why twist and anguish and almost suffocate with humiliation at the mere mention of money? Its on a par with not pump shipping[1] before your wife. Very American, I expect; and the more I see of that race the more I thank God for my British blood, which does at any rate preserve one from wearing 3 waistcoats; enamel buttons on one's overcoat, and keeping one's eyes perpetually shut— like Ezra Pound.

Morgan and Herbert Read[2] were dining here last night, and Read, who

---

1. Virginia misconstructed this now obsolescent term for urinating.
2. The art historian and critic, who was then an Assistant Keeper in the Victoria and Albert Museum.

has been in the Wyndham Lewis pigsty without wallowing in it, had some amazing stories of the brutes. Lewis now paints in a shed behind a curtain— rites are gone through before you enter; but this is all very dull and out of date, and I'm sure Oscar Wilde did it all much better. Morgan was very charming, and we went a walk in Richmond Park together and talked entirely about very very minute domestic details: the cat; the maid; the cousin; and Miss Partridge of Ashstead. He is finishing his novel,[1] and utterly refuses to stay with the Asquiths or dine with Lady Colefax.

Margery was here the other night—your sister I mean, not Marjorie Strachey who ramps in Gordon Square—a menagerie without cages. The animals prowl in and out, and Nessa was laying the law down the other night with some force. If only she could never see any of her friends, she says, life might be tolerable: but there's Karin, there's Mary Hutch: there's the telephone, there's Kitty Maxse falling over the bannisters and killing herself —ought one to write to Susan Lushington [her sister]? No, one would say the wrong thing. Still it seems a pity that Kitty did kill herself: but of course she was an awful snob. No, one couldn't go on with people like that. One had to make a break somewhere. Then, of course, in comes Angelica [Bell]; all the beads are upset on the floor; et cetera, et cetera.

I'm sending you my novel tomorrow—a little reluctantly. It has *some* merit, but its too much of an experiment. I am buoyed up, as usual, by the thought that I'm now, at last, going to bring it off—next time. I suppose one goes on thinking this for ever; and so burrowing deeper and deeper into whatever it is that perpetually fascinates. Why don't you come back and explain it?—you are the only person who ever does; so for God's sake, get perfectly cured, and moderate your activity. It will accumulate in the cistern, and you can draw it off at leisure. I mean, you'll paint your master-piece if you have a rest. But then nothing except painting and writing is really interesting: and as one's time is limited, how can one sit and smile?

I wish you would consider, seriously, bringing out a series of modern paintings, with introductions, through the Hogarth Press.[2] The Press takes up all my time, and I ought to be translating Kots Russian,[3] instead of running on like the kitchen tap. I think it is now firm on its legs, and might branch out: I think a shop and gallery combined must come next, but this waits for you.

Yrs V.W.

Sussex

1. *A Passage to India* (1924).
2. In 1923 the Hogarth Press published a book of Duncan Grant's paintings, with an introduction by Roger Fry.
3. Virginia was collaborating with S. S. Koteliansky on two further books, which the Hogarth Press published in 1923: *Tolstoi's Love Letters;* and *Talks with Tolstoi,* by A. B. Goldenveizer.

Sunday [29 October 1922]

My Violet,

Considering you pay handsomely for the books, I don't see why you should thank us. Yes, Leonard is standing[1]; we are in the midst of an awful rush; and I suppose the Election will kill the books. What a bore L. G. [Lloyd George] didn't sit on his chair a little longer!

I didn't send my book to Gerald,[2] as I thought he wouldn't like it.

I shall come up and have tea one day, when we have done doing up parcels and writing bills—its rather a large undertaking, without help, but great fun.

I go on having a temperature, but my heart seems quite recovered.

Yr

V.W.

Leonard sends his love, and hopes to see you. He hasn't got to go to Manchester to canvass, I'm glad to say, as there is no chance of his getting in against Herbert Fisher.

I've heard nothing about Kitty [Maxse], and couldn't face the memorial service—my black being incomplete. How on earth did it happen?

Berg

1305: To David Garnett   *Hogarth House, Paradise Road,*
Richmond, Surrey

Oct 29 1922

My dear Bunny,

I am writing to express the real, yet queer, pleasure which your fox lady [*Lady into Fox*] has given me.

I was fascinated, and read on as quick as I could, in spite of knowing the end. I think it succeeds completely. The marriage of your own peculiar humour with the Eighteenth Century style is very seductive. But the interesting thing is I think your capacity for incident. Something is always happening; and it is, apparently effortless, and alive, and more like Defoe than any one else.

1. For the Combined English Universities as Labour candidate. Virginia's cousin, H. A. L. Fisher, was one of the two sitting members for the seat.
2. Gerald Duckworth, Virginia's half-brother, had published *The Voyage Out* and *Night and Day*. *Jacob's Room* was published on 27 October by the Hogarth Press, and printed for them by R. & R. Clark of Edinburgh.

Do go on, and drop the 18th Century and do it completely off your own bat.

You must have a fund of stories in your head. All we battered old novelists find nothing so hard as perpetual story telling, and there you are doing it as a fountain bubbles.

This is not worth sending you, but unless I write now I shan't, for we are worried and harassed by the elections and the books.

We want to discuss your letter. Leonard will arrange a meeting if he can.

This is only to thank you for the pleasure, for I don't often like a book so much.

Yours ever
Virginia Woolf

Berg

1306 : To Philip Morrell   *Hogarth House, Paradise Road,*
                                  Richmond, Surrey

29th Oct. 1922

My dear Philip

It was extraordinarily nice of you to write to me, and your letter gave me so much pleasure that I am promptly disobeying your command not to inflict one of my disagreeable and sarcastic replies upon you.

I should very much like to think that you are right about Jacob's Room. Certainly you have picked out the things I most like myself. When I wrote it I thought it was better than my other books. I am now, of course, getting all sorts of opinions, of the most opposite kinds, and can't quite remember my original view.

I expect to be fearfully sat upon by reviewers, or ignored; and so I shall keep your letter to encourage me. I want to get a great deal further next time, than I have this. And as I was doubtful how far Jacob would convey anything to anybody, I am more than usually glad of your praises. And aren't you hypocritically pretending to be merely agricultural? But I must not be sarcastic: please rub your eyes and see me sincere and grateful.

Now I am afraid I must bore you with the Eliot fund affairs. I have heard from Aldington who thinks that we had better go on with the fund, and add to the circular the postscript which Ottoline sent me.

I suppose that you have all the forms ready printed at Garsington; and it would be easy to have the postscript (enclosed) added on the blank page, or inserted as a slip—As you have had all the trouble and expense of the original printing, Shall we print a slip at the Hogarth Press, and send it to you—or what? I am telling Aldington that this is being done, and that he should write for forms to you or Ottoline. Aldington also wants to know the address of Ella A. Abbot who has contributed, but sends no address. She is unknown to me.

What a bore this business is! It leaves me no room nor time to talk of anything else. Our summer got so disorganised for various reasons that it was useless to ask you to Rodmell; nor did I think you would come, or I might have risked it—the risk being that you would have found a bed like a board, inefficient service, no bath, arm chair; and a tumult of ill assorted visitors. Perhaps another time we shall be better ordered. Leonard is in the middle of his election, and there is now a ghastly fear that he has some chance of getting in. Herbert Fisher has offended all the schoolteachers, apparently.[1]

Love to Ottoline, and please ask her why it is that I must go to tea with Lady Colefax, and buy white gloves, a new hat, and shoes, instead of dropping into 44 Bedford Square,[2] precisely as I am, dirty, dowdy, and disreputable. Doesn't the thought sting her conscience and remind her of her duties!

Yours ever
Virginia Woolf

Texas

1307: TO KATHERINE ARNOLD-FORSTER
*Hogarth House, Paradise Road,
Richmond, Surrey*

Oct 29 1922

Dearest Bruin,

It was a great pleasure to get your letter, for I wasn't at all sure that you would find anything good to say of my offspring. It seems to affect people violently: with delight or disgust. I never know which its going to be; and am quite at sea, as to what I did write. Anyhow, though I expect a good deal of abuse from the reviewers, I rest in the praises of that faithful Cornish thick haired brute. Did you recognise some of your own scenery?

We are chaotic in this house, doing up Dostoevsky [*Stavrogin's Confession*], and Jacob in brown paper, writing election addresses, interviewing lady agents, and now I must talk to Miss Mary Butts[3] about *her* novel—an indecent book, about the Greeks and the Downs.

Is there any chance of seeing Will?

1. Fisher had been President of the Board of Education until the fall of Lloyd George's government earlier this month.
2. The Morrells' former London house.
3. See p. 552, note 6.

But I must ask you to explain a passage which puzzles both Leonard and me:

"Of course you're quite right about cruelty—it does really spoil the very best of the writing—but this is so very many degrees further into the heart of the matter."

I see its very profound; but did I say it? or does it refer to the poor old Criterion? Am I cruel? is Dostoevsky? You must explain. Fame has come to me with her arms full: Lady Colefax has invited me to tea.

Excuse this wretched scrawl: I am rather in a rush.

We have put your pound in store.

Now write me another letter, or come and see me, or send your husband, for whom I cherish an unrequited affection.

Yours
V.W.

Mark Arnold-Forster

1308: To Richard Aldington *Hogarth House, Paradise Road, Richmond, Surrey*

Oct. 29th 1922

Dear Mr Aldington,

I have written to the Morrells and told them that you agree that it is best to go on sending out the circulars with the postscript added. They will get the new version ready.

Would you communicate with Mr Pound?

I am sorry that I don't know who Ella Abbott is—she is not in the telephone book.

Yours sincerely
Virginia Woolf

I shall be here till Christmas if you want to settle anything further.

Texas

1309: To C. P. Sanger *Hogarth House, Paradise Road, Richmond*

30th Oct. 1922

My dear Charlie,

I think a close study of Jacob's Room, should you ever wish to approach the book again, will reveal many passages which a trained mind would have pinched much closer together: and others where the mistakes are glaring. What about lilacs in April, fountains in Neville's Court, tulips in August etc etc etc. I am not going to pick them all out for your benefit. What I do feel is that education helps one to be drastic with oneself, instead of sloppy, and as age increases I do more and more believe in thought as an element of fiction. You are quite right, I am sure, in having grave doubts about the form of Jacob's Room. So have I. It would take too long to explain why I had this time to use it, and what I hope next time to do with it. I am getting the most contradictory opinions daily, and feel quite at sea as to the success or failure of the whole. But as you ought to know, I have a humble respect, not to say veneration, for your judgment, and so if you found good in it, I am immensely encouraged.

It is no joke publishing ones own book, and there is this cursed election on top of it. Otherwise, it would be much nicer to see you and Dora than to write to you. There is now a ghastly chance that Leonard may get in. Herbert Fisher has made himself so unpopular. Directly the fuss is over, I shall try to get you to come and see us.

Ever so many thanks for writing.

Yours ever,
Virginia Woolf

Daphne Sanger

1310: TO DORA SANGER   [*Hogarth House, Richmond*]
Enclosed with preceding letter
[30 October 1922]

My dear Dora,

I ought to have answered your letter before.

But your own views of politeness are, if I may say so, so rudimentary, that I can never behave properly to you.

I hope the Gyles visit will become annual.[1]

Even more than seeing you, I enjoyed your complete rout by that apparently insignificant woman—She has gone up miles in my respect: you have sunk.

Why do you accuse Leonard of indifference to public affairs? Here he is slaving all day to make the world safe for democracy or some trash like that. Its on the cards he will be Woolf M.P. before long, and I may dedicate my life to tea parties on the terrace. What have you and Charlie done compared with this? I have been telling Charlie on the other page that you must come and see us. I suppose you'll say you haven't time for frivolity, and make off

1. Mrs Gyles kept a guest-house at Southease, near Rodmell, where the Sangers had stayed during the summer of 1922.

with my matches again, having first said all the disagreeable things you can think of, because you are upset about the Chinese rice pickers and their famines and earthquakes.

I have had another very mild attack, but nothing to count. I think I am naturally 99.

Yours ever
(with apologies for not writing more
seriously)

Virginia Woolf

What about the Californian Bee?[1] Could we borrow a sprout?

Daphne Sanger

1311: To Lady Ottoline Morrell

Hogarth House, Paradise Road,
Richmond, Surrey

Nov. 1st 1922

Dearest Ottoline

It gives me great pleasure that you should like Jacob. I had many doubts whether it would mean anything to anybody. Its all very well writing the things one enjoys writing—and I did this—but one does want, too, that *some* people should like it as well. Naturally, I am very glad that you should be one of them. I am rather anxious about it from a base commercial point of view. We have just ordered a second edition of a thousand; and now I look forward to sneers and jeers in all quarters, and a loss of so many pounds— This, as you see, is a hint to you, who receive so many such hints, to be good enough to tell people to spend 7/6 on it. However, if we get through the General Election safely, I daresay it will be all right.

Lady Colefax gave me 10/. That is why I went. She had Paul Valery[2] lecturing, to a room full of feathers and white gloves. Lytton and I sat together and I took a great dislike, you will be glad to hear, to Aldous, another of the captives, in spats and grey trousers.

It was all very full of furs and thick handsome clothes—not an atmosphere I find congenial at the start—but who knows? I shall become domesticated like the rest perhaps. There was Edmund Gosse, George Moore, Arnold Bennett, etc etc. However the French was beautiful: beauty is not the note of our great men.

1. A vegetable core, which moved up and down in a jar of water, and when sugar and ginger were added, it made ginger beer.
2. The French poet (1871-1945). His poems, *La Jeune Parque* (1917) and *Charmes* (1922), had established his international reputation.

I have brutally told Aldington to write to you for Eliot forms. I think we must let him and Pound muddle through it as they can. We have done our best, and Tom I suppose may get something out of it. I will despatch forms when they are ready.

But this is really to thank you for your letter—a great pleasure to get.

Texas

Ever yours
Virginia Woolf

1312: TO KATHERINE ARNOLD-FORSTER

*Hogarth House, Paradise Road,
Richmond, Surrey*

Nov 1st [1922]

Dearest Ka,

Leonard says he is not quite sure, but thinks you write to Registrar of University, enclose £1.1. and ask to be put on voting list. Many thanks for your emendation, which is very interesting, and I think true (I mean universally speaking.)

I've just had a letter from Mrs Robert Lynd, 5 Seaview Terrace, St Ives, apologising humbly for her husband, because the Daily News treats me with contempt in a review. Robert Lynd the Editor, was away. If you see her, please assure her that I don't mind, and its perfectly all right. (I have written to her; but as they're so polite, would like it made sure). But I don't suppose you know them—nor do I.

We have just ordered a second edition of Jacob, thus sacrificing a certain profit for a possible greater; and now the Election looks as if it would kill all books, and we are rather apprehensive. So please persuade Saxon or anyone else to buy it, if you can honestly recommend the investment.

Publishing one's own books is very nervous work, and we don't know how this is going. So, besides being incoherent and having to scratch out every other word, I am also blatantly advertising.

No sign of Will; but our chaos here is still too great for rational conversation. L. has to go to Manchester.

Yr V.W.

Mark Arnold-Forster

1313: TO CLIVE BELL

*Hogarth House, Paradise Road,
Richmond, Surrey*

Tuesday [7 November 1922]

Dearest Clive,

I assure you with my hand on my heart that the talk about J's Room did nothing but intrigue and interest me.

I wish I had known Mary earlier. Then I should never have got so encrusted with vanity, or the appearance (for its not much more) of vanity that my good brother in law thinks that unless praise is spread smooth and thick I wilt and pine and crack and craze and finally have to remove to a nursing home.

J. is nothing but an experiment, as I've always said; an interesting experiment; and nothing more: unless indeed, being stirred up by a little discussion and criticism, which is the blood of life, I can push on further next time. The direction of that however must wait till I can somehow nail you to the wall, and then proceed to pour out endlessly. As I've been having tea with Violet, my wits are dispersed to the five winds. No sense will come.

Perhaps you're lunching with your Paramour on Thursday?

Yr V.W.

Quentin Bell

1314: To Clive Bell   [*Hogarth House, Richmond*]

Postcard
[7? November 1922]

Like a donkey, I went off leaving the drawings for your book[1] at Nessa's, in a roll. Would you take them with you to Tidmarsh, and hand over to Partridge, who will bring them here.

V.W.

Quentin Bell

1315: To Will Arnold-Forster

Hogarth House, Paradise Road,
Richmond, Surrey

Nov. 7th [1922]

Dear Will,

I wish I had got wind of your state before, for then I would have come with the greatest pleasure. But tomorrow I can't manage, and you'll be off, I suppose, on Thursday, to the far superior charms of Tregerthen. Let me know if by any chance you stay on.

I should have made you tell me why Jacob is just the book for you—but the egoism of authoresses is proverbially bad for invalids, so no doubt all's for the best.

Leonard is off to Liverpool, on a goose's errand, for the Conservative students break up the meetings and he is only to speak to a few old ladies in a drawing room.

1. *The Legend of Monte della Sibilla.*

That is my terrible destiny in 30 minutes. Adrian, my brother, is coming to speak to the 12 Co-operators of Richmond, good working women who mind the pot and smack the baby, upon the possibilities of psycho-analysis. Ka will see the joke. You, who probably think me much like other people and my brothers and sisters equally capable of addressing Co-operators will see nothing in it at all.

As I will not remain an invalid much longer, ring me up, and let me arrive with my cheerful good sense and sound labour party politics. I went to a meeting here,—was so appalled by the stuff people talk that I am going to drop my vote in the gutter. How you and Leonard see anything solid where to me it is all phantasies and moonshine, only mudcoloured moonshine, I can't conceive. Bonar Law[1] seems to me precisely the same as Lloyd George —and so on.

> But goodbye.
> Yours Virginia Woolf

Mark Arnold-Forster

1316: To Dora Carrington   *Hogarth House, Paradise Road, Richmond, Surrey*

[8 November 1922]

Dearest Carrington,

I would have written yesterday, but had to rush off to the Womens Guild. It is quite untrue that we didn't enjoy our weekend.[2] As for the great argument anyhow I think it proved that if we have to part it wont be for personal reasons on our side, or on Ralph's. Certainly we didn't think that he gave us notice either because he disliked us or was tired of the Press. The difficulties on both sides seem to me purely and simply practical ones— However, I don't suppose you want to revive the argument—this is only to show that it is just as desirable for Hogarth to be connected with Tidmarsh as for Tidmarsh to be connected with Hogarth. If the Press dies, poor creature, we shall still expect to be invited to stay.

I meant to ask your advice about sending my book to Gerald. I wrote to him 6 weeks ago but had no answer. Ralph says you have sent him a copy, which remind me to repay. Hope Johnstone[3] has some messages from Gerald, he says; and I shall get him to come here.

1. Andrew Bonar Law (1858-1923), the Conservative leader, had become Prime Minister on the fall of the Lloyd George Coalition Government in October. He was confirmed in office by the General Election in November.
2. The Woolfs had stayed with Lytton Strachey, Carrington and Ralph Partridge at Tidmarsh on the 4th and 5th of November.
3. John Hope-Johnstone, formerly editor of *The Burlington Magazine*, and a close friend of Gerald Brenan.

Please excuse illiteracy; I have had to scribble all day to finish an article[1] and this leaves one very much out of language. Not however, out of affection, which is always very strong for Carringtonia; so you must come and see me, and Leonard joins in this.

Ever
VW.

Robert H. Taylor

1317: To Ralph Partridge　　　　*Hogarth* [*House, Richmond*]

Friday [10 November 1922]

My dear Ralph,

　　I think I had better explain why you made me so angry this evening by asking me to see that Leonard did not sell the press during the weekend to Constables, and why I was further indignant with you for going on to suggest that we were ready, as you said, to "sell the press to the highest bidder." I suspect that you didn't mean either of these remarks seriously.

　　But I think I may have left you with the impression that I am myself in favour of amalgamation with some big firm in order to increase the publicity of my own books and profits. If you do think this, you are quite wrong; but the fault (being angry) may be mine.

　　What did make my blood boil was your assumption that Leonard and I are quite ready to be bamboozled with a bargain which would destroy the character of the press for the sake of money or pride or convenience; and that you must protect its rights. After all we have given the press whatever character it may have, and if you're going to tell me that you care more about it than I do, or know better what's good for it, I must reply that you're a donkey. You will retaliate by telling me that I'm another to take your chance remarks seriously. No doubt I am; but I was left with a feeling that you would base some weekend discussions upon the assumption that the Woolves are out to make a good bargain, and that Virginia, consumed with vanity, and blown with ambition, is going to persuade Leonard etc and etc— In short, that the days of an independent Hogarth are doomed.

　　This was not at all my meaning, I assure you.

Yours ever
Virginia Woolf

Tell Carrington, if she is not sick altogether of these fiery quadrupeds [the Woolfs], that she never did give me the receipt for the toffee; which might sweeten my temper.

Robert H. Taylor

1. Review of *Modern English Essays*, edited by Ernest Rhys (*TLS*, 30 November 1922).

Postcard
[10 November 1922]

Leonard will communicate with you about the Poem. We had already got the information from Bunny. L. will also answer the question about the New Republic. Your card was swept from me, so I can't remember what it was.

                                                                                        V.W.

Quentin Bell

1319: To Vanessa Bell   *Hogarth* [*House, Richmond*]

Sunday [12 November 1922]

Dearest,

Here is 15/- which I consider dirt cheap for the hat. It is thought to be very becoming.

Would you possibly take me one day this week to buy an outfit—or anyhow tell me where the shop is?

Our proposal about the woodcuts is that you and Duncan should receive half profits, and produce as many woodcuts as would make a little book, in time to be published in the spring—[1]

What about calling on Kate [Katharine Stephen?]?

Adrian and Karin are here playing bridge.

                                                                                        Yr

                                                                                          B

Please let me know what I owe for the table. Could it be sent? Also what measurement is right for your chair.

Berg

1320: To Lady Robert Cecil   *Hogarth House, Paradise Road,*
                                                          Richmond, [*Surrey*]

[12 November 1922]

Dear Nelly,

I have been trying to buy some notepaper, and so answer your letter, but I have little hope of doing that. For one thing it is Sunday evening. We are back here, and have been for a month, and every day seems wasted in this weather.

1. They never published this book.

I envy you and [Lady] Gwendolen [Cecil] very much. (I would send her my love, but I reflect that my clothes are wholly unsuitable for that.) One of these days, when I have bought a new skirt, I shall ask her to tea. Meanwhile Leonard and I say that though we are committed to keeping a secretary and a printing press going here, there is no reason why you should not come to us. Please consider it. We have a spare room—not comfortable, or very clean, but you could put up with it perhaps, and we should very much enjoy having you. Please consider it and suggest a time. We should like to see your dog too.

Leonard has been meeting Lord Robert. He has seen his constituents, and they seem cordial; but if he does get in (I'm talking of Leonard) I shall divorce him. Unfaithfulness is not with women only. In fact, politics seems worse to me than mistresses. Are those your sentiments? Sidney Webb is safe, so they say[1]; and if England is governed by Sidney Webb surely the rest of us may fold our hands!

I read the book of Job last night—I dont think God comes well out of it —How I wish you were here to tell me stories of your childhood, and what happened when the man asked how a cob differed from a horse.

I'm sitting on the edge of a party playing Bridge—very cold, dismal, faced with the appalling problem of buying some clothes. Nessa has sold me a hat for 10/6—but who will sell me a skirt, and until I get a skirt, Lady Gwendolen will not come to tea.

Now my dear Nelly, when will [you] come and see us?

Yrs aff.

V.W.

Hatfield

1321: To Lady Ottoline Morrell

*Hogarth House, Paradise Road,
Richmond, Surrey*

13th Nov. 22

Dearest Ottoline:

I am afraid these have taken a long time,[2] but we are rather busy just now. I have kept a few, and shall now begin pestering some of the mild cold ladies I meet at tea parties. But my career is running to an end. I can't forever appear in the same skirt; already glances of derision are levelled at it; and I foresee that I must retire to the suburbs until May, when I shall buy a new one.

I sometimes think with some horror that you are taking my hint to advertise my book seriously. Please don't. I didn't mean that. I think we are

1. Sidney Webb won the Seaham division of Durham from a Liberal by a majority of nearly 12,000.
2. The 'postscript' to the Eliot Fund letter, which the Hogarth Press had printed.

safe not to lose on it now, and I have a great dread of becoming a bore to Ottoline, who is not without her troupe of them already.

I met old Mr [Augustine] Birrell the other day, who talked of you affectionately, as I did; but said you were very depressed. I hope this is one of the misunderstandings old men make.

Ever yours
V.W.

I'll send the forms [Eliot Fund pledges] tomorrow. I see they must be put in a parcel.

Texas

1322: TO PHILIP MORRELL   *Hogarth House, Paradise Road,*

Richmond, Surrey

16th Nov. 1922

Dear Philip.

Please excuse me for bothering you with the Eliot fund again; but I know Ottoline is in London.

I'm sending you this pledge of Logan's to keep; and shall send you any others I get; as they had better be together in one place, I think.

No answer is required.

Ever yours
Virginia Woolf

We are much relieved not to have got into Parliament, and yet to have done creditably.[1]

Texas

1323: TO JANET CASE   *Hogarth House, [Richmond]*

Sunday [19 November 1922]

My dear Janet,

It was very nice of you to read Jacob, and to like some of it. I'm so

1. The result of the election for the Combined English Universities was:

Sir Martin Conway (Unionist)	1,093
H. A. L. Fisher (Nat. Lib.)	1,009
Strong, J. (Indep.)	813
Woolf, Leonard (Labour)	366
Faraday, W. B. (Indep. Unionist)	206
Lawrence, S. L. (Indep. Unionist)	90

Conway and Fisher, the sitting Members, were re-elected.

confused by contradictory opinions, that I can't remember in the least what it is about. However, I've no doubt its very clever!

I am trying to write against a conversation about chess, which is now going forward between Leonard and Oliver Strachey. Then I have to get up and pour out tea. Then we talk about Ray's failure. I thought she had succeeded marvellously: but she was positive she would get in: the poll completely dismayed her.[1]

We had one terrible night of hope. Mr Strang [Strong] withdrew. All the teachers then came over to Leonard. Thank God, Mr Strang thought better of it, and they returned to him, or we should have been within an ace of getting in.

But this is mere gossip and triviality beside the solid and prodigious fact of your house. I can't believe it has really happened—Is it coal black? perfect in every way? A view of trees from each window? Forest rides as near you as Eton Street is near me? And all the blue china and cups without handles already unpacked—not a single one of course broken; and Emphie acclaimed by divine right the Despot of Minstead [New Forest], with complete control and knowledge of all domestic arrangements within 5 miles, including births, deaths and marriages, none of which take place without her consent, and it is said she is getting up an anti-staghunt agitation, which meets with grave opposition from old Colonel Lascelles whom I used to know.

I am dribbling; and must stop.

Yr V.W.

Sussex

1324: To Vanessa Bell   *Hogarth House, Paradise Road,*
                                Richmond, Surrey
Thursday [23 November 1922]

Dearest,

I have made so bold as to ask Roger to meet us and you at 46 Gordon Square on Saturday next at 6. p.m. *If this is utterly abhorrent to you, say so, beforehand*

The thing is that Heinemann has made us rather a tempting proposal about the Press[2]; but it is essential to get Roger and you to give us your

---

1. Ray (Mrs Oliver) Strachey had stood for Parliament as an Independent candidate for the Brentford and Chiswick division of Middlesex, in a straight fight against a Unionist. She lost by over 2,000 votes.
2. Heinemann, the established publishers, had offered to take the Hogarth Press into 'a kind of partnership' (*Downhill all the Way*, p. 79), with James Whitall as business manager. The Woolfs turned down the offer because 'we were really much too small a fly to enter safely into such a very large web' (p. 81).

opinion about it, as it depends a good deal upon our contributors—especially the artists, whether we ought to reject or accept.

I've asked Morgan for Tuesday.

Yr
B.

I owe you 5/. I was rather ashamed of myself as usual for chivvying you out of your pictures at 5/. when they are probably worth £5.5.5.

Berg

1325: To R. C. Trevelyan   *Hogarth House, Paradise Road,*
Richmond, Surrey

23rd Nov. 1922

Dear Bob,

It was extremely nice of you to write to me. I think that there is a great deal in all that you say about Jacob's Room—I mean in your criticisms. Of course, the effort of breaking with strict representation is very unsettling, and many things were not controlled as they should have been. It is true, I expect, that the characters remain shadowy for the most part; but the method was not so much at fault as my ignorance of how to use it psychologically. But this is too difficult to explain in writing—(at this moment at least—and I hope we shall see you). I'm sorry about the obscurity—if you mean that the actual sentences were obscure, and not only the approaches, and transitions, and situations generally. I think there is no excuse for needless difficulty—it is bad writing merely;—I shan't tolerate it again, I hope.

Anyhow, I am awfully pleased that you liked much of it, and think it a fruitful experiment, for this encourages me to go on, as I wish to do.

I hope you will come here soon, and then, if it didn't bore you, I should like very much to get you to tell me more of your views. Why don't you write a poem which brings in and leaves out what you wish? And then we would publish it—but I expect this is a silly remark, for I don't know enough of your problems as a poet.

I am ashamed to send this letter, because I have not time to write properly, but I was so pleased with yours that I wanted to answer it.

Leonard sends his love, and hopes to see you. Having got through his election, he now has to serve on a jury at the Old Bailey—we're afraid its the Ilford murder case. He might as well be in Parliament.

Yours ever,
Virginia Woolf

Sussex

1326: To H. G. Wells　　　　*Hogarth House, Paradise Road,*
　　　　　　　　　　　　　　　Richmond, Surrey

26th Nov. [1922]

Dear Mr Wells,

Miss [Ethel] Sands has suggested that you might be willing to give us the great pleasure of meeting you. We wondered whether you would come to a very small dinner on Tuesday, 5th December, at 7.45, at my sister's house, 46 Gordon Square. (I think perhaps you have met her husband, Clive Bell.) Dress, of course, is not necessary.

My husband wishes to be remembered to you.[1]

　　　　　　　　　　　　　　　　　　　　Yours sincerely
University of Illinois　　　　　　　　　　　　Virginia Woolf

1327: To Lady Ottoline Morrell
　　　　　　　　　　　　　　　Hogarth House, Paradise Road,
　　　　　　　　　　　　　　　Richmond, Surrey

Nov 30 [1922]

Dearest Ottoline,

I have only succeeded in finding that Lady Cunard lives at Carlton House Terrace. I'll try and get the number from Mary Hutchinson tomorrow. Mary H: is distributing notices, and will do the Jowitts. I will do Maynard and Lytton.

I have become like one of those dreary drudges who always say that they are too busy to breathe. It is a dull and disgraceful state to be in; but for the last week or so, quite true of me, I'm ashamed to say.

That old silly Sybil Colefax never mentioned you on her orange note paper; or perhaps I could have put off my pressing engagement. I'm sorry I didn't; but one tea party a week is as much as I have the head for. I don't mean that one requires a real head; but a head that knows where to stop, which for me, trained at Bedford Square, is a perpetual dilemma. What can one say to Mr Percy Lubbock? By no means all one thinks. That is the strain and misery to me. But they are all very nice and kind and Morgan Forster and I simply cannot make out what it is that is wrong. Perhaps it is wrong with Morgan and me. He has been with Elizabeth Bibesco, motoring all night, eating hot lobster, and hearing all her stories of love and sorrow: but, he says, it is no more interesting than old ladies at Weybridge, and costs £10,000 a year.

Please excuse this scrawl.

　　　　　　　　　　　　　　　　　　　　Your ever
Texas　　　　　　　　　　　　　　　　　　　　V.W.

1. Leonard had known Wells since the middle of the War, when they were both members of the League of Nations Union.

1328: To Maynard Keynes   *Hogarth House, Paradise Road,*
                               Richmond, Surrey

[3? December 1922]

Dear Maynard,

You will be indignant no doubt to receive the enclosed, which is the most muddled appeal ever written. Still I don't see how you can deny that it meets all your objections; and I'm afraid you'll have to contribute.

Yours ever
Virginia Woolf

King's

Printed

ELIOT FELLOWSHIP FUND

It has been known for some time to Mr T. S. Eliot's friends that the effort of Bank work in which he is at present engaged is injuring his health and must seriously interfere with his creative powers. It is impossible that he should continue to produce good poetry unless he has more leisure than he can now hope to obtain, but his literary work is of too high and original a quality to afford by itself a means of livelihood. For this reason it is proposed to raise a special fellowship fund to enable him to give up his post at the Bank and devote his whole time to literary work. It is estimated that at least £300 a year for a period of not less than 5 years will be required, and it is hoped that many admirers of good literature will be glad to contribute to a fund which has for its aim the preserving of the talent of one of the most original and distinguished writers of our day.

Subscribers are asked to pledge themselves to contribute a sum of *£10 a year, or £5 in special cases, for not less than 5 years, and arrangements will, if possible, be made to send to each subscriber a copy of all Mr Eliot's works as published.

The Committee for England will consist of Lady Ottoline Morrell, Garsington Manor, Oxford; Mrs Leonard Woolf, Hogarth House, Richmond; Mr H. T. J. Norton, Merton House, Cambridge; and Mr Richard Aldington, Malthouse Cottage, Padworth, Reading, who is acting as Treasurer of the fund. Another Committee is also working in collaboration with this Committee, both in France and America. Subscribers are asked to sign both the annexed forms and to return them as soon as possible to any of the Committee.

October 1922

*Donations of £25 and over will also be accepted but annual subscriptions are preferred. In the event of the necessary amount not being raised within 3 months all money received will, if desired, be repaid to the subscribers.

POSTSCRIPT

Since the scheme in the accompanying circular was proposed it has come to the knowledge of the Committee that circumstances have arisen which make it necessary that Mr Eliot should be allowed to use his own discretion as to continuing or relinquishing his present work at the Bank.

It is however certain that any addition to his income would not only remove from him considerable anxiety which the expense of illness has brought upon him but would make it possible for him to give more time to writing than he can now do. Under these circumstances the Committee propose to continue the scheme in its present form without imposing or implying any condition that Mr Eliot should give up his work at the Bank.

1329: TO LYTTON STRACHEY   *Hogarth House, Paradise Road,*
                            Richmond, Surrey
Sunday, Dec. 3rd [1922]

Here at last is the letter you have been so anxiously waiting. It is worth keeping as a specimen of English.

I'm not sure, though, that it leaves you with a leg to stand on. All your objections are met, (if you will read carefully) and so . . . Cheques payable to me, or Aldington, or Philip.

When are we going to see you again?

                                                    Yr
                                                    V.W.

Berg

1330: TO JACQUES RAVERAT   *Hogarth House, Paradise Road,*
                            Richmond, Surrey
Dec. 10 1922

My dear Jacques,

It was very nice to get your letter—to which Gwen's handwriting adds an unmistakable smack of that lost but unforgotten woman. I'm glad you liked Jacob better than the other novels; one always wishes the last to be best. I'm not blind, though, to its imperfections—indeed it is more an experiment than an achievement. Is your art as chaotic as ours? I feel that for us writers the only chance now is to go out into the desert and *peer* about, like devoted scapegoats, for some sign of a path. I expect you got through your discoveries sometime earlier. All this, however, we will chatter about endlessly when we meet.

But when? I say the end of March. This depends, for us, upon arrangements with the Nation, for which Leonard has to write a weekly article on foreign politics. Still, we do mean to come, and have promised to take a boat from Marseilles and go on to Spain to stay with a solitary eccentric young man called Brenan, who is trying to learn to write upon a mountain near Granada. Do you know him? Ought we to arrange about rooms? Perhaps Gwen would tell me sometime closer to March. I heard praises of your pictures from Roger Fry the other night. He thinks you are now doing the interesting things—but I don't know if his praises, or any one's praises, mean much to you. We are so lonely and separated in our adventures as writers and painters. I never dare praise pictures, though I have my own opinions. Raspail was spelt wrong owing to Duncan and Vanessa, whom I consulted. A letter more or less means nothing to them. Toads are (essentially) insects, I maintain. Women may be worse, or may be better, than men, but surely the opinions of the writer of Jacobs Room on that point, or any other, are not *my* opinions. This is a very old quarrel though.

I'm glad you are fat; for then you are warm and mellow and generous and creative. I find that unless I weigh 9½ stones I hear voices and see visions and can neither write nor sleep. It is a necessity, I suppose, to part with youth and beauty, but I think there are compensations.

Please write again, if it doesn't bore you. I enjoyed your letter so much, and imagine your whole existence, no doubt a little wrong, as I walk with my dog, in Richmond Park.

The Hogarth Press is branching out in January with 2 partners.[1] Haven't you some writing up your sleeve?

Yours ever,
Virginia Woolf

Sussex

1331: TO RICHARD ALDINGTON *Hogarth House, Paradise Road, Richmond, Surrey*

19th Dec. 1922

Dear Mr Aldington,

I am quite ready to ask Lady Ottoline to sign a cheque, and I think it would be a very good time to give it, however it is done. But after what Mr Eliot told me, I'm sure he won't take a penny unless we can assure him that no conditions are attached to it.

If you will let me have a line to say that this is so, I will communicate with Lady Ottoline at once.

He was also refusing, when I saw him, to take money from people who

---

1. Ralph Partridge (who left the Press in March 1923), and Marjorie Thomson, who joined them in January. She was living with C. E. M. Joad, the philosopher, and used his name.

were earning their livings, as he is. Should I be at liberty to give him the names of the donors if he insisted upon knowing?

Yours sincerely,
Virginia Woolf

Texas

1332: To R. C. Trevelyan [*Monk's House, Rodmell*]

21st Dec. 1922

Dear Bob,

I wonder if you would be so very kind as to lend me Earlham, by Percy Lubbock,[1] which I'm told you have. Logan says it is a masterpiece, and I can't get it from Mudies [Library]. I enclose stamps, and would promise to return within a fortnight. Address,

Monks House,
Rodmell,
Lewes.

but don't bother to answer if you haven't got it. I'm taking your translations down to read. I don't think you ought to use the word "quire" for "choir", it suggests to me, as a publisher, 24 sheets post 8vo. I've only looked in.

Yours ever,
Virginia Woolf

Sussex

1333: To Richard Aldington Monk's House, Rodmell, Lewes, [Sussex]

[21? December 1922]

Dear Mr Aldington,

I think it would be best to send Mr Eliot a cheque for £50 at once, and am writing to Lady Ottoline by this post. I shall meet his objections as best I can—but I'm afraid you are right in thinking that recent events will make him refuse, whatever one may say or do.

However, one can but try.

Yours truly
Virginia Woolf

Texas

1. Recollections of his childhood in Norfolk (1922).

1334: To Lady Ottoline Morrell   *Monks House, Rodmell,*
[21? December 1922]   *Lewes, [Sussex]*

Dearest Ottoline,

The affairs of the Eliot fund once more! Aldington writes to suggest that we should pay over some money to Tom at once. There is £77 in the Bank.

So do you agree to sending him a cheque for £50 now?

If so, would you sign the enclosed cheque and return it to me? I will then fill it up, and send on to him. I feel rather doubtful that he'll take it. Still we can but try.

Its a dismal and howling day down here. I suppose you have somehow conjured a party up at Garsington. I sat next a young Mr Sackville¹ at dinner the other night, who talked of you incessantly, with the greatest admiration and gratitude.

Ever yr aff

We go back to Hogarth House on the 1st.   V.W.

Texas

1335: To Vanessa Bell   *Monk's House, [Rodmell,*
Dec. 22nd [1922]   *Sussex]*

Dearest,

I searched the curiosity shops of Lewes yesterday, and only found this curious phallic emblem (don't ask your father in law what that means) reminding me slightly of the bowl which figures in some of your still lives. Anyhow, being glass, it is easily broken. It is meant to hold scent: but why not try it as a candlestick? (failing the other use, which, as I say, don't investigate at the breakfast table)

I can hardly imagine Cleeve House,² with Dolphin captive all day. I suppose the children tide you over, and exhibit you only in those maternal aspects which may well disarm suspicion.

I left you in black despair. Must you really become wandering again? Six months in France—six at Charleston—I shall never see you. But that, as you will remark, is not really the point. Seriously, I think you ought to prevent Maynard before it is too late.³ I can't believe that he realises what the

1. Edward Sackville-West (1901-65), later Lord Sackville, the novelist and music critic. He had just left Oxford.
2. At Seend, Wiltshire, the home of Clive Bell's parents.
3. Lydia Lopokova had rejoined the Diaghilev ballet earlier in the year, and Maynard Keynes had fallen in love with her. She was separated from her husband, and Keynes persuaded her to live in Gordon Square, near his own house. They did not marry until 1925.

effects would be. I can foresee only too well Lydia stout, charming, exacting; Maynard in the Cabinet; 46 the resort of the dukes and prime ministers. M. being a simple man, not analytic as we are, would sink beyond recall long before he realised his state. Then he would awake, to find 3 children, and his life entirely and for ever controlled.

That is how it appears to me, without considering my own grievances. If you dont put your view before him, he will have a case against you when the catastrophe arrives. Moreover, Lydia is far better as a Bohemian un-attached, hungry, and expectant, than as a matron with nothing to hope, and all her rights secure.

There's not much news. Fragments of gossip return to my mind—but I cant help thinking your own pouch is full, and the contents not shared equitably. Lord Esher has forbidden Brett[1] to live with Gertler—not that they ever lived, save in the sense of sharing the same saucepan. So he lodges 2 doors off. We have been elected to that horrid muling puling society which meets on Thursdays—Murry, Sydney, Brett, Gertler, and Koteliansky. The absurd creatures model themselves, I gather, upon the Apostles: first you are looked at; then voted for. Sydney's wife was black-balled. So it is a very great compliment. But what I say is, if you can't be clever, isn't it better to be beautiful? Did I tell you that Sydney has discovered that we are all responsible for the sins of all? It is the new gospel—and accounts for the miserable quality of their conversation. But none of this interests Dolphin. I am still rather stupid in the head, or I should be writing Punch and Judy.

I have laid down the law to Lottie, with the usual result—she is perfectly angelic and as humble as a caterpillar. I think I shall keep her like this, and be a real lady in future. However Nelly tells me she was even worse with Jo-an.[2] Once they had such a scene that Jo-an went to Roger and said either she must leave or Lottie, upon which Roger chose Lottie, according to Nellie. But I don't think you quite appreciate the difficulties of being a Socialist. Did you know that I'm a Socialist?

Ralph became so sad and so charming and pathetic that I almost relented. But when I think of his remark about Lytton I stiffen my bristles. Its all very distressing, as I feel slightly responsible for that marriage, and so feel that one is hauling up a life belt—leaving Carrington to flounder in the middle of the channel embraced by a cuttlefish.[3] And if it is true that we are all responsible for the sins of all, surely we ought to sink together? What is

1. Dorothy Brett, Lord Esher's daughter.
2. Joan Fry, Roger's sister, who kept house for him at Durbins, near Guildford.
3. Within a few months of their marriage, Ralph Partridge and Carrington found themselves in difficulties. Ralph was constantly unfaithful, and Carrington was maintaining a clandestine correspondence with Gerald Brenan, the young writer who lived in Spain and was much in love with her. Virginia did not know these details, but she sensed the strain, and sided with Carrington.

your opinion? I am constantly surprised by moral doctrines rolled out, most unexpectedly, from your deep seas.

If Julian has got the book I sent, let me have it; as I rather want it. Give him my love, and tell him I insist upon having a letter of thanks, giving me a full account of his views upon English literature. I want to see him.

Now write me a letter of love.

Yr
B.

We have just settled with a German firm to reproduce Duncan's designs for Luce.[1] They are very cheap, and if good, we might start doing pictures. How much does your man charge for photographing pictures? A block wd cost about 10/- we think.

Berg

1336: To Dora Carrington   *Monk's House, Rodmell,*
                                             near Lewes, Sussex

Xmas Day [1922]

My dear Carrington,

I don't know which was nicer—your letter, or your sweets—both completely unlike anything else in the habitable globe. I have written so many letters, that you must not expect any flowers from me—Leonard is sending you and Ralph with our love some cooking apples—rather a mangy present; but then the old serpent, I mean,—you know who I mean [Lytton] —often takes an apple with his tapioca.

No: all friendships remain intact.[2] Its a great blessing—but then at our time of life, to break even a ten penny mug over a dispute would be in the highest degree idiotic. Besides, who knows?—something may be rigged up yet. I don't despair. The Toads[3] may turn out hollow frauds. But I don't mean to open my mouth again until I have something sensible to say.

[Edward] Shanks is coming to call. That is all our news. He was riding his pony in a gale, looking precisely like a plum pudding; There's no drink to give him, so we shall stew over the fire as before.

Lottie's rump is cured. She is now angelicity itself, and made a mouse out of marzipan with a tail of string which she put in my cup at tea—The

1. In 1923 the Hogarth Press published an edition of the *Poems* of Gordon Hannington Luce, with decorations by Duncan Grant. Luce, who was born in 1889, taught English for many years in the University of Rangoon, and was a friend of Maynard Keynes, who financed the first edition of his poems (1920). At Cambridge Luce had been an Apostle.
2. After the arguments with Ralph about his future at the Hogarth Press.
3. Marjorie Thomson and C. E. M. Joad.

excitement in the kitchen is still intense. Then we had the rector singing carols in the cabbages for the sake of the blind—altogether, a very Merry Christmas—

It isn't as if the Hogarth Press were settled down irretrievably. I expect it to grow all over the place, and certainly I shall call upon you, in some capacity.

I wonder whether marriage was much discussed during the weekend—Maynards I mean.[1]

But you must come in January, 1923.

Yr
V.W.

Oh did you hear that I wrote to Thomas Gage? He has accepted a packet of Bromo; suitably inscribed.[2]

Robert H. Taylor

1337: To Gerald Brenan   *Monk's House, Rodmell,*
                                Near Lewes, Sussex

Christmas Day 1922

Dear Gerald,

Very stupidly I came away without your letter, though I have been putting off writing till Christmas, hoping to have time and some calmness. It interested me, very much, and now I can't take it up and answer it as I had meant. But no doubt this is as well. What one wants from a letter is not an answer. So I shall ramble on, until the cook goes off to tea with Mrs Dedman, when I must scramble the eggs.

First however, we certainly hope to come to you about the end of March, or beginning of April. This depends on things that can't be settled now; so may we leave it, and write definitely later? Apart from talking to you, as we want to do, at leisure, fully, at night, at dawn, about people, books, life, and so on and so on, my eyes are entirely grey with England—nothing but England for 10 years; and you can't imagine how much of a physical desire it becomes to feed them on colour and crags—something violent and broken and dry—not perpetually sloping and sloppy like the country here. (This is a very wet Christmas day).

I have been thinking a great deal about what you say of writing novels. One must renounce, you say. I can do better than write novels, you say. I

1. Maynard Keynes did not marry Lydia Lopokova until August 1925.
2. 'Tom Gage' briefly appears in *Jacob's Room* as a name on a tombstone, alongside that of Berta Ruck's. Lytton and Carrington wrote Virginia a fake letter from Tom Gage, claiming the loss of his job as lavatory-attendant at Oxford Circus, as a consequence of her use of his name.

don't altogether understand. I don't see how to write a book without people
in it. Perhaps you mean that one ought not to attempt a 'view of life'?—one
ought to limit oneself to one's own sensations—at a quartet for instance;
one ought to be lyrical, descriptive: but not set people in motion, and attempt
to enter them, and give them impact and volume? Ah, but I'm doomed!
As a matter of fact, I think that we all are. It is not possible now, and never
will be, to say I renounce. Nor would it be a good thing for literature were it
possible. This generation must break its neck in order that the next may have
smooth going. For I agree with you that nothing is going to be achieved by
us. Fragments—paragraphs—a page perhaps: but no more. Joyce to me
seems strewn with disaster. I can't even see, as you see, his triumphs. A
gallant approach, that is all that is obvious to me: then the usual smash and
splinters (I have only read him, partly, once). The human soul, it seems to
me, orientates itself afresh every now and then. It is doing so now. No one
can see it whole, therefore. The best of us catch a glimpse of a nose, a shoulder,
something turning away, always in movement. Still, it seems better to me to
catch this glimpse, than to sit down with Hugh Walpole, Wells, etc. etc.
and make large oil paintings of fabulous fleshy monsters complete from top
to toe. Of course, being under 30, this does not apply to you. To you,
something more complete may be vouchsafed. If so, it will be partly because
I, and some others, have made our attempts first. I have wandered from the
point. Never mind. I am only scribbling, more to amuse myself than you,
who may never read, or understand: for I am doubtful whether people, the
best disposed towards each other, are capable of more than an intermittent
signal as they forge past—a sentimental metaphor, leading obviously to
ships, and night and storm and reefs and rocks, and the obscured, uncom-
passionate moon. I wish I had your letter for I could then go ahead; without
so many jerks.

   You said you were very wretched, didn't you? You described your liver
rotting, and how you read all night, about the early fathers; and then walked,
and saw the dawn. But were wretched, and tore up all you wrote, and felt
you could never, never write—and compared this state of yours with mine,
which you imagine to be secure, rooted, benevolent, industrious—you did
not say dull—but somehow unattainable, and I daresay, unreal. But you
must reflect that I am 40: further, every 10 years, at 20, again at 30, such
agony of different sorts possessed me that not content with rambling and
reading I did most emphatically attempt to end it all; and should have been
often thankful, if by stepping on one flagstone rather than another I could
have been annihilated where I stood. I say this partly in vanity that you
may not think me insipid; partly as a token (one of those flying signals out
of the night and so on) that so we live, all of us who feel and reflect, with
recurring cataclysms of horror: starting up in the night in agony: Every
ten years brings, I suppose, one of those private orientations which match
the vast one which is, to my mind, general now in the race. I mean, life has

to be sloughed: has to be faced: to be rejected; then accepted on new terms with rapture. And so on, and so on; till you are 40, when the only problem is how to grasp it tighter and tighter to you, so quick it seems to slip, and so infinitely desirable is it.

As for writing, at 30 I was still writing, reading; tearing up industriously. I had not published a word (save reviews). I despaired. Perhaps at that age one is really most a writer. Then one cannot write, not for lack of skill, but because the object is too near, too vast. I think perhaps it must recede before one can take a pen to it. At any rate, at 20, 30, 40, and I've no doubt 50, 60, and 70, that to me is the task; not particularly noble or heroic, as I see it in my own case, for all my inclinations are to write; but the object of adoration to me, when there comes along someone capable of achieving—if only the page or paragraph; for there are no teachers, saints, prophets, good people, but the artists—as you said—But the last sentence is hopelessly unintelligible. Indeed, I am getting to the end of my letter writing capacity. I have many more things to say; but they cower under their coverlets, and nothing remains but to stare at the fire, and finger some book till the ideas freshen within me, or they once more become impartible.

I think, too, there is a great deal of excitement and fun and pure pleasure and brilliance in one's fellow creatures. I'm not sure that you shouldn't desert your mountain, take your chance, and adventure with your human faculties—friendships, conversations, relations, the mere daily intercourse. Why do young men hold books up before their eyes so long? French literature falls like a blue tint over the landscape.

But I am not saying what I mean, and had better stop. Only you must write to me again—anything that occurs to you—And what about something for the Hogarth Press?

Leonard adds his wishes to mine for the future.

Yours
Virginia Woolf

P.S.

I add a postscript, which is intended to explain why I say that one must not renounce. I think I mean that beauty, which you say I sometimes achieve, is only got by the failure to get it; by grinding all the flints together; by facing what must be humiliation—the things one can't do—To aim at beauty deliberately, without this apparently insensate struggle, would result, I think, in little daisies and forget-me-nots—simpering sweetnesses— true love knots—But I agree that one must (we, in our generation must) renounce finally the achievement of the greater beauty: the beauty which comes from completeness, in such books as War and Peace, and Stendhal I suppose, and some of Jane Austen; and Sterne; and I rather suspect in Proust, of whom I have only read one volume. Only now that I have written this, I doubt its truth. Are we not always hoping? and though we fail every time, surely we do not fail so completely as we should have failed if we were

599

not in the beginning, prepared to attack the whole. One must renounce, when the book is finished; but not before it is begun. Excuse me for boring on: you may have said nothing of the kind. I was wondering to myself why it is that though I try sometimes to limit myself to the thing I do well, I am always drawn on and on, by human beings, I think, out of the little circle of safety, on and on, to the whirlpools; when I go under.

George Lazarus

1338: To Vanessa Bell   *Monk's House, [Rodmell, Sussex]*

Wednesday [27 December 1922]

Here is a sketch for Punch and Judy.[1] It will want a good deal of alteration. However I think you and Duncan had better see what can be done with it.

I have made some of the characters appear in front of the house—but perhaps this can't be managed. It takes about 10 minutes to read aloud.

It is very dismal here today, except that we had our second turkey. Did I tell you we bought 2, the size of young chickens?

What happened to you? Waits and carols and mistletoe? Were you a success? Did Angelica behave?

I'm involved once more in awful doings with poor Tom. I believe we are sending him £50 for Christmas; but I expect he will refuse it.

We come back on Monday.

Possibly I might look in to tea on Monday. I will if I can.

                                        V.W.

Berg

1339: To V. Sackville-West   *Hogarth House, Paradise Road, Richmond*

Dec. 28th [1922]

Dear Mrs Nicolson,

I hope you will not think me very grasping if I complain that 'Knole', which you said was being sent to me, has never arrived.[2]

1. For the Bell children.
2. Virginia first met Vita Sackville-West (Mrs Harold Nicolson) on 14 December 1922, dining with Clive. Four days later Virginia dined with Vita at her house in Ebury Street, with Clive and Desmond as the other guests. Vita had just published the history of her family, *Knole and the Sackvilles*.

No doubt they got the address wrong. It should be
> Hogarth House
> Paradise Road
> Richmond.

I have been reading some of your poems in the new Georgian book[1] with great pleasure; and so can't help dunning you in this way in order that I may get more from your last book.

> Yours sincerely
> Virginia Woolf

Berg

1340: To R. C. Trevelyan

Monk's House, Rodmell, Lewes, [Sussex]

Dec. 29th 1922

Dear Bob,

I return Percy Lubbock [*Earlham*] with many thanks. I have read every word with great interest, trying to make out why in spite of every appearance to the contrary, and Logan and so on, it seems to me a thoroughly bad book —not a book at all in fact. I really cannot say why. Percy is obviously intelligent, scrupulous, devout, meritorious, well read, a scholar, a gentleman, I daresay a Christian—I could go on adding up his qualities—Moreover his style is by no means despicable. He is never slipshod, sentimental, or trite— indeed he is often subtle and illuminating. What, then, can it be? I suspect something hopelessly prosaic, timid, tepid, in his goal. The spirit of Earlham is undoubtedly the family butler. Everybody is combed and clipped into their nice, portly, respectable waistcoats and flounces—that, to me, is the heart of the mischief—this conspiracy to misrepresent the human soul in the interests of respectability and, I suppose, of the defunct Henry James, until what with the mildew and the mould and the tone and the mellowness and the setting sun—the rooks cawing and so on and so on, nothing approaching bone or blood is left. And why should Percy, who is comparatively young, enter this conspiracy? It makes me long for glaring suburbs, brass bands— Brighton Piers. Oh the smugness of it! Never a venture or an oath or one word more important than another. Still, I exaggerate—but really it is queer, how good it is and how bad, and why; and whether Percy himself is corrupt; or whether—perhaps I am quite wrong from start to finish. I've just met him, and felt a little of this in talking to him.

We go back to Richmond on Monday, and hope you and Bessie [Mrs Trevelyan] will come and see us sometime. I want to discuss your Aeschylus with you—I give way about the spelling of quire. Nor should I yield to

1. The fifth and last volume of *Georgian Poetry* (1920-22), an anthology of contemporary verse edited by Edward Marsh.

Logan. If he thinks Earlham a masterpiece, he is not to be trusted about the letter K.

I hope you are writing a poem. I am dipping into Georgian Poetry 1922, and get bored to death with apple trees and acorns. Surely there are more amusing things to talk about than these!

Yours ever
Virginia Woolf

Bertha Ruck and I are now great friends[1]: Tom Gage turned out to be Lytton-Carrington.

Sussex

1. Berta Ruck (Mrs Oliver Onions), the popular novelist, had complained through her husband's solicitor that Virginia had used her name in *Jacob's Room*, pronouncing her dead. Virginia replied that she had never heard of Miss Ruck. They corresponded, then met, and the incident dissolved in laughter.

Index

The numbers are page-numbers, except in the 'Letters to' section at the end of individual entries, where the letter-numbers are given in italics.

Abbreviations: V. stands for Virginia Woolf. L. for Leonard Woolf. VB. for Vanessa Bell.

4; his poems, 124; contemplates journalism, 159; considers going to Russia, 245n; quoted on Keynes, 247n; V. on his character, 273; opens bookshop, 437; engaged, 461; on *Jacob's Room*, 571; *Lady into Fox* 571n, 574-5

Letters to: Nos. *798, 853, 1137, 1236, 1302, 1305*

Garnett, Edward and Constance, 94n, 114, 175

Garsington Manor, Oxford: Morrells buy, 25n; farm for C.O.s., 113, 150n, 167; alleged unpopularity of, 152; Woolfs stay at, 158; K. Mansfield at, 174; Woolfs stay again, 196, 197-8; and again, 263, 270; and again, 370-1, 379; 'a floating palace', 518; V. stays again, 539; V's 'Garsington novel', 543

Gaskell, Elizabeth, 64, 66

Geall, Mrs (daily help), 253, 276, 283, 296, 299, 324

Genlis, Madame F. de, 82

Georgian Poetry, 203n, 601n

Gertler, Mark: loves Carrington, 128n; V. on his paintings, 195, 300; V. dines with, 252; admires VB., 255; invited to Asheham, 274, 277, 280; V.'s alleged indiscretion, 286-9, 297, 330, 431, 486; and Brett, 595

Gibbs, F. W., 462

Gibson, Hugh, 349

Gill, Eric and Mary, 18

Gill, Winifred, 157

Glasgow: V. in, 19, 23

Glasgow, George, 513n

Glazebrook family (Monk's House), 384

Glenconner, Lady, 407

Godrevy, Cornwall, 48

Goha le Simple, 438, 440

Goldenveizer, A. B., 573n

Gordon, General (*Eminent Victorians*), 173, 205, 281

Gordon, John, 341

Gordon Square, Bloomsbury, 247n, 344, 411, 426-7, 527n, 544n

Gore, Bishop Charles, 360n

Gore-Brown, Eric, 487n

Gorki, Maxim, 432

Gosse, Edmund, 579

Gozzi, Carlo, 109

Grafton Gallery, 10, 15

Graham, Stephen, 405n

Grant, Duncan: at V.'s wedding, 3; works for Omega, 15n; in Paris 71; farms in Suffolk, 83; gives V. a painting, 84; applies for exemption from war-service, 94, 97-100, 102; exempted, 106; proposed move to Sussex, 117; moves to Charleston, 118; exhibits at Omega, 130; 130; woodcuts for Hogarth Press, 168; 181, decorates Hutchinson house, 171; refuses to be war-artist, 245n; father of Angelica, 263n; V.'s description of in 1919, 331; a-political, 340; V. proposes as art-critic for *Athenaeum*, 341; V. invites to design papers, 349; life at Charleston, 363; paints hat for V., 368; *Night and Day* dedication, 394; gives V. a picture, 421-2; painting style changes, 469; illustrates Luce, 596n; *mentioned*, xxiii, 7n, 50, 88, 227-8, 273, 294, 302, 326, 372, 429, 432, 491, 584

Letters to: Nos. *717, 736, 747, 809, 825, 932, 964, 998, 1039, 1120*

Grant, Henrietta Anne, 72n

Gravé, Madame (dressmaker), 257, 348, 472

Graves, Robert, 552

Greek Literature: V. reads, 132; Aeschylus, 141; quotes Anthology, 134; Homer, 558; Sophocles, 220-1, 282, 446; Plato, 389, 446; grammar, 437

Green, M. M., 263n

Green, Miss (secretary), 446n, 471, 513, 517

Grey, Sir Edward, xviii, 281

Grizel (dog), 560

Grys, Mrs le, 50

Gunn (Asheham bailiff), 46, 96, 114, 117, 226, 312, 349, 382, 386

Gurnard's Head, Cornwall, 120, 165, 325, 354, 460, 462, 463

Gyles, Mrs (Southease), 578

Hamill, Dr, 541

Hamilton, Agnes (Molly), 144, 180, 266, 377, 418

Hamilton, Margot, 377, 418

Omega Workshops: Roger Fry founds, 15, 16; VB. at, 28, 39; publish Fry translations, 73n; furniture of, 78; quarrel between Fry and Lewis, 85n; design clothes, 92, 111, 136, 157; list of customers, 115; club in association with, 116n, 151; exhibitions, 125, 187, 195, 285; D. Grant exhibits at, 130; scheme for loaning pictures, 166, 260; chair-covers, 249, 255, 259; influence of, 291; publish woodcut book, 296-7; reprint *Kew Gardens*, 366; close down, 396n; dispersal of stock, 450

Orchardleigh, Somerset, 233, 343
Osborne, Guendolen Godolphin, 64, 69
Osgood, Alice (maid), 320-1
Owen's School, Islington, 376n

Palatine Review, 158
Paley, G. A., 13n
Partridge, Ralph: meets Lytton Strachey, 423n; may join Hogarth Press, 439n; joins, 446, 451; and Carrington, 442, 459; marries her, 470-1; works at Hogarth Press, 487, 495, 554; resigns from Press, 582-3, 596; relations with Carrington, 595n; *mentioned*, xxii, 453, 533
    Letter to: No. *1317*
Pater, Charlotte and Clara, 307
Patmore, Coventry, 467
Pearsall Smith, Logan: 301, 357-8, 359, 364n; *Stories from Old Testament*, 430, 432-3; 586, 602
Pelican Press, 368, 460
Pelman Institute, 271
Phoenix Society (drama), 515n
Picasso, Pablo, 356, 361, 364
Pisa, Italy, 7-8
Pissarro, Lucien, 240
Pitcher (Charleston gardener), 363
Plato, 389, 446
Plomer, William, xx
Popham, Brynhild, *see* Olivier
Porter, Frederick, 475
Post-Impressionist Exhibition, Second, 10n, 15
Potter, Betty, 487, 518-19, 524
Pound, Ezra: 296; helps Eliot Fellowship Fund, q.v.; V.'s bias against, 572

Poynter, Sir Edward, 235
Prelude (K. Mansfield): promised to Hogarth Press, 168; printing, 196, 209, 289n; cover-design, 244, 246; first copies, 248; binding, 258; V. on its merits, 262
Pretious, Ivy Gladys (Mrs Charles Tennyson), 319
Prewett, Frank, 479
Priest, Alfred, 378n
Primmer, Mrs, 362
Prince of Wales (Edward VIII), 445
Prothero, Mrs George, 322
Proust, Marcel, 396, 499, 525, 566

Quakers, 75, 232, 245n
Quantock Hills, Somerset, 3
Quaritch (bookseller), 258
Queen's Dolls House, xviii, 515
Queen Victoria (Lytton Strachey): 363, 390, 423; dedicated to V., 456; published 464; V.'s copy of 497n

Ransome, Mr (Asheham), 22
Rathbone, Mrs William, 291, 505
Raverat, Gwen (Darwin), 121, 410, 454
    Letter to No. *661*
Raverat, Jacques: his paintings, 255, 257, 592; VB. on, 410; V.'s revived friendship with, 549, 553-5; on *Jacob's Room*, 591
    Letters to: Nos. *1280*, *1330*
Ray, Mr (tenant of Charleston), 96
Read, Herbert, 572-3
Reading, Lord, 180
Reid, John R., 378n
Renoir, Pierre Auguste, 260
Ribblesdale, Lord, 144, 360
Rice, Estelle, 241
Richards, Arthur, 451
Richmond, Bruce: 224, 233, 267, 290, 302, 339; 392, 403; V. on his character, 306-7; wants to rent Asheham, 338
Richmond, Elena, 302, 306-7, 342; V. on her character, 505
Richmond, Surrey: Woolfs live on The Green, 50; move to Hogarth House, q.v.; Co-op. Guild of, 138-9, 152, 155, 223, 582
Ritchie, Lady (Aunt Anny), 4n, 47n, 105, 207, 319; Mrs Hilbery in *Night and Day*, 406, 474

V. abuses 350; praises *Night and Day*, 394; Woolfs stay with, 401, 404; at Tidmarsh with R. Partridge 423; *Queen Victoria*, q.v.; *Books and Characters*, 501n, 534n; *Son of Heaven*, 519; contributes to Eliot Fund, 550-1, 591; V.'s admiration for, 553; reaction to *Jacob's Room*, 568-9

Letters to: Nos. *641, 644, 653, 656, 685, 687-8, 711, 718, 723, 732, 745, 775, 859, 899, 914, 918, 924, 935, 978, 1012, 1051, 1082, 1087, 1097, 1100, 1122, 1165, 1173-4, 1187, 1212, 1215, 1220, 1277, 1298, 1329*

Strachey, Marjorie ('Gumbo'): intends becoming publisher, 14; at Asheham, 21, 27, 146-8; in Manchester, 72; and Josiah Wedgwood, 149, 206, 261; dismissed from school, 341; dines with Eliot, 347; falls downstairs, 451; starts Bloombury school, 544n; *mentioned*, 203, 457

Strachey, Oliver, 286, 292, 294, 298, 347, 349, 349, 527

Strachey, Mrs Oliver (Rachel, 'Ray'), 12n, 63, 84, 102, 199, 204, 298, 357, 451-2, 587

Strachey, Pernel, 82, 109, 112, 177, 383n

Strachey, Philippa ('Pippa'), 103, 511
   Letter to: No. *1225*

Strutt, W. M., 81

Studd, Arthur (Peter), 322, 522

Studland, Dorset, 17, 20

Sturgeon, George and Flora (L.'s sister), 57, 280, 425

Suffield House, Richmond, 60n, 398n, 405, 411, 557

Sullivan, J. W. N., 499n

Suret, Louis, 107n

Sydney-Turner, Saxon: V.'s affection for, 126-7, 128, 192-4, 362; sample of his conversation, 508-9; at Asheham, 22; works in Treasury, 79n; his friendship with Thoby Stephen, 126; in love with Barbara Hiles, 126, 128, 129, 130-1, 192, 194; V. talks to his father, 134; melancholic, 137, 143; Asheham lent to, 140; alone with V., 192-4; Barbara prefers him to Bagenal,

211-12; but she married Bagenal, 218; his unhappiness, 222; not a snob, 238-9; ageing, 244; happy again, 284, 292; dismal again, 299, 302, 313-14; like an undertaker, 331; mania for trains, 404; corrects *The Voyage Out*, 418; his London flat, 451; in Finland, 480n, 497; his father dies, 506, 509

Letters to: Nos. *646, 742, 777, 790, 803, 805, 810, 813-14, 821, 862, 871, 889, 910, 1005, 1052, 1057, 1081, 1115, 1172, 1190*

Sylvester, Prof James, 426

Talland House, St Ives, 48, 460n, 461, 550

Tarragona, Spain, 4-5

Taylor, Cecil, 408

Tchekov, Anton, 437, 459n; Notebooks, 466n, letters, 521

Temple, Inner (London), 4, 10, 35

Templeton, Mrs (Strachey housekeeper) 53

Tennant, Laura (Mrs Alfred Lyttelton), 154

Tennyson, Mr and Mrs Charles, 319

Tennyson, Hallam, 493

Thackeray, W. M.: *Pendennis*, 9; sale of MSS, 172, 219n, 225, 233, 248, 258; picture of, 475

Thomas, Jean, 24, 33, 77, 125, 194

Thorndike, Sybil, 519

Three Jews (L.'s story), 155

Thynne, Beatrice, 18, 64, 84-5, 86, 91, 413

Tidmarsh (L. Strachey's house), 205n, 262, 582

Tim (dog), 121, 151

Times Literary Supplement, The, 12-13, 23, 135, 224, 233, 267, 339

Timworth, Suffolk, 29

Toledo, Spain, 8

Tolstoy, Leo, 94n, 432, 573n

Tonks, Henry, 522

Torre, Don Claudio de la, 454

Tournier, Miss, 60n, 63

Tree, Iris, 72

Tree, Viola, 72

Tregerthen, Cornwall; V.'s cottages at, 340, 350, 351, 354, 356; give up, 380, 382; Woolfs visit, 463

Trevelyan, George, 13

Trevelyan, R. C. ('Bob'): character, 120, 499; visits Asheham, 111, 113; V. stays with, 152; lectures at Richmond, 157; congratulated on play, 175; dines at Hogarth House in air-raid, 202; *Night and Day*, 391; his *Death of Man*, 410, 419-20 412; corrects V.'s novels, 419; on *Jacob's Room*, 588

Trevelyan, Mrs R. C. ('Bessy'), 78, 494
Tribunal, The (journal), 240*n*
Trissie (Selwood, VB.'s cook), 162, 188, 219, 245, 252, 271, 275, 305
Turner, J. M. W., 260
Turner, W. J., 455*n*, 470
Twickenham: mental home at, 32-4; Woolfs househunting in, 52
Two Stories (V's and L.'s), 155, 159, 161, 162, 165, 167, 168, 170, 282
Tyro, The (journal), 467

Ulysses: see Joyce, James
Union of Democratic Control, 65
Uppington, Mrs (Rodmell helper), 544, 568

Valencia, Spain, 7*n*, 8
Valéry, Paul, 579
Vandervelde, Lalla and Emile, 117, 141, 143, 197
Vaucluse, France, 478
Vaughan, Barbara, 223
Vaughan, Emma ('Toad'): wedding present to V., 11; visits Asheham, 24-5; works for German prisoners, 150, 156, 186; gives V. bookbinding tools, 185-6
Vaughan, Halford, 201
Vaughan, Janet, 202
Vaughan, Margaret ('Madge'): V. 'drops', xx; 65, 88, 202, 386; *A Child of the Alps*, 434, 473; visits V. at Richmond, 471
Vaughan, Margaret ('Marny') 24-5, 150, 186; V.'s sketch of her conversation and character, 199-202
Vaughan, William Wyamar, xx, 88, 471*n*
Vaughan Williams, Hervey, 291

Vaughan Williams, Ralph and Adeline, 114, 201, 307
Venereal Disease, lecture on, 138-9
Venice: Woolfs on honeymoon in, 8-9; V. detests, 24
Venning, Dr, 223
Vere, Aubrey de, 428
Veronese, Paolo, 260
Verrall, Helen, 26
Verrall, Jacob, 388
Versailles, Treaty of, 377
Vesci, Viscount and Lady de, 302
Victoria and Albert Museum, 284
Vildrac, Charles, 417
Village in the Jungle, The (L.'s novel): finished, 4; V. praises, 11; accepted for publication, 13; published, 18; success, 36
Voyage Out, The (V.'s novel): finished, 4; V. fears non-acceptance, 17; accepted by Duckworth, 20*n*, 23*n*; proofs, 28; publication announced, 56; published while V. mad, 57; sales, 68*n*, 84; praised by Lytton Strachey, 82; criticised by Forster, 82; V. thinks 'long and dull', 56; 'tumult of life', 82; praised by K. Mansfield, 107*n*; form 'too loose?', 400; U.S. publishers, 401, 403; re-issued, 418, 419; corrections to, 418, 419
Vuillard, Edouard, 260

Wadhams, Judge, 231
Wagner, 26
Wain, John, 249*n*
Walberswick, Suffolk, 384
Walkley, A. B., 503*n*
Walpole, Hugh, 598
War, First World: V.'s attitude to, xvi-xvii; outbreak, 50-1; V. sickened by jingoism, 57, 71; Dardanelles, 67; 'preposterous masculine fiction', 76; semolina, 85; end predicted in 1916, 95; V. helps conscientious objectors, 97-100; air-raids, 112, 185, 202, 214; Asquith and Lloyd George, 133; war-weariness, 178; food-shortages 226, 227-8; peace near, 283; Armistice Day, 290; celebrations, 292-4
War and Peace (journal), 69, 233, 244

Ward, Mrs Bessie, 138-9

Ward, Mrs Humphry, 62, 68, 221, 261, 268, 281, 307, 309, 341, 427

Warre-Cornish, Blanche, 547

Waterlow, John, 103

Waterlow, Sydney: V. sometimes ridicules him, xix-xx, 67, 72, 551; her excuse, 455; secretary Post-Impressionist exhibition, 16n; divorced, 25, 27; remarries, 67n, 72; Woolfs visit in London, 78, 79; 'ponderous devotion', 83; has a son, 103; introduces Middleton Murry to V., 107; at Asheham, 114; 'crisis' with, 136; not an Apostle, 138; at Asheham again, 177; 'his absurdity loveable', 181; weekend with, 252; dines with V., 302; 'colony' at Oare, 326, 407; at Paris Peace Conference, 350; no literary judgement, 383; pompous but innocent, 410-11; sense of insecurity, 355-6, 553; his marriage in trouble, 493; 'improved', 549; bathing, 551
  Letters to: Nos. 1164, 1176, 1279

Watson, Sir William, 141

Watts, G. F., 104, 322

Weaver, Harriet, 215n, 231n, 242.
  Letter: to: No. 933

Webb, Beatrice and Sidney: Woolfs meet, 53; 'attack at great length', 76; predict end of war, 78, 95; Beatrice 'young and crude', 102; Woolfs, weekend with, 101-2, 104; offer L. job, 132; they stay at Asheham, 273, 277; Beatrice has 'barren heart', 277; make V. feel ignorant, 288; Woolfs lunch with, 357, 422; Sidney stands for Parliament, 422n; elected, 585; fails to find Hogarth House, 447-8; Beatrice thinks V. amoral, 529, 547

Wedgwood, Josiah, 149, 206, 247, 261

Weiss, Professor, 458, 467

Wells, H. G.: child by Amber Blanco White, 130n; writes for L., 327; L. consults on school, 441; party for Charlie Chaplin, 486; invites Woolfs to stay weekend, 516, 519-20; V. invites to dine, 589; his novels, 598
  Letter to: No. 1326

West, Rebecca, 245, 247, 542, 548

Weyman, Stanley, 412

Weymouth, Viscount, 84n

Whitall, James, 545n, 565, 587n

White, Amber Blanco, 92, 130, 137

Whitehead, Evelyn, 78, 133

Whitham, John Mills, 146, 236, 403

Willard, Frances, 12n

Wilson, Hester (Cox), 102

Wilson, Mona, 407n

Wilson, Romer, 466

Wilson, President Woodrow, 133, 313

Wise Virgins, The (L's novel): begins, 6; progress, 23; accepted for publication, 36, 38-9

Wissett, Suffolk: 83, 95, 106; V. visits 106-7; Ottoline Morrell at, 156n

Wolfe, Edward, 303, 366n

Wooler, Bella (servant), 90

Wooler, Northumberland, 51, 274

Woolf, Cecil (L.'s brother): killed, 209; poems published, 225

Woolf, Clara (sister), 511n

Woolf, Edgar (brother), 89n

Woolf, Herbert (brother), and Freda, 115, 176, 512

Woolf, Leonard: summary of his relationship with V., xiii-xiv; and of his career 1912-22, xxi-xxii; marriage, 1, 3; honeymoon, 2-9; refuses secretaryship Hoxton charity, 8; Secretary Post-Impressionist Exhibition, 10; stays with L. Strachey, 12; malaria, 14; studies Co-operation, 17, 23n, 27n; with V. visits northern and Midland cities, 18-19, 28; cares for V. during 1913 madness, 32-6; leaves Cliffords Inn, 35n; strain of V.'s illness, 40; stays with Lytton, 40-5; Fabian Society commissions report from him, 53n, 68; move to Hogarth House, 57; intends book on diplomacy, 68; his work in wartime, 83, 118; exempted from war-service, 95, 102; on Labour international committee, 95; invited to serve Council Civil Liberties, 110; with V. in Cornwall, 118-20; Sec. Labour committee, 132, 135; launches Hogarth Press, 147, 151ff (see separate heading); lectures in north, 187,